Morte Arthure

THE ALLITERATIVE

Morte Arthure

A CRITICAL EDITION

Edited, with an Introduction,
Notes, and Glossary, by
VALERIE KRISHNA

Preface by Rossell Hope Robbins

Burt Franklin & Co., Inc., Publishers
New York

Library of Congress Cataloging in Publication Data

Morte Arthure.
The alliterative Morte Arthure.
(Middle-English Texts & Contexts 1)
Includes bibliographical references.
1. Arthurian romances. I. Krishna, Valerie
II. Title.
PR2065.M3 1976 821'.1 76-28813
ISBN 0-89102-039-X

This book has been printed on
Warren 66 Antique Offset,
chosen for its high
degree of permanency, good quality,
and acid-free characteristics.

Designer: Ernst Reichl

Contents

Illustrations and Maps follow p. 140

ACKNOWLEDGEMENTS   I am grateful to the City University of New York Faculty Research Award Program for supporting this project; to the Reverend D. N. Griffiths, Vice-Chancellor and Librarian, and the staff of the Lincoln Cathedral Library for allowing me to consult the Thornton manuscript and for their courtesy and assistance during my work; and to Mr. A. V. B. Norman of the Wallace Collection, London, for generously supplying me with information on fourteenth-century arms and armor. My thanks are due also to Jess B. Bessinger, Jr., for his encouragement and guidance in this project; to Thelma Sargent for her meticulous editing of the manuscript; to Rossell Hope Robbins for his careful reading of the manuscript and his valuable suggestions; and to Kumar Krishna for unwavering and unselfish support and applause.

Preface

Although the *Alliterative Morte Arthure* is one of the major works of the later fourteenth century, the only scholarly edition of the work is over one hundred years old. Several selections have appeared recently as college texts, and a complete version (in regularized spelling), directed primarily to students, has become available. Dr. Valerie Krishna's new edition, therefore, with its full apparatus and glossary, permits the intensive reading the poem deserves.

Most readers start their study of Middle English literature with Chaucer. Such an approach is fully justified, for Chaucer is head and shoulders England's greatest writer before Shakespeare, not merely for what he accomplished in the art of storytelling or for his skilled rhetoric, which turned the traditional genres on their head, but for his dominant and decisive position in making London English a mainstream literary vehicle for succeeding generations. But Chaucer could never have become outstanding had he been alone; artists thrive best in company. Gower, whose *Confessio Amantis* is only now receiving its due respect, was his contemporary; his style often equals Chaucer's, and some readers find his narrative techniques superior. Hoccleve overlapped Chaucer, as did Lydgate, whose courtly poems (like the *Complaint of the Black Knight* or the *Temple of Glass*), written under Chaucer's influence, are among his best, free from the prosiness of his later works. Also contemporary were the two or three unknown poets who translated the other parts of the *Roman de la Rose:* their renditions were apparently good enough to pass for Chaucer's until only recently. And one glimpses the names of others, like Sir Lewis Clifford, a friend of both Chaucer and Deschamps, praised as the

"amorous Clifford" (surely implying a writer of court love lyrics), or Scogan, tutor to the sons of Henry IV.

Establishing Chaucer in his circle stresses the importance of the royal court of Richard II, which attracted and fostered such writers. If it had not been for the patronage of Edward III, Lionel Duke of Clarence, Henry Duke of Lancaster, and Richard II himself, there would have been no Chaucer, no fellow Chaucerians, and perhaps no "King's English" as the term is understood today.

But the second half of the fourteenth century is exceptional because it had more than Chaucerian verses to represent it. Without Chaucer, it is not inconceivable that the poets of the nobility at the court would have continued to write French *formes fixes* (as Gower did). Without Chaucer, it is not inconceivable that the poets of the nobility in the provinces would have continued to write rhetorical alliterative verse (like the author of *Sir Gawain and the Green Knight*). And when one moves to poetry written outside the influence of the nobility, or before Chaucer, one enters another completely different tradition (that of the *Alliterative Morte Arthure*), which too might have continued.

Sir Gawain and the Green Knight has long been known and admired by modern readers. But only recently have readers come to see in that poem a similar degree of urbane sophistication that they find, for example, in *Troilus and Criseyde*. It is not only that both authors were familiar with all the devices in the whole repertory of rhetoric, appreciating the nuances of the game of making love like gentlefolk, but that the audiences of both poets were equally well-informed. It takes a highly educated group of lords and ladies to enjoy the comedy of the most courteous knight of legend, a renowned wooer, taxed to his wit's end to avoid offending a lively lady who offers surrender. In other words, this audience was little different from the elite coterie who enjoyed Chaucer's *Parliament of Fowls* or the Prologue to the *Legend of Good Women*. Those close to the court, like the Warwicks, the Beauchamps, even the Duke of Lancaster himself, had to return constantly to their own estates, far away from Westminster, and I think they would have equally enjoyed Machaut in French and Chaucer in nonarchaic East Midland, as well as anonymous poets (like the author of *Sir Gawain and the Green Knight*) in the restricted dialects of their own provincial estates. The language, diction, and

style of the latter, however, are different, and *Sir Gawain and the Green Knight* shows the survival, after many centuries of neglect, of the native Old English style. Whether or not this "revival" was in conscious political opposition to the royal palace fashions may be moot: at any rate it formed some sort of alternate culture.

Outside the magnates of the court circle were the English-speaking gentry, the knights and gentlemen of the county families who by the end of the fourteenth century formed the local administrative corps of the provinces. At the baronial halls, the audience was predominantly English-speaking, although the knights themselves understood French. The retainers, the ostlers, the household servants, possibly a cleric or two, were not familiar with the "high style" of either Chaucer or the Gawain poet. It is an interesting exercise in the influence of audience on style to observe how the French "society romances" were rendered into English for the gentry and their entourage. *Ywain and Gawain,* for example, written between 1325 and 1350, substitutes stories of battles for the talk of the niceties of lovemaking and the manners of knightly conduct, so prominent in the French original of Chrétien de Troyes. A later example of the removal of the court-oriented ploys in *Sir Gawain and the Green Knight* is seen in *Sir Gawain and the Carl of Carlisle,* a decade or so before 1400. The popular English version lacks both sophistication and refinement of feeling, yet it is a boisterous enough story to entertain men (and women) with glasses of ale in hand.

Between 1350 and 1400, this half century unique in artistic creativity, comes also the *Alliterative Morte Arthure,* which I suppose may be considered aesthetically inferior only to Chaucer and to *Sir Gawain and the Green Knight*. It is undoubtedly a masterpiece. But what kind of man composed it, where was it recited, and what was its audience? Answers to these questions, which affect the location of the poem on the map of Middle English literature and thereby give a reader sighting points to comprehend the literary renaissance of the late fourteenth century, are not easy.

The *Alliterative Morte Arthure* is composed in the alliterative measure, and the dialect is apparently northwestern; its milieu is neither London nor the palace. In theme it is more epic than romance, more *chanson de geste* than *roman courtois*. It bypasses love because love is not germane to its topic, yet it is not ignorant of love and

love conventions. The murdered duchess is described in mannered formulas:

> She was flower of all France, of full five realms,
> And one of the fairest that ever was framed;
> Lauded by lords as the loveliest jewel
> From Genoa to Garonne, by Jesu in Heaven!
>   (860–63)

And the attack on the giant is prefaced with a fashionable *locus amoenus,* a grove by a flower-bedecked riverside:

> The friths were embellished with blooms in abundance,
> With falcons and pheasants of fabulous hues;
> There flashed all the birds that fly upon wing,
> There warbled the cuckoo full clear in the copse
> —They give vent to their joy with all manner of mirth.
> Sweet was the sound of the nightingales' notes
> —They vied with the thrushes, three hundred at once;
> That such sighing of water and singing of birds
> Might soothe one of sorrow who had never been sound.
>   (924–33)

And the Wheel of Fortune clearly implies knowledge of a European tradition; this poem is certainly not "burel" as is *Sir Gawain and the Carl of Carlisle.*

On the other hand, what concerned the author of *Sir Gawain and the Green Knight* or the author of the *Knight's Tale* was not the concern of the poet of the *Alliterative Morte Arthure.* Here, stress is laid on the old epic devices of the challenge or taunt, the boasting of the hero to inspire awe or fear, the "coach's speech" to the warriors, and the list of those dead in combat. The situations are traditional—the order of battle, the battle itself, and the caste divisions between "us" (who rejoice in our courage) and "them" (who are cowards and traitors).

Stylistic indications seem to suggest a date about 1360. It is undoubtedly a pre-Chaucerian piece, when the influence of the French *dits amoreux* had not yet been felt, when lords still identified with battle, and when heroic feudalism was still admired:

> "Think on that valiant prince who invests us ever
> With lordship and lands wherever we like,

Who has dealt us out dukedoms and dubbed us knights,
Gave us goods and gold and guerdons untold,
Hounds and fine horses and boundless delights
That would gladden any lord that lives under God;
Think on the great renown of the Round Table,
And let it never be reft us for any Roman on earth;
Do not waver weakly or spare any weapons,
But look that you each one fight faithfully, knights!
I will be boiled alive and quartered asunder
If I do not pay my debt before wrath departs!"

(1726–37)

The spirit is aristocratic: there is no love of the lowborn, and often archers and footsoldiers are ignored.

Yet within this society that harks back to an earlier period come unexpected moral reservations. For example, how do others see Arthur's great crusade? A stranger might question the motives of Gawain:

"Where ride you, robber, who bid battle so freely?
Here you will pick up no plunder—fight when you please!"

(2533–34)

And are there doubts as to the morality of Arthur's conduct in war?

Cloister and house of God they hammer to earth,
Churches and chapels, painted chalk-white;
Sturdy stone steeples lie in the streets,
Chimneyed chambers and many fine inns;
They battered and beat down plastered walls
—The pain of the people was pity to hear!

(3038–43)

The *Alliterative Morte Arthure* belongs to the domestic courts of the local aristocracy before the influence of the royal court began to spread. It is provincial, preserving earlier values, ignoring the continental fashions, yet geared to the thinking of noblemen. To study this poem opens up one more vista of that rich half century; and one can move from here to *Sir Gawain and the Green Knight* and on to Chaucer and then to the Chaucerian epigones, where at every successive stage love themes more and more displace those of war.

Dr. Valerie Krishna comes to edit this poem with a valuable

background. Her original intention was to publish a translation—
which has given her an unequaled command of the whole poem. This
awareness, along with her meticulous annotations and glossary, will I
think make Dr. Krishna's edition a standard scholarly reference for
many years to come.

Rossell Hope Robbins

Introduction

MANUSCRIPT

The *Morte Arthure* is preserved in only one known manuscript, a folio paper volume containing seventy-six other works of varying length, among them the alliterative romances *The Awntyrs off Arthure at the Terne Wathelyne, Syr Degravante,* and *Syr Ysambrace.*[1] The manuscript is preserved in the library of Lincoln Cathedral and identified as 91 (formerly A.1.17 and A.5.2). Though the handwriting varies considerably, the manuscript is thought to be the work of a single person, the fifteenth-century Yorkshire scribe Robert of Thornton, whose signature appears at the end of *Morte Arthure.* The handwriting and watermarks fix the date of the MS as 1430–40.[2] The poem, which appears on ff. 53–98, is written in a clear, cursive hand, with no punctuation except for the marking of the caesura by a colon or by parallel vertical lines. The work is divided into sections by large decorated capital letters, but not always logically; capitalization is also irregular.[3] The conventional abbreviations are used.

SPELLING AND SOUNDS

Due in part, perhaps, to the poem's original dialect differing from that of Robert of Thornton,[4] spelling is extremely variable throughout. Both *þ* and *th* are used interchangeably for [θ, ð], generally *þ* for the voiced and *th* for the voiceless consonant (*þe, furth*). The symbol *ȝ* is used for three sounds: (1) the initial semivowel [j] (*ȝorke*); final [s] and [z] in both nouns and verbs, alternatively with *s* (*lykeȝ, lykes, tuskes, bryddeȝ*); (3) the voiceless fricative before *t* (*wiȝtnesse*). The sound [ʃ] is spelled most frequently *sch* (*scholde*),

1

but also *ch* (*wyrchipe*), and in unstressed positions *s* (*sall, sulde*). [Ch] is generally written *ch*, but occasionally *sch* (*schalke* 'chalk'). For both [u] and [v], *v* is usually used initially and *u* medially (*vnfaire, seuen*); *w* is used occasionally for medial [v] or [u] (*ewyn*). Both *qw* and *wh* are used for the sound derived from OE [hw] (*qwen, when*). Both *k* and *c* are used for [k] (*fawcon, frekely*).

The letter *i* is used interchangeably with *y*, and both are frequently placed after vowels to indicate length (*theis, ruydly*). The letters *e, i,* and *y* are used interchangeably throughout for the unstressed vowel before final consonants in verbs and nouns (*maylys, lyppeʒ, takyn, landis*). The letter *e* is added indiscriminately to many nouns and adjectives as a final letter. Long and short *i* and long and short *e* are written indiscriminately as *i, y, e, ei, ey, ie,* and *ye* (*riste, ryotte, slely, weife, weyne, fegure, feghte, drisside*). Apparently this interchangeability of *i* and *e* is a northern characteristic.[5] Long and short *a* are written as *a, o, au,* and, occasionally, *e* (*lange, mon, landis, laundez, keste*). Both long and short *o* are written *o* or *u*, short *o* occasionally *a* (*forth, furth, fute, farlande*). Long and short *u* are written *u, o, ou, ow* (*sonne, spoures, hownte*). The sound derived from OE *oʒ, uʒ*, long and short, is frequently written *ow, ew, eu* (*enewe, bewes* 'boughs,' *fewle*), in addition to the more common *ogh, ugh*. The doubling of vowels to show length is common. For more information on sounds, see below, "Dialect."

The text of the poem is printed as it stands in the manuscript, with the following modifications: punctuation is inserted, capitalization is normalized (including *ff* [printed as such in Brock's edition]), the scribal curl after *m* and *n* and the stroke through *ll* (both shown as final *e* [italicized] in Brock) are not reproduced, and conventional abbreviations are expanded without notice. Where *ʒ* stands for *z*, it is printed as *z*. The text is printed in verse paragraphs, sometimes corresponding to manuscript divisions marked by decorated capitals and sometimes not. The caesura is not shown.

FORMS AND INFLECTIONS

Nouns. The plural ending is *s, es, is, ys, z, ez, iz, yz* (*presoners, lates, feris, landys, landez,* etc.). Uninflected plurals are occasionally found,

:specially in expressions of quantity or measurement (*seuen wyntyre, all theire kene wapen, sextie horse*). The possessive ending is written ike the plural. The uninflected possessive is common, especially with proper names (*Arthur landes, Bedwyne knyghtez*). The random use of final *e* makes it impossible to determine other noun inflections.

Adjectives. The random use of final *e* makes it impossible to determine whether there are any remnants of the adjectival inflections (*with . . . pryse men, of full gret lordes*). As in other alliterative poetry, absolute adjectives are fairly common (*that ryall, the bolde, that wlonke*) and are occasionally coupled with prepositional phrases (*steryn in stour*) to create elegant descriptive variations reminiscent of those in OE poetry (*heard under helm* [*Bwf,* 342]). The superlative is also used in this way (*wyghteste of hanndes*). (See the discussion under "Rhetorical Style.")

Personal Pronouns. The form *scho, cho* is used throughout for the nominative third person singular feminine. The northern *they, them,* and their spelling variants are used throughout for the nominative and dative third person plural; the OE derivatives *hie, hem,* and their variants are never used. The second person singular nominative and dative forms are used interchangeably with the second person plural forms in the address of a single person, apparently without connotations of intimacy or disrespect. Though there are some passages in which the two forms appear to be used with a careful social distinction (for example Arthur, in appointing Mordred regent, addresses him throughout the passage in the second person singular, and Mordred addresses Arthur in the plural [649–92]), the distinction breaks down in such places as lines 127 and 136–39, where the senator, speaking in fear of Arthur's lion-like visage addresses the King in the singular; and in 247–302, in the passage in which the men make their battle vows, where Cador addresses the King as *ʒow,* and King Angus addresses Arthur as *thow.* No rule can be drawn, therefore, for the use of these pronouns in the poem.

The plural of majesty is used rarely in the *Morte Arthure.* Arthur usually refers to himself with the singular pronoun. Most of the instances in which he does use the plural may be interpreted as collective references to himself and his men; for example, *Thus hafe we*

euydens to aske þe emperour þe same (286) and *Now may we reuell and riste, fore Rome es oure awen* (3207). It may be significant that the only example that can be identified definitely as a plural of majesty occurs in an arrogant statement that Arthur makes when he is at his zenith, just after the capitulation of Rome and just before the dream prophesying his downfall: *We sall be ouerlynge of all þat on the erthe langez. / We will by þe Crosse Dayes encroche þeis londez / And at þe Crystynmesse daye be crowned theraftyre* (3211–13).

A construction that appears frequently in the poem is the intensification of a pronoun (sometimes a noun) by *selfe, selfen, selve, selven*. According to Mustanoja, though this combination was used in OE and early ME with intensifying force, in the course of time this quality dropped away and *selfe* became a redundancy.[6] In the *Morte Arthure* this expression appears to be used in both ways (as well as reflexively, of course).

The nonexpression of pronouns, personal and relative, is another characteristic feature of the *Morte Arthure*. However, as Mustanoja has noted,[7] it is often difficult to determine whether a given illustration represents the nonexpression of the subject pronoun or the nonexpression of the relative pronoun, as the following examples illustrate: *And that es Sir Mordrede, þat þow has mekyll praysede / [who/he] Sall be thy dictour, my dere, to doo whatte the lykes* (711–12); *Drechede with a dragon, and syche a derfe beste / [who/he] Has mad me full wery* (811–12). There are also many situations in which the nonexpression of the subject pronoun may be interpreted as the nonexpression of a coordinating conjunction between two verbs: *Thane þe Conquerour kyndly carpede to þose lordes [he/and] Rehetede þe Romaynes with realle speche* (220–21); *Sir Cador of Cornewayle to þe Kyng carppes [he/and] Lughe on hym luffly with lykande lates* (247–48). Nonexpression of the object pronoun is also fairly common: *Be sekyre of þi sowdeours, and sende [them] to þe mowntes* (551); *Schirreues scharply schiftys the comouns / Rewlys [them] before þe ryche of the Rounde Table* (725–26).

Demonstrative Pronouns. The plural of *this* is usually *these*, with a number of spelling variants, occasionally *thire* and its variants. The plural forms of *that* are *tho* and *those* and their variants. Both demonstrative pronouns are used where formal ModE requires the definite

article (*This ilke kyde conquerour* [65]; *That comlyche conquerour* [71]; *thes cheualrous knyghttez* [1619]; *thas lordlyche byernes* [2281]), although, according to Mustanoja, by the beginning of the thirteenth century these forms had assumed a definitely demonstrative character.[8] This usage seems to parallel colloquial ModE.

Verbs. The infinitive is occasionally written with an *en* (*wonnen, drenschen*), more frequently without any ending, or simply with a scribal *e* (*schewe*). The present participle has the northern ending *and*(*e*) or *aund*(*e*) (*lykande, chawngawnde*), with only one example of *ynge* (*chawngynge*). The past participle of strong verbs ends in *n, en;* there is no trace of the OE prefix in the past participles. In the present indicative, the first person singular has either the ending *e* (*I loue*) or no ending (*I sall*); very rarely *s* or *es* (*I . . . dyghttes*). The second and third person singular ends in *es, ys, is, ez* (*thow ocupyes, Syr Cador . . . comforthes*). In the plural, in instances in which the personal pronoun or noun immediately precedes the verb, the ending is usually *e* (*we fynde, they schounte, ʒe mayntene*). Where the noun or pronoun and the verb are separated by another word or words, the verb ending is northern *es*, with numerous spelling variants (*Schirreues scharply schiftys*). The northern ending *en* appears in both constructions (*they swappen, The pryce schippez of the porte prouen*).

The preterite ending of weak verbs is *ed*(*e*) and its variants *t*(*e*), *d*(*e*), *id*(*e*), *yd*(*e*); in those verbs whose stem ends in a dental, the ending is often dropped (*He command*).[9] Strong verbs in the preterite have no ending in the singular, *e* in the plural (*þey knewe*), very rarely *en* (*þey sprangen*). The present and preterite subjunctive ending is usually *e*, singular and plural, occasionally *en* (*ʒife we . . . withstonden*), though this last may be simply the indicative used as the subjunctive. Northern apocopated forms are occasionally found (*tase, mase, bus, has*).[10]

The impersonal construction of verbs was very popular in ME and was used not only with impersonal but also with personal verbs inherited from OE (e.g., *seem*), as well as with many verbs borrowed from OF and ON.[11] Though the personal construction became increasingly dominant as the ME period wore on, in the *Morte Arthure*, it is the impersonal construction that seems to predominate with many

common verbs (*wham þem lykys* [186]; *vs no skathe lympe* [1643]; *Me thoughte* [3230]), the personal appearing only rarely (*they no skathe lymppen* [3119], *þow dremyde* [815]). However, since these verbs are in a state of transition, many of these constructions may be interpreted alternatively as personal constructions with the dative pronoun functioning as the nominative.

Another common feature of the poem is the appearance of many verbs in a form that can be described only as a cross between the imperative and subjunctive moods. These are usually found in exclamations that come at the end of speeches or descriptive passages, usually accompanied by the verb *lyke,* and often used impersonally (*taste wham þem lykys* [186]; *saile when þe lykes* [381]; *chalange who lykes* [2524]).

Occasionally the verb is unexpressed, especially *be, do,* and *go* (*That will he neuer* [do] *for no wye of all þis werlde ryche* [515]; *Qwen all was schyppede that sholde* [be] *they schounte no lengere* [736]. There is a scarcity of verbs in some of the long descriptive passages, which consist, for the most part, of noun clauses linked by a loose syntax. The description of the feast (176–219) is the most striking example; others are the catalogue of Arthur's conquests (25–51) and the description of Arthur's arming just before his fight with the giant (900–915).

The present tense alternates throughout, apparently indiscriminately, with the preterite. Mustanoja, who uses the term "historical present" for this verb use, notes its spectacular increase around the middle of the fourteenth century, possibly under the influence of OF poetry, and suggests that it is used in an effort to create vividness.[12] It is difficult to detect any such rationale for its use in the *Morte Arthure,* as the following example illustrates: *Than Sir Priamous þe prynce in presence of lordes / Presez to his penown and pertly it hentes / Reuertede it redily and awaye rydys* (2916–18). If the present tense is intended to convey vividness, it is difficult to see why in this, a typical example, it is not sustained throughout and why such an important verb as *Reuertede,* describing Priamus' swinging his banner around in order to carry it over to Gawain's side, should be in the preterite.

VOCABULARY

In addition to basic grammatical features such as the feminine and third personal plural pronouns and the present participle, which may be the work of the scribe rather than the original poet, the vocabulary of the *Morte Arthure* contains a substantial number of Scandinavian words, supporting the theory of a north midlands origin. Many of these words alternate with native synonyms or cognates, the choice between the native and the ON word obviously dictated, in many cases, by the alliteration: *Vnsaughtely he* saide *hym þese sittande wordez* (1501), *Then* carpys *the Conquerour crewell wordez* (132); *Sir Arthure . . .* Wente *to hys wardrop and warp of hys wedez* (900–01), *Then blythely fro Bareflete he* buskes *on þe morne* (1223); *Schirreues scharply* schiftys *the comouns* (725), *Scathyll Scottlande by skyll he* skyftys *as hym lykys* (32).

A very great proportion of the vocabulary of the *Morte Arthure* is of French origin. According to Matthews,[13] the percentages of OF words recorded in four selected passages (22, 15, 18, and 15 percent) are not only much higher than those for ME poetry in general, but also much higher than those of other ME alliterative poetry (*Sir Gawain,* 8, 10, *Patience,* 5, both passages of several hundred lines), decreasing the likelihood that the OF words were chosen solely for their alliterative qualities. Matthews also notes that many of these words are either not recorded at all in the *OED* or the *MED,* or are recorded as appearing in *Morte Arthure* only, and that many more recorded elsewhere are rare. This unusually high percentage, along with the French forms of some of the proper names (*Cayon* [2380], *Cadors* [4188]) and the numerous complimentary references to France, has led Matthews to posit an unknown French work as the source of the poem.

DIALECT

There is disagreement about the dialectical area in which the *Morte Arthure* was composed. Though the northern scribe, Robert Thornton, changed many of the forms in the MS from which he copied to northern forms, he did not change them all, and the text as it survives is mixed.[14] A southern provenance is precluded by the

complete absence of such characteristics as *est* and *eth* verb inflections in the present indicative second and third person singular and
plural, the plural pronoun forms *hem* and *her,* and the preverb *i* in
the present participle of strong verbs. Some of the more common
non-northern forms that stand in the text and that suggest a midland
dialect for the original poem are (1) *sore* (1173), *brode* (116), with
the vowel descended from OE *ā* rounded to *ō,* in addition to northern
sare (134), *brade* (106); (2) *en* verb inflections in the present
plural, *þey chaungen* (168), in addition to the northern *es, ez, fers
feghtande folke folowes* (4257); (3) *ȝife* (1668), *myche* (4062),
along with the northern forms with hard consonants, *gyffe* (1503),
mekill (1236).

Two notable attempts have been made to further localize this midland dialect. S. O. Andrew [15] (whose purpose it was to refute the contention of F. J. Amours and others that the original poem was in a
northern dialect), after citing evidence that the underlylng dialect is
midlands and admitting that there are no specifically west-midland
dialect characteristics in the poem, goes on to localize the original
poem as northwest midland on the basis of the following evidence.
(1) In line 3064 the pronoun *he* appears, where, Andrew maintains,
the feminine pronoun is required. This could only mean that Thornton was copying a text which contained the western pronoun *ho,*
which Thornton mistook for *he* and failed to change to *scho, cho* as
he had all other occurrences of the pronoun. (2) Western preterites
with *e* endings are found: *bere* (1486), *breke* (4146 [incorrectly
cited as 4147 by Andrew]). (3) Though there are no instances of
the western forms *mon, bonk,* and the like, Thornton's unusual *blank*
for *blonk* (1799, 1860) suggests an *over*-correction resulting from
the habitual changing of *o*'s to *a*'s in such words; thus, many western
forms with *o* must have stood in the original. (4) Though there are
no instances of the western plural pronouns *her* or *hem* in the poem,
in a number of cases the northern forms *their, them* occur after the
plural verb ending *en,* as in *faken þeire coblez* (742). Since the *en*
ending is preferred in alliterative poetry before words beginning with
h or a vowel, Andrew maintains, *her* and *hem* must have stood in the
original. These spurious arguments have been influential. J. P. Oakden, after cataloguing the northern and midland features in the dialect

and admitting that there are no specific west-midland characteristics in the poem, appears to acknowledge the possibility of a west-midland origin based on Andrew's conjectural feminine pronoun and the supposed implications of *blank*.[16]

Andrew's arguments have been attacked by Angus McIntosh,[17] who points out that, as Andrew himself admits, no specifically west-midland forms are to be found in the poem (he admits that *mony* occurs, but states that he has found this form in other texts known to be east midland) and that all of Andrew's arguments rest upon ingenious but unconvincing conjectures. To McIntosh's observation may be added the following points, which further undermine Andrew's case: (1) It is by no means certain that a feminine pronoun stood in the original at line 3064. The poet frequently uses pronouns to refer to remote or obscure antecedents (see, for example, line 3072, in which *Thay* refers, not to the people of the city, who have been the subject of the preceding four lines, but to Sir Florent and his followers, mentioned only in a prepositional phrase). There is no reason to suppose that the poet is not referring to the Duke, rather than the Duchess here; the Duke is the logical person to surrender the city, and the Duchess is mentioned as having only been sent out to plead for mercy. (2) The words *bere* (1486) and *breke* (4146) are not preterite forms; the former is in the historical present and the latter in the present tense as it is used to signify future time.[18]

McIntosh maintains not only that a west-midland provenance has not satisfactorily been proven, but also that what evidence exists actually points to an *east*-midland origin. By a very complicated process he concludes that the original MS of the *Morte Arthure* was at least two steps removed from Thornton's MS and that it contained the following forms that he has found common in texts known to be specifically east midland: *swych* and its spelling variants, *iche, miche, schall þoghe, ȝif, aȝeynez, dethe, throughe, chirche,* and *–lyche, –lich*.[19]

The assumption of a west-midland provenance for the *Morte Arthure,* and for all the other alliterative poems as well, has also been attacked by J. R. Hulbert, who contends that many of the characteristics cited by commentators as evidence of a west-midland origin are not dialectical features exclusive to that area.[20]

AUTHOR

A great part of the early scholarship on the *Morte Arthure* centered on a hotly debated question of authorship. The starting point of this debate is a reference in the rhymed chronicle (c. 1400) of the Scottish poet Andrew of Wyntoun. In speaking of other poets who have dealt with the history of Arthur, Andrew mentions a person with the mysterious name "Huchon (var. Hucheon, Huchown) of þe Aule Reale," who, he says, "made a gret Gest of Arthure / And the Awntyr of Gawane / Þe Pistil [Epistle] als of Suet Susane" (4311-13). The latter is a known ME alliterative poem based upon the Biblical story of Susannah; the other two works have not been identified with certainty. It was proposed by John Pinkerton in 1792 that, *Huchon* being an alternate form of *Hew*, this poet is to be identified with Sir Hew of Eglintoun, a Scottish poet mentioned by Dunbar as preceding Wyntoun.[21] In 1878 Moritz Trautmann attempted to show that Huchon, whose identification he accepted as Sir Hew of Eglintoun, wrote not only the *Pistil of Susan* but also the *Morte Arthure,* which he identifies with the "gret Gest of Arthure" mentioned by Wyntoun.[22] George Neilson, a Scotsman, not only accepted Trautmann's conclusions but went on to assert, on the basis of metrical similarities, that Huchon, or Sir Hew, had written not only the *Pistil of Susan* and the *Morte Arthure,* but almost all of the extant alliterative poetry as well (*Sir Gawain and the Green Knight* is identified with the "Awntyr of Gawane") and that *Aule Ryale* is a reference to the royal hall, or king's hall, of Scotland.[23] Neilson's claims are denied by Henry N. MacCracken, who also systematically disproves all of Trautmann's metrical arguments for the connection of *Susan* and *Morte Arthure* and concludes that the only fact that is certain is that a poet named Huchon wrote the *Pistil of Susan.*[24] The author of the *Morte Arthure,* therefore, remains unknown, but in the literature he is frequently referred to as Huchon.

The Huchon debate has long since died down, and the only thing that can be said with certainty today concerning the author is that correspondences between details that appear in the *Morte Arthure* and *The Awntyrs off Arthure at the Terne Wathelyne* (a short alliterative poem in stanza form that appears in the Thornton manuscript) suggest a special relationship that may indicate a common authorship.

These correspondences are summarized by Matthews:

> Some uncommon resemblances occur in the heraldic devices used in the two poems. The device borne by Gawain is usually described in romances as a double-headed eagle or a lion—*Sir Gawain and the Green Knight* is unique in making it a pentangle. In both *Morte Arthure* and *Awntyrs of Arthure,* however, this device is slightly different from normal—one or more 'griffones of golde.' More striking is their agreement about Mordred's device. Descriptions of the traitor's arms are rare in the romances, but heraldic authorities say that they were very similar to Gawain's. . . . It is persuasive evidence of the connection of *Morte Arthure* and *Awntyrs of Arthure,* therefore, that they agree in describing his arms as a saltire engrailed, the former mentioning 'þe sawturoure engrelede' (l. 4182), the latter 'a sawtire engrelede of siluer fulle schene' (l. 307).

> Equally curious correspondences occur in topographical and personal names. The campaign in Italy that forms an unusual part of *Morte Arthure* is briefly alluded to in one line of *Awntyrs:* 'Ther salle in tuskayne be tallde of that tresone' (l. 291); and a similar passing reference is made to Fortune's wheel: 'Maye no mane stere hym [Arthur] of strenghe whilles þe whele standis' (l. 266). The ghost of Guenevere's mother, prophesying the death of Gawain, tells him that 'in a slake þou salle be slayne' (l. 298); in *Morte Arthure,* the uncommon Norse loanword 'slake' . . . is used just before Gawain lands for his final battle . . . (l. 3719). This prophecy contains further topographical details that make it fairly sure what was the source:

> > And ther salle the Rownde Tabille losse the renowne
> > Be-syde ramessaye, fulle ryghte as a rydynge,
> > And at Dorsett salle dy the doghetyeste of all.
> > (ll. 293–295)

The riding beside Romsey (seven miles from Southampton and still nearer to Winchester) corresponds to the battle between Southampton and Winchester in *Morte Arthure,* and although Dorset is incorrect . . . the name must derive from a line in *Morte Arthure* . . . 'Thane drawes he to Dorsett, and dreches no langere' (l. 4052).[25]

DATE

The date of composition of the *Morte Arthure* is also uncertain and still being debated. The latest possible date is 1440—established as the latest date for the copying of the Thornton MS.[26] The dating of one of the likely sources, the *Voeux de Paon,* at 1310 fixes the earliest limits. Neilson, who regards Edward III as the model for Arthur and the poem as a criticism of the Hundred Years' War, suggests the date 1365, which has gained wide acceptance.[27] Harvey Eagleson supports Neilson's date with the rather weak argument that the description of Lady Fortune's costume (3251–59) accords with the feminine costume of that date in England.[28] Eagleson's entire case seems to be based upon the identification of the *lappes* of line 3254 with the long, trailing sleeves which he says were popular in the dress of that date. Finlayson undermines Eagleson's case by showing that *lappes* may refer to any long, trailing fold of a garment and that, even if the word could be proved to refer to the sleeves this fact would be of no help in dating the poem, since such sleeves are not peculiar to the costume of 1365.[29] Finlayson also attacks Neilson's arguments by showing that many of the place names and historical references that are supposed to be drawn directly from the contemporary events of Edward's reign could as well have been taken by the poet from a secondary source and need not be contemporaneous with the writing of the poem. In support of his argument Finlayson shows that a number of the references are found in the Chandos Herald's *Life of the Black Prince,* written in 1385. Finlayson's main concern is to show that the 1365 date is not necessarily the only possible date, rather than to propose a new date. He does not maintain that the references must have come from the *Life of the Black Prince,* only that they might have. Though his evidence is mainly negative, Finlayson does suggest the last quarter of the fourteenth century as his preference for the date.

EDITIONS

The *Morte Arthure* was published for the first time in 1847 by J. O. Halliwell in a limited edition of 75 copies, under the title *The Alliterative Romance of the Death of King Arthur.* It was edited again

in 1865 for the Early English Text Society by George Perry (O.S. 8).
A revision of Perry's edition was produced by Edmund Brock in 1871,
and this text was reprinted by the Early English Text Society in 1961,
making it the only text of the entire poem available in recent years.
Unfortunately, the critical apparatus accompanying Brock's edition
is meager: the glossary is inadequate, the text is accompanied by only
a few cryptic notes, and the Introduction consists of only a rudimen-
tary discussion of meter. The edition of Mary M. Banks, which appeared in 1900 (London: Longmans, Green, and Co.) is accompanied by a more ample Introduction and set of notes, primarily
explanatory rather than textual, and a glossary that presents a few
advances over that of Brock. Miss Banks' edition was supplemented a
few years later by an article in which she discusses some of the cruxes
and textual problems presented by the poem.[30]

In spite of their shortcomings, the editions of both Brock and
Banks have the virtue of presenting a fairly conservative text. In the
very year, however, that Banks' edition appeared, there also appeared
a lengthy article by Franz Joseph Mennicken [31] in which it was contended that the *Morte Arthure* MS. was extremely corrupt. Mennicken
proposed regularizing the meter and the alliteration of the text through
extensive emendation, with hundreds of changes proposed. A number
of similar articles appeared following Mennicken,[32] and under the influence of these scholars Erik Björkman published his edition in 1915
(Heidelberg: Carl Winters). Björkman's edition contained a much
more ample critical apparatus than any of the earlier editions, including (1) a generous introduction with an extensive bibliography, a
summary of dialectical and orthographic forms, a brief discussion of
versification, and a summary of the poem; (2) a more complete
glossary than had ever been available and the only one until now
with derivations cited; and (3) extensive notes, with discussions of
textual problems and full references to every scholarly work on the
poem through 1915 (all of this, however, in German). Unfortunately,
Björkman accepted and printed a great number of the emendations
proposed by Mennicken and others (however, with the original MS
readings and all other proposed emendations printed at the bottom of
every page of text). In 1935 J. L. N. O'Loughlin demonstrated that
the German scholars were too rigid in their alliterative and metrical
requirements, and most of the changes they favored were unnecessary.

(See below, "Alliteration and Meter," for a detailed discussion of O'Loughlin's work.) O'Loughlin's study undermines the value of Björkman's edition, which is marred also by his adoption of the theory of this school on the pronunciation of final *e* and emending accordingly (see below, "Alliteration and Meter").

The desirability of a conservative handling of the text suggested by O'Loughlin was further supported by the discovery in 1934 of the Winchester MS. of Malory's *Le Morte d'Arthur*. Malory's Book V in the Winchester version proved to be much closer to its source, the *Morte Arthure*, than the Caxton version perviously known. The Winchester MS. supported a number of the MS readings that had been emended by Björkman. It must be mentioned, however, that, whereas the Winchester MS. was generally regarded as supporting the case for a conservative handling of the text, it seems to have affected O'Loughlin in the opposite way. Curiously, he reverses himself and regards the passages in which the Winchester MS. does not coincide with the *Morte Arthure* as indications of rampant corruption of the alliterative poem.[33] However, in the closest comparison of the two works published to date,[34] William Matthews argues against assuming that Malory's deviations from the Thornton MS. must result from his following a more correct text of the *Morte Arthure*. As Matthews shows, Malory's instances of more nearly perfect alliteration are not necessarily derived from another alliterative text, as alliteration is to be found throughout *all* of Malory's work, even in places where he was translating directly from the French. Malory, according to Matthews, simply had a fondness for and facility in alliteration, and there is no reason to suppose that his deviations from the Thornton MS. are not simply his own inventions.

John Finlayson, in his edition of the *Morte Arthure*, published in 1967 (London: Edward Arnold), recognized the need for a conservative handling of the text and accordingly reproduced the manuscript readings very closely. However, Finlayson's edition, though it has a good general introduction and some interesting notes, contains an abridged text, amounting to about half the original, and no discussion of textual and editorial problems.

O'Loughlin's contention that many of the emendations proposed by Mennicken and Holthausen were based on overly rigid metrical and alliterative requirements is accepted here, and emendations are cor

sidered only in cases where no sense can be made of the MS reading. To O'Loughlin's argument might be added the observation that the very obviousness of many of the emendations proposed for the purpose of regularizing the alliteration may actually be evidence against the case for emendation. The very ease with which a line such as *For it is sakles of syn sa helpe me oure Lorde* (3992) can be regularized to *For it is sakles of syn sa save me oure Lorde* (see 1687 for this B-verse) could indicate a conscious effort on someone's part to avoid the regular alliteration. Since such instances of irregularity of alliteration where regularity would be easy are so frequent in *Morte Arthure,* it is possible that some subtle effect is being attempted that could only be apparent to someone more finely attuned to alliterative poetry than we are.[35]

Therefore, in the text printed here, in instances in which the alliteration fails according to the pattern noted by O'Loughlin (see below, "Alliteration and Meter") or in which it falls upon a prefix that might be stressed, either naturally or artificially, the line is accepted as it stands in the MS, and no comment is made in the notes. The other problematical passages are discussed, and the MS reading is retained wherever possible. Where an emendation is made, an attempt is made to account for the scribal error.

THE STORY

The poem begins with Arthur, already the triumphant conqueror of a great part of western Europe, celebrating his victories surrounded by faithful knights and vassals. A challenge to his supremacy comes in the form of messengers from the Emperor Lucius demanding that the King pay homage as a vassal of Rome. Arthur delays his answer, first entertaining the Roman embassy with an elaborate feast and then calling his men to council. After his prominent vassals swear to support him and urge him to war, Arthur imperiously hurls the challenge back at the messengers and orders them to return to Rome.

Arthur and Lucius rally their armies, the allies of Lucius consisting primarily of barbarians and Saracens, and Arthur sets sail from Britain, leaving Mordred as regent. On the sea Arthur dreams of a battle between a dragon and a bear, which ends with the dragon

victorious, apparently a forecast of the adventure that immediately follows. Upon landing in Brittany, Arthur fights and slays single-handed the giant of St. Michael's Mount, who has carried off and devoured many people of that land, including the Duchess of Brittany herself.

Learning that the Emperor has reached France, Arthur sends a party of knights, including Gawain, to him, demanding that he leave the King's lands. Insults are exchanged, Gawain slays the Emperor's uncle, and the Britons flee, beating back the pursuing Romans with the help of a party of reinforcements. Arthur is delighted with the victory and sends a group of knights to Paris with the Roman prisoners that have been taken. The party is ambushed, and, after a fierce fight against heavy odds in which many Britons are killed, Arthur's men are victorious, but Arthur rebukes the leader, Cador, for engaging in a battle against such great odds. Finally, after some more skirmishing, the battle with the Emperor takes place: Arthur's knights fulfill the vows they had made in council, Lucius is slain, and Arthur is victorious, but Kay, Bedevere, and many other British knights are slain. Arthur sends the bodies of his enemies back to Rome with a scornful message and buries his men with great honors.

After his victory over Lucius, Arthur decides to make war on the Duke of Lorraine, who he claims is a disloyal vassal. He settles down to a siege of the city of Metz, sending Gawain and other knights out on a foraging expedition. Gawain, looking for adventure, encounters and fights Priamus, a Saracen knight, in a joust that ends with the two knights becoming friends and Priamus apparently converting to Christianity.

A battle against the Duke's forces and the siege of the city both end in victory for Arthur, who then marches down into Italy, conquering city after city in a campaign that ends with the Romans, including an emissary of the Pope, offering Arthur the Imperial crown. Just at this moment of greatest triumph, Arthur has a second dream, in which he sees eight of the nine great heroes or "worthies" of history in various positions on Lady Fortune's wheel. He himself is set atop the wheel, befriended briefly by Fortune, and then hurled down and crushed. His sages tell him that the dream portends the end of his triumphs and counsel him to shrive himself and prepare for his death. The morning after the dream, Arthur encounters a knight of his

court, Cradok, dressed in humble clothes like a pilgrim and traveling to Rome, who informs him of Mordred's seizure of the crown and adultery with Guinevere.

Arthur hastens back to Britain and engages in a sea battle with Mordred's heathen allies. After their victory, Gawain and his men rashly go ashore and engage in a battle against heavy odds, which ends with the slaying of Gawain by Mordred. Arthur grievously laments Gawain's death, realizes that his own fortunes are at an end, and vows vengeance on Mordred. In a final battle, Arthur receives his death wound at Mordred's hand, but continues fighting until he slays Mordred in turn. Arthur is taken to Glastonbury, where he is shriven, dies, and is buried with great magnificence.

SOURCES

In general outline, the story told in the *Morte Arthure* is the last segment of the chronicle version of Arthur's life told originally by Geoffrey of Monmouth and retold by Wace, Laȝamon, and other chroniclers such as Peter of Langtoft, Robert of Gloucester, and Robert Mannyng of Brunne. However, the immediate source of the *Morte Arthure* is uncertain. It may have been one of these or another version of the chronicle story now lost. Paul Branscheid, in the earliest study of the poem's sources—a detailed comparison of the text with the known chronicle versions—concludes that the poet depended most heavily on Geoffrey himself, with many borrowings from Laȝamon.[36] Branscheid's case rests mainly on general resemblances and is weak. William Matthews notes that the use of Laȝamon as a source is especially unlikely, as there are none of the verbal correspondences that one would expect between two alliterative poems with the same subject.[37] In fact, as J. L. N. O'Loughlin points out, the appearance of the rare word *lothyn* 'shaggy' in the *Morte Arthure* (1097) and at a corresponding place in Mannyng's version of the story may point to Mannyng as the immediate source.[38] Tania Vorontzoff notes that in the section of Malory's work thought to be based on the *Morte Arthure,* alliterative phrases appear that do not appear in the *Morte Arthure* itself, and she conjectures that Malory must have followed another now lost English alliterative poem, which was also the source

of the *Morte Arthure*.[39] Vorontzoff's argument is weakened by a recent study in which Matthews shows that Malory himself was adept at alliteration and used it throughout his work.[40] Because of the poem's unusually large French vocabulary (see above, "Vocabulary"), Matthews argues for a now lost French version of the chronicle story as the immediate source.[41]

To the basic chronicle story, someone has made extensive additions. One is the episode in which Gawain, on a foraging expedition during Arthur's siege of Metz, jousts with and overcomes the Saracen knight Priamus (2513–2715).[42] R. H. Griffith has shown this section to be derived from the French romance *Fierabras* (or its English version *Sir Ferumbras*), in which Charlemagne's paladin Oliver jousts with the Saracen knight Fierabras, who, in the middle of the fight, suddenly decides to convert to Christianity.[43] In addition to some minor resemblances, the two accounts show striking parallels: (1) the sudden conversion of the Saracen (*MA,* 2587–88); (2) the Christian's pretense (carried to great lengths in *Fierabras*) that he is of low status (2620–31); (3) the healing of both men's wounds by a magic balm which the Saracen carries (2704–13); and (4) the Saracen's informing the Christian that an army is in ambush near at hand (2650–67). In line with Griffith's suggestion, it may be significant that British Museum Egerton 3028, a mid-fourteenth-century manuscript written in England, contains an abridgment of Wace's *Roman de Brut,* bound together with a version of *Fierabras.*

The Gawain-Priamus story stands out as an addition, perhaps because its romantic tone contrasts with that of the rest of the poem (see below, "Genre"). Matthews emphasizes, however, that this much-discussed episode is only a part of the long segment (2386–3083) recounting Arthur's invasion of Lorraine and besieging of Metz, itself the largest addition to the poem. Matthews brings into focus this whole section, which Griffith regards as "useless" and merely a frame for the Gawain story. As would be expected of such a substantial addition, it is an important part of the structure of the work, since it is the section in which Arthur turns from fighting a defensive war to waging a war of aggression. In discussing its source, Matthews does not discount Griffith's theory of *Fierabras* as an influence on the Gawain-Priamus episode, but he emphasizes the resemblance of the larger sequence to a French Alexandrian romance, *Li Fuerres de*

Gadres, which recounts a foraging expedition in the Vale of Jehose-
phat by a party of Alexander's knights during the siege of Tyre. The
outline of both stories is the same: siege, foraging expedition, the
encounter of an enemy leading a large host, the overcoming of
superior forces, return to the siege, and reduction of the city. Matthews
also notes a number of similar details: the rashness of both leaders
(*MA,* 2428–47), the cruelty of the siege (3036–43), the desire of the
knights to fight, though outnumbered, to avoid reproach when they
return to their comrades (2727–28), the youth slain in battle (2952–
88), and some unusual names (*Vale of Josephas,* 2876; *Ferraunt,*
2760, 2765; *Floridas,* 2755, 2778, 2780).[44]

The other long section added to the chronicle story is the dream
of Fortune (3218–3455). Matthews also finds parallels for this
sequence in the Alexandrian literature: the description of the Nine
Worthies set up on Fortune's wheel appears to be based on a similar
description in another Alexandrian tale in Old French, the *Voeux du
Paon* (*The Vows on the Peacock*). This work is also, according to
Matthews, the source of the four vows made by Arthur's prominent
vassals in the council scene (added to the original three in the chronicles) that are later fulfilled on the battlefield (320–94; 2050–94;
3084–3175). These four are based on a similar pattern of vows and
fulfillment in the French work.

A possible source of details in the poem is contemporary history.
George Neilson notes that particulars of Arthur's battles parallel those
of the battles of Edward III,[45] but it is uncertain whether these were
drawn from contemporary events, as Neilson maintains, or from later
chronicle accounts, as suggested by John Finlayson (see further
discussion above, "Date").[46]

GENRE

The *Morte Arthure* eludes neat classification. Perhaps because
Arthurian subjects are usually associated with romances and because
there are a few romantic elements in the poem, A. C. Baugh and
others assume that it is a romance.[47] Its tone is, however, predom-
nantly heroic and is so recognized by such critics as George Kane
(though he treats it in a chapter on romance and actually calls it a
romance)[48] and Dorothy Everett.[49] Both point out resemblances to

Old English heroic poetry: the emphasis on generosity as one of the prime virtues of a king; the loyalty of the men to their lord, stronger even than blood ties (see lines 4142–54); the stylized boasts, threats, and insults exchanged before battle, reminiscent of the OE *bēots;* the council of advisors called by Arthur before declaring war on Lucius, resembling the Anglo-Saxon *witan;* and the speeches with which the leaders fire up their men before battle. Cador's speech rousing his greatly outnumbered men just before the encounter with the Roman host is singled out as especially striking in its resemblance to the speeches made by Byrhtnoth's men in *The Battle of Maldon* (*MA,* 1726–37).[50] However, most of these "heroic" details may in fact be only the universal accompaniments of any kind of literary description of warfare. They are paralleled as closely by descriptions of contemporary events in the chronicles of Froissart as they are by OE poetry.[51]

Eric Auerbach defines a romance as the story of a solitary knightly adventure in a setting detached from any political or historical reality. Its purpose is to test a knight's personal perfection in chivalric virtue, in deeds of arms or courtly love.[52] Though many of the virtues so tested are the same as the knightly virtues of heroic poetry (courage, strength, loyalty), in a romance they are put to little social or political purpose and are tried in a setting of magic and mystery, rather than of war or conquest. By Auerbach's definition, most of the adventures in the *Morte Arthure* are not romantic, but heroic. There is no courtly love in the poem and few solitary adventures. Most of the deeds of arms serve a political purpose: in the first part of the poem the defense of Arthur's kingdom against Roman aggression; in the second, the widening of Arthur's conquests; and in the third, the defense of the kingdom against treachery. Most of the deeds are part of battles, social and collective rather than individual undertakings (though they may be described as duels between leaders).

Two adventures in the *Morte Arthure* are undertaken by solitary knights: Arthur's battle with the giant of St. Michael's Mount just before the war with Lucius and Gawain's encounter with Priamus just after Lucius' defeat. These have been regarded as romantic interludes in an otherwise heroic poem, and the Gawain-Priamus episode, at least, is romantic. It is motivated by the desire for adventure, with Gawain going out all alone in the early morning, *wondyrs to seke*

His opponent is engaged because he looks like a worthy adversary, not because he is an enemy in war; the jousting is a test to determine who is the better man, not a battle which will have any political consequences; and the wounds that are inflicted are healed with a magic balm. Arthur's adventure with the giant, however, is not romantic in Auerbach's sense. The poet has, of course, changed a collective expedition into a singlehanded venture (in the chronicles, Kay and Bedevere accompany Arthur throughout), and there are some romantic trappings—the idealized nature setting (see below, "Rhetorical Style"), the abduction of a lady, and the suggestion of the supernatural in the giant's ghoulish nature. However, the poet's purpose in having Arthur undertake this adventure alone is not to subject his hero to a ritualized test but, as Finlayson points out, to glorify him as a great Christian hero and defender of his people.[53] His adversary is not only a supernatural being and lady's abductor, but an imperialistic aggressor, the oppressor of Arthur's people, and the murderer of Christian children. The slaying is thus a political and social act and the adventure heroic.

The most important recent study of the *Morte Arthure* characterizes the work as a tragedy. William Matthews sees the poem as primarily the story of the rise and fall of a great king, with the fall brought about not only by capricious Fortune, but also by the change that takes place in the hero's character. According to Matthews, Arthur, in the course of his military successes, becomes overconfident and corrupted by power; his wars change from defensive to aggressive; and he is finally destroyed, in part by his own pride. The King's transformation, in Matthews' view, is shown by the following contrasts. (1) Arthur embarks on a war with Lucius to defend his own kingdom against Lucius' imperial ambitions. Once the Romans are overcome, Arthur decides to bring the Duke of Lorraine under his yoke, behaving toward the Duke exactly as Lucius had toward him. In the war in Lorraine he besieges the city of Metz in a brutal and unmerciful manner (*MA,* 3036–53). (2) Arthur, early in the poem, rebukes Cador for his rashness (1922–27). Yet, during the siege of Metz Arthur behaves rashly in exposing himself openly to assault, is rebuked by one of his men, and replies with unmistakable *hubris* that as an anointed king he is invincible (2428–47). (3) The first solitary adventure, Arthur's encounter with the giant just before the war with

Lucius, is a heroic and righteous defense of the King's people against an evil. The second solitary adventure, Gawain's joust with Priamus just after the victory over Lucius, is a purposeless and private ritual which, "placed as it is at the point where Arthur's wars cease to be just . . . serves as an emphasis to the altered nature of the subsequent wars." [54] (4) In the battles against Lucius, Arthur fights Saracens and pagans, who are allied with the Emperor. After the siege of Metz, when he turns his aggressions toward Italy itself, he fights the Church, since the chief emissary who comes to surrender Rome is a Cardinal. This ambiguous picture of Arthur, as both great king and aggressive imperialist, is modeled, Matthews believes, on the picture of Alexander the Great drawn in some of the poem' sources, and may be a criticism as well of the imperial policies of Edward III.[55]

Matthews' theory brings together the heroic and romantic elements of the *Morte Arthure,* makes plain the symmetry of the poem and demonstrates that it is a work with form and balance and not simply a spinning out of miscellaneous battles and other adventures Matthews is correct in noting that there are parallels everywhere Arthur not only resembles Lucius in the second part of the poem, but in a few details he parallels the giant as well. His shaving the conquered Roman senators as a mark of humiliation after his victory parallels the giant's demanding a yearly tribute of the beards of noble kings (998–1004; 233–35). The senators kneeling to Arthur in their kirtles recalls the old woman's advice to Arthur to kneel before the giant clad only in his kirtle (1025; 2312). Arthur's reigning in triumph after his victories *as lorde in his awen* 'lord unto himself' echoes the giant's living outside of law, *as lorde in his awen* (997; 3092).

ALLITERATION AND METER

The unrhymed alliterative long line of ME poetry resembles the OE alliterative line, from which it is descended, in several respects There is a fixed number of stresses (sometimes called "lifts") in each line, usually four, but occasionally five or more, and a varying number of unstressed syllables. The chief ornamental and linking device alliteration. The line is divided syntactically in the middle by a slight

pause, or caesura, with two stresses (occasionally three) falling in the first half-line, the A verse, and two in the second half-line, the B verse. The two halves are linked by alliteration, which falls generally on the stress words. The most common alliterative pattern is aa/ax.

There are a number of important differences between the ME alliterative line and the "classic" OE type, exemplified by *Beowulf*.[56] (1) Stress and alliteration are not so restricted as they are in OE verse (where they are confined to long syllables primarily in nouns, adjectives, and non-finite verbs) but may fall on any of the main words that receive natural stress in a line, frequently the finite verb (a rare occurrence in OE poetry). (2) English having changed by the fourteenth century from a synthetic language, which is highly inflected, to an analytic language, in which many inflections are lost and meaning must be put into auxiliary words such as prepositions and articles, the rhythm of the line changed from falling (trochaic or dactylic) to rising (iambic or anapestic). (3) The long lines are strongly end-stopped, the caesura marking a slight pause but rarely the full stop that it often marks in OE poetry. Enjambment, frequent in OE, is rare. (4) Though the most common alliterative pattern is, as in OE, aa/ax, heavier alliteration is frequent, perhaps because of the need for increased alliteration to unite the longer line that resulted from the increase in articles and prepositions in the language. Alliteration is more irregular than in OE, and licenses, such as extended verses and unusual alliterative patterns, are more frequent. (5) Ornament other than increased alliteration is common: one alliterating sound often continues through two or more lines; stanzas, end rhyme, and decorative repetition of words are common; there are more alliterating consonant groups (to the OE *st, sp, sc*, which alliterate exclusively with themselves, are added such clusters as *sl, sw, br, ch, pr, tr, gr*); and there is more vocalic alliteration on the same vowel, rather than different vowels, as in OE, perhaps for appeal to the eye as well as the ear.[57] (6) With the caesura rarely marking a full stop, the substance of the narrative tends to be contained in the A verse, making it heavier than the B verse in content as well as alliteration.

The *Morte Arthure* is conservative in its alliteration, which is lighter than that of any other ME alliterative poem. The patterns that appear in it parallel the patterns in *Beowulf* more closely than do those of any other ME work. Heavy ornamental alliteration occurs

less frequently in the *Morte Arthure* than in, for example, the poems of the *Gawain* group. The pattern ax/ax is the second most common pattern in the *Morte Arthure,* as it is in *Beowulf* (though to be sure, it occurs in a much lower percentage of lines). The pattern xa/ax is the third most common pattern. These austere patterns, common in OE poetry, appear much less frequently in both the heavy alliterating poems of the *Gawain* group and in lighter alliterating poems of what might be termed the *Alexander* group, which tend to have an extremely high percentage of aa/ax lines (e.g., *The Destruction of Troy,* over 99 percent). The *Morte Arthure* also preserves the OE tendency toward a high percentage of lines with vocalic alliteration, in addition to the OE practice of alliterating on different vowels. In these respects also it is the most conservative of the ME poems. In keeping with this conservatism, the *Morte Arthure* contains none of the lettered devices so striking in poems such as *Sir Gawain* and *Pearl*—complex stanza form, ornamental repetition of words, and end rhyme.

In contrast to this conservatism, the alliteration of the *Morte Arthure* also has two striking features that are a part of the ME, rather than the OE, alliterative tradition. The alliteration frequently extends through two or more lines, a rare practice in OE, and in this respect the *Morte Arthure* is the outstanding ME poem.[58] Groups of two, three, four, and even more lines linked by a single alliterating sound are common, and in one instance the alliteration carries through no fewer than ten lines (2483–92). (2) The alliteration of new consonant clusters is also common, the following sounds alliterating with themselves often, though not exclusively: *sk, pr, ch, gr, tr, fl, cl, fr, gl,* and, a particular favorite, *sw.*

Another characteristic feature of the *Morte Arthure*'s alliteration is that there are a great number of lines in which it fails in the B verse. Early critics, particularly Franz Joseph Mennicken and his followers, assumed that such lines were corrupt and expended a staggering amount of scholarly energy trying to reconstruct their "original" readings. (See above, "Editions.") In an attack on this wholesale emendation, which included hundreds of proposed changes, J. L. N. O'Loughlin points out that, in a large percentage of the instances in which the alliteration fails, it fails according to a pattern in one of the B verses of a couplet (two lines that alliterate on one sound and form a syntactic unit).[59] O'Loughlin advocates dispensing

with emendation in all such cases, since the pattern suggests conscious design. Further, O'Loughlin points out that many more presumably corrupt lines do alliterate properly if one assumes that stress falls naturally on the prefix of certain words (as it does in ModE *rescued;* see *reschowede,* 363) or that a prefix was artificially stressed for the sake of alliteration, as perhaps in *command,* 626, *auenture,* 642, *reherse,* 3206. (Alliteration normally falls on the root syllable, if it is stressed, not the prefix.) [60]

There has also been much study of whether the *Morte Arthure* contains such alliterating combinations as h + vowels, $v + w$, $f + v$, $w + wh$ (< OE *hw*), and $w + qw$.[61] However, because there are a number of lines in the poem with the light alliterating pattern ax/ax and because the alliteration sometimes fails, it is impossible to know whether or not the poet intends to alliterate these sounds. For example, in line 1736, *I walde be wellyde all qwyke and quarterede in sondre,* it cannot be determined whether this is an example of (a)aa/ax alliteration, with *w* and *qw* alliterating, or simply xa/ax alliteration. Similarly, *And syche a vennymous flayre flowe fro his lyppez* (772) may be only an example of xa/ax alliteration, rather than aa/ax with alliteration of *v* and *f. And wyesly by þe woddez voydez his oste* may be a case of the alliteration failing in the second verse rather than an example of the aa/ax pattern with *w* and *v* alliterating.

Like the alliteration, the meter of ME alliterative poetry has evolved from that of OE. Its half-lines, or verses, are classified into categories derived from three of the five original types devised by Eduard Sievers for OE poetry: [62]

A (falling rhythm):   *Bwf* 745a: fét ond fólma

                                   MA 1989a: Fíttes his fóte-men

B (rising rhythm):   *Bwf* 857a: þætte súð ne nórð

                                   MA 2017a: This tráytour has tréunt

C (clashing rhythm):   *Bwf* 921a: of brýdbúre

                                   MA 3206a: Than this róy róyall

$$\text{x} \quad \text{x} \quad / \quad \text{x} \quad / \quad \text{x}$$

BA (rising-falling: *MA* 3221a: And fore slewthe of slomowre
rhythm [only in

$$\text{x} \quad / \quad \text{x} \quad \text{x} \quad / \quad \text{x}$$

ME])   *MA* 3238b: with montayngnes enclosyde [63]

In the *Morte Arthure,* as in all ME alliterative poetry, type B is more common than type A (in contrast to OE, in which type A prevails), since ME nouns are usually preceded by articles and prepositions. Most common is type BA, the combination of types A and B covering the many lines in ME poetry that begin with articles and prepositions and end with nouns or verbs in which the inflections are still sounded. The OE types D and E are not found in ME, because the OE poetic compounds they were created to account for do not exist in ME. Types D and E had actually disappeared very late in OE.[64]

Noting the poet's preference for feminine line endings, shown by the prevalence of type BA, early critics sought to regularize all the B verses by insisting that final scribal *e,* appearing in many words in the MS (see above, "Spelling and Sounds"), must have been sounded.[65] Marie Borroff has demonstrated that final *e* following a syllable of primary stress was not pronounced in the north by the end of the thirteenth century or in the north midlands by the end of the fourteenth (though it continued to be pronounced in the more conservative south, as illustrated by Chaucer's verse).[66] This silencing is indicated not only by the scribal omission of the letter in words where it was once pronounced, but also by the addition of random, superfluous *e*'s in words where they are unjustified etymologically. The latter practice presumably arose by analogy with the former, indicating that *e* must have been silent in the former group. The rhyming by the Gawain poet of words in both etymological groups is further proof of the silencing of final *e.* Though Borroff recognizes the preference of the alliterative poets for feminine line endings, she maintains that the masculine line ending, which appears in type B, is an infrequent but legitimate variant.

In both OE and ME poetry a verse may be expanded by increasing the usual number of unstressed syllables. In OE this usual number, one or two, may be stretched to as many as four or five, as in the following type B verse:

$$\text{x} \quad \text{x} \quad \text{x} \quad \text{x} \quad \text{x} \quad / \quad \text{x} \quad (\text{x}) \quad /$$
þara þe hit mid mundum bewand   (Bwf, 1461b).

In ME the number of unstressed syllables is usually two or three, occasionally stretched to four in the *Morte Arthure:*

    x   x   x x / x x /
    Bot þou arte a meruailous man   (260a)
    x x x x / x x   x /
    Bot euer þe senatour forsothe   (487a).

Again as in OE poetry, verses may be expanded in ME by the addition of stressed syllables, with or without alliteration. Such extended verses, termed "hypermetric" half lines, are common in the *Morte Arthure* and the other ME poems, often with the extra stresses alliterating and contributing to a lavish alliterative effect. The extra stresses almost invariably occur in the A verse:

    x   /   x   / x x x x /
    And bryng the bouxsomly as a beste   (*MA,* 107a)
    x /   / x x x   / x
    The king blyschit on the beryn   (*MA,* 116a).

About 4.3 percent of the A verses in the *Morte Arthure* are extended with alliteration, a low percentage compared with the more highly decorative verse of the *Gawain* group.

FORMULAS AND RHETORICAL STYLE

Another characteristic for which the *Morte Arthure* has always been recognized is its highly formulaic nature. J. P. Oakden long ago called attention to the frequent repetition of identical or near identical half-lines—particularly second half-lines, or B verses—in the ME alliterative poems, condemning them as empty "tags," and singling out the *Morte Arthure* as a particular offender.[67] After 1953, when F. P. Magoun began to apply Milman Parry's theory of the oral-formulaic nature of Homeric verse to OE poetry,[68] such repetitious half-lines began to be recognized as oral formulas. In 1957 R. A. Waldron initiated the study of formulas in ME alliterative poetry, using the opening lines of the *Morte Arthure* as his example.[69] Waldron's work was expanded in 1963 by John Finlayson [70] and in 1965 by Karl H. Göller,[71] with both studies based upon the *Morte Arthure,* a further testimony to its strongly formulaic nature.[72]

Both the first half lines and the second half lines of the *Morte Arthure* are formulaic, but it is the B verses that stand out as particularly stereotyped. Though there are many lines in the poem in which an essential syntactical element, such as a verb or an object, occurs in the B verse (*Thane gudly Sir Gawayne gydes his knyghttez,* 3005), in a great number of lines the basic syntactical structure of a clause is completed in the A verse, and the rest of the line is a nonessential element, such as an appositive, a nonrestrictive modifier, or a prepositional phrase (*Gas in at þe gayneste, as gydes him telles,* 3006; *I sall be at journée with gentill knyghtes,* 372; *They turne in by Thebay, terauntez full hugge,* 583). The poet has a habit of using a limited number of favorite formulas to fill in these syntactically nonessential B verses. When to this feature is added the poet's fondness for ending lines with certain favorite words, with one word used in a number of different formulas, the effect is indeed repetitious. For example, there are 120 B verses consisting of several formulas ending in the word *selfe* or *selven,* 96 ending in *lord* or *lordes,* 93 ending in *lyke* or *lykes,* 64 ending in *ryche.*[73]

In spite of their steroetyped nature, however, it is a mistake to regard these B verses as empty tags or mere fillers. In the first place, even the most repetitious are sometimes used with more subtlety than is apparent at first glance. For example, in the line *And so into Lumberddye, lykande to schewe* (498), the "tag" *lykande to schewe* 'lovely to see' is actually a dramatic expression of the Roman ambassadors' relief and happiness at finally reaching sight of their own lands after their fearful flight from Arthur's kingdom. Similarly, when Arthur takes leaves of Guinevere, to comfort her he tells her that he has made one of her favorite knights, Mordred, *Ouerlyng of Ynglande vndyre thy seluen* (after telling Mordred that he has full sovereignty). Here the *seluen* formula, one of the most frequently repeated B verses in the poem, is used to enhance the picture of Arthur's solicitude for Guinevere and to add a human touch to the passage by showing the King pretending that he has left the kingdom in her charge, with Mordred only a spokesman under her command. A third example is line 803, in which the poet exclaims, referring to the "loathly" bear that has just been slain by the dragon, *Lette hym fall in the flode, fleete whare hym lykes.* The B verse, another one of the most common formulaic phrases in the poem, seems inappropriate, a likely candi-

date for condemnation as an empty tag, for it is meaningless to say "float where he likes" or "where pleases him" of a creature who has just been slain. However, the line is pointed and emphatic if another meaning of *lykes* is considered: "to wherever befits him, is appropriate to him, to where he deserves (being such a loathly creature)."

Admittedly, the B-verse formulas are not always used with such subtlety. However, they may function in other ways. In close succession, where their stereotyped quality is even more evident than usual, they are like a refrain that helps to set the mood of a passage. In the description of the feast, the repetition of the *ynewe* 'in plenty' formula and the *taste wham þem lykys* formula enhance the picture of abundance and luxury. In the passage in which Arthur's men make their vows to support him in war, the oft-repeated *feghte (saile) when þe lykes* 'fight when you please' formula, which comes at the end of almost every speech, emphasizes the men's loyalty to Arthur and the supremacy of his will. The repetition of the *Saracens ynewe* 'Saracens in hosts' formula and its variants in the battle scenes is a constant reminder of the enemies' superior force and the courage of Arthur's men in facing such a foe (Arthur's men are vastly outnumbered in almost every battle). The formula *by þa fresche (salte) stremes* that crops up often and seemingly inappropriately in the battle scenes may set up a poignant contrast between the beauty of the landscape and the gruesomeness of the slaughter.

At the very least these stereotyped verses enhance the graphic qualities of the descriptions or serve as decoration. An example of the first is the fact that the warriors never merely strike at their foes; they always strike *with perilous wapyns* or *with growndene swerdes*, details that make the action vivid. When Bedevere is slain, the reader is told not only that it is *With a burlyche brannde*, but also that the weapon is *brode at þe hiltes* (2239), "With a stout (or hard) blade, broad at the hilt." These details, the broadness and hardness of the sword and the allusion to the hilt, particularize and concretize Bedevere's pain dramatically.

As in all alliterative poetry, the poet is aiming at solemnity, formality, and an elevated style. Thus, even if these stereotyped verses had no function other than the decorative, they would still be very much in keeping with the spirit and the other rhetorical techniques of the poem. The retardation of narrative pace, the amplification, and

the stylization that result from the use of such verses are, of course, considered desirable qualities in highly rhetorical works, contributing to an elevated tone.

Elegant variation is another rhetorical technique contributing to the poem's elevated style. It is produced by the device inherited from OE poetry of designating characters not only by their names or titles, but by a variety of synonyms for *man, warrior,* or *being*,[74] by a variety of absolute adjectives (*that hende* 'gracious one,' *this gentill*), and by nouns or absolute adjectives followed by prepositional phrases (*steryn in stour* 'fierce in battle' [*MA,* 377], comparable to OE *hearde under helm* 'hardy in helmet' [*Bwf,* 342]). In addition to providing elegant variation, this technique may aggrandize and idealize a subject through the laudatory nature of the diction. This device stylizes, rather than individualizes, characters, and the complimentary epithets tend to be the same for all characters.

Many passages in the poem are formal rhetorical "set pieces." Sometimes the laudatory epithets are used in a series to make up the conventional rhetorical passage known as the encomium. The most notable in the *Morte Arthure* is Mordred's lament for the death of Gawain (3875–85). This passage is not only an excellent example of a formal rhetorical type but also of the rhetorical ideals of amplification, idealization, and decoration. A theme, Gawain's heroic qualities, is sounded in the first line and amplified through eleven lines in variations of the traditional alliterative construction, absolute adjective followed by prepositional phrase (*hardyest of hande, happyeste in armes, hendest in hawle,* and so on). Other encomiums in the poem are King Angus's compliment to Arthur (289–91), the Roman senator's laudation of Arthur (530–37), and the templar's description of the duchess who has been carried off by the giant (860–63).

Another conventional rhetorical passage in the *Morte Arthure* is the description of costume or armor. Here again the poet aggrandizes his subject through amplification, in this case through an enumeration of details. As Benson points out, amplification through particularizing and specifying is characteristic of ME alliterative poetry.[75] That is, rather than using a generality, such as "He clothed himself in fine armor," or a simile, such as "His garb was as gay as a peacock" or "as rich as an emperor's," the alliterative poet achieves his effects by the enumeration of an abundance of concrete, usually

visual, details, with the grandeur (or humility) of a character implied by the details rather than actually stated. Four such descriptions are found in the *Morte Arthure:* the arming of Arthur before his fight with the giant (900–15); Lady Fortune and her costume (3250–59); the second arming of Arthur as he goes off alone just after the dream of Fortune (3456–65); and Sir Cradok in his humble pilgrim's dress (3468–75). The last two are juxtaposed to point up the contrast between Arthur's vainglory and the humility of the man who already knows of the destruction of the Arthurian kingdom. Similar descriptions of costume or armor are found in *Pearl* (193–228) and *Sir Gawain* (566–89).

The details that are enumerated within this stylized framework are realistic. The armor is identifiable as the "mixed armor" of the fourteenth century, a combination of the old mail shirt and the newer plates of solid armor protecting strategic parts of the body (full suits of plate armor are fifteenth century and later): on the arm the *bracer*, on the shoulder the *ailette*, on the upper arm the *rerebrace*, on the elbow the *couter*, on the forearm the *vambrace*, on the abdomen and loins the *paunce*, on the leg the *schynbawde*. The visored *basinet* is an innovation perfected in the second half of the fourteenth century.[76] The garments worn with the armor are also conventional fourteenth-century style—two garments worn beneath the mail and one above, all richly embroidered, the topmost garment emblazoned with the heraldic device of the wearer.[77] The scalloping at the edge of the surcoat also called *dagging* or *jagging*, is another true-to-life and contemporary detail, the decoration having been in vogue in the last quarter of the fourteenth century.[78]

The descriptions of the battles are also a mixture of realistic detail and stylization. The prominent part played by archers and foot soldiers in the great battle (1989–91) is a non-aristocratic and down-to-earth touch that recalls the type of warfare waged by the English under the Edwards. The disposal of Arthur's army before the battle with Lucius, according to George Neilson, resembles Edward III's disposal of his troops at Crécy (1985–2005).[79] The brigands, "genators," or light horsemen, and Genoan soldiers mentioned as Arthur's foes were all prominent participants in the battles against Edward III.[80] These and other details parallel contemporary warfare so closely that Neilson declared the battle scenes to be directly

inspired by specific battles of Edward III. The general sequence which the battles follow is also realistic—the cavalry charge with lance, followed up by an attack with the sword, sometimes further followed by an attack with the knife.

In spite of the numerous realistic details, the dominant mode of the battle descriptions is stylization. Though the battles are collective enterprises, they are usually described as duels between prominent knights, not as action involving collective tactics or strategy. The sense of magnitude of the action surrounding the principals is conveyed by the rush of formulaic phrases describing specific but conventional details such as the smashing of helms, the killing of horses, and the hewing down of men. Victory comes not as a result of tactics but as a result of one dueller slaying another.

Other stylized elements found in the battle scenes and common to other heroic poetry are the victory against impossible odds, the boasts and insults exchanged between enemies before battle, the speeches with which the leader fires up his men and gets them ready for the fight, the collection of booty after victory, and the passionate lamentation for knights who are slain, which includes weeping, swooning, and elaborate eulogizing on the battlefield.

Another formal rhetorical set piece is the nature description, of which there are four examples in the *Morte Arthure*. Three are of an ideal spring landscape and are used as settings for the two solitary adventures in the poem.[81] (The second adventure is framed by two nature descriptions, one at the beginning and one at the end, and the first, though it has an extended description only at the beginning, has a one-line allusion to nature just at its conclusion [1197]); both adventures therefore seem to be clearly framed and set off in this way from the rest of the poem.) The fourth description, which forms the setting for Arthur's dream of fortune, is a combination of wilderness landscape, "the usual opening of a significant dream"[82] and an otherworldly, ideal landscape set in the middle of the wilderness, its elements made of precious metals, resembling the elements of the dream landscape in *Pearl*.

In addition to these larger rhetorical passages, a notable feature of the style of the *Morte Arthure* is the poet's fondness for word play. Appearing frequently is *adnominatio,* the use of homonyms or near homonyms with very different meanings in close proximity, the con-

trast between them resulting in an ironic incongruity, as in *Bryne Bretayne the brade and bryttyn thy knyghtys* (106). Alliteration undoubtedly promotes the appearance of this feature.

The poet makes extensive use of ambiguity. First of all, as has been pointed out by Matthews,[83] words are used to describe the King, his actions, and his men, which can yield either a favorable or an unfavorable interpretation, suggesting the poet's view of Arthur as an Alexander figure, admirable yet sinful. The two outstanding examples of this ambiguous diction are the repeated use of the word *cruel* to designate Arthur and his actions and the use of the words *riot, riotous* in descriptions of Arthur's knights and their activities. In ModE these words are no longer ambiguous but primarily derogatory, but their use in the poem can be understood if they are compared with ModE words that retain this ambiguity. *Cruel* is similar to ModE *fierce,* which can suggest, on the one hand, savage ferocity and on the other, zealous bravery. The ME noun *riot* may mean either *band* or *revelry;* both ModE words possess some of the ambiguity of the original, *band* suggesting either lawless mob or loyal company and *revelry* both gaiety and debauchery.[84]

The poet's fondness for ambiguity is also illustrated by Arthur's elaborate and sometimes overdone punning. This practice is at its most effective in Arthur's characterization of the coffins containing the bodies of Lucius and his other enemies as treasure coffers that he is sending over the mountains in response to Rome's demands for tribute. (2342–51). It is less effective in Arthur's tedious references to the giant which he has slain as the *saynt* of St. Michael's Mount whom he has purportedly gone to the top of the mountain to *seke* (which means both "visit" and "assault, attack"; see 1162–73 and note to 1171).

Simile and metaphor are rarely used by the alliterative poets.[85] Similes are very scarce in the *Morte Arthure* and often feeble and one-dimensional when used. The exception to this sparsity is in the description of the giant, where there are no fewer than thirteen similes (most likening the giant to an animal). Line 4285 also contains an interesting comparison (Arthur, after all his knights have been slain, likens himself to a woeful widow who longs for her man), the effectiveness of which is perhaps a happy accident, in view of the weakness of most of the other comparisons (for example, line 2922, in which

Priamus' men, deserting the Duke's army to come over to Gawain's side are likened to sheep pouring out of a fold).

In sum, the *Morte Arthure* is a mysteriously anachronistic work. In its epic form, it has more in common with the *Iliad* or the *Chanson de Roland* than with fourteenth-century Arthurian romances. In the conservative quality of its alliteration, its highly formulaic style, and the poet's avoidance of lettered techniques, it is closer to *Beowulf* than is any other fourteenth-century work. As such, it is the pivotal work in the evolution of Middle English alliterative poetry.

Notes

[1] For the complete list of works that appear in this MS see Sir Frederick Madden, ed., *Syr Gawayne* (London: Bannatyne, 1839), pp. l–lix. A detailed account of the manuscript, including a list of the contents, also appears in the facsimile reprint *The Thornton Manuscript*, intro. D. S. Brewer and A. E. B. Owen (London: Scolar Press, 1975), pp. vii–xx.

[2] Madden, p. 1; J. L. N. O'Loughlin, "The English Alliterative Romances," in *Arthurian Literature in the Middle Ages: A Collaborative History*, ed. R. S. Loomis (Oxford: Clarendon Press, 1959), p. 521; Margaret S. Ogden, *The "Liber de Diversis Medicinis"* (London: E.E.T.S. O.S. 207, 1938, rev. rpt. 1969), pp. x–xi.

[3] Including the use of *ff* for capital F.

[4] See below, "Dialect," and Angus McIntosh, Untitled Review of Ogden's *Liber de Diversis Medicinis*, *RES*, 15 (1939), 336–38.

[5] William Matthews, *The Ill-Framed Knight* (Berkeley: University of California Press, 1966), p. 78.

[6] Tauno F. Mustanoja, *A Middle English Syntax: Part I, Parts of Speech* (Helsinki: Société Néophilologique, 1960), pp. 145–48. For the indiscriminate use of the inflected form *selven,* see p. 147.

[7] *Ibid.,* pp. 121, 203–06.

[8] *Ibid.,* pp. 170–71.

[9] See Fernand Mossé, *A Handbook of Middle English,* trans. James A. Walker (Baltimore: Johns Hopkins Press, 1952), p. 156.

[10] *Ibid.,* pp. 78–79.

[11] *A Middle English Syntax,* pp. 112–113; 434–36.

[12] *Ibid.,* pp. 485–88.

[13] William Matthews, *The Tragedy of Arthur* (Berkeley: University of California Press, 1960), pp. 181–82, 211–12.

[14] Thornton dealt similarly with other texts; see Angus McIntosh, "The Textual Transmission of the Alliterative *Morte Arthure*," in *English and Medieval Studies Presented to J. R. R. Tolkien,* ed. Norman Davis and C. L. Wrenn (London: Allen & Unwin, 1962), p. 231.

[15] "The Dialect of *Morte Arthure,*" *RES,* 4 (1928), 418–23.

[16] *Alliterative Poetry in Middle English,* Vol. I: *The Dialectical and Metrical Survey* (Manchester: Manchester University Press, 1930; rpt. as one volume with *A Survey of the Traditions,* Hamden, Conn.: Archon Books, 1968), pp. 63–67.

[17] "The Textual Transmission of the Alliterative *Morte Arthure,*" pp. 231–41.

[18] See *A Middle English Syntax,* pp. 483–84 on the present used for the future.

[19] Another MS copied by Thornton has certain unusual characteristics in common with the MS of *Morte Arthure.* McIntosh concludes that the two MSS underlying the two Thornton MSS must have been written by the same scribe and that any

further unusual features peculiar to the *Morte Arthure* MS must derive from an even earlier MS, which must have been closer to the original version of the poem.

20 "The 'West Midland' of the Romances," *MP*, 19 (1921), 1–16.

21 Quoted in Henry N. MacCracken, "Concerning Huchown," *PMLA*, 25 (1910), 512.

22 "Der Dichter Huchown und seine Werke," *Anglia*, 1 (1878), 109–49.

23 *Huchown of the Awle Ryale* (Glasgow: J. Maclelose, 1902).

24 "Concerning Huchown," pp. 507–34.

25 *The Tragedy of Arthur*, pp. 157–58.

26 J. L. N. O'Loughlin, "The English Alliterative Romances," p. 521.

27 *Huchown of the Awle Ryale*, pp. 59–66.

28 "Costume in the Middle English Romances," *PMLA*, 47 (1932), 344–45.

29 "*Morte Arthure:* The Date and a Source for the Contemporary References," *Speculum*, 42 (1967), 624–38.

30 "Notes on the 'Morte Arthure' Glossary," *MLQ*, 6 (1903), 64–69.

31 "Versbau und Sprache in Huchowns Morte Arthure," *Bonner Beiträge zur Anglistik*, 5 (1900), 33–144.

32 Karl Luick, Review of Mennicken's "Versbau und Sprache in Huchowns Morte Arthure," *Beiblatt zur Anglia*, 12 (1901), 33–49; F. Holthausen, Review of Banks' Edition of *Morte Arthure*, *Beiblatt zur Anglia*, 12 (1901), 235–37; F. Holthausen, "Zum alliterierenden Morte Arthure," *Beiblatt zur Anglia*, 24 (1913), 250–52.

33 "The English Alliterative Romances."

34 *The Ill-Framed Knight.*

35 One cannot be completely sure, however, that the author is the source of this effort. Though scribes are known for their tendencies to increase or regularize alliteration, as George Kane has now shown (*Piers Plowman: The A Version* [London: Athlone Press, 1960], Introduction, pp. 141, 145–46, 165), they are unpre-

dictable and are capable of decreasing alliteration as well. "An enthusiastic [scribal] alliterator . . . might remove alliteration in a hard reading smoothed over by him ([*PP*] V, 59) or, erratically, in an easy reading (VII, 29), but oversupply it elsewhere" (Jess B. Bessinger, Jr., Untitled review of Kane's *Piers Plowman: The A Version, JEGP*, 60 [1961], p. 574). One cannot with certainty, therefore, distinguish scribal from authorial tendencies on the basis of heavy or light alliteration.

36 "Über die Quellen des stabreimenden Morte Arthure," *Anglia*, 8 (1885), 179–236.

37 *The Tragedy of Arthur*, p. 4.

38 "The English Alliterative Romances," p. 523.

39 "Malory's Story of Arthur's Roman Campaign," *Medium Aevum*, 6 (1937), 99–121. See also E. V. Gordon and Eugène Vinaver, "New Light on the Text of the Alliterative *Morte Arthure, ibid.,* 81–98.

40 *The Ill-Framed Knight*, Appendix H, pp. 223–38.

41 *The Tragedy of Arthur*, pp. 181–82, 211–12.

42 Branscheid and Moritz Trautmann regarded this section as the poet's most extensive and notable addition to the chronicle story. Trautmann (pp. 141–42) thought that this episode might be the "Awntyre of Gawayne" mentioned by the Scottish chronicler Wyntoun as one of the poet Huchown's works (see above, "Author"). Branscheid (pp. 200–01, 216) conjectures that the source of this segment was a French romance, now lost, with Sir Florent as the hero, because of Florent's being the leader of the expedition.

43 "Malory, *Morte Arthure*, and *Fierabras*," *Anglia*, 32 (1909), 389–98.

44 *The Tragedy of Arthur*, pp. 44–51.

45 *Huchown of the Awle Ryale*, pp. 58–66.

[46] *"Morte Arthure:* The Date and a Source for the Contemporary References," pp. 624–38.

[47]"The Middle English Period," Vol. I, Part II of *A Literary History of England,* ed. Albert C. Baugh (New York: Appleton, 1948), p. 191. The poem is often referred to as a romance in the critical literature.

[48] *Middle English Literature,* (London: Methuen, 1951), pp. 69–73.

[49] *Essays on Middle English Literature,* (Oxford: Clarendon Press, 1955), pp. 61–62.

[50] *Ibid.,* p. 62.

[51] Larry D. Benson, "The Alliterative *Morte Arthure* and Medieval Tragedy," *TSL,* 6 (1966), 75–87; John Finlayson, "The Concept of the Hero in 'Morte Arthure,'" in *Chaucer und seine Zeit: Symposion für Walter F. Schirmer* (Buchreihe der *Anglia,* Zeitschrift für englische Philologie, Band 14), ed. Arno Esch (Tübingen: Max Niemeyer, 1968), pp. 249–74.

[52] *Mimesis: The Representation of Reality in Western Literature,* trans. Willard Trask (Garden City, N. Y.: Doubleday, 1957), pp. 116–24.

[53] "Arthur and the Giant of St. Michael's Mount," *Medium Aevum,* 33 (1964), 117–20.

[54] John Finlayson, ed., *Morte Arthure* (London: Edward Arnold, 1967), p. 81, n.

[55] *The Tragedy of Arthur,* Chap. 5.

[56] The following discussion is heavily indebted to Larry D. Benson, *Art and Tradition in Sir Gawain and the Green Knight* (New Brunswick: Rutgers University Press, 1965), pp. 112–17, and to J. P. Oakden, *Alliterative Poetry in Middle English: The Dialectical and Metrical Survey,* Chap. 7.

[57] *The Dialectical and Metrical Survey,* pp. 177–78.

[58] *Ibid.,* pp. 155–57.

[59] "The Middle English Alliterative *Morte Arthure,"* *Medium Aevum,* 4 (1935), 153–68.

[60] It is impossible to know whether this was an artificial displacement for the sake of the alliteration, like the artificial stress in the end-rhymes of *Sir Gawain;* whether such words were actually pronounced with the stress on the prefix; or whether there were two pronunciations from which the poet could choose. See Marie Borroff, *Sir Gawain and the Green Knight: A Stylistic and Metrical Study* (New Haven: Yale University Press, 1962), pp. 150–71.

[61] Karl Schumacher, "Studien über den Stabreim in der Mittelenglischen Alliterationsdichtung," *Bonner Studien zur Englischen Philologie,* 11 (1914), 67–92.

[62] See Eduard Sievers, "Old Germanic Metrics and Old English Metrics," trans. Gawaina D. Luster, rpt. in *Essential Articles for the Study of Old English Poetry,* ed. Jess B. Bessinger, Jr., and Stanley J. Kahrl (Hamden, Conn.: Archon Books, 1968).

[63] J. R. R. Tolkien and E. V. Gordon, eds., *Sir Gawain and the Green Knight,* 2d ed., rev. Norman Davis (Oxford: Clarendon Press, 1967), pp. 147–49.

[64] Oakden, *The Dialectical and Metrical Survey,* p. 133.

[65] Karl Luick, "Die Englische Stabreimzeile im XIV, XV, und XVI Jahrhundert," *Anglia,* 11 (1889), 585–97; Franz J. Mennicken, "Versbau und Sprache in Huchowns Morte Arthure."

[66] *Sir Gawain and the Green Knight: A Stylistic and Metrical Study,* pp. 154–58, 183–89.

[67] *Alliterative Poetry in Middle English,* Vol. II: *A Survey of the Traditions* (Manchester: Manchester University Press, 1935, rpt. as one volume with *The Dialectical and Metrical Survey,* Hamden, Conn.: Archon Books, 1968), pp. 381–91.

[68] "The Oral-Formulaic Character of

Anglo-Saxon Narrative Poetry," *Speculum*, 28 (1953), 446–67.

[69] "Oral-Formulaic Technique and Middle English Alliterative Poetry," *Speculum*, 32 (1957), 792–804.

[70] "Formulaic Technique in *Morte Arthure*," *Anglia*, 81 (1963), 372–93.

[71] "Stab und Formel im Alliterierenden *Morte Arthure*," *Neophilologus*, 49 (1965), 57–67.

[72] The question of why the presumably lettered poets of the "Alliterative Revival" should be using oral-formulaic techniques is a difficult one. For a consideration of this problem see Larry D. Benson, *Art and Tradition in Sir Gawain and the Green Knight*, pp. 122–66.

[73] James D. Johnson, *Formulaic Diction and Thematic Composition in the Alliterative Morte Arthure*, Unpbl. Diss. University of Illinois, 1969, Appendix B. Exactly how many formulas are to be distinguished in each of these word groups is a complex question and depends upon how one defines the formula. See Johnson, Chapter II for a detailed consideration of this question.

[74] Marie Borroff has characterized a group of these nouns (*berne, freke, gome, lede, renk, hathel, schalke, segge, tulk,* and *wye*) as "elevated and archaic synonyms for "man, warrior," and discussed in detail their rhetorical function in *Sir Gawain and the Green Knight* (*Sir Gawain and the Green Knight: A Stylistic and Metrical Study*). There is some doubt whether these nouns are used in the *Morte Arthure* in the way Borroff says they are used in *Sir Gawain*. They often seem to have a more general denotation than "man, warrior," and they are not necessarily more elevated, as Borroff claims, than their nonalliterating counterparts such as *lord, knight,* or *king*. For a detailed discussion of this question see Valerie Krishna, "Archaic Nouns in the *Alliterative Morte Arthure*," *NM* 76 (1975), 439–45.

[75] *Art and Tradition in Sir Gawain and the Green Knight*, pp. 151–53.

[76] F. H. Kelly and R. Schwabe, *A Short History of Costume and Armor, Chiefly in England* (1931; rpt. New York: B. Blom, 1968), pp. 55–82.

[77] *Ibid.*, pp. 59–60.

[78] *Ibid.*, p. 26.

[79] *Huchown of the Awle Ryale*, pp. 60–66.

[80] *Ibid.*, pp. 60–66.

[81] John Finlayson, "Rhetorical 'Descriptio' of Place in the Alliterative *Morte Arthure*," *MP*, 61 (1963), 1–11.

[82] *Ibid.*, p. 7.

[83] *The Tragedy of Arthur*, pp. 112–13.

[84] This interpretation rejects the theory of Laila Gross that *riot* is a variant spelling of *realté* 'royal dignity' ("The Meaning and Oral-Formulaic Use of *Riot* in the Alliterative *Morte Arthure*," *Annuale Medievale*, 9 [1968], 98–102).

[85] J. P. Oakden, *Alliterative Poetry in Middle English: A Survey of the Traditions*, pp. 399–401.

The Poem

Now grett glorious Godd, thurgh grace of Hym seluen,
And the precyous prayere of Hys prys Modyr,
Schelde vs fro schamesdede and synfull werkes,
And gyffe vs grace to gye and gouerne vs here,
In this wrechyd werld, thorowe vertous lywynge, 5
That we may kayre til Hys courte, the kyngdom of Hevyne,
When oure saules schall parte and sundyre fra the body,
Ewyre to belde and to byde in blysse wyth Hym seluen;
And wysse me to werpe owte som worde at this tym
That nothyre voyde be ne vayne, bot wyrchip till Hym selvyn, 10
Plesande and profitabill to the popule þat them heres.
    ȝe that liste has to lyth or luffes for to here
Off elders of alde tym and of theire awke dedys,
How they were lele in theire lawe and louede God Almyghty,
Herkynes me heyndly and holdys ȝow styll, 15
And I sall tell ȝow a tale þat trewe es and nobyll,
Off the ryeall renkys of the Rownnde Table,
That chefe ware of cheualrye and cheftans nobyll,
Bathe ware in thire werkes and wyse men of armes,
Doughty in theire doyngs and dredde ay schame, 20
Kynde men and courtays and couthe of courte thewes;
How they whanne wyth were wyrchippis many,
Sloughe Lucyus þe lythyre, that Lorde was of Rome,
And conqueryd that kyngryke thorowe craftys of armes;
Herkenes now hedyrwarde and herys this storye. 25
    Qwen that the kyng Arthur by conqueste hade wonnyn
Castells and kyngdoms and contreez many,
And he had couerede the coroun of the kyth ryche,
Of all that Vter in erthe aughte in his tym:

41

Orgayle and Orkenay and all this owte iles,   *30*
Irelande vttirly, as occyane rynnys;
Scathyll Scottlande by skyll he skyftys as hym lykys,
And Wales of were he wane at hys will;
Bathe Flaundrez and Fraunce fre til him seluyn,
Holaund and Henawde they helde of hym bothen,   *35*
Burgoyne and Brabane and Bretayn the Lesse,
Gyan and Gothelande and Grace the ryche;
Bayon and Burdeux he beldytt full faire,
Turoyn and Tholus, with toures full hye;
Off Peyters and of Prouynce he was prynce holdyn,   *40*
Of Valence and Vyenne, off value so noble,   f.53ᵛ
Of Ouergne and Anyou, thos erledoms ryche—
By conqueste full cruell þey knewe hym fore lorde;
Of Nauerne and Norwaye and Normaundye eke,
Of Almayne, of Estriche, and oþer ynowe;   *45*
Danmarke he dryssede all by drede of hym seluyn,
Fra Swynn vnto Swetherwyke, wiþ his swerde kene.
        Qwenn he thes dedes had don, he doubbyd hys knyghtez,
Dyuysyde dowcherys and delte in dyuerse remmes,
Mad of his cosyns kyngys ennoyntede,   *50*
In kyth there they couaitte crounes to bere.
        Whene he thys rewmes hade redyn and rewlyde the popule,
Then rystede that ryall and helde þe Rounde Tabyll;
Suggeourns þat seson to solace hym seluen
In Bretayn þe Braddere, as hym beste lykes.   *55*
Sythyn wente into Wales with his wyes all,
Sweys into Swaldye with his snell houndes,
For to hunt at þe hartes in thas hye laundes,
In Glamorgan with glee, thare gladchipe was euere.
        And thare a citée he sette, be assentte of his lordys,   *60*
That Caerlyon was callid, with curius walles,
On the riche reuaré þat rynnys so faire,
There he myghte semble his sorte to see whenn hym lykyde.
        Thane aftyre at Carlele a Cristynmese he haldes,
This ilke kyde conquerour, and helde hym for lorde,   *65*

37 Grace *Holthausen*] Grece   42 Ouergne *Banks*] Eruge
47 swerde] swrede   64 Carlele] Carlelele

Wyth dukez and duspers of dyuers rewmes,
Erles and ercheuesqes and oþer ynowe,
Byschopes and bachelers and banerettes nobill,
Þat bowes to his banere, buske when hym lykys.
Bot on the Cristynmes Daye, when they were all semblyde,   *70*
That comlyche conquerour commaundez hym seluyn
Þat ylke a lorde sulde lenge and no lefe take
To the tende day fully ware takyn to þe ende.
Thus on ryall araye he helde his Rounde Table,
With semblant and solace and selcouthe metes;   *75*
Whas neuer syche noblay in no manys tym
Mad in mydwynter in þa weste marchys.
    Bot on the Newȝere Daye, at þe none euyne,
As the bolde at the borde was of brede seruyde,
So come in sodanly a senatour of Rome,   *80*
Wyth sexten knyghtes in a soyte, sewande hym one.   f.54ʳ
He saluȝed the souerayne, and the sale aftyr,
Ilke a kyng aftyre kyng, and mad his enclines;
Gaynour in hir degré he grette as hym lykyde,
And syne agayne to þe gome he gaffe vp his nedys: *85*
"Sir Lucius Iberius, the Emperour of Rome,
Saluz the as sugett, vndyre his sele ryche;
It es credens, Sir Kyng, with cruell wordez;
Trow it for no trufles: his targe es to schewe.
Now in this Newȝers Daye, with notaries sygne,   *90*
I make the somouns in sale to sue for þi landys,
That on Lammesse Daye thare be no lette founden,
Þat thow bee redy at Rome with all thi Rounde Table,
Appere in his presens with thy price knyghtez,
At pryme of the daye, in payne of ȝour lyvys,   *95*
In þe kydd capytoile, before þe kyng selvyn,
When he and his senatours bez sette as them lykes,
To ansuere anely why thow ocupyes the laundez
That awe homage of alde till hym and his eldyrs;
Why thow has redyn and raymede and raunsound þe pople,   *100*
And kyllyde doun his cosyns, kyngys ennoynttyde;
Thare schall thow gyffe rekkynyng for all thy Round Table
Why thow arte rebell to Rome and rentez them wytholdez.

Ʒiff thow theis somouns wythsytte, he sendes thie thies wordes:
He sall the seke ouer þe see wyth sexten kynges,   105
Bryne Bretayn þe Brade and bryttyn thy knyghtys,
And bryng the bouxsomly as a beste with brethe whare hym lykes,
That thow ne schall rowte ne ryste vndyr the heuene ryche,
Þofe thow for reddour of Rome ryne to þe erthe;
For if thow flee into Fraunce or Freselaund owþer,   110
Þou sall be feched with force and ouersette fore euer!
Thy fadyr mad fewtée, we fynde in oure rollez,
In the regestre of Rome, who-so ryghte lukez.
Withowttyn more trouflyng the trebute we aske
That Iulius Cesar wan with his ientill knyghttes."   115
   The Kyng blyschit on the beryn with his brode eghn,
Þat full brymly for breth brynte as the gledys,
Keste colours as Kyng, with crouell lates,
Luked as a lyon, and on his lyppe bytes.   f.54ᵛ
The Romaynes for radnesse ruschte to þe erthe,   120
Fore ferdnesse of hys face, as they fey were;
Cowchide as kenetez before þe Kyng seluyn:
Because of his contenaunce confusede them semede.
Then couerd vp a knyghte and criede ful lowde,
"Kyng corounede of kynd, curtays and noble,   125
Misdoo no messangere for menske of þi seluyn,
Sen we are in thy manrede and mercy þe besekes.
We lenge with Sir Lucius, that Lorde es of Rome,
That es þe meruelyousteste man þat on molde lengez;
It is lefull till vs his likyng till wyrche;   130
We come at his commaundment; haue vs excusede."
   Then carpys þe Conquerour crewell wordez:
"Haa, crauaunde knyghte, a cowarde þe semez!
Þare [is] some segge in this sale, and he ware sare greuede,
Thow durste noghte for all Lumberdye luke on hym ones."   135
"Sir," sais þe Senatour, "so Crist mott me helpe,
Þe voute of thi vesage has woundyde vs all!
Thow arte þe lordlyeste lede þat euer I one lukyde;
By lukyng, withowttyn lesse, a lyon the semys!"
"Thow has me somond," quod þe Kyng, "and said what þe lykes;   140
   135 for] full

'ore sake of thy soueraynge I suffre the þe more;
en I [was] coround in kyth, wyth crysum enoyntede,
Vas neuer creature to me þat carpede so large.
ot I sall tak concell at kynges enoyntede,
)ff dukes and duspers and doctours noble, 145
)ffe peres of þe parlement, prelates and oþer,
)ff þe richeste renkys of þe Rounde Table;
)us schall I take avisemente of valiant beryns,
Vyrke aftyre the wytte of my wyes knyghttes;
To warpe wordez in waste no wyrchip it were, 150
Ne wilfully in þis wrethe to wreken my seluen.
'orþi sall þow lenge here and lugge wyth þise lordes,
This seuenyghte in solace, to suggourne ȝour horses,
To see whatte lyfe þat wee leede in thees lawe laundes,
'orby þe realtée of Rome, þat recheste was euere." 155
He command Sir Cayous, "Take kepe to thoos lordez,
To styghtyll þa steryn men as theire statte askys,
That they bee herberde in haste in thoos heghe chambres,
Sythin sittandly in sale seruyde theraftyr. f.55ʳ
That they fynd na fawte of fude to thiere horsez, 160
Nowthire weyn, ne waxe, ne welthe in þis erthe,
Spare for no spycerye, bot spende what þe lykys,
That there be largesce on lofte and no lake founden.
If þou my wyrchip wayte, wy, be my trouthe,
Pou sall haue gersoms full grett, that gayne sall þe euere." 165
        Now er they herberde in hey and in oste holden,
Hastyly wyth hende men within thees heghe wallez;
In chambyrs with chympnes þey chaungen þeire wedez,
And sythyn the chauncelere þem fecchede with cheualrye noble.
Sone þe Senatour was sett, as hym wele semyde; 170
At þe Kyngez ownn borde twa knyghtes hym seruede,
Singulere sothely, as Arthure hym seluyn,
Richely on þe ryghte hannde at the Round Table,
Be resoun þat þe Romaynes whare so ryche holden,
As of þe realeste blode þat reynede in erthe. 175
        There come in at þe fyrste course, befor þe Kyng seluen,
Bareheuedys þat ware bryghte, burnyste with syluer,

169 cheualrye] chelualrye

All with taghte men and town in togers full ryche,
Of saunke reall in suyte, sexty at ones;
Flesch fluriste of fermyson with frumentée noble,
Therto wylde to wale and wynlyche bryddes,
Pacokes and plouers in platers of golde,
Pygges of porke despyne þat pasturede neuer,
Sythen herons in hedoyne, hyled full faire,
Grett swannes full swythe in silueryn chargeours,
Tartes of turky—taste wham þem lykys—
Gumbaldes grathely, full gracious to taste,
Seyne bowes of wylde bores with þe braune lechyde,
Bernakes and botures in baterde dysches,
Þareby braunchers in brede—bettyr was neuer—
With brestez of barowes þat bryghte ware to schewe;
Seyn come þer sewes sere, with solace þerafter—
Ownd of azure all ouer and ardant þem semyde—
Of ilke a leche þe lowe launschide full hye,
Þat all ledes myghte lyke þat lukyde þem apon;
Þan cranes and curlues craftyly rosted,
Connygez in cretoyne, colourede full faire,
Fesauntez enflureschit in flammande siluer,
With dariells endoride and daynteez ynewe;
Þane clarett and creette, clergyally rennen,
With condethes full curious, all of clene siluyre,
Osay a[n]d algarde and oþer ynewe,
Rynisch wyne and rochell—richere was neuer—
Vernage of Venyce vertuouse and Crete,
In faucetez of fyn golde—fonode whoso lykes.
The Kyngez cope-borde was closed in siluer,
In grete goblettez ouergylte, glorious of hewe;
There was a cheeffe buttlere, a cheualere noble,
Sir Cayous þe curtaise, þat of þe cowpe seruede:
Sexty cowpes of suyte fore þe Kyng seluyn,
Crafty and curious, coruen full faire,
In euerilk a party pyghte with precyous stones,
That nan enpoyson sulde goo preuely þervndyre,
Bot þe bryght golde for brethe sulde briste al to peces,

183 neuer] ncuer neuer   199 endoride Björkman] endordide

Or ells þe venym sulde voyde thurghe vertue of þe stones.   215
And the Conquerour hym seluen, so clenly arayede,
In colours of clene golde cleede, wyth his knyghttys,
Drissid with his dyademe on his deesse ryche,
Fore he was demyd þe doughtyeste þat duellyde in erthe.

    Thane þe Conquerour kyndly carpede to þose lordes,   220
Rehetede þe Romaynes with realle speche:
"Sirs, bez knyghtly of contenaunce, and comfurthes ȝour seluyn;
We knowe noghte in þis countré of curious metez,
In thees barayne landez, bredes none oþer;
Forethy, wythowttyn feynyng, enforce ȝow þe more   225
To feede ȝow with syche feble as ȝe before fynde."
"Sir," sais þe Senatour, "soo Criste motte me helpe,
There ryngnede neuer syche realtée within Rome walles!
There ne es prelatte, ne pape, ne prynce in þis erthe,
That he ne myghte be wele payede of þees pryce metes."   230

    Aftyre theyre welthe þey wesche and went vnto chambyre,
Dis ilke kydde Conquerour, with knyghtes ynewe;
Sir Gaywayne þe worthye Dame Waynour he ledys;
Sir Owghtreth on the toþer syde, of Turry was lorde.

Thane spyces vnsparyly þay spendyde thereaftyre: 235
Maluesye and muskadell, þase meruelyous drynkes,
Raykede full rathely in rossete cowpes,
Till all þe riche on rawe, Romaynes and oþer.
Bot the soueraingne sothely, for solauce of hym seluen,
Assingnyde to þe Senatour certaygne lordes,   240
To lede to his leueré, whene he leue askes,
With myrthe and with melodye of mynstralsy noble.

    Thane þe Conquerour to concell cayres thereaftyre,
Wyth lordes of his lygeaunce þat to hym selfe langys;
To þe geauntes toure iolily he wendes,   245
Wyth justicez and iuggez and gentill knyghtes.

    Sir Cador of Cornewayle to þe Kyng carppes,   f.56ʳ
Lughe on hym luffly with lykande lates:
"I thanke Gode of þat thraa þat vs þus thretys!
ȝow moste be traylede, I trowe, bot ȝife ȝe trett bettyre.   250
Þe lettres of Sir Lucius lyghttys myn herte!

225 ȝow þe] þe ȝow   230 he ne] ne he

We hafe as losels liffyde many longe daye,
Wyth delyttes in this land with lordchipez many,
And forelytenede the loos þat we are layttede;
I was abaischite, be oure Lorde, of oure beste bernes,   255
Fore gret dule of deffuse of dedez of armes.
Now wakkenyse þe were! Wyrchipide be Cryste!
And we sall wynn it ag[a]yne be wyghtnesse and strenghe!"
      "Sir Cadour," quod þe Kyng, "thy concell es noble;
Bot þou arte a meruailous man with thi mery wordez;   260
For thow countez no caas, ne castes no forthire,
Bot hurles furthe appon heuede, as thi herte thynkes.
I moste trette of a trew towchande þise nedes,
Talke of thies tythdands þat tenes myn herte:
Þou sees þat þe Emperour es angerde a lyttill;   265
Yt semes be his sandismen þat he es sore greuede;
His senatour has sommonde me and said what hym lykyde,
Hethely in my hall, wyth heynȝous wordes,
In speche disspyszede me and sparede me lyttill—
I myght noghte speke for spytte, so my herte trymblyde!   270
He askyde me tyrauntly tribute of Rome,
That tenefully tynt was in tym of myn elders,
There alyenes, in absence of all men of armes,
Couerd it of comons, as cronicles telles.
I have title to take tribute of Rome;   275
Myne ancestres ware emperours and aughte it þem seluen,
Belyn and Brene and Bawdewyne the Thyrde;
They ocupyede þe Empyre aughte score wynnttyrs,
Ilkane ayere aftyre oþer, as awlde men telles;
Thei couerde þe capitoile and keste doun þe walles,   280
Hyngede of þeire heddys-men by hundrethes at ones.
Seyn Constantyne, our kynsmane, conquerid it aftyre,
Þat ayere was of Ynglande and Emperour of Rome,
He þat conquerid þe crosse be craftez of armes
That Criste was on crucifiede, þat Kyng es of Heuen.   285
Thus hafe we euydens to aske þe Emperour þe same,
That þus regnez at Rome, whate ryghte þat he claymes."
      Þan answarde Kyng Aungers to Arthure hym seluyn,

277 Brene *Branscheid*] Bremyn

"Thow aughte to be ouerlynge ouer all oþer kynges,
Fore wyseste and worthyeste and wyghteste of hanndes,   f.56ᵛ 290
The knyghtlyeste of counsaile þat euer coron bare;
I dare saye fore Scottlande þat we them schathe lympyde:
When þe Romaynes regnede þay raunsound oure eldyrs,
And rade in theire ryotte and rauyschett oure wyfes,
Withowttyn reson or ryghte refte vs oure gudes.   295
And I sall make myn avowe deuotly to Criste,
And to þe haly vernacle, vertuus and noble,
Of this grett velany I sall be vengede ones,
On ʒone venemus men, wyth valiant knyghtes!
I sall the forthire of defence, fosterde ynewe,   300
Fifty thowsande men, wythin two eldes,
Of my wage for to wende whare so the lykes,
To fyghte wyth thy faamen, þat vs vnfaire ledes!"
     Thane the burelyche Beryn of Bretayne þe Lyttyll
Counsayles Sir Arthure, and of hym besekys   305
To ansuere þe alyenes wyth austeren wordes,
To entyce the Emperour to take ouere the mounttes.
He said, "I make myn avowe verreilly to Cryste
And to þe haly vernacle þat voide schall I neuere,
For radnesse of na Romayne þat regnes in erthe,   310
Bot ay be redye in araye and at areste founden.
No more dowtte the dynte of theire derfe wapyns,
Þan þe dewe þat es dannke when þat it doun falles:
Ne no more schoune fore þe swape of theire scharpe suerddes,
Then fore þe faireste flour þatt on the folde growes!   315
I sall to batell the brynge of brenyede knyghtes
Thyrtty thosannde be tale, thryftye in armes,
Wythin a monethe daye into whatte marche
Þat þow wyll sothelye assygne, when thy selfe lykes."
     "A! A!" sais þe Walsche kyng, "wirchipid be Criste!   320
Now schalle we wreke full wele þe wrethe of oure elders!
In West Walys iwysse syche wonndyrs þay wroghte,
Þat all for wandrethe may wepe þat on þat were thynkes.
I sall haue the avanttwarde wytterly my seluen,
Tyll þat I haue venquiste þe Vicounte of Rome,   325
Þat wroghte me at Viterbe a velanye ones,

As I paste in pylgremage by the Pounte Tremble;
He was in Tuskayne þat tyme and tuke of oure knyghttes,
Areste them vnryghttwyslye and raunsound þam aftyre;
I sall hym surelye ensure þat saghetyll sall we neuer,　　　　　　*330*
Are we sadlye assemble by oure selfen ones,
And dele dynttys of dethe with oure derfe wapyns!
And I sall wagge to þat were, of wyrchipfull knyghtes,
Of Wyghte and of Walschelande and of the weste marches,
Twa thosande in tale, horsede one stedys,　　　　　　f.57ʳ *335*
Of þe wyghteste wyes in all ȝone weste landys!"
　　　Syre Ewan fytz Vryence þane egerly fraynez—
Was cosyn to þe Conquerour, corageous hym selfen—
"Sir, and we wyste ȝour wyll, we walde wirke þeraftyre:
Ȝif þis journée sulde halde or be ajournede forthyre,　　　　　　*340*
To ryde one ȝone Romaynes and ryott theire landez,
We walde schape vs therefore to schippe whene ȝow lykys."
　　　"Cosyn," quod þe Conquerour, "kyndly þou asches;
Ȝife my concell accorde to conquere ȝone landez,
By þe kalendez of Iuny we schall encountre ones,　　　　　　*345*
Wyth full creuell knyghtez, so Cryste mot me helpe!
Thereto make I myn avowe devottly to Cryste,
And to the holy vernacle, vertuous and noble,
I sall at Lammesse take leue to lenge at my large
In Lorayne or Lumberdye, whethire me leue thynkys;　　　　　　*350*
Merke vnto Meloyne and myne doun þe wallez,
Bathe of Petyrsande and of Pys and of þe Pounte Tremble;
In þe Vale of Viterbe vetaile my knyghttes,
Suggourne there sex wokes and solace my selfen;
Send prekers to þe price toun and plaunte there my segge,　　　　　　*355*
Bot if þay profre me þe pece be processe of tym."
　　　"Certys," sais Sir Ewayn, "and I avowe aftyre,
And I þat hathell may see euer with myn eghn,
Þat ocupies thin heritage, þe Empyere of Rome,
I sall auntyre me anes hys egle to touche,　　　　　　*360*
Þat borne es in his banere of brighte golde ryche,
And raas it from his riche men and ryfe it in sondyre,
Bot he be redily reschowede with riotous knyghtez!

337 Vryence *Brock*] Vryenee

I sall enforsse ʒowe in þe felde with fresche men of armes,
Fyfty thosande folke apon faire stedys, 365
On thi foomen to foonde, there the faire thynkes,
In Fraunce or in Friselande—feghte when þe lykes!"
    "By oure Lorde," quod Sir Launcelott, "now lyghttys myn herte!
I loue Gode of þis loue þis lordes has avowede.
Nowe may lesse men haue leue to say whatt them lykes, 370
And hafe no lettyng be lawe, bot lystynnys þise wordez:
I sall be at journée with gentill knyghtes,
On a jamby stede, full jolyly graythide,
Or any journée begane to juste with hym selfen,
Emange all his geauntez, Genyuers and oþer, 375
Stryke hym styfflye fro his stede, with strenghe of myn handys,
For all þa steryn in stour þat in his stale houys!
Be my retenu arayede, I rekke bott a lyttill
To make rowtte into Rome with ryotous knyghtes; f.57ᵛ
Within a seuenyghte daye, with sex score helmes, 380
I sall be seen on the see—saile when þe lykes!"
    Thane laughes Sir Lottez and all on lowde meles:
"Me likez þat Sir Lucius lannges aftyre sorowe;
Now he wylnez þe were, hys wanedrethe begynnys!
It es owre weredes to wreke the wrethe of oure elders. 385
I make myn avowe to Gode and to þe holy vernacle,
And I may se þe Romaynes, þat are so ryche halden,
Arayede in þeire riotes on a rounde felde,
I sall at þe reuerence of þe Rounde Table,
Ryde thrughte all þe rowtte, rerewarde and oþer, 390
Redy wayes to make and renkkes full rowme,
Rynnande on rede blode as my stede ruschez!
He þat folowes my fare and fyrste commes aftyre
Sall fynde in my farewaye many fay leuyde!"
    Thane þe Conquerour kyndly comforthes þese knyghtes, 395
Alowes þaim gretly theire lordly avowes:
"Alweldande Gode wyrchip ʒow all,
And latte me neuere wanntte ʒow, whylls I in werlde regne;
My menske and my manhede ʒe mayntene in erthe,
Myn honour all vtterly in oþer kyngys landes; 400

400 all vtterly] all ow vtterly

My wele and my wyrchipe, of all þis werlde ryche,
ȝe haue knyghtly conqueryde, þat to my coroun langes;
Hym thare be ferde for no faees þat swylke a folke ledes,
Bot euer fresche for to fyghte in felde when hym lykes;
I acounte no kynge þat vndyr Criste lyffes; 405
Whills I see ȝowe all sounde, I sette be no more."

  Qwhen they tristily had tretyd, þay trumppede vp aftyre,
Descendyd doune with a daunce of dukes and erles.
Thane þey semblede to sale and sowpped als swythe,
All þis semly sorte, wyth semblante full noble. 410

  Thene the roy reall rehetes thes knyghttys,
Wyth reuerence and ryotte of all his Rounde Table,
Till seuen dayes was gone—þe Senatour askes
Answere to þe Emperour with austeryn wordez.

  Aftyre þe Epiphanye, when þe purpos was takyn, 415
Of peris of þe parlement, prelates and oþer,
The Kyng in his concell, curtaise and noblee,
Vtters þe alienes and ansuers hym seluen:
"Gret wele Lucius, thi lorde, and layne noghte þise wordes;
Ife þow be lygmane lele, late hym wiet sone 420
I sall at Lammese take leue and loge at my large
In delitte in his laundez, wyth lordes ynewe,
Regne in my realtée and ryste when me lykes,
By þe reyuere of Reone halde my Rounde Table,
Fannge the fermes, in faithe, of all þa faire rewmes, 425
For all þe manace of hys myghte and mawgrée his eghne!
And merke sythen ouer the mounttez into his mayne londez, f.58ʳ
To Meloyne the meruaylous, and myn doun the walles;
In Lorrayne ne in Lumberdye lefe schall I nowthire
Nokyn lede appon liffe þat þare his lawes ȝemes; 430
And turne into Tuschayne, whene me tyme thynkys,
Ryde all þas rowme landes wyth ryotous knyghttes;
Byde hy[m] make reschewes, fore menske of hym seluen,
And mette me fore his manhede in þase mayne landes.
I sall be foundyn in Fraunce—fraiste when hym lykes— 435
The fyrste daye of Feuerȝere, in thas faire marches;
Are I be fechyde wyth force or forfette my landes,
Þe flour of his faire folke full fay sall be leuyde!

I sall hym sekyrly ensure, vndyre my seele ryche,
To seege þe cetée of Rome wythin seuen wyntyre,   440
And that so sekerly ensege apon sere halfes,
That many a senatour sall syghe for sake of me one!
My sommons er certified, and thow arte full seruyde
Of cundit and credense—kayre whene the lykes;
I sall thi journaye engyste, enjoyne them my seluen,   445
Fro this place to þe porte, there þou sall passe ouer;
Seuen dayes to Sandewyche I sette at the large,
Sexty myle on a daye—þe somme es bott lyttill.
Thowe moste spede at the spurs and spare noghte thi fole;
Thow weyndez by Watlyng Strette and by no waye ells;   450
Thare thow nyghes on nyghte nedez moste þou lenge:
Be it foreste or felde, found þou no forthire;
Bynde thy blonke by a buske with thy brydill euen,
Lugge þi selfe vndyre lynde, as þe leefe thynkes;
There awes none alyenes to ayer appon nyghttys,   455
With syche a rebawdous rowtte to ryot thy seluen.
Thy lycence es lemete in presence of lordys;
Be now lathe or lette, ryghte as þe thynkes,
For bothe þi lyffe and thi lym lygges þerappon,
Þofe Sir Lucius had laide þe lordchipe of Rome;   460
For be þow founden a fute withowte þe flode merkes,
Aftyr þe aughtende day, when vndroun es rungen,
Þou sall be heuedede in hye and with horsse drawen,
And seyn heyly be hangede, houndes to gnawen!
The rente ne rede golde þat vnto Rome langes   465
Sall noghte redily, renke, raunson thyn one!"
        "Sir," sais þe Senatour, "so Crist mot me helpe,
Might I with wirchip wyn awaye ones,
I sulde neuer fore emperour þat on erthe lenges,
Efte vnto Arthure ayere on syche nedys;   470
Bot I am sengilly here, with sex sum of knyghtes;
I beseke ȝow, Sir, that we may sounde passe:
If any vnlawefull lede lette vs by þe waye,
Within thy lycence, lorde, thy loosse es enpeyrede."
"Care noghte," quod the Kyng; "thy coundyte es knawen   f.58ᵛ 475

451 nyghes *Banks*] nyghttes   464 to gnawen] to gw gnawen

Fro Carlele to þe coste, there thy cogge lengges;
Þoghe thy cofers ware full, cramede with syluer,
Thow myghte be sekyre of my sele sexty myle forthire."
They enclined to þe Kyng, and coungé þay askede,
Cayers owtt of Carelele, catchez on theire horsez;   480
Sir Cadore þe curtayes kende them the wayes,
To Catrike þem cunvayede and to Crist þem bekennyde.

     So þey spede at þe spoures, þey sprangen þeire horses,
Hyres þem hakenayes hastyly þereaftyre;
So fore reddour þey reden and risted them neuer,   485
Bot ȝif they luggede vndire lynd whills þem lyghte failede;
Bot euere þe Senatour forsothe soghte at þe gayneste.
By þe sevend day was gone þe cetée þai rechide;
Of all þe glee vndire Gode so glade ware þey neuere,
As of þe sounde of þe see and Sandwyche belles.   490
Wythowttyn more stownntyng þey schippide þeire horsez,
Wery, to þe wane see þey went all att ones;
With þe men of þe walle they weyde vp þeire ankyrs,
And fleede at þe fore flude; in Flaundrez þey rowede,
And thorughe Flaundres þey founde, as þem faire thoghte, 495
Till Akyn in Almayn, in Arthur landes;
Gosse by þe Mount Goddarde full greuous wayes,
And so into Lumberddye, lykande to schewe.
They turne thurghe Tuskayne, with towres full heghe,
In Pis appairells them in precious wedez;   500
The Sonondaye in Suters þay suggourne þeire horsez,
And sekes þe seyntez of Rome, be assente of knyghtes;
Sythyn prekes to þe pales, with portes so ryche,
Þare Sir Lucius lenges, with lordes enowe;
Lowttes to hym lufly, and lettres hym bedes,   505
Of credence enclosyde, with knyghtlyche wordez.

     Then þe Emperour was egree and enkerly fraynes;
Þe answere of Arthure he askes hym sone,
How he arayes þe rewme and rewlys þe pople,
ȝif he be rebell to Rome whate ryghte þat he claymes. 510
"Thow sulde his ceptre haue sesede and syttyn aboun,
Fore reuerence and realtée of Rome þe noble;

476 Carlele] Carlelele   500 Pis *Branscheid*] pris

By sertes þow was my sandes and senatour of Rome;
He sulde, fore solempnitée, hafe seruede þe hym seluen!"
   "That will he neuer for no wye of all þis werlde ryche,   *515*
Bot who may wynn hym of werre, by wyghtnesse of handes;
Many fey schall be fyrste appon þe felde leuyde,
Are he appere in this place profre when þe likes.
I saye the, Sir, Arthure es thyn enmye fore euer,
And ettells to bee ouerlyng of þe Empyre of Rome,   *520*
That alle his ancestres aughte, bot Vtere hym selfe.   f.59ʳ
Thy nedes this Newe Ʒere I notifiede my selfen,
Before þat noble of name and neynesom of kynges;
In the moste reale place of þe Rounde Table,
I somounde hym solempnylye, one-seeande his knyghtez.   *525*
Sen I was formyde, in faythe, so ferde was I neuere,
In all þe placez ther I passede of pryncez in erthe.
I wolde foresake all my suyte of segnourry of Rome,
Or I efte to þat soueraygne whare sente one suyche nedes!
He may be chosyn cheftayne, cheefe of all oþer,   *530*
Bathe be chauncez of armes and cheuallrye noble,
For whyeseste and worthyeste and wyghteste of hanndez;
Of all the wyes þate I watte in this werlde ryche,
The knyghtlyeste creatoure in Cristyndome halden,
Of kyng or of conquerour crownede in erthe;   *535*
Of countenaunce, of corage, of crewelle lates,
The comlyeste of knyghtehode þat vndyre Cryste lyffes.
He maye be spoken in dyspens despysere of syluere,
That no more of golde gyffes þan of grette stones,
No more of wyne þan of watyre þat of þe welle rynnys,   *540*
Ne of welthe of þis werlde bot wyrchipe allone.
Syche contenaunce was neuer knowen in no kythe ryche,
As was with þat conquerour in his courte halden;
I countede at this Crystynmesse of kyngez enoynttede
Hole ten at his table þat tym with hym selfen.   *545*
He wyll werraye iwysse—be ware Ʒif þe lykes;
Wage many wyghtemen and wache thy marches,
That they be redye in araye and at areste foundyn;
For Ʒife he reche vnto Rome, he raunsouns it for euere!

515 wye *Brock*] waye

I rede þow dresce the þerfore, and drawe no lytte langere;　　　550
Be sekyre of þi sowdeours and sende to þe mowntes;
Be þe quartere of þis ȝere, and hym quarte stannde,
He wyll wyghtlye in a qwhyle on his wayes hye."
　　　"Bee estyre," sais þe Emperour, "I ettyll my selfen
To hostaye in Almayne with armede knyghtez;　　　555
Sende freklye into Fraunce, þat flour es of rewmes,
Fande to fette þat freke and forfette his landez;
For I sall sette kepers, full conaunde and noble,
Many geaunte of Geen, justers full gude,
To mete hym in the mountes and martyre hys knyghtes,　　　560
Stryke þem doun in strates and struye them fore euere!
There sall appon Godarde a garette be rerede,
That schall be garneschte and kepyde with gude men of armes,
And a bekyn abouen to brynne when þem lykys,
Þat nane enmye with hoste sall entre the mountes;　　　565
There schall one Mounte Bernarde be beyldede anoþere,
Buschede with banerettes and bachelers noble;　　　f.59ᵛ
In at the portes of Pavye schall no prynce passe,
Thurghe the perelous places, for my pris knyghtes."
　　　Thane Sir Lucius lordlyche lettres he sendys　　　570
Onone into þe Oryente, with austeryn knyghtez,
Till Ambyganye and Orcage and Alysaundyre eke,
To Inde and to Ermonye, as Ewfrates rynnys,
To Asye and to Affrike and Ewrope þe large,
To Irritayne and Elamet and all þase owte ilez,　　　575
To Arraby and Egipt, till erles and oþer,
That any erthe ocupyes in þase este marches,
Of Damaske and Damyat, and dukes and erles,
For drede of his daungere they dresside þem sone;
Of Crete and of Capados the honourable kyngys　　　580
Come at his commandmente clenly at ones,
To Tartary and Turky, when tythynngez es comen;
They turne in by Thebay, terauntez full hugge,
The flour of þe faire folke of Amazonnes landes—
All thate faillez on þe felde be forfette fore euere!　　　585
Of Babyloyn and Baldake the burlyche knyghtes,
Bayous with theire baronage bydez no langere;

Of Perce and of Pamphile and Preter Iohne landes,
Iche prynce with his powere appertlyche graythede;
The Sowdane of Surrye assemblez his knyghtes,   590
Fra Nylus to Nazarethe, nommers full huge;
To Garyere and to Galelé þey gedyre all at ones,
The sowdanes that ware sekyre sowdeours to Rome;
They gadyrede ouere þe Grekkes See with greuous wapyns,
In theire grete galays, wyth gleterande scheldez;   595
The kynge of Cyprys on the see þe Sowdane habydes,
With all þe realls of Roodes arayede with hym one.
They sailede with a syde wynde oure þe salte strandez,
Sodanly þe Sarezenes, as them selfe lykede;
Craftyly at Cornett the kynges are aryefede,   600
Fra þe ceté of Rome sexti myle large.
Be that the Grekes ware graythede, a full gret nombyre,
The myghtyeste of Macedone, with men of þa marches;
Pulle and Pruyslande presses with oþer,
The legemen of Lettow with legyons ynewe.   605
Thus they semble in sortes, summes full huge,
Sowdanes and Sarezenes owt of sere landes;
The Sowdane of Surry and sextene kynges,
At the cetée of Rome assemblede at ones.
      Thane yschewes þe Emperour, armede at ryghtys,   610
Arayede with his Romaynes appon ryche stedys;
Sexty geauntes before, engenderide with fendez,
With weches and warlaws to wacchen his tentys,
Ayware whare he wendes, wyntres and ȝeres.
Myghte no blonkes them bere, thos bustous churlles,   f.60ʳ 615
Bot couerde camellez of tourse, enclosyde in maylez.
He ayerez oute with alyenez, ostes full huge,
Ewyn into Almayne, þat Arthure hade wonnyn;
Rydes in by þe ryuere and ryottez hym seluen,
And ayerez with a huge wyll all þas hye landes.   620
All Westwale of werre he wynnys as hym lykes,
Drawes in by Danuby and dubbez hys knyghtez;
In the contré of Coloine castells enseggez,
And suggeournez þat seson wyth Sarazenes ynewe.
      At the vtas of Hillary, Syr Arthure hym seluen   625

In his kydde councell commande þe lordes:
"Kayere to ȝour cuntréz and semble ȝour knyghtes,
And kepys me at Constantyne clenlyche arayede;
Byddez me at Bareflete apon þa blythe stremes,
Baldly within borde, with ȝowre beste beryns;   630
I schall menskfully ȝowe mete in thos faire marches."
He sendez furthe sodaynly sergeantes of armes
To all hys mariners on rawe, to areste hym schippys.
Wythin sexten dayes hys fleet whas assemblede,
At Sandwyche on þe see—saile when hym lykes.   635
        In the palez of Ȝorke a parlement he haldez,
With all þe perez of þe rewme, prelates and oþer;
And aftyre þe prechynge, in presence of lordes,
The Kyng in his concell carpys þes wordes:
"I am in purpos to passe perilous wayes,   640
To kaire with my kene men to conquere ȝone landes,
To owttraye myn enmy, ȝif auenture it schewe,
That ocupyes myn heritage, þe Empyre of Rome.
I sett ȝow here a soueraynge—ascente ȝif ȝowe lykys—
That es me sybb, my syster son, Sir Mordrede hym seluen,   645
Sall be my leuetenaunte, with lordchipez ynewe,
Of all my lele legemen þat my landez ȝemes."
He carpes till his cosyne þane, in counsaile hym seluen:
"I make the kepare, Sir Knyghte, of kyngrykes manye,
Wardayne wyrchipfull, to weilde al my landes,   650
That I haue wonnen of werre, in all þis werlde ryche.
I wyll þat Waynour, my weife, in wyrchipe be holden,
That hire wannte noo wele ne welthe þat hire lykes;
Luke my kydde castells be clenlyche arrayede,
There cho maye suggourne hire selfe wyth semlyche berynes;   655
Fannde my forestez be frythede o frenchepe for euere,
That nane werreye my wylde botte Waynour hir seluen,
And þat in þe seson whene grees es assignyde,
That cho take hir solauce in certayne tymms.
Chauncelere and chambyrleyn chaunge as þe lykes;   660
Audytours and offycers ordayne thy seluen,
Bathe juréez and juggez and justicez of landes;
Luke thow justifye them wele that injurye wyrkes.   f.60ᵛ

If me be destaynede to dye at Dryghtyns wyll,
I charge the my sektour, cheffe of all oþer,   665
To mynystre my mobles fore mede of my saule
To mendynauntez and mysese in myschefe fallen;
Take here my testament of tresoure full huge:
As I trayste appon the, betraye thowe me neuer!
As þow will answere before the austeryn Jugge,   670
That all þis werlde wynly wysse as Hym lykes,
Luke þat my laste wyll be lelely perfournede.
Thow has clenly þe cure that to my coroune langez
Of all my wer[l]dez wele, and my weyffe eke;
Luke þowe kepe the so clere there be no cause fonden   675
When I to contré come, if Cryste will it thole;
And thow haue grace gudly to gouerne thy seluen,
I sall coroune þe, knyghte, kyng with my handez."
     Þan Sir Modrede full myldly meles hym seluen,
Knelyd to þe Conquerour and carpes þise wordez: 680
"I beseke ȝow, Sir, as my sybbe lorde,
Þat ȝe will for charyté cheese ȝow anoþer;
For if ȝe putte me in þis plytte, ȝowre pople es dyssauyde;
To presente a prynce astate my powere es symple.
When oþer of werre wysse are wyrchipide hereaftyre,   685
Than may I forsothe be sette bott at lyttill.
To passe in ȝour presance my purpos es takyn,
And all my purueaunce apperte fore my pris knyghtez."
     "Thowe arte my neuewe full nere, my nurrée of olde,
That I haue chastyede and chosen, a childe of my chambyre;   690
For the sybredyn of me, foresake noghte þis offyce;
That thow ne wyrk my will, thow watte whatte it menes."
     Nowe he takez hys leue and lengez no langere,
At lordez, at legemen, þat leues hym byhynden.
And seyne þat worthilyche wy went vnto chambyre,   695
For to comfurthe þe Qwene, þat in care lenges.
Waynour, waykly wepande, hym kyssiz,
Talkez to hym tenderly with teres ynewe:
"I may wery the wye thatt this werre mouede,

667 mendynauntez] mendynauantez   670 answere] ansuere answere
689 nurrée] nurrree   692 watte whatte] whatte watte

That warnes me wyrchippe of my wedde lorde;   700
All my lykyng of lyfe owte of lande wendez,
And I in langour am lefte, leue ȝe, for euere.
Whyne myghte I, dere lufe, dye in ȝour armes,
Are I þis destanye of dule sulde drye by myne one?"
   "Grefe þe noghte, Gaynour, fore Goddes lufe of Hewen,   705
Ne gruche noghte my ganggyng: it sall to gude turne.
Thy wonrydez and thy wepyng woundez myn herte;
I may noghte wit of þis woo, for all þis werlde ryche!
I haue made a kepare, a knyghte of thyn awen,
Ouerlyng of Ynglande, vndyre thy seluen,   710
And that es Sir Mordrede, þat þow has mekyll praysede,
Sall be thy dictour, my dere, to doo whatte the lykes."
Thane he takes hys leue at ladys in chambyre,   f.61ʳ
Kysside them kyndlyche and to Criste beteches;
And then cho swounes full swythe, whe[n] he hys swerde aschede,   715
Twys in a swounyng, swelte as cho walde.
He pressed to his palfray, in presance of lordes,
Prekys of the palez with his prys knyghtes;
Wyth a reall rowte of þe Rounde Table
Soughte towarde Sandwyche—cho sees hym no more.   720
   Thare the grete ware gederyde, wyth galyarde knyghtes,
Garneschit on þe grene felde and graythelyche arayede;
Dukkes and duzseperez daynttehely rydes,
Erles of Ynglande, with archers ynewe;
Schirreues scharply schiftys the comouns,   725
Rewlys before þe ryche of the Rounde Table;
Assingnez ilke a contrée to certayne lordes,
In the southe on þe see banke, saile when þem lykes.
   Thane bargez them buskez and to þe baunke rowes,
Bryngez blonkez on bourde and burlyche helmes;   730
Trussez in tristly trappyde stedes,
Tentez and othire toylez and targez full ryche,
Cabanes and clathe-sekkes and coferez full noble,
Hekes and haknays and horsez of armez;
Thus they stowe in the stuffe of full steryn knyghtez.   735
   Qwen all was schyppede that scholde they schounte no lengere,

703 whyne] whyne ne 704 by myne one] by myne[?] honoure one 734 hekes *Banks*] hukes

Bot ventelde them tyte, as þe tyde rynnez;
Coggez and crayers þan crossez þaire mastez,
At the comandment of þe Kynge vncouerde at ones.
Wyghtly on þe wale þay wye vp þaire ankers,   740
By wytt of þe watyre-men of þe wale ythez;
Frekes on þe forestavne faken þeire coblez,
In floynes and fercostez and Flemesche schyppes;
Tytt saillez to þe toppe and turnez þe lufe,
Standez appon stere-bourde, sternly þay songen.   745
The pryce schippez of the porte prouen theire depnesse,
And fondez wyth full saile ower þe fawe ythez;
Iolly withowttyn harme þay hale in bottes;
Schipemen scharply schoten þaire portez,
Launchez lede apon lufe, lacchen þer depez;   750
Lukkez to þe lade-sterne when þe lyghte faillez,
Castez coursez be crafte when þe clowde rysez,
With þe nedyll and þe stone one þe nyghte tydez;
For drede of þe derke nyghte þay drecchede a lyttill,
And all þe steryn of þe streme strekyn at onez.   755
        The Kynge was in a gret cogge, with knyghtez full many,
In a cabane enclosede, clenlyche arayede;
Within on a ryche bedde rystys a littyll,
And with þe swoghe of þe see in swefnyng he fell.
Hym dremyd of a dragon, dredfull to beholde,   760
Come dryfande ouer þe depe to drenschen hys pople,
Ewen walkande owte of the weste landez,   f.61ᵛ
Vanderande vnworthyly ouere the wale ythez;
Bothe his hede and hys hals ware halely all ouer
Dundyde of azŭre, enamelde full faire;   765
His scoulders ware schalyde all in clene syluere,
Schreede ouer all þe schrympe with schrinkande poyntez;
Hys wombe and hys wenges of wondyrfull hewes,
In meruaylous maylys he mountede full hye;
Whaym þat he towchede he was tynt for euer.   770
Hys feete ware floreschede all in fyne sabyll,
And syche a vennymous flayre flowe fro his lyppez,
That the flode of þe flawez all on fyre semyde.

742 forestavne *Björkman*] forestayne   750 lede] *possibly* lode

Thane come of þe oryente, ewyn hym agaynez,   775

A blake, bustous bere abwen in the clowdes,

With yche a pawe as a poste and paumes full huge,

With pykes full perilous—all plyande þam semyde;

Lothen and lothely lokkes and oþer,

All with lutterde legges, lokerde vnfaire,   780

Filtyrde vnfrely, with fomaunde lyppez,

The foulleste of fegure that fourmede was euer.

He baltyrde, he bleryde, he braundyschte þerafter;

To bataile he bounnez hym with bustous clowez;

He romede, he rarede, that roggede all þe erthe,   785

So ruydly he rappyd at to ryot hym seluen.

    Thane the dragon on dreghe dressede hym aȝaynez,

And with hys d[i]nttez hym drafe on dreghe by þe walkyn;

He fares as a fawcon: frekly he strykez;

Bothe with feete and with fyre he feghttys at ones.

The bere in the bataile þe bygger hym semyde,   790

And byttes hym boldlye wyth balefull tuskez;

Syche buffetez he hym rechez with hys brode klokes,

Hys brest and his brayell whas blodye all ouer.

He rawmpyde so ruydly that all þe erthe ryfez,

Rynnande on reede blode as rayne of the heuen.   795

He hade weryede the worme by wyghtnesse of strenghte,

Ne ware it fore the wylde fyre þat he hym wyth defendez.

    Thane wandyrs þe worme awaye to hys heghttez,

Commes glydande fro þe clowddez and cowpez full euen,

Towchez hym wyth his talounez and terez hys rigg,   800

Betwyx þe taile and the toppe ten fote large.

Thus he brittenyd the bere and broghte hym o lyfe—

Lette hym fall in the flode, fleete whare hym lykes.

So they þryng þe bolde kyng bynne þe schippe-burde,

Þat nere he bristez for bale, on bede whare he lyggez.   805

    Than waknez þe wyese kyng, wery foretrauaillede,

Takes hym two phylozophirs that folowede hym euer,   f.6

In the seuyn scyence the suteleste fonden,

The cony[n]geste of clergye vndyre Criste knowen.

He tolde þem of ṅys tourmente þat tym þat he slepede: 8

778 lokkes] lokes lokkes   804 þring *Holthausen*] bring

"Drechede with a dragon, and syche a derfe beste,
Has mad me full wery; ȝe tell me my swefen,
Ore I mon swelte as swythe, as wysse me oure Lorde!"
"Sir," saide þey son thane, thies sagge philosopherse,
"The dragon þat þow dremyde of, so dredfull to schewe,   *815*
That come dryfande ouer þe deepe to drynchen thy pople,
Sothely and certayne, thy seluen it es,
That thus saillez ouer þe see with thy sekyre knyghtez;
The colurez þat ware castyn appon his clere wengez,
May be thy kyngrykez all, that thow has ryghte wonnyn;   *820*
And the tatterede taile with tonges so huge,
Betakyns þis faire folke that in thy fleet wendez;
The bere that bryttenede was abowen in þe clowdez
Betakyns the tyrauntez þat tourmentez thy pople;
Or ells with somme gyaunt some journée sall happyn,   *825*
In syngulere batell by ȝoure selfe one,
And þow sall hafe þe victorye, thurghe helpe of oure Lorde,
As þow in thy visione was opynly schewede.
Of this dredfull dreme ne drede the no more;
Ne kare noghte, Sir Conquerour, bot comforth thy seluen;   *830*
And thise þat saillez ouer þe see, with thy sekyre knyghtez."
    With trumppez then trystly they trisen vpe þaire saillez,
And rowes ouer the ryche see, this rowtte all at onez;
The comely coste of Normandye they cachen full euen,
And blythely at Barflete theis bolde are arryfede,   *835*
And fyndys a flete there of frendez ynewe,
The floure and þe faire folke of fyftene rewmez;
Fore kyngez and capytaynez kepyde hym fayre,
As he at Carelele commaundyde at Cristynmesse hym seluen.
    Be they had taken the lande and tentez vpe rerede,   *840*
Comez a templere tyte and towchide to þe Kynge:
Here es a teraunt besyde that tourmentez thi pople,
A grett geaunte of Geen, engenderde of fendez;
He has fretyn of folke mo than fyfe hondrethe,
And als fele fawntekyns of freeborne childyre.   *845*
This has bene his sustynaunce all this seuen wyntteres,

---

811 and] and and   821 tatterede *Branscheid*] tathesesede
840 rerede] rerer rerc [*next letter illegible*] [*both crossed out*] rerede

And ȝitt es that sotte noghte sadde, so wele hym it lykez!
In þe contrée of Constantyne ne kynde has he leuede,
Withowttyn kydd castells enclosid wyth walles,
That he ne has clenly dystroyede all the knaue childyre,　　　850
And them caryede to þe cragge and clenly deworyd!
The Duchez of Bretayne todaye has he takyn,　　　　　　　—
Beside Reynes as scho rade with hire ryche knyghttes;　　　f.62ᵛ
Ledd hyre to þe mountayne thare þat lede lengez,
To lye by that lady aye whyls hir lyfe lastez.　　　　　　855
We folowede o ferrom, moo then fyfe hundrethe
Of beryns and of burgeys and bachelers noble,
Bot he couerde the cragge—cho cryede so lowde,
The care of þat creatoure couer sall I neuer!
Scho was flour of all Fraunce, or of fyfe rewmes,　　　　860
And one of the fayreste that fourmede was euere,
The gentileste jowell ajuggede with lordes
Fro Geen vnto Geron, by Ihesu of Heuen!
Scho was thy wyfes cosyn—knowe it if þe lykez—
Comen of þe rycheste that rengnez in erthe;　　　　　　86
As thow arte ryghtwise Kyng, rewe on thy pople,
And fande for to venge them that thus are rebuykyde!"
　　　　"Allas!" sais Sir Arthure, "so lange haue I lyffede;
Hade I wyten of this, wele had me chefede;
Me es noghte fallen faire, bot me es foule happynede,　　　87
That thus this faire ladye this fende has dystroyede!
I had leuere thane all Fraunce this fyftene wynter
I hade bene before thate freke a furlange of waye,
When he that ladye had laghte and ledde to þe montez;
I hadde lefte my lyfe are cho hade harme lymppyde.　　　87
Bot walde þow kene me to þe crage thare þat kene lengez;
I walde cayre to þat coste and carpe wythe hym seluen,
To trette with that tyraunt fore treson of londes,
And take trewe for a tym, till it may tyde bettyr."
　　　　"Sire, see ȝe ȝone farlande, with ȝone two fyrez?　　　8
Þar filsnez þat fende—fraiste when the lykes—
Appone the creste of the cragge, by a colde welle,
That enclosez þe clyfe with þe clere strandez;
Ther may thow fynde folke fay wythowttyn nowmer,

Mo florenez, in faythe, than Fraunce es in aftyre;   885
And more tresour vntrewely that traytour has getyn
Thane in Troye was, as I trowe, þat tym þat it was wonn."
    Thane romyez the ryche kynge for rewthe of þe pople,
Raykez ryghte to a tente and restez no lengere;
He welterys, he wristeles, he wryngez hys handez;   890
Thare was no wy of þis werlde that wyste whatt he menede.
He calles Sir Cayous, þat of þe cowpe serfede,
And Sir Bedvere þe bolde, þat bare hys brande ryche:
'Luke ȝe aftyre euensang be armyde at ryghttez,
On blonkez by ȝone buscayle, by ȝone blythe stremez,   895
Fore I will passe in pilgremage preuely hereaftyre,
In the tyme of suppere, whene lordez are servede,   f.63ʳ
For to seken a saynte be ȝone salte stremes,
In Seynt Mighell Mount, there myraclez are schewede."
Aftyre euesange, Sir Arthure hym se[l]fen   900
Wente to hys wardrop and warp of hys wedez,
Armede hym in a acton with orfraeez full ryche,
Abouen on þat a jeryn of Acres owte ouer,
Abouen þat a jesseraunt of jentyll maylez,
A jupon of Ierodyn, jaggede in schredez;   905
He brayedez one a bacenett, burneschte of syluer,
The beste þat was in Basill, wyth bordurs ryche;
The creste and þe coronall enclosed so faire
Wyth clasppis of clere golde, couched wyth stones;
The vesare, þe aventaile, enarmede so faire,   910
Voyde withowttyn vice, with wyndowes of syluer;
His gloues gaylyche gilte and grauen at þe hemmez,
Vith graynez and gobelets, glorious of hewe.
He bracez a brade schelde and his brande aschez,
Bounede hym a broun stede and on þe bente houys;   915
He sterte till his sterep and stridez on lofte,
Streynez hym stowttly and sterys hym faire,
Brochez þe baye stede and to þe buske rydez,
And there hys knyghtes hym kepede full clenlyche arayede.
    Than they roode by þat ryuer þat rynnyd so swythe,   920
Þare þe ryndez ouerrechez with reall bowghez;
The roo and þe raynedere reklesse thare ronnen,

In ranez and in rosers, to ryotte þam seluen;
The frithez ware floreschte with flourez full many,
Wyth fawcouns and fesantez of ferlyche hewez;   *925*
All þe feulez thare fleschez that flyez with wengez,
Fore thare galede þe gowke one greuez full lowde:
Wyth alkyn gladchipe þay gladden þem seluen;
Of þe nyghtgale notez þe noisez was swette—
They threpide wyth the throstills, thre hundreth at ones;   *930*
Þat whate swowyng of watyr and syngyng of byrdez,
It myghte salue hym of sore þat sounde was neuere.

       Than ferkez this folke and on fotte lyghttez,
Festenez theire faire stedez o ferrom bytwene;
And thene the Kyng kenely comandyde hys knyghtez   *933*
For to byde with theire blonkez and bowne no forthyre:
"Fore I will seke this seynte by my selfe one,
And mell with this mayster mane þat this monte ȝemez;
And seyn sall ȝe offyre, aythyre aftyre oþer,
Menskfully at Saynt Mighell full myghtty with Criste."   *94*

       The Kyng coueris þe cragge wyth cloughes full hye,
To the creste of the clyffe he clymbez on lofte;   *f.63*
Keste vpe hys vmbrer and kenly he lukes,
Caughte of þe colde wynde to comforthe hym seluen.
Two fyrez he fyndez, flawmande full hye;   *94*
The fourtedele a furlang betwene þus he walkes;
The waye by þe welle strandez he wandyrde hym one,
To wette of þe warlawe, whare þat he lengez.
He ferkez to þe fyrste fyre, and euen there he fyndez
A wery wafull wedowe, wryngande hire handez,   *95*
And gretande on a graue grysely teres;
Now merkyde on molde sen myddaye it semede.
He saluȝede þat sorowfull with sittande wordez,
And fraynez aftyre the fende fairely thereaftyre.

       Thane this wafull wyfe vnwynly hym gretez,   *95*
Couerd vp on hire kneess and clappyde hire handez;
Said "Carefull careman, thow carpez to lowde;
May ȝone warlawe wyt, he worows vs all!
Weryd worthe þe wyghte ay that þe thy wytt refede,
That mase the to wayfe here in þise wylde lakes.   *9*

I warne þe fore wyrchipe þou wylnez aftyr sorowe;
Whedyre buskes þou, berne? Vnblysside þow semes.
Wenez thow to britten hym with thy brande ryche?
Ware thow wyghttere than Wade or Wawayn owthire,
Thow wynnys no wyrchip, I warne the before. 965
Thow saynned the vnsekyrly to seke to þese mountez;
Siche sex ware to symple to semble with hym one,
For and thow see hym with syghte, the seruez no herte
To sayne the sekerly, so semez hym huge!
Thow arte frely and faire and in thy fyrste flourez, 970
Bot thow arte fay, be my faythe, and þat me forthynkkys.
Ware syche fyfty on a felde or one a faire erthe,
The freke walde with hys fyste fell ȝow at ones!
Loo, here the duchez dere—todaye was cho takyn—
Depe doluen and dede, dyked in moldez; 975
He hade morthirede this mylde be myddaye war rongen,
Withowttyn mercy one molde—I not watte it ment.
He has forsede hir and fylede, and cho es fay leuede;
He slewe hir vnslely and slitt hir to þe nauyll.
And here haue I bawmede hir and beryede þeraftyr; 980
For bale of þe botelesse, blythe be I neuer.
Of alle þe frendez cho hade, þere folowede none aftyre,
Bot I, hir foster modyr of fyftene wynter;
To ferke of this farlande, fande sall I neuer,
Bot here be founden on felde till I be fay leuede." 985
　　Thane answers Sir Arthure to þat alde wyf, f.64ʳ
'I am comyn fra þe Conquerour, curtaise and gentill,
As one of þe hathelest of Arthur knyghtez,
Messenger to þis myx, for mendemente of þe pople,
To mele with this maister man that here this mounte ȝemez; 990
To trete with this tyraunt for tresour of landez,
And take trew for a tym, to bettyr may worthe."
　　"ȝa, thire wordis are bot waste," quod this wif thane,
'For bothe landez and lythes full lyttill by he settes;
Of rentez ne of rede golde rekkez he neuer, 995
For he will lenge owt of lawe, as hym selfe thynkes,
Withowten licence of lede, as lorde in his awen.

977　watte] watte watte

Bot he has a kyrtill one, kepide for hym seluen,
That was sponen in Spayne with specyall byrdez,
And sythyn garnescht in Grece full graythly togedirs.   *1000*
It es hyded all with har hally al ouere,
And bordyrde with the berdez of burlyche kyngez,
Crispid and kombide, that kempis may knawe
Iche kyng by his colour, in kythe there he lengez;
Here the fermez he fangez of fyftene rewmez: *1005*
For ilke Esterne ewyn, howeuer that it fall,
They send it hym sothely for saughte of þe pople,
Sekerly at þat seson, with certayne knyghtez.
And he has aschede Arthure all þis seuen wynntter:
Forthy hurdez he here, to owttraye hys pople,   *1010*
Till þe Bretons kyng haue burneschte his lyppys,
And sent his berde to that bolde wyth his beste berynes.
Bot thowe hafe broghte þat berde, bowne the no forthire,
For it es buteless bale thowe biddez oghte ells;
For he has more tresour to take when hym lykez   *1015*
Than euere aughte Arthure or any of hys elders;
If thowe hafe broghte þe berde he bese more blythe
Thane þowe gafe hym Burgoyne or Bretayne þe More.
Bot luke nowe for charitée þow chasty thy lyppes,
That the no wordez eschape, whateso betydez;   *1020*
Luke þi presante be priste, and presse hym bott lytill,
For he es at his sowper, he will be sone greuyde;
And þow my concell doo, þow dosse of thy clothes,
And knele in thy kyrtyll, and call hym thy lorde.
He sowppes all þis seson with seuen knaue childre,   *1025*
Choppid in a chargour of chalke-whytt syluer,
With pekill and powdyre of precious spycez,
And pyment full plenteuous of Portyngale wynes;
Thre balefull birdez his brochez þey turne,
Þat byddez his bedgatt, his byddyng to wyrche;   *1030*
Siche foure scholde be fay within foure hourez,
Are his fylth ware filled that his flesch ȝernes."   f.64

     "ȝa, I haue broghte þe berd," quod he, "the bettyr me lykez;
Forthi will I boun me, and bere it my seluen;

1001 ouere] ouere ouerc [*after* ouyrc *crossed out*]

Bot, lefe, walde þow lere me whare þat lede lengez, 1035
I sall alowe þe and I liffe, oure Lorde so me helpe."
"Ferke fast to þe fyre," quod cho, "that flawmez so hye;
Thare fillis þat fende hym, fraist when the lykez;
Bot thow moste seke more southe, sydlyngs a lyttill,
For he will hafe sent hym selfe sex myle large." 1040
To þe sowþe of þe reke he soghte at þe gayneste,
Sayned hym sekerly with certeyne wordez,
And sydlyngs of þe segge the syghte had he rechid,
Iow vnsemly þat sott satt sowpand hym one;
Ie lay lenand on lang, lugand vnfaire, 1045
De thee of a manns lymme lyffe vp by þe haunche;
Iis bakke and his bewschers and his brode lendez
Ie bekez by þe bale-fyre, and breklesse hym semede.
Dare ware rostez full ruyd and rewfull bredez,
Beerynes and bestaile brochede togeders, 1050
Cowle full cramede of crysmed childyre,
Sum as brede brochede, and bierdez þam tournede.
And þan this comlych kyng, bycause of his pople,
Iis herte bledez for bale, one bent ware he standez.
Thane he dressede one his schelde, schuntes no lengere, 1055
Braundesch[t]e his bryghte swerde by þe bryghte hiltez,
Raykez towarde þe renke reghte with a ruyd will,
And hyely hailsez þat hulke with hawtayne wordez:
"Now, allweldand Gode, þat wyrscheppez vs all,
Giff the sorowe and syte, sotte, there thow lygges, 1060
For the fulsomeste freke that fourmede was euere;
Foully thow fedys the, þe Fende haue thi saule!
Iere es cury vnclene, carle, be my trowthe,
Taffe of creatours all, thow curssede wriche!
Because that þow killide has þise cresmede childyre, 1065
Thow has marters made, and broghte oute of lyfe,
That here are brochede on bente and brittened with thi handez,
I sall merke þe thy mede, as þou has myche serfed,
Thurghe myghte of Seynt Mighell, þat þis monte zemes;
And for this faire ladye, þat þow has fey leuyde, 1070
And þus forced one foulde, for fylth of þi selfen.

1041 sowþe Banks] sowre

Dresse the now, dogge-sone—the Deuell haue þi saule—
For þow sall dye this day, thurghe dynt of my handez!"
    Than glopned þe gloton and glored vnfaire;
He grenned as a grewhounde, with grysly tuskes;   1075
He gaped, he groned faste, with grucchand latez,
For grefe of þe gude kyng þat hym with grame gretez.
His fax and his foretoppe was filterede togeders,
And owte of his face come ane halfe fote large;
His frount and his forheued all was it ouer,   1080
As þe fell of a froske, and fraknede it semede;
Huke-nebbyde as a hawke, and a hore berde,
And herede to þe hole eyghn with hyngande browes;   f.65
Harske as a hunde-fisch hardly whoso lukez,
So was þe hyde of þat hulke hally al ouer.   1085
Erne had he full huge and vgly to schewe,
With eghne full horreble and ardauunt forsothe;
Flatt-mowthede as a fluke, with fleryand lyppys,
And þe flesche in his fortethe fowly as a bere.
His berde was brothy and blake, þat till his brest rechede,   1090
Grassede as a mereswyne, with corkes full huge,
And all falterd þe flesche in his foule lippys,
Ilke wrethe as a wolfe-heuede, it wraythe owtt at ones.
Bulle-nekkyde was þat bierne and brade in the scholders,
Brok-brestede as a brawne, with brustils full large,   109.
Ruyd armes as an ake with rusclede sydes,
Lym and leskes full lothyn, leue ȝe forsothe.
Schouell-foted was þat schalke, and schaylande hym semyde,
With schankez vnschaply, schowand togedyrs;
Thykke theese as a thursse, and thikkere in þe hanche,   110
Greesse growen as a galte, full gry[s]lych he lukez.
Who þe lenghe of þe lede lelly accountes,
Fro þe face to þe fote was fyfe fadom lange.
    Thane stertez he vp sturdely on two styffe schankez,
And sone he caughte hym a clubb all of clene yryn;   110
He walde hafe kyllede þe Kyng with his kene wapen,
Bot thurghe þe crafte of Cryste ȝit þe carle failede;
The creest and þe coronall, þe claspes of syluer,

1079 come *Björkman*] fome

Clenly with his clubb he crassched doune at onez.
The Kyng castes vp his schelde and couers hym faire,   *1110*
And with his burlyche brande a box he hym reches;
Full butt in þe frunt the fromonde he hittez,
That the burnyscht blade to þe brayne rynnez.
He feyed his fysnamye with his foule hondez,
And frappez faste at his face fersely þeraftyre;   *1115*
The Kyng chaungez his fote, eschewes a lyttill—
Ne had he eschapede þat choppe, cheuede had euyll;
He folowes in fersly and festenesse a dynte
Hye vpe on þe hanche with his harde wapyn,
That he hillid þe swerde halfe a fote large—   *1120*
The hott blode of þe hulke vnto þe hilte rynnez;
Ewyn into inmette the gyaunt he hyttez,
Iust to þe genitales and jaggede þam in sondre.
      Thane he romyed and rared, and ruydly he strykez
Full egerly at Arthur, and on the erthe hittez;   *1125*
A swerde lenghe within þe swarthe he swappez at ones,
That nere swounes þe Kyng for swoughe of his dynttez.
Bot ȝit the Kyng sweperly full swythe he byswenkez,
Swappez in with the swerde þat it þe swange brystedd;
Bothe þe guttez and the gorr guschez owte at ones,   *1130*
Þat all englaymez þe gresse one grounde þer he standez.
Thane he castez the clubb and the Kyng hentez: f.65ᵛ
On þe creeste of þe cragg he caughte hym in armez,
And enclosez hym clenly, to cruschen hys rybbez—
So hard haldez he þat hende þat nere his herte brystez.   *1135*
Þane þe balefull bierdez bownez to þe erthe,
Kneland and cryande, and clappide þeire handez:
"Criste comforthe ȝone knyghte, and kepe hym fro sorowe,
And latte neuer ȝone fende fell hym o lyfe."
      ȝitt es þe warlow so wyghte, he welters hym vnder,   *1140*
Wrothely þai wrythyn and wrystill togederz,
Welters and walowes ouer within þase buskez,
Tumbellez and turnes faste and terez þaire wedez;
Vntenderly fro þe toppe þai tiltin togederz,
Whilom Arthure ouer and oþerwhile vndyre;   *1145*

1123 genitales *Brock*] genitates

Fro þe heghe of þe hyll vnto þe harde roche,
They feyne neuer are they fall at þe flode merkes.
Bot Arthur with ane anlace egerly smyttez,
And hittez euer in the hulke vp to þe hiltez;
Þe theeffe at þe dede-thrawe so throly hym thryngez,   1150
Þat three rybbys in his syde he thrystez in sunder.
    Then Sir Kayous þe kene vnto þe Kyng styrtez:
Said "Allas, we are lorne—my lorde es confundede;
Ouerfallen with a fende—vs es full hapnede!
We mon be forfeted, in faith, and flemyde for euer!"   1155
Þay hafe vp hys hawberke þan and handilez þervndyr
His hyde and his haunche eke, on heghte to þe schuldrez,
His flawnke and his feletez and his faire sydez,
Bothe his bakke and his breste and his bryghte armez;
Þay ware fayne þat þey fande no flesche entamed,   1160
And for þat journée made joye, þir gentill knyghttez.
    "Now certez," saise Sir Bedwere, "it semez, be my Lorde,
He sekez seyntez bot selden, þe sorer he grypes,
Þat þus clekys this corsaunt owte of þir heghe clyffez,
To carye forthe siche a carle at close hym in siluer.   1165
Be Myghell, of syche a makk I hafe myche wondyre
That euer owre soueraygne Lorde suffers hym in Heuen;
And all seyntez be syche þat seruez oure Lorde,
I sall neuer no seynt bee, be my fadyre sawle!"
    Thane bourdez þe bolde kyng at Bedvere wordez: 1170
"Þis seynt haue I soghte, so helpe me owre Lorde!
Forthy brayd owtte þi brande, and broche hym to þe herte;
Be sekere of this sergeaunt, he has me sore greuede.
I faghte noghte wyth syche a freke þis fyftene wyntyre;
Bot in þe montez of Araby I mett syche anoþer: 1175
He was þe forcyer be ferre þat had I nere funden—
Ne had my fortune bene faire, fey had I leuede.
Onone stryke of his heuede, and stake it thereaftyre,
Gife it to thy sqwyere, fore he es wele horsede,
Bere it to Sir Howell, þat es in harde bandez,   1180
And byd hym herte hym wele, his enmy es destruede.   f.6
Syne bere it to Bareflete, and brace it in yryne,
And sett it on the barbycane, biernes to schewe.

My brande and my brode schelde apon þe bent lyggez,
On þe creeste of þe cragge, thare fyrste we encontrede,   1185
And þe clubb þarby, all of clene iren,
Þat many Cristen has kyllyde in Constantyne landez;
Ferke to the farlande, and fetche me þat wapen,
And late founde till oure flete, in flode þare it lengez.
If thow wyll any tresour, take whate the lykez;   1190
Haue I the kyrtyll and þe clubb, I coueite noghte ells."
      Now þey caire to þe cragge, þise comlyche knyghtez,
And broghte hym þe brade schelde and his bryghte wapen,
Þe clubb and þe cotte alls, Syr Kayous hym seluen,
And kayres with [the] Conquerour, the kyngez to schewe   1195
That in couerte þe Kyng helde closse to hym seluen,
Whills clene day fro þe clowde clymbyd on lofte.
      Be that to courte was comen clamour full huge;
And before þe comlyche kyng they knelyd all at ones:
"Welcom, our liege lorde, to lang has thow duellyde—   1200
Gouernour vndyr Gode, graytheste and noble,
To wham grace es graunted and gyffen at His will;
Now thy comly come has comforthede vs all.
Thow has in thy realtée reuengyde thy pople;
Thurghe helpe of thy hande, thyne enmyse are struyede,   1205
That has thy renkes ouerronne and refte them theire childyre;
Whas neuer rewme owte of araye so redyly releuede!"
      Than þe Conquerour Cristenly carpez to his pople:
"Thankes Gode," quod he, "of þis grace, and no gome ells,
For it was neuer manns dede, bot myghte of Hym selfen,   1210
Or myracle of Hys Modyr, þat mylde es till all."
He somond þan þe schippemen scharpely þeraftyre,
To schake furthe with þe schyremen to schifte þe gudez,
All þe myche tresour þat traytour had wonnen,
To comouns of the contré, clergye and oþer: 1215
Luke it be done and delte to my dere pople,
That none pleyn of theire parte, o peyne of ȝour lyfez."
He comande hys cosyn, with knyghtlyche wordez,
To make a kyrke on þe cragg, ther the corse lengez,
And a couent therein, Criste for to serfe,   1220
In mynde of þat martyre, þat in þe monte rystez.

Qwen Sir Arthur the Kyng had kylled þe gyaunt,
Than blythely fro Bareflete he buskes on þe morne;
With his batell on brede, by þa blythe stremes,
Towarde Castell Blanke he chesez hym the waye;   *1225*
Thurghe a faire champayne, vndyr schalke hyllis,
The Kyng fraystez a furth ouer the fresche strandez,
Foundez with his faire folke ouer as hym lykez;   f.66ᵛ
Furthe stepes that steryn and strekez his tentis
One a strenghe by a streme, in þas straytt landez.   *1230*
    Onone aftyre myddaye, in the mene-while,
Þare comez two messangers of tha fere marchez,
Fra þe Marschall of Fraunce, and menskfully hym gretes,
Besoghte hym of sucour and saide hym þise wordez:
"Sir, thi marschall, þi mynistre, thy mercy besekez,   *1235*
Of thy mekill magestée, fore mendement of thi pople,
Of þise marchez-men, that thus are myskaryede,
And thus merred amang, maugrée theire eghne.
I witter þe þe Emperour es entirde into Fraunce,
With ostes of enmyse, orrible and huge;   *1240*
Brynnez in Burgoyne thy burghes so ryche,
And brittenes thi baronage, that bieldez þarein;
He encrochez kenely by craftez of armez,
Countrese and castells þat to thy coroun langez,
Confoundez thy comouns, clergy and oþer: *1245*
Bot thow comfurth them, Sir Kyng, couer sall they neuer!
He fellez forestez fele, forrayse thi landez,
Frysthez no fraunchez, bot fraiez the pople;
Þus he fellez thi folke and fangez theire gudez:
Fremedly the Franche tung fey es belefede.   *1250*
He drawes into douce Fraunce, as Duchemen tellez,
Dresside with his dragouns, dredfull to schewe;
All to dede they dyghte with dynttys of swerddez,
Dukez and dusperes þat dreches tharein.
Forthy the lordez of the lande, ladys and oþer,   *1255*
Prayes the for Petyr luffe, þe Apostyll of Rome,
Sen thow arte presant in place, þat þow will profyre make
To þat perilous prynce, be processe of tym.

1248 fraiez *Brock*] fraisez

He ayers by ȝone hilles, ȝone heghe holtez vndyr,
Hufes thare with hale strenghe of haythen kyngez;   *1260*
Helpe nowe for His lufe, that heghe in Heuen sittez,
And talke tristly to them þat thus vs destroyes."
    The Kyng biddis Sir Boice, "Buske the belyfe;
Take with the Sir Berill and Bedwere the ryche,
Sir Gawayne and Sir Geryn, these galyarde knyghtez,   *1265*
And graythe ȝowe to ȝone grene wode, and gose on þer nedes:
Saise to Syr Lucius, to vnlordly he wyrkez,
Thus letherly agaynes law to lede my pople;
I lette hym or oghte lange, ȝif me þe lyffe happen,
Or many lyghte sall lawe þat hym ouere lande folowes.   *1270*
Comande hym kenely wyth crewell wordez,
Cayre owte of my kyngryke with his kydd knyghtez:
In caase that he will noghte, þat cursede wreche,
Com for his curtaisie, and countere me ones.   f.67ʳ
Thane sall we rekken full rathe whatt ryghte þat he claymes,   *1275*
Thus to ryot þis rewme and raunsone the pople.
Thare sall it derely be delte with dynttez of handez—
The Dryghtten at Domesdaye dele as Hym lykes!"
    Now thei graythe them to goo, theis galyarde knyghttez,
All gleterande in golde, appon grete stedes,   *1280*
Towarde þe grene wode, with grownden wapyn,
To grete wele the grett lorde, that wolde be grefede sone.
    Thise hende houez on a hill by þe holte eyues,
Behelde þe howsyng full hye of hathen kynges:
They herde in theire herbergage hundrethez full many   *1285*
Hornez of olyfantez full helych blawen;
Palaisez proudliche pyghte, þat palyd ware ryche,
Of pall and of purpure, with precyous stones;
Pensels and pomell of ryche prynce armez,
Pighte in þe playn mede, þe pople to schewe.   *1290*
And than the Romayns so ryche had arayede their tentez,
On rawe by þe ryuer, vndyr þe round hillez,
The Emperour for honour ewyn in the myddes,
Wyth egles al ouer, ennelled so faire;

1265 Geryn *Björkman*] Gryme   1281 with] þat with
1294 ennelled so faire] enamellede [?] so faire *crossed out*

And saw hym and þe Sowdane, and senatours many   *1295*
Seke towarde a sale with sextene kyngez,
Syland softely in, swettly by them selfen,
To sowpe withe þat soueraygne full selcouthe metez.
     Nowe they wende ouer the watyre, þise wyrchipfull knyghttez,
Thurghe þe wode to þe wone there the wyese rystez;   *1300*
Reght as þey hade weschen and went to þe table,
Sir Wawayne þe worthy vnwynly he spekes:
"The myghte and þe maiestée þat menskes vs all,
That was merked and made thurghe þe myghte of Hym seluen,
Gyffe ȝow sytte in ȝour sette, Sowdane and oþer,   *1305*
That here are semblede in sale—vnsawghte mott ȝe worthe!
And þe fals heretyke þat Emperour hym callez,
That ocupyes in erroure the Empyre of Rome,
Sir Arthure herytage, þat honourable kyng,
That all his auncestres aughte but Vtere hym one,   *1310*
That ilke cursynge þat Cayme kaghte for his brothyre
Cleffe on þe, cukewalde, with croune ther thow lengez,
For the vnlordlyeste lede þat I on lukede euer!
My lorde meruailles hym mekyll, man, be my trouthe,
Why thow morthires his men, þat no mysse serues,   *1315*
Comouns of þe countré, clergye and oþer,
Þat are noghte coupable þerin, ne knawes noght in armez.
Forthi the comelyche kynge, curtays and noble,
Comandez þe kenely to kaire of his landes,
Ore ells for thy knyghthede encontre hym ones;   f.67ᵛ *1320*
Sen þow couettes the coroune, latte it be declarede!
I hafe dyschargide me here—chalange whoo lykez—
Before all thy cheualrye, cheftaynes and oþer;
Schape vs an ansuere, and schunte þow no lengere,
Þat we may schifte at þe schorte and schewe to my lorde."   *1325*
     The Emperour ansuerde wyth austeryn wordez:
"Ȝe are with myn enmy, Sir Arthur hym seluen;
It es non honour to me to owttray hys knyghttez,
Þoghe ȝe bee irous men þat ayres on his nedez;
Bot say to thy soueraygne I send hym thes wordez,   *1330*
Ne ware it for reuerence of my ryche table,

     1302 worthy] worthethy

Þou sulde repent full rathe of þi ruyde wordez—
Siche a rebawde as þowe rebuke any lordez,
Wyth theire retenuz arrayede, full reall and noble—
Here will I suggourne whills me lefe thynkes,   *1335*
And sythen seke in by Sayne with solace þeraftere,
Ensegge al þa cetése be þe salte strandez,
And seyn ryde in by Rone, þat rynnez so faire,
And of all his ryche castells rusche doun þe wallez;
I sall noghte lefe in Paresche, by processe of tyme,   *1340*
His parte of a pechelyne—proue when hym lykes!"
     "Now certez," sais Sir Wawayne, "myche wondyre haue I
Þat syche an alfyn as thow dare speke syche wordez!
I had leuer then all Fraunce, that heuede es of rewmes,
Fyghte with the faythefully on felde be oure one."   *1345*
Thane answers Sir Gayous full gobbede wordes—
Was eme to þe Emperour and erle hym selfen—
"Euere ware þes Bretouns braggers of olde!
Loo, how he brawles hym for hys bryghte wedes,
As he myghte bryttyn vs all with his brande ryche;   *1350*
Ʒitt he berkes myche boste, ʒone boy þere he standes!"
     Than greuyde Sir Gawayne at his grett wordes,
Graythes towarde þe gome with grucchande herte;
With hys stelyn brande he strykes of hys heuede,
And sterttes owtte to hys stede, and with his stale wendes.   *1355*
Thurghe þe wacches þey wente, thes wirchipfull knyghtez,
And fyndez in theire farewaye wondyrlyche many;
Ouer þe watyre þey wente by wyghtnesse of horses,
And tuke wynde as þey walde by þe wodde hemmes.
Thane folous frekly one fote frekkes ynewe,   *1360*
And of þe Romayns arrayed appon ryche stedes,
Chasede thurghe a champayne oure cheualrous knyghtez,
Till a cheefe forest, on scalke-whitte horses.
Bot a freke all in fyne golde, and fretted in sable,
Come forþermaste on a freson, in flawmande wedes;   *1365*
A faire floreschte spere in fewtyre he castes,
And folowes faste on owre folke and freschelye ascryez.
     Thane Sir Gawayne the gude, appone a graye stede,   f.68ʳ
He gryppes hym a grete spere and graythely hym hittez;

Thurghe þe guttez into þe gorre he gyrdes hym ewyn,   *1370*
That the grounden stele glydez to his herte;
The gome and þe grette horse at þe grounde lyggez,
Full gryselyche gronande, for grefe of his woundez.
Þane presez a preker in, full proudely arayede,   *1375*
That beres all of pourpour, palyde with syluer;
Byggly on a broune stede he profers full large—
He was a paynyme of Perse þat þus hym persuede.
Sir Boys, vnabaiste all, he buskes hym agaynes,
With a bustous launce he berez hym thurghe,
Þat þe breme and þe brade schelde appon þe bente lyggez;   *1380*
And he bryngez furthe the blade and bownez to his felowez.

      Thane Sir Feltemour of myghte, a man mekyll praysede,
Was mouede on his manere and manacede full faste;
He graythes to Sir Gawayne graythely to wyrche,
For grefe of Sir Gayous, þat es on grounde leuede.   *1385*
Than Sir Gawayne was glade: agayne hym he rydez,
Wyth Galuth his gude swerde graythely hym hyttez;
The knyghte on þe coursere he cleuede in sondyre—
Clenlyche fro þe croune his corse he dyuysyde,
And þus he killez þe knyghte with his kydd wapen.   *1390*

      Than a ryche man of Rome relyede to his byerns:
"It sall repent vs full sore and we ryde forthire!
Ȝone are bolde bosturs þat syche bale wyrkez;
It befell hym full foule þat þam so fyrste namede."

      Thane þe riche Romayns retournes þaire brydills   *1395*
To þaire tentis in tene, telles theire lordez
How Sir Marschalle de Mowne es on þe monte lefede,
Forejustyde at that journée for his grett japez.
Bot thare chasez on oure men cheuallrous knyghtez,
Fyfe thosande folke appon faire stedes,   *1400*
Faste to a foreste ouer a fell watyr,
That fillez fro þe falow see fyfty myle large.
Thare ware Bretons enbuschide, and banarettez noble,
Of þe cheualrye cheefe of þe kyngez chambyre,
Seese them chase oure men and changen þeire horsez,   *1405*
And choppe doun cheftaynes that they moste chargyde.

      Thane þe enbuschement of Bretons brake owte at ones,

Brothely at baner, and Bedwyne knyghtez
Arrestede of þe Romayns þat by þe fyrthe rydez
All þe realeste renkes þat to Rome lengez; *1410*
Thay iche on þe enmyse and egerly strykkys,
Erles of Ingland, and "Arthure!" ascryes;
Thrughe brenes and bryghte scheldez brestez they thyrle,
Bretons of the boldeste, with theire bryghte swerdez.
Thare was Romayns ouerredyn and ruydly wondyde, f.68ᵛ *1415*
Arrestede as rebawdez with ryotous knyghttez;
The Romaynes owte of araye remouede at ones,
And rydes awaye in a rowtte, for reddoure it semys.
        To þe Senatour Petyr a sandesmane es commyn,
And saide, "Sir, sekyrly, ȝour seggez are supprysside." *1420*
Than ten thowsande men he semblede at ones,
And sett sodanly on our seggez, by þe salte strandez;
Than ware Bretons abaiste and greuede a lyttill,
Bot ȝit the banerettez bolde and bachellers noble
Brekes that battailles with brestez of stedes; *1425*
Sir Boice and his bolde men myche bale wyrkes.
The Romaynes redyes þam, arrayez þam better,
And al toruscheez oure men withe theire ryste horsez,
Arestede of the richeste of þe Rounde Table,
Ouerrydez oure rerewarde and grette rewthe wyrkes. *1430*
        Thane the Bretons on þe bente habyddez no lengere,
Bot fleede to þe foreste and the feelde leuede;
Sir Beryll es born down and Sir Boice taken,
The beste of our bolde men vnblythely wondyde;
Bot ȝitt our stale on a strenghe stotais a lyttill, *1435*
All tostonayede with þe stokes of þa steryn knyghtez;
Made sorowe fore theire soueraygne, þat so þare was nomen,
Besoughte Gode of socure, sende whene Hym lykyde.
        Than commez Sir Idrus, armede vp at all ryghttez,
Wyth fyue hundrethe men appon faire stedes; *1440*
Fraynez faste at oure folke freschely þareaftyre,
Sif þer frendez ware ferre, þat on þe felde foundide.
Thane sais Sir Gawayne, "So me God helpe,
We hafe bene chased todaye and chullede as hares,

1425 battailles] baitailles   1427 þam *O'Loughlin*] þan

Rebuyked with Romaynes appon þeire ryche stedez,   *1445*
And we lurkede vndyr lee as lowrande wreches!
I luke neuer on my lorde þe dayes of my lyfe,
And we so lytherly hym helpe þat hym so wele lykede."
    Thane the Bretons brothely brochez theire stedez,
And boldly in batell appon þe bent rydes;   *1450*
All þe ferse men before frekly ascryes,
Ferkand in þe foreste, to freschen þam selfen.
The Romaynes than redyly arrayes them bettyre,
One rawe on a rowm felde, reghttez theire wapyns,
By þe ryche reuere, and rewles þe pople;   *1455*
And with reddour Sir Boice es in areste halden.
    Now thei semblede vnsaughte by þe salte strandez:
Saddly theis sekere menn settys þeire dynttez;
With lufly launcez on lofte they luyschen togedyres,
In lorayne so lordlye on leppande stedes.   *1460*
Thare ware gomes thurghegirde with grundyn wapyns,
Grisely gayspand with grucchande lotes;
Grete lordes of Greke greffede so hye.
Swyftly with swerdes they swappen thereaftyre,   f.69r
Swappez doun full sweperlye swelltande knyghtez,   *1465*
That all swellttez one swarthe that they ouerswyngen;
So many sweys in swoghe, swounande att ones.
    Syr Gaweayne the gracyous full graythelye he wyrkkes:
The gretteste he gretez wyth gryeslye wondes;
Wyth Galuth he gyrdez doun full galyard knyghtez—   *1470*
Fore greefe of þe grett lorde so grymlye he strykez.
He rydez furthe ryallye and redely thereaftyre,
Thare this reall renke was in areste halden;
He ryfez þe raunke stele, he ryghttez þeire brenez,
And refte them the ryche man and rade to his strenghes.   *1475*
The Senatour Peter thane persewede hym aftyre,
Thurghe þe presse of þe pople, wyth his pryce knyghttes;
Apperrtly fore þe prysonere proues his strenghes,
Wyth prekers the proudeste that to þe presse lengez.
Wrothely on the wrange hande Sir Gawayne he strykkes,   *1480*
Wyth a wapen of were vnwynnly hym hittez;

    1465 knyghtez] knynghtez

The breny one þe bakhalfe he brystez in sondyre—
Bot ȝit he broghte forthe Sir Boyce, for all þeire bale biernez.
    Thane þe Bretons boldely braggen þeire tromppez,
And fore blysse of Sir Boyce was broghte owtte of bandez,   *1485*
Boldely in batell they bere doun knyghtes;
With brandes of broun stele þey brettened maylez;
Þay stekede stedys in stour with stelen wapyns,
And all stewede with strenghe þat stode þem agaynes.
    Sir Idrus fitz Ewayn þan "Arthur!" ascryeez,   *1490*
Assemblez on þe Senatour wyth sextene knyghttez,
Of þe sekereste men þat to oure syde lengede.
Sodanly in a soppe they sett in att ones,
Foynes faste att þe forebreste with flawmande swerdez,
And feghttes faste att þe fronte freschely þareaftyre,   *1495*
Felles fele on þe felde appon þe ferrere syde,
Fey on þe faire felde by þa fresche strandez.
Bot Sir Idrus fytz Ewayn anters hym seluen,
And enters in anly and egyrly strykez,
Sekez to þe Senatour and sesez his brydill;   *1500*
Vnsaughtely he saide hym þese sittande wordez:
"Ȝelde þe, Sir, ȝapely, ȝife þou þi lyfe ȝernez;
Fore gyftez þat þow gyffe may þou ȝeme now þe selfen.
Fore dredlez dreche þow or droppe any wylez,
Thow sall dy þis daye thorowe dyntt of my handez!"   *1505*
"I ascente," quod þe Senatour, "so me Criste helpe;
So þat I be safe broghte before þe Kyng seluen,
Raunson me resonabillye, as I may ouerreche
Aftyre my renttez in Rome may redyly forthire."
Thane answers Sir Idrus with austeryn wordez: *1510*
"Thow sall hafe condycyon, as þe Kyng lykes,
When thow comes to þe kyth there the courte haldez,   f.69ᵛ
In caase his concell bee to kepe the no langere,
To be killyde at his commandment his knyghttez before."
Þay ledde hym furthe in þe ròwte and lached ofe his wedes,   *1515*
Lefte hym wyth Lyonell and Lowell, hys brothire.
    O lawe in þe launde þan, by þe lythe strandez,
Sir Lucius lyggemen loste are fore euer.
The Senatour Peter es prysoner takyn;

Of Perce and of Porte Iaffe full many price knyghtez,　　　　*1520*
And myche pople wythall perischede þam selfen—
For presse of þe passage they plungede at onez.
Thare myghte men see Romaynez rewfully wondyde,
Ouerredyn with renkes of the Round Table.
In þe raike of þe furthe they righten þeire brenys,　　　　*1525*
Þat rane all on reede blode redylye all ouer.
They raughte in þe rerewarde full ryotous knyghtez
For raunsone of rede golde and reall stedys;
Radly relayes and restez theire horsez,
In rowtte to þe ryche kynge they rade al at onez.　　　　*1530*
　　　　A knyghte cayrez before and to þe Kynge telles,
"Sir, here commez thy messangerez with myrthez fro þe mountez;
Þay hafe bene machede todaye with men of þe marchez,
Foremaglede in þa marras with meruailous knyghtez.
We hafe foughten, in faithe, by ȝone fresche strandez,　　　　*1535*
With þe frekkeste folke that to þi foo langez;
Fyfty thosaunde on felde of ferse men of armez,
Wythin a furlange of waye, fay ere bylefede.
We hafe eschewede þis chekke thurghe chance of oure Lorde,
Of tha cheualrous men that chargede thy pople.　　　　*1540*
The cheefe chaunchelere of Rome, a cheftayne full noble,
Will aske þe chartyre of pesse, for charitée, hym selfen.
And the Senatour Petire to presoner es takyn;
Of Perse and of Porte Iaffe paynymmez ynewe
Commez prekande in the presse with thy prysse knyghttez,　　　　*1545*
With pouerté in thi preson theire paynez to drye.
I beseke ȝow, Sir, say whate ȝowe lykes,
Whethire ȝe suffyre them saughte or sone delyuerde.
Ȝe may haue fore þe Senatour sextie horse chargede
Of siluer be Seterdaye, full sekyrly payede;　　　　*1550*
And for þe cheefe chauncelere, þe cheualere noble,
Charottez chokkefull charegyde with golde;
The remenaunt of þe Romaynez be in areste halden,
Till thiere renttez in Rome be rightewissly knawen.
I beseke ȝow, Sir, certyfye ȝone lordez,　　　　*1555*
Ȝif ȝe will send þam ouer þe see or kepe þam ȝour selfen.

　　1522 they plungede] they plungede they plungede

All ȝour sekyre men, forsothe, sounde are byleuyde,
Saue Sir Ewayne fytz Henry es in þe side wonddede."
    "Crist be thankyde," quod the Kyng, "and hys clere Modyre,   f.70ʳ
That ȝowe comforthed and helpede be crafte of Hym selfen;   1560
Skilfull skomfyture he skiftez as Hym lykez;
Is none so skathlye may skape ne skewe fro His handez.
Desteny and doughtynes of dedys of armes,
All es demyd and delte at Dryghtynez will.
I kwn the thanke for thy come—it comfortes vs all.   1565
Sir Knyghte," sais þe Conquerour, "so me Criste helpe,
I ȝif the for thy thyȝandez Tolouse þe riche,
The toll and þe tachementez, tauernez and oþer,
Þe town and þe tenementez, with towrez so hye,
That towchez to þe temporaltée, whills my tym lastez.   1570
    Bot say to þe Senatour I sende hym þes wordez:
Thare sall no siluer hym saue bot Ewayn recouer;
I had leuer see hym synke on the salte strandez,
Than the seegge ware seke, þat es so sore woundede.
I sall disseuere that sorte, so me Criste helpe,   1575
And sett them full solytarie, in sere kyngez landez.
Sall he neuer sownde see his seynowres in Rome,
Ne sitt in þe assemblé in syghte wyth his feris;
For it comes to no kyng þat Conquerour es holden,
To comon with his captifis fore couatys of siluer.   1580
It come neuer of knyghthede—knawe if ȝif hym lyke—
To carpe of coseri when captyfis ere takyn;
It aughte to no presoners to prese no lordez,
Ne come in presens of pryncez whene partyes are mouede.
Comaunde ȝone constable, þe castell þat ȝemes,   1585
That he be clenlyche kepede, and in close halden;
He sall haue maundement tomorne, or myddaye be roungen,
To what marche þay sall merke, with mauger to lengen."
    Þay conuaye this captyfe with clene men of armez,
And kend hym to þe constable, alls þe Kynge byddez;   1590
And seyn to Arthure þey ayr and egerly hym towchez
The answere of þe Emperour, irows of dedez.
Thane Sir Arthur, on erthe atheliste of oþere,
At euen at his awen borde auantid his lordez:

"Me aughte to honour them in erthe ouer all oþer thyngez   *1595*
Þat þus in myn absens awnters þem selfen;
I sall them luffe whylez I lyffe, so me our Lorde helpe,
And gyfe þem landys full large whare them beste lykes;
Thay sall noghte losse on þis layke, ȝif me lyfe happen,
Þat þus are lamede for my lufe be þis lythe strandez."   *1600*

    Bot in þe clere daweyng, þe dere kynge hym selfen
Comaundyd Sir Cadore, with his dere knyghttes,
Sir Cleremus, Sir Cleremonde, with clene men of armez,
Sir Clowdmur, Sir Clegis, to conuaye theis lordez;
Sir Boyce and Sir Berell, with baners displayede,   *1605*
Sir Bawdwyne, Sir Bryane, and Sir Bedwere þe ryche,
Sir Raynalde and Sir Richere, Rawlaund childyre,
To ryde with þe Romaynes in rowtte wyth theire feres.
"Prekez now preualye to Parys the ryche,   *f.70ᵛ*
Wyth Petir the pryssonere and his price knyghttez;   *1610*
Beteche þam þe proueste, in presens of lordez,
O payne and o perell þat pendes theretoo;
That they be weisely wachede and in warde holden,
Warded of warantizez with wyrchipfull knyghttez,
Wagge hym wyghte men, and woonde for no siluyre—   *1615*
I haffe warnede þat wy, be ware ȝif hym lykes."

    Now bownes þe Bretons, als þe Kynge byddez,
Buskez theire batells, theire baners displayez;
Towardez Chartris they chese, thes cheualrous knyghttez,
And in the champayne lande full faire þay eschewede: *1620*
For þe Emperour of myghte had ordand hym selfen
Sir Vtolfe and Sir Ewandyre, two honourable kyngez,
Erles of þe Orient, with austeryn knyghttez,
Of þe awntrouseste men þat to his oste lengede,
Sir Sextynour of Lyby and senatours many,   *1625*
The Kyng of Surrye hym selfe, with Sarzynes ynowe,
The Senatour of Sutere, wyth sowmes full huge,
Whas assygnede to þat courte be sent of his peres,
Traise towarde Troys þe treson to wyrke,
To hafe betrappede with a trayne oure traueland knyghttez,   *1630*
That hade persayfede þat Peter at Parys sulde lenge,

    1629 þe treson] þe treson the treson

In presonne with þe prouoste, his paynez to drye.
Forthi they buskede them bownn, with baners displayede,
In the buskayle of his waye, on blonkkes full hugge;
Planttez them in the pathe with powere arrayede,   *1635*
To pyke vp þe presoners fro oure pryse knyghttez.
    Syr Cadore of Cornewalle comaundez his peris,
Sir Clegis, Sir Cleremus, Sir Cleremownnde þe noble,
"Here es þe close of Clyme, with clewes so hye:
Lokez the contrée be clere, the corners are large;   *1640*
Discoueres now sekerly skrogges and oþer,
That no skathell in þe skroggez skorne vs hereaftyre;
Loke ȝe skyfte it so þat vs no skathe lympe,
For na skomfitoure in skoulkery is skomfite euer."
    Now þey hye to þe holte, thes harageous knyghttez,   *1645*
To herken of þe hye men, to helpen theis lordez;
Fyndez them helmede hole and horsyde on stedys,
Houande on þe hye waye by þe holte hemmes.
With knyghttly contenaunce Sir Clegis hym selfen
Kryes to þe companye and carpes thees wordez: *1650*
"Es there any kyde knyghte, kaysere or oþer,
Will kyth for his kyng lufe craftes of armes?
We are comen fro þe Kyng of þis kythe ryche,
That knawen as for conquerour, corownde in erthe,
His ryche retenuz here all of his Round Table,   *1655*
To ryde with þat reall in rowtt where hym lykes;
We seke justyng of werre, ȝif any will happyn,
Of þe jolyeste men ajuggede be lordes,
If here be any hathell man, erle or oþer,
That for þe Emperour lufe will awntere hym selfen."   f.71ʳ *1660*
    And ane erle þane in angere answeres hym son:
"Me angers at Arthure, and att his hathell bierns,
That thus in his errour ocupyes theis rewmes,
And owtrayes þe Emperour, his erthely lorde.
The araye and þe ryalltéz of þe Rounde Table   *1665*
Es wyth rankour rehersede in rewmes full many;
Of oure renttez of Rome syche reuell he haldys,
He sall ȝife resoun full rathe, ȝif vs reghte happen,

1647 horsyde] horsesyde   1653 kythe *Brock*] lythe   1668 He] ne

That many sall repente that in his rowtte rydez,
For the reklesse roy so rewlez hym selfen!"　　　　　　　　167

　　"A!" sais Sir Clegis þan, "so me Criste helpe,
I knawe be thi carpyng a cowntere þe semes!
Bot be þou auditoure or erle or Emperour thi selfen,
Appon Arthurez byhalue I answere the sone:
The renke so reall þat rewllez vs all,　　　　　　　　162
The ryotous men and þe ryche of þe Rounde Table,
He has araysede his accownte and redde all his rollez,
For he wyll gyfe a rekenyng that rewe sall aftyre,
That all þe ryche sall repente þat to Rome langez,
Or þe rereage be requit of rentez þat he claymez.　　　　　　164
We crafe of ȝour curtaisie three coursez of werre,
And claymez of knyghthode, take kepe to ȝour selfen!
Ȝe do bott trayne vs todaye wyth trofeland wordez;
Of syche trauaylande men trecherye me thnykes.
Sende owte sadly certayne knyghttez,　　　　　　　　16
Or say me sekerly sothe—forsake ȝif ȝowe lykes."

　　Þane sais þe Kynge of Surry, "Alls saue me oure Lorde,
Ȝif þow hufe all þe daye, þou bees noghte delyuerede,
Bot thow sekerly ensure with certeyne knyghtez,
Þat þi cote and thi breste be knawen with lordez,　　　　　　16
Of armes of ancestrye entyrde with londez."
"Sir Kyng," sais Sir Clegys, "full knyghttly þow askez;
I trowe it be for cowardys thow carpes thes wordez.
Myn armez are of ancestrye enueryd with lordez,
And has in banere bene borne sen Sir Brut tyme;　　　　　　16
At the cité of Troye þat tymme was ensegede,
Ofte seen in asawtte with certayne knyghttez,
Fro þe Borghte broghte vs and all oure bolde elders
To Bretayne þe Braddere, within chippe-burdez."

　　"Sir," sais Sir Sextenour, "saye what þe lykez,　　　　　　17
And we sall suffyre the, als vs beste semes;
Luke thi troumppez be trussede, and trofull no lengere,
For þoghe þou tarye all þe daye, the tyddes no bettyr.
For there sall neuer Romayne þat in my rowtt rydez
Be with rebawdez rebuykyde whills I in werlde regne!"　　　　17

　　1698 fro] for fro

Thane Sir Clegis to þe Kyng a lyttill enclinede,
Kayres to Sir Cadore and knyghtly hym tellez,
"We hafe founden in ȝone firthe, floresched with leues,
Þe flour of þe faireste folke þat to þi foo langez: f.71ᵛ 1710
Fifty thosandez of folke of ferse men of armez,
Þat faire are fewteride on frounte vndyr ȝone fre bowes;
They are enbuschede on blonkkes, with baners displayede,
In ȝone bechen wode appon the waye sydes.
Thay hafe the furthe forsette all of þe faire watyre,
That fayfully of force feghte vs byhowys; 1715
For thus vs schappes todaye, schortly to tell,
Whedyre we schone or schewe—schyft as þe lykes."
"Nay," quod Cador, "so me Criste helpe,
It ware schame þat we scholde schone for so lytyll.
Sir Lancelott sall neuer laughe, þat with þe Kyng lengez, 1720
That I sulde lette my waye for lede appon erthe;
I sall be dede and vndone ar I here dreche,
For drede of any doggeson in ȝone dym schawes!"
Syr Cador thane knyghtly comforthes his pople,
And with corage kene he karpes þes wordes: 1725
'Thynk on þe valyaunt prynce þat vesettez vs euer
With landez and lordcheppez, whare vs beste lykes;
That has vs ducherés delte and dubbyde vs knyghttez,
Gifen vs gersoms and golde and gardwynes many,
Grewhoundez and grett horse and alkyn gamnes, 1730
That gaynez till any gome that vndyre God leuez.
Thynke on riche renoun of þe Rounde Table,
And late it neuer be refte vs fore Romayne in erthe;
Feyne ȝow noghte feyntly, ne frythes no wapyns,
Bot luke ȝe fyghte faythefully, frekes, ȝour selfen; 1735
walde be wellyde all qwyke and quarterde in sondre,
Bot I wyrke my dede, whils I in wrethe lenge."
Than this doughtty duke dubbyd his knyghttez,
oneke and Askanere, Aladuke and oþer,
That ayerez were of Esex and all þase este marchez, 1740
Iowell and Hardelfe, happy in armez,
Sir Heryll and Sir Herygall, þise harageouse knyghttez.
han the souerayn assignede certayne lordez,

Sir Wawayne, Sir Vryell, Sir Bedwere þe ryche,
Raynallde and Richeere and Rowlandez childyre: *1745*
"Takez kepe on this prynce with ȝoure price knyghtez,
And ȝife we in þe stour withstonden the better,
Standez here in this stede, and stirrez no forthire;
And ȝif þe chaunce falle þat we bee ouercharggede,
Eschewes to som castell, and chewyse ȝour selfen,   *1750*
Or ryde to þe riche Kyng, ȝif ȝow roo happyn,
And bidde hym com redily to rescewe hys biernez." ,
     And than the Bretons brothely enbrassez þeire scheldez,
Braydez one bacenetez and buskes theire launcez;
Thus he fittez his folke and to þe felde rydez,   *1755*
Fif hundreth on a frounte fewtrede at onez.
With trompes þay trine, and trappede stedes,   f.72ᵛ
With cornettes and clarions and clergiall notes;
Schokkes in with a schakke and schontez no langere,
There schawes ware scheen vndyr þe schire eyuez.   *1760*
And thane the Romaynez rowtte remowes a lyttill,
Raykes with a rerewarde þas reall kynghttez;
So raply þay ryde thare that all þe rowte ryngez
Of ryues and raunke stele and ryche golde maylez.
     Thane schotte owtte of þe schawe schiltrounis many,   *1765*
With scharpe wapynns of were schotand at ones;
The Kyng of Lebe before the wawarde he ledez,
And all his lele ligemen o laundon ascriez.
Thane this cruell kyng castis in fewtire,
Kaghte hym a couerde horse and his course haldez,   *1770*
Beris to Sir Berill and brathely hym hittes—
Throwghe golet and gorger he hurtez hym ewyne;
The gome and þe grette horse at þe ground liggez,
And gretez graythely to Gode and gyffes Hym þe saule.
Thus es Berell the bolde broghte owtte of lyue,   *1775*
And byddez aftyre beryell þat hym beste lykez.
     And thane Sir Cador of Cornewayle es carefull in herte,
Because of his kynysemane, þat þus es myscaryede;
Vmbeclappes the cors and kyssez hym ofte,
Gerte kepe hym couerte with his clere knyghttez.   *1780*

    1768 lele ligemen] ligemen lele ligemen

Thane laughes the Lebe Kyng and all on lowde meles,
"ȝone lorde es lyghttede—me lykes the bettyre;
He sall noghte dere vs todaye, the Deuyll haue [his] bones!"
"ȝone kyng," said Cador, "karpes full large,
Because he killyd þis kene—Criste hafe þi saule: *1785*
He sall hafe corne-bote, so me Criste helpe;
Or I kaire of þis coste, we sall encontre ones.
So may þe wynde weile turnne, I quytte hym or ewyn,
Sothely hym selfen or summ of his ferez."
      Thane Sir Cador þe kene knyghttly he wyrkez,   *1790*
Cryez "À Cornewale!" and castez in fewtere,
Girdez streke thourghe þe stour on a stede ryche;
Many steryn mane he steride by strenghe of hym one.
Whene his spere was sprongen, he spede hym full ȝerne,
Swappede owtte with a swerde that swykede hym neuer,   *1795*
Wroghte wayes full wyde and wounded knyghttez,
Wyrkez in his wayfare full werkand sydez,
And hewes of þe hardieste halsez in sondyre,
That all blendez with blode thare his blanke rynnez.
So many biernez the bolde broughte owt of lyfe,   *1800*
Tittez tirauntez doun and temez theire sadills,
And turnez owte of þe toile when hym tyme thynkkez.
      Thane the Lebe Kynge criez full lowde
One Sir Cador the kene, with cruell wordez,
"Thowe hase wyrchipe wonne and wondyde knyghttez;   f.72ᵛ *1805*
Thowe wenes for thi wightenez the werlde es thy nowen.
I sall wayte at thyne honnde, wy, be my trowthe;
I haue warnede þe wele, be ware ȝif the lykez!"
With cornuse and clariones þeis newe-made knyghttez
Lythes vnto þe crye and castez in fewtire;   *1810*
Ferkes in on a frounte one feraunte stedez,
Fellede at þe fyrste come fyfty att ones.
Schotte thorowe the schiltrouns and scheuerede launcez,
Laid doun in þe lumppe lordly biernez.
And thus nobilly oure newe men notez þeire strenghez—   *1815*
Bot new notte es onon þat noyes me sore.
      The Kyng of Lebe has laughte a stede þat hym lykede,

1797 in his *Brock*] his in   1801 and temez] and temez and temez

And comes in lordely in lyonez of siluere,
Vmbelappez þe lumpe and lattes in sondre—
Many lede with his launce þe liffe has he refede.   *1820*
Thus he chaces þe childire of þe Kyngez chambire,
And killez in þe champanyse cheualrous knyghttez;
With a chasyng spere he choppes doun many.
Thare was Sir Alyduke slayne and Achinour wondyde,
Sir Origg and Sir Ermyngall hewen al to pecez.   *1825*
And ther was Lewlyn laughte and Lewlyns brothire,
With lordez of Lebe, and lede to þeire strenghez.
Ne hade Sir Clegis comen and Clemente þe noble,
Oure newe men hade gone to noghte and many ma oþer.
    Þane Sir Cador þe kene castez in fewtire   *1830*
A cruell launce and a kene and to þe Kynge rydez,
Hittez hym heghe on þe helme with his harde wapen,
That all þe hotte blode of hym to his hande rynnez.
The hethen harageous kynge appon þe hethe lyggez,
And of his hertly hurte helyde he neuer.   *183.*
Thane Sir Cador þe kene cryez full lowde,
"Thow has corne-botte, Sir Kyng, þare God gyfe þe sorowe;
Thow killyde my cosyn, my. kare es the lesse.
Kele the nowe in the claye, and comforthe thi selfen!
Thow skornede vs lang ere with thi skornefull wordez,   *184.*
And nowe has þow cheuede soo, it es thyn awen skathe.
Holde at þow hente has, it harmez bot lyttill,
For hethynge es hame-holde, vse it who-so will."
    The Kyng of Surry þan es sorowfull in herte,
For sake of this soueraygne, þat þus was supprissede;   *184.*
Semblede his Sarazenes and senatours manye:
Vnsaughtyly þey sette thane appon oure sere knyghttez.
Sir Cador of Cornewaile he cownterez them sone,
With his kydde companye clenlyche arrayede;
In the frount of þe fyrthe, as þe waye forthis,   *185.*
Fyfty thosande of folke was fellide at ones.
Thare was at þe assemblé certayne knyghttez
Sore wondede sone appone sere halfes;   f.7.
The sekereste Sarzanez that to þat sorte lengede,
Behynde the sadylls ware sette sex fotte large.   *185.*

They scherde in the schiltrone scheldyde knyghttez,
Schalkes they schotte thrughe schrenkande maylez,
Thurghe brenys browden brestez they thirllede,
Brasers burnyste bristez in sondyre,
Blasons blode and blankes they hewen,   *1860*
With brandez of browne stele brankkand stedez.
The Bretons brothely brittenez so many,
The bente and þe brode felde all on blode rynnys.
Be thane Sir Cayous þe kene a capitayne has wonnen,
Sir Clegis clynges in and clekes anoþer,   *1865*
The capitayne of Cordewa, vndire þe Kynge selfen,
That was keye of þe kythe of all þat coste ryche;
Vtolfe and Ewandre Ioneke had nommen,
With þe Erle of Affryke and oþer grette lordes;
The Kyng of Surry the kene to Sir Cador es ȝelden,   *1870*
Þe Synechall of Soter to Segramoure hym selfen.
        When þe cheualrye saw theire cheftanes were nommen,
To a cheefe foreste they chesen theire wayes,
And felede them so feynte, they fall in þe greues,
In the ferynne of þe fyrthe, fore ferde of oure pople.   *1875*
Thare myght men see the ryche ryde in the schawes,
To rype vpe the Romaynez ruydlyche wondyde;
Schowttes aftyre men, harageous knyghttez,
Be hunndrethez they hewede doun be þe holte eyuys.
Thus oure cheualrous men chasez þe pople;   *1880*
To a castell they eschewede, a fewe þat eschappede.
        Thane relyez þe renkez of þe Rounde Table,
For to ryotte þe wode þer þe duke restez;
Ransakes the ryndez all, raughte vp theire feres,
That in þe fightyng before fay ware byleuyde.   *1885*
Sir Cador garte chare theym and couere them faire,
Kariede them to þe Kyng with his beste knyghttez;
And passez vnto Paresche with presoners hym selfen,
Betoke theym the proueste, pryncez and oþer;
Tase a sope in the toure and taryez no langere,   *1890*
Bot tournes tytte to þe Kynge and hym wyth tunge telles.
        "Syr," sais Sir Cador, "a caas es befallen;
We hafe cowntered today, in ȝone coste ryche

With kyngez and kayseres, krouell and noble,
And knyghtes and kene men, clenlych arayede.   *1895*
They hade at ʒone foreste forsette vs þe wayes,
At the furthe in þe fyrthe, with ferse men of armes;
Thare faughtte we, in faythe, and foynede with sperys,
One felde with thy foomen and fellyd them on lyfe.
The Kyng of Lebe es laide and in þe felde leuyde,   f.73ᵛ *1900*
And manye of his legemen þat þare to hym langede.
Oþer lordez are laughte of vncouthe ledes;
We hafe lede them at lenge, to lyf whilles þe lykez.
Sir Vtolfe and Sir Ewaynedyr, theis honourable knyghttez,
Be a nawntere of armes Ioneke has nommen,   *1905*
With erlez of þe Oryentte and austeren knyghttez,
Of awncestrye þe beste men þat to þe oste langede;
The Senatour Carous es kaughte with a knyghtte,
The Capitayne of Cornette, that crewell es halden,
The Syneschall of Suter vnsaughte wyth þes oþer,   *1910*
The Kyng of Surry hym selfen and Sarazenes [ynowe].
Bot fay of ours in þe felde a fourtene knyghttez,
I will noghte feyne ne forbere, bot faythfully tellen;
Sir Berell es one, a banerette noble,
Was killyde at þe fyrste come with a kyng ryche;   *1915*
Sir Alidoyke of Towell, with his tende knyghtez,
Emange þe Turkys was tynte and in tym fonden;
Gude Sir Mawrell of Mauncez and Mawren his broþer,
Sir Meneduke of Mentoche, with meruailous knyghttez."
     Thane the worthy Kyng wrythes and wepede with his eughne,   *1920*
Karpes to his cosyn Sir Cador theis wordez:
"Sir Cador, thi corage confundez vs all!
Kowardely thow castez owtte all my beste knyghttez.
To putte men in perille, it es no pryce holden,
Bot þe partyes ware puruayede and powere arayede;   *1925*
When they ware stade on a strenghe, þou sulde hafe withstonden,
Bot ʒif thowe wolde all my steryn stroye for þe nonys!"
     "Sir," sais Sir Cador, "ʒe knowe wele ʒour selfen
ʒe are kyng in þis kythe, karpe whatte ʒow lykys;
Sall neuer vpbrayde me, þat to þi burde langes,   *1930*

1904 Vtolfe *Branscheid*] Vtere   1908 Carous *Branscheid*] Barous

That I sulde blyn fore theire boste thi byddyng to wyrche;
When any stirttez to stale, stuffe þam þe bettere,
Ore thei will be stonayede and stroyede in ȝone strayte londez.
I dide my delygens todaye, I doo me one lordez,
And in daungere of dede fore dyuerse knyghttez;   1935
I hafe no grace to þi gree, bot syche grett wordez—
Ȝif I heuen my herte, my hape es no bettyre."

    Þofe Sir Arthure ware angerde, he ansuers faire;
"Thow has doughttily donn, Sir Duke, with thi handez,
And has donn thy deuer with my dere knyghttez;   1940
Forthy thow arte demyde, with dukes and erlez,
For one of þe doughtyeste þat dubbede was euer.
Thare es non ischewe of vs on this erthe sprongen;
Thow arte apparant to be ayere, are one of thi childyre—
Thow arte my sister sone, forsake sall I neuer."   f.74ʳ 1945
Thane gerte he in his awen tente a table be sette,
And tryede in with tromppez trauaillede biernez;
Serfede them solempnely with selkouthe metez,
Swythe semly in syghte with sylueren dischees.

    Whene the senatours harde saye þat it so happenede,   1950
They saide to þe Emperour, "Thi seggez are suppryssede;
Sir Arthure, thyn enmy, has owterayede þi lordez,
That rode for þe rescowe of ȝone riche knyghttez.
Thow dosse bot tynnez þi tym and turmenttez þi pople;
Thow arte betrayede of þi men that moste thow on traystede,   1955
That schall turne the to tene and torfere for euer."
Than the Emperour irus was angerde at his herte,
For oure valyant biernez siche prowesche had wonnen.
With kyng and with kaysere to consayle they wende,
Souerayngez of Sarazenez and senatours manye;   1960
Thus he semblez full sone certayne lordez,
And in the assemblé thane he sais them theis wordez:
"My herte sothely es sette—assente ȝif ȝowe lykes—
To seke into Sexon, with my sekyre knyghttez,
To fyghte with my foomen, if fortune me happen,   1965
Ȝif I may fynde the freke within the four haluez;
Or entir into Awguste, awnters to seke,
And byde with my balde men within þe burghe ryche;

Riste vs and reuell and ryotte oure selfen,
Lende þare in delytte in lordechippez ynewe,   *1970*
To Sir Leo be comen with all his lele knyghtez,
With lordez of Lumberdye, to lette hym þe wayes."
    Bot owre wyese Kyng es warre to waytten his renkes,
And wyesly by þe woddez voydez his oste;
Gerte felschen his fyrez, flawmande full heghe,   *1975*
Trussen full traystely and treunt thereaftyre.
Seþen into Sessoyne he soughte at the gayneste,
And at the surs of þe sonne disseuerez his knyghttez;
Forsette them the cité appon sere halfez,
Sodaynly on iche halfe, with seuen grett stales.   *1980*
Anely in the vale a vawewarde enbusches:
Sir Valyant of Vyleris, with valyant knyghttez,
Before þe Kyngez visage made siche avowez
To venquyse by victorie the Vescownte of Rome;
Forthi the Kyng chargez hym, what chaunce so befall,   *1985*
Cheftayne of þe cheekke, with cheualrous knyghttez.
And sythyn meles with mouthe, þat he moste traistez;
Demenys the medylwarde menskfully hym selfen:
Fittes his fotemen alls hym faire thynkkes,
On frounte in the forebreste the flour of his knyghtez;   *1990*
His archers on aythere halfe he ordaynede þeraftyre
To schake in a sheltrone, to schotte when þam lykez.   f.74ᵛ
He arrayed in þe rerewarde full riall knyghtez,
With renkkes renownnd of þe Round Table,
Sir Raynalde, Sir Richere, that rade was neuer,   *1995*
The riche Duke of Rown wyt[h] ryders ynewe.
Sir Cayous, Sir Clegis, and clene men of armes,
The Kyng casts to kepe be þaa clere strandes;
Sir Lott and Sir Launcelott, þise lordly knyghttez,
Sall lenge on his lefte hande, with legyones ynewe,   *2000*
To meue in þe morne-while, ȝif þe myste happynne;
Sir Cador of Cornewaile and his kene knyghtez,
To kepe at þe karfuke, to close in þer oþere;
He plantez in siche placez pryncez and erlez,
That no powere sulde passe be no preué wayes.   *2005*

    1984 Vescownte] vescowte vescownte

Bot the Emperour onone, with honourable knyghtez
And erlez enteres the vale, awnters to seke,
And fyndez Sir Arthure with hostez arayede;
And at his income, to ekken his sorowe,
Oure burlyche bolde Kyng appon the bente howes,   *2010*
With his bataile on brede and baners displayede.
He hade þe ceté forsett appon sere halfes,
Bothe the clewez and þe clyfez with clene men of armez,
The mosse and þe marrasse, the mounttez so hye,
With gret multytude of men, to marre hym in þe wayes.   *2015*
    When Sir Lucius sees, he sais to his lordez,
"This traytour has treunt this treson to wyrche;
He has the ceté forsett appon sere halfez,
All þe clewez and the cleyffez with clene men of armez;
Here es no waye, iwys, ne no wytt ells,   *2020*
Bot feghte with oure foomen, for flee may we neuer."
Thane this ryche mane rathe arayes his byernez,
Rewlede his Romaynez and reall knyghtez;
Buschez in the avawmewarde the Vescounte of Rome,
Fro Viterbe to Venyse theis valyante knyghtez;   *2025*
Dresses vp dredfully the dragone of golde,
With egles alouer, enamelede of sable;
Drawen dreghely the wyne and drynkyn thareaftyre,
Dukkez and dusseperez, dubbede knyghtez;
For dauncesyng of Duchemen and dynnyng of pypez,   *2030*
All dynned fore dyn that in þe dale houede.
    And thane Sir Lucius on lowde said lordlyche wordez:
"Thynke on the myche renownn of ȝour ryche fadyrs,
And the riatours of Rome, þat regnede with lordez,
And the renkez ouerrane all that regnede in erthe,   *2035*
Encrochede all Cristyndome be craftes of armes—   f.75ʳ
In eueriche a viage the victorie was halden;
Insette all þe Sarazenes within seuen wyntter,
The parte fro the Porte Iaffe to Paradyse ȝatez.
Thoghe a rewme be rebelle, we rekke it bot lyttill;   *2040*
It es resone and righte the renke be restreynede.
Do dresse we tharefore and byde we no langere,
Fore dredlesse withowttyn dowtte, the daye schall be ourez!"

Whene þeise wordez was saide, the Walsche kyng hym selfen
Whas warre of this wyderwyn þat werrayede his knyghttez;   *2045*
Brothely in the vale with voyce he ascryez,
"Viscownte of Valewnce, enuyous of dedys,
The vassallage of Viterbe todaye schall be reuengede;
Vnuenquiste fro þis place voyde schall I neuer!"
Thane the Vyscownte valiante, with a voute noble,   *2050*
Auoyeddyde the avawewarde, enuerounde his horse;
He drissede in a derfe schelde, endenttyd with sable,
With a dragone engowschede, dredfull to schewe,
Deuorande a dolphyn with dolefull lates,
In seyne that oure soueraygne sulde be distroyede,   *2055*
And all don of dawez with dynttez of swerddez—
For thare es noghte bot dede thare the dragone es raissede.
     Thane the comlyche kyng castez in fewtyre,
With a crewell launce cowpez full euen,
Abowne þe spayre a spanne, emange þe schortte rybbys,   *2060*
That the splent and the spleen on the spere langez;
The blode sprente owtte and sprede as þe horse spryngez,
And he sproulez full spakely, bot spekes he no more.
And thus has Sir Valyantt halden his avowez,
And venqwyste þe Viscownte, þate victor was halden.   *2065*
     Thane Sir Ewayne fitz Vriene full enkerlye rydez
Onone to the Emperour, his egle to towche;
Thrughe his brode bataile he buskes belyfe,
Braydez owt his brande with a blyth chere,
Reuerssede it redelye and awaye rydys;   *2070*
Ferkez in with the fewle in his faire handez,
And fittez in freely one frounte with his feris.
     Now buskez Sir Launcelot and braydez full euen
To Sir Lucius the lorde and lothelye hym hyttez;
Thurghe pawnce and platez he percede the maylez,   *2075*
That the prowde pensell in his pawnche lengez;
The hede hayled owtt behynde ane halfe fote large,
Thurghe hawberke and hanche, with þe harde wapyn,
The stede and the steryn mane strykes to þe grownde,

2049 fro] for   2050 voute *Mennicken*] uoyse   2056 swerddez] swreddez
2060 þe spayre] þe spayre the spayere   2066 Sir Ewayne fitz Vriene] Sir Ewayne Sir ftiz Vriene

Strake down a standerde and to his stale wendez. 2080

    "Me lykez wele," sais Sir Loth, "ȝone lordez are delyuerede!

The lott lengez nowe on me, with leue of my lorde;

Today sall my name be laide and my life aftyre,

Bot some leppe fro the lyfe that on ȝone lawnde houez!" f.75ᵛ

Thane strekez the steryn and streynys his brydyll, 2085

Strykez into the stowre on a stede ryche,

Enjoynede with a geaunt and jaggede hym thorowe;

Jolyly this gentill forjustede anoþer,

Wroghte wayes full wyde, werrayande knyghtez,

And wondes all wathely that in þe waye stondez; 2090

Fyghttez with all the frappe a furlange of waye,

Felled fele appon felde with his faire wapen,

Venqwiste and has the victorie of valyaunt knyghtez,

And all enverounde the vale and voyde when hym likede.

    Thane bowmen of Bretayne brothely thereaftyre 2095

Bekerde with bregaundez of ferre in tha laundez;

With flonez fleterede þay flitt full frescly þer frekez,

That flowe o ferrome in flawnkkes of stedez.

Fichene with fetheris thurghe þe fyne maylez—

Siche flyttyng es foule þat so þe flesche derys. 2100

Dartes the Duchemen dalten aȝaynes,

With derfe dynttez of dede dagges thurghe scheldez;

Qwarells qwayntly swappez thorowe knyghtez,

With iryn so wekyrly, that wynche they neuer:

So they scherenken fore schotte of þe scharppe arowes, 2105

That all the scheltron schonte and schoderide at ones.

Thane riche stedes rependez and rasches on armes—

The hale howndrethe on hye appon heythe lygges;

Bott ȝitte þe hathelieste on hy, haythen and oþer,

All hoursches ouer hede harmes to wyrke. 2110

And all theis geauntez before, engenderide with fendez,

Ioynez on Sir Ionathal and gentill knyghtez;

With clubbez of clene stele clenkkede in helmes,

Craschede doun crestez and craschede braynez,

Kyllede cou[r]sers and couerde stedes,

Choppode thurghe cheualers on chalke-whytte stedez; 2115

2108 heythe *Björkman*] heyghe   2112 Ionathal *O'Loughlin*] Ienitall

Was neuer stele ne stede mighte stande them aʒaynez,
Bot stonays and strykez doun that in þe stale houys,
Till þe Conquerour come with his kene knyghttez,
With crewell contenaunce he cryede full lowde,   2120
"I wende no Bretons walde bee basschede for so lyttill,
And fore barelegyde boyes þat on the bente houys!"
He clekys owtte Collbrande, full clenlyche burneschte,
Graythes hym to Golapas, þat greuyde moste,
Kuttes hym euen by þe knees clenly in sondyre.   2125
"Come down," quod the Kyng, "and karpe to thy ferys;
Thowe arte to hye by þe halfe, I hete þe in trouthe:
Thow sall be handsomere in hye, with þe helpe of my Lorde!"
With þat stelen brande he strake ofe his hede.
Sterynly in þat stoure he strykes anoþer;   2130
Thus he settez on seuen with his sekyre knyghttez—   f.76r
Whylles sexty ware seruede soo ne sessede they neuer.
And thus at the joynynge the geauntez are distroyede,
And at þat journey forjustede with gentill lordez.
    Than the Romaynes and the rennkkez of þe Rounde Table   2135
Rewles them in arraye, rerewarde ande oþer;
With wyghte wapynez of werre thay wroghten on helmes,
Rittez with raunke stele full ryalle maylez.
Bot they fitt them fayre, thes frekk byernez,
Fewters in freely one feraunte stedes,   2140
Foynes ful felly with flyschande speris,
Freten of orfrayes feste appon scheldez;
So fele fay es in fyghte appon þe felde leuyde,
That iche a furthe in the firthe of rede blode rynnys.
By that swyftely one swarthe þe swett es byleuede,   2145
Swerdez swangen in two sweltand knyghtez,
Lyes wyde opyn, welterande on walopande stedez;
Wondes of wale men, werkande sydys,
Facez fetteled vnfaire in filterede lakes,
All craysed, fortrodyn with trappede stedez,   2150
The faireste on folde that fygurede was euer,
Alls ferre alls a furlang, a thosande at ones.
    Be than the Romaynez ware rebuykde a lyttill,

2133 joynynge] joynenynge   2151 on folde *Branscheid*] fygured folde

Withdrawes theym drerely and dreches no lengare;
Oure prynce with his powere persewes theyme aftyre,   *2155*
Prekez on þe proudeste with his price knyghttez.
Sir Kayous, Sir Clegis, Sir Cleremond the noble
Enconters them at þe clyffe with clene men of armes;
Fyghttes faste in þe fyrth, frythes no wapen,
Felled at þe firste come fyfe hundrethe at ones.   *2160*
And when they fande theym foresett with oure fers knyghtez,
Fewe men agayne fele mot fyche them bettyre,
Feghttez with all þe frappe, foynes with speres,
And faughte with the frekkeste þat to Fraunce langez.
Bot Sir Kayous þe kene castis in fewtyre,   *2165*
Chasez one a coursere and to a kyng rydys;
With a launce of Lettowe he thirllez his sydez,
That the lyuer and þe lunggez on þe launce lengez;
The schafte sc[h]odyrde and schott in the schire byerne,
And soughte thorowowte þe schelde and in þe schalke rystez.   *2170*
    Bot Kayous at the income was kepyd vnfayre
With a cowarde knyghte of þe kythe ryche;
At þe turnyng that tym the traytoure hym hitte,
In thorowe the felettes, and in þe flawnke aftyre,
That the boustous launce þe bewells attamede,   *2175*
Þat braste at þe brawlyng and brake in þe myddys.
Sir Kayous knewe wele, be þat kyde wounde,
That he was dede of þe dynte and don owte of lyfe;   f.76ᵛ
Than he raykes in arraye and one rawe rydez,
One this reall his dede to reuenge;   *2180*
"Kepe the, cowarde," he calles hym sone,
Cleues hym wyth his clere brande clenliche in sondire.
"Hadde thow wele delte thy dynt with thi handes,
I hade forgeffen þe my dede, be Crist now of Hewyn."
He weyndes to þe wyese kyng and wynly hym gretes: *2185*
"I am wathely woundide—waresche mon I neuer;
Wirke nowe thi wirchipe, as þe worlde askes,
And brynge me to beryell—byd I no more.
Grete wele my ladye, þe Qwene, ȝife þe werlde happyne,
And all þe burliche birdes þat to hir boure lengez,   *2190*

2157 Sir Cleremond the noble *Björkman*] with clene men of armez   2181 he] and

And my worthily weife, þat wrethide me neuer,
Bid hire, fore hir wyrchipe, wirke for my saulle."
The Kyngez confessour come, with Criste in his handes,
For to comforthe the knyghte, kende hym þe wordes;
The knyghte coueride on his knees with a kaunt herte,   *2195*
And caughte his Creatoure, þat comfurthes vs all.
     Thane remmes þe riche kynge fore rewthe at his herte,
Rydes into rowte, his dede to reuenge;
Presede into þe plumpe, and with a prynce metes,
That was ayere of Egipt in thos este marches,   *2200*
Cleues hym with Collbrande clenlyche in sondyre;
He broches euen thorowe þe byerne and þe sadill bristes,
And at þe bake of þe blonke þe bewells entamede.
Manly in his malycoly he metes anoþer,
The medill of þat myghtty, þat hym myche greuede;   *2205*
He merkes thurghe the maylez the myddes in sondyre,
That the myddys of þe mane on þe mounte fallez,
Þe toþer halfe of þe haunche on þe horse leuyde—
Of þat hurte, alls I hope, heles he neuer.
He schotte thorowe þe schiltrouns with his scharpe wapen,   *2210*
Schalkez he schrede thurghe and schrenkede maylez,
Baneres he bare downne, bryttenede scheldes,
Brothely with brown stele his brethe he þare wrekes;
Wrothely he wryththis by wyghtnesse of strenghe,
Woundes þese whydyrewyns, werrayede knyghttes,   *2215*
Threppede thorowe þe thykkys thryttene sythis,
Thryngez throly in the thrange and chis euen aftyre.
     Thane Sir Gawayne the gude, with wyrchipfull knyghttez,
Wendez in the avawewarde be tha wodde hemmys;
Was warre of Sir Lucius, one launde there he houys,   *2220*
With lordez and liggemen that to hym selfe lengede.
Thane the Emperour enkerly askes hym sonne,
"What will thow, Gawayne, wyrke with thi wapyn?
I watte be thi waueryng thow willnez aftyre sorowe;   *f.77ᵛ*
I sall be wrokyn on thi wrethe, fore all thi grete wordez!"   *2225*
He laughte owtte a lange swerde and luyschede one faste,
And Sir Lyonell in the launde lordely he hym strykes:
Hittes hym on þe hede, þat þe helme bristis,

Hurttes his herne-pane an hannde-brede large.
Thus he layes one þe lumppe and lordlye þem serued,   2230
Wondide worthily wirchipfull knyghttez;
Fighttez with Florent, that beste es of swerdez,
Till þe fomande blode till his fyste rynnes.
     Thane þe Romayns releuyde, þat are ware rebuykkyde,
And all torattys oure men with theire riste horsses;   2235
Fore they see þaire cheftayne be chauffede so sore,
They chasse and choppe doun oure cheualrous knyghttes.
Sir Bedwere was borne thurghe, and his breste thyrllede,
With a burlyche brannde, brode at þe hiltes;
The ryall raunke stele to his herte rynnys,   2240
And he rusches to þe erthe—rewthe es the more.
     Thane þe Conquerour tuke kepe and come with his strenghes
To reschewe þe ryche men of þe Rounde Table,
To owttraye þe Emperour, ȝif auntire it schewe,
Ewyn to þe egle, and "Arthure!" askryes.   2245
The Emperour thane egerly at Arthure he strykez,
Awkwarde on þe vmbrere and egerly hym hittez;
The nakyde swerde at þe nese noyes hym sare,
The blode of [the] bolde kyng ouer þe breste rynnys,
Beblede at þe brode schelde and þe bryghte mayles.   2250
Oure bolde kyng bowes þe blonke be þe bryghte brydyll,
With his burlyche brande a buffette hym reches,
Thourghe þe brene and þe breste with his bryghte wapyn:
O slante doun fro þe slote he slyttes at ones.
Thus endys þe Emperour of Arthur hondes,   2255
And all his austeryn oste þareofe ware affrayede.
Now they ferke to þe fyrthe, a fewe þat are leuede,
For ferdnesse of oure folke, by þe fresche strandez;
The floure of oure ferse men one ferant stedez
Folowes frekly on þe frekes, thate frayede was neuer.   2260
     Thane þe kyde conquerour cryes full lowde,
"Cosyn of Cornewaile, take kepe to þi selfen
That no captayne be kepyde for non siluer,
Or Sir Kayous dede be cruelly vengede."
"Nay," sais Sir Cador, "so me Cryste helpe,   2265

2248 nese] nesse nese

Thare ne es kaysere ne kyng þat vndire Criste ryngnes
Þat I ne schall kill colde dede be crafte of my handez!"
Thare myghte men see chiftaynes on chalke-whitte stedez
Choppe doun in the chaas cheualrye noble;
Romaynes þe rycheste and ryall kynges   *2270*
Braste with ranke stele theire rybbys in sondyre;   f.77ᵛ
Braynes forebrusten thurghe burneste helmes,
With brandez forbrittenede one brede in þe laundez;
They hewede doun haythen men with hiltede swerdez
Be hole hundrethez on hye, by þe holte eyuyes.   *2275*
Thare myghte no siluer thaym saue ne socoure theire lyues,
Sowdane ne Sarazene ne senatour of Rome.
        Thane releuis þe renkes of the Rounde Table
Be þe riche reuare that rynnys so faire;
Lugez thaym luflye by þa lyghte strandez,   *2280*
All on lawe in þe lawnde, thas lordlyche byernes.
Thay kaire to þe karyage and tuke whate them likes,
Kamells and cokadrisses and cofirs full riche,
Hekes and hakkenays and horses of armes,
Howsyng and herbergage of heythen kyngez;   *2285*
They drewe owt of dromondaries dyuerse lordes,
Moyllez mylke whitte and meruayllous bestez,
Olfendes and arrabys and olyfauntez noble,
Þer are of þe Oryent, with honourable kynges.
        Bot Sir Arthure onone ayeres þeraftyre   *2290*
Ewyn to þe Emperour, with honourable kyngis;
Laughte hym vpe full louelyly with lordlyche knyghttez,
And ledde hym to þe layere thare the Kyng lygges.
Thane harawdez heghely, at heste of the lordes,
Hunttes vpe the haythemen that on heghte lygges: *2295*
The Sowdane of Surry and certayne kynges,
Sexty of þe cheefe senatours of Rome.
Thane they bussches and bawmede þaire honourliche kyngis,
Sewed them in sendell sexti-faulde aftire,
Lappede them in lede, lesse that they schulde   *2300*
Chawnge or chawffe, ȝif þay myghte escheffe;
Closed in kystys clene vnto Rome,

2280 lugez] lugegez 2283 cokadrisses *Banks*] sekadrisses 2288 olfendes *Holthausen*] elfaydes

With theire baners abowne, theire bagis therevndyre,
In whate countré þay kaire that knyghttes myghte knawe
Iche kynge be his colours, in kyth whare [he] lengede.   2305
  Onone on þe secounde daye, sone by þe morne,
Twa senatours ther come, and certayne knyghttez,
Hodles fro þe hethe, ouer þe holte eyues,
Barefote ouer þe bente, with brondes so ryche;
Bowes to þe bolde kyng and biddis hym þe hiltes,   2310
Whethire he will hang theym or hedde or halde theym on lyfe.
Knelyde before þe Conquerour in kyrtills allone;
With carefull contenaunce þay karpide þese wordes:
"Twa senatours we are, thi subgettez of Rome,
That has sauede oure lyfe by þeise salte strandys,   2315
Hyd vs in þe heghe wode, thurghe þe helpyng of Criste,
Besekes the of socoure, as Soueraygne and Lorde;
Grante vs lyffe and lym with leberall herte,   f.78r
For His luffe that the lente this lordchipe in erthe."
"I graunte," quod [the] gude kyng, "thurghe grace of my selfen: 2320
I giffe ȝowe lyffe and lyme and leue for to passe,
So ȝe doo my message menskefully at Rome,
That ilke charge þat I ȝow ȝiffe here before my cheeffe knyghttez."
"Ȝis," sais the senatours, "that sall we ensure,
Sekerly be oure trowhes thi sayenges to fullfill;   2325
We sall lett for no lede þat lyffes in erthe,
Fore pape, ne for potestate, ne prynce so noble,
That ne sall lelely in lande thi letteres pronounce,
For duke ne for dussepere, to dye in þe payne."
  Thane the banerettez of Bretayne broghte þem to tentes,   2330
There barbours ware bownn, with basyns on lofte,
With warme watire, iwys, they wette them full son;
They schouen thes schalkes schappely theraftyre,
To rekken theis Romaynes recreaunt and ȝolden;
Forthy schoue they them to schewe, for skomfite of Rome.   2335
They coupylde þe kystys on kameles belyue,
On asses and arrabyes, theis honourable kynges—
The Emperoure for honoure all by hym one,
Euen appon an olyfaunte, hys egle owtt ouere—

2332 watire] wartire

Bekende them the captyfis, the Kynge dide hym selfen,   *2340*
And all byfore his kene men karpede thees wordes:
"Here are the kystis," quod the Kyng, "kaire ouer þe mownttez:
Mette full monée, þat ȝe haue mekyll ȝernede,
The taxe and þe trebutte of tene schore wynteres,
That was tenefully tynte in tym of oure elders;   *2345*
Saye to þe Senatoure þe ceté þat ȝemes,
That I sende hym þe somme, assaye how hym likes.
Bott byde them neuere be so bolde, whylls my blode regnes,
Efte for to brawlle þem for my brode landez,
Ne to aske trybut ne taxe be nakyn tytle,   *2350*
Bot syche tresoure as this, whilles my tym lastez."
    Nowe they raike to Rome the redyeste wayes,
Knylles in the Capatoylle and comowns assembles,
Souerayngez and senatours the ceté þat ȝemes,
Bekende them the caryage, kystis and oþer,   *2355*
Alls þe Conquerour comaunde with cruell wordes.
"We hafe trystily trayuellede þis tribute to feche,
The taxe and þe trewage of fowre score wynteris,
Of I[n]glande, of Irelande, and all þir owtt illes,
That Arthure in the Occedente ocupyes att ones.   *2360*
He byddis ȝow neuere be so bolde, whills his blode regnes,
To brawle ȝowe fore Bretayne ne his brode landes,
Ne aske hym trebute ne taxe be nonkyns title,
Bot syche tresoure as this, whills his tyme lastis.
We haffe foughtten in France, and vs es foule happenede,   f.78ᵛ *2365*
And all oure myche faire folke faye are byleuede;
Eschappide there ne cheuallrye, ne cheftaynes noþer,
Bott choppede downn in the chasse, syche chawnse es befallen.
We rede ȝe store ȝowe of stone and stuffen ȝour walles:
Ȝow wakkens wandrethe and werre—be ware ȝif ȝow lykes."   *2370*
    In the kalendez of Maye this caas es befallen:
The roy ryalle renownde, with his Rownde Table,
One the coste of Costantyne, by þe clere strandez,
Has þe Romaynes ryche rebuykede for euer.
Whene he hade foughtten in Fraunce and the felde wonnen,   *2375*
And fersely his foomen fellde owtte of lyfe,

2349 brawlle] [?] brawllee 2366 byleuede] byleude leuede 2368 chawnse] chanse chawnse

He bydes for þe beryenge of his bolde knyghtez
That in batell with brandez ware broughte owte of lyfe.
He beryes at Bayone Sir Bedwere þe ryche;
The cors of Kayon þe kene at Came es beleuefede,   2380
Koueride with a crystall clenly all ouer—
His fadyre conqueride þat kyth knyghtly with hondes.
Seyn in Burgoyne he bade to bery mo knyghttez,
Sir Berade and Bawdwyne, Sir Bedwar þe ryche,
Gud Sir Cador at Came, as his kynde askes.   2385
Thane Sir Arthure onone, in þe Auguste þeraftyre,
Enteres to Almayne wyth ostez arrayed;
Lengez at Lusscheburghe, to lechen hys knyghttez,
With his lele liggemen, as lorde in his awen.
And on Christofre Daye a concell he haldez,   2390
Withe kynges and kaysers, clerkkes and oþer;
Comandez them kenely to caste all þeire wittys,
How he may conquere by crafte the kythe þat he claymes.
Bot the Conquerour kene, curtais and noble,
Karpes in the concell theys knyghtly wordez: 2395
"Here es a knyghte in theis kleuys, enclosside with hilles,
That I haue cowayte to knawe, because of his wordez:
That es Lorayne þe lele, I kepe noghte to layne;
The lordchipe es louely, as ledes me telles.
I will that ducherye devyse and dele as me lykes,   2400
And seyn dresse wyth þe Duke, if destyny suffre;
The renke rebell has bene vnto my Rownde Table,
Redy aye with Romaynes to ryotte my landes;
We sall rekken full rathe, if reson so happen,
Who has ryghte to þat rente, by ryche Gode of Heuen!   2405
Than will I by Lumbardye, lykande to schawe,
Sett lawe in þe lande, þat laste sall euer;
The tyrauntez of Tuskayn tempeste a littyll,
Talke with þe temperall, whills my tym lastez.
I gyffe my protteccione to all þe Pope landez,   2410
My ryche pensell of pes my pople to schewe;   f.79ʳ
It es a foly to offende oure fadyr vndire Gode,
Owþer Peter or Paule, þa postles of Rome.

2403 to] and   2408 Tuskayn *Brock*] Turkayn

ȝif we spare the spirituell, we spede bot the bettire;
Whills we haue for to speke, spille sall it neuer."   *2415*
      Now they spede at þe spurres, withowttyn speche more,
To þe marche of Meyes, theis manliche knyghtez,
That es [in] Lorrayne alofede, as London es here,
Ceté of þat seynȝowre, that soueraynge es holden.
The Kyng ferkes furthe on a faire stede,   *2420*
With Ferrer and Ferawnte and oþer foure knyghtez;
Abowte the ceté þa seuen they soughte at þe nextte,
To seke them a sekyre place to sett withe engeynes.
Thane they bendyde in burghe bowes of vyse,
Bekyrs at þe bolde kyng with boustouse lates;   *2425*
Allblawsters at Arthure egerly schottes,
For to hurte hym or his horse with þat hard wapen.
The Kynge schonte for no schotte, ne no schelde askys,
Bot schewes hym scharpely in his schene wedys;
Lenges all at laysere and lokes on the wallys,   *2430*
Whare þey ware laweste the ledes to assaille.
"Sir," said Sir Ferrer, "a foly thowe wirkkes,
Thus nakede in thy noblaye to neghe to þe walles,
Sengely in thy surcotte, this ceté to reche,
And schewe þe within, there to schende vs all.   *2435*
Hye vs hastylye heynne, or we mon full happen,
For hitt they the or thy horse, it harmes for euer."
"Ife thow be ferde," quod the Kyng, "I rede thow ryde vttere,
Lesse þat þey rywe the with theire rownnd wapyn!
Thow arte bot a fawntkyn—no ferly me thynkkys,   *2440*
Þou will be flayede for a flye þat on thy flesche lyghttes.
I am nothyng agaste, so me Gode helpe:
Þof siche gadlynges be greuede, it greues me bot lyttill;
Thay wyn no wirchipe of me, bot wastys theire takle—
They sall wante or I weende, I wagen myn hevede.   *2445*
Sall neuer harlott haue happe, thorowe helpe of my Lorde,
To kyll a corownde kyng with krysom enoynttede!"
      Thane come þe herbariours, harageous knyghtez,
The hale batells on hye harrawnte theraftyre;

2419 Ceté *Brock*] Pety   2421 Ferrer and *Brock*] ferrannde
2445 *Indecipherable extra letter in* hevede   2447 with] with with

And oure forreours ferse, appon fele halfes, 2450
Come flyeande before one ferawnte stedes,
Ferkande in arraye theire ryall knyghttez,
The renkez renownde of þe Rounnd Table.
All þe frekke men of Fraunce folowede thareaftyre,
Faire fittyde on frownte, and on the felde houys. 2455
Thane the schalkes scharpelye scheftys theire horsez, f.79ᵛ
To schewen them semly in theire scheen wedes;
Buskes in batayle with baners displayede,
With brode scheldes enbrassede and burlyche helmys,
With penouns and pensells of ylke prynce armes, 2460
Appayrellde with perrye and precious stones;
The lawnces with loraynes and lemande scheldes,
Lyghtenande as þe leuenyng and lemand al ouer.
　　Thane the price men prekes and proues þeire horsez,
Satills to þe ceté appon sere halfes; 2465
Enserches the subbarbes sadly thareaftyre,
Discoueris of schotte-men and skyrmys a lyttill;
Skayres þaire skottefers and theire skowtte-waches,
Brittenes theire barrers with theire bryghte wapyns,
Bett down a barbycan and þe brygge wynnys; 2470
Ne hade the garnyson bene gude at þe grete ȝates,
Thay hade wonn that wone be theire awen strenghe.
Than withdrawes oure men and drisses them bettyre,
For dred of þe drawe-brigge dasschede in sondre;
Hyes to þe harbergage thare the Kyng houys, 2475
With his batell on heghe, horsyde on stedys.
Thane was þe Prynce puruayede and þeire places nommen,
Pyghte pauyllyons of palle and plattes in seegge;
Thane lenge they lordly, as þem leefe thoghte,
Waches in ylke warde, as to þe werre falles, 2480
Settes vp sodaynly certayne engynes.
　　One Sonondaye be þe soone has a flethe ȝolden,
The Kyng calles on Florente, þat flour was of knyghttez:
"The Fraunchemene enfeblesches, ne farly me thynkkys;
They are vnfondyde folke in þe faire marches, 2485
For them wantes þe flesche and fude that them lykes.
Here are forestez faire appon fele halues,

And thedyre feemen are flede with freliche bestes.
Thow sall foonde to þe fell and forraye the mountes;
Sir Forawnt and Sir Florydas sall folowe thi brydyll.   2490
Vs moste with some fresche mette refresche oure pople,
That are feedde in þe fyrthe with þe froyte of þe erthe.
Thare sall weende to þis viage Sir Gawayne hym selfen,
Wardayne full wyrchipfull, and so hym wele semes;
Sir Wecharde, Sir Waltyre, theis wyrchipfull knyghtes,   2495
With all wyseste men of þe weste marches;
Sir Clegis, Sir Clarybalde, Sir Clarymownde þe noble,
The Capytayne oo Cardyfe clenlyche arrayede.
Goo now, warne all þe wache, Gawayne and oþer,
And weendes furthe on ȝour waye withowttyn moo wordes."   2500
    Now ferkes to þe fyrthe thees fresche men of armes,
To þe fell so fewe, theis fresclyche byernes,
Thorowe hopes and hymland, hillys and oþer,   f.80ʳ
Holtis and hare woddes with heslyn schawes,
Thorowe marasse and mosse and montes so heghe;   2505
And in the myste [of] mornyng one a mede falles,
Mawen and vnmade, maynoyrede bott lyttyll,
In swathes sweppen down, full of swete floures.
Thare vnbrydills theis bolde and baytes þeire horses,
To þe grygynge of þe daye, þat byrdez gan synge,   2510
Whylls the surs of þe sonne, þat sonde es of Cryste,
That solaces all synfull þat syghte has in erthe.
    Thane weendes owtt the wardayne, Sir Gawayne hym selfen,
Alls he þat weysse was and wyghte, wondyrs to seke;
Than was he warre of a wye, wondyre wele armyde,   2515
Baytand on a wattire banke by þe wodde eyuis,
Buskede in brenyes bryghte to behalde,
Enbrassede a brode schelde on a blonke ryche,
Withowttyn ony berne, bot a boye one,
Houes by hym on a blonke and his spere holdes.   2520
He bare gessande in golde thre grayhondes of sable,
With chapes and cheynes of chalke-whytte slyuer,

2506 myste of mornyng *Brock*] myste mornyng   2510 þat byrdez] þat byrdez that byrdes
2514 wyghte] wyghte wyghte   2519 withowttyn *Brock*] with birenne
2521 gessande *Banks*] gessenande   2522 and *Björkman*] a

A charebocle in þe cheefe, chawngawnde of hewes,
And a cheefe anterous, chalange who lykes.
    Sir Gawayne glyftes on the gome with a glade will;   *2525*
A grete spere fro his grome he grypes in hondes,
Gyrdes ewen ouere þe streme on a stede ryche,
To þat steryn in stour, one strenghe þare he houys.
Egerly one Inglisce "Arthure!" he askryes;
The toþer irouslye ansuers hym sone,   *2530*
On a launde of Lorrayne with a lowde steuen,
That ledes myghte lysten þe lenghe of a myle:
"Whedyr prykkes thow, pilouur, þat profers so large?
Here pykes thowe no praye, profire when þe lykes!
Bot thow in þis perell put of the bettire,   *2535*
Thow sall be my presonere, for all thy prowde lates!"
"Sir," sais Sir Gawayne, "so me Gode helpe,
Siche glauerande gomes greues me bot lyttill!
Bot if thowe graythe thy gere, the will grefe happen,
Or thowe goo of þis greue, for all thy grete wordes!"   *2540*
    Than þeire launces they lachen, thes lordlyche byernez,
Laggen with longe speres one lyarde stedes;
Cowpen at awntere be kraftes of armes,
Till bothe þe crowell speres brousten att ones.
Thorowe scheldys þey schotte and scherde thorowe ma[y]les,   *2545*
Bothe schere thorowe schoulders a schaftmonde large.
Thus worthylye þes wyes wondede ere bothen—
Or they wreke þem of wrethe awaye will þey neuer.
Than they raughte in the reyne and agayne rydes,
Redely theis rathe mene rusches owtte swerdez,   f.80ᵛ *2550*
Hittes one hellmes full hertelyche dynttys,
Hewes appon hawberkes with full harde wapyns;
Full stowttly þey stryke, thire steryn knyghttes,
Stokes at þe stomake with stelyn poyntes,
Feghtten and floresche withe flawmande swerdez,   *2555*
Till þe flawes of fyre flawmes one theire helmes.
    Thane Sir Gawayne was greuede and grychgide full sore;
With Galuthe his gude swerde grymlye he strykes:
Clefe þe knyghttes schelde clenliche in sondre—

2535 perell] pererell

Who lukes to þe lefte syde when his horse launches   *2560*
With þe lyghte of þe sonne men myghte see his lyuere.
Thane granes þe gome fore greefe of his wondys,
And gyrdis at Sir Gawayne, as he by glentis;
And awkewarde egerly sore he hym smyttes:
An alet enamelde he oches in sondire,   *2565*
Bristes þe rerebrace with the bronde ryche,
Kerues of at þe coutere with þe clene egge,
Ane[n]tis þe avawmbrace, vayllede with siluer.
Thorowe a dowble vesture of veluett ryche
With þe venymous swerde a vayne has he towchede,   *2570*
That voydes so violently þat all his witte changede;
The vesere, the aventaile, his vesturis ryche,
With the valyant blode was verrede all ouer.
Thane this tyrante tite turnes þe brydill,
Talkes vntendirly and sais "Þow arte towchede;   *2575*
Vs bus haue a blode-bande or thi ble change,
For all þe barbours of Bretayne sall noghte thy blode stawnche;
For he þat es blemeste with þis brade brande blyne schall he neuer."
     "Ȝa," quod Sir Gawayne, "thow greues me bot lyttill;
Thowe wenys to glopyne me with thy gret wordez;   *2580*
Thow trowes with thy talkyng þat my harte talmes.
Thow betydes tourfere or thowe hyen turne,
Bot thow tell me tytte, and tarye no lengere,
What may staunche this blode þat thus faste rynnes."
"Ȝise, I say þe sothely, and sekire þe my trowthe: *2585*
No surgyon in Salarne sall saue þe bettyre;
Withthy þat thowe suffre me, for sake of thy Cryste,
To schewe schortly my schrifte and schape for myn ende."
"Ȝis," quod Sir Gawayne, "so me God helpe,
I gyfe þe grace and graunt, þofe þou hafe grefe seruede,   *2590*
Withthy thowe say me sothe what thowe here sekes,
Thus sengilly and sulayne all þi selfe one;
And whate laye thow leues one, layne noghte þe sothe,
And whate legyaunce and whare þow arte lorde."
     "My name es Sir Priamus; a prynce es my fadyre,   *2595*
Praysede in his partyes with prouede kynges;

2568 vayllede *Holthausen*] vrayllede

In Rome thare he regnes he es riche halden.
He has bene rebell to Rome and reden theire landes,
Werreyand weisely wyntters and ȝeres;   f.81ʳ
Be witt and be wyssdome and be wyghte strenghe,   2600
And be wyrchipfull werre, his awen has he wonn.
He es of Alexandire blode, ouerlyng of kynges,
The vncle of his ayele, Sir Ector of Troye;
And here es the kynreden that I of come,
And Iudas and Iosue, þise gentill knyghtes.   2605
I ame apparaunt his ayere, and eldeste of oþer,
Of Alexandere and Aufrike and all þa owte landes;
I am in possessione and plenerly sessede
In all þe price cetées that to þe porte langes;
I sall hafe trewly the tresour and the londes,   2610
And bothe trebute and taxe whills my tym lastes.
I was so hawtayne of herte, whills I at home lengede,
I helde nane my hippe heghte vndire heuen ryche;
Forthy was I sente hedire with seuen score knyghttez,
To asaye of this werre, be sente of my fadire,   2615
And I am for cirqwitrye schamely supprisede,
And be aw[n]tire of armes owtrayede fore euere.
Now hafe I taulde the þe kyne that I ofe come,
Will thow, for knyghthede, kene me thy name?"
        "Be Criste," quod Sir Gawayne, "knyghte was I neuer;   2620
With þe kydde Conquerour a knafe of his chambyre,
Has wroghte in his wardrope wynters and ȝeres,
One his long armour that hym beste lykid;
I poyne all his pavelyouns þat to hym selfe pendes,
Dyghttes his dowblettez for dukes and erles,   2625
Aketouns auenaunt fore Arthure hym selfen,
That he vsede in werre all this aughte wynttter.
He made me ȝomane at ȝole, and gafe me gret gyftes,
And c. pound and a horse and harnayse full ryche;
Gife I happe to my hele that hende for to serue,   2630
I be holpen in haste, I hette the forsothe."
        "Giffe his knafes be syche, his knyghttez are noble!
There es no kyng vndire Criste may kemp with hym on;
He will be Alexander ayre, that all þe erthe lowttede,

Abillere þan euer was Sir Ector of Troye.   2635
Now fore the krisome þat þou kaghte þat day þou was crystenede,
Whethire thowe be knyghte or knaffe, knawe now þe sothe."
          "My name es Sir Gawayne, I graunt þe forsothe,
Cosyn to þe Conquerour, he knawes it hym selfen;
Kydd in his kalander a knyghte of his chambyre,   2640
And rollede the richeste of all þe Rounde Table.
I ame þe dussepere and duke he dubbede with his hondes,
Deynttely on a daye before his dere knyghtes;
Gruche noghte, gude sir, þofe me this grace happen:
It es þe gifte of Gode, the gree es Hys awen."   2645
"Petire!" sais Priamus, "Now payes me bettire   f.81ᵛ
Thane I of Provynce warre prynce and of Paresche ryche;
Fore me ware leuer preuely by prykkyd to þe harte,
Than euer any prikkere had siche a pryse wonnyn.
Bot here es herberde at hand, in ȝone huge holtes,   2650
Halle bataile one heyghe—take hede ȝif the lyke—
The Duke of Lorrayne the derfe, with his dere knyghtes,
The doughtyest of Dolfinede and Duchemen many,
The lordes of Lumbardye, that leders are halden,
The garnyson of Godard gaylyche arrayede,   2655
The wyese of þe Westuale, wirchipfull biernez,
Of Sessoyn and Surylande Sarazenes enewe;
They are nowmerde full neghe and namede in rollez,
Sexty thowsande and ten, forsothe, of sekyre men of armez;
Bot ȝif thow hye fro þis hethe, it harmes vs bothe,   2660
And bot my hurtes be son holpen, hole be I neuer.
Take heede to þis hanseman þat he no horne blawe,
Are thowe heyly in haste beese hewen al to peces;
For they are my retenuz, to ryde whare I wyll,
Es non redyare renkes regnande in erthe;   2665
Be thow raghte with þat rowtt, thow rydes no forþer,
Ne thow bees neuer rawnsonede for reches in erthe."
          Sir Gawayn wente or þe wathe com whare hym beste lykede,
With this wortheliche wye, that wondyd was sore;
Merkes to þe mountayne there oure men lenges,   2670
Baytaynde theire blonkes þer on þe brode mede:
Lordes lenande lowe on lemand scheldes,

With lowde laghttirs on lofte for lykyng of byrdez,
Of larkes, of lynkwhyttez, þat lufflyche songen;
And some was sleghte one slepe with sleyghte of þe pople,   *2675*
Þat sange in þe seson in the schenne schawes,
So lawe in þe lawndez so lykand notes.

  Thane Sir Whycher whas warre þaire wardayne was wondyde,
And went to hym wepand and wryngande his handes;
Syr Wycherd, Sir Walthere, theis weise men of armes,   *2680*
Had wondyre of Sir Gawayne, and wente hym agayns,
Mett hym in the mydwaye and meruaile them t[h]oghte
How he maisterede þat man, so myghtty of strenghes.
Be all þe welthe of þe werlde, so woo was þem neuer:
"For all oure wirchipe, iwysse, awaye es in erthe!"   *2685*

  "Greue ȝow noghte," quod Gawayne, "for Godis luffe of Heuen;
For this es bot gosomer and gyffen on erles;
Þoffe my schouldire be schrede and my schelde thyrllede,
And the wielde of myn arme werkkes a littill,
This prissonere, Sir Priamus, þat has perilous wondes,   *2690*
Sais þat he has saluez sall soften vs bothen."
Thane stirttes to his sterape sterynfull knyghttez,
And he lordely lyghttes and laghte of his brydill,
And lete his burlyche blonke baite on þe flores;
Braydes of his bacenette and his ryche wedis,   f.82ʳ *2695*
Bownnes to his brode schelde and bowes to þe erthe—
In all the bodye of that bolde es no blode leued.

  Than preses to Sir Priamous precious knyghtes,
Auyssely of his horse hentes hym in armes;
His helme and his hawberke þay taken of aftyre,   *2700*
And hastily for his hurtte all his herte chawngyd,
They laide hym down in the lawndez and laghte of his wedes,
And he lenede hym on lange, or how hym beste lykede.
A fyole of fyne golde they fande at his gyrdill,
Þat es full of þe flour of þe fouur well,   *2705*
Þat flowes owte of Paradice when þe flode ryses,
That myche froyt of fallez, þat feede schall vs all;
Be it frette on his flesche, þare synues are entamede,

2675 sleyghte *Banks*] slaughte 2680 Wycherd] Wychere
2687 gosomer] gosesomer 2704 fyole *Mennicken*] foyle

The freke schalle be fische-halle within fowre howres.
They vncouere þat cors with full clene hondes;   *2710*
With clere watire a knyghte clensis theire wondes,
Keled theym kyndly and comforthed þer hertes.
And whene þe carffes ware clene, þay clede them aȝayne;
Barell-ferrers they brochede and broghte them the wyne,
Bothe brede and brawn and bredis full ryche.   *2715*
    When þay hade eten anon they armede after;
Thane tha awntrende men "As armes!" askryes.
With a claryoune clere thire knyghtez togedyre,
Callys to concell and of this case tellys:
"Ȝondyr es a companye of clene men of armes,   *2720*
The keneste in contek þat vndir Criste lenges;
In ȝone oken wode an oste are arrayede,
Vndirtakande men of þiese owte londes,
As sais vs Sir Priamous, so helpe Seynt Peter!
Go men," quod Gawayne, "and grape in ȝoure hertez,   *2725*
Who sall graythe to ȝone greue to ȝone gret lordes;
Ȝif we gettlesse goo home, the Kyng will be greuede,
And say we are gadlynges, agaste for a lyttill.
We are with Sir Florente, as todaye falles,
That es floure of Fraunce, for he fleede neuer;   *2730*
He was chosen and chargegide in chambire of þe Kyng,
Chiftayne of þis journée with cheualrye noble;
Whethire he fyghte or he flee, we sall folowe aftyre;
Fore all þe fere of ȝone folke forsake sall I neuer!"
    "Fadyre," sais Sir Florent, "full faire ȝe it tell.   *2735*
Bot I ame bot a fawntkyn, vnfraystede in armes;
Ȝif any foly befall, þe fawte sall be owrs,
And fremdly o Fraunce be flemede for euer.
Woundes noghte, ȝour wirchip, my witte es bot symple;
Ȝe are owre wardayne, iwysse, wyrke as ȝowe lykes;   *2740*
Ȝe are at the ferreste noghte passande fyve hundrethe,
And þat es fully to fewe to feghte with them all,
Fore harlottez and hansemene sall helpe bott littill—   *f.82ᵛ*
They will hye theym hyen, for all þeire gret wordes.
I rede ȝe wyrke aftyre witte, as wyesse men of armes,   *2745*
And warpes wylily awaye, as wirchipfull knyghtes."

"I grawnte," quod Sir Gawayne, "so me Gode helpe;
Bot here are galyarde gomes þat of þe gre seruis,
The kreuelleste knyghttes of þe Kynges chambyre,
That kane carpe with the coppe knyghtly wordes—   2750
We sall proue todaye who sall the prys wyn."
    Nowe ferriours fers vnto þe fyrthe rydez,
And fongez a faire felde and on fotte lyghttez;
Prekes aftyre þe pray, as pryce men of armes.
Florent and Floridas, with fyve score knyghttez,   2755
Folowede in þe foreste, and on þe way fowndys,
Flyngande a faste trott, and on þe folke dryffes.
Than felewes fast to oure folke wele a fyve hundreth
Of freke men to þe fyrthe, appon fresche horses;
One Sir Feraunt before, apon a fayre stede,   2760
Was fosterede in Famacoste—the Fende was his fadyre.
He flenges to Sir Florent, and pristly he kryes,
"Why flees thow, falls knyghte? The Fende hafe þi saule!"
Thane Sir Florent was fayne, and in fewter castys;
One Fawuell of Fryselande to Feraunt he rydys,   2765
And raghte in þe reyne on þe stede ryche,
And rydes towarde the rowte, restes he no lengere:
Full butt in þe frounte he flysches hym euen,
And all disfegoures his face with his fell wapen;
Thurghe his bryghte bacenette his brayne has he towchede,   2770
And brusten his neke-bone, þat all his breste stoppede.
    Thane his cosyn askryede and cryede full lowde,
"Thowe has killede colde dede þe kynge of all knyghttes!
He has bene fraistede on felde in fyftene rewmes;
He fonde neuer no freke myghte feghte with hym one.   2775
Thow schall dye for his dede with my derfe wapen,
And all þe doughtty for dule þat in ȝone dale houes!"
    "Fy," sais Sir Floridas, "thow fleryande wryche!
Thow wenes for to flay vs, floke-mowthede schrewe!"
Bot Floridas with a swerde, as he by glenttys,   2780
All þe flesche of þe flanke he flappes in sondyre,
That all þe filthe of þe freke and fele of þe guttes
Foloes his fole fotte, whene he furthe rydes.
    2765 to] te

Than rydes a renke to reschewe þat byerne,
Þat was Raynalde of þe Rodes and rebell to Criste,   2785
Peruertede with paynyms þat Cristen persewes;
Presses in prowdly, as þe praye wendes,
Fore he hade in Prewsslande myche pryce wonnen—
Forthi in presence thare he profers so large.
Bot thane a renke, Sir Richere of þe Rounde Table,   2790
One a ryall stede rydes hym aȝaynes;
Thorowe a rownnde rede schelde he ruschede hym sone,   f.83ʳ
That the rosselde spere to his herte rynnes;
The renke relys abowte and rusches to þe erthe,
Roris full ruydlye, bot rade he no more.   2795
      Now all þat es fere and vnfaye of þes fyve hundreth
Falles on Sir Florent, a fyve score knyghttes;
Betwyx a plasche and a flode, appon a flate lawnde,
Oure folke fongen theire felde and fawghte them agaynes.
Than was lowde appon lofte "Lorrayne!" askryede,   2800
When ledys with longe speris lasschen togedyrs,
And "Arthure!" on our syde, when theyme oghte aylede.
Than Sir Florent and Floridas in fewtyre þey caste,
Fruschen on all þe frape and biernes affrayede,
Fellis fyve at þe frounte thare they fyrste enteride,   2805
And, or they ferke forthire, fele of þese oþere.
Brenyes browdden they briste, brittenede scheldes,
Bettes and beres down the best þat þem byddes;
All þat rewlyd in the rowtte they ryden awaye,
So rewdly they rere theys ryall knyghttes.   2810
      When Sir Priamous, þat prince, persayuede theire gamen,
He hade peté in herte þat he ne durste profire;
He wente to Sir Gawayne and sais hym þese wordes:
"Thi price men fore thy praye putt are all vndyre;
They are with Sarazenes ouersette, mo þan seuen hundreth   2815
Of þe Sowdanes knyghtes owt of sere londes;
·Walde þow suffire me, Sir, for sake of thi Criste,
With a soppe of thi men suppowell theym ones?"
"I grouche noghte," quod Gawayne, "þe gree es þaire awen!
They mon hafe gwerddouns full grett graunt of my lorde;   2820
Bot the freke men of Fraunce fraiste them selfen—

Frekes faughte noghte þeire fill this fyftene wynter.
I will noghte stire with my stale halfe a stede lenghe,
Bot they be stedde with more stuffe than on ȝone stede houys."
    Than Sir Gawayne was warre, withowttyn þe wode hemmes, *2825*
Wyes of þe Westfale appon wyght horsez,
Walopande wodely, as þe waye forthes,
With all þe wapyns, iwys, þat to þe werre longez.
The erle Antele the Olde the avawmwarde he buskes,
Ayerande on ayther hande heghte thosande knyghtez; *2830*
His pelours and pauysers passede all nombyre
That euer any prynce lede puruayede in erthe.
Than þe Duke of Lorrayne dresesse thareaftyre,
With dowbill of þe Duchemen, þat doughtty ware holden;
Paynymes of Pruyslande, prekkers full noble, *2835*
Come prekkande before with Priamous knyghttez.
Than saide the erle Antele to Algere, his broþer,
"Me angers ernestly at Arthures knyghtez,
Thus enkerly on an oste awnters þem selfen;
They will be owttrayede anon, are vndron ryng, f.83ᵛ *2840*
Thus folily on a felde to fyghte with vs all;
Bot they be fesede in faye ferly me thynkes.
Walde they purposse take and passe on theire wayes,
Prike home to theire prynce and theire pray leue,
They myghte lenghen theire lyefe and lossen bott littill— *2845*
It wolde lyghte my herte, so helpe me oure Lorde!"
"Sir," sais Sir Algere, "thay hafe littill vsede
To be owttrayede withe oste—me angers þe more;
The fayreste schall be full feye þat in oure floke ryddez
Alls fewe as they bene, are they the felde leue." *2850*
    Than gud Gawayne, gracious and noble,
All with glorious gle he gladdis his knyghtes:
"Gloppyns noghte, gud men, for gleterand scheldes,
Þofe ȝone gadlyngez be gaye on ȝone gret horses;
Banerettez of Bretayne, buskes vp ȝour hertes! *2855*
Bees noghte baiste of ȝone boyes, ne of þaire bryghte wedis.
We sall blenke theire boste for all theire bolde profire,
Als bouxom as birde es in bede to hir lorde.
Ȝeffe we feghte todaye, þe felde schall be owrs,

The fekill faye sall faile and falssede be distroyede! 2860
ȝone folk is one frountere, vnfraistede theym semes;
Thay make faythe and faye to þe Fend seluen!
We sall in this viage victoures be holden,
And avauntede with voycez of valyant biernez,
Praysede with pryncez in presence of lordes, 2865
And luffede with ladyes in dyuerse londes;
Aughte neuer siche honoure none of oure elders—
Vnwyn ne Absolon ne non of thies oþer.
When we are moste in destresse Marie we mene,
That es oure maisters seyne, þat he myche traistez, 2870
Melys of þat mylde Qwene that menskes vs all—
Who-so meles of þat Mayde myskaries he neuer."
  Be þese wordes ware saide, they ware noghte ferre behynd
Bot the lenghe of a launde, and "Lorayne!" askryes.
Was neuer siche a justyng at journé in erthe, 2875
In the Vale of Iosephate, as gestes vs telles,
When Iulyus and Ioatall ware juggede to dy,
As was when þe ryche men of þe Rownde Table
Ruschede into þe rowte one ryall stedes;
For so raythely þay rusche with roselde speris, 2880
That the raskaille was rade, and rane to þe grefes,
And karede to þat courte as cowardes for euer.
  "Peter!" sais Sir Gawayne; "This gladdez myn herte,
That ȝone gedlynges are gon that made gret nowmbre;
I hope that thees harlottez sall harme vs bot littill, 2885
Fore they will hyde them in haste within ȝone holte euis.
Thay are fewere one felde þan þay were fyrste nombird, f.84ʳ
Be fourtty thousande, in faythe, for all theyre faire hostes!"
Bot one Iolyan of Iene, a geante full howge,
Has jonede on Sir Ierant, a justis of Walis; 2890
Thorowe a jerownde schelde he jogges hym thorowe,
And a fyn gesserawnte of gentill mayles—
Ioynter and gemows he jogges in sondyre.
One a jambé stede þis jurnée he makes;
Thus es þe geante forjuste, that errawnte Iewe, 2895
And Gerard es jocunde, and joyes hym þe more.
  Than the genatours of Genne enjoynes att ones,

And frykis on þe frowntere well a fyve hundreth;
A freke highte Sir Federike, with full fele oþer,
Ferkes on a frusche and fresclyche askryes,   2900
To fyghte with oure forreours, þat on felde houis.
And thane the ryalle renkkes of þe Rownde Table
Rade furth full ernestly and rydis them agaynes,
Mellis with the medillwarde, bot they ware ill machede,
Of siche a grett multytude was meruayle to here.   2905
Seyne at þe assemblé the Sarazenes discoueres
The soueraynge of Sessoyne, that saluede was neuer;
Gyawntis forjustede with gentill knyghtes,
Thorowe gesserawntes of Iene jaggede to þe herte.
They hewe thorowe helmes hawtayne biernez,   2910
Þat þe hiltede swerdes to þaire hertes rynnys.
Than þe renkes renownd of þe Rownd Table
Ryffes and ruyssches down renayede wreches;
And thus they dreuen to þe dede dukes and erles,
All þe dreghe of þe daye, with dredfull werkes.   2915
        Than Sir Priamous þe prynce, in presens of lordes,
Presez to his penown and pertly it hentes,
Reuertede it redily and awaye rydys,
To þe ryall rowte of þe Rownde Table;
And heyly his retenus raykes hym aftyre,   2920
For they his reson had rede on his schelde ryche.
Owte of þe scheltrone þey schede, as schepe of a folde,
And steris furth to þe stowre and stode be þeire lorde.
Seyne they sent to þe Duke and saide hym þise wordes:
"We hafe bene thy sowdeours this sex ȝere and more;   2925
We forsake þe todaye be serte of owre lorde;
We sewe to oure soueraynge in sere kynges londes.
Vs defawtes oure feez of þis foure wyntteres:
Thow arte feble and false and noghte bot faire wordes.
Oure wages are werede owte and þi werre endide;   2930
We maye with oure wirchipe weend whethire vs lykes.
I red þowe trette of a trewe and trofle no lengere,
Or þow sall tyne of thi tale ten thosande or euen."
        "Fy à debles!" saide þe Duke; "The Deuell haue ȝour bones!
The dawngere of ȝon doggez drede schall I neuer.   f.84ᵛ 2935

We sall dele this daye, be dedes of armes,
My dede, and my ducherye, and my dere knyghtes.
Siche sowdeours as ȝe I sett bot att lyttill,
That sodanly in defawte forsakes theire lorde."
    The Duke in his scheltrone dreches no lengere,   *2940*
Drawes hym a dromedarie, with dredfull knyghtez;
Graythes to Sir Gawayne, with full gret nowmbyre
Of gomes of Gernaide, that greuous are holden;
Thas fresche horsede men to þe frownt rydes,
Felles of oure forreours be fourtty at ones—   *2945*
They hade foughtten before with a fyve hundrethe;
It was no ferly, in faythe, þofe they faynt waxen.
Thane Sir Gawayne was grefede and grypys his spere,
And gyrdez in agayne with galyarde knyghttez;
Metes þe Marches of Mees and melles hym thorowe,   *2950*
As man of þis medill-erthe þat moste hade greuede.
Bot on Chastelayne, a childe of þe Kynges chambyr,
Was warde to Sir Wawayn of þe weste marches,
Cheses to Sir Cheldrike, a cheftayne noble,
With a chasyng he chokkes hym thurghe—   *2955*
This chekke hym eschewede be chauncez of armes.
So þay chase þat childe, eschape may he neuer;
Bot on Swyan of Swecy, with a swerde egge,
The swyers swyre-bane he swappes in sondyre;
He swounande diede and on þe swarthe lengede,   *2960*
Sweltes ewynne swiftly, and swanke he no more.
    Þan Sir Gawayn gretes with his gray eghne—
The guyte was a gude man, begynnande of armes;
Fore the charry childe so his chere chawngide,
That the chillande watire on his chekes rynnyde.   *2965*
"Woo es me," quod Gawayne, "that I ne weten hade;
I sall wage for that wye all þat I welde,
Bot I be wroken on that wye that thus has hym wondyde."
He dresses hym drerily and to þe Duke rydes,
Bot one Sir Dolphyn the derfe dyghte hym agaynes,   *2970*
And Sir Gawayne hym gyrd with a grym launce,

2940 in his scheltrone dreches *Branscheid*] in his schelde and dreches
2944 horsede] horsesede   2950 Marches *Branscheid*] maches

That the grounden spere glade to his herte.
And egerly he hente owte and hurte anoþer,
An haythen knyghte, Hardolfe, happye in armes;
Sleyghly in at the slotte slyttes hym thorowe, 2975
That the slydande spere of his hande sleppes.
Thare es slayne in þat slope, be sleyghte of his hondes,
Sexty slongen in a slade of sleghe men of armes.
Þofe Sir Gawaynne ware wo, he wayttes hym by,
And was warre of þat wye that the childe wondyde, 2980
And with a swerde swiftly he swappes hym thorowe,
That he swyftly swelte and on þe erthe swounes.
And thane he raykes to þe rowte and ruysches one helmys, f.85ʳ
Riche hawberkes he rente and rasede schyldes,
Rydes on a rawndoune and his rayke holdes, 2985
Thorowowte þe rerewarde he holdes wayes;
And thare raughte in the reyne this ryall þe ryche,
And rydez into þe rowte of þe Rownde Table.
    Þane oure cheualrous men changen theire horsez,
Chases and choppes down cheftaynes noble, 2990
Hittes full hertely on helmes and scheldes,
Hurtes and hewes down haythen knyghtez;
Ketell-hattes they cleue euen to þe scholdirs—
Was neuer siche a clamour of capitaynes in erthe.
Thare was kynges sonnes kaughte, curtays and noble, 2995
And knyghtes of þe contré, that knawen was ryche;
Lordes of Lorayne and Lumbardye bothen
Laugh[t]e was and lede in with oure lele knyghttez.
Thas þat chasede that daye, theire chaunce was bettire—
Swiche a cheke at a chace escheuede theym neuer. 3000
    When Sir Florent be fyghte had þe felde wonen,
He ferkes ine before with fyve score knyghttez;
Theire prayes and þeire presoneres passes one aftyre,
With pylours and pauysers and pryse men of armes.
Thane gudly Sir Gawayne gydes his knyghttez, 3005
Gas in at þe gayneste, as gydes hym telles,
Fore greffe on a garysone of full gret lordes
Sulde noghte gripe vpe his gere, ne swyche grame wirche.

2977 sleyghte *Mennicken*] elagere   2989 cheualrous] cheualrours

Forethy they stode at the straytez and with his stale houede,
Till his prayes ware paste the pathe that he dredis;   *3010*
When they the ceté myghte see that the Kyng seggede—
Sothely the same daye was wit[h] asawte wonnen—
An hawrawde hyes before, the beste of the lordes,
Hom at þe herbergage, owt of tha hyghe londes,
Tornys tytte to þe tente and to the Kyng telles   *3015*
All the tale sothely, and how they hade spede:
"All thy forreours are fere, that forrayede withowttyn,
Sir Florent and Sir Floridas and all thy ferse knyghtez;
Thay hafe forrayede and foghten with full gret nowmbyre,
And fele of thy foomen has broghte owt of lyffe.   *3020*
Oure wirchipfull wardayne es wele escheuyde,
For he has wonn todaye wirchip for euere;
He has Dolfyn slayne and þe Duke takyn;
Many dowghty es dede be dynt of his hondes.
He has presoners price, pryncez and erles,   *3025*
Of þe richeste blode þat regnys in erthe;
All thy cheuallrous men faire are eschewede;
Bot a childe Chasteleynne myschance es befallen."
"Hawtayne," sais þe Kyng, "harawde, be Criste,
Thow has helyd myn herte, I hete the forsothe;   *3030*
I ȝife the in Hamptone a hundreth pownde large."   f.85ᵛ
        The Kynge þan to assawte he sembles his knyghtez,
With somercastell and sowe appon sere halfes;
Skyftis his skotiferis and skayles the wallis,
And iche wache has his warde with wiese men of armes.   *3035*
Thane boldly þay buske and bendes engynes,
Payses in pylotes and proues theire castes;
Mynsteris and masondewes they malle to þe erthe,
Chirches and chapells chalke-whitte blawnchede.
Stone [s]tepells full styffe in þe strete ligges,   *3040*
Chawmbyrs with chymnés and many cheefe inns;
Paysede and pelid down playsterede walles—
The pyne of þe pople was peté for to here.
        Thane þe Duchez hire dyghte with damesels ryche,
The Cowntas of Crasyn, with hir clere maydyns,   *3045*
Knelis down in þe kyrnelles thare the Kyng houede,

On a couerede horse comlyli arayede.
They knewe hym by contenaunce and criede full lowde,
"Kyng crownede of kynde, take kepe to þese wordes!
We beseke ȝow, Sir, as soueraynge and lorde,   *3050*
That ȝe safe vs todaye, for sake of ȝoure Criste;
Send vs some socoure and saughte with the pople,
Or þe ceté be sodaynly with assawte wonnen."
He weres his vesere with a vowt noble;
With vesage vertouous, this valyante bierne   *3055*
Meles to hir myldly with full meke wordes:
"Sall no mysse do ȝow, ma dame, þat to me lenges;
I gyf ȝow chartire of pes, and ȝoure cheefe maydens,
The childire and þe chaste men, the cheualrous knyghtez;
The Duke es in dawngere, dredis it bott littyll.   *3060*
He sall be demyd full wele, dout ȝow noghte elles."
     Thane sent he on iche a syde to certayne lordez,
For to leue þe assawte, the ceté was ȝolden;
With þe Erle eldeste son he sent hym þe kayes,
And seside þe same nyghte, be sent of þe lordes.   *3065*
The Duke to Douere es dyghte, and all his dere knyghtez,
To duelle in dawngere and dole þe dayes of hys lyue.
Thare fleede at the ferrere ȝate folke withowttyn nombyre,
For ferde of Sir Florent and his fers knyghtez;
Voydes the ceté and to the wode rynnys,   *3070*
With vetaile and vessell and vestoure so ryche.
Thay buske vpe a banere abown þe brode ȝates—
Of Sir Florent, in fay, so fayne was he neuer;
The knyghte houys on a hyll, behelde to þe wallys,
And saide, "I see be ȝone syngne the ceté es oures."   *3075*
Sir Arthure enters anon, with hostes arayede,
Euen at þe vndrone etles to lenge.
In iche leueré on lowde the Kynge did crye,
Of payne of lyf and lym and lesyng of londes,   f.86^r
That no lele ligemane, that to hym lonngede,   *3080*
Sulde lye be no ladysse, no be no lele maydyns,
Ne be no burgesse wyffe, better ne werse,

3047 couerede horse comlyli arayede] couerede comlily arayede horse comlyli arayede
3061 be demyd *Branscheid*] idene þe

Ne no biernez mysebide, that to þe burghe longede.
        When þe Kyng Arthure had lely conquerid,
And the castell couerede of þe kythe riche,   3085
All þe crowell and kene, be craftes of armes,
Captayns and constables knewe hym for lorde.
He deuysede and delte to dyuerse lordez
A dowere for þe Duchez and hir dere childire;
Wroghte wardaynes by wytte to welde all þe londez,   3090
That he had wonnen of werre, thorowe his weise knyghtez.
Thus in Lorayne he lenges, as lorde in his awen,
Settez lawes in the lande, as hym leefe t[h]oghte.
And one þe Lammese Day to Lucerne he wendez,
Lengez thare at laysere with lykyng inowe;   3095
Thare his galays ware graythede, a full gret nombyre,
All gleterand as glase, vndire grene hyllys,
With cabanes couerede for kynges anoyntede,
With clothes of clere golde for knyghtez and oþer.
Sone stowede theire stuffe and stablede þeire horses,   3100
Strekes streke ouer þe strem into þe strayte londez.
Now he moues his myghte with myrthes of herte,
Ouere mowntes so hye, þase meruailous wayes;
Gosse in by Goddarde, the garett he wynnys,
Graythes the garnison grisely wondes.   3105
When he was passede the heghte, than the Kyng houys
With his hole bataylle, behaldande abowte,
Lukand one Lumbarddye, and one lowde melys,
"In ȝone lykand londe, lorde be I thynke."
        Thane they cayre to Combe, with kyngez anoyntede,   3110
That was kyde of þe coste, kay of all oþer.
Sir Florent and Sir Floridas þan fowndes before,
With freke men of Fraunce well a fyve hundreth;
To þe ceté vnsene thay soghte at þe gayneste,
And sett an enbuschement, als þem selfe lykys.   3115
Thane ischewis owt of þat ceté, full sone be þe morne,
Slely discouerours, skyftes theire horses;
Than skyftes þes skouerours and skippes on hyllis,
Diskoueres for skulkers that they no skathe lymppen.

3093 t[h]oghte] toht toghte   3117 slely *Banks*] slal

Pouerall and pastorelles passede on aftyre,   *3120*
With porkes to pasture at the price ȝates;
Boyes in þe subarbis bourden full heghe,
At a bare synglere that to þe bente rynnys.
Thane brekes oure buschement and the brigge wynnes,
Brayedez into þe burghe with baners displayede;   *3125*
Stekes and stabbis thorowe that them aȝayne-stondes;   *f.86ᵛ*
Fowre stretis or þay stynte they stroyen fore euere.
    Now es the Conquerour in Combe and his courte holdes
Within þe kyde castell, with kynges enoynttede;
Reconsaillez the comouns þat to þe kyth lengez,   *3130*
Comfourthes þe carefull with knyghtly wordez;
Made a captayne kene a knyghte of hys awen,
Bot all þe contré and he full sone ware accordide.
The Syre of Melane herde saye þe ceté was wonnen,
And send to Arthure sertayne lordes,   *3135*
Grete sommes of golde, sexti horse chargegid,
Besoghte hym as souerayne to socoure þe pople,
And saide he wolde sothely be sugette for euer,
And make hym seruece and suytte for his sere londes;
For Plesaunce, for Pawnce, and for Pownte Tremble,   *3140*
For Pyse, and for Pavy, he profers full large,
Bothe purpur and palle and precious stonys,
Palfrayes for any prynce and prouede stedes;
And ilke a ȝere for Melan a melion of golde,
Mekely at Martynmesse to menske with his hordes;   *3145*
And euer withowttyn askyng he and his ayers
Be homagers to Arthure, whills his lyffe lastis.
The Kyng be his concell a condethe hym sendis,
And he es comen to Combe, and knewe hym as lorde.
    Into Tuskane he tournez, when þus wele tymede,   *3150*
Takes townnes full tyte, with towrres full heghe;
Walles he welte down, wondyd knyghtez,
Towrres he turnes and turmentez þe pople,
Wroghte wedewes full wlonke wrotherayle synges,
Ofte wery and wepe and wryngen theire handis;   *3155*

3126 stabbis] stablis   3140 For Plesaunce, for Pawnce, and for Pownte Tremble
                          Banks] For plesaunce of Pawnce and of Pownte Tremble

And all he wastys with werre, thare he awaye rydez,
Thaire welthes and theire wonny[n]ges, wandrethe he wroghte.
Thus they spryngen and sprede and sparis bot lyttill,
Spoylles dispetouslye and spillis theire vynes,
Spendis vnsparely þat sparede was lange,   3160
Spedis them to Spolett with speris inewe.
Fro Spayne into Spruyslande the worde of hym sprynges,
And spekynngs of his spencis—disspite es full hugge.
Towarde Viterbe this valyant avires the reynes;
Avissely in þat vale he vetailles his biernez,   3165
With vernage and oþer wyne and venyson baken;
And one the Vicounte londes he visez to lenge.
Vertely the avawmwarde voydez theire horsez,
In the Vertennon Vale, the vines imangez;
Thare suggeournes this souerayne with solace in herte,   3170
To see when the senatours sent any wordes.
Reuell with riche wyne, riotes hym selfen,
This roy with his ryall men of þe Rownde Table,
With myrthis and melodye and manykyn gamnes—   f.87
Was neuer meriere men made on this erthe.   3175
     Bot one a Seterdaye at none, a seuenyghte thareaftyre,
The konyngeste cardynall that to the courte lengede,
Knelis to þe Conquerour and karpes thire wordes:
Prayes hym for þe pes and profyrs full large,
To hafe peté of þe Pope, þat put was atvndyre;   3180
Besoghte hym of surrawns, for sake of oure Lorde,
Bot a seuenyghte daye to þay ware all semblede,
And they schulde sekerlye hym see the Sonondaye þeraftyre,
In the ceté of Rome, as soueraynge and lorde;
And crown hym kyndly with krysomede hondes,   3185
With his ceptre and swerde, as soueraynge and lorde.
Of this vndyrtakyng ostage are comyn,
Of ayers full auenaunt awughte score childrenne,
In toges of tarsse full richelye attyryde,
And betuke them the Kynge and his clere knyghttes.   3190
When they had tretide thiere trewe, with trowmpynge þerafter,
They tryne vnto a tente, whare tables whare raysede;

3186 With his ceptre and swerde *Björkman*] With his ceptre

The Kynge hym selfen es sette, and certayne lordes,
Vndyre a sylure of sylke, sawghte at the burdez;
All the senatours are sette sere be þam one,   3195
Serfed solemply with selcouthe metes.
The Kyng myghtty of myrthe, with his mylde wordes,
Rehetez the Romaynes at his riche table,
Comforthes the Cardynall so knyghtly hym seluen;
And this roye ryall, as romawns vs tellis,   3200
Reuerence the Romayns in his riche table.
The tawghte men and þe conynge, when them tym thoghte,
Tas theire lefe at þe Kynge and tornede agayne:
To þe ceté þat nyghte thaye soughte at þe gayneste,
And thus the ostage of Rome with Arthure es leuede.   3205
　　　Than this roy royall rehersys theis wordes:
"Now may we reuell and riste, fore Rome es oure awen!
Make oure ostage at ese, þise auenaunt childyren,
And luk ȝe honden them all that in myn oste lengez.
The Emperour of Almayne and all theis este marches,   3210
We sall be ouerlynge of all þat on the erthe lengez!
We will by þe Crosse Dayes encroche þeis londez,
And at þe Crystynmesse Daye be crowned theraftyre;
Ryngne in my ryalltés, and holde my Rownde Table,
Withe the rentes of Rome, as me beste lykes;   3215
Syne graythe ouer þe grette see with gud men of armes,
To reuenge the Renke that on the Rode dyede."
　　　Thane this comlyche Kynge, as cronycles tellys,
Bownnys brathely to bede with a blythe herte;
Of he slynges with sleghte and slakes gyrdill,   3220
And fore slewthe of slomowre on a slepe fallis.
Bot be ane aftyre mydnyghte all his mode changede:
He mett in the morne-while full meruaylous dremes.   f.87ᵛ
And when his dredefull drem whas drefen to þe ende,
The Kynge dares for dowte, dye as he scholde;   3225
Sendes aftyre phylosophers, and his affraye telles:
"Sen I was formede, in fayth, so ferde whas I neuer!
Forthy rawnsakes redyly and rede me my swefennys,
And I sall redily and ryghte rehersen the sothe.

3199 knyghtly] kynghtly　3208 auenaunt] auenaumt　3212 encroche] encroche encroche

Me thoughte I was in a wode willed myn one,   *3230*
That I ne wiste no waye whedire þat I scholde,
Fore woluez and whilde swynne and wykkyde bestez
Walkede in that wasternne, wathes to seche;
Thare lyouns full lothely lykkyde þeire tuskes,
All fore lapynge of blude of my lele knyghtez.   *3235*
Thurghe þat foreste I flede, thare floures whare heghe,
For to fele me for ferde of tha foule thyngez;
Merkede to a medowe with montayngnes enclosyde,
The meryeste of medillerthe that men myghte beholde.
The close was in compas castyn all abowte   *3240*
With clauer and clereworte clede euen ouer;
The vale was enuerownde with vynes of siluer,
All with grapis of golde, gretter ware neuer;
Enhorilde with arborye and alkyns trees,
Erberis full honeste and hyrdez þerevndyre;   *3245*
All froytez foddenid was þat floreschede in erthe,
Faire frithed in frawnke appon tha free bowes;
Whas thare no downkynge of dewe that oghte dere scholde:
With þe drowghte of þe daye all drye ware þe flores.
　　　Than discendis in the dale, down fra þe clowddez,   *3250*
A duches dereworthily dyghte in dyaperde wedis,
In a surcott of sylke full selkouthely hewede,
All with loyotour ouerlaide lowe to þe hemmes,
And with ladily lappes the lenghe of a ȝerde,
And all redily reuersside with rebanes of golde;   *3255*
Bruchez and besauntez and oþer bryghte stonys
With hir bake and hir breste was brochede all ouer;
With kelle and with corenall clenliche arrayede,
And þat so comly of colour on knowen was neuer.
Abowte cho whirllide a whele with hir whitte hondez,   *3260*
Ouerwhelme all qwayntely þe whele as cho scholde;
The rowell whas rede golde with ryall stonys,
Raylide with reches and rubyes inewe;
The spekes was splentide all with speltis of siluer,
The space of a spere lenghe springande full faire;   *3265*
Thereone was a chayere of chalke-whytte siluer,

3242 enuerownde *Brock*] euen rownde   3263 reches *Mennicken*] reched

And chekyrde with charebocle, chawngynge of hewes.
Appon þe compas ther clewide kyngis one rawe,
With corowns of clere golde þat krakede in sondire;
Sex was of þat setill full sodaynliche fallen,   *3270*
Ilke a segge by hym selfe, and saide theis wordez:
'That euer I rengnede on þir roo me rewes it euer!
Was neuer roye so riche that regnede in erthe;   f.88ʳ
Whene I rode in my rowte, roughte I noghte ells,
Bot reuaye and reuell and rawnson the pople;   *3275*
And thus I drife forthe my dayes, whills I dreghe myghte,
And therefore derflyche I am dampnede for euer.'
     The laste was a lityll man that laide was benethe;
His leskes laye all lene and latheliche to schewe,
The lokkes lyarde and longe, the lenghe of a ȝerde,   *3280*
His lire and his lygham lamede full sore;
Þe tone eye of þe byeryn was brighttere þan siluer,
The toþer was ȝalowere then the ȝolke of a naye.
'I was lorde,' quod the lede, 'of londes inewe,
And all ledis me lowttede that lengede in erthe;   *3285*
And nowe es lefte me no lappe my lygham to hele,
Bot lightly now am I loste, leue iche mane the sothe.'
     The secunde sir, forsothe, þat sewede them aftyre,
Was sekerare to my sighte and saddare in armes;
Ofte he syghede vnsownde and said theis wordes: *3290*
'On ȝone see hafe I sitten als souerayne and lorde,
And ladys me louede to lappe in theyre armes;
And nowe my lordchippes are loste and laide for euer.'
     The thirde thorowely was throo and thikke in the schuldyrs,
A thra man to thrette of, there thretty ware gaderide;   *3295*
His dyadem was droppede down, dubbyde with stonys,
Endente all with diamawndis and dighte for þe nonis;
'I was dredde in my dayes,' he said, 'in dyuerse rewmes,
And now dampnede to þe dede, and dole es the more.'
     The fourte was a faire mane and forsy in armes,   *3300*
Þe fayreste of fegure that fourmede was euer:
'I was frekke, in my faithe,' he said, 'whills I one fowlde regnede,

3272 þir roo *Björkman*] þe þir rog   3282 Þe tone eye *Brock*] Þe two eyne
3300 forsy] forsesy

Famows in ferre londis and floure of all knyges;
Now es my face defadide, and foule es me hapnede,
For I am fallen fro ferre and frendles byleuyde.'   330.
    The fifte was a faire man þan fele of þies oþer,
A forsy man and a ferse, with fomand lippis;
He fongede faste on þe feleyghes and falded his armes,
Bot ȝit he failede and fell a fyfty fote large;
Bot ȝit he sprange and sprente and spradden his armes,   3310
And one þe spere-lenghe spekes, he spekes þire wordes:
'I was in Surrye a syr and sett be myn one,
As souerayne and seyngnour of sere kynges londis;
Now of my solace I am full sodanly fallen,
And for sake of my syn, ȝone sete es me rewede.'   3315
    The sexte hade a sawtere semliche bownden,
With a surepel of silke sewede full faire,
A harpe and a hande-slynge with harde flynte stones;
What harmes he has hente he halowes full sone:
'I was demede in my dayes,' he said, 'of dedis of armes,   3320
One of the doughtyeste that duellede in erthe;
Bot I was merride one molde in my moste strenghethis,   f.88ᵛ
With this mayden so mylde, þat mofes vs all.'
    Two kynges ware clymbande and clauerande one heghe,
The creste of þe compas they couette full ȝerne;   3325
'This chaire of charbokle,' they said, 'we chalange hereaftyre,
As two of þe cheffeste chosen in erthe.'
The childire ware chalke-whitte, chekys and oþer,
Bot the chayere abownne cheuede they neuer;
The forthirmaste was freely, with a frount large,   3330
The faireste of fyssnamy þat fourmede was euer;
And he was buskede in a blee of a blewe noble,
With flourdelice of golde floreschede al ouer;
The toþer was cledde in a cote all of clene siluer,
With a comliche crosse coruen of golde,   3335
Fowre crosselettes krafty by þe crosse ristes,
And therby knewe I the kyng, þat crystnede hym semyde.
    Than I went to þat wlonke and wynly hire gretis,
And cho said, 'Welcom iwis; wele arte thow fownden;

3307 forsy] forsesy   3308 falded Björkman] fayled

The aughte to wirchipe my will, and thow wele cowthe, *3340*
Of all the valyant men that euer was in erthe;
Fore all thy wirchipe in werre by me has thow wonnen.
I hafe bene frendely, freke, and fremmede till oþer,
That has þow fownden in faithe, and fele of þi biernez:
Fore I fellid down Sir Frolle with frowarde knyghtes; *3345*
Forethi the fruytes of Fraunce are freely thynne awen.
Thow sall þe chayere escheue, I chese þe my selfen,
Before all þe cheftaynes chosen in this erthe.'
Scho lifte me vp lightly with hir lene hondes,
And sette me softely in the see, þe septre me rechede; *3350*
Craftely with a kambe cho kembede myn heuede,
That the krispane kroke to my crownne raughte;
Dressid one me a diademe that dighte was full faire,
And syne profres me a pome pighte full of faire stonys,
Enamelde with azoure, the erth thereon depayntide, *3355*
Serkylde with the salte see appone sere halfes,
In sygne þat I sothely was souerayne in erthe.
Than broght cho me a brande with full bryghte hiltes,
And bade me 'Brawndysche þe blade, þe brande es myn awen;
Many swayn with þe swynge has the sw[e]tte leuede, *3360*
For whills thow swanke with the swerde, it swykkede þe neuer.'
    Than raykes cho with roo and riste when hir likede,
To þe ryndes of þe wode—richere was neuer;
Was no pomarie so pighte of pryncez in erthe,
Ne nonne apparayll so prowde, bot Paradys one. *3365*
Scho bad þe bewes scholde bewe down and bryng to my hondes
Of þe beste that they bare one brawnches so heghe;
Than they heldede to hir heste all holly at ones,
The hegheste of iche a hirste, I hette ȝow forsothe.
Scho bade me fyrthe noghte þe fruyte, bot fonde whills me likede: *f.89ʳ*
 Fonde of þe fyneste, thow frelich byerne, *3371*
And reche to þe ripeste and ryotte thy seluen.
Riste, thow ryalle roye, for Rome es thyn awen!
And I sall redily roll þe roo at þe gayneste,
And reche the þe riche wyne in rynsede coupes.' *3375*
Thane cho wente to þe welle by þe wode euis,

3356 Serkylde *Brock*] Selkylde

That all wellyde of wyne and wondirliche rynnes;
Kaughte vy a coppe-full and couerde it faire;
Scho bad me dereliche drawe and drynke to hir selfen.

    And thus cho lede me abowte the lenghe of an owre,   3380
With all likyng and luffe þat any lede scholde;
Bot at þe myddaye full ewyn all hir mode chaungede,
And mad myche manace with meruayllous wordez.
When I cryede appon hire, cho kest down hir browes:
'Kyng, thow karpes for noghte, be Criste þat me made!   3385
For thow sall lose this layke and thi lyfe aftyre;
Thow has lyffede in delytte and lordchippes inewe!'
Abowte scho whirles the whele and whirles me vndire,
Till all my qwarters þat whille whare qwaste al to peces,
And with that chayere my chyne was chopped in sondire!   3390
And I hafe cheueride for chele sen me this chance happenede.
Than wakkenyde I iwys, all wery fordremyde,
And now wate thow my woo, worde as þe lykes."

    "Freke," sais the philosophre, "thy fortune es passede;
For thow sall fynd hir thi foo—frayste when the lykes.   3395
Thow arte at þe hegheste, I hette the forsothe;
Chalange nowe when thow will, thow cheuys no more.
Thow has schedde myche blode and schalkes distroyede,
Sakeles, in cirquytrie, in sere kynges landis.
Schryfe the of thy schame and schape for thyn ende;   3400
Thow has a schewynge, Sir Kynge—take kepe ȝif the lyke;
For thow sall fersely fall within fyve wynters.
Fownde abbayes in Fraunce—þe froytez are theyn awen—
Fore Froill and for Ferawnt and for thir ferse knyghttis,
That thowe fremydly in Fraunce has faye beleuede.   3405
Take kepe ȝitte of oþer kynges and kaste in thyne herte,
That were conquerours kydde and crownnede in erthe:
The eldeste was Alexandere, þat all þe erthe lowttede,
The toþer Ector of Troye, the cheualrous gume;
The thirde Iulyus Cesare, þat geant was holden,   3410
In iche jorné jentill, ajuggede with lordes;
The ferthe was Sir Iudas, a justere full nobill,
The maysterfull Makabee, the myghttyeste of strenghes;

3397 no] no no

The fyfte was Iosue, þat joly mane of armes,
Þat in Ierusalem oste full myche joye lymppede;   3415
The sexte was Dauid þe dere, demyd with kynges
One of þe doughtyeste þat dubbede was euer;
For he slewe with a slynge, be sleyghte of his handis,
Golyas the grette gome, grymmeste in erthe,
Syne endittede in his dayes all the dere psalmes,   f.89ᵛ 3420
Þat in þe sawtire ere sette with selcouthe wordes;
The two clymbande kynges, I knawe it forsothe,
Sall Karolus be callide, the kyng son of Fraunce;
He sall be crowell and kene, and conquerour holden,
Couere be conqueste contres ynewe;   3425
He sall encroche the crowne that Crist bare hym selfen,
And þat lifeliche launce that lepe to his herte,
When he was crucyfiede one Crose, and all þe kene naylis,
Knyghtly he sall conquere to Cristyn men hondes.
The toþer sall be Godfraye, that Gode schall reuenge   3430
One þe Gud Frydaye with galyarde knyghtes;
He sall of Lorrayne be lorde, be leefe of his fadire,
And syne in Ierusalem myche joye happyn,
For he sall couer the Crosse be craftes of armes,
And synne be corownde kynge with krysome enoynttede;   3435
Sall no duke in his dayes siche destanye happyn,
Ne siche myschefe dreghe when trewthe sall be tryede.
Forethy Fortune þe fetches to fulfill the nowmbyre,
Alls nynne of þe nobileste namede in erthe:
This sall in romance be redde with ryall knyghttes,   3440
Rekkenede and renownde with ryotous kynges,
And demyd on Domesdaye, for dedis of armes,
For þe doughtyeste þat euer was duelland in erthe;
So many clerkis and kynges sall karpe of ȝoure dedis,
And kepe ȝoure conquestez in cronycle for euer.   3445
Bot the wolfes in the wode and the whilde bestes,
Are some wikkyd men that werrayes thy rewmes,
Es entirde in thyn absence to werraye thy pople,
And alyenys and ostes of vncouthe landis.
Thow getis tydandis, I trowe, within ten dayes,   3450
That some torfere es tydde, sen thow fro home turnede;

I rede thow rekkyn and reherse vnresonable dedis,
Ore the repenttes full rathe all thi rewthe werkes.
Mane, amende thy mode, or thow myshappen,
And mekely aske mercy for mede of thy saule."   3455

      Thane rysez the riche Kyng and rawghte on his wedys,
A reedde acton of rosse, the richeste of floures,
A pesane and a paunson and a pris girdill;
And one he henttis a hode of scharlette full riche,
A pauys pillion hatt, þat pighte was full faire   3460
With perry of þe Oryent and precyous stones;
His gloues gayliche gilte and grauen by þe hemmys
With graynes of rubyes full gracious to schewe.
His bede grehownde and his bronde ande no byerne ells,
And bownnes ouer a brode mede, with breth at his herte;   3465
Furth he stalkis a stye by þa still euys,
Stotays at a hey strette, studyande hym one.

      Att the surs of þe sonne he sees there commande,
Raykande to Romewarde the redyeste wayes,
A renke in a rownde cloke with righte rowmme clothes,   3470
With hatte and with heyghe schone homely and rownde;
With flatte ferthynges the freke was floreschede all ouer,
Manye schredys and schragges at his skyrttes hynnges;   f.90ᵛ
With scrippe ande with slawyn and skalopis inewe,
Both pyke and palme alls pilgram hym scholde.   3475
The gome graythely hym grette and bade gode morwen;
The Kyng lordelye hym selfe, of langage of Rome,
Of Latyn corroumppede all, full louely hym menys:
"Whedire wilnez thowe, wye, walkande thyn one?
Qwhylls þe werlde es o werre, a wawhte I it holde.   3480
Here es ane enmye with oste vndire ȝone vynes:
And they see the, forsothe, sorowe the betyddes;
Bot ȝif thow hafe condethe of þe Kynge selfen,
Knaues will kill the and keppe at thow haues;
And if þou halde þe hey waye, they hente the also,   3485
Bot if thow hastyly hafe helpe of his hende knyghttes."

      Than karpes Sir Cradoke to the Kynge selfen:
"I sall forgyffe hym my dede, so me Gode helpe,
Onye grome vndire Gode that one this grownde walkes.

Latte the keneste come that to þe Kyng langes,   3490
I sall encountire hym as knyghte, so Criste hafe my sawle!
For thow may noghte reche me, no areste thy selfen,
Þoffe þou be richely arayede in full riche wedys.
I will noghte wonde for no werre to wende whare me likes,
Ne for no wy of this werlde þat wroghte es on erthe!   3495
Bot I will passe in pilgremage þis pas vnto Rome,
To purchese me pardone of the Pape selfen,
And of paynes of Purgatorie be plenerly assoyllede.
Thane sall I seke sekirly my souerayne lorde,
Sir Arthure of Inglande, that auenaunt byerne;   3500
For he es in this empire, as hathell men me telles,
Ostayande in this Oryente with awfull knyghtes."
         "Fro qwyn come þou, kene man," quod þe Kynge than,
"That knawes Kynge Arthure and his knyghttes also?
Was þou euer in his courte, qwylls he in kyth lengede?   3505
Thow karpes so kyndly, it comforthes myn herte.
Well wele has þou wente and wysely þou sechis,
For þou arte Bretowne bierne, as by thy brode speche."
"Me awghte to knowe þe Kynge: he es my kydde lorde,
And I calde in his courte a knyghte of his chambire;   3510
Sir Craddoke was I callide in his courte riche,
Kepare of Karlyon, vndir the Kynge selfen:
Nowe am I cachede owtt of kyth with kare at my herte,
And that castell es cawghte with vncowthe ledys."
         Than the comliche kynge kaughte hym in armes,   3515
Keste of his ketill-hatte and kyssede hym full sone,
Saide, "Welcom, Sir Craddoke, so Criste mott me helpe!
Dere cosyn of kynde, thowe coldis myn herte;
How faris it in Bretayne, with all my bolde beryns?
Are they brettenede or brynte or broughte owte of lyue?   3520
Ken þou me kyndely whatte caase es befallen;
I kepe no credens to crafe—I knawe the for trewe."
         "Sir, thi wardane es wikkede and wilde of his dedys,
For he wandreth has wroghte sen þou awaye passede: f.90ᵛ
He has castells encrochede and corownde hym seluen,   3525
Kaughte in all þe rentis of þe Rownde Tabill;
He devisede þe rewme and delte as hym likes,

Dubbede of þe Danmarkes dukes and erlles,
Disseueride þem sondirwise and cités dystroyede.
To Sarazenes and Sessoynes appon sere halues,   *3530*
He has semblede a sorte of selcouthe berynes;
Soueraynes of Surgenale and sowdeours many,
Of Peyghtes and paynyms and prouede knyghttes,
Of Irelande and Orgaile owtlawede berynes.
All thaa laddes are knyghttes þat lange to þe mowntes,   *3535*
And ledynge and lordechipe has all, alls them selfe likes;
And there es Sir Childrike a cheftayne holdyn,
That ilke cheualrous man, he chargges thy pople;
They robbe thy religeous and ravische thi nones,
And redy ryddis with his rowtte to rawnsone þe pouere;   *3540*
Fro Humbyre to Hawyke he haldys his awen,
And all þe cowntré of Kentt be couenawnte entayllide;
The comliche castells that to the corown langede,
The holttes and the hare wode and the harde bankkes—
All þat Henguste and Hors hent in þeire tym;   *3545*
Att Southampton on the see es seuen skore chippes,
Frawghte full of ferse folke owt of ferre landes,
For to fyghte with thy frappe when þow them assailles.
Bot ȝitt a worde witterly, thowe watte noghte þe werste:
He has weddede Waynore, and hir his wieffe holdis,   *3550*
And wonnys in the wilde bowndis of þe weste marches,
And has wroghte hire with childe, as wittnesse tellis.
Off all þe wyes of þis worlde, woo motte hym worthe,
Alls wardayne vnworthye women to ȝeme.
Thus has Sir Modrede merrede vs all!   *3555*
Forthy I merkede ouer thees mowntes to mene þe the sothe."
      Than the burliche kynge, for brethe at his herte,
And for this botelesse bale, all his ble chaungede.
"By þe Rode," sais þe Roye, "I sall it revenge!
Hym sall repente full rathe all his rewthe werkes!"   *3560*
All wepande for woo he went to his tentis;
Vnwynly this wyesse kynge he wakkenysse his beryns,
Clepid in a clarioune kynges and othire,
Callys them to concell and of þis cas tellys:

     3539 ravische] ravichse

"I am with treson betrayede, for all my trewe dedis; 3565
And all my trauayle es tynt, me tydis no bettire!
Hym sall torfere betyde þis tresone has wroghte,
And I may traistely hym take, as·I am trew lorde.
This es Modrede, þe mane that I moste traystede,
Has my castells encrochede and corownde hym seluen, 3570
With renttes and reches of the Rownde Table;
Has made all hys retenewys of renayede wrechis,
And devysed my rewme to dyverse lordes,
To sowdeours and to Sarazenes owtte of sere londes.
He has weddyde Waynore and hyr to wyefe holdes; f.91ʳ 3575
And a childe es eschapede, the chaunce es no bettire.
They hafe semblede on the see seuen schore chippis,
Full of ferrom folke to feghte with myn one;
Forthy to Bretayne the Brode buske vs byhouys,
For to brettyn the beryne that has this bale raysede. 3580
Thare sall no freke men fare bott all one fresche horses,
That are fraistede in fyghte and floure of my knyghttez;
Sir Howell and Sir Hardolfe here sall beleue,
To be lordes of the ledis that here to me lenges;
Lokes into Lumbardye þat thare no lede chaunge, 3585
And tendirly to Tuskayne take tente alls I byde;
Resaywe the rentis of Rome qwen þay are rekkenede;
Take sesyn the same daye that laste was assygnede,
Or elles all þe ostage withowttyn þe wallys,
Be hynggyde hye appon hyghte all holly at ones." 3590
        Nowe bownes the bolde kynge with [his] beste knyghtes,
Gers trome and trusse and trynes forth aftyre:
Turnys thorowe Tuskayne, taries bot littill,
Lyghte noghte in Lumbarddye bot when þe lyghte failede;
Merkes ouer the mowntaynes full mervaylous wayes, 3595
Ayres thurghe Almaygne evyne at the gayneste,
Ferkes evyne into Flawndresche with hys ferse knyghttes.
Within fyftene dayes his flete es assemblede,
And thane he schoupe hym to chippe and schownes no lengere,
Scherys with a charpe wynde ouer þe schyre waters. 3600
By þe roche with ropes he rydes on ankkere,
Thare the false men fletyde and one flode lengede,

With chefe chaynes of chare chokkode togedyrs,
Charggede evyn chekefull of cheualrous knyghtes,
And in þe hynter one heghte helmes and crestes;   3605
Hatches with haythen men hillyd ware tharevndyre,
Prowdliche purtrayede with payntede clothys,
Iche a pece by pece prykkyde tyll oþer—
Dubbyde with dagswaynnes dowblede they seme;
And thus þe derfe Danamarkes had dyghte all theyre chippys,   3610
That no dynte of no darte dere them ne schoulde.
       Than the Roye and þe renkes of the Rownde Table
All ryally in rede arrayes his chippis;
That daye ducheryes he delte and doubbyde knyghttes,
Dresses dromowndes and dragges and drawen vpe stonys;   3615
The toppe-castells he stuffede with toyelys, as hym lykyde.
Bendys bowes of vys brothly þareaftyre;
Tolowris tentyly takell they ryghtten,
Brasen hedys full brode buskede one flones,
Graythes for garnysons gomes arrayes;   3620
Gryme gaddes of stele, ghywes of iryn,
Stiȝttelys steryn one steryne with styffe men of armes;
Mony lufliche launce appon lofte stondys,
Ledys one leburde, lordys and oþer,
Pyghte payvese one porte, payntede scheldes,   3625
One hyndire hurdace one highte helmede knyghtez.
Thus they scheften fore schotys one thas schire strandys,   f.91ᵛ
Ilke schalke in his schrowde—full scheen ware þeire wedys.
The bolde kynge es in a barge and abowtte rowes,
All bare-heuvede for besye with beueryn lokkes,   3630
And a beryn with his bronde and ane helme betyn,
Mengede with a mawntelet of maylis of siluer,
Compaste with a coronall and couerde full riche;
Kayris to yche a cogge to comfurthe his knyghttes:
To Clegys and Cleremownde he cryes one lowde,   3635
"O Gawayne, O Galyran, thies gud mens bodyes."
To Loth and to Lyonell full louefly he melys,
And to Sir Lawncelot de Lake lordiche wordys:
"Lat vs couere þe kythe—the coste es owre ownn—

3607 purtrayede] prutrayede   3622 stiȝttelys *Brock*] stirttelys   3633 couerde] couererde

And gere them brotheliche blenke, all ȝone blod-hondes,   3640
Bryttyn them within bourde and brynne them þareaftyre;
Hewe down hertly ȝone heythen tykes!
Thay are harlotes halfe, I hette ȝow myn honnde!"
        Than he coueres his cogge and caches one ankere,
Kaughte his comliche helme with þe clere maylis,   3645
Buskes baners one brode, betyn of gowles,
With corowns of clere golde, clenliche arraiede;
Bot þare was chosen in þe chefe a chalke-whitte Mayden,
And a Childe in hir arme, þat Chefe es of Hevyne;
Withowtten changyng in chace, thies ware þe cheefe armes   3650
Of Arthure þe auenaunt, qwhylls he in erthe lengede.
        Thane the marynerse mellys and maysters of chippis;
Merily iche a mate menys till oþer:
Of theire termys they talke, how þay ware tydd,
Towyn trvssell one trete, trvssen vpe sailes,   3655
Bet bonettez one brede, bettrede hatches,
Brawndeste brown stele, braggede in trompes,
Standis styffe one the stamyn, steris one aftyre,
Strekyn ouer þe streme thare stryvynge begynnes.
        Fro þe wagande wynde owte of þe weste rysses,   3660
Brethly bessomes with byrre in beryns sailles;
With hir bryngges one burde burliche cogges,
Qwhylls þe bilyge and þe beme brestys in sondyre;
So stowttly þe forsterne one þe stam hyttis,
Þat stokkes of þe stere-burde strykkys in peces.   3665
Be than cogge appon cogge, krayers and oþer,
Castys crepers one crosse als to þe crafte langes.
Thane was hede-rapys hewen þat helde vpe þe mastes;
Thare was conteke full kene and crachynge of chippys:
Grett cogges of kampe crasseches in sondyre;   3670
Mony kaban clevede, cabills destroyede.
Knyghtes and kene men killide the braynes;
Kidd castells were corven with all theire kene wapen,
Castells full comliche þat coloured ware faire.
Vptyhes eghelyng þay ochen þareaftyre: 3675
With þe swynge of þe swerde sweys þe mastys,

3663 bilyge *Banks*] bilynge   3675 vptyhes *OED*] vptynes

Ovyrefallys in þe firste frekis and othire;
Frekke in þe forchipe fey es byleuefede.
Than brothely they bekyre with boustouse tacle;
Bruschese boldlye on burde brynyede knyghtes,
Owt of botes one burd was buskede with stonys,
Bett down of þe beste, brystis the hetches;
Som gomys thourghegyrde with gaddys of yryn:
Gomys gayliche clede englaymes wapen.
Archers of Inglande full egerly schottes,
Hittis thourghe þe harde stele full hertly dynttis.
Sone hotchen in holle the heþene knyghtes—
Hurte thourghe þe harde stele, hele they neuer.
Than they fall to þe fyghte, foynes with sperys,
All the frekkeste one frownte þat to þe fyghte langes;
And ilkon frechely fraystez theire strenghes,
Were to fyghte in þe flete with theire fell wapyn.

  Thus they dalte þat daye, thire dubbide knyghtes,
Till all þe Danes ware dede and in þe depe throwen.
Than Bretons brothely with brondis they hewen,
Lepys in vpone lofte lordeliche berynes;
When ledys of owt-londys leppyn in waters,
All oure lordes one lowde laughen at ones.
Be thane speris whare sprongen, spalddyd chippys,
Spanyolis spedily sprentyde ouer burdez;
All þe kene men of kampe, knyghtes and oþer,
Killyd are colde dede and castyn ouer burdez.
Theire swyers sweyftly has þe swete leuyde;
Heþen heuande on hatche in þer hawe ryses,
Synkande in þe salte see seuen hundrethe at ones.
Thane Sir Gawayne the gude, he has þe gree wonnen,
And all þe cogges grete he gafe to his knyghtes,
Sir Geryn and Sir Grisswolde and othir gret lordes,
Garte Galuth, a gud gome, girde of þaire hedys.
Thus of þe false flete appon þe flode happenede,
And thus þeis feryne folke fey are beleuede.

  ȝitt es þe traytoure one londe with tryede knyghttes,
And all trompede they trippe one trappede stedys,

3684 englaymes *Björkman*] englaymous

Since the Thornton Manuscript contains no illustrations, the following illustrations have been taken from manuscripts containing Wace's version of the Arthurian story and Lydgate's account of Lady Fortune and are reprinted with the permission of the British Museum and the John Rylands Library.

King Arthur arrives at court.
(From Wace, *Roman de Brut,* British Museum MS. Egerton 3028, folio 42).

Messengers from Rome appear at King Arthur's banquet.

(From MS. Egerton 3028, folio 43).

Arthur and King Hoel discuss plans in a tower.
(From MS. Egerton 3028, folio 45).

The Emperor Lucius rides out of Rome.
(From MS. Egerton 3028, folio 47).

King Arthur asleep on board ship.
(From MS. Egerton 3028, folio 48).

King Arthur encounters the giant of St. Michael's Mount.
(From MS. Egerton 3028, folio 49).

King Arthur battles the Emperor of Rome.
(From MS. Egerton 3028, folio 51).

The queue of

Lady Fortune
and her wheel.

(From Lydgate,
Siege of Troy,
Rylands
English MS. 1,
folio 28).

King Arthur is mortally wounded.
(From MS. Egerton 3028, folio 53).

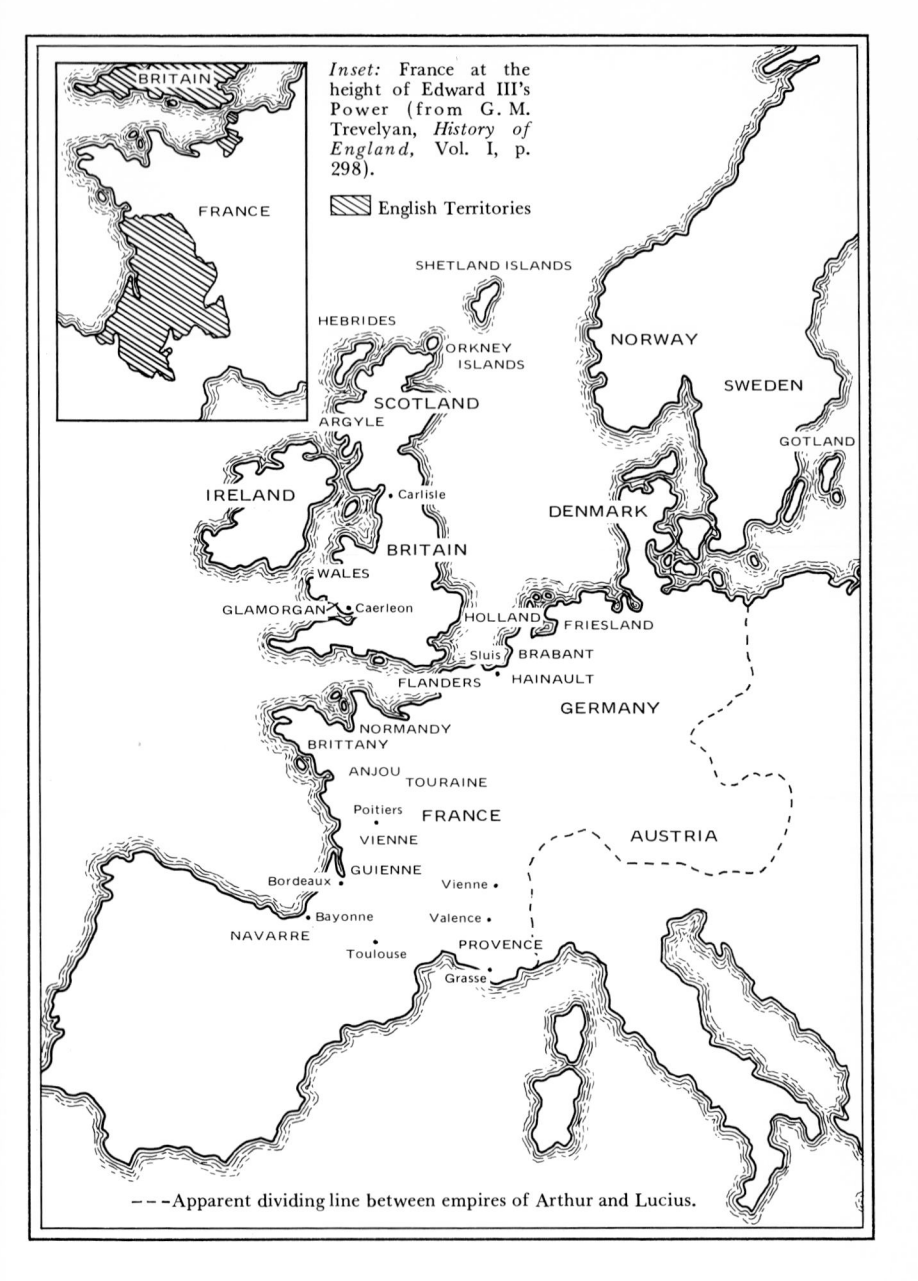

Inset: France at the height of Edward III's Power (from G. M. Trevelyan, *History of England*, Vol. I, p. 298).

English Territories

Arthur's Empire at the beginning of *Morte Arthure* (from a 1360 map [*Rand McNally World Atlas*, 1965, p. 154]). Note concentration of names in areas of Edward III's conquests (see inset).

Localities in the *Morte Arthure*

Schewes them vndir schilde one þe schire bankkes—
He ne schownttes for no schame but schewes full heghe. 3715
Sir Arthure and Gawayne avyede them bothen,
To sexty thosandez of men þat in theire syghte houede.
Be this the folke was fellyde, thane was þe flode passede;
Thane was it slyke a slowde in slakkes full hugge,
That let þe Kyng for to lande in the lawe watyre; 3720
Forthy he lengede on laye for lesyng of horsys,
To loke of his legemen and of his lele knyghtes,
ȝif any ware lamede or loste, life ȝife they scholde.
    Than Sir Gawayn þe gude a galaye he takys,
And glides vp at a gole with gud men of armes; 3725
When he growndide, for grefe he gyrdis in þe watere,
That to þe girdyll he gos in all his gylte wedys;
Schottis vpe appon þe sonde in syghte of þe lordes,
Sengly with hys soppe—my sorowe es the more.
With baners of his bagys, beste of his armes, f.92ᵛ 3730
He braydes vp on the banke in his bryghte wedys;
He byddys his baneoure, "Buske þow belyfe
To ȝone brode batayle that one ȝone banke houes,
And I ensure ȝow sothe I sall ȝowe sewe aftyre.
Loke ȝe blenke for no bronde, ne for no bryghte wapyn, 3735
Bot beris down of þe beste and bryng them o dawe;
Bees noghte abayste of theire boste, abyde on þe erthe.
ȝe haue my baneres borne in batailles full hugge;
We sall fell ȝone false, þe Fende hafe theire saules!
Fightes faste with þe frape, þe felde sall be owres; 3740
May I þat traytoure ouertake, torfere hym tyddes,
That this treson has tymbyrde to my trewe lorde.
Of siche a engendure full littyll joye happyns,
And þat sall in this journée be juggede full euen."
    Now they seke ouer þe sonde þis soppe at þe gayneste, 3745
Sembles one þe sowdeours and settys theire dyntys:
Thourghe þe scheldys so schene schalkes þey towche,
With schaftes scheueride schorte of þas schene launces;
Derfe dynttys they dalte with daggande sperys.
One þe danke of þe dewe many dede lyggys: 3750

3720 in *Branscheid*] and   3721 horsys] horsesys

Dukes and duszeperis and dubbide knyghttys;
The doughttyeste of Danemarke vndone are for euer.
Thus thas renkes in rewthe rittis theire brenyes,
And rechis of þe richeste vnreken dynttis;
Thare they thronge in the thikke and thristis to þe erthe   3755
Of the thraeste men thre hundrethe at ones.

    Bot Sir Gawayne for grefe myghte noghte agayne-stande,
Vmbegrippys a spere and to a gome rynnys,
Þat bare of gowles full gaye with gowtes of syluere;
He gyrdes hym in at þe gorge with his grym launce,   3760
Þat þe grownden glayfe graythes in sondyre;
With þat boystous brayde he bownes hym to dye—
Þe Kyng of Gutlande it was, a gude man of armes.
Thayre avawwarde than all voydes þareaftyre,
Alls venqueste verrayely with valyant beryns.   3765
Metis with medilwarde, that Modrede ledys;
Oure men merkes them to, as them myshappenede.
For hade Sir Gawayne hade grace to halde þe grene hill,
He had wirchipe, iwys, wonnen for euer.

    Bot þan Sir Gawayne, iwysse, he waytes hym wele   3770
To wreke hym on this werlaughe þat þis werre mouede;
And merkes to Sir Modrede amonge all his beryns,
With the Mownttagus and oþer gret lordys.
Þan Sir Gawayne was greuede and with a gret wyll
Fewters a faire spere and freschely askryes: 3775
"Fals fosterde foode, the Fende haue thy bonys!
Fy one the, felone, and thy false werkys!
Thow sall be dede and vndon for thy derfe dedys,
Or I sall dy this daye, ȝif destanye worthe!"

    Thane his enmye, with oste of owtlawede beryns,   f.93ʳ 3780
All enangylls abowte oure excellente knyghttez,
That the traytoure be tresone had tryede hym seluen;
Dukes of Danemarke he dyghttes full sone,
And leders of Lettowe, with legyons inewe;
Vmbylappyde oure men with launcez full kene.   3785
Sowdeours and Sarazenes owte of sere landys,
Sexty thosande men semlyly arrayede,
Sekerly assembles thare one seuen schore knyghtes,

Sodaynly in dischayte by tha salte strandes.
Thane Sir Gawayne grette with his gray eghen, 3790
For grefe of his gud men that he gyde schulde;
He wyste that þay wondyde ware and wery forfoughtten,
And what for wondire and woo, all his witte faylede.
And thane syghande he saide, with sylande terys,
"We are with Sarazenes besett appon sere halfes. 3795
I syghe noghte for my selfe, sa helpe oure Lorde;
Bot for to [see] vs supprysede, my sorowe es the more.
Bes dowghtty todaye, ȝone dukes schall be ȝoures;
For dere Dryghttyn this daye, dredys no wapyn.
We sall ende this daye alls excellent knyghttes, 3800
Ayere to endelesse joye with angells vnwemyde.
Þofe we hafe vnwittyly wastede oure selfen,
We sall wirke all wele in þe wirchipe of Cryste.
We sall for ȝone Sarazenes, I sekire ȝow my trowhe,
Souppe with oure Saueoure solemply in Heuen, 3805
In presence of þat precious Prynce of all oþer,
With prophetes and patriarkes and apostlys full nobill,
Before His freliche face that fourmede vs all.
Ȝondire to ȝone ȝaldsons, he þat ȝeldes hym euer,
Qwhylls he es qwykke and in qwerte, vnquellyde with handis, 3810
Be he neuer mo sauede, ne socourede with Cryste,
Bot Satanase his sawle mowe synke into Helle!"
        Than grymly Sir Gawayne gryppis hys wapyn;
Agayne þat gret bataille he graythes hym son:
Radly of his riche swerde he reghttes þe cheynys, 3815
In he schokkes his schelde, schountes he no lengare;
Bot alls vnwyse, wodewyse, he wente at þe gayneste,
Wondis of thas wedirwyns with wrakfull dynttys—
All wellys full of blode thare he awaye passes;
And þofe hym ware full woo, he wondys bot lyttill, 3820
Bot wrekys at his wirchip þe wrethe of hys lorde.
He stekys stedis in stoure and sterenefull knyghttes,
That steryn men in theire sterapes stone-dede þay lygge;
He ryvys þe ranke stele, he rittes þe mayles—
Thare myghte no renke hym areste, his reson was passede. 3825
He fell in a fransye for fersenesse of herte;

He feghttis and fellis down þat hym before standis—
Fell neuer fay man siche fortune in erthe.
Into þe hale bataile hedlyngs he rynys,
And hurtes of þe hardieste þat one the erthe lenges.   3830
Letande alls a lyon he lawnches them thorowe,
Lordes and ledars that one the launde houes.   f.93ᵛ
Ʒit Sir Gawayne for wo wondis bot lyttill,
Bot woundis of thas wedirwyns with wondirfull dyntes,
Alls he þat wold wilfully wasten hym selfen;   3835
And for wondsom and will all his wit failede,
That wode alls a wylde beste he wente at þe gayneste;
All walewede one blode, thare he awaye passede—
Iche a wy may be warre be wreke of anoþer.

  Þan he moues to Sir Modrede amange all his knyghttes,   3840
And mett hym in þe myde-schelde and mallis hym thorowe;
Bot the schalke for the scharpe he schownttes a littill,
He schare hym one þe schorte rybbys a schaftmonde large:
The schafte schoderede and schotte in the schire beryn,
Þat þe schadande blode ouer his schanke rynnys,   3845
And schewede on his schynbawde, þat was schire burneste.
And so they schyfte and schove, he schotte to þe erthe;
With þe lussche of þe launce he lyghte one hys schuldyrs,
Ane akere lenghe one a launde, full lothely wondide.
Than Gawayne gyrde to þe gome and one þe groffe fallis—   3850
Alls his grefe was graythede, his grace was no bettyre—
He schokkes owtte a schorte knyfe schethede with siluere,
And scholde haue slottede hym in, bot no slytte happenede:
His hand sleppid and solde o slante one þe mayles,
And þe toþer slely slynges hym vndire;   3855
With a trenchande knyfe the traytoure hym hyttes,
Thorowe þe helme and þe hede, one heyghe one þe brayne:
And thus Sir Gawayne es gon, the gude man of armes,
Withowttyn reschewe of renke and rewghe es þe more;
Thus Sir Gawayne es gon, that gyede many othire—   3860
Fro Gowere to Gernesay, all þe gret lordys,
Of Glamour, of Galys londe, þis galyarde knyghtes,
For glent of gloppynyng glade be they neuer.

3863 gloppynyng] gloppyngnyng

Kyng Froderike of Fres faythely þareaftyre
Fraynes at the false mane of owre ferse knyghte: 3865
"Knew thow euer this knyghte in thi kithe ryche,
Of whate kynde he was comen? Beknowe no þe sothe;
Qwat gome was he this with the gaye armes,
With þis gryffoune of golde, þat es one growffe fallyn?
He has grettly greffede vs, so me Gode helpe, 3870
Gyrde down oure gude men and greuede vs sore;
He was þe sterynneste in stoure that euer stele werryde,
Fore he has stonayede oure stale and stroyede for euer!"
Than Sir Mordrede with mouthe melis full faire:
"He was makles one molde, mane, be my trowhe; 3875
This was Sir Gawayne the gude, þe gladdeste of othire,
And the graciouseste gome that vndire God lyffede,
Mane hardyeste of hande, happyeste in armes,
And þe hendeste in hawle vndire heuen riche,
Þe lordelieste of ledyng qwhylls he lyffe myghte, 3880
Fore he was lyone allossede in londes inewe;
Had thow knawen hym, Sir Kyng, in kythe thare he lengede, f.94ʳ
His konynge, his knyghthode, his kyndly werkes,
His doyng, his doughtynesse, his dedis of armes,
Thow wolde hafe dole for his dede þe dayes of thy lyfe." 3885
Ȝit þat traytour alls tite teris lete he fall,
Turnes hym furthe tite, and talkes no more,
Went wepand awaye and weries the stowndys,
Þat euer his werdes ware wroghte siche wandrethe to wyrke.
Whene he thoghte on þis thynge, it thirllede his herte: 3890
For sake of his sybb blode sygheande he rydys;
When þat renayede renke remembirde hym seluen
Of reuerence and ryotes of þe Rownde Table,
He remyd and repent hym of all his rewthe werkes;
Rode awaye with his rowte, ristys he no lengere, 3895
For rade of oure riche kynge, ryve þat he scholde.
Thane kayres he to Cornewaile, carefull in herte,
Because of his kynsemane that one the coste ligges;
He taries tremlande ay, tydandis to herken.
Than the traytoure treunted þe Tyseday þaraftyre, 3900
Trynnys in with a trayne treson to wirke;

And by þe Tambire þat tide his tentis he reris,
And thane in a mette-while a messangere he sendes,
And wraite vnto Waynor how the werlde chaungede,
And what comliche coste the Kyng was aryuede,   3905
One floode foughten with his fleete and fellyd them o lyfe;
Bade hir ferken oo ferre and flee with hir childire,
Whills he myghte wile hym awaye and wyn to hir speche,
Ayere into Irelande, into þas owte-mowntes,
And wonn thare in wildernesse, within þa wast landys.   3910
Than cho ȝermys and ȝeȝes at ȝorke in hir chambire,
Gronys full grysely with gretand teres,
Passes owte of þe palesse with all hir pryce maydenys,
Towarde Chestyre in a charre thay chese hir þe wayes,
Dighte hir ewyn for to dye, with dule at hir herte;   3915
Scho kayres to Karelyone and kawghte hir a vaile,
Askes thare þe habite in þe honoure of Criste,
And all for falsede and frawde and fere of hir louerde.

    Bot whene oure wiese kyng wiste þat Gawayne was landede,
He al towrythes for woo, and, wryngande his handes,   3920
Gers lawnche his botes appon a lawe watire,
Londis als a lyon with lordliche knyghtes,
Slippes in in the sloppes o slante to þe girdyll,
Swalters vpe swyftly with his swerde drawen,
Bownnys his bataile and baners displayes,   3925
Buskes ouer þe brode sandes with breth at his herte,
Ferkes frekkly one felde þare þe feye lygges.
Of the traytours men one trappede stedis,
Ten thosandez ware tynte, þe trewghe to acownt,
And certane on owre syde seuen score knyghtes,   3930
In soyte with theire souerayne vnsownde are beleuede.
Þe Kyng comly ouerkeste knyghtes and othire,   f.94ᵛ
Erlles of Awfrike and Estriche berynes,
Of Orgaile and Orekenay, þe Iresche kynges,
The nobileste of Norwaye, nowmbirs full hugge,   3935
Dukes of Dánamarke and dubbid knyghtes;
And the Guthede kynge in the gay armes
Lys gronande on þe grownde and girde thorowe even.

3911 ȝeȝes Mennicken] ȝee

The riche kynge ransakes with rewthe at his herte,
And vp rypes the renkes of all þe Rownde Tabyll; *3940*
Ses them all in a soppe in sowte by them one,
With the Sarazenes vnsownde enserclede abowte;
And Sir Gawayne the gude in his gaye armes,
Vmbegrippede the girse and one grouffe fallen,
His baners brayden down, betyn of gowlles, *3945*
His brand and his brade schelde all blody beronen;
Was neuer oure semliche kynge so sorowfull in herte,
Ne þat sanke hym so sade bot þat sighte one.

     Than gliftis þe gud kynge and glopyns in herte,
Gronys full grisely with gretande teris; *3950*
Knelis down to þe cors and kaught it in armes,
Kastys vpe his vmbrere and kyssis hym sone,
Lokes one his eye-liddis, þat lowkkide ware faire,
His lippis like to þe lede and his lire falowede.
Þan the corownde kyng cryes full lowde, *3955*
"Dere kosyn o kynde, in kare am I leuede,
For nowe my wirchipe es wente and my were endide;
Here es þe hope of my hele, my happynge of armes—
My herte and my hardynes hale one hym lengede,
My concell, my comforthe, þat kepide myn herte. *3960*
Of all knyghtes þe kynge þat vndir Criste lifede,
Þou was worthy to be kyng, þofe I þe corown bare;
My wele and my wirchipe of all þis werlde riche
Was wonnen thourghe Sir Gawayne and thourghe his witt one."

     "Allas!" saide Sir Arthure, "Nowe ekys my sorowe; *3965*
I am vttirly vndon in myn awen landes.
A, dowttouse, derfe dede, þou duellis to longe!
Why drawes þou so one dreghe? Thow drownnes myn herte!"
Than swe[l]tes the swete kyng and in swoun fallis,
Swafres vp swiftely and swetly hym kysses, *3970*
Till his burliche berde was blody berown,
Alls he had bestes birtenede and broghte owt of life;
Ne had Sir Ewayne comen and othire grete lordys,
His bolde herte had brousten for bale at þat stownde.

     "Blyne," sais thies bolde men, "thow blondirs þi selfen; *3975*

3942 enserclede *Brock*] enserchede

Þis es botles bale, for bettir bees it neuer.
It es no wirchipe, iwysse, to wryng thyn hondes;
To wepe als a woman it es no witt holden.
Be knyghtly of contenaunce, als a kyng scholde,
And leue siche clamoure, for Cristes lufe of Heuen!"   3980

    f.95ʳ

"For blode," said the bolde kyng, "blyn sall I neuer,
Or my brayne tobriste, or my breste oþer!
Was neuer sorowe so softe that sanke to my herte;
Itt es full sibb to my selfe, my sorowe es the more.
Was neuer so sorowfull a syghte seyn with myn eyghen;   3985
He es sakles supprysede for syn of myn one."
Down knelis þe Kyng and kryes full lowde;
With carefull contenaunce he karpes thes wordes:
"O rightwis, riche Gode, this rewthe Thow beholde,
Þis ryall, rede blode ryn appon erthe;   3990
It ware worthy to be schrede and schrynede in golde,
For it es sakles of syn, sa helpe me oure Lorde."
Down knelis þe Kyng with kare at his herte,
Kaughte it vpe kyndly with his clene handis,
Keste it in a ketill-hatte and couerde it faire,   3995
And kayres furthe with þe cors in kyghte þare he lenges.
    "Here I make myn avowe," quod the Kynge than,
"To Messie, and to Marie, the mylde Qwene of Heuen,
I sall neuer ryvaye, ne racches vncowpyll
At roo ne raynedere þat rynnes appone erthe;   4000
Neuer grewhownde late glyde, ne gossehawke latt flye,
Ne neuer fowle see fellide þat flieghes with wenge;
Fawkon ne formaylle appon fiste handill,
Ne ȝitt with gerefawcon rejoyse me in erthe;
Ne regne in my royaltez, ne halde my Rownde Table,   4005
Till thi dede, my dere, be dewly reuengede;
Bot euer droupe and dare, qwylls my lyfe lastez,
Till Drighten and derfe dede hafe don qwate them likes."
    Than kaughte they vpe þe cors with kare at theire hertes,
Karyed one a coursere with þe Kynge selfen;   4010
The waye vnto Wynchestre þay wente at the gayneste,
Wery and wandsomdly, with wondide knyghtes.

    3985 eyghen] eyne eyghen

Thare come þe prior of þe plas and professide monkes,
Apas in processione and with the Prynce metys;
And he betuke þam the cors of þe knyghte noble.   4015
"Lokis it be clenly kepyd," he said, "and in þe kirke holden,
Done for derygese, as to þe ded fallys,
Menskede with messes for mede of þe saule;
Loke it wante no waxe, ne no wirchipe ells,
And at þe body be bawmede and one erthe holden;   4020
ʒiff þou kepe thi couent encroche any wirchipe
At my comyng agayne, ʒif Crist will it thole,
Abyde of þe beryeng till they be broughte vndire,
Þat has wroghte vs this woo and þis werre mouede."
Þan sais Sir Wychere þe wy, a wyese mane of armes,   4025
"I rede ʒe warely wende and wirkes the beste;
Soiorne in this ceté and semble thi berynes,
And bidde with thi bolde men in thi burghe riche;
Get owt knyghttez of contres that castells holdes,
And owt of garysons grete gude men of armes,   4030
For we are faithely to fewe to feghte with them all,
Þat we see in his sorte appon þe see bankes."
With krewell contenance thane the Kyng karpis theis wordes:
"I praye the, kare noghte, Sir Knyghte, ne caste þou no dredis;   f.95ᵛ
Hadde I no segge bot my selfe one vndir sone,   4035
And I may hym see with sighte or one hym sette hondis,
I sall even amange his mene malle hym to dede!
Are I of þe stede styre halfe a stede lenghe,
I sall [stryke] hym in his stowre and stroye hym for euer;
And þareto make I myn avowe devottly to Cryste,   4040
And to Hys Modyre Marie, þe mylde Qwene of Heuen,
I sall neuer soiourne sounde, ne sawghte at myne herte,
In ceté ne in subarbe sette appon erthe,
Ne ʒitt slomyre ne slepe with my slawe eyghne,
Till he be slayne þat hym slowghe, ʒif any sleyghte happen;   4045
Bot euer pursue the payganys þat my pople distroyede,
Qwylls I may pare them and pynne, in place þare me likes."
Thare durste no renke hym areste of all þe Rownde Table,
Ne none paye þat Prynce with plesande wordes,

4039 stryke *Brock*]

Ne none of his ligemene luke hym in the eyghne, 4050
So lordely he lukes for losse of his knyghttes.

    Thane drawes he to Dorsett and dreches no langere,
Derefull dredlesse with drowppande teris;
Kayeris into Kornewayle with kare at his herte:
The trays of þe traytoure he trynys full euene, 4055
And turnys in be þe Treyntis þe traytoure to seche,
Fyndis hym in a foreste þe Frydaye thereaftire;
The Kyng lyghttes one fott and freschely askryes,
And with his freliche folke he has þe felde nomen.

    Now isschewis his enmye vndire þe wode eyuys, 4060
With ostes of alynes full horrebill to schewe.
Sir Mordrede the Malebranche, with his myche pople,
Foundes owt of the foreste appon fele halfes,
In seuen grett batailles semliche arrayede,
Sexty thowsande men—the syghte was full hugge— 4065
All fyghtande folke of þe ferre laundes,
Faire fettede one frownte be tha fresche strondes.
And all Arthurs oste was amede with knyghtes,
Bot awghtene hundrethe of all, entrede in rolles;
This was a mache vnmete, bot myghttis of Criste, 4070
To melle with þat multitude in þase man londis.
Than the royall roy of þe Rownde Table
Rydes one a riche stede, arrayes his beryns,
Buskes his avawmwarde, als hym beste likes;
Sir Ewayne and Sir Errake and othire gret lordes, 4075
Demenys the medilwarde menskefully thareaftyre,
With Merrake and Meneduke, myghtty of strenghes;
Idirous and Alymere, þire auenaunt children,
Ayers with Arthure, with seuen score of knyghtes;
He rewlis þe rerewarde redyly thareaftyre, 4080
The rekeneste redy men of þe Rownde Table,
And thus he fittis his folke and freschely askryes,
And syen comforthes his men with knyghtlyche wordes:
"I beseke ȝow, Sirs, for sake of oure Lorde,
That ȝe doo wele todaye and dredis no wapen; 4085
Fighttes fersely nowe and fendis ȝoure seluen,
Fellis down ȝone feye folke, the felde sall be owrs; f.96ʳ

They are Sarazenes, ȝone sorte—vnsownde motte they worthe!
Sett one them sadlye, for sake of oure Lorde.
Ȝif vs be destaynede to dy todaye one this erthe,   4090
We sall be hewede vnto Heuen, or we be halfe colde.
Loke ȝe lett for no lede lordly to wirche:
Layes ȝone laddes lowe be the layke ende.
Take no tente vnto me, ne tale of me rekke;
Bes besy one my baners with ȝoure brighte wapyns,   4095
That they be strenghely stuffede with steryn knyghtes,
And holden lordly one lofte, ledys to schewe;
Ȝif any renke them arase, reschowe them sone.
Wirkes now my wirchipe, todaye my werre endys;
Ȝe wotte my wele and my woo—wirkkys as ȝow likys.   4100
Crist comly with crown comforthe ȝow all,
For þe kyndeste creatours that euer kynge ledde;
I gyffe ȝow all my blyssyng with a blithe will,
And all Bretowns bolde—blythe mote ȝe worthe."
     They pype vpe at pryme tyme, approches them nere: 4105
Pris men and priste proues theire strenghes;
Bremly the brethemen bragges in troumppes,
In cornettes comlyly, when knyghttes assembles,
And thane jolyly enjoynys þeis jentyll knyghttes;
A jolyere journé ajuggede was neuer,   4110
Whene Bretons boldly enbraces theire scheldes,
And Cristyn encroyssede them and castis in fewtire.
     Þan Sir Arthure oste his enmye askryes,
And in they schokke theire scheldes, schontes no lengare;
Schotte to þe schiltrons and schowttes full heghe,   4115
Thorowe scheldis full schene schalkes they touche.
Redily thas rydde men of the Rownde Table
With ryall raunke stele rittys theire mayles;
Bryneys browdden they briste and burneste helmys,
Hewes haythen men down, halses in sondre.   4120
Fyghtande with fyne stele, þe feye blod rynnys;
Of þe frekkeste of frounte, vnfers ere belevede.
     Ethyns of Argayle and Irische kynges
Enverounes oure avawmwarde with venymos beryns;
Peghttes and paynymes with perilous wapyns,   4125

With speres disspetousely disspoylles oure knyghttes,
And hewede down the hendeste with hertly dynttys;
Thorow the holle batayle they holden theire wayes.
Þus fersly they fyghte appon sere halfes,
That of þe bolde Bretons myche blode spillis;　　　　　　4130
Thare durste non rescowe them for reches in erthe,
Þe steryn ware þare so stedde and stuffede wit[h] othire;
He durste noghte stire a steppe, bot stodde for hym seluen,
Till thre stalis ware stroyede be strenghe of hym one.
　　　"Idrous," quod Arthure, "ayre the byhoues;　　　4135
I see Sir Ewayne ouersette with Sarazenes kene.
Redy the for rescows, arraye thee sone;　　　　　　f.96ᵛ
Hye þe with hardy men in helpe of thy fadire.
Sett in one the syde and socoure ȝone lordes:
Bot they be socourrede and sownde, vnsawghte be I euer."　　4140
Idrous hym ansuers ernestly þareaftyre:
"He es my fadire, in faithe—forsake sall I neuer;
He has me fosterde and fedde and my faire bretheren.
Bot I forsake this gate, so me Gode helpe,
And sothely all sybredyn bot thy selfe one;　　　　　　4145
I breke neuer his biddyng for beryn one lyfe,
Bot euer bouxvm as beste blethely to wyrke.
He comande me kyndly, with knyghtly wordes,
That I schulde lelely one þe lenge and one noo lede ells;
I sall hys comandement holde, ȝif Criste wil me thole.　　4150
He es eldare than I, and ende sall we bothen:
He sall ferkke before, and I sall come aftyre;
ȝiffe hym be destaynede to dy todaye one þis erthe,
Criste comly with crown take kepe to hys saule."
　　　Þan remys the riche kyng with rewthe at his herte,　4155
Hewys hys handys one heghte and to þe heuen lokes:
"Qwythen hade Dryghttyn destaynede at his dere will,
Þat he hade demyd me todaye to dy for ȝow all;
That had I leuer than be lorde all my lyfe tym
Off all þat Alexandere aughte qwhills he in erthe lengede."　4160
Sir Ewayne and Sir Errake, þes excellente beryns,
Enters in one þe oste and egerly strykes;

　　4140　euer] neuer

The ethenys of Orkkenaye and Irische kynges,
Þay gobone of þe gretteste with growndene swerdes,
Hewes one þas hulkes with þeire harde wapyns,   4165
Layed down þas ledes with lothely dynttys;
Schuldirs and scheldys þay schrede to þe hawnches,
And medills thourghe mayles þay merken in sondire—
Siche honoure neuer aughte none erthely kyng
At theire endyng daye, bot Arthure hym seluen.   4170
So þe droughte of þe daye dryede theire hertes,
That bothe drynkles they dye—dole was þe more.
     Now mellys oure medillwarde and mengen togedire
Sir Mordrede þe Malebranche, with his myche pople;
He had hide hym behynde within thas holte eyuys,   4175
With halle bataile on hethe—harme es þe more;
He hade sene þe conteke al clene to þe ende,
How oure cheualrye cheuyde be chaunces of armes;
He wiste oure folke was forfoughtten, þat þare was feye leuede;
To encowntere þe Kyng he castes hym sone.   4180
Bot the churles chekyn hade chaungyde his armes:
He had sothely forsaken þa sawturoure engrelede,
And laughte vpe thre lyons all of whitte siluyre,
Passande in purpre of perrie full riche,
For þe Kyng sulde noghte knawe þe cawtelous wriche;   4185
Because of his cowardys he keste of his atyre,   f.97r
Bot the comliche kyng knewe hym full swythe,
Karpis to Sir Cadors þes kyndly wordez:
"I see þe traytoure come ȝondyr trynande full ȝerne:
Ȝone ladde with þe lyones es like to hym selfen;   4190
Hym sall torfere betyde, may I touche ones,
For all his treson and trayne, alls I am trew lorde.
Today Clarente and Caliburne sall kythe them togedirs,
Whilke es kenere of kerfe or hardare of eghge;
Fraiste sall we fyne stele appone fyne wedis.   4195
Itt was my derlyng daynteuous and full dere holden,
Kepede fore encorownmentes of kynges enoynttede;
One dayes when I dubbyde dukkes and erlles,
It was burliche borne be þe bryghte hiltes;
I durste neuer dere it in dedis of armes,   4200

Bot euer kepide clene, because of my seluen.
For I see Clarent vnclede, þat crowne es of swerdes,
My wardrop of Walyngfordhe I wate es distroyede;
Wist no wy of wone bot Waynor hir seluen;
Scho hade þe kepynge hir selfe of þat kydde wapyn,   4205
Off cofres enclosede þat to þe crown lengede,
With rynges and relikkes and þe Regale of Fraunce,
That was fownden on Sir Froll when he was feye leuyde."
　　Than Sir Marrike in malyncoly metys hym sone,
With a mellyd mace myghtyly hym strykes;   4210
The bordour of his bacenett he bristes in sondire,
Þat þe schire rede blode ouer his brene rynnys.
The beryn blenkes for bale, and all his ble chaunges,
Bot ȝitt he byddys as a bore and brymly he strykes;
He braydes owte a brande, bryghte als euer ony syluer,   4215
Þat was Sir Arthure awen and Vtere his fadirs,
In þe wardrop of Walyngfordhe was wonte to be kepede;
Þarewith þe derfe dogge syche dynttes he rechede,
Þe toþer withdrewe one dreghe and durste do non oþer;
For Sir Marrake was man merrede in elde,   4220
And Sir Mordrede was myghty and [in] his moste strenghis;
Come non within þe compas, knyghte ne non oþer,
Within þe swyng of swerde, þat ne he þe swete leuyd.
　　Þat persayfes oure Prynce and presses to faste,
Strykes into þe stowre by strenghe of hys handis,   4225
Metis with Sir Mordrede, he melis vnfaire:
"Turne, traytoure vntrewe—þe tydys no bettyre;
Be gret Gode, thow sall dy with dynt of my handys!
The schall rescowe no renke, ne reches in erthe."
The Kyng with Calaburn knyghtly hym strykes: 4230
Þe cantell of þe clere schelde he kerfes in sondyre,
Into þe schuldyre of þe schalke a schaftmonde large,
Þat þe schire rede blode schwede one þe maylys.
He schodirde and schrenkys and schontes bott lyttill,
Bott schokkes in scharpely in his schene wedys: f.97ᵛ 4235
The felone with þe fyn swerde freschely he strykes;
The felettes of þe ferrere syde he flassches in sondyre,

4221 in *Brock*]

Thorowe jopown and jesserawnte of gentill mailes—
The freke fichede in þe flesche an halfe fotte large;
That derfe dynt was his dede, and dole was þe more   *4240*
That euer þat doughtty sulde dy, bot at Dryghttyns wyll.
    ȝitt with Calyburn his swerde full knyghttly he strykes,
Kastes in his clere schelde and coueres hym full faire;
Swappes of þe swerde hande, als he by glentes:
Ane inche from þe elbowe he ochede it in sondyre,   *4245*
Þat he swounes one þe swarthe and one swym fallis;
Thorowe bracer of brown stele and þe bryghte mayles,
That the hilte and þe hande appon þe hethe ligges.
Thane frescheliche þe freke the fente vpe rerys,
Brochis hym in with the bronde to þe bryghte hiltys,   *4250*
And he brawles one the bronde and bownes to dye.
"In faye," says þe feye kynge, "sore me forthynkkes
That euer siche a false theefe so faire an ende haues."
Qwen they had fenyste þis feghte, thane was þe felde wonen,
And the false folke in þe felde feye are byleuede;   *4255*
Till a foreste they fledde and fell in the greuys,
And fers feghtande folke folowes them aftyre,
Howntes and hewes down the heythen tykes,
Mourtherys in the mowntaygnes Sir Mordrede knyghtes;
Thare chapyde neuer no childe, cheftayne ne oþer,   *4260*
Bot choppes them down in the chace—it chargys bot littyll.
    Bot when Sir Arthure anon Sir Ewayne he fyndys,
And Errake þe auenaunt and oþer grett lordes,
He kawghte vp Sir Cador with care at his herte,
Sir Clegis, Sir Cleremonde, þes clere men of armes,   *4265*
Sir Lothe and Sir Lyonell, Sir Lawncelott and Lowes,
Marrake and Meneduke, þat myghty ware euer.
With langoure in the launde thare he layes them togedire,
Lokede on theyre lighames and with a lowde steuen,
Alls lede þat liste noghte lyfe and loste had his myrthis,   *4270*
Than he stotays for made and all his strenghe faylez,
Lokes vpe to þe lyfte and all his lyre chaunges,
Downne he sweys full swythe and in a swoun fallys,
Vpe he coueris one kneys and kryes full often:

4246 swarthe] swrathe   4249 rerys] rererys

"Kyng comly with crowne, in care am I leuyde;   4275
All my lordchipe lawe in lande es layde vndyre,
That me has gyfen gwerdons, be grace of Hym seluen,
Mayntenyde my manhede be myghte of theire handes,
Made me manly on molde and mayster in erthe,
In a tenefull tym this torfere was reryde,   4280
That for a traytoure has tynte all my trewe lordys.
Here rystys the riche blude of the Rownde Table,
Rebukkede with a rebawde, and rewthe es the more!   f.98ʳ
I may helples one hethe house be myn one,
Alls a wafull wedowe þat wanttes hir beryn;   4285
I may werye and wepe and wrynge myn handys,
For my wytt and my wyrchipe awaye es for euer;
Off all lordchips I take leue to myn ende.
Here es þe Bretons blode broughte owt of lyfe,
And nowe in þis journée all my joy endys."   4290
      Thane relyes þe renkes of all þe Rownde Table:
To þe ryall roy thay ride þam all;
Than assembles full sone seuen score knyghtes,
In sighte to þaire souerayne, þat was vnsownde leuede.
Than knelis the crownede kynge and kryes one lowde,   4295
"I thanke þe, Gode, of Thy grace, with a gud wyll,
That gafe vs vertue and witt to vencows þis beryns;
And vs has grauntede þe gree of theis gret lordes.
He sent vs neuer no schame, ne schenchipe in erthe,
Bot euer ȝit þe ouerhande of all oþer kynges.   4300
We hafe no laysere now þese lordys to seke,
For ȝone laythely ladde me lamede so sore;
Graythe vs to Glasthenbery—vs gaynes non oþer—
Thare we may ryste vs with roo and raunsake oure wondys.
Of þis dere day werke, þe Dryghtten be loued,   4305
That vs has destaynede and demyd to dye in oure awen."
      Thane they holde at his heste hally at ones,
And graythes to Glassthenberye þe gate at þe gayneste;
Entres þe Ile of Aueloyne, and Arthure he lyghttes,
Merkes to a manere there, for myghte he no forthire;   4310
A surgyn of Salerne enserches his wondes,

     4280   reryde] rereryde   4311   surgyn *Brock*] susgyn

The Kyng sees be asaye þat sownde bese he neuer,
And sone to his sekire men he said theis wordes:
"Doo calle me a confessour, with Criste in his armes;
I will be howselde in haste, whate happe so betyddys.   *4315*
Constantyn, my cosyn, he sall the corown bere,
Alls becomys hym of kynde, ȝife Criste will hym thole;
Beryn, fore my benyson, thowe berye ȝone lordys,
That in baytaille with brondez are broghte owte of lyfe;
And sythen merke manly to Mordrede children,   *4320*
That they bee sleyghely slayne and slongen in watyrs;
Latt no wykkyde wede waxe, no wrythe one this erthe—
I warne fore thy wirchipe, wirke alls I bydde.
I foregyffe all greffe, for Cristez lufe of Heuen;
ȝife Waynor hafe wele wroghte, wele hir betydde."   *4325*
He saide *In manus* with mayne one molde whare he ligges,
And thus passes his speryt, and spekes he no more.

    The baronage of Bretayne thane, bechopes and othire,   f.98ᵛ
Graythes them to Glasthenbery with gloppynnande hertes,
To bery thare the bolde kynge and bryng to þe erthe,   *4330*
With all wirchipe and welthe þat any wy scholde.
Throly belles thay rynge and *Requiem* syngys,
Dosse messes and matyns with mournande notes:
Relygeous reueste in theire riche copes,
Pontyficalles and prelates in precyouse wedys,   *4335*
Dukes and dusszeperis in theire dule-cotes,
Cowntasses knelande and claspande theire handes,
Ladys languessande and lowrande to schewe;
All was buskede in blake, birdes and othire,
That schewede at the sepulture, with sylande teris—   *4340*
Whas neuer so sorowfull a syghte seen in theire tym.

    Thus endis Kyng Arthure, as auctors alegges,
That was of Ectores blude, the kynge son of Troye,
And of Sir Pryamous the prynce, praysede in erthe;
Fro thythen broghte the Bretons all his bolde eldyrs   *4345*
Into Bretayne the Brode, as þe *Bruytte* tellys.

Notes

ABBREVIATIONS USED IN THE NOTES

(References cited in the Bibliography are shortened here)

Ackerman = Ackerman, Robert W., *An Index of Arthurian Names in Middle English,* Stanford, Stanford University Press, 1952.

Amours = Amours, F. J., *Scottish Alliterative Poems.*

Atlas of Britain = *Atlas of Britain,* Oxford, Clarendon Press, 1963.

Awntyrs off Arthure = Gates, Robert J., ed., *The Awntyrs off Arthure at the Terne Wathelyne.*

Banks, *MA* = Banks, Mary M., ed., *Morte Arthure.*

Banks, "Notes on the 'MA,' " = Banks, Mary M., "Notes on the 'Morte Arthure' Glossary."

Benson = Benson, Larry D., *Art and Tradition in Sir Gawain and the Green Knight.*

Beowulf = Klaeber, Fr., ed., *Beowulf and the Fight at Finnsburg,* 3d. ed., Boston, D. C. Heath, 1950.

Björkman, "Etymological Notes" = Björkman, Erik, "Etymological Notes."

Björkman, *MA* = Björkman, Erik, ed., *Morte Arthure.*

Björkman, "Notes on the 'MA' " = Björkman, Erik, "Notes on the 'Morte Arthure' and Its Vocabulary."

Blair = Blair, Peter Hunter, *An Introduction to Anglo-Saxon England,* London, Cambridge University Press, 1962.

Branscheid = Branscheid, P., "Über die Quellen des Stabreimenden Morte Arthure."

Brock, *MA* = Brock, Edmund, ed., *Morte Arthure.*

Chaucer = Robinson, F. N., ed., *The Works of Geoffrey Chaucer,* 2d. ed., Boston, Houghton Mifflin, 1957.

Dickens and Wilson = Dickens, Bruce, and R. M. Wilson, *Early Middle English Texts,* London, Bowes and Bowes, 1951.

EDD = Wright, Joseph, ed., *The English Dialect Dictionary,* London, Henry Frowde, 1898–1905.

Everett, *MA* = Everett, Dorothy, *Essays on Middle English Literature,* Oxford, Clarendon Press, 1955.

Finlayson, *MA* = Finlayson, John, ed., *Morte Arthure.*

Finlayson, "Rhetorical *Descriptio* of Place" = Finlayson, John, "Rhetorical *Descriptio* of Place in the Alliterative *Morte Arthure.*

Froissart = Bourchier, Sir John, Lord Berners, trans., *The Chronicle of Froissart,* Vol. III, *Great Britain,* London, D. Nutt, 1901–03.

Gardner = Gardner, John, trans., *The Alliterative Morte Arthure, The Owl and the Nightingale, and Five Other Middle English Poems.*

161

Geoffrey = Thorpe, Lewis, ed. and trans., *Geoffrey of Monmouth: The History of the Kings of Britain,* London, Penguin, 1966.

Giraldus = Williams, W. Llewelyn, ed., *Giraldus Cambrensis: The Itinerary through Wales and the Description of Wales,* London, Everyman, 1930.

Gist = Gist, Margaret A., *Love and War in the Middle English Romances.*

Godefroy = Godefroy, P., ed., *Dictionnaire de l'ancienne langue française,* 10 vols., Paris, F. Vieweg, 1881–1902.

Griffith = Griffith, R. H., "Malory, *Morte Arthure,* and Fierabras."

Holthausen = Holthausen, F., "Review of Banks" edition of *Morte Arthure* (untitled).

Loomis, *Arthurian Legends* = Loomis, R. S., *Arthurian Legends in Medieval Art.*

Malory = Vinaver, Eugène, ed., *The Works of Sir Thomas Malory,* 2d. ed., 3 vols., Oxford, Clarendon Press, 1967.

Manly = Manly, John Matthews, "Chaucer and the Rhetoricians," in *Chaucer Criticism: The Canterbury Tales,* ed. Richard J. Schoeck and Jerome Taylor, Notre Dame, Notre Dame University Press, 1960.

Matthews = Matthews, William, *The Tragedy of Arthur.*

MED = Kurath, Hans, and Sherman M. Kuhn, eds., *Middle English Dictionary,* Ann Arbor, University of Michigan Press, 1952—.

Mennicken = Mennicken, Franz, "Versbau und Sprache in Huchowns Morte Arthure."

Mossé = Mossé, Fernand, *A Handbook of Middle English,* trans. J. A. Walker, Baltimore, Johns Hopkins Press, 1952.

Mustanoja = Mustanoja, Tauno F., *A Middle English Syntax,* Vol. I, *Parts of Speech,* Helsinki, Société Néophilologique, 1960.

Neilson = Neilson, George, *Huchown of the Awle Ryale.*

Oakden = Oakden, J. P., *Alliterative Poetry in Middle English.*

OED = Murray, James, *A New English Dictionary on Historical Principles,* Oxford, Clarendon Press, 1888–1928; Introduction and Supplement by W. A. Craigie and C. T. Onions, 1933.

O'Loughlin = O'Loughlin, J. L. N., "The Middle English Alliterative *Morte Arthure.*"

Oman = Oman, Charles, *A History of the Art of War in the Middle Ages,* Vol. II, 1924; rpt. New York, Burt Franklin, 1969.

Patience = Anderson, J. J., ed., *Patience.*

Pearl = Gordon, E. V., ed.. *Pearl.*

Sayers = Sayers, Dorothy, trans., *The Song of Roland: A New Translation,* Baltimore, Penguin, 1965.

Schumacher = Schumacher, Karl, "Studien über den Stabreim in der Mittelenglischen Alliterationsdichtung."

Sir Gawain = Tolkien, J. R. R., and E. V. Gordon, eds., *Sir Gawain and the Green Knight,* 2d. ed. Norman Davis.

Tatlock = Tatlock, J. S. P., *The Legendary History of Britain.*

Trautmann = Trautmann, Moritz, "Der Dichter Huchown und seine Werke."

Vegetius = Vegetius, "The Military Institutions of the Romans," in *The Roots of Strategy,* ed. Thomas R. Phillips, Harrisburg, Pa., The Military Publishing Co., 1940.

Waldron = Waldron, R. A., "Oral Formulaic Technique in Middle English Alliterative Poetry."

Webster = *Webster's New International Dictionary,* 2d. ed., Springfield, Mass., Merriam, 1953.

1–25. The invocation and the brief summary of the story to come are standard rhetorical introductory devices often used in the fourteenth century (Manly, pp. 274–76). Matthews considers the invocation as particularly important in establishing the serious moral and religious tone that he believes dominates the poem and colors the poet's attitude toward Arthur's military conquests (pp. 21, 112).

1. *thurgh grace of Hym seluen.* For the periphrastic use of *of* + personal pronoun as a possessive (apparently for emphasis), see Mustanoja, p. 158; for *self, seluen,* etc., as a reinforcing word with nouns and pronouns, see Mustanoja, pp. 145–48. This construction is very common in the poem.

3. *Schelde vs fro schamesdede and synfull werkes.* This appears to be the only example in the poem of the alliteration of *sh* and *s*. A number of emendations of *synfull* have been proposed (see Björkman, *MA,* Notes, p. 129). However, the MS reading is retained here, since, as Oakden notes, even those poets who make a practice of alliterating *sh* only with itself "do not hesitate on occasion to allow it to alliterate with *s*" (p. 165).

schamesdede, 'a death of shame, a shameful death' (*often written as one word*). For a similar use of this expression see *Cursor Mundi,* 1619, "He suar

his ath þat þai suld all thole schammes deid" and *The Merchant's Tale,* 1133, "God yeve yow bothe on shames deeth to dyen!"

13. *awke.* Literally, 'untoward.' This is the poet's first hint of an ambivalent attitude toward Arthur and the Round Table (see Matthews, pp. 112–13 and Introduction, "Formulas and Rhetorical Style," on the use of ambiguous language in the description of the King).

23. *Lucyus.* See note to line 86.

26–51. The syntax of this passage is tangled, unlike that of most of the rest of the poem. It is difficult to determine where the subordinate clause, with which the passage begins, ends, and there are several series of noun clauses which are not clearly attached to verbs or independent clauses. The reason for the poet's difficulty here is perhaps that he is not accustomed to managing a complex hypotactic syntax. The syntax throughout most of the poem is paratactic and cumulative, and the subordinate clauses that do appear are usually short.

Though Arthur is supposed to have conquered half of Europe, the poet's geography is the most specific and detailed in the area of Edward III's conquests—western France; see Map I.

37. MS: *Grece* (emend. *Grace,* 'Grasse' Holthausen, p. 256). Greece

163

is not only anomalous in the geography of Arthur's empire (see Map I), but also mentioned in line 602 as a country allied with Lucius.

41. *Vyenne.* Either the district around Poitiers or the town north of Valence on the Rhône River. Ackerman (p. 240) is mistaken in identifying this as 'Vienna,' which, like Greece, is far from the area of most of the named localities.

42. MS:?*Eruge* (unknown) (emend. *Ouergne,* 'Auvergne' Banks, *MA,* Notes, p. 131). Banks suggests that the scribe omitted an *Ou* by haplography (*Of [Ou]ergne*) and then transposed the *g* and the *n,* producing a word printed *Eruge* by most editors, *n* and *u* having been confused. Banks derives her emendation from Laȝamon, who mentions *Auvergne* and *Anjou* together.

47. "*Swynn* was an old roadstead . . . where Edward III won a victory over Philip's fleet. Just about that time the name was changed from Swynn . . . to Sluse and Sluys. It lay just between Zeeland and Flanders. . . . Minot uses both names in commemorating Edward's victory" (Banks, *MA,* Notes, p. 131).

48 ff. This ceremonious dubbing, which contrasts with the hasty and desperate dubbing of new young knights on the battlefield in lines 1738–45, results both from the acquisition of new wealth in the King's recent conquests and from his desire to reward and decorate the heroes of his campaigns. Lucius also dubs knights after his victories in Westphalia (621–22).

49. 'Created dukedoms and dealt (them) out in diverse realms.' The object pronoun after *delte* is unexpressed.

57. *Swaldye.* There is no information on this locality in any of the earlier editions of the poem. Ackerman identifies it simply as a place in Wales where a hunt is held, taking his information from this line. The name is very likely a corruption of *Sudwallia,* a Latin name used in England for South Wales (Tatlock, p. 62). The term *Sudgualensis,* 'South Welsh,' appears in Geoffrey's description of the festivities at Caerleon, the ultimate source of this passage, and might have suggested *Sudwallia* or *Swaldye* to the *Morte Arthure* poet or to one of his sources.

61. *Caerlyon.* The Arthurian city given the greatest prominence in the chronicles, in Geoffrey at its most splendid as the scene of Arthur's Pentecostal crown-wearing (Tatlock, p. 69). Here the great feast, which is shifted to Carlisle (see note to line 64), derives from the chronicle description of the crown-wearing at Caerleon. The expression *curius walles* suggests some knowledge on the poet's part of Giraldus' description of the city: "[Caerleon] was of undoubted antiquity, and handsomely built of masonry, with courses of bricks, by the Romans. Many vestiges of its former splendour may yet be seen; immense palaces . . . a tower of prodigious size, remarkable hot baths, relics of temples, and theatres, all enclosed within fine walls, parts of which remain standing. You will find on all sides, both within and without the circuit of the walls, subterraneous buildings, aqueducts, underground passages; and what I think worthy of notice, stoves contrived with wonderful art, to transmit the heat insensibly through narrow tubes passing up the side walls" (pp. 50–51).

62. *the riche reuare.* The Usk.

63. *semble his sorte to see.* 'Gather his retinue around his throne.'

64. MS: *Carlelele* (emend. *Carlele,* 'Carlisle.' Dittography is fairly common in this MS; see, e.g., *horsesede,* 2944, *reryde,* 4280, *worthethy,* 1302). Though Branscheid (p. 222) and Björkman (*MA,* Notes, p. 130) believe this to be

a mistake for Caerleon and suggest emending accordingly, *Carlele* is undoubtedly correct. It is mentioned elsewhere in the poem (476, 480, 839), and, as Banks points out (*MA*, Notes, p. 135), the route followed by the Roman ambassadors in their departure from Britain involves northern cities out of the way of Caerleon (see Map II). Matthews is puzzled by the mention of Carlisle and suggests that its choice "may have to do with the area in which the poem was composed" (p. 21). Matthews, Branscheid, and Björkman seem to regard the choice of Carlisle as unusual, apparently not realizing that Arthur did have traditional associations with this city, as well as with Caerleon; Froissart states that Arthur was known to have often held court at Carlisle (Vol. I, p. 48).

65. *and helde hym for lorde.* Several emendations have been proposed for this half line, both because its alliteration was assumed to be faulty and because its meaning is difficult to determine. For example, Björkman (*MA,* Notes, p. 130) suggests *and kende* (proclaimed) *hym for lorde,* Mennicken (p. 137) *and kidde* (made known) *hym for lorde.* However, emendation is unnecessary because the alliteration fails according to the pattern noted by O'Loughlin (see Introduction, "Alliteration and Meter") and because, according to the *MED, hold* is used reflexively with the meaning 'to remain (in a state or condition)' (*holden* v 1 13a). The literal meaning of the half line is 'and remained lord,' meaning 'reinforced his position as lord (with this public and politic celebration of his victories).'

67. *ercheuesqes.* The regular ME form is *archebishop* or *erchebischop* [OE *ercebiscop* (from L)]. *Ercheuesqes* is a nonce word, and, being derived from OF, supports Matthews' theory that the immediate source of the poem was an OF work (pp. 181–182).

70. *Bot.* Often used in this work to mark a transition to something new or supplemental rather than to something contradictory. The meaning in its fullest sense is 'furthermore, morever' (*MED but* conj 7). See 239 for a similar construction; in both cases the poet uses the word to introduce some further act of hospitality on the part of the King.

73. *takyn,* 'enjoyed.' See *OED take* v 11.

80. *So* merely indicates sequence here. See Mustanoja, p. 336, and *The General Prologue,* 30–31: 'And shortly, whan the sonne was to reste / So hadde I spoken with hem everichon.'

86. *Lucius Iberius.* The Emperor Lucius was apparently invented by Geoffrey, who calls him *Lucius Tiberius.* For speculation about the coinage of this "wholly unhistorical and also improbable name," see Tatlock, *Speculum,* 6 (1930), 216. The attempt at a reconquest of Britain by the Romans in the sixth century also derives from Geoffrey.

87. The meaning is either 'Greets you as (his) subject (in this document) under his great seal' or 'Greets you as (his) subject (that is) under his great insignia.'

88. *It.* The senator is referring to the document in his hand.

89. *his targe is to schewe.* 'His (official) seal is (here) to see' (perhaps with double meaning, 'His shield of battle is uncovered,' that is, he is ready to strike [Gardner, Notes, p. 283]). For the meaning 'seal,' see *OED targe* sb[1] 2: 'A name applied in the reigns of the first three Edwards to the King's private or privy seal (perh. bearing a shield as its device).' Björkman must be incorrect in proposing 'charter' as the meaning here (*MA,* Notes, p. 131), since it would not be the document itself, which could be drawn up by anyone, but the Emperor's

official seal that would attest to the validity of the messengers' claim.

91–103. The syntax of this passage (especially lines 91–95), like that of 26–51, is confused. *That* in line 92 means 'so that,' and the causal connection with 91 is important, as it emphasizes the messenger's concern for legality; he has been careful to serve the summons in public, before witnesses in Arthur's own court (*in sale,* 91), so that it cannot be ignored or legally set aside. Line 94 has either a subject pronoun or a coordinating conjunction unexpressed (see Introduction, under *Personal Pronouns*). The word *kyng* in line 96 refers to Lucius. In line 103 the pronoun *them* is apparently dative (from them) and refers to Lucius and his senators.

107. 'And lead you, meek as any beast that breathes, wherever it pleases him.'

123. 'Because his countenance seemed disturbed to them' (*Because of* = because). For another possible interpretation of this construction, see note to line 133.

124–131. Gist (pp. 171–77) notes that an envoy's safety being endangered by a hot-headed member of the host court is a common situation in the ME romances. Usually, however, it is some high-principled leader, often the King himself, who intervenes and saves the envoy and the honor of the court. It is significant that here it is Arthur, rather than some young, rash knight, who imperils the envoys, and it is the envoy himself who is forced to interject the appeal to honor and legality. By deliberately changing this stock situation, the poet is going out of his way to set the stage for the ruthlessness and rashness that Arthur displays in the second half of the poem and that lead ultimately to his downfall (see Matthews, pp. 40–41).

It is not certain whether the speaker in this passage is the same *Senator* who speaks in lines 136–39 (and who seems to be the same person who delivers the first speech). The speaker here is called *a knyghte* (124), and Brock indicates in his marginal summary that these are two different speakers. However, there is a strong likelihood that this speech is delivered by *the Senator*. The Senator is the only member of the delegation who speaks throughout the entire episode and the only one who is given any individuality and, as leader, is the logical person to challenge Arthur and remind him of his legal responsibilities: he delivers a similar speech in lines 467–74. Except for the expression *a knyghte,* the only possible indication that a second speaker is called for is the expression *woundyde vs all* (137). Brock perhaps understood this as 'stricken us all,' that is to say, 'all of us, not only this man who has just spoken,' and felt it necessary for the previous speech to be delivered by another person. However, *all* functions as an adverb as well as a noun, with the meaning 'entirely, quite,' an interpretation that makes a second speaker unnecessary.

126. *for menske of þi seluyn.* 'For the sake of, in the name of your own honor.'

127. *in thy manrede.* 'Dependent on thee'? (or perhaps 'among thy vassals, in thy court').

133. *þe semez. Seem,* like many ME verbs, is in a state of transition between the impersonal and the personal construction, hence the dative pronoun *þe* functioning as a nominative. See Introduction, *Verbs,* Mustanoja, pp. 112–13, 434–36, and lines 123, 139, 186, etc.

140. *said what þe lykes.* A variation on a formula that is common in this poem: verb + unemphatic word, such as a preposition + pronoun + the verb

lyke. The verb means not only 'is pleasing, is agreeable,' but also 'is fitting, is appropriate,' hence 'spoken what is proper for you to speak,' that is, 'spoken as ordered by your sovereign.' *Lyke* is used frequently in this work in this sense of 'suits, fits'; see, e.g., line 803 and Introduction, "Formulas and Rhetorical Style."

154–55. The punctuation of these lines is different from that of all the other editions of the poem, where there is a full stop and a closing quotation mark at the end of 154, attaching 155 to 156 as an introductory, modifying element. Apparently these lines have been a source of confusion to past editors, for none of them glosses the word (or words) *Forby* at the beginning of 155. Björkman, though he prints *For by,* appears not to have been satisfied with it, for in his notes to these lines he proposes emending *for* to *then,* apparently having in mind the reading 'Then, in accordance with (*MED bi* prep 8b [a]) the splendor of Rome . . . he commanded Sir Kay. . . .' However, if 155 is regarded as attached to 154 and line 156 considered the beginning of a new sentence, a more satisfactory reading results, without the need for emendation. *Forby* in this context means 'in comparison with' (*MED forbi* 3 [b]), and the line simply continues Arthur's statement on the humble manner of life in his lands.

156. *Cayous.* This knight has a prominent role in the *Morte Arthure,* as in many other Arthurian works, where he appears often with *Sir Bedevere.* Both knights have very ancient literary connections with Arthur, predating Geoffrey, the three appearing together in the *Life of St. Cadocus,* dated between 1067 and 1086 (Tatlock, pp. 185–86).

161. *waxe.* This word puzzled Björkman, who suggests the emendation *wastel* 'fine bread or cake' (*MA,* Notes, p. 132).

There is no reason, however, for not assuming that the poet is simply referring to candle wax. See also line 4019.

161. *weyn.* As Björkman points out (*MA,* Notes, p. 132), there is no need to emend to *wyne* (suggested by Holthausen, p. 236), as the scribe uses *ey* and *ei* for long *i* elsewhere in the MS: *weyffe,* 674, *weisely,* 1613.

164. *my wyrchip.* Arthur is referring to his honor in entertaining the visitors. He is emphasizing the grandeur of his kingdom by promising to confer riches on Sir Kay in the proper manner of a feudal lord, but in return not for winning a great battle or performing an heroic deed, but simply for entertaining the guests fittingly.

176–230. This passage, describing in enormous detail the great feast with which Arthur entertains the Roman ambassadors, is original with this poem (setting aside the question of an unknown source) and illustrates one of the poet's great talents—precise, concrete, and elaborate description. It also exemplifies the poet's ambiguous presentation of Arthur as both a splendid and gracious monarch and a person capable of becoming so carried away with his splendor and power that he surpasses all bounds (see Matthews, p. 22). A human touch is Arthur's mock modesty (222–26).

The syntax of this passage is loose, like that of the catalogue of Arthur's victories in lines 26–51. Verbs are scarce, and the passage consists for the most part of noun clauses, here describing the different types of food and drink that are being served, casually strung together—one might almost say piled on top of one another as food is piled on the table. Such long series of noun clauses are favorite descriptive devices of this poet, appearing also in the description of Arthur's arming before his fight with the giant (900–15) and, in

the form of appositives, in the speeches in praise of Arthur (289–91, 530–37) and Gawain (3875–85).

180. *frumentée.* 'A potage made of boiled, hulled grain mixed with milk or almond mild and sweetened' (*MED frumente*). The quotations in the *MED* indicate that frumenty usually accompanied venison.

184. *hedoyne.* Unknown; no suggestions or glosses given by any of the editors or commentators.

185. The verb is unexpressed in this line and in 187; in both lines a verb such as *were served, were brought,* or *appeared* is necessary for completion of the construction. For the non-expression of verbs in ME see Introduction, *Verbs,* and Mustanoja, p. 510).

189. *baterde,* 'hammered, embossed.' Banks ("Notes on the 'MA,'" p. 64) is incorrect in interpreting this as 'done up with batter or pastry.' See *OED batter* v[1] 1b.

199. MS: *endordide* (emend. *endoride,* 'glazed, covered' Björkman [*MA,* Notes, p. 132], from OF *endorer,* 'to glaze or gild').

214. *for brethe.* 'Because of (the poison's) vapor.' Precious stones were believed to be a protection against poison in the Middle Ages.

225. *enforce ʒow þe more.* 'Try all the harder' (since we know nothing more in our lands than this humble fare).

230. *That he.* 'Who.' A relative pronoun equivalent found occasionally in colloquial ModE as well as in ME and apparently a survival of the OE relative construction *þe* or *þæt* + personal pronoun.

231. *welthe.* 'pleasure.' See *OED wealth* 1.
  chambyre. Specifically, the presence chamber. See *OED chamber* sb 1b.

234. *Sir Owghtreth.* This person does not appear elsewhere in the poem. Branscheid (p. 227) suggests that the phrase *of Turry was lorde* means that someone named 'Turry' was Sir Uhtred's wife, a speculation that throws no light on the mystery of his identity. Branscheid also suggests the possibility of striking out the name altogether and replacing it with the name of one of Arthur's known knights. O'Loughlin (p. 159) offers the most plausible interpretation: he identifies *Turry* as 'Turin' and suggests that *Owghtreth* (*Uhtred*) is one of Lucius' ambassadors, who is assigned, out of courtesy, to escort the Queen, along with Gawain.

239. *Hym seluen* refers to the Senator, rather than King Arthur, here.

241. The object pronoun is unexpressed in this line, a common construction in ME and in this poem particularly. See Introduction, *Personal Pronouns,* Mustanoja, p. 144, and *Sir Gawain,* 1289).

245. *þe geauntes toure.* Geoffrey's *giganteam turrim,* at the entrance to the palace at Caerleon (ix.15), translated by Thorpe as 'gigantic tower.'

247–405. Though a council scene appears in the chronicles (Geoffrey ix.15–20), the *Morte Arthure* poet (or the author of his immediate source) has enlarged so considerably upon it that there is little resemblance to the original scene. To the speeches made by Arthur and three followers, Cador, Hoel, and Anguselus, are added the four speeches of the Welsh King, Ewain, Lancelot, and Lot, in which vows are made that are fulfilled later in the battle with Lucius (2051–94). The scene is an important one in Matthews' discussion of the sources of the *Morte Arthure,* for it parallels the pattern of feast, vows, and fulfillment of vows in the fourteenth-century verse romance of Jacques de Longuyon, *Les Voeux du Paon,* the

source also of the dream of fortune sequence and an interpolation in several of
the ME Alexandrian romances
(Chap. 2).

247. Sir Cador follows up his bellicose
speech in praise of war with a victory
over great odds (1601–1891), after
which, in spite of his triumph, he is rebuked by Arthur for his rashness.

250. An obscure line, perhaps with
traylede and *trett* as punning words. The
sense appears to be 'You will be dragged
(to Rome?), I swear, unless you negotiate (or bargain) better (than they).'

263–64. '(Though you may be head-
strong) I must call a truce (in my heart)
concerning these matters (and) talk
over these tidings that trouble my heart.'

277. MS: *Bremyn* (emend. *Brene*,
'Brennius,' Branscheid [p. 184] and
Banks [*MA*, Notes, p. 134], who suggest
that the scribe interpolated *yn* because
of its presence in the other two names
in this line). The scribe's habit of sub-
stituting *m* for *n* is illustrated by *Came*,
'Caen,' 2380. See note to line 1265.
Belinus and Brennius are brothers and
rulers of Britain, who appear in Geoffrey's Book III. Baldwin the Third is
unknown; perhaps he was invented for
the sake of the alliteration.

288–319. The chronicle works have
only these two speeches. The names
of the speakers are the same, though
reversed in order, but otherwise there
is little resemblance. The assertion in
the first speech that Arthur ought to be
overlord of all other kings may derive
from the reiteration in the first chronicle
speech of the Sybilline Prophecy that
three times someone born of British
blood would hold the Empire of Rome.
For the most part, the two speeches in
the chronicle version are much more
aggressive. It may be that the *Morte
Arthure* poet began in a low key in
order to build a dramatic crescendo of

bellicosity through all six speeches: the
speakers begin with legal arguments and
accounts of enemy atrocities and end
with vivid descriptions of the atrocities
they themselves intend to commit.

288. *Kyng Aungers.* King of Scotland
and brother of Lot, called *Auguselus*
by Geoffrey, *Angel* by Laȝamon, and
Angwysshaunce by Malory (see Ackerman, p. 20).

290. *Fore.* 'being.' See *OED for* prep
VI. This usage is represented in ModE
in such expressions as 'gave him up for
lost, left him for dead.'

292. *them.* There is no need to emend
the MS reading to *then,* as proposed by
Björkman (*MA*, Notes, p. 134). *Them*
is the dative here meaning 'of them,
from them.'

300–301. 'I shall furnish you for defense, fully trained, fifty thousand men
in the prime of life.'

301. Because the alliteration is faulty
in this line and the second half-line,
wythin two eldes, difficult to translate,
numerous emendations have been proposed. Branscheid (p. 228) suggests *Fifty
thowsande men, within two monethes*
(not much of an improvement on the
alliteration); Schumacher (p. 193) *Fifty
thowsande men, within four eldes,* without offering a meaning for the second
half-line; Björkman (*MA*, Notes,
p. 135) *Twenty thousand men, within
two eldes.* However, the alliteration fails
here according to the pattern noted by
O'Loughlin (see Introduction) and,
moreover, Banks (*MA*, Notes, p. 134)
has offered a reasonable translation of
the second half-line: 'within the right
limits of old age and youth.' The *OED*
gives the meaning of *eld* as 'age' and of
within elde as 'of age.' It is reasonable
to suppose that *within two eldes* means
'of age, but not over age.'

304. *the burelyche Beryn of Bretayne
þe Lyttyll.* King Hoel of Brittany.

320. *þe Walsche kyng.* Brock is incorrect in identifying this speaker as Arthur in his marginal paraphrase. He is identified later in the poem (2064) as *Sir Valyant* in the passage in which his fulfillment of this vow is described.

322. *wonndyrs.* For a remarkably similar use of this word [OE *wundor*], see the *Peterborough Chronicle,* entry for 1137 (describing the anarchy under King Stephen): "Þa the suikes [traitors] undergæton [perceived] ðat he milde man was and softe and god, and na justise ne dide, þa diden he [they] alle wundor."

328. *tuke of.* 'Laid hold of.' Björkman (*MA,* Notes, p. 135) is incorrect in interpreting this expression as 'killed.' It is illogical for a statement that the men have been killed to precede a statement that they are held for ransom. Perhaps Björkman believed that the villainy referred to here consisted in demanding ransom for someone who had already been killed, but it is clear from the passage that it consisted of attacking a party that was on a peaceful pilgrimage. This asyndetic construction, in which the same action is described in two or more variant, parallel expressions, unconnected by conjunctions, is typical of this poem: 'laid hold of our men / Seized them unjustly.'

348–56. Arthur's own vow is fulfilled in lines 3164–75. Noteworthy is the bellicose tone of the passage, contrasted with the calm, legalistic tone of the King's preceding speech: now that his men have begun to declare their commitment to war, after he has given them the legal justification for doing so, the King is shrewdly encouraging their aggressiveness by giving vent to his own.

369. 'I praise God for the love these lords have avowed.'

374. *hym selfen.* Lucius.

375. *Genyuers.* The notorious giants from Genoa in Lucius' army (mentioned also in 559, 843, 863, 2889, 2897, 2909) may derive from the Genoan mercenaries who fought with France against Edward III at Crécy and other important battles.

391. *renkkes.* Branscheid (p. 228) is right in correcting Brock's mistaken gloss of this word as 'men.' The word, from OF *renc,* is the same as ModE *rink* and means 'path, track, way' (see *OED rink*).

406. *I sette be no more.* 'I esteem, value nothing more.' See also line 994.

413. This line has a structure that is extremely unusual in the *Morte Arthure* —a strong caesura, marking an abrupt shift and linking the second half-line with the following line. This construction is so unusual that Brock has tried to deal with it by marking the break with a colon, a punctuation mark that he uses nowhere else in this position in the poem. Branscheid (p. 228) has attempted to regularize the construction by suggesting that the word *Till,* with which the line begins, means not 'until,' but 'after,' an interpretation not substantiated by the entries under *till* in the *OED.* It is likely that the poet has deliberately used this unusual construction for a dramatic effect, suggesting the abruptness of the Senator's interruption of the festivities.

450. *Watlyng Strette.* This name has been used for various old Roman roads and is most commonly attributed, according to Blair (pp. 28 [map], 255–256) to the route running from London to Chester, through Shrewsbury, very likely the route referred to here (see Map II).

450–66. Arthur's instructions to the envoys parallel very closely the legal procedure by which a criminal was instructed to pass into exile during the Middle Ages. Neilson (p. 43), in his discussion of this point, quotes from

he thirteenth century legal treatise of Henry de Bracton: "His [the criminal's] port of embarcation being chosen, there ought to be computed for him the reasonable days' journey to that port, and he ought to be forbidden to quit the king's highway, and he should tarry nowhere for two nights . . . but should ever hold on by the direct road to the port, so that he may be there by his given day. . . . If he do otherwise he shall be in peril." It is obvious therefore that Arthur is sending the envoys away like common criminals and that his entire speech, not merely the last four lines, is insulting.

451. MS: *nyghttes* (emend. *nyghes* 'sink down' [OE *hnīgan*] Banks ["Notes on the 'MA,' " p. 67]). The appearance of *nyghte* in the same line is very likely the source of the scribal error.

458–59. The subject pronoun is unexpressed: 'Let (it) be now annoyance or hindrance, whatever (it) seems to thee, for both thy life and thy limb depend upon it.' *It* refers to the *lycence,* or passage permit.

462. *aughtende.* The northern form of *eighth,* influenced by ON *attundi* (see *OED eightin*).

vndroun. This word had many designations in the fourteenth century, from nine AM to mid-afternoon. It is impossible to be sure what time is meant here.

466. *thyn one.* By analogy with the intensifying *selfe,* the original dative pronoun has been supplanted by the possessive (see Mustanoja, p. 294).

468–74. This speech resembles that made in lines 125–32, which may also have been made by the Senator (see note). Both show the speaker as fearful and a trifle obsequious, but nevertheless plucky enough to try to save himself by an appeal to law and to Arthur's concern for his reputation as a sovereign with a commitment to uphold the law.

471. *with sex sum.* Either 'part of a company of six' or 'along with a company of six.' (The expression survives in ModE in expressions such as *twosome, foursome.*) In either case the number given is inconsistent with that of line 81, where the Senator arrives with a company of sixteen.

483–500. This rapid summation of the Roman ambassadors' return journey contrasts markedly with the leisurely and elaborate descriptions in the poem, such as those of the feast and the council. Its rapid movement underlines the Romans' urgency, just as the leisurely movement of the description of the feast emphasizes its elaborateness and ceremoniousness. See Map II.

500. MS: *pris* (emend. *Pis* 'Pisa' Branscheid, p. 229, and Björkman, *MA,* Notes, p. 137). See *Pys,* 352, and *Pyse,* 3141. The letters *pr* appearing in the word *precious* in the same line may have caused the scribe to write *pris.*

515. MS: *no waye* (emend. *no wye* Brock, *MA,* p. 17, n., Mennicken, p. 50, and Björkman, *MA,* Notes, p. 138). No sense can be made of the line or of line 516, containing the relative pronoun *who,* which needs an antecedent, if *waye* is retained.

518. The MS *profre when þe likes* resembles the imperative exclamations, such as *saile when þe lykes* (381) that Arthur's men make in their council-scene speeches. This resemblance suggests a reading such as 'war when you wish' here. However, according to the *OED proffer* is a transitive verb only and cannot be used by itself to convey the full meaning 'do battle.' Since there is no object in the line, it must be assumed that the object is an unexpressed pronoun. Though Mustanoja does not mention any instances of an unexpressed reflexive pronoun, the OED gives one example of the use of *proffer* in the reflexive sense with an unexpressed

pronoun, with the meaning 'to project.' The verb is therefore apparently being used here with the same construction, but with its more common meaning, 'to present.' The meaning therefore is 'present (himself) whenever you wish.'

523. *neynesom of kynges.* See note to line 471. Line 545 indicates that the poet is using the -*sum* construction in the sense of 'along with a company of so many,' rather than 'one of a company of so many.'

550. *drawe no lytte langere.* Though the general sense of this expression is obvious, the literal translation is difficult. The verb *drawe* itself means 'protract' or 'delay' and does not need the addition of *lytte* 'delay' (*OED lite* n), to say nothing of the modifying *langere.* 'Protract no longer delay' seems to be the literal, but certainly redundant, translation (see Björkman, "Notes on the 'MA,' " pp. 36–37).

552. *and hym quarte stannde.* 'If (good) health remain with him.' See *OED quarte* a & sb¹ B.

556. This line, together with 1344, was used by Trautmann (p. 147) as evidence establishing a Scottish nationality for the *Morte Arthure* poet. Trautmann reasoned that an Englishman would not have made complimentary remarks about France during the period of the Hundred Years' War. However, it is even more unlikely that a Scottish poet would have used an expression such as *Scathyll* 'harmful, wicked' *Scotland* (32). If Matthews' theory of a French source is correct, it is likely that these phrases, like the numerous nonce words of French derivation, have been carried over from the French work.

570–616. The Romans in *Morte Arthure,* like those in the chronicles and popular romances of the period, though technically Christian (see the mention of the Pope at line 3180) are given a strong heathen coloration, reminiscent of both classical paganism and Islam. The Roman alliance against Arthur with the emperors of Islam and other barbaric potentates gives a crusade-like tone to Arthur's war (Tatlock, p. 493).

572. *Ambyganye and Orcage.* Unidentified countries subject to Lucius. Ackerman (p. 10) speculates that *Ambyganye* may be Amazonia. Malory (V.2) calls them *Ambage* and *Arrage.*

575. *Irritayne and Elamet.* Ackerman (pp. 79, 83), acknowledging O'Loughlin as his source (personal communication), tentatively identifies these as Hyrcania, near the Caspian Sea, and the lands of the Elamites, a Biblical people.

587. *Bayous.* Men of Bayous. See Finlayson, *"Morte Arthure:* The Date and a Source for the Contemporary References," *Speculum,* 42 (1967), p. 631.

588. *Pamphile.* A region of Asia Minor.

Preter (from *presbyter*) *Iohne* was a legendary medieval Christian prince and priest of fabulous wealth and power who ruled kingdoms in Africa and Asia (see *OED Prester John*).

592. *Garyere.* Ackerman (p. 100) states in a footnote that O'Loughlin has suggested that "the MS reading is Gaddrys and that the reference is to the town of Gadda." The MS reading is clearly *Garyere;* perhaps Ackerman meant to say that O'Loughlin has proposed an emendation to *Gaddrys. Garyere* has not been identified.

594. *þe Grekkes See.* The eastern Mediterrean.

623. *Coloine.* Incorrectly printed by Brock as *Colome.*

625. *the vtas of Hillary.* Literary, 'the octaves of Hillary,' *octaves* designating a festival day plus the seven days following it, the usual period of celebration of

a holiday. St. Hilary's feast day is January 13. The scene describing Arthur's preparation for war and those that follow it take place not after Lucius' preparation and invasion, as the text may suggest, but concurrently with them.

642. *ʒif auenture it schewe.* 'If fortune decree it.'

645. *me sybb.* 'Kin to me.'

658. *in þe seson whene grees es assignyde.* 'In the season when game is deemed fat (and fit to kill).'

662. *bathe.* The *MED* notes that *both* is often used in ME as a correlative conjunction for more than two items.

667. *mysese.* Holthausen (p. 236) suggests emending this word to *myselse* 'leprous'; however, as Banks points out ("Notes on the 'MA,' " p. 67)), *mysese* occurs frequently in *Piers Plowman* in the sense 'unfortunate.' Here the adjective is used as a noun.

678. Arthur, who has no legitimate children, is promising here to make Mordred his heir. His enigmatic statement in line 692 seems to refer to this promise.

683. The word *plytte* is from OF *ploit,* 'manner of being, trim, condition, state.' This word originally had neutral or good connotations. Its modern connotations (and its spelling) derive from a confusion between it and OE *pliht,* 'danger, risk.' Though he tries to refuse the office, Mordred could hardly have described his appointment as regent as a *plight,* in the modern sense.

692. See note to line 678.

708. *I may noghte wit of þis woo.* 'I can observe nothing of this woe,' that is, 'I cannot (stand to) witness this woe.'

734. MS: *hukes* (emend. *hekes,* 'horses,' Banks [*MA,* p. 175]). See line 2284.

737. *ventelde.* The *OED* cites *ventel* with only this quotation and the meaning 'to set sail.' Though this is the only example given, the gloss is reasonable since there was an OF *venteler* with this meaning. Emendation, suggested by several editors and commentators, is therefore unnecessary.

742. MS: *forestayne* (emend. *forestavne,* 'stem, prow,' Björkman *MA,* Notes, p. 742).

765. *oundyde.* From OF *ondé,* with the English past participial ending. Also used by Chaucer, who prefers the French form: "Hir heer, that oundy was and crips" (*HF,* 1386) (see *OED oundy*).

766. *schalyde.* The *OED,* on the basis of this line alone, derives a verb *shale* from the noun *shale* = *shell,* meaning 'encased, as in a shell.' It seems equally justifiable to derive a verb *shale* from the noun *shale* = *scale* (*OED shale* sb 3: 'A scale [of a fish, of metal, of a scaly disease, etc.']), meaning 'covered with scales.' Though it is true that the dragon is likened to a crustacean in line 767, the scaly covering that is traditionally associated with dragons is suggested by the *meruaylous maylys* of 769 and by the dragon's being referred to as a *worme* 'serpent' in 796 and 798. Banks, Brock, and Finlayson gloss the word as 'scaled,' but without explanatory notes; Björkman glosses 'umschlossen wie von einer Schale,' explaining that he is following the *OED*.

clene. There is no need to emend to an alliterating word such as *schire,* as suggested by Mennicken (p. 108), as the alliteration fails according to the pattern noted by O'Loughlin, and *clene* is used to modify *siluyr* in 201.

767. *schreede.* 'Shredded'; from the noun *shred,* 'a length or end of gold or silver thread or lace.'

schrympe. 'Crustacean' (*OED shrimp* 1 b).

This strange line describes a most decorative feature of the dragon's appearance: silver, which forms the scales of the shoulder area, is shredded into particles or flecks (*poyntez*), which are scattered over the rest of the animal's body, most thickly near the shoulder area and dwindling (*schrinkande*) in density (or size) toward the tail area.

768. Note the care with which the description proceeds: the belly and the wings are the parts that would be noticed as the dragon ascended.

769. *maylys*. The silver scales, likened to the individual metal rings or plates of which mail is composed.

769–770. Branscheid (p. 229) speculates that there is a line missing between these two which mentions the dragon's 'tattered tail.' Malory (v.4) reads 'and his wombe was lyke mayles of a merveylous hew, and his tayle was fulle of tatyrs, and his feete were florysshed as hit were fyne sable,' and the King's sages, in interpreting the dream, refer to the dragon's *tatterede taile* (821).

772. MS: *flayre*. Because *flare* in its ModE sense, 'a sudden outburst of flame' does not appear elsewhere until the nineteenth century, Banks (*MA*, Gloss., p. 169) and the *OED* and the *MED* understand this as 'odor, smell, stench' [OF *flair*]. However, in spite of lack of other recorded instances of the word, Björkman (*MA*, Notes, p. 142), on the basis of Malory's paraphrase *flame of fyre* (v.4) concludes that the word must mean 'a sudden outburst of flame' (*OED flare* sb), an interpretation substantiated by the general sense of lines 773–74, where the intensifying comparative structure *syche . . . that* is used: 'And such a deadly flame darted from his mouth / That the sea appeared all on fire (or one fire) from the sparks.' There is no way in which an odor or stench can cause fire and sparks.

778. *Lothen*. Björkman ("Notes on the 'MA,'" pp. 50–51) points out that *lothen* (which appears also in 1097, in the description of the giant) is wrongly connected by Brock and Banks with OE *lāð* and glossed as 'hateful, hideous, disgusting.' Björkman derives the word from ON *loðinn* 'hairy, shaggy, rough.' The *en* ending is difficult to account for if the word is considered as derived from *lāð*, as the regular ME forms are *lothly, lothsom*, and their variants.

793. *brayell*. Brock emends to *brathelle*, but corrects his emendation in a note (*MA*, p. xiv), restoring *brayell*, which he takes to mean 'the fur of the bear's belly.' Banks, Björkman, and Finlayson retain *brayell*, Björkman and Finlayson glossing it as 'waist, belly,' Banks leaving it unglossed. The *MED* defines the word as 'the belly or rump of an animal,' giving this line as the single example of its use in this sense and interpolating 'a bear's' in brackets after the word *his* in the quotation. However, it is certainly the dragon's body that is referred to here. Except for the meaning inferred from this line, all the citations having to do with animals under this word in both the *OED* and the *MED* relate to the bodies of hawks and falcons, animals to which the dragon is likened throughout the passage. Moreover, the *brode klokes* of the previous line must belong to the bear and, therefore, the animal's body that is bloodied by them must be the dragon's.

798. *hys heghttez*. Though neither the *OED* nor the *MED* mentions it, *heghttez* might be a technical term drawn from falconry, similar to *pitch*, which is also used with the possessive pronoun. The importance of the expression as a technical term comes from the fact that it is his pitch, that is, the height that a falcon is able to reach that determines, in part, the impetus of his plummet and thus of the bird's striking power.

802.   *o lyfe.* "[I]t is not necessary to emend to *of* as some suggest; *O* for *of* is quite common" (Banks, "Notes on the 'MA,' " p. 67). See lines 1139 and 3906 for the MS spelling *o*. The "some" to whom Banks refers is Holthausen (p. 236).

804.   MS: *bryng* (emend. *þryng* 'press' Holthausen, p. 275). To speak of someone's bringing the King into the ship at this point makes no sense. If the pronoun subject of this verb, *they,* is understood as referring to the two beasts, or the King's visions of them, to say that they have pressed him, or tormented him, is consistent with the King's assertions in lines 810 to 814 that he has been tormented by these visions. Moreover, the connection of lines 804 and 805 by the word *þat* 'so that' demands that 804 describe an action that causes the King to nearly burst with anguish, a demand hardly satisfied by the word *bryng.*

806.   *wery foretrauaillede.* Though it is possible that these are coordinate adjectives, it is more likely that *wery* is used in the quasi-adverbial sense here (*OED weary* 7c), meaning 'grievously, most, very' or 'wearily.'

811.   The beginning of the quotation is abrupt, and Björkman (*MA,* Notes, p. 143) suggests the addition of *I was* at the beginning of the line. However, it may be that the poet is aiming at an abrupt, incoherent effect, reflecting Arthur's disturbed state of mind.

815–17.   The strange ambiguity of these lines reflects, according to Matthews (p. 113), the poet's view of Arthur as both courageous conqueror and cruel warlord, whose fate is to bring devastation upon his own knights.

821.   This is the line that corresponds to the one supposedly left out of Arthur's own account of his dream. See note to lines 769–70.

MS: *tathesesede* (emend. *tatterede* 'tattered, many-tongued' Branscheid, p. 229, 233). Branscheid, Brock, and Björkman have misread this word as *tachesesede,* due to the resemblance of *th* and *ch* in this MS (see *Glasthenbery,* line 4303). Branscheid proposes that *tachesesede* is a misspelling of *tacherede,* in turn a corruption of *tatterede.* This explanation appears far-fetched, but it is made more convincing by Malory's use of *totattered* here and *tatyrs* in the place corresponding to the supposedly omitted line between 769 and 770 (v. 4) and by Björkman's partial accounting for the corruption process by comparing this word with similar examples elsewhere in the MS (*MA,* Notes, p. 143). Björkman cites line 4303, which has (according to Björkman's reading) *Glaschenbery,* for *Glastonbury,* in which the *t* has been transformed into a *th* (as in *comforth,* 830) and then written, by mistake, as *ch* (actually *th*). The fact that dittography is common in this MS accounts for the extra syllable. (No detailed explanation is given by Björkman or Branscheid on the use of *s* for *r.*)

824–828.   The ambiguous significance of Arthur's dream is a part of the legend that antedates Geoffrey. See Elaine C. Southward, "Arthur's Dream," *Speculum,* 18 (1943), 249–51.

825–26.   *Or ells with somme gyaunt some journée sall happyn / In syngulere batell by ȝoure selfe one.* Literally, 'Or else that against a certain giant a certain battle must come to pass of single-handed combat by you, all alone.' It is certain that *In syngulere batell* modifies *journée* (which must be translated as 'battle' or 'day of battle' rather than simply 'day,' because of the phrase *with somme gyaunt*), but the expression 'a battle of, in, by, or with single-handed combat,' though it makes sense, is clumsy in ModE (see Mustanoja, p. 388 for an account of the versatility of the prepo-

sition *in* in adjectival expressions in ME).

869. *wele had me chefede.* Literally, 'well had it befallen me.' As Björkman notes ("Notes on the 'MA,'" p. 38), Banks is incorrect in glossing this as 'attained to.' See *OED cheve* 4b.

881. *filsnez,* 'lurks.' Apparently because the MS reading is a nonce word, Mennicken (p. 141) proposes emending it to *filles* (as in 1038) or *felles* [OE *fēōlan* 'betake oneself']. However, as Banks has noted ("Notes on the 'MA,'" p. 65), the *OED* has accounted for the word by deriving it from ON *fylgsni* 'hiding place,' and there is no need for emendation.

890. Arthur's dramatic emotional reaction to the sufferings of his people was apparently a desirable characteristic of the great and heroic leader. Later, he actually faints and weeps on the battlefield on learning of the death of some of his dearest warriors (3949–74). Gawain also weeps for his men in 3790–91. The warriors in the *Chanson de Roland* also weep and swoon and agonize uninhibitedly.

890 ff. Apparently, Arthur does not wish to tell his men that he is going on such a dangerous mission alone, hence his pretense at going on a pilgrimage. However, the word play and the ironic allusions to the "pilgrimage" and the seeking out of the "saint" on the mountain are carried through the passage by Arthur and his men, with varied effects ranging from the tragically ironic (1068, Arthur's reference to the giant's having served God well by making so many martyrs) to the comic (1163, Bedevere's teasing reference to the strange type of saint which Arthur seeks out). See note to line 1171.

891. *whatt he menede,* 'how he suffered.' Brock has glossed *menede* incorrectly as 'meant.' For *what* in the sense

of 'how, to what extent, in what way,' see *OED what* adv II 4.

892–93. In the chronicles it is Bedevere who is the cup-bearer; Kay is seneschal. Their offices in this poem may have been assigned to them purely for the sake of the alliteration.

899. Legends and miracles have clustered around Mont-Saint-Michel since ancient times, and a local tale of a giant's abduction of a lady named Helène is the ultimate source of this episode; an island near the Mount called Tombelène is the legendary site of the lady's tomb (Banks, *MA,* Notes, p. 138).

The geography of the area in which the giant-killing episode takes place is unclear. Line 840 suggests that Arthur and his army set up camp near Barfleur. However, lines 880–81 indicate that the giant's dwelling place can be seen from the camp—an impossibility if the camp is at Barfleur. The camp might be set up nearer to Mont-Saint-Michel, though the journey taken by Arthur, Kay, and Bedevere toward the giant's dwelling place, which seems substantial and which involves travel along a river (the Vire?), suggests that the camp is a fair distance away.

900–15. This passage may be compared with the arming of Gawain (*Sir Gawain,* 566–618). Both passages are lavish in their descriptions of the richness and splendor of the costume and the battle gear. Though it is difficult to ascertain exactly the nature of all the garments, Arthur, like Gawain, wears two garments under his hauberk and one over, all of them precious. The helmets of both warriors have clasps, visors, and coronals and are decorated with gems and gold.

902. *acton.* This first garment that Arthur dons is, like Gawain's *dublet,* a kind of tight-fitting, jacket-like piece of clothing, made to support the hauberk

(see *OED acton*). Where Arthur's garment is richly embroidered, Gawain's is made of precious Silk from Turkey (*dere Tars*).

903. *jeryn* [OF *giron* 'tunic']. Apparently a looser and lighter garment than the *acton*. Gawain's second garment is a *capados*, a garment lined with fur.

of Acres. The poet is seeking to emphasize the precious quality of the objects described by having them come from far-away and exotic places, in this case a city in Palestine. He may also be trying to impart a religious tone to his description, as Acre was the site of a famous battle during the Crusades, in 1189.

905. *jupon.* At first, like the *giron*, padded and worn under the armor, later evolving into a sleeveless surcoat or tabard worn outside the armor, frequently still quilted and often emblazoned with the coat of arms of the wearer. The jupon or surcoat of the Black Prince is a short-sheeved, quilted jacket, lavishly embroidered with fleurs-de-lys and rampant lions.

schredez. See *OED shred* sb 4 and line 767 and note.

Ierodyn. Unknown. Very likely a place; see *Acres,* line 903.

906. *bacenett.* The visored basinet is a common type of late fourteenth-century helmet.

913. *gobelets.* Apparently an ornamental representation of a goblet (Björkman, *MA,* Gloss. p. 213).

920–32. This is the first of four such nature descriptions, none of which is found in the chronicle versions of the story. The author makes skillful use of the description by contrasting the beauty of the landscape and the happiness and exuberance of the animals and birds with Arthur's sorrow at the sad fate of his people. For a detailed examination of all four passages see Finlayson, "Rhetorical 'Descriptio' of Place."

921. *ryndez.* Björkman ("Notes on the 'MA,' " pp. 51–52) argues against the *OED*'s definition of *ryndez* as 'banks or brakes' [Norw. *rind* 'bank, ridge'], maintaining that "a bank or brake can have no 'royal boughs' " and that the word can be explained as the poetical extension of the word for bark to refer to the entire tree. However, it is as plausible for a poet to speak figuratively of the banks of a river having boughs which overhang the water as it is for him to use the word for bark to refer to an entire tree.

931–32. 'So that, what with the sighing of water and singing of birds, it might cure that person of distress who had never (before) been sound.' See *OED what* pron D II 2.

935 ff. In the chronicles, it is Bedevere who ventures first into the giant's territory, meets and converses with the old woman, and learns of the whereabouts of the giant as well as further details of his atrocities. The poet's having Arthur undertake this part of the adventure himself not only enhances Arthur's heroism but also allows the highlighting of some of Arthur's personal traits—his gentleness with the old woman, his ironic humor, and his compassion.

938. *mell.* The word means both 'to negotiate, deal, treat' and 'to mingle in combat' (*OED mell* v 6, 8), and Arthur is surely using it with this double meaning, speaking overtly of conversing or negotiating, but referring indirectly to his secret intention to do battle with the giant.

It is not clear whether Arthur is referring openly to the giant in the expression 'the overlord who governs this mount' or whether he is pretending to refer to St. Michael. Lines 896–99 and 937 suggest that he is keeping secret from his men the fact that he intends to confront the giant. However, lines 878–79, 938, and 989–92 suggest that the pretense that he is making (to both his

men and the old woman) is that he is going to bargain with the giant and make some sort of treaty with him in order to relieve the people's suffering.

964.   As this line sugggests *Wade* was apparently a hero well known to readers of romance in the Middle Ages. Chaucer alludes to him twice (*MT*, 1424, *Tr*, iii, 614), and he appears in the OE *Widsith*, 22. According to Speght (1598 ed. of Chaucer), he had a boat named *Guingelot*, which may have something to do with his connection with Gawain here, as Gawain's horse is named *Gringolet* in *Sir Gawain*. See Robinson's detailed note, *MT*, 1424.

998 ff.   The detail of the giant's kirtle being bordered with the beards of kings is taken from the short account that Arthur gives in the chronicles of his slaying of the giant Ritho (Geoffrey x.3). The *Morte Arthure* poet has combined the two giants.

1010.   *hurdez,* 'lies hidden.' See *OED hoard* v 3. The *OED* is incorrect in citing this line under *herd* v[1] 2: 'to join oneself to any band or company.'

1033.   *the bettyr me lykez.* The full meaning is 'After hearing this story, I see that it is so much the better that I have brought the beard.'

1040.   'For he will have the scent (of you) six miles off.'

1041.   MS: *sowre.* Several emendations have been proposed: Banks *sowþe* (*MA*, Gloss., p. 191), Björkman *sowþre,* glossed as 'side' (*MA*, Notes, p. 145), Brock *sowrs* 'source' (*MA*, Gloss, p. 196). Banks' emendation is the least complicated, and it is consistent with the old woman's suggestion in line 1039.

1045.   *lugand.* Finlayson's proposed emendation to *lukande* (*MA*, Notes, p. 49) is unnecessary, since 'repose' [ModE *lodge*] fits the context very well here.

1047.   *bewschers.* A nonce word of uncertain etymology. Björkman ("Etymological Notes," pp. 501–02) speculates that it is derived from OE *bōȝ* 'limb' (with OE *oȝ* spelled *ew* as elsewhere in the MS: *ynewe,* 1360) and OE *scearu* 'groin,' with the meaning 'buttocks.'

1079.   MS: *fome* (emend. *come,* 'came, stood out,' Björkman, *MA*, p. 32).

1083.   *hole eyghn.* There is no need to emend to *eyghn holes,* as do Björkman and Finlayson, if *hole* is understood as 'hollow' [OE *holh*] rather than 'hole, socket.'

1090.   *brothy.* Holthausen (p. 251) suggests an emendation to *brostly* 'bristly'; Banks (*MA*, Gloss., p. 160) glosses it as 'rough,' without an explanation; Björkman ("Notes on the 'MA,'" p. 38) tries to derive it from OSw *brāþ* 'meat,' with the full meaning 'full of rags of flesh'; Brock and Finlayson gloss it as 'frothy, foamy.' However, the meaning of *brothy* is simply 'of the nature of broth' (*OED*), not quite the same thing as 'frothy' or 'foamy,' and there is no reason why this meaning should not be presumed to apply here: the giant's beard is covered or saturated with the soup that he has been eating.

1091.   *corkes,* 'carcass.' The use of *o* for *a* is found also in *cobles* 'cables' (742).

1092–93.   Obscure. Perhaps 'And all tangled together was the flesh (of his victims?) in his vile mouth, (so that) each fold (of flesh), like an outlaw, writhed out individually' (see OED *wolf's head* 2); or 'as in a wolf's head, each fold (of flesh) writhed out individually.'

1112.   *fromonde.* Literally 'stranger, alien, barbarian'; derivation by Björkman ("Notes on the 'MA,'" p. 39) on the basis of present-day Norw. dial. *framand* 'strange,' Icel. *framandi* 'strange.'

1122. *inmette.* Misread by Brock, who prints *jumette* (unknown) but corrects himself in his glossary.

1148. *anlace.* According to Finlayson, this weapon symbolizes 'trust in God when all arms have failed' (*MA,* Notes, p. 52). (Arthur uses his sword in the chronicle versions [Geoffrey x.3]). That Divine Providence is given credit for Arthur's victory is shown by lines 1117, 1136–39, 1209–11 (but see line 1177, where Arthur refers to his fortunes).

1162–65. These first four lines of Bedevere's speech, in which reference is facetiously made to Arthur's "saint," are obscure, very likely because of the word-play. Malory may have had trouble understanding these lines, as he omits them, though he picks up the speech again at line 1166 and renders it in the same spirit as the original (v.5). Finlayson (*MA,* note, p. 53) is incorrect in translating *grypes* as 'is gripped by'; the sense is simply 'gets' (1163).

1163. ?'He will seek out saints but seldom, the more dearly he gets them' or 'He seeks out saints but seldom the more grievously he grips them.'

1171. *soghte.* In this passage there is a great deal of word play on *seke, soghte* (as earlier on *mell;* see note to line 938). As well as 'visit, approach, go to a person to approach him for help,' a meaning appropriately used with *seynt* (see *General Prologue,* 17, and line 502, in which the Romans *sekes þe Seyntez of Rome*), the word also has the meaning 'get, attack' (*OED seek* v 5, 6). Arthur and his men are undoubtedly using the word with both meanings. Whether *seynt* also has a double meaning is unknown.

1173. Here Arthur seems to be punning on *sergeaunt,* which means a servant of either God or Satan.

1175. *Araby.* Not a reference to Arabia, but to a mountain in Wales vari-ously called *Arabe, Araby, Aravia, Ravin,* and *Erith,* identified with Mount Snowdon and traditionally regarded as the place where Arthur slays the giant Ritho. In the chronicles it is Ritho who has the kirtle decorated with the beards of kings (Geoffrey, x.3). Since the *Morte Arthure* poet has transferred this and other details to the giant of St. Michael's Mount, he makes only a pass-ing allusion to the other giant.

1176–77. It is not clear which of the two giants Arthur is referring to here. Perhaps, as in Geoffrey (x.3), the im-plication is that the giant of Mount Arabe was the strongest he had ever en-countered until he fought the giant of St. Michael's Mount.

þat had I nere funden. 'That I had faced at close quarters.'

1180. *Sir Howell.* King of Britanny and father of the duchess who has been murdered by the giant; perhaps he is also the noble of Britanny who makes his vow at the council in 304–19, called Hoel in Geoffrey. The 'cruel bondage' is, of course, the oppression of Britanny by the giant.

1195–96. 'And go off with the con-queror to show to the kings / That which the King had in secret kept hid-den to himself.' The reference is to Arthur's having concealed his real mis-sion under the pretense of 'visiting a saint.'

1197. The hint of a nature description in this line serves to mark the end of the adventure. Gawain's solitary adven-ture (2501–2678) is framed by two nature descriptions.

1198. *to courte.* It is not clear just where "court" is at this point, perhaps Barfleur.

1225. *Castell Blanke.* This unknown locality seems to be original with the *Morte Arthure* poet. The chronicle ver-sions have variants of Geoffrey's *Au-*

gustodunum (x.4), modern Autun. Branscheid (p. 223) suggests that the name *Augustodunum* was the source of *Castell,* without a clear explanation, and that the *Albam fluvium* mentioned a few lines later in Geoffrey (modern *Aube*) was the source of *Blanke.*

1228. MS: *Foundez with his faire folke ouer as hym lykez.* The alliteration fails according to the pattern noted by O'Loughlin, and the suggested emendations (Mennicken [p. 138], *as hym faire thynkez;* Björkman ["Notes on the 'MA,' " p. 40] *fare* or *ferk ouer as hym lykez*) are unnecessary. Further, the assertion that a verb is needed here is incorrect. Björkman apparently understood *Foundez* as 'tries' (*OED found* v[1] 3); however, though it is often used with this meaning in ME along with the infinitive of another verb, the word can as well be an intransitive verb meaning simply 'go, proceed' (*OED found* v[1] 1), making another verb unnecessary.

1229. *strekez.* See *OED streek* v 7; the northern form of *strech* [OE *streccan,* ModE *stretch*]. This instance is the only record in the *OED* of the word's being used for the action of pitching a tent.

1230. In the chronicles, this river is the Aube (Geoffrey, x.4) (see note to line 1225).

1248. MS: *fraisez,* unknown (emend. *fraiez,* Brock, *MA,* Gloss., pp. 160–61). Brock's gloss of 'frighten' is imprecise. For the meaning 'attack, assail,' see *MED fraien* v (1) 1 (a).

1252. *his dragouns.* Not emblems on a banner, but bannerlike objects themselves. Though the heraldic device of a dragon was often used on banners, helmets, and other objects (Arthur and Lucius both use the dragon emblem), the banner also often took the actual form of a dragon, resulting in the word's being used in a manner parallel to *banner* or *flag:* "Baneres, penouns, pensellis, dragunnes in whiche ben depaynted dyuers armes of diuers schappe and diuers coloures" (Vegetius [1] 57 b; quoted in *MED dragoun* n 2 [b]). Tatlock describes the object thus: "From . . . historical precedents as well as Geoffrey's words it is entirely clear how he pictured his dragon-ensign, as a gold head fixed to a staff and a hollow body of fabric to swell out and struggle in the wind" (p. 330). A similar object is shown in the French miniature reproduced on the paperback cover of Thorpe's translation of Geoffrey.

1265. MS: *Gryme* (emend. *Geryn* Björkman, *MA,* Notes, p. 148). The name *Gerin* (*Geryn, Guerinus*) appears at this point in the chronicles (Geoffrey, x. 4), as well as in the *Morte Arthure* itself at line 3708; here and there in the MS, *m* appears for *n*.

1281. *þat with. Þat* is syntactically superfluous and must be deleted. As suggested by Mennicken (pp. 83, 141), the scribe may have picked up this word from the next line, where it appears in the same position.

1283. *eyues.* Incorrectly printed by Brock throughout as *eynes* and glossed as 'narrow passages, passes [OE *eng*].' The word, not a plural, is actually the ancestor of ModE *eaves* [OE *efes*] and is frequently used in ME for the edge or border of a wood (see *Sir Gawain,* 1178). The combination *ey* or *ei* is used for *e* frequently in this MS: *theis,* 104; *seyn,* 3985.

1286. *hornez of olyfantez.* Branscheid (p. 229) has rightly corrected Brock's apparent assumption (*MA,* Notes, p. xv) that this expression implies a naive belief on the poet's part that elephants have horns like cattle. Most of Branscheid's note consists of the argument that *Oliphant,* the name of Roland's horn, came to be synonymous with the word *horn* in its general sense, an interpretation that suggests the reading

'sounds of horns' or 'trumpetings of horns' (see *MED horn* n 5 b for this meaning of *hornez*). However, two more colorful readings are possible. If *hornez* is understood as "trumpetings,' *olyfantez* can be read as 'elephants,' giving the reading 'trumpetings' or 'buglings of elephants.' Alternatively, if *hornez* is understood as 'horns,' *olyfantez* can be understood as 'ivory' (*OED elephant* 4 a [the *ez* accounted for as a remnant of the Latin nominative *elephantus*]), giving the reading 'bugles' or 'trumpets of ivory,' with the quotations in the *OED* verifying the existence of such instruments. All three readings are equally plausible.

1287. *palaisez,* 'palisades.' Though all the editors gloss this word as 'palaces,' it is difficult to see how this meaning is appropriate here. The passage describes an encampment, and the Romans are housed in pavilions. For the meaning 'palisades,' see *OED palis* sb 1.

1301. *Reght as þey hade weschen.* The pronoun reference is uncertain, making it unclear whether Gawain speaks after he and his party have joined the Emperor's feast or whether he simply bursts in upon the Emperor and his companions after *they* have washed their hands in preparation for the feast.

1330. Branscheid correctly points out (p. 229) that Lucius' speech reads more smoothly if this line is removed from its position and inserted after line 1334. However, it may be that the poet is intentionally breaking the continuity of the speech to emphasize Lucius' anger.

1341. *pechelyne,* 'haycock.' O'Loughlin (p. 161) offers this plausible gloss of the MS *pechelyne,* a word that has taxed the ingenuity of several commentators. See *EDD pike* sb[1] and v[1] 14, note on *pikelins* for the meaning 'haycock.' Other speculations are summarized by Björkman ("Notes on the 'MA,' " p. 41): Banks, 'spot, stain'; Skeat, 'fish-

ing line'; Björkman, 'peachlet,' as in 'not a fig.' Another possibility is 'crumpet' (*EDD pikelin* sb); however, the image of Lucius leveling everything on the landscape from castles to haycocks is the most appealing.

1343. *alfyn,* 'oaf, clumsy person.' The former name of the chess piece now called the Bishop, which had the form of an elephant in eastern countries (*MED alfyn*). The use of the word in this disparaging sense derives from the formerly awkward and limited moves of the piece.

1346–47. *Sir Gayous.* Because the full name *Gaius Quintilianus,* as far as is known, is given only in Geoffrey (with only *Quintilianus* or its variants in the other chronicles), Branscheid (p. 193) concludes that Geoffrey must have been a direct source for the *Morte Arthure.* Björkman, however, thinks that the spelling of the name suggests a French source.

Gayous is the Emperor's *nephew* in Geoffrey and the other chronicles. Only here is he the Emperor's *eme* 'uncle,' perhaps simply for purposes of alliteration.

1366. *in fewtyre he castes.* The *fewter* is a felt-lined socket for a lance or spear attached to the saddle, designed to absorb some of the shock of the weapon's impact. The expression 'to cast in fewter' (with or without 'lance' or 'spear' as the object of the verb) means to place a weapon in its attack position. See *OED fewter* sb; *MED feuter* n.

1382. *Sir Feltemour.* The source of this name is unknown. Laȝamon, Wace, and Robert of Gloucester call this man *Marcell,* Geoffrey (x.4), *Marcellus Mutius.* Branscheid (p. 193) suggests that *Feltemour* is a corruption of *Marcellus Mutius,* but it is difficult to see how this can be so. Geoffrey's name is acually more similar to the name *Marschalle de Mowne* in line 1397. Since the

death of *Sir Marschalle* is not mentioned in the description of the skirmish, it is tempting to suppose that he and the man in 1382 are the same and that the name *Sir Feltemour* is a mistake. Adding to the confusion is the assertion that *Sir Marschalle* has been laid low *for his grett japez,* suggesting an identification with *Sir Gayous.*

1397. See note to line 1382. There is no need to emend the MS *monte* to *molde* as suggested by Mennicken (p. 116) and printed by Björkman; the formula with *monte* is used in 2207.

1402. MS: *fillez.* The only example in the *MED* of the intransitive use of the verb *fill* in the sense 'becomes filled' (*MED fillen* v 1 [c]). The earliest example cited in the *OED* is from Shakespeare.

1408. *Bedwyne.* Not mentioned elsewhere in the *Morte Arthure* or in the chronicles. Branscheid (p. 235) suggests that this name may have been miswritten for *Baldwin,* a name appearing in lines 1606 and 2384.

1419. *Senatour Petyr.* Geoffrey's *Petreius Cocta,* who plays a comparable role in the skirmish at Autun (x.4).

1422. *sett . . . on.* This use of *set on* in the sense of 'attack' is earlier than any of the examples in the *OED,* which has only the concrete sense 'place on' and the intransitive use in the sense 'go forward' as early as this poem.

1427. MS: *redyes þan.* There is no alternative but to accept O'Loughlin's emendation to *redyes þam* (p. 161), as *ready* is never used intransitively (*OED*).

1436. *stokes.* The emendation to *strokes* suggested by Brock (*MA,* p. 43) is unnecessary. See *OED stoke* sb².

1437. *theire soueraygne.* Sir Boice.

1442. 'If their friends were far off, who were fighting in the field.' The sense of Idrus' inquiry seems to be 'Where is the battle?' Gawain confesses that the Britons have been temporarily routed, then proceeds to rally his men for another assault on the Romans.

1448. 'If we so miserably serve him (Arthur) who favored him (Boice) so well.'

1460. *lorayne,* 'trappings.' See *OED lorain* sb. Arthur and his men do not invade Lorraine until 2416 ff. Finlayson is incorrect in printing *Lorayne.*

1461–62. 'Then were those run through with whetted weapons / Horridly gaping, with grieving looks.'

1494. MS: *faste.* Because the word *faste* appears also in 1495, O'Loughlin (p. 161) proposes emending to *firste.* Björkman deletes *faste* in this line; Banks, Brock, and Finlayson retain the original reading, kept also here.

1503. *Fore gyftez þat þow gyffe may þou ʒeme now þe selfen.* O'Loughlin (p. 161) correctly calls attention to the fact that, if a comma is used in this line, it should fall after *gyffe,* not after *may.* Banks and Brock print a comma after *may,* Finlayson a caesural space. Only Björkman prints the line correctly.

It is difficult to understand the reason for the proposals of Branscheid (p. 230) and O'Loughlin (p. 162) to emend *now* to *not* (printed by Björkman and Finlayson). Sir Idrus is clearly inviting the Senator to surrender himself to be ransomed. That he threatens the Senator in 1510–14 with the possibility that Arthur may choose to kill him instead of exchanging him for ransom does not contradict the sense of lines 1502–05, which is 'There is no way to save yourself but by surrendering your person for ransom, for if you try to escape I shall kill you here and now.'

1509. The relative pronoun is unexpressed in this line.

1529. *Radly relayes and restez theire horsez.* Though the *OED* does not re-

cord *relay* used as a verb in the sense 'exchange horses' until the nineteenth century, this meaning appears inevitable here. The word is recorded as a noun with the meaning 'fresh horses' in the early fifteenth century (*OED relay* sb 1).

1534. *foremaglede.* The *EDD* cites *maggled* as an obsolete Scottish variant of *mangled.* The word is of French origin, with an Anglo-Saxon intensive prefix.

1558. Because *Ewayne fytz Henry* is mentioned nowhere else in the poem, Branscheid (p. 184) suggests emendation to *Ewayne fytz Vrien,* a name that appears in 337 and 2066.

1559–88. Arthur's speech, in which he again ascribes victory to God, generously rewards the messenger, debates the propriety of a king's accepting ransom, and announces plans to exile his prisoners, contrasts with his attitude near the end of the great battle with Lucius, when he instructs his men to spare no one for ransom (2262–64).

1592. A reference to the Emperor's answer in 1326–41. Gawain and his party were originally sent out as messengers, but, with the battle and its subsequent events intervening, only now come around to delivering the Emperor's answer to Arthur's message.

1612. The *payne* and the *perell* refer to the magistrate's responsibility for the prisoners.

1634. The pronoun *his* refers to Sir Cador, the leader of the party.

1689–91. The King of Syria is insulting Sir Clegis by pretending not to recognize his coat of arms. Sir Clegis responds (1692–99) by tracing his ancestry and his heraldic charge back to the days of Brutus, the legendary grandson of Aeneas and founder of Britain.

1776. 'And awaits the burial that best befits him.'

1786. *corne-bote,* 'requital.' See Banks, "Notes on the 'MA,' " p. 65. The expression comes from the exacting of payment for corn when the price is highest; the sense is 'something which one pays dearly for.'

1788. 'May the wind shift so to my advantage, that I requite him before nightfall.'

1797. MS: *his in.* Brock's proposed transposition of these two words must be accepted (*MA,* Notes, p. xv).

1807. *honnde.* See *MED hōnd*(*e* n 4 (c). Björkman's reading *hounde* is an error.

1838. 'That you killed my kinsman, my grief is the less (now that I have killed you).'

1842–43. 'Hold on to what you have received; it harms us but little / For scorn returns to its source, use it who will.'

1883. *þe duke.* Sir Berill.

1904. MS: *Sir Vtere.* Since *Sir Vtolfe* and *Sir Ewandyre* appear together twice elsewhere (1622, 1868), it is reasonable to emend *Vtere* to *Vtolfe. Vtere,* Arthur's father, is mentioned early in the poem (29, 521, 1310) and again at the end (4216). No other person of that name appears in the work. See Branscheid, p. 230.

1908. MS: *Barous* (emend. *Carous* Branscheid, pp. 230, 235). The hard *c* is needed for the alliteration, which rarely fails in the first half-line, and the name *Quintus Carusius* appears in this episode in Geoffrey (x.5).

1911. MS: *and Sarazenes.* The second half-line is obviously incomplete, having only one main stress. Mennicken's proposed emendation *and Sarazenes ynowe* (pp. 36, 55) is reasonable, as this formula appears many times in the poem.

1922–27. Arthur's rebuke to Cador for fighting when greatly outnumbered

contrasts with his own rashness later in approaching too close to the walls of Metz, when he himself is rebuked by Sir Ferrar (2428–47).

1964. MS: *Sexon; Sessoyne* at line 1977. This locality has been the source of confusion. Because Geoffrey's battle (x.6) takes place near Autun, in a locality named *Siesia* (which Tatlock pinpoints as *Saussy,* "an obscure place thirty-five miles southwest of Langres . . . on the way to Autun" [p. 103]), it has been assumed that this battle must also take place near Autun (identified with *Awguste,* 1967, and perhaps with *Castell Blanke,* through *Augustodunum* [see line 1225 and note]). However, there is no definite statement in the *Morte Arthure* that either Lucius or Arthur has moved out of northern France at this point. In 1223–25 it is stated only that Arthur moves from Barfleur *Towarde Castell Blanke* and that he makes camp in an unnamed locality near chalk cliffs. Even if Castell Blanke were to be identified with Autun, there is no indication that Arthur has done more than set out for the place. Lucius' camp is near Arthur's camp (1259–60) and is the locale where the skirmish involving Gawain and the messengers takes place. The second skirmish occurs somewhere on the route between the first unnamed locality and Paris, to which Arthur's men are supposed to convey their prisoners. Again the locale is vague: Arthur's men are said to have set out toward Chartres (1619) and Lucius' men toward Troyes (1629). Arthur takes no part in these two initial skirmishes, and nowhere is it actually stated that he has moved from the place in northern France where he originally made camp. After the second skirmish, Lucius announces plans to march into either *Sexon* (1964) or *Awguste* (1967). Arthur, learning of these plans, breaks up his camp and marches into *Sessoyne,* ambushing Lucius. Nowhere is it stated that either has reached *Awguste* (Autun). Since it is possible that both are still in northern France, it is reasonable to identify Soissons, a town northeast of Paris, as *Sessoyne,* the locality of the great battle. After the battle (which the poet, incidentally, inaccurately places at Cotentin [2373] in a confused passage containing a number of other errors) Arthur finally moves east, to Luxemburg (2388), Lorraine and Metz (2398, 2417), and from there down toward Italy. There is difficulty with the geography, to be sure, but there is no reason to compound the confusion by assuming that a place near Autun must be the locale of the great battle simply because it is so in Geoffrey. [Note: In a recent paper, William Matthews rejects Soissons and identifies *Sessoyne* (Geoffrey's *Siesia*) as Val-Suzon, a town "37 miles southwest of Langres on the direct line to Autun" ("Where Was Siesia-Sessoyne?" *Speculum,* 49 [1974], 680–86)].

1975. MS: *felschen.* No satisfactory explanation of this word has been given. Brock glosses 'renovate,' Banks 'make good,' neither of which fits the sense of the line. Björkman (*MA,* Notes, p. 154) suggests emendation to *flaschen* 'to give out flame or sparks.' The *MED* cites only this line under *felschen,* calling it a scribal error. However, the *MED* lists another verb, *flashen,* which has the meaning 'to sprinkle or splash (water on something),' a meaning that fits very well in this line. The transposition of the *l* can be accounted for by metathesis, and the use of *e* for *a* is a fairly common practice in this MS: see *keste* for *kaste* (118, 280).

1981–2005. Arthur's disposal of his army for the battle with Lucius parallels Edward III's disposal of his troops at Crécy (Matthews, pp. 185–86; Neilson, pp. 59–60). Similarities are the three battalions, the archers in two divisions, one on each side of the men-at-arms,

and the dismounted knights and footmen in the front lines.

2001.   ȝif þe myste happynne. 'If the need arise.'

2003.   'To keep watch at the cross-road, to enclose there the rest (of the enemy).'

2039.   According to Matthews (p. 36) the reference to the Gates of Paradise may derive from the Alexandrian litera-ture. Alexander's conquests were said to have extended all the way to the Earthly Paradise in the east.

2044–94.   In this passage, King Val-iant of Wales, Sir Ewain, Sir Lancelot, and Sir Lot fulfill the vows made at the council of war (320–94).

2049.   'I shall never quit this place un-less I am conquered' (O'Loughlin, p. 163).

2058.   the comlyche kyng. Valiant, the Welsh king.

2070.   'Pulled it (the eagle insignia) down swiftly and rides away.'

2071.   the fewle. Finlayson (MA, Note, p. 69) is mistaken in identifying this as a reference to Sir Ewain's sword, "in an imaginative metaphor which recalls Old English kennings." The word refers to the Emperor's eagle insignia, which Sir Ewain has just ripped down.

2073–80.   All commentators have ac-cepted without question the assumption that Lancelot kills Lucius in this pas-sage. Since Arthur kills Lucius in lines 2251–56, it is presumed that the poet has been careless. Banks (MA, Notes, p. 146) tries to save the situation by proposing two Luciuses, the one whom Lancelot kills "probably Lucius Catel-lus, a great general mentioned by Geof-frey." A simpler explanation is possible. Lancelot has vowed merely to strike Lucius from his horse (376) not to kill him, and, though he wounds Lucius

grievously in this passage, it is not stated with certainty that he kills him. The passage declares only that he has struck Lucius with his lance, as he had vowed to do. It may be that the word hede in line 2077—The hede hayled owtt be-hynde ane halfe fote large—has been assumed to refer to Lucius' head, the line suggesting that he has been be-headed. However, considering the mean-ing of hayled (MED hālen v (4) d 'to extend in space, stretch, reach'), it is more logical to assume that hede refers to the head of the lance with which Lucius has been struck, for it makes no sense to say that Lucius' head stretched out behind the space of half a foot. To be sure, even if this interpretation is correct, Lucius has suffered a wound that one would expect to be a death wound. However, Gawain inflicts a similar wound on Mordred (3840–46), but Mordred lives on for an undeter-mined length of time, actually fighting another battle and slaying Arthur. Simi-larly, Lucius might survive long enough to engage Arthur and finally be slain by him.

2098.   This line appears in the MS as 2100. Since flyttyng 'strife,' the subject of 2099, cannot be thought of as flying into flanks of steeds, Mennicken's pro-posed transposition of the line (p. 53) to give flowe the subject flonez 'arrows, darts' in 2097 must be accepted.

2110.   ouer hede. Finlayson (MA, Note, p. 71) is incorrect in interpreting this as 'over the heads (of their fallen comrades).' This is a common idiom meaning 'rashly, headlong'; see line 261 and MED hēd n (1) 3 (c).

2112.   MS: sir Ienitall. The scribe may have picked up the spelling of this im-possible name from the word gentill in the second half-line. O'Loughlin's pro-posed emendation (p. 163) to Ionathal, a name found in the corresponding pas-sage in Geoffrey (x.6) is reasonable.

2128. Finlayson (*MA*, Note, p. 71) is incorrect in interpreting *handsomere* as 'easier to handle'; the sense is 'You will be handsomer without your head': see next line.

2149. MS: *Facez fetteled vnfaire in filterede lakes.* All editors understand *filterede lakes* as 'muddied pools.' However, all the examples in the *MED* cited under *feltered* 'tangled, matted' refer to hair, as does the word in line 780 of this poem. The *MED*'s definition 'of a puddle: stirred up, muddy' derives only from this line. Since this line is the only example of the use of the word to modify something other than hair and since *lakes* may be a variant of *locks* (*a* is sometimes used for *o* in this MS: *farland*, 880, 1188), it is more likely that the expression means 'matted locks' than 'muddied pools.'

2151. MS: *fygured folde.* The emendation *on folde* proposed by Branscheid must be accepted. *The fairests fygured folde* makes no sense; *fygured* must have been picked up by the scribe from the second half-line, *that fygurede was euer.*

2157. MS: *with clene men of armez.* The MS reading is identical with 2158B, and, as Björkman points out ("Notes on the 'MA,' " p. 43), one of these must be incorrect. Björkman proposes emending to *Sir Cleremond the noble,* which appears as 1638B and 2497B; Sir Clegis and Sir Cleremond appear together also in 3635 and 4265. Finlayson prints *sir Bedevere the ryche,* from Malory. Björkman also suggests changing 2158B to *on the creste of the cragge.*

2167. *Lettowe.* On weapons and armor from foreign places see note to line 903 on *Acres.*

2187. 'Pay now your respects, as custom demands.'

2283–84. Kay is apparently referring to the fact that his own death blow has

been clumsily delivered in contrast to the quick and clean death which he deals the other man in 2182.

2189. *ȝife þe werlde happyne,* 'if fortune befall you.' The emendations of *werlde* suggested by Mennicken (*werde* 'fate,' p. 142), Holthausen (*qwerte* 'health,' p. 274), and Brock (*welthe, MA,* Notes, p. xv) are unnecessary. See *OED world* sb 3 c.

2204. *malycoly,* 'fury.' See *OED melancholy* sb 2.

2207. *mounte.* The emendation to *molde* suggested by Mennicken (p. 142) is unnecessary.

2217. *and chis euen aftyre,* 'and followed straight after.' The emendations of *chis* that have been proposed by Björkman (*thrichis* 'pushes, rushes' from OE *þryccan,* "Notes on the 'MA,' " p. 44), Banks (*thris* 'three [more times],' "Notes on the '*MA,*' " p. 65), and Holthausen (*thrichis,* p. 275) are unnecessary.

2260. *thate frayede was neuer.* Mennicken (p. 142) felt this half-line to be corrupt, since it characterizes Lucius' men, and suggested either the emendation of *never* to *ever* or the transposition of this and the second half-line of 2259. However, no emendation is necessary, since line 2260 can be understood as indicating that Lucius' followers had never *before* known fear (for the preterite as the prevailing tense of the past with *ever* and *never,* see Mustanoja, pp. 498–99).

2262–64. See note to lines 1559–1588.

2283. MS: *sekadrisses.* Since the alliteration calls for hard *c* in this line, the emendation *cokadrisses* 'cockatrices' (Banks, "Notes on the 'MA,' " p. 68) or *cokadrilles* 'crocodiles' (Brock, *MA,* Gloss., p. 190) must be accepted. Either word may be translated 'croco-

dile,' since *cockatrice* was used interchangeably with *cokadrille* (see *OED,*
cockatrice; Björkman, *MA,* Notes,
p. 157; and Brock, *MA,* Notes, p. 190).
As to the inappropriateness of crocodiles
in the heathen camp, Brock suggests
that "they are not more out of place
than camels and elephants are when
crossing the Alps with coffins on their
backs" (*MA,* Gloss., p. 190). In any
case, the poet may not have had a clear
idea of the animal but simply desired
to make his description exotic with an
allusion to some kind of unusual beast.
Sekadriss is unknown.

2288. MS: *Elfaydes.* Unknown
(emend. *olfendes* 'camels,' Holthausen,
p. 236).

2300. *lesse that they schulde,* 'so that
they might the less.' The suggested
emendations of *lesse* to *lest* (Björkman,
MA, Notes, pp. 155–56) or *leste* 'last,
stay' (Mennicken, p. 142, an emendation requiring extensive changes in the
next line) are unnecessary.

2328–29. *That ne sall lelely in lande*
thi letteres pronounce / For duke ne for
dussepere, to dye in þe payne. Mennicken's suggested interpolation of *we*
after *That* in 2328 (p. 142 [the line
mistakenly cited as 2327]) is unnecessary if *That* is regarded as a relative
pronoun with the subject pronoun *those*
unexpressed (see Mustanoja, pp. 138–
44) and the entire clause as an absolute
infinitive (see Mustanoja, pp. 543–44).

2330–35. Shaving was a mark of humiliation (Björkman, *MA,* Notes,
p. 158); see the giant episode, lines
998–1004, 1009–18.

2342–51. Arthur's ironic punning is
most effective in this passage, as he suggests that the coffins that he is sending
over the mountains to Rome are the
treasure chests containing the tribute
which Rome demanded from him.

2355. *caryage.* In the original, the
ironic double meaning of Arthur's
speech is carried through in this word,
which means 'tribute, tax,' as well as
'cargo' (see *MED cariāge* 4 [b]).

2358. *fowre score wynteris.* Because
fowre does not alliterate and because it
is inconsistent with the *tene schore wyn-*
teres of line 2344, Branscheid (p. 231)
and Mennicken (p. 139) suggest emending to *tene.* However, though the messenger is presumably referring in 2358
to the tribute that Arthur's court owed
and had not paid for four score winters,
Arthur in 2344 is referring to something
else—the tribute from Rome to his own
kingdom that was lost in his ancestors'
day. The disparity between the numbers
may, therefore, be intentional, as Arthur makes it clear that in sending the
bodies over the mountains he is not only
giving the Romans the "payment" which
they have demanded, but also making
up for his own, much older, grievance.

2371–85. There are defective lines in
this passage, perhaps because it is the
linking passage between the traditional
chronicle version of the story and an
interpolated episode from another
source. In 2373–74 the poet names
Cotentin (MS: *Costantyne*) as the
place where the great battle with the
Romans has taken place, but line 1977
indicates that it takes place in *Soissons*
(*Sessoyne*); it is the battle with the
giant that takes place in Cotentin (834–
35, 848, 1187). Also, after mentioning
that Arthur buries Sir Kay at *Caen*
(MS: *Came*) in 2380, the poet states in
2385 that Arthur buries *Cador* at *Caen*
(MS: *Came*), after entering Burgundy.
However, no mention has been made of
Cador's death in this battle—he reappears in 4188—and in any case *Caen*
is in Normandy, not in Burgundy. The
phrase *as his kynde askes* echoes line
2382, further suggesting that 2385 is
merely a repetition of the description of
Kay's burial. Similarly, in 2384 *Sir Bed-*

war is mentioned as one of the knights who is buried in Burgundy; either *Bedwar* is a person distinct from *Bedwere* and a person not mentioned earlier as having been killed, or this is a confused repetition of 2379, where *Bedwere's* burial is mentioned. Neither is *Sir Bawdwyne* or *Sir Berade*, also said to be buried in 2384, mentioned earlier as among those slain (though a *Sir Bawdwyne* is a member of the party led by Cador that skirmishes with the Romans [see line 1606]). Branscheid (p. 231) suggests that *Berade* may be a corruption of *Berill*, a member of Cador's party killed in the earlier skirmish (1771–76). Another irregularity is the form of Sir Kay's name at 2380—*Kayon*, a French form; everywhere else the Latin form *Cayous* is used. All these defects point to some difficulty on the poet's part, perhaps brought about by the problems that he faced in joining his extensive interpolation to the main story at this point (see Branscheid, p. 199, and Banks, *MA*, Notes, p. 147).

2381.   Relics were often enclosed in crystal. See *MED cristal* a (a).

2386–3083.   This long episode, recounting Arthur's siege of Metz and the adventure of Gawain and Priamus, is the most extensive interpolation in the chronicle version of the story, in which it is merely mentioned that Arthur subdued a few nearby cities throughout the winter, set out for Rome the next summer, and immediately learned of Mordred's treachery (Geoffrey, x.13). For theories on the source of this episode, see Introduction, "Sources." It is in this section, according to Matthews (passim) that Arthur changes from just defender of his own kingdom to imperialistic aggressor, setting the stage for his final downfall.

2386.   *Auguste* is either a corruption like those mentioned in the note to lines 2371–85, or, as in line 1967, it refers

to the town of Autun (see note to line 1225), in Latin *Augustodunum*. The month of *August* is unsatisfactory here, since the battle takes place in early May (2371), after which Arthur enters Germany (2386–87), holds a council on St. Christopher's Day, July 25 (2390), and finally fulfills the promise of line 421 to enter Roman lands by Lammas Day, August 1 (3094) (see O'Loughlin, p. 164). However, *Autun* is not much more satisfactory, since it is quite a distance out of the way of the route from Caen to Luxemburg.

2396–2405.   This speech marks the turning point in Arthur's attitude. He is now no longer defending his kingdom from outside aggression, but has taken on a role similar to that of Lucius, becoming the aggressor who seeks to annex the lands of another and to demand tribute and cynically asking his advisors to find a legal justification for his intended aggression (see Matthews, p. 132).

2419.   MS: *Pety* (emend. *Ceté,* printed by all editors).

2421.   MS: *Ferawnte.* In line 2760, someone called *Feraunt* is named as an enemy. Branscheid (p. 212) suggests that an emendation to *Florent* is in order, though admitting that *Forawnt,* named in 2490 to accompany Florent on the foraging expedition, may be identical with this *Ferrant.* Matthews (p. 49) suggests that this unusual name is derived from the names of horses in *Fierabras* and the *Voeux du Paon,* likely sources for this episode, a theory supported by *ferant* 'iron-grey' being a common adjective for *steeds* in the *Morte Arthure* (1811, 2259, 2451).
  and oþer foure. See *OED other* adj, pron (sb) 5 d for this construction.

2423.   *a sekyre place.* One of the major problems in besieging a city was the protection of the men attempting to break down the wall, a laborious process,

from the weapons of the enemy atop the wall (Oman, Vol. II, p. 16).

2428–47. Arthur's rashness in approaching too close to the walls unprotected and in arrogantly rebuking Sir Ferrar contrasts with his earlier criticism of Sir Cador's rashness (1922–27). For Matthews (p. 132) this arrogant attitude that Arthur assumes after his victory over Lucius is, in part, the cause of his ultimate downfall.

2449. *harrawnte,* 'hurrying.' Interpretation from Banks ("Notes on the 'MA,' " p. 66), who derives the word from OF *errant, arrant.* The *MED* gives the meaning 'shouting, yelling,' deriving the word from OF *harer* 'to incite, set on' (*MED harraunte* adj, with only this instance cited).

2462. *loraynes.* See note to line 1460.

2482. *One Sonondaye be þe soone has a flethe ʒolden,* 'On Sunday, when the sun had begun to stream down.' Several attempts have been made to interpret or emend this difficult line. Most commentators agree that *be* means 'when' here, as it does in several other lines in the poem (488, 840, 976, 2873). Branscheid (p. 231) suggests emending *flethe* to *seethe,* translating 'am Sonntag als die Sonne eine schwüle Hitze abgab,' thus accounting for the fatigue of the Frenchmen in the next line. Holthausen emends extensively (p. 236) to *be the souerain has an asawt ʒolden,* translating 'als der Herrscher einen Angriff gemacht hatte.' Björkman ("Notes on the 'MA,' " p. 45) suggests retaining the line as it stands, interpreting *flethe* as 'flood' and translating 'on a Sunday when the Saône was flooded,' not a very satisfactory interpretation, since it has no relation to the fatigue of the Frenchmen. Banks (*MA,* Notes, p. 147) has an enigmatic note suggesting, without explanation, that *flethe* means, or ought to mean, 'parley.' The *MED* (*flēth* n [1]) derives the word from OI *flœor,* 'flood

tide, flooding' and suggests the meaning 'a flood of light.' The *MED*'s is the most satisfactory interpretation, since it allows the line to stand without emendation and also makes sense in context, accounting for the fatigue of the men.

2482–3083. This interlude, in which Gawain goes off alone to seek adventure and finds it in the best style of the romance tradition, balances the adventure of Arthur and the giant at the beginning of the poem. The relative frivolity of Gawain's adventure in contrast to Arthur's may be an intentional contrast meant to point up the shift in preoccupation from defense to conquest and victory for their own sake (see Finlayson, *MA,* Note, p. 81). For a discussion of the sources of this episode see Introduction, "Sources."

2484. The designation of Arthur's followers as Frenchmen rather than Britons, as elsewhere in the poem, along with the French forms of many of the names (e.g., *Cayon,* 2380) suggests a French source for this episode (Branscheid, pp. 216–17).

2490. *Sir Forawnt.* See note to line 2421.

2501–12. See note to lines 920–932. This description of the landscape sets the stage for Gawain's romantic adventure, as that of lines 920–32 marks the beginning of Arthur's. The end of the adventure is marked by another description of nature in lines 2670–77. There is only the hint of such a description at the end of Arthur's adventure in line 1197.

2502. *fewe.* Banks' suggested emendation to *fawe* is unnecessary ("Notes on the 'MA,' " p. 65), since *e* stands for *a* frequently in the MS (e.g., *keste,* 118).

2503. *hymland,* 'borderland.' The translation is from Holthausen's interpretation of *hymland* as a variant of *hemland* (p. 237). Other suggestions

are *hyȝlande* 'highland' (emend. Banks, "Notes on the 'MA,' " p. 66); *hymland* 'a fenland covered with fogs' from ModE Dial. *hime* 'hoarfrost' (Björkman, "Notes on the 'MA,' " p. 45).

2506.   MS: *myste mornyng.* This must be emended, to either *mysty mornynge, myste of mornynge* (both Brock, *MA,* Notes, p. xvi), or *mornyng myste* (Branscheid, p. 231).

2511–12.   MS: *Whylls,* 'with.' If *Whylls* is regarded as a preposition (Björkman, *MA,* Notes, p. 160), there is no need to delete the relative pronoun *That,* with which 2512 begins, an emendation favored by O'Loughlin (p. 165).

2519.   MS: *With birenne. Birenne* unknown (emend. *withouten* Brock, *MA,* Notes, p. xvi). Malory has *withoute* (v.9).

2520.   MS: *blonke,* 'steed.' There is no reason for emending to *bonk* as suggested by O'Loughlin (p. 166).

2521.   MS: *gessenande,* (emend. *gessande,* a variant of *jessant* [for similar superfluous syllables in the MS, see, e.g., *rereys* 'rears,' 4249], an heraldic term meaning 'lying over' or 'issuing' [Banks, "Notes on the 'MA,' " p. 66]). However, because the word does not alliterate (alliteration being on hard *g* in this line) and because the alliteration does not carry through two lines as is usual when the alliteration fails in one, O'Loughlin (p. 166) is in favor of emending to *glessenande* 'glistening.' Finlayson prints *gessenande,* glosses it as 'glistening,' and translates it as *jessant* in a footnote.

2522.   *chapes.* Specifically, 'the metal tip of a sword sheath' (Brock, *MA,* Gloss., p. 146). Brock assumes that these were actual heraldic devices, but it is more likely that they were ornamental trim at the edge of the shield.

2531.   *launde,* 'meadow.' It is not necessary to emend to *launge* 'language,' a

change originally suggested by Mennicken (p. 142) and printed by Björkman and Finlayson.

2543.   *at awntere,* 'madly.' For this adverbial construction, modeled on OF, see Mustanoja, p. 365.

2556.   'Till sparks of fire flew from their helms.' The *MED* cites this line under *flaumen* v 1 (a), 'to emit flames, to be afire, to blaze,' apparently understanding *flawes of fyre* as 'gushes of fire,' rather than 'sparks.' The line should be cited under *flaumen* v 1 (c) 'to give off (fire, light, sparks),' with *flawes* understood as 'sparks.' It makes no sense to say that the helmets were flaming, but the image of sparks given off by the clash of metal on metal is realistic and vivid.

2565.   *alet.* A small plate of steel protecting the shoulder, 'square, round, pentagonal, and shieldlike; sometimes plain, but generally ornamented with the family arms, or the cross of St. George' (Brock, *MA,* Notes, p. xvi), hence the enameling.

  oches, 'slices.' According to the *OED* (*oche* v) found only in this work; from OF *oschier, ocher* 'to notch, nick, cut a deep notch in.'

2566.   *rerebrace.* The upper arm plate.

2567.   *coutere.* The elbow plate.

2568.   *avawmbrace.* The forearm plate. Gawain is wearing the mixed armor, mail and plate combined, of the last half of the fourteenth century.

  MS: *vrayllede.* Unknown (emend. *vayllede* 'covered.' Holthausen, p. 251).

2576.   *blode-bande,* 'bandage for stopping the flow of blood.' See *OED blood* sb 19.

2587–88.   Presumably, Priamus is referring to his desire to convert to Christianity, an incident derived, perhaps, from *Sir Fierabras.* However, the abruptness and unmotivated quality of Pri-

amus' statement has led O'Loughlin (p. 166) to suppose that some lines are missing at this point. O'Loughlin reconstructs the "missing" lines from an alliterative sentence in Malory in which Priamus expresses his desire to convert: *Yet woll I beleve on thy Lorde that thou belevyst on, and take the for thy labour tresour inow* (v.10 [misprinted as 16 in Vinaver's one-volume edition]). Unfortunately, one cannot be sure that alliterating lines in Malory have their source in *Morte Arthure,* as it is now known that Malory himself was adept at alliteration (see Introduction, "Editions"). The ending *inow,* though, is strongly suggestive of the *Morte Arthure,* as lines ending in *enowe* 'enough' are very common.

2597–98. These two lines appear to contradict each other, perhaps due simply to the poet's carelessness (see Finlayson, *MA,* Note, p. 85).

2622–31. Gawain's refusal to reveal his nobility probably derives from Oliver's similar reluctance in *Fierabras,* which is carried to elaborate lengths.

2630–31. Branscheid (p. 232) is in favor of assigning these two lines to Priamus, rather than Gawain, as he cannot understand how Gawain, who has just stated that he is one of Arthur's knights, can speak of a desire to serve Arthur. It is true that Priamus does go on to serve Arthur by joining his side in the battle. However, line 2631 makes no sense as part of a speech by Priamus, as it is Gawain who is extolling Arthur's munificence, about which Priamus cannot be expected to know anything. The problem can be resolved if it is assumed that Gawain is referring to continuing in Arthur's service, if he is lucky enough to survive, rather than joining it for the first time. (See E. V. Gordon and Eugène Vinaver, "New Light on the Text of the Alliterative *Morte Arthure,*" *Medium Aevum,* 6 [1937], 96.)

2646–49. Priamus means that he is pleased that the one who has overcome him is a worthy opponent—a nobleman and a knight; it would have been most humiliating for him to have been overcome by a squire or a page, which Gawain had been pretending to be. The *pryse* of line 2649 is Priamus himself, not 'glory,' as translated by Finlayson (*MA,* Note, p. 87).

any prikkere, 'any common horseman, just any horseman.'

2670–77. See note to lines 2501–12.

2675. MS: *slaughte* (emend. *sleyghte,* 'skill,' Banks "Notes on the 'MA,'" p. 68).

pople. For this word used of animals see *OED people* sb 1 c.

2680. MS: *Sir Wychere.* A *Sir Whycher* appears in line 2678; one of the two must be emended, as the same man cannot meet Gawain twice. *Wycherd* is chosen here because the name is coupled with *Sir Walter* in line 2495.

2704. MS: *foyle* (emend. Mennicken *fyole* 'vial, flask' p. 142).

2705. *þe fouur well.* The four great rivers of the Orient (Tigris, Euphrates, Ganges, and Nile), believed to flow out of the Earthly Paradise (see Mandeville's *Travels,* Chap. XXXIII). Matthews (pp. 35–36) relates this allusion to the motif common in Alexandrian literature of Alexander's conquests in Asia, his approach to the Earthly Paradise, and the healing of his wounded men by the waters of the four rivers of Paradise. The gates of the Earthly Paradise are mentioned in lines 2038–39.

2720–24. As Branscheid points out (p. 214, note 5), Brock has misunderstood this passage in his marginal summary, which reads 'The scouts bring news of the army in the wood.' At line 2724, the speaker can only be Gawain,

who is telling his men what Priamus has revealed to him in lines 2650–67.

2725–51. Arthur's men are greatly outnumbered, and Gawain's rashness in urging battle is emphasized by having a younger man, Florent, urge a prudent retreat. According to Vegetius, the authority on war in the Middle Ages, avoidance of an engagement under such circumstances is no dishonor, but a mark of prudence (pp. 142–43), and Cador is rebuked by Arthur early in the poem for engaging in just this sort of battle (1922–27). Though Florent is technically the leader of the group, Gawain is the more experienced man, and his judgment is deferred to here. (Perhaps the less experienced Florent has been named leader because this was originally meant to be merely a foraging expedition; however, it may be significant that Gawain was not named as leader, for this is the second time that he accompanies a troop under someone else's leadership and behaves rashly [see 1263–1355]). In 2733–34, when Gawain asserts that he will follow Florent in whatever he decides to do, he is assuming that Florent will decide to fight, having never before fled battle. When Florent surprises Gawain by urging retreat his argument is quickly dismissed.

2730. *floure of Fraunce.* See note to line 2484.

2735. *Fadyre.* For *fader* used as a title of respect for a secular leader see *MED fāder* n 6.

2760. *Sir Feraunt.* See note to line 2421.

2765. For other mention of the famed horses of Friesland see 110 and 367.

2768. *flysches,* 'slashes.' A rare word, apparently imitative like *splash, dash* (see *OED flish* v and *MED flishen*). See also *fleschez,* 926, and *flassches,* 4237.

2793. *rosselde,* 'reddened.' See Godefroy *roseler, -eller, rousseller* 'tomber de la rosée, faire de la rosée'; *rousselet* adj 'un peu roux.' Earlier speculations are Björkman ("Notes on the 'MA,' " p. 46), 'tempered, hardened,' from OF *rostel* 'grill,' OE *rostian* 'to roast'; Brock (*MA,* Gloss., p. 186) 'brandished, shaken,' from ModE *rustle,* Sw *ruskla.*

2814–17. Priamus' pity and desire to come to the aid of Arthur's men, as well as Gawain's tough response, points up Gawain's recklessness.

2819. *I grouche noghte.* The sense is 'I grudge them not the honor of this battle.'

2829–30. Apparently, there are 24,000 knights in Antele's army alone, 8,000 in each flank.

2869. *Marie we mene,* 'We think on Mary.' See *OED mean* v[1] 4a.

2870. *oure maisters seyne.* Arthur carries the image of Mary as an heraldic emblem (see 3648–49) in the *chief,* the top part of his shield.

2875–77. Matthews (p. 35) and Banks ("Notes on the 'MA,' " p. 69) note that this must be a reference to the battle in the *Fuerres de Gadres* that takes place in the Vale of Jehosaphat.

2880. See note to line 2793.

2897. *genatours.* Specifically, light horsemen, mounted on jennets, lightly armored and equipped with two javelins. Such cavalry fought in the Castilian army against the Black Prince in 1367 (see Oman, Vol. II, pp. 180–181 and pl. xxvii). There is no need to emend to *geantes* 'giants,' as suggested by Mennicken (p. 142).

2917. *his penown.* Priamus' banner, which is being flown by his men, who are serving as hired soldiers to the Duke of Lorraine. Priamus, apparently

simply out of friendship and admiration for his new companion, Sir Gawain, and the court he represents, has decided to come over to Arthur's side.

2918. *Reuertede it,* 'Swung it around.' See line 2070, where Sir Ewain fulfills his vow and *reuerssede* Lucius' eagle, performing a similar action.

2921. *reson,* 'sign, insignia.' See *OED reason* sb¹ 4 b.

2926. *be serte.* Literally, 'by reason of the service due our lord'; see *OED serte* (aphetic OF *desert*); see also line 513. There is no need to emend to *sente,* as suggested by Mennicken (p. 143).

2940. MS: *The Duke in his schelde and dreches no lengere.* The line appears to be corrupt. Emend. *schelde and* to *scheltrone* 'troop, legion' Branscheid (p. 233) and Mennicken (p. 143).

2947. *no ferly . . . þofe.* See *OED though* adv and conj 4 a: 'After negative or interrogative phrases with *wonder, marvel . . .* where *if* or *that* is now substituted.'

2950. MS: *maches.* Branscheid (p. 233), Mennicken (p. 143), Banks ("Notes on the 'MA,' " p. 67), and Björkman ("Notes on the 'MA,' " p. 46) agree on the emendation *marches* 'marquis.' Malory has *marquesse* (v.11).

2952–68. Matthews (pp. 48–49) in his argument in favor of the influence of the *Fuerres de Gadres* on the Gawain episode, notes the resemblance between the Chastelaine incident and the episode involving Pirrus, Emenides' nephew: young Pirrus slays Gastinel, then is slain by Gadifer, and finally is avenged by Emenides, who slays Gadifer.

2955. *chokkes,* 'thrusts.' See *MED chokken* v; not the same word as ModE *choke.*

2958. Björkman ("Notes on the

'MA,' " p. 46) suggests that Swecy may be Sweden.

2964. *charry.* The *MED* under *chārī* adj gives the meaning 'cherished,' with only this line cited. 'Sad' is equally appropriate here and the more common meaning.

2976. *slydande,* 'slippery.' See *OED sliding* ppl a 2. The *OED* has this line cited under 3, 'flowing, gliding,' but 2 'slippery [with blood]' makes better sense, explaining why the spear slipped from Gawain's hand.

2977. MS: *elagere.* Unknown (emend. *sleyghte,* 'skill,' Mennicken [p. 139]. See line 3418 for the same formula.

2985. *on a rawndoune,* 'headlong.' See *OED random* sb, a, & adv 1.

2999–3000. 'Those who ran (away) that day, their fate was better / (For) in their flight they never had to suffer such a setback.'

3004. *With pylours and pauysers.* It is not clear whether these *pylours and pauysers* are Arthur's men who are conducting the prisoners (*with* is frequently used in the sense 'by means of' in this poem; see, e.g., line 178) or whether they themselves are captives. The mention of *pelours and pauysers* on the Duke's side in line 2831 suggests the latter. *Pelour* (not to be confused with *pilouur* 'robber' of line 2533; see *OED piller*) derives from *OED pile* sb¹ 'dart, shaft, arrow, javelin,' according to Banks ("Notes on the 'MA,' " p. 67). *Pauyser* refers to the bearer of a large shield protecting more than one person; see *OED pavis, pavise* sb.

3029–31. Arthur's response is a significant contrast to his rebuke of Cador in 1921–27, where Cador reports having engaged in the same type of battle against fantastic odds.

3033. *somercastell.* 'A small tower on top of an elephant, horse, or . . . en-

gine to help the besiegers gain access to the top of the walls, the name deriving from OF *somer* "a horse load" ' (see *OED somer* and *summer* sb 2).

sowe. Specifically, 'a moveable structure having a strong roof, used to cover men advancing to the walls of a besieged town or fortress, and to protect them while engaged in . . . mining or other operations' (*OED sow* sb 1 4), apparently so called because of its resemblance in shape to a pig. The quotations under this entry in the *OED* name other war engines called after animals, such as the battering ram.

3037.   *Payses*. Meaning uncertain. Though the *OED* gives the meaning 'To drive, bear down . . . by impact of a heavy body, or generally by force, to force' (*OED peise* v 3), it bases this definition on only three examples, this line, line 3042, and a third citation that is unclear. Though it appears that this is the meaning intended in 3042, 3037 is not clear. The word is followed by a preposition in 3037, and the *OED* indicates that the word is transitive with this meaning. However, even if this meaning is correct for 3042, the fact remains that it is a very unusual use of the word, which generally means 'to poise, weigh in a balance.' Quite possibly, the word in 3037 means 'poise their missiles' or 'sling their missiles into catapults.'

3042.   See note to line 3037.

3054.   *weres*. An obscure word and a puzzle to earlier editors. For the meaning 'raises' see *OED vere* v and *Pearl* 253–54: *That juel þenne in gemmeȝ gente / Vered vp her vyse wyth yȝen graye*. Though the *OED* characterizes this word as of obscure origin, Gordon, in his glossary to *Pearl* derives it from OF *ver-*, stem of pres. sg. of *vertir*.

3061.   MS: *He sall idene þe. Idene* is an unknown word, and, in spite of Brock's ingenious efforts to explain this

line as it stands in the MS (*idene* = *iþenli* 'frequently'; *þe* = *thee* 'thrive': 'He shall frequently thrive' [a translation which does not fit the context well], *MA*, Notes, pp. xvi–xvii), it is undoubtedly corrupt. The best choice is Branscheid's proposal *he shall be demyd* (pp. 233–34), though it must be noted that Branscheid based his proposed emendation on a clause that he found in this place in Malory, *he salle be demyd full wele*, which unfortunately does not appear in the Winchester MS. Other conjectures of Branscheid are *denie* 'deny' and *deine* 'esteem,' neither of which fits the context well. Mennicken (p. 139) suggests *dwelle þer*.

3064.   *he*. The Duke of Lorraine. See Introduction, "Dialect."

3117.   MS: *Slal*. Unknown. Banks (*MA*, Gloss., p. 190) suggests *slely*, a variant of *slily*. Mennicken (p. 107) suggests *skathel* 'baneful.'

3122.   MS: *bourden*, 'give chase with a spear.' See *MED bourden* v (2). All editors gloss this incorrectly as 'jest.'

3122–23.   The purpose of these lines appears to be to show that the city was caught unaware by Arthur's men.

3140.   MS: *For plesaunce of Pawnce and of Pownte Tremble*. Emend. Banks (*MA*, Notes, p. 149) *For Plesaunce, for Pawnce, and for Pownte Tremble. Plesaunce* is Piacenza; *Pawnce* may be *Ponte*, near Turin, or *Pallanze* (Pallance). The scribe may not have realized that *Pleasaunce* was a proper noun and may have attempted to correct the line by changing *for* to *of*.

3154.   MS: *Wroghte wedewes full wlonke wrotherayle synges*. Björkman (*MA*, Notes, p. 167) proposes emending *synges* to the infinitive *syngen*, giving the reading 'Made widows . . . wail'; this emendation is unnecessary if it is assumed that the relative pronoun

is unexpressed, a common construction in ME (see Mustanoja, pp. 204–05).

3162. MS: *Spruyslande,* 'Prussia.' It is not necessary to emend to *Pruysland,* as *Spruyslande* is recorded elsewhere as a variant of *Pruysland* (see Björkman, *MA,* Notes, pp. 167–68).

3164–75. Here Arthur fulfills the vow he made in lines 353–55, to refresh his men in the Vale of Viterbo. The Viscount mentioned in 3167 must be the enemy of the Welsh king, Valiant, whom Valiant has slain in lines 2044–65, in fulfillment of his vows.

3166. *vernage.* A strong and sweet wine of Italy.

3168. MS: *Vertely,* 'quickly.' A nonce word, according to the *OED,* which derives it from OF *vertement* 'readily,' related to *verte* 'green, youthful, energetic.'

3186. MS: *With his ceptre.* The verse is corrupt, as it contains only one main word or stress. Emend. *and swerde* Björkman ("Notes on the 'MA,'" p. 46); other possibilities are *With his ceptre on the see* 'throne,' *Semlyche with his ceptre* (both Mennicken, p. 54) and *With his ceptre full semely* (Holthausen, p. 237).

3187. *vndyrtakyng,* 'pledge.' See *OED undertaking* vbl sb 3. This is the only example cited of the word with this meaning before the eighteenth century.
 ostage. For *hostage* as a collective noun see *MED hōstāge* n (1).

3190. *betuke them the Kynge.* See *MED bitāken* v 1 for a number of examples with the receiver expressed as an indirect object noun, without preposition. The subject is unexpressed.

3205. MS: *ostage.* See note to line 3187.

3212. *Crosse Dayes.* Specifically, the three days preceding Ascension Day (also called Rogation Days). This date

is anomalous, as Arthur has entered Italy some time after Lammas Day, August 1, and Ascension Day is forty days after Easter, which, long before the fourteenth century, had been regularized throughout the Roman Catholic world and could occur at the latest on April 25. The only way to save the poet's chronology is to assume that one winter has already passed since Arthur's invasion of Italy, an assumption that is reasonable from a realistic point of view, but inconsistent with the chronology of the rest of the poem, for Arthur appears to have carried out his vow and accomplished all he had planned to do between New Year's Day and Lammas.

3214. *in my ryalltés,* 'in royal splendor.' See *OED rialty.* The plural is common in phrases of this type.

3222–3455. This remarkable passage foreshadows Arthur's downfall with a marvelously detailed dream, which balances the dream that foreshadows his triumph over the giant at the beginning of the poem. In contrast to the earlier dream, this is not a part of the chronicle tradition that furnishes the bulk of source material for the poem. The description of Nine Worthies of history resembles that in *The Parlement of Thre Ages,* based in part on the *Voeux du Paon,* the source of other details in the poem. Lady Fortune and her wheel is a common medieval motif. The richly dressed lady and the gold and silver landscape are reminiscent of *Pearl.*

3230. *willed,* 'lost." See *OED will* v[3].

3233. *wathes,* prey.' See *OED waith* sb[1] 2.

3244. *Enhorilde,* 'bordered.' See *MED enorlen* v.

3245. *honeste,* 'fair, beautiful.' See *MED honest(e* adj 3.

3246. *foddenid.* The *MED* has only this example under *fodenen* v, and it

may be that the word should be emended to *foddemid* 'produced,' as suggested by Björkman ("Notes on the 'MA,' " p. 46).

3255. *redily*, 'carefully, lovingly.' See *OED redly* and *redely* (not the same word as *readily*).

3263. MS: *reched*. Unknown (emend. *reches*, 'opulence' Mennicken, p. 143).

3272. MS: *rog*. Unknown (emend. *roo*, 'wheel' Björkman, *MA*, Notes, p. 169).

3276. MS: *drife*. The sense requires the past tense, and Bjorkman (*MA*, Notes, p. 169) suggests the emendation *drafe*. However, the *MED* records *drife* as a variant of the normal singular preterite form.

3281. *lire*, 'flesh.' See *OED lire* sb¹. An equally plausible translation is *face;* see *OED leer* sb¹ 2.

3282. MS: *Þe two eyne of Þe byeryn.* In view of the next line, this must be considered a scribal error and emended by *Þe tone eye.* See Brock, Intro., p. xvii.

3282–83. As Matthews notes (p. 38), this weird characteristic of Alexander appears also in *The Wars of Alexander:*

With grete glesenand aȝen grymly he lokis,
Þat ware as blyckenand briȝt as blesand sternes,
ȝit ware þai sett vn-samen of serelypy hewys;
Þe tane to brene at a blisch as blak as a cole,
As any ȝare ȝeten gold ȝalow was þe tothire (603–07).

3302. *I was frekke, in my faithe.* 'I was heroic, by my faith.' All earlier editors, as indicated by their omission of a comma after *frekke,* and also the *MED* understand this as 'zealous in my faith.' This meaning is inconsistent with the

rest of this speech and the speeches of all the other Worthies, which consist of boasts about the power which they formerly enjoyed. Since, as pointed out by Mustanoja (pp. 350–52), prepositions were often interchangeable in ME, *in my faithe* may be the common exclamation *on my faith*, yielding a line more consistent with the rest of the passage.

3307. The foam is apparently a reference to the man's exertion in clutching the wheel.

3317. *surepel.* The *OED* lists this as a nonce word with the meaning 'a cover for a book,' reconstructing it from AF **surepel* from *sur* 'over' and *pell* 'parchment.'

3324–29. The poet does not allow the last two Worthies, Charlemagne and Godfrey de Bouillon, to attain the chair, apparently in order to avoid anachronism, as Arthur was supposed to have lived several centuries before these two. In lines 3423–35 the sage who is interpreting Arthur's dream refers to them in the future tense.

3328. Probably a reference to their exertions. See note to 3307.

3336. This heraldic device of Godfrey's is shown in a miniature depicting the Nine Worthies in a fourteenth-century manuscript of *Chevalier Errant* (Bibliothèque National, Fr. 12559), reproduced in Loomis, *Arthurian Legends,* Fig. 13.

3345. Though Frollo is not mentioned earlier in the *Morte Arthure,* Geoffrey (ix.11) and the other chroniclers recount in detail the story of Arthur's victory over him. See also line 3404.

3352. *That the krispane kroke to my crownne raughte.* A difficult line. Finlayson (*MA*, Note, p. 95) translates 'so that the crisped curl reached to my crown,' explaining "In the Nine Heroes tapestry in the Cloisters Museum, New

York, Arthur is depicted with a long curl descending from the bottom rim of his crown to the centre of his forehead." It is not clear how 'reached to my crown' describes such a picture. Moreover, since a diadem is placed on Arthur's head in the next line, it is reasonable to assume that he is not wearing a crown while Fortune is combing his hair, and that *crowne* must therefore refer to the top of the head. The *MED* notes that *crōk* may designate 'a head of curly hair, locks,' as well as 'a curl.' If *to* is understood as 'toward,' a picture emerges of hair being combed in such a way that it curls up and points toward the crown of the head.

3404. *Froill, Ferawnt.* Enemies of Arthur slain in battle. See line 3345 and note and lines 2760 and 2765. This Ferawnt is not to be confused with another man of the same name who is an ally of Arthur and who appears in line 2421.

3408–39. The men named here are, with Arthur, the conventional Nine Worthies, or Nine Heroes, of history, three pagans, three Jews, and three Christians. They were a popular subject in fourteenth and fifteenth century literature and art, beginning with their description in the *Voeux du Paon.* For a detailed survey of the Nine Worthies motif see Loomis, *Arthurian Legends,* pp. 37–40.

3423–35. See note to lines 3324–29. Both Charlemagne and Godfrey are traditionally credited with having brought back noted relics from Jerusalem. Godfrey was a leader in the First Crusade and was actually crowned King of Jerusalem in 1099. He figures as the hero of two *chansons de geste, Chanson d'Antioche* and *Chanson de Jérusalem* (Finlayson, *MA,* Note, p. 98).

3458. *pesane,* 'gorget.' See *OED pisane.* From OF *pisainne, pizane,* the feminine form of the adjective *pisain,*

pizain 'Pisan,' used at first to qualify the words *gorgerette, helme,* etc., later used by itself to designate a piece of armor. That it was frequently used for a piece of neck armor is clear from the numerous quotations in the *OED* stating that a knight's neck was struck 'through ventail and pisan.' The word appears in *Sir Gawain,* 204.

paunson, 'breastplate.' All editors assume that this word is identical with *pawnce* (used in line 2075) and identify it as a piece of armor covering the belly. The form of the word is unaccounted for, however, as it is not listed in the *OED* as a variant of *pauncer, pauncher* (as is *paunce*) and it resembles none of the variants in the other languages that are cited, though it appears that it must have some relationship to *pauncer.*

3460. *pauys pillion hatt.* The MS reading is a puzzle, and no satisfactory interpretations have been offered. The *ketill-hatte* of 3516 must be Arthur's, as it could hardly belong to Cradok, who is dressed like a pilgrim. Accordingly, the expression *pauys pillion hatt,* unless the poet has been careless, must be a description of the kettle helm. The word *pauys,* like the word *pesane* (see note to line 3458) is an expression derived from the name of a city (here Pavia) used to describe a piece of knightly equipment made in that city, specifically a shield (see 3625). Though all the examples given in the *OED* are of shields, and though the word is used as a noun and not an adjective, it is reasonable to assume that, like *pesane,* it was originally an adjective and that it was used to describe more than one piece of knightly equipment, here the kettle helm. The term *pillion hatt* is used for a hat of felt worn by the clergy. Since whatever Arthur is wearing is studded with precious stones, it is unlikely that it is a cap of felt. Very possibly the pillion hat resembled the

kettle helm in shape closely enough for the term to be used figuratively for the helmet.

3464. *bede,* 'hunting.' The *MED* derives this nonce word from OI *beiddr,* ppl of beiða 'hunt.'

3466. *stye,* 'path.' See *OED* sty sb¹.

3470–75. Cradok's humble attire contrasts with the rich garb that Arthur is wearing. Several emblematic elements—palm, staff, mantle, pouch, and scallop shells—identify Cradok as a pilgrim. Presumably, Cradok is not recognized because of his humble clothes, Arthur because he is wearing a kettle helm.

rownde, 'coarse.' See *OED round* a 2 b, 'of cloth, made with thick thread.' This meaning is chosen over 3 c, where the *OED* cites this line, 'cut circularly at bottom so as to have no train or skirts,' because the earliest examples, aside from this citation, are sixteenth century and because Cradok's cloak is irregular at the bottom (see line 3473).

3472. *ferthynges.* There is no evidence in either the *OED* or the *MED* that this word means anything other than 'farthing, a coin worth one-fourth of a penny,' Brock's gloss of 'round spots' notwithstanding. It must be assumed that Cradok has farthings attached to his clothes. They may, like the accoutrements in 3474–75, be symbols of his status as a pilgrim; as coins of small denomination they may be meant as a contrast to the *besauntez* 'golden coins of Byzantium,' with which Fortune's clothing is adorned.

3474. *skalopis.* See *OED scallop, scollop* sb 1 c, 'A pilgrim's cockle shell, worn as a sign that he had visited the shrine of St. James at Compostela.'

3475. *hym scholde,* 'he had to (be).' The impersonal construction must have developed by analogy with *seem* (see Mustanoja, pp. 433–36). For the ellipsis of the verb *to be* see *OED shall* 27, 29.

3487. *Sir Cradoke.* A variant of *Caradoc,* the name of a knight associated with Arthur's court in a number of romances, most notably *Le Livre de Caradoc,* a continuation of Chrétien de Troyes' *Perceval* (Björkman, *MA,* Notes, pp. 171–72).

3516. *ketill-hatte.* See note to line 3460.

3532. *Surgenale.* Since Mordred has both Saxons and Saracens in his army, this name might be a variant of either *Sargans,* a city in Switzerland, southeast of Zurich on the Rhine River, or *Sergen,* a city in Turkey near the Black Sea.

3537. *Sir Childrike.* The Saxon prince who is similarly allied with Mordred in Geoffrey (xi.1) and the other chronicles. Branscheid (pp. 204, 215) and Björkman (p. 172) assume that this is the same Cheldrike who is apparently slain in lines 2954–55 and who now reappears through the carelessness of the poet. However, in Geoffrey there are also two Childriks; the first is slain by Cador on the Isle of Thanet (ix.5).

3538. *cheualrous,* 'brutal.' See *MED chevalrous* adj (c).

3541. *Hawyke.* A city in southern Scotland on the River Teviot. It is difficult to understand the reason for Branscheid's suggested emendation to *Berwick* (p. 204). The pronoun *he* in this line refers to Childrike, and the entire passage, through line 3545, follows Geoffrey closely (xi.1, *a flumine Humbro ad Scotium*). This, with Kent, is the territory that Mordred has ceded to Childrike in return for his military aid against Arthur. The carving up of the kingdom in this way is emphasized throughout the passage as a mark of Mordred's irresponsibility and contrasts with Arthur's consolidation of many lands at the beginning of the poem.

3545. *Henguste and Hors.* The two Saxon princes who were brought by the

British king Vortigern to aid him in his wars with the Picts and the Scots. According to Geoffrey (vi.12) Hengest gave his daughter Renwein in marriage to Vortigern and received Kent in exchange. Their ultimate betrayal of Vortigern was the beginning of the Saxon conquest of Britain.

3578. *myn one,* 'none else but me.' See *OED one* numeral, a, pron, 27 d: 'After pronouns, almost = *self, selves.* Hence, after the analogy of *my–,* northern writers used *mine . . . ane,* etc.'

3583. *Sir Howell and Sir Hardolfe.* A *Howell* and a *Hardelfe* are mentioned together in line 1741 as two of the men whom Cador knights just before the rash battle with Lucius' allies. It is unlikely that these are the same two. Presumably, new knights are young men, not likely to be left in charge in Arthur's absence over older, more seasoned men. Howell may be the King of Britanny, whose people were plagued by the giant, named in line 1180, who in turn is possibly to be identified with the Baron of Britain the Little (see line 304 and note). Hardolfe is not to be confused with the heathen knight of the same name who is slain by Gawain (2974–75).

3591. MS: *with beste knyghtes.* This verse is lacking a syllable, and *his* or *the* must be interpolated before *beste* (see Björkman, *MA,* Notes, p. 172).

3592. *trome,* 'forces.' See *OED trume* sb. There is no need to emend to *trompe* as suggested by Björkman (*MA,* Notes, p. 172).

3600. *scherys,* 'shears.' The earliest examples given in the *OED* of this word describing the movement of a ship are sixteenth century (*OED shear* v 8) and seventeenth century (*OED sheer* v²).

3603. *chaynes of chare,* 'wagon chains.' Meaning suggested by Holthau-

sen (p. 237), who identifies *chare* with ModE *car* (CFr *char*). As suggested by Finlayson (*MA,* Note, p. 100) the enemy ships were likely chained together to form a defense boom (see *OED chain* sb 6). The syntax of 3603–05 is obscure, as a word for 'boats' is not used; the image of boats is to be understood from the context, but the modifying lines 3604–05 have no noun to qualify.

3604. *cheualrous.* See note to line 3538.

3607. MS: *clothys,* 'pennons?' See *MED clōth* n 1 b (g). The picture in 3607–08 is not clear. Perhaps the ships are flying the pennons of the various heathen forces strung together like signal flags.

3608. *pece by pece.* This antedates the earliest example given in the *OED* of the use of this expression, derived from OF *pièce à pièce,* which is sixteenth century.

3613. *in rede.* It has been suggested that this is an allusion to a ship of Edward III called the Red Cog (see Björkman, *MA,* Notes, p. 173).

3615. MS: *drawen.* There is no need to emend to *drawes* as suggested by Björkman (*MA,* Notes, p. 173) for consistency with *dresses* if it is assumed that both verbs have an unexpressed subject pronoun *they* (see Mustanoja, pp. 138–44). Both *es* and *en* are used for the present tense plural verb ending. Björkman apparently assumed that the King was the subject of these verbs.

stonys. For use as missiles. See line 3681.

3616. *toyelys,* 'weapons.' See *OED tool* sb 1 b. *Toyel* is a common variant.

3618. *tolowris,* 'rope-men.' The *OED* lists this nonce word with the suggestion that it means the tillers of crossbows. However, the syntax requires an agent noun, not an object. Björkman's sugges-

tion of 'men who toll or pull, pullers' (*MA*, Notes, p. 178) is better. See *OED toll, tole* v[1] 3.

3620.   *Graythes*, 'gear.' See *MED greith(e* n (c).

3626.   *hurdace*, 'rampart.' See *MED hurdis* n (c).

3630.   *besye*, 'bustle.' See *MED bisi* adj as n; found also in *Patience*, 157: Þer watʒ busy ouer-borde bale 'bundles' to kest.

3632.   *mawntelet*. See *OED mantelet, mantlet*. This must be a long ventail (the throat protector made of chain mail which is attached to the helmet, often extending to slightly below the shoulders). Brock's *mawncelet* is an incorrect reading.

3636.   The connection with the previous line is not clear, and the B verse, *thies gud mens bodyes,* is especially puzzling. A possible interpretation is 'these (referring to the King's knights or warriors) embody (see *OED body* v) good resources (see *OED mean* sb[2]).' None of the earlier editors has a comment on this line or a gloss of any of the words in it.

3647.   Arthur bears the heraldic device of three crowns, representing England, Scotland, and Brittany, in the Nine Worthies iconography in Loomis, *Arthurian Legends,* Figs. 11, 12, 13, 14, 15, and 17.

3648.   *chosen*, 'seen.' See *MED chēsen* v 9.

3648–49.   *chalke-whitte Mayden*. See lines 2869–70, where Gawain mentions that Arthur bears the Virgin and Child as his heraldic device, a tradition beginning ın Geoffrey (ix.4). In a fifteenth century mural from Switzerland pictured in Loomis (*Arthurian Legends,* Fig. 17), which shows the three Christian Worthies, Arthur also carries a shield with a divided field—half showing the three crowns and half the Virgin and Child.

3662.   *one burde*, 'on their sides.' See *MED bōrd* n 6 (c).

3672.   MS: *killide the braynes,* 'smashed skulls.' There is no need to emend *braynes* to *berynes,* as suggested by Branscheid (p. 234), as the earliest meaning of *kill* is 'strike, hit, beat, knock.' See *OED kill* v 1, where two examples are listed with the expression 'kill the head.'

3675.   MS: *vptynes*. Unknown (emend. *OED vptyhes,* a variant of *uptie* = *tie* sb 2: 'A rope or chain by which a yard is suspended.' Brock has mistakenly printed this word as *vpcynes.*

3681.   *one burd*, 'alongside.' See note to line 3662.

3684.   MS: *englaymous*. The syntax requires emendation to the 3 pr pl *englaymes,* 'enslime,' suggested by Björkman (*MA*, Notes, p. 173). The emended form appears in line 1131.

3694.   In line 3528 it is mentioned that the Danes are allied with Mordred.

3700.   Spaniards are not mentioned elsewhere as Mordred's allies. Neilson (pp. 60–61) thinks this is a slip on the poet's part resulting from his using a chronicle account of Edward III's sea battle with the Spaniards off Winchelsea as the source for this episode.

3704.   *hawe*. See *MED aue* n (variant *hawe*), 'terror.' This word, as well as the entire line, has been a puzzle to earlier editors.

3706.   Gawain has not been mentioned before as the leader of this battle.

3708.   *Sir Geryn* may be the same man who is mentioned in 1265 (see note). Sir Griswold has not been mentioned before.

3709. *Galuth, a gud gome.* Gawain's sword.

3719. *slowde.* Meaning uncertain, according to the *OED.* Björkman (*MA,* Notes, p. 174) suggests a relation to dial. *slud* 'mud, mire' (see *EDD slud* sb and v 1).

slakkes. It is apparent from the context that this is *OED slake* sb³ 2: 'A stretch of muddy ground left exposed by the tide; a mud flat,' though there are no examples in the *OED* that are earlier than the nineteenth century.

3720. MS: *and* (emend. *in* Branscheid, p. 235).

3721. Muddy ground was always a danger to cavalry, and defending armies often took up a position surrounded in part by a marsh (Oman, Vol. II, pp. 112–16).

3735. Gawain shifts here from addressing his flag-bearer to addressing his entire army.

3743. This obscure line may be a reference to Mordred's bastard birth (not mentioned elsewhere in the poem, except, perhaps, in line 3776).

3759. *gowtes.* See *MED goute* n (2) (c) and *Webster goutte, 'Her.* A bearing consisting of a drop-shaped figure.' Incorrectly read by Brock as *gowces.*

3761. *graythes,* 'shatters.' See *MED greithen* v 4 (c).

3763. See 3937–38 and note.

3773. The Montagues were a noble family that served all three Edwards. William Montague was Marshall of England under Edward III, fought with him against the Scots, and played a prominent role in both the Battle of Crécy and the Battle of Poitiers (Matthews, p. 184).

3776. *foode,* 'bastard.' See *MED fōde* n (2).

3836. *for wondsom and will.* The *OED* lists *wondsom* as an adjective but *will,* in this line, as a rare noun (derived from the more common adjective), meaning 'bewilderment,' and for the use of *for* in this line refers to *for* prep 10. Since *will* is more common as an adjective and since here it parallels an adjective, it is difficult to see why the *OED* lists it as a rare noun. Both words are adjectives, and *for* is being used here in the sense 'as' (see OED *for* 19 b), as in the ModE expressions 'for certain, for dead.'

3842. *the scharpe,* 'the sharp weapon.' See *OED sharp* a and sb¹ B 1.

3843. *a schaftmonde large,* 'a six-inch span.' See *OED shaftment.*

3846. *schynbawde,* 'greave.' Though Banks (*MA,* Gloss., p. 189) suggests that this word is 'probably miswritten for "schynbande,"' Amours (p. 352; quoted in Björkman, *MA,* Notes, p. 175) supports the MS reading with a Latin quotation containing the word *schynbaldes* (with the alteration of *l* with a vowel sound as in *faute, fault*). Though two MSS of *The Awntyrs off Arthure* contain the reading *schynbandes,* 295, both the *OED* and Gates, in his edition of the poem, accept the Thornton MS reading *schynbawdes.* The *OED* points out, however, that the second element of the word is of unknown derivation.

3863. *glent.* See *MED glent* n 1 (c). Though *glent* more commonly means 'glimpse, glance,' the *MED* derives the meaning 'a glancing blow' from *glenten* v 2: 'to strike a glancing blow.' An alternate translation of the line, using the more common meaning, is 'After a glimpse of that woe never more will know joy.'

3869. See Gates, *The Awntyrs off Arthure,* 508–09: *Gawyne was gaily graþed in grene / Withe his griffons of*

golde engreled fulle gay. As noted by Matthews (p. 157), in all the other romances (except *Sir Gawain*, in which he bears the pentangle), Gawain's arms are a double-headed eagle or a lion. The two poems also agree in their description of Mordred's arms: see line 4182 and note.

3899. Mordred is apparently waiting for tidings that Arthur has learned of Gawain's death.

3903. *in a mette-while.* See *OED met* ppl adj 'measured'; literally, 'in a measured time.'

3905. *And what comliche coste the Kyng was aryuede.* See *MED arīven* v 1 (b) for the transitive use of this verb.

3908. *wyn to hir speche,* 'speak to her, face to face.' See *OED win* v¹ 12; *speech* sb¹ 2 b.

3911. MS: *ȝee* (emend. *ȝeȝes,* 'weeps.' Mennicken, p. 144) for parallelism with *ȝermys* 'wails'; see *OED yeie.*

3917–18. That is, Guinevere is taking the veil, not because of a desire to serve Christ, but in order to get sanctuary.

3921. See lines 3717–21 and notes.

3924. *Swalters,* 'splashes.' There is no need to emend to *swafres* 'staggers,' suggested by Björkman (*MA,* Notes, p. 176) or to *swaifels* 'swings,' suggested by Holthausen (p. 275). See *OED swalter* v and *swatter* v.

3937. *the Guthede kynge,* 'the Gotland king.' Struck down by Gawain in lines 3758–63. Because of the resemblance of *c* and *t* in this MS (see note to line 821), the word was mistakenly printed as *guchede* by Banks and Brock and tentatively defined by Brock as 'spotted' (*MA,* Notes, p. xvii). Björkman ("Notes on the 'MA,' " pp. 47–48) properly prints the word and derives it

from *Gut* + OE *þeōd* 'people, race'; *Gutlande* appears in 3763.

3967–68. Arthur is referring to his own death here, implying either that he is dying of grief and imploring death to hasten or that he has nothing left to live for and wishing for death to come to him.

3970. *Swafres,* 'staggers.' See *OED swaver* v.

3981. *For blode,* 'By Christ's blood.' See *MED blōd* n (1) 5 (c). For the use of *for* = *by* in oaths, see *MED for* prep 2 (d). Another possible translation is 'by my blood.'

4012. *wandsomdly.* The *OED* lists this as a nonce word, with the meaning 'reluctantly, falteringly,' deriving it from *wonde* v, 'to shrink or flinch for fear, to hesitate.' More likely it is an adverb derived from *OED wansome* a, 'miserable, unhappy.'

4020. *one erthe,* 'above earth.' There is no need to emend to *on bere* 'on the bier,' as suggested by Mennicken (p. 140).

4047. *pare,* 'injure.' See *OED pair* v² and Banks, "Notes on the 'MA,' " p. 67.

4052. This allusion to Dorset is believed to be the source of the (inaccurate) detail in *The Awntyrs off Arthure,* 295, *In Dorset shal dy þe doughetest of alle.* See Matthews, p. 158, and Gates, Introduction.

4056. MS: *þe Treyntis.* Though it has been speculated that this is a mistake for *Tambire* 'Tamar' (see line 3902 and Branscheid, p. 207), it very likely refers to the small stream named *Trent,* also called *Piddle,* that flows into Poole Bay at Wareham in Dorset (see *Atlas of Britain,* p. 56).

4062. *Mordrede the Malebranche.* This unfamiliar designation for Mordred, which appears also in 4174, is ac-

companied by other puzzling facts in this section: the reappearance of the supposedly buried Cador (4188, 4264; see note to 4188 [but see also note to 2371–85]) and the mention of Arthur's second sword *Clarente* (4193, 4202) and its storage place, Arthur's *wardrop* at Wallingford (4203, 4217)—neither of which is mentioned elsewhere in the poem or, as a matter of fact, in any Arthurian literature in ME (Ackerman, p. 59). Branscheid (p. 210) who was struck also by the frequent mention of Danes in Mordred's army and by the signs of a "Gaweinkultus" (3875–89, 3943–4024), concludes that all these elements derive from a yet undiscovered source for this last section of the *Morte Arthure* (3591–4346).

4075.   *Sir Ewayne and Sir Errake.* Both appear frequently in English and French romances of the period and are mentioned together in *The Awntyrs off Arthure*, 654. Sir Ewain may be the same man who is mentioned in 337.

4077.   *Merrake and Meneduke.* Not mentioned before this (the *Sir Meneduke of Mentoche* of line 1919 has been killed), these two continue to play an important part in this last battle (see 4209, 4220, 4267), further supporting the theory of a yet undiscovered source for this last section.

4078.   *Idirous.* Mentioned earlier in the poem (1439, 1490, 1498, 1510), this man continues to play a role in the last battle (4135, 4141). That he is the son of Ewain is consistent with the earlier part of the poem, where he is called *Idrus fitz Ewayne* (1490–98). *Sir Alymere* is not mentioned elsewhere.

4123.   *Ethyns.* Björkman ("Notes on the 'MA,' " p. 49) criticizes the gloss of this word as 'giants' by both Brock and Banks, stating that the word, here and in 4163, "certainly means 'heathens,' not 'giants,' " without explanation. However, in describing Ewain and Eric's

battle with the *ethenys*, the poet uses the word *hulkes* to refer to the enemy (4165), a word that is used four times elsewhere in the poem, all referring to the giant of St. Michael's Mount (1058, 1085, 1121, 1149). The gloss 'giants' is therefore probably correct.

4157.   *Qwythen,* 'Why not.' Though the sense of this word has always been clear, commentators have had difficulty in accounting for its form. Brock (*MA,* Gloss., p. 183) and Banks ("Notes on the 'MA,' " p. 68) take it as a scribal error for *qwyne* 'why not' (= O that . . . !). Holthausen (p. 237) suggests *Quoth then.* Björkman ("Notes on the 'MA,' " p. 49) states that it is equivalent to ODan *hveden* 'why.' The *OED* solves the problem without the necessity for emendation by understanding the word as = *why then ne,* listing it with *why ne* (usually spelled as one word) under *why* adv 4 a.

dere, 'dread.' See *MED dēre* adj (2) and *Cleanness* 214: *Dryȝten with his dere dom hym drof to þe abyme.*

4163.   See note to line 4123.

4181.   *charles chekyn,* 'churl's son.' All earlier editors understand *chekyn* as 'chicken' (coward?) and *charles* as a variant of or error for 'churlish.' O'Loughlin (p. 68) goes so far as to account for the error by suggesting that the last three letters of *churlesche* have been suppressed by haplography. However, *chiken* in the sense of 'chick, young bird' is often used, as is *chike,* as a disparaging word for human beings, meaning 'offspring' (see *MED chiken* n 3). This is undoubtedly the way it is used here. *Churles* is possessive, as in *fendes chike* (under *MED chik* n).

4182.   *The Awntyrs off Arthure* also mentions Mordred's device as being a *sauter engreled* (307 [all MSS except Lambeth, which has *englorid*]). Matthews (p. 157) considers this a striking coincidence and proof of a connection

between the two poems, since descriptions of traitors' arms are rare in literature, and since Mordred's arms, when they are described, usually have an eagle as the main device.

4188. *Sir Cadors.* See note to lines 2371–85 for a discussion of the contradiction between Cador's presumed burial at line 2385 and his reappearance here. Even if the name *Cador* at 2385 could be proven a mistake for *Kayous* (Cador's death is never described), it is nevertheless strange that he, a prominent knight early in the poem, is not mentioned again until this point.

4193. *Clarente.* See note to line 4062.

4196. *Itt.* The sword Clarent.

4201. *because of my seluen,* 'for my own purposes.'

4203. *Walyngfordhe.* See note to line 4062.

4207. *Regale of Fraunce.* The title of a renowned jewel which a king of France was said to have offered at the St. Thomas shrine at Canterbury (see *OED regal* a and sb¹ A 5).

4208. *Sir Froll.* See note to line 3404.

4209. *in malyncoly,* 'maddened.' See note to line 3404.

4210. *mellyd,* 'battered.' A puzzle to earlier editors. Brock glosses '(?) made like a *mall* or hammer, hammer-headed'; Björkman, 'mit einem Hammer oder Kolben schlagen, hämmern'; Banks, 'hammer-headed (?), beaten with a hammer (?).' 'Hammer-headed' obviously does not follow from the past participial form. 'Forged' is possible, but, since the mace is a weapon used for smashing, it is reasonable to assume that it is described as 'battered' from its use in battle.

4221. MS: *and his moste strenghis.* The interpolation of *in* before *his* is an obvious one, printed, with brackets, by all editors.

4240. *his.* Arthur's.

4249. *fente.* A puzzle to earlier editors. Brock gives no gloss. Banks suggests 'opening of the mantle at the chest?' (*MA,* Gloss., p. 168), 'the binding of any part of the dress' ("Notes on the 'MA,' " p. 65), both meanings from the *OED.* Björkman glosses 'Schlitz an einem Kleidungsstücke' (*MA,* Gloss, p. 206). Holthausen (p. 251) proposes emending to *fence,* with an extension to 'shield.' The *MED* cites this line under *fente* n (b): 'a slit in a robe,' with only one other example. However, the *MED* lists as variants of *fēnd* 'fiend' the spellings *fent, feont, veont, faynt.* This is the reading adopted here, with *fente* 'fiend' referring to Mordred. The picture of Arthur heaving Mordred to his feet to deal him his death blow is much more graphic and poetically appealing than the picture of him lifting up a part of his armor to do so as he lies dying. Moreover, line 4251 suggests that Mordred falls on the sword, necessitating that he be lifted after having fallen to the sod in line 4246.

4251. *brawles,* 'sprawls.' See *MED braulen* v (2).

4264. *Cador.* See notes to lines 2386–3083 and 4188.

4265–66. See lines 3635–38, where these same knights, with the exception of *Lowes,* are also catalogued together just before the sea battle.

4278. *theire.* There is no need to emend to *thine,* as suggested by Björkman (*MA,* Notes, p. 179). Arthur is saying that God has upheld his honor through the might of his (Arthur's) men's hands.

4284. *helples,* 'hopeless.' See *MED helplēs* adj (e).

4303. *Glasthenbery.* The chronicles state that Arthur was taken to *Avalon* (see 4309), a place which, in Laʒamon, became a magical spot where Arthur's wounds would be healed. By the twelfth century *Avalon* had become identified with *Glastonbury,* though it is not known how (for some ingenious theories see Loomis, "The Legend of Arthur's Survival"). The *Morte Arthure* poet includes both, by making Avalon the place where Arthur stops on his way to Glastonbury when his strength fails him and he is too weak to go on. There is no hint in the *Morte Arthure* that either place is magical or that Arthur's wounds will heal and he will return to life, as there is in Laʒamon.

4309. *Ile of Aueloyne.* See note to 4303.

4314. *Criste.* Björkman must be mistaken in identifying this as 'Kruzifix' (*MA,* Notes, p. 179); surely it is a reference to the Host. See the next line and 2193.

4316. *Constantyn.* The son of Cador and Arthur's successor in the chronicles. The fact that he has not been mentioned elsewhere in the *Morte Arthure* underlines the fact that all of Arthur's prominent knights have been lost, and only a person as yet obscure is left to be successor. Originally, Arthur has expected either Mordred (678) or Cador (1944) to be his successor.

4318. It is not known whom Arthur is addressing here, but that he does not use a name emphasizes that all the more familiar knights are now dead. See note to line 4316.

4320–23. The advice to do away with Mordred's children is likely seen by Arthur not as an act of revenge, for in line 4324 he declares that he forgives all offenses, but one of prudence that will aid in the restoration of a stable kingdom. Whatever the reader may think of Arthur's moral state, it is clear from this last speech that he considers himself at peace with God.

4326. *In manus.* 'Into Thy hands (O God, I commend my spirit)' (Finlayson, *MA,* Note, p. 120).

4343–46. As in the opening lines of *Sir Gawain,* the poet is taking pains to establish his hero's connection, and that of the British, with the oldest heroes of antiquity, the royal house of Troy. One of its scions, Brutus, was presumed to be founder of Britain. Priamus is King Priam of Troy, not to be confused with the pagan prince of the same name in the Gawain episode of the *Morte Arthure.*

Glossary

In the Glossary and the Index of Names, *y* is alphabetized as *i*, consonantal *u* as *v*, vocalic *v* as *u*, consonantal *i* as *j*, and *þ* as *th*. Initial *ȝ* appears immediately after *w*. Every occurrence of every form is recorded, with the exception of frequently recurring forms, which are indicated by the abbreviation *etc*. Line references to emended readings are italicized. The head word in each entry is the form closest to its ModE cognate.

ABBREVIATIONS USED IN THE GLOSSARY

AF Anglo-French
Dan Danish
Icel Icelandic
L Latin
LG Low German
ME Middle English
MBreton Middle Breton
MDu Middle Dutch
MedL Medieval Latin
MHG Middle High German
MLG Middle Low German
ModDu Modern Dutch
ModE Modern English

ModF Modern French
ModG Modern German
MSw Middle Swedish
N Northern
Norw Norwegian
ODan Old Danish
OE Old English
OF Old French
OHG Old High German
ON Old Norse
ONF Old Northern French
OSw Old Swedish
Scand Scandinavian

a   *interj.* ah, aha 320, 1671, 3967 [natural interj.].

a   *indef. art.* a 16, 60, 64, 72, etc.; **an(e)** (*before vowels*) an 1079, 1148, 2229, etc.; some 1912 [OE *ān*]. See ONE, ILKE.

abaischite, abaiste, abayste, basschede, baiste *pp.* ashamed, abashed 255; confounded, disconcerted 1424, 2121, 2856, 3737 [AF *abahir, abaïss-*].

abbayes *n. pl.* abbeys, monasteries 3403 [OF *ab(b)aïe*].

abyde *v.* to remain, wait, await 4023; **habydes** *3 sg.* 596; **habyddez** *3 pl.* hesitate, wait 1431; *abyde on þe erthe,* stand your ground 3737 [OE *abīdan*].

abillere *adj. compar.* stronger, more powerful 2635 [OF *(h)able*].

abouen(n), aboun, abowen, abown(n)(e), abwen *adv.* aloft, on top, up, above 564, 775, 823, 904, 2060, 2303, etc.; in a higher place 511; *abouen on,* on top of 903 [OE *abufan*].

abowte *adv.* about, round about, around 2422, 2794, 3107, 3240, etc. [OE *abūtan*].

absence, absens *n.* absence 273, 1596, 3448 [OF *absence*].

abwen. See ABOUEN(N).

accorde *v.* to agree, consent 344; **accordide** *pp.* in accord 3133 [OF *acorder*].

ac(c)ounte, acownt *v.* to value, esteem, look up to 405; tell 3929; **accountes** *3 sg.* 1102[OF *aconter, acunter*].

accownte *n.* account 1677 [OF *acont, acunt*].

acton *n.* jacket worn under mail, usually quilted 902 (*see note*), 3457; **aketouns** *pl.* 2626 [OF *aketon, auqueton*].

affraye *n.* fear, terror 3226 [OF *esfrei, effrey*].

affrayede. See FRAIEZ.

aftyr(e) *prep.* after, in pursuit of (*sometimes following its object*) 83, 231, 279, 383, etc.; according to 149, 2745; about 954; *adv.* behind 393, 982, 2733, etc.; afterward, later, then 64, 82, 282, 329, etc.; throughout 885; ever after 1678; in pursuit 2217, 4257 [OE *æfter*].

agayne, aʒayne *adv.* again 258, 2549, 2949; back 4022; *syne agayne* back again 85 [OE *ongegn*]. See next.

agayn(e)s, agaynez, aʒaynes, aʒaynez, agayne *prep.* toward

211

774, 786, 1386, (after pron. obj.) 2681, 2799, (with pron. obj. unexpressed) 1378, 2101, 2791, etc.; against, counter to 1268, 1489, 2162, (after pron. obj.) 2117 [prec. with gen. ending].

agaynestande v. to hold back 3757; **aȝaynestondes** 3 pl. resist, stand up against 3126 [AGAYNE, adv. + STAND].

agast(e) pp. frightened, terrified 2442, 2728 [OE gǣstan].

ay(e) adv. always, ever, continually 20, 311, 855, 959, 2403, etc. [ON ei, ey].

ayele n. grandfather 2603 [OF aiel].

ayer(e), ayers, etc. See AYRE, AYR(E).

aylede pa. t. troubled, afflicted 2802 [OE eglan].

ayre, ayere n. heir, inheritor 279, 283, 1944, 2200, 2606, etc.; uninfl. pl. 3801; **ayers, ayerez** pl. 1740, 3146; offspring 3188 [OF (h)eir].

ayr(e), ayer(e) v. intr. to go, journey, be off, move about 455, 470, 1591, 3909, etc.; **ayres, ayer(e)s, ayerez** 3 sg. 617, 1259, 1329, 2290, etc.; **ayers** 3 pl. 4079; **ayerande** pres. p. 2830; trans. **ayerez** 3 sg. traverses [OF errer, eirer].

aythyre adj. either, both 1991, 2830; pron. aythyre aftyre oþer, each in turn, one after the other 939 [OE ǣgþer, red. from ǣghwæþer].

ayware adv. everywhere 614 [OE ǣghwǣr].

ajournede pp. put off, delayed 340 [OF ajorner, ajurner].

ajuggede pp. deemed, esteemed 862, 1658, 3411, 4110 [OF ajuger].

ake n. oak 1096 [OE āc].

akere: ane akere lenghe, a furlong (away) 3849 [OE acer].

aketouns. See ACTON.

alde. See OLDE.

alegges 3 pl. declare, affirm 4342 [late AF alegger].

alet n. ailette, steel plate of armor worn at the shoulder 2565 [OF alete].

alfyn n. oaf 1343 (see note) [OF alfin].

algarde n. wine from Algarve, Portugal 202.

alienes, alyenes, alyenez, alyenys, alynes n. pl. aliens 273, 306, 455, 617, etc.; dat. pl. to the aliens 418 [OF alien].

alkyn, alkyns adj. every sort of, every kind of, all kinds of 928, 1730, 3244 [OE alles cynnes, alra cynna].

all, al, alle adj. all 30, 56, 70, 93, etc.; (after n.) 820, 1064, 1884, etc.; both 958; n. all, everything, everyone 29, 178, 323, 406, etc.; adv. entirely, fully 201, 214, 382, 400, etc.; al(l) ouer(e), all over, everywhere 193, 764, 793, 1001, etc. [OE al(l)].

allas interj. alas! 868, 1153, 3965 [OF alas].

allblawsters n. pl. soldiers armed with arbalests, crossbowmen 2426 [AF allblaster].

allone adj. alone, only 541, 2312 [ALL, adv. + ONE, adj.].

allossede pp. celebrated, renowned 3881 [OF aloser].

alls. See AS.

allweldand, alweldande *pres. p.*
all-ruling, almighty 397, 1059
[OE *eallwealdende*].

almyghty *adj.* almighty 14 [OE
ælmihtig].

alofede. See next.

alowe *v.* to praise, laud 1036;
alowes *3 sg.* 396; **alofede** *pp.*
celebrated 2418 [OF *alouer*].

als. See AS, SWYTHE.

also *adv.* also, too 3504 [OE
alswā].

alweldande. See ALLWELDAND.

am(e) *1 sg. pres.* am 471, 640,
702, etc.; (*as auxil.*) 987, 3305
[OE *am*].

amede *pp.* reckoned, estimated
4068 [OF *esmer*, with infl. of
Picard *amer*].

amende *v.* to amend, rectify 3454
[OF *amender*].

**among(e), amang(e), emange,
imangez** *prep.* among, surrounded by, in the midst of 375,
1917, 2060, 3169, 3772, etc.;
adv. all this time 1238 [OE (*on*)
gemang, on mong, etc.; -*ez* =
adv. gen. ending].

ancestres, auncestres *n. pl.* ancestors 276, 521, 1310 [OF
ancestre].

ancestrye, awncestrye *n.* ancestry
1691, 1694, 1907 [OF *an-
ces*(*s*)*erie*, with infl. of *ancestre*].

and(e) *conj.* and 2, 3, 4, 7, 8, 9,
etc.; if 134, 339, 358, 387, 552,
etc.; but 2507 (*often abbr. in
MS*) [OE *and*].

ane. See ONE, adj. & pron.

anentis *prep.* next to, near 2568
[OE *on efen, on emn* + adv. gen.
-*es*].

anes. See ONES.

angells *n. pl.* angels 3801 [OE

ængel, from L *angelus*].

anger *n.* anger 1661 [ON *angr*].

angers *3 sg. impers.* me angers, it
angers me, I am angered 1662; it
grieves me, I am grieved 2838,
2848; **angerde** pp. 265, 1938,
1957 [ON *angra*].

any, ony(e) *adj.* any 374, 473,
577, 1015, etc.; as *n.* 1932 [OE
ænig].

ank(k)ere *n.* anchor 3601, 3644;
ankyrs *pl.* 493, 740 [OE *ancor*].

anlace *n.* dagger 1148 (*see note*)
[OF *alenas*].

anly, anely *adv.* only 98; alone,
singly 1499, 1981 [OE *ænlīce*,
adv.].

**anoyntede, en(n)oyntede, enoynt-
tede, ennoynttyde** *pp.* anointed,
sanctified 50, 101, 142, 144,
544, etc. [OF *enoint*, pp. of
enoindre].

anon, onon(e) *adv.* straightway, at
once, just, soon 571, 1178, 1231,
1816, 2006, etc. [OE *on ān, on
āne*].

anoþer(e) *pron.* another 566, 682,
1175, 1865, etc. [OE *ān ōþer*].

answere, ansuere *n.* reply, response 414, 508, 1592 [OE
andswaru].

answere, ansuere *v.* to explain 98;
account 670; answer, reply 306,
1674; **answer(e)s, ansuers** *3 sg.*
418, 986, 1346, etc.; **answarde,
ansuerde** *pa. t.* 288, 1326 [OE
an(*d*)*swarian, -swerian*].

anterous *adj.* bold, daring 2524;
awntrouseste *superl.*   1624 [OF
aventeros].

anters. See AUNTYRE.

apas *adv.* at a considerable pace,
quickly 4014 [*a*, prep. (OE
an) + OF *pas*].

apon(e), appon(e)　*prep.* upon, on, onto 195, 261, 365, 441, 455, etc.; in 669; over 750 [OE *uppon*].

apostyll　*n.* apostle 1256; **apostlys, postles** *pl.* 2413, 3807 [OE *apostol,* from L].

appairelles　*3 pl. refl.,* dress, deck 500; **appayrellde,** *pp.* 2461 [OF *aparailler*].

apparayll　*n.* array, embellishment 3365 [OF *aparail*].

apparant, apparaunt　*adj.* manifest, obvious (applied to one who will undoubtedly inherit) 1944, 2606 [OF *aparant*].

appere　*v. subj.* 94, 518 [OF *apareir, aper-*].

apperte　*adj.* plain, apparent 688 [OF *apert*].

appertly, appertlyche, pertly　*adv.* plainly, boldly 589, 1478, 2917 [from prec.].

approches　*3 pl.* approach 4105 [OF *aproch(i)er*].

araye(s).　See ARRAYE, n. & v.

araysede　*pp.* made up (an account) 1677 [ON *reisa*].

arase　*v. subj.* throw to the ground 4098 [OF *araser*].

arborye　*n.* shrubs 3244 [OF *arboirie*].

archers　*n. pl.* archers, bowmen 724, 1991, 3685 [AF *archer*].

ardant, ardauunt　*adj.* flaming 193, 1087 [OF *ardant*].

ar(e), or　*prep.* before 2933; *adv.* before, formerly 254, 2234, 2540, 3053; *conj.* before, until 331, 374, 437, 518, 529, etc. [OE *ǣr,* ON *ár*].

are, er(e)　*pres. pl.* are 127, 166, 387, 443, etc.; (*as auxil.*) have 600, 835, 1237, 1306, etc. [OE (*e*)*aron*].

are.　See OR, conj.

areste　*n.* projection on the side of the breastplate on which the lance rests when ready for a charge; *at areste,* ready for battle 311, 548; custody, bondage, captivity 1456, 1473, 1553 [OF *arest*].

areste　*v.* to capture 3492 (*with pron. obj. unexpressed*); **areste, ar(r)estede** *pa. t.* 329, 1409, 1429; **arrestede,** *pp.* 1416; commandeer 633; stop, restrain 3825, 4048 [OF *arester*].

aryefede, aryuede.　See ARRYFEDE.

arme　*n.* arm 2689, 3649; **armes, armez** *pl.* 703, 1096, 1133, 1159, etc. [OE *earm*].

armede, armyde　*pa. t.* armed 902, 2716; *pp.* 555, 610, 894, 1439, etc. [OF *armer*].

armes, armez　*n. pl.* weapons 2107; heraldic arms 1289, 1691, 1694, 2460, etc.; warfare 19, 24, 256, 284, etc.; *in, of armes, armez* in, of warfare 1317, 1741, 1905, etc.; *As armes!* To arms! 2717 [OF *armes*]. See CRAFTE, DEDE., n.[1].

armour　*n.* armor 2623 [OF *armeüre* (13th C. *armure*)].

arowes　*n. pl.* arrows 2105 [OE *earh*].

arraby(e)s　*n. pl.* Arabian horses 2288, 2337 [OF *ar(r)abi*].

ar(r)aye　*n.* array, disposition, arrangement, martial order 74, 311, 548, 2136, 2179, etc.; *owte of araye,* in disarray, in disorder 1207, 1417; display 1665 [OF *arei*].

arraye　*v.* to dress, arm, prepare for battle) 4137; **ar(r)ayes** *3 sg.* 2022, 3613; **arrayes, arrayez** *3 pl.* 1427, 1453 (*refl.*), 3620;

ar(r)ayede, arraiede *pp.* dressed, garbed 216; armed, fitted out, furnished 654, 757, 1291, etc.; marshaled, deployed 378, 388, 597, 611, 628, etc.; assembled 1334, 1925; arrayed 3647; **arayes** *3 sg.* rules, controls 509 [OF *areier*].

ar(r)estede. See ARESTE, V.

arryfede, aryefede *pp.* arrived 600, 835; **ryve** *infin.* 3896; *trans.* **aryuede** *pp.* gained, come to 3905 (*see note*) [OF *ariver*].

arte *2 sg. pres.* art, are 103, 138, 260, 443, 689, etc. [OE *eart*].

as, als, alls *prep.* as, like 87, 107, 117, 119, 122, etc.; *adv.* also, as well 1194; *conj.* as, just as 32, 55, 79, 84, 97, etc.; as if, as though 121, 716, 3225, 3261, etc.; so 1251, 1508, 2724; where 31, 573; to the extent that 866; as being 175, 988; while 118, 392, 737, etc.; when 1329; since 670; so (in asseveration) 669, 813, 887, 1687, etc. [red. from ALSO].

asaye *n.* experience 4312 [AF *asay*].

asaye. See ASSAYE.

asawt(t)e. See ASSAWTE.

ascente. See ASSENT(T)E, n. & v.

ascrye(e)z, askryes *3 sg.* cries out, shouts 1490, 2046, 2245, 2529, etc.; **ascryes, askryes** *3 pl.* 1412, 2717, 2874; **askryede** *pp.* 2800; *3 pl.* espy, discover, notice 1451, 4113; **askryede** *pa. t.* 2772; *3 sg.* attacks (with a battle cry) 1367, 3900, 3775, 4058; **ascriez** *3 pl.* 1768 [OF *escrier*].

aske *v.* to ask, call for, request, demand, inquire 114, 286, 1542, 2350, etc.; **asches** *2 sg.* 343;

askes, askys, aschez *3 sg.* 157, 241, 413, 508, etc.; **askede, askyde, aschede** *pa. t.* 271, 479, 715, 1009, etc. [OE *āscian*]. See LEUE, n.

askyng *vbl. n.* asking 3146 [from prec.].

askyres, askryede, etc. See ASCRYE(E)Z.

assaye, asaye *v.* to assess (*subj.*) 2347 (*with pron. obj. unexpressed*); venture, make an attempt (at something difficult) 2615 [OF *as(s)ayer*].

assaille *v.* to assault, attack 2431; **assailles** *2 sg.* 3548 [OF *asail(l)ir*].

assawte, asawt(t)e *n.* battle, assault 1697, 3012, 3032, 3053, etc. [OF *as(s)aut*].

assemble, semble *v. trans.* to assemble, bring together 4027; **sembles, semblez, assemblez** *3 sg.* 590, 1961, 3032; **assembles** *3 pl.* 2353; **semble** *imper. pl.* 627; **semblede** *pa. t.* 1421; *pp.* 3531, 3577; *intr.* come together, gather 63, 331; *3 pl.* 4108, 4293; *pa. t.* 409, 1846, **assemblede** 609; *pp.* 634, 1306, 3182, 3598, **semblyde** 70; come together in battle, meet in conflict 967; *3 sg.* 1491; **sembles** *3 pl.* 3746; *pa. t.* 1457; *assembles . . . on 3 pl.* move in on 3788 [OF *assembler*].

assemblé *n.* assembly, council 1578, 1962; hostile encounter, clash 1852, 2906 [OF *as(s)emblee*].

assente, ascente, sent *v.* to assent 1506, 1628; *subj.* 644, 1963 [OF *assenter*].

assent(t)e, ascente, sent *n.* assent 60, 502, 2615, 3065 [from prec.].

asses *n. pl.* asses 2337 [OE *assa*].

assygne v. to assign, appoint, specify 319; **assingnez** 3 pl. 727; **assignede, assingnyde** pa. t. 240, 1743; **assignyde, assygnede** pp. 658 (see note), 1628, 3588 [OF assigner].

assoyllede pp. absolved 3498 [OF a(s)souldre, a(s)soill-].

astate n. office, position 684 [OF estate].

at, att prep at 9, 33, 64, 78, etc.; after verb) 58; through, by 664, 1564; of, from 144, 694, 713, 1441, etc.; to 940, 1165 (expressing purpose); in 389; on 1372, 1773, 2203; at the time of 494, 1008, 1150 [OE æt]. See ONES, REUERENCE.

at conj. = THAT what, that 1842, 3484, 4020 [N dial. var.].

atheliste adj. superl. most noble 1593 [OE æþele].

atyre n. attire, apparel 4186 [from OF atirer, v.].

attamede. See ENTAMEDE.

attyryde pp. attired 3189 [OF atirer].

atvndyre. See PUTTE.

auctors n. pl. authorities 4342 [OF autor, L auctor].

auditoure n. accountant, auditor 1673; **audytours** pl. court officers 661 [AF auditour].

aughte, awughte adj. eight 278, 2627, 3188 [OE eahta].

aughte. See AWE.

aughtende adj. eighth 462 [OE eahtoþa, ON attundi].

auncestres. See ANCESTRES.

auntyre, awntere v. (usually refl.) to venture, risk, expose to danger 360, 1660; **anters** 3 sg. 1498; **awnters** 3 pl. 1596, 2839; **awntrende** pres. p. daring, brave 2717 [OF aventurer].

auntire, awntere, etc. See AUENTURE.

austeren, austeryn adj. stern, harsh, severe 306, 414, 571, 670, 1326, etc. [OF austere with infl. from STERYN].

avanttwarde, avawewarde, avawm(e)warde, avawwarde, vawewarde, wawarde n. vanguard, front line 324, 1981, 2024, 2051, 2219, 2829, 3168, etc. [ONF avantwarde, vauntward, vaumward, etc.].

avauntede, auantid pa. t. praised, celebrated 1564; pp. 2864 [OF ava(u)nter].

avawewarde, avawm(e)warde. See AVANTTWARDE.

avawmbrace n. vambrace, plate of armor protecting the forearm 2568 [AF avantbras].

auenaunt adj. noble, splendid, beautiful 2626, 3188, 3208, 3500, etc. [OF avenaunt].

aventaile n. the lower movable front of the helmet for the admission of air; in the visored basinet, the lower part of the visor which has slits for breathing 910, 2572 [AF *aventail = OF esventail].

auenture, auntire, aw[n]tire n. fortune, good fortune 642, 2244, 2617; adventure, a nawntere = an awntere, an adventure 1905; **awnters** pl. 1967, 2007; at awntere, recklessly, madly 2543 [OF aventure].

avyede pa. t. took (their) way, set out 3716 [OF avier].

avires 3 sg. turns 3164 [OF avirer].

avisemente n. advice, counsel 148 [OF avisement].

avissely, auyssely adv. warily,

carefully 2699; deliberately, in a leisurely manner 3165 [from OF *avisé,* pp. of *aviser*].

auoyeddyde *pa. t.* drew apart from 2051 [AF *avoider*].

avowe *n.* vow 296, 308, 347, 386, 3997, etc.; **avowes, avowez** *pl.* 396, 1983, 2064 [from next].

avowe *v.* to vow 357; **avowede** *pp.* avowed, declared 369 [OF *avouer*].

awaye *adv.* away 468, 798, 1418, 2070, etc.; along, on (his) way 3156, 3819, 3838 [OE *on weg*].

awe *v.* to owe 99; **aughte, awghte** *pa. t.* ought 289, 1595, 3509; **awes** *3 sg. impers.* (it) behooves 455; *pa. t.* 1583, 3340; *pa. t.* possessed, owned, had 29, 276, 521, 1015, 2867, etc. [OE *āgan*].

awen. See OWNN.

awfull *adj.* awesome, inspiring dread 3502 [from ON *agi,* n.].

awghte. See AWE.

awghtene *adj.* eighteen 4069 [OE *e(a)htatēne*].

awke *adj.* perverse, strange 13 (*see note*) [ON *afug*].

awk(e)warde *adv.* with a backward stroke 2247, 2564 [from prec.].

awlde. See OLDE.

awncestrye. See ANCESTRYE.

awntere, awntire, awnters, etc. See AUNTYRE, AUENTURE.

awntrende. See AUNTYRE.

awntrouseste. See ANTEROUS.

awughte. See AUGHTE.

azure, azoure *n.* azure, blue 193 (referring to flames), 765, 3355 [OF *azur*].

bacenett(e) *n.* a light, conical helmet 906 (*see note*), 2695, 2770 **bacenetez** *pl.* 1754 [OF *bacinet*].

bachel(l)ers *n. pl.* young knights 68, 567, 857, 1424 [OF *bacheler*].

bagis, bagys *n. pl.* heraldic emblems 2303, 3730 [OF *bage*].

baye *adj.* bay, red-brown 918 [OF *bai*].

baiste. See ABAISCHITE.

baite *v. intr.* to graze 2694; *trans.* **baytes** *3 pl.* put (a horse) to graze 2509; **baytand, baytande** *pres. p.* grazing (a horse) 2516, 2671 [ON *beita*].

bake, bakke *n.* back 1047, 1159, 2203, 3257 [OE *bæc*].

baken *pp.* baked 3166 [OE *bacan*].

bakhalfe *n.* back portion 1482 [BAKE + HALFE].

balde, baldly. See BOLDE, BOLDLY(E).

bale *n.* torment, anguish, pain 805, 981, 1054, 3974, etc.; trouble, woe 1014, 1393, 1426, 3558, etc.; *adj.* baleful, deadly 1483 [OE *balu*].

bale-fyre *n.* bonfire 1048 [OE *bǣlfȳr*].

balefull *adj.* deadly, injurious 791; wretched, miserable 1029, 1136 [from BALE].

baltyrde *pa. t.* hopped about clumsily 782 [prob. ON; cf. Dan *baltre,* Scot. dial. *balter*].

bandez *n. pl.* shackles, bondage 1180, 1485 [ON *band*].

baneoure *n.* flag-bearer 3732 [OF *baneour*].

banere *n.* banner 69, 361, 1695, 3072; **baneres, baners** *pl.* 1605, 1618, 1633, 2212, etc.; *at baner,* under (their) banners 1408 [OF *ban(i)ere*].

banerette *n.* banneret, baronet 1914; **banerettes, banerettez,**

banarettez *pl.* 68, 567, 1403, 1424, etc. [OF *baneret*].

banke, baunke *n.* shore, bank 728, 729, 2516, 3731, etc.; **bankes, bankkes** *pl.* 3544, 3714, 4032 [of Scand. orig.; cf, ON *bakki*].

barayne *adj.* barren 224 [OF *baraigne*].

barbycan(e) *n.* watchtower 1183, 2470 [OF *barbacane*].

barbours *n. pl.* barbers 2331, 2577 [AF *barbour*].

bare. See BORE.

bare. See BERE, *v.*

barefote *adj.* barefoot 2309 [OE *bærfōt*].

bare-heuvede *adj.* bareheaded (as mark of respect) 3630 [from OE *bær* + HEUEDE].

bareheuedys *n. pl.* boars' heads 177 [from BARE, n. + HEUEDE].

barelegyde *adj.* barelegged 2122 [from OE *bær* + ON *leggr*].

barell-ferrers *n. pl.* vessels (casks, jars, or leather bottles) in which water or wine was carried on horseback on military expeditions 2714 [*barell* (= OF *baril*) + OF *ferr(i)ere*].

barge *n.* boat, bark 3629; **bargez** *pl.* 729 [OF *barge*].

baronage *n.* body of barons, peerage 587, 1242, 4328 [OF *barnage*].

barowes *n. pl.* barrows, boars 191 [OE *bearg, bearh*].

barrers *n. pl.* barricades 2469 [AF *barrere*].

basyns *n. pl.* basins 2331 [OF *bacin*].

basschede. See ABAISCHITE.

batail(l)e, batayl(l)e, etc. See BAT(T)ELL.

baterde *pp.* embossed, hammered

189; **bettrede** *pa. t.* hammered down 3656 [OF *bat(t)re*].

bathe. See BOTHE.

bat(t)ell, batail(l)e, batayl(l)e *n.* battle 316, 783, 790, 1486, etc.; **batailles** *pl.* 3738; combat 826; army, battalion 1224, 2011, 2068, 2476, etc.; **batells, bat(t)ailles** *pl.* 1425, 1618, 2449, etc.; *in batell,* in battle array 1450 [OF *bataille*].

baunke. See BANKE.

bawmede *pp.* anointed (a body) 980, 2298, 4020 [OF *balsamer, v., baume, n.*].

be, bee *v.* to be 111, 230, 250, etc.; *subj.* 10, 92, 93, 158, etc.; *imper. sg.* 546, 551, 1173, etc.; **bes(e), bees, bez** *3 sg.* 1016; *3 pl.* 97; *imper. pl.* 222, 3798; **bene** *3 pl. subj.* 2850; *pp.* 846, 873, 1177, 1444, etc.; *future,* shall be, will be 585, 981, 1553, 1971, etc.; **bees(e)** *2 sg.* 1688, 2663, 2667, etc.; *3 sg.* 3976, 4312 [OE *bēon*].

be. See BY.

beblede *pp.* bloodied, covered with blood 2250 [from OE *be-* + *blēdan*].

because, bycause *conj.* because 1053, 1785; *because of, because that,* because 123, 1065; because of, on account of 1778, 3898, 4186; for the purpose of 4201 (*see note*) [BY + CAUSE].

bechen *adj.* beech 1713 [OE *bēcen*].

bechopes. See BYSCHOPES.

becomys *3 sg.* is suitable to, befits 4317 [OE *becuman*].

bed(d)e *n.* bed 758, 805, 2858, etc. [OE *bedd*].

bede *adj.* hunting 3464 [see note].

bedes. See BID.

bedgatt *n.* going to bed 1030 [BED(D)E + GATE, act of going].

bee. See BY.

beerynes. See BERNE.

bees(e). See BE.

befall *v. trans.* to befall, fall to 1985; **befell** *pa. t.* 1394; **befallen** *pp.* 3028, (*with pron. obj. unexpressed*) 1892, 2368; *intr.* come to pass 2737; *pp.* 2371, 3521 [OE *befeallan*].

befor(e), byfore *prep.* in front of, ahead of, in the presence of 96, 122, 176, 523, 1199, 1514 (*after noun*), etc.; *adv.* at hand 226; ahead 1451, 2451, 3002, 3013; up front, in the lead 612, 2111, 2760, 2836, etc.; in advance, beforehand 965, 1531, 1767, 2946; earlier 1885 [OE *beforan*].

begynnes, begynnys *3 sg.* begins 384, 3659; **begane** *pa. t* (*subj.*) 374; **gan** *pa. t.* 2510; **begynnande** *pres. p.* 2963 [OE *beginnan*].

behynd(e), byhynden *prep.* in back of 694, 1855; *adv.* in back 2077, 2873; in the rear 4175 [OE *behindan*].

beholde, behalde *v.* to behold, look 760, 3239, 3989; **behelde** *pa. t.* 1284, 3074; **behaldande** *pres. p.* 3107 [OE *behealdan*].

beyldede. See BELDE.

bekende, bekennyde *pa. t.* handed over, entrusted, commended 482, 2340, 2355 [OE *be-* + *cennan*].

bekerde. See BEKYRE.

bekez *3 sg.* warms 1048 [uncertain; N and Scot. form, rel. to OE *bacan*].

bekyn *n.* beacon 564 [OE *bēcen*].

bekyre *v.* to skirmish, fight, attack 3679; **bekerde** *pa. t.* 2096; **bekyrs** *3 pl.* assaults, besieges 2425 [uncertain].

beknowe *imper. sg.* declare 3867 [OE *becnāwan*].

belde *v. intr.* to shelter, lodge, dwell 8; **bieldez** *3 pl.* 1242; *trans.* **beldytt** *pa. t.* built, built up 38; **beyldede** *pp.* 566 [OE *beldan*].

beleue *v. intr.* to be left, remain 3583; *trans.* **belefede, bylefede, belevede, byleuyde, beleuefede,** etc. *pp.* left 1250, 1538, 1557, 1885, 2145, 2366, etc.; [OE *belǣfan*].

belyfe, belyue *adv.* quickly, with haste 1263, 2068, 2336, 3732 [BY + LYFE, n.].

belles *n. pl.* bells 490, 4332 [OE *belle*].

beme *n.* beam 3663 [OE *bēam*].

bendes, bendys *3 pl.* bend (a bow) 3036, 3617; **bendyde** *pa. t.* 2424 [OE *bendan*].

benethe *adv.* underneath 3278 [OE *beneoþan*].

benyson *n.* blessing 4318 [OF *beneison*].

bente *n.* field, grassy field, plain 915, 1054, 1067, 1184, 1380, etc. [OE *beonot-,* grass, in place names].

berde *n.* beard 1012, 1013, 1016, 1033, etc.; **berdez** *pl.* 1002 [OE *beard*].

bere *n.* bear 775, 790, 802, 823, etc. [OE *bera*].

bere *v.* to wear, carry as a heraldic device 51, 4316; **beres** *3 sg.* 1375; **bare** *pa. t.* 291, 3426, 3759, 3962; carry, bear 615, 1034, 1180, 1182; *pa. t.* 893, 2521, 3367; **borne** *pp.* 361, 1695, 3738, 4199; **berez** *3 sg.* thrusts (with a sword) 1379; *pp.* 2238; **beris** *3 sg.* rushes, charges 1771; *bere doun* overwhelm, overthrow 1486; *beres down 3 pl.* 2808;

beris down imper. pl. 3736; *pa. t.* cut down, threw down 2212; *pp.* 1433 [OE *beran*].

bery(e) *v.* to bury 2383, 4330, 4318; **beryes** *3 sg.* 2379; **beryede** *pp.* 980 [OE *byrgan*]

beryell *n.* burial 1776, 2188 [incorrectly formed as sg. of OE *byrgels,* tomb].

beryeng(e) *vbl. n.* burial 2377, 4023 [from BERY(E)].

beryn(e). See BERNE.

berkes *3 sg.* barks 1351 [OE *beorcan*].

bernakes *n. pl.* wild geese, barnacle geese 189 [OF *bernaque*].

berne, beryn(e), bierne, byerne, byeryn *n.* man, warrior, baron, knight 116, 304, 962, 2169, 2202, etc.; **be(e)ryn(e)s, byernes, biernez, byernez** etc. *pl.* 148, 255, 630, 1183, 1662, etc.; **beryns** *poss.* 3661; any man 4146; creature 1094 [OE *beorn* (poetic), with infl. from OF *baron, barun*].

beronen, berown *pp.* wet, flooded 3946, 3971 [OE *berinnan*].

besauntez *n. pl.* golden coins (originally of Byzantium) or ornaments resembling golden coins 3256 [OF *besan*].

beseke *v.* to beseech, beg, urge 472, 681, 1547, 1555, etc.; **besekez, besekys** *3 sg.* 305, 1235; **besekes** *1 pl.* 127, 2317; **beso(u)ghte** *pa. t.* 1234, 1438, 3137, 3181, etc. [OE *besēcan*].

besett *pp.* beset, surrounded 3795 [OE *besettan*].

besy, besye *adj.* busy, diligent 4095; *as n.* busyness 3630 [OE *bisig*].

beside, besyde *prep.* near, by 853; *adv.* nearby 842 [OE *be sīdan*].

bessomes *3 sg.* sweeps with force or violence 3661 [from OE *besema,* sweeping implement].

bestaile *coll. n.* domesticated beasts 1050 [OF *bestaille*].

beste *n.* beast 107, 811, 3837, etc.; **bestes, bestez** *pl.* 2287, 2488, 3232, etc. [OF *beste*].

beste *adj. superl.* best, noblest, finest 255, 630, 907, 1012, etc. (*often as n.*); *adv.* best 55, 1598, 1727, 1776, etc. [OE *betst*].

betakyns *3 sg.* betokens, signifies 822, 824 [OE *betācnian*].

beteche *v.* to deliver, entrust, commend to 1611; **beteches** *3 sg.* 714 (*with pron. obj. unexpressed*) [OE *betæcan*].

betyde, betydde *v.* to befall, occur 3567, 4191; *3 sg. impers. subj.* 4325; **betyd(d)es, betydez, betyddys** *3 sg. future* 1020, 2582, 3482, 4315 [OE *be- + tīdan*].

betoke, betuke *pa. t.* handed over, delivered, entrusted to 1889, 3190, 4015 [OE *be- + TAKE*].

betraye *v.* to betray 669; **betrayede** *pp.* 1955, 3565 [OE *be- + OF traïr*].

betrappede *pp.* entrapped 1630 [OE *betræppan*].

bett *v.* to beat, strike 2470; **bettes** *3 pl.* 2808; **bet(t)** *pa. t.* beat 3682; whipped 3656; **betyn** *pp.* embossed, inlaid, damascened 3631, 3646, 3945 [OE *bēatan*].

better(e), bettir(e), bettyr(e) *adj. compar.* better 190, 1453, 3082, 3576, etc.; *adv.* better 250, 992, 1033, 1427, etc.; (*the*) *bettere, bettire,* etc., the better, better, more 1782, 1932, 2414, 2535, etc. [OE *betera, be(t)tra*].

bettrede. See BATERDE.

betuke. See BETOKE.

betwene, bytwene *prep.* between (*with pron. obj. unexpressed*) 934, 946 [OE *betweonan*].

betwyx *prep.* between 801, 2798 [OE *betwux*].

beueryn *adj.* beaver-colored, reddish-brown 3630 [from OE *beofor,* n.].

bewe *v. intr.* to bow 3366; **bowes** *3 pl.* bow, bow down, give allegiance 69, 2310; *3 sg.* bends, sinks 2696; *trans. 3 sg.* turns 2251 [OE *būgan*].

bewells *n. pl.* bowels 2175, 2203 [OF *boël*].

bewes. See BOWES.

bewschers *n. pl.* ?buttocks (*see note*) 1047 [uncertain].

by, be(e) *prep.* by, by means of, through 26, 32, 43, 46, 139, 174, 258, etc.; (in oaths) 164, 255, 368, 863, 1063, etc.; by virtue of 531; with 60, 502, 3081; near, next to 327, 424, 497, 619, 622, 882, etc.; to 453, 787; at 2125; *be this, be that, by that,* by this (that) time, by the time that, by then, when 602, 1198, 2145, 2510, 3718; *conj.* by the time that, when, before 488, 840, 976, 2482, 2873, 4093 [OE *bi, be*]. See FORBY, TALE, n², SETT(E), v.

bid, bidde, byd(e), bydde *v.* to bid, command 433, 1181, 1752, 2192, 2348, etc.; **biddis, bydes, byddez,** etc. *3 sg.* 1263, 1590, 1617, 2361, etc.; **bad(e)** *pa t.* 2383, 3359, 3366, 3370, etc.; **biddez** *2 sg.* offer, give 1014; **biddis, bedes** *3 pl.* 505, 2310; *3 sg.* offers battle, challenges 4214; *3 pl.* engages (in combat) 2808; ask, entreat 2188 [comb.

of OE *biddan* and OE *bēodan*].

bidding, byddyng *vbl. n.* bidding, command 1030, 1931, 4146 [from prec.].

byde, bidde *v. intr.* dwell 8; stay, tarry 936, 1968, 4028; delay 2042; **bydez** *3 pl.* 587; *trans.* **byddez** *3 sg.* awaits 1776 (*with* AFTYR(E); *3 & imper. pl.* 629, 1030 [OE *bīdan*].

bieldez. See BELDE.

bierdez. See BIRDE.

byeryn, bierne, byerne, etc. See BERNE.

byfore. See BEFOR(E).

bygger *adj. compar.* mightier, stronger in battle 790; **byggly** *adv.* with great force or violence 1376 [uncertain].

byhalue *n.* behalf 1674 [OE *be healfe*].

byhoues, byhouys, byhowys, bus *3 sg. impers.* it behooves 1715, 2576, 3579, 4135, etc. [OE *behōfian*].

bylefede, byleuyde. See BELEUE.

bilige *n.* the bottom of a ship's hull 3663 [corruption of *bulge* (OF *boulge*)].

bynde *v.* to bind, tie 453; **bownden** *pp.* 3316 [OE *bindan*].

bynne *prep.* within 804 [OE *binnan*].

birde *n.* woman, bride 2858; **birdes, birdez, bierdez, byrdez** *pl.* women 999, 1029, 1052, 1136, 2190, 4339 [OE *brȳd*].

byrdez, bryddes *n. pl.* birds 931, 2510, 2673 [OE *byrd*].

byrre *n.* force, momentum 3661 [ON *byrr*].

birtenede. See BRITTEN.

byschopes, bechopes *n. pl.* bishops 68, 4328 [OE *bisceop*].

byswenkez *3 sg.* strains, exerts

himself 1128 [OE *beswincan*].

byt(t)es *3 sg.* bites 119, 791 [OE *bītan*].

blade *n.* blade, sword 1113, 1381, 3359 [OE *blæd*].

blake *adj.* black 775, 1090, 4339 [OE *blāc*].

blanke, blonke *n.* horse, steed 453, 1799, 2203, 2251, 2518, etc.; **blankes, blonk(k)es, blonkez** *pl.* 615, 730, 895, 936, 1634, etc. [OE *blanca*].

blasons *n. pl.* shields 1860 [OF *blason*].

blawe *v.* to blow 2662; **blawen** *pp.* 1286 [OE *blāwan*].

blawnchede *pp.* whitened, whitewashed 3039 [cf. OF *blanchir*].

ble, blee *n.* color, complexion 2576, 3558, 4213; shade, hue 3332 [OE *blēo*].

bledez *3 sg.* bleeds 1054 [OE *blēdan*].

blemeste *pp.* wounded, injured 2578 [OF *blemir, blemiss-*].

blendez *3 sg.* blends, mingles 1799 [OE *blandan*].

blenke *v. trans.* to thwart 2857; *intr.* turn aside, flinch 3640, 3735; **blenkes** *3 sg.* 4213 [OE *blencan*].

bleryde *pa. t.* stuck out (his) tongue 782 [uncertain].

blethely. See BLYTHELY.

blewe *adj.* blue, azure 3332 [OF *bleu*].

blyn(e) *v.* to cease, leave off 1931, 2578, 3975, 3981 [OE *blinnan*].

blyschit *pa. t.* glared 116 [OE *blyscan*].

blysse *n.* joy, blessedness, beatitude 8, 1485 [OE *bliss*].

blyssyng *vbl. n.* blessing 4103 [from OE *blētsian*].

blithe, blyth(e) *adj.* quiet, calm, gentle 629, 895, 1224; happy 981, 1016, 2069, 3219, 4103, etc. [OE *blīþe*].

blythely, blethely *adv.* smoothly, easily 835; happily 1223, 4147 [OE *blīþelīce*].

blod(e), blude *n.* blood 175, 392, 795, 1121, etc.; lineage 4343; Christ's blood 3981 (*see note*); *as coll. n.* lusty men, young bloods 2509 [OE *blōd*].

blode-bande *n.* a bandage for stopping bleeding 2576 (*see note*) [prec. + OF *bande*].

blod-hondes *n. pl.* bloodhounds (*fig.*), hunters for blood 3640 [BLOD(E) + OE *hund*].

blody(e), blodé *adj.* bloody 793, 1860, 3946, 3971 [OE *blōdig*].

blondirs *2 sg. refl.* confound (yourself), distract (yourself) in understanding 3975 [uncertain].

blonke, blonkes, etc. See BLANKE.

blude. See BLOD(E).

body(e) *n.* body 7, 2697, 4020 [OE *bodig*].

boy *n.* boy, knave, wretch 1351; **boyes** *pl.* 2122, 2856, 3122; page 2519 [obscure].

boystous. See BUSTOUS.

bolde, balde *adj.* brave, valiant, bold 804, 893, 1170, 1393, 1775, 1424 (*after n.*), etc.; *as n.* 79, 835, 1012, 1800, etc.; **boldeste** *superl.* 1414 [OE *bald*].

boldly(e), boldely, baldly *adv.* bravely 630, 1450, 1486, 4111; fiercely 791, 3036; boldly 1484, 3680 [OE *baldlīce*].

bones, bonys *n. pl.* bones 1783, 2934, 3776 [OE *bān*].

bonettez *n. pl.* pieces of canvas laced to the foot or the top of a sail to catch more wind 3656 [OF *bonet*].

borde, bourde, burde *n.* table 79, 171, 1594, 1930; *at the burdez,* at table 3194; *on, within bo(u)rde,* on shipboard 630, 730, 3680; *on(e) burd(e),* on (their) sides 3662 (*see note*); at (their) sides, alongside 3681; *ouer burdez,* overboard 3700, 3702 [OE *bord*].

bordyrde *adj.* bordered 1002 [from next].

bordour *n.* ornamental strip along the edge of an object 4211; **bordurs** *pl.* 907 [OF *bordure*].

bore, bare *n.* boar 3123, 4214; **bores** *pl.* 188 [OE *bār*].

borne. See BERE, V.

boste *n.* clamor, outcry 1351; boast 1931, 2857, 3737 [uncertain].

bosturs *n. pl.* boasters 1393 [from prec.].

bot, bott, botte *prep.* except 516, 521, 541, 657, 983, etc.; except for 4070; *adj.* only 2687, 3182; *adv.* only, but 378, 448, 616, 686, 830, etc.; *conj.* but, nevertheless, however, yet, unless 10, 70, 78, 144, 162, 214, 311, 363, etc.; and, then 239, 260, 998, 1364, 1571, 1601, 2006, etc.; *bot ȝif(e),* if, unless 250, 356, 486, 2539, 2660, etc. [OE *būtan*].

botes, bottes *n. pl.* small boats 748, 3681, 3921 [OE *bāt*].

bothe, bothen, bathe *adj.* both 34, 35, 459, 531, 764, 789, etc.; (more than two) 352, 662, 3142; *adv.* both 19 [ON *baþir*].

botles, botelesse, buteless *adj.* beyond help or remedy 3558, 3976; *as n.* 981; useless, unavailing 1014 [OE *bōtlēas*].

bottes. See BOTES.

botures *n. pl.* bitterns, small herons 189 [OF *butour*].

boun, bounnez, etc. See BOWNE.

bourde. See BORDE.

bourden *3 pl.* tilt at, charge with a spear 3122 (*see note*) [OF *border, bourder,* from *behorder,* to fence, tilt].

bourdez *3 sg.* banters 1170 [OF *bourder*].

boure *n.* ladies' chamber 2190 [OE *būr*].

boustous. See BUSTOUS.

bouxom, bouxvm, bouxsomly *adj.* submissive, meek 107; obedient 4147 (*with v.* to be *unexpressed*); obliging, amiable 2858 [OE **būhsum,* from stem of *būgan,* v.].

bowes, bowghez, bewes *n. pl.* shoulders 188; boughs 921, 1711, 3247, 3366 [OE *bōg*].

bowes. See BEWE.

bowes of vys(e) *n. pl.* arbalests, crossbows 2424, 3617 [OE *boga* + OF *vis*].

bowghez. See BOWES.

bowmen *n. pl.* bowmen, archers 2095 [OE *boga* + MAN].

bownden. See BYNDE.

bowndis *n. pl.* borders, borderlands 3551 [AF *bounde*].

bowne, boun *v. intr.* to go, hasten 936; **bown(n)es, bownez** *3 sg.* 1381, 3465, 3591; *3 sg.* falls, falls down 2696, 3762 (*refl.*), 4251; **bownez** *3 pl.* 1136; *refl.* ready oneself, betake onself, hasten 1013, 1034; **bounnez, bownnys** *3 sg.* 783, 3219; *trans. & intr. 3 sg.* makes ready, prepares 3925; *3 pl.* 1617; **bounede** *pa. t.* 915 [from next].

bownn *adj.* ready, prepared, armed 1633, 2331, [ON *búinn*].

box *n.* blow 1111 [unknown].

brace *v.* to gird, encircle 1182; **bracez** *3 sg.* fastens on, fixes 914 [OF *bracier*].

bracer *n.* piece of armor covering the arm 4247; **bracers** *pl.* 1859 [OF *brasseure*].

brade. See BRODE.

braggers *n. pl.* braggarts 1348 [from *brag*, v. (see next)].

bragges, braggen *3 pl.* sound, blare, blow (trumpets) 1484, 4107; **braggede** *pa. t.* 3657 [from *brag*, n. (origin uncertain)].

brayd *v. trans.* to draw, pull 1172; **braydes, bray(e)dez** *3 sg.* 906, 2069, 2695, 4215; **braydez** *3 pl.* 1754; **brayden,** *pp.* flung 3945; **browd(d)en** *pp.* interlocked, braided, linked 1858, 2807, 4119; *intr. 3 sg.* moves quickly, rushes 2073, 3125 (*coll. n.*), 3731 [OE *bregdan*].

brayde *n.* blow 3762 [OE *bræd*].

brayell *n.* belly 793 (*see note*) [OF *braiel*].

brayne *n.* brain 1113, 2770, 3857, 3982; **braynes, braynez** *pl.* 2114, 2272; skull 3672 [OE *brægn*].

brake *pa. t.* burst (forth) 1407 [OE *brecan*].

brand(e), brannde, bronde *n.* sword 893, 914, 963, 1111, 1172, etc. **brandes, brondez, brondis,** etc. *pl.* 1487, 1861, 2273, 2309, 2378, etc. [OE *brand, brōnd*].

brankkand *pres. p.* prancing 1861 [obscure; cf. MHG *brangen*, adorn, vaunt onself].

brasen *adj.* hard as brass 3619 [OE *bræsen*].

braste. See BRISTE.

brathely. See BROTHLY.

braunchers *n. pl.* young birds 190 [OF *branchier*].

braune. See BRAWN(E).

brawlyng *vbl. n.* quivering, vibration 2176 [from OF *brauler*].

brawl(l)e *v. refl.* to strive, contend, fight 2349, 2362; **brawles** *3 sg.* boasts loudly 1349; cries out 4251 [uncertain; cf. ModDu *brallen*, brag, boast, ModG dial. *brallen*, shout].

brawnches *n. pl.* branches 3367 [OF *branche*].

brawndysche *v. trans.* to brandish, flourish (a weapon) 3359; **braundesch[t]e, brawndeste** *pa. t.* 1056, 3657; *intr.* **braundyschte** *pa. t.* flourished (his) limbs, swaggered 782 [OF *brandir, brandiss-*].

brawn(e), braune *n.* flesh, meat 188, 2715; boar, swine 1095 [OF *braon*].

brede *n.*[1] breadth; *on(e) brede, one brode,* spread out, abroad, wide open 1224, 2011, 2273, 3646, 3656 [OE *brædu, brædo*, n.; *brād*, adj].

brede *n.*[2] bread, food 79, 2715; **bredes** *pl.* 224; pastry crust 190; meat 1052; **bredis, bredez** *pl.* 1049, 2715 [OF *brēad*].

bregaundez *n. pl.* foot soldiers, mercenaries 2096 [OF *briga(u)nd*].

breke *v.* to violate 4146 (*future*); **brekes** *3 pl.* break through, break out 1425, 3124; **brake** *pa. t.* 2176 [OE *brecan*].

breklesse *adj.* without breeches, naked 1048 [from OE *brēc*].

breme *adj.* (*as n.*) fierce, bold 1380; **bremly** *adv.* boldly, vigorously 4107 [OE *brēme*].

breny, brené *n.* mail-shirt, armor 1482, 2253, 4212; **breny(e)s, bryneys, brenes, brenez** *pl.* 1413,

1419, 1474, 1482, 1525, 1858,
etc. [OE *byrne,* OF *brunie*].

brenyede, brynyede   *pp.* mailed,
armored 316, 3680 [from prec.].

brest(e)   *n.* breast 793, 1090,
1159, 1690, etc.; **brestez** *pl.* 191,
1413, 1425, 1858; heartbeat
2771 [OE *brēost*].

brestys.   See BRISTE.

brethe   *n.*¹ breath 107 (*see note*);
vapor 214 (*see note*) [OE *brǣþ,*
brēþ].

breth(e)   *n.*² wrath, anger, rage
117, 2213, 3465, 3557, 3926
[ON *brǽþi*].

brethemen   *n. pl.* trumpeters 4107
[BRETHE, n.¹ + MAN].

brethly   *adv.* madly, wildly 3661
[from BRETHE, n.²].

brettyn, brettened.   See BRITTEN.

bryddes.   See BYRDEZ.

brydill, brydyll   *n.* bridle 453,
1500, 2085, 2251, etc.; **brydills**
pl. 1395 [OE *brīdel*].

brigge, brygge   *n.* drawbridge
2470, 3124 [OE *brycg*].

brighte, bryghte   *adj.* bright, shining 177, 214, 361, 1056, etc.;
beautiful, magnificent 191; gaudy,
showy 1349, 2856; fair 1159;
brighttere *compar.* brighter 3282
[OE *beorht, berht*].

brymly   *adv.* arrogantly, fiercely
117, 4214 [from BREME].

bryne, brynne   *v.* to burn, burn up
106, 564, 3641; **brynnez** *3 sg.*
1241; **brynte** *pa. t.* 117; *pp.* 3520
[OE *byrnan, birnan*].

bryneys.   See BRENY.

bryng(e)   *v.* to lead (as a beast)
107; **bryngez** *3 pl.* 730; bring,
draw 316, 2188, 3366, 4330
(*with pron. obj. unexpressed*);
bryngez, bryngges *3 sg.* 1381,
3662; **broght(e)** *pa. t.* 1193,

1483, 1698, etc.; *pp.* 1013, 1016,
1033, etc.; bro(u)ghte (hym) *o*
lyfe, oute of lyfe, owte of lyue,
etc., sent (him) from life, killed
(him) 802, 1066, 1775, 1800,
2378, etc. (*o = of*); *bryng them*
o dawe, send them from (life's)
days, kill them 3736 (*dawe =*
days); *broughte vndire,* brought
down, destroyed 4023 [OE
bringan].

brynyede.   See BRENYEDE.

briste   *v.* to burst, burst open,
break 214, 2807, 4119; **bristes,**
bristez, bristis, etc. *3 sg.* 805,
1135, 1482, 2228, etc.; **brestys,**
brystis, etc. *3 pl.* 1859, 3663,
3682; **braste, brystedd** *pa. t.*
1129, 2176, 2271; **brousten**
pa. t. pl. 2544; **brousten, brusten**
pp. 2771, 3974 [OE *berstan*].

britten, bryttyn, brettyn   *v.* to cut,
destroy, butcher, cut to pieces
106, 963, 1350, 3580, 3641;
brittenes *3 sg.* 1242; *3 pl.* 1862,
2467; **brittenede, brettened,** etc.
pa. t. 802, 1487, 2212, 2807;
birtenede, bryttenede *pp.* 823,
1067, 3520, 3972 [OE *brytnian*].

broche   *v.* to stab, spit, skewer
1172; **broches, brochis** *3 sg.*
2202, 4250; **brochede** *pp.* 1050,
1052, 1067; **brochede** *pa. t.*
pierced, broke open 2714;
brochez *3 sg.* spurs 918, 1449;
pp. embroidered, brocaded 3257
[OF *brocher*].

brochez, bruchez   *n. pl.* skewers,
spits 1029; brooches, ornaments
3256 [OF *broche*].

brode, brade   *adj.* big, huge, wide,
great 914, 1047, 1094, 1184,
1193, 1380, etc.; (of eyes) staring, glaring 116; (of claws)
extended 792; (of speech) plain,

straightforward 3508; *one brode,* see BREDE, n.¹ [OE *brād*].

brok-brestede   *adj.* with a chest striped like a badger 1095 [from OE *bróc* +¹ BREST(E)].

bronde, brondez,   etc. See BRAND(E).

broþer, brothire, brothyre   *n.* brother 1311, 1516, 1826, 1918, etc.; **bretheren** *pl.* 4143 [OE *brōþor, brōþur*].

brothy   *adj.* ?covered with broth 1090 (*see note*) [from OE *broþ*].

brothly, brothely, brotheliche, brathely   *adv.* quickly, swiftly, hastily 1449, 1753, 3219, 3617, etc.; fiercely, violently 1408, 1771, 1862, 2046 etc. [ON *bráþliga*].

broun.   See BROWN(E).

brousten.   See BRISTE.

browd(d)en.   See BRAYD.

browes   *n. pl.* eyebrows 1083, 3384 [OE *brū*].

brown(e), broun   *adj.* brown 915, 1376; gleaming, shining 1487, 1861, 2213, 3657, etc. [OE *brūn*].

bruchez.   See BROCHEZ.

Bruytte.   *Brut,* the story of Britain 4346.

bruschese   *3 pl.* dash, rush 3680 [perh. from OF *brosser*].

brusten.   See BRISTE.

brustils   *n. pl.* bristles 1095 [OE *brystl;* cf. *byrst*].

buffette   *n.* blow 2252; **buffetez** *pl.* 792 [OF *buffet*].

bullenekkyde   *adj.* bull-necked 1094 [from ON *bole* + OE *hnecca*].

burde, burdez.   See BORDE.

burgeys   *n. pl.* freemen, citizens 857; **burgesse** *poss.* 3082 [OF *burgeis*].

burghe   *n.* castle, city, walled town 1968, 2424, 3083, 3125, etc.; **burghes** *pl.* 1241 [OE *burg, burh*].

burliche, bur(e)lyche   *adj.* stately, noble, goodly 304, 1002, 2190, 3557, etc.; strong, stout 586, 730, 1111, 2010, 2239, etc.; thick 3971; *adv.* in a stately manner, ceremoniously 4199 [OE *borlíce,* excellently].

burnyscht, burnyste, burneschte, burneste   *pp.* burnished, shining, gleaming 177, 906, 1113, 1859, 2272, etc.; polished 1011, 2123 [OF *burnir, burniss-*].

bus.   See BYHOUES.

buscayle, buskayle   *n.* copse, thicket 895, 1634 [OF *boschaille*].

buschement.   See ENBUSCHEMENT.

buschez, buschede,   etc. See BUSKE, V.

buske   *n.* bush 453; thicket, grove, wood 918; **buskez** *pl.* 1142 [ON *busk-r*].

buske   *v. intr.* (*often refl.*) to make ready, move, go, set out 69, 1263, 3036, 3579, 3732; **buskes** *2 sg.* 962; *3 sg.* 1223, 1378, 2068, 2073, etc.; *3 pl.* 2458; **buskede** *pa. t.* 1633; *trans. 3 sg.* makes ready, prepares 4074; **buskez, bussches** *3 pl.* 729, 1618, 1754, 2298; **buskede, buschede** *pp.* provided, furnished 567, 3681; *pp.* dressed, attired 2517, 3332, 4339; **buschez** *3 sg.* sets, places 2024; *pa. t.* 3619; *3 sg.* hurries forward, dispatches 2829; *3 sg.* raises 3646; *buske vpe,* raise up 3072; *buskes vp* (*imper. pl.*), brace up 2855 [ON *búask*].

bustous, boustous(e), boystous

adj. massive, enormous 615; powerful, fierce, savage 775, 783, 1379, 2175, 2425, etc. [uncertain].

buteless. See BOTLES.

butt. See FULL BUTT.

buttlere *n.* cupbearer, seneschal 208 [AF *butuiller*].

c. one hundred 2629.

caas(e). See CASE.

cabane, kaban *n.* cabin (on a ship) 757, 3671; **cabanes** *pl.* 3098; *pl.* tents, pavilions 733 [OF *cabane*].

cabills, coblez *n. pl.* cables, ropes 742, 3671 [OF *ca(a)ble*].

caches, cachede, etc. See CATCHEZ.

caffe. *n.* refuse 1064 [OE *ceaf*].

caire, cayre, kaire, kay(e)re *v.* to go, proceed 6, 444, 627, 641, 877, 1192, etc.; **cayres, kayris, kayeris,** etc. *3 sg.* 243, 1531, 1707, 3634, etc.; **cayers,** etc. *3 pl.* 480, 1195; *kaire of,* depart from, leave 1319, 1787; **karede** *pa. t.* went back 2882 [*ON keyra*].

call(e) *v.* to call, call out 1024; **calles, callez** *3 sg.* 1307, 2181, 2483; **callid(e), calde** *pp.* 61, 3423, 3510; summon 4314; *3 sg.* 892, 3564; **callys** *3 pl.* 2719 [late OE *ceallian* from ON *kalla*].

camellez, kamells, kameles *n. pl.* camels 616, 2283, 2336 [OE *camel,* from L *camēlus*].

cantell *n.* corner 4231 [ONF *cantel*].

capitoile, capytoile, capatoylle *n.* the Capitol in Rome 96, 280, 2353 [OF *capitoile*].

captayne, capitayne, capytayne *n.* chieftain 1864, 1866, 1909,

2263, etc.; **captayns, captaynez,** etc. *pl.* 838, 2994, 3087 [OF *capitaine*].

captyfe *n.* prisoner, captive 1589; **captifis, captyfis** *pl.* 1580, 1582, 2340 [OF *captif*].

cardynall *n.* cardinal 3177, 3199 [OF *cardinal*].

care, kare *n.* sorrow, grief 696, 859, 1838, 3513, etc. [OE *caru*].

care, kare *v.* to worry, be anxious 475, 830, 4034 [OE *carian*].

carefull *adj.* troubled, concerned, sorrowful 957, 1777, 2313, 3897, 3988; *as n.* 3131 [OE *carful*].

careman *n.* man 957 [ON *karmann,* var. of *karlmann*].

carffes. See KERFE.

caryage, karyage *n.* baggage train 2282, 2355 [OF *cariage*].

carye *v.* to carry, drag 1165; **karyed** *pa. t.* 4010 (*with pron. obj. unexpressed*); **caryede, kariede** *pp.* 851, 1887 [ONF *carier*].

carle *n.* churl 1063, 1107, 1165 [ON *karl*].

carpe, karpe *v.* to speak, say 877, 1582, 1929, 2126, etc.; **carpes, karpes,** etc. *2 sg.* 957, 1693, 3506; *3 sg.* 132, 237, 639, 648, etc.; **carpede, karpide,** etc. *pa. t.* 143, 220, 2313, 2341; *2 sg.* chatter, prate 3385 [ON *karpa*].

carpyng *vbl. n.* speech, discourse 1672 [from prec.].

case, caas(e) *n.* chance, fate, occurrence 261, 1892, 2371; *in caase (that),* in the event that 1273, 1513; situation, circumstances, plight 2719, 3521, 3564 [OF *cas*].

caste, kest(e) *v. intr.* to take

thought, deliberate 3406; **castes** *2 sg. trans.* to calculate or conjecture as to the future, forecast 4034; **cast(e)s** *3 sg.* resolves, decides 1998, 4180; **castez** *3 pl.* chart (a course) 752; *caste all theire wittys,* contrive, devise, scheme 2392; **castis, kastys,** etc. *3 sg.* casts, throws, throws down, throws away 1110, 1132, 1769, 3952, etc.; *3 pl.* 3667; **keste** *pa. t.* 280, 943, 3516, 4186, etc.; **castyn** *pp.* 3702; *keste colours,* flashed fire 118; *3 sg.* thrusts 4243; *pa. t.* placed 3995; *pp.* laid out 3240; *pp.* painted 819; *castez owtte* (*2 sg.*), bring down 1923; *kest down,* drew down 3384 [ON *kasta*]. See FEWTIRE.

castell *n.* castle 1585, 1750, 1881, etc.; **castell(e)s** *pl.* 27, 623, 654, etc.; *pl.* towers, topcastles 3673, 3674 [ONF *castel*].

castes *n. pl.* acts of casting or firing 3037 [from CASTE, v.].

catchez *3 pl.* chase, urge on, press 480; **kaghte** *pa. t.* 1770; **cachede** *pp.* 3513; **cachen** *3 pl.* catch, snatch, fetch, reach, take; **caughte, kawghte,** etc. *pa. t.* 1105, 1133, 1908, 3378, etc.; *pa. t.* got, received 1311, 2196, 2636, etc.; **cawghte, kaughte** *pp.* captured 2995, 3514; *caches one* (*3 sg.*), draws up 3644; *caughte of* (*pa. t.*), caught a breath of, breathed in 944 [ONF *cach(i)er,* with pa. t. and pp. by anal. with LAC(C)HEN]. See VAILE.

cause *n.* charge, accusation 675 [OF *cause*].

cawtelous *adj.* crafty, deceitful 4185 [OF *cauteleux*].

ceptre. See SEPTRE.

certayne, certaygne, certeyn, certane, sertayne *adj.* steadfast, trustworthy, trusty 240, 1008, 1685, 1689, 1697, etc.; solid, dependable 2481; fixed, definite 659; fixed, as in a formula or prayer 1042; chosen, particular 727, 2296, 2307, etc.; *adv.* certainly, in truth 817, 3930 [OF *certain*].

certez, certys *adv.* certainly, verily 357, 1162, 1342 [pl. of OF *cert, certain*].

certyfye *v.* to assure, inform with certainty 1555; **certified** *pp.* attested [OF *certifier*].

ceté, cetees, etc. See CITÉ(E).

chaas, chace, etc. See CHASSE, n. & v.

chaynes, cheynes, cheynys *n. pl.* chains 2522, 3815; *chaynes of chare,* wagon chains 3603 (*see note*) [OF *chaeine, chaaine,* etc.].

chaire, chayere *n.* chair, seat, throne 3266, 3326, 3329, 3347, etc. [OF *chaëre*].

chalange *v.* to challenge 1322, 2524 (*with pron, obj. unexpressed*); demand, lay claim to 3326; take up a challenge 3397 [OF *chalanger*].

chalke-whitte, chalke-whytt(e), schalke-whitte *adj.* (of silver) shining, untarnished, lustrous 1026, 2522, 3266; white as chalk 1363, 2116, 2268, 3039, etc. [OE *calc* + *hwīt*].

chambire, chambyr(e) *n.* presence chamber, household, hall 231, 690, 1404, 1821, 2621, etc.; private room 713, 3911; **chambres, chambyrs, chawmbyrs** *pl.* rooms 158, 168, 3041; *vnto chambyre,* to his (private) room 695 [OF *chambre*].

chambyrleyn *n.* the head of officers serving in a king's chamber 660 [OF *chamberlain*].

champayne *n.* open country, plain, field 1226, 1362; *as adj.* 1620; **champanyse** *pl.* 1822 [OF *champaigne*].

chance, chaunce, chawnse *n.* fortune, fate, chance 1539, 1749, 1985, 2368, etc.; **chaunces, chauncez** *pl.* 2956, 4178; *pl.* exploits 531 [OF *chaunce*].

change, chaunge, chawnge, chaungen *v.* to change, shift 660; **chaungez** *3 sg.* 1116; **cha(u)ngen** *3 pl.* 168, 2989; **cha(u)ngede, chawngide** *pa. t.* 2964, 3222, 3382, 3558, etc.; **chawngynge, chawngawnde** *pres. p.* 2523, 3267; **chaungyde** *pp.* 4181; take over 1405; decay 2301; go astray 3585; fade 2576; *3 sg.* 4213, 4272; *pa. t.* changed for the worse 2701 [OF *cha(u)ng(i)er*].

changyng *vbl. n.* change 3650 [from prec.].

chapells *n. pl.* chapels 3039 [OF *chapele*].

chapes *n. pl.* metal plates on a scabbard 2522 [OF *chape*].

chapyde. See ESCHAPE.

charbokle, charebocle *n.* ruby 2523, 3267 [OF *charbocle*].

chare *v.* to care for, take care of 1886 [OE *carian*].

chare. See CHAYNES.

charge *n.* task, commission, office 2323 [OF *charge*].

charge *v.* to appoint 665; **chargez** *3 sg.* 1985; **chargegide** *pp.* 2731; **chargges** *3 sg.* burdens, oppresses 3538; **chargede** *pa. t.* 1540; **chargegid, chargyde** *pp.* 1549, 1552, 3136, 3604, etc.; *pa. t.* attacked, rushed upon 1406 (*see note*); *3 sg.* matters 4261 [OF *charg(i)er*].

chargour *n.* large bowl 1026; **chargeours** *pl.* platters, chargers

185 [AF *chargeour*].

charyté, charitée: *for charyté, for charitée,* for kindness, at God's will, God willing 682, 1019, 1542 [OF *par charité*].

charottez *n. pl.* chariots, wagons 1552 [OF *chariot, charrette*].

charpe. See SCHARP(P)E.

charre *n.* chariot, cart 3914 [OF *charre*].

charry *adj.* sad 2964 [OE *carig*].

chartire, chartyre *n.* charter, treaty 1542, 3058 [OF *chartre*].

chasse, chace, chaas *n.* pursuit of an enemy, rout 2269, 2368, 3000, 3650, 4261 [OF *chace*].

chas(s)e *v. trans.* to pursue with hostile intent, chase, attack, harass 2237, 2957; **chaces** *3 sg.* 1821; **chases** *3 pl.* 1399, 1880, 2990; **chasede** *pa. t.* 1362; *pp.* 1444; *chasyng spere,* hunting spear 1823, 2955; *intr. 3 sg.* gives chase 2166; *pa. t.* ran 2999 [OF *chac(i)er, chassier*].

chaste *adj.* innocent 3059 [OF *chaste*].

chasty *v.* to curb, discipline 1018; **chastyede** *pp.* trained 690 [OF *chastier*].

chaunce, chawnse, etc. See CHANCE.

chauncelere, chaunchelere *n.* escort 169; chief administrative officer of a ruler 660 [AF *chanceler*].

chaunge, etc. See CHANGE.

chawffe *v.* to decompose 2301; **chauffede** *pp.* aroused, angered 2236 [OF *chaufer*].

chawmbyrs. See CHAMBIRE.

chawnge, etc. See CHANGE.

cheekke. See CHEKKE.

cheese. See CHESE.

chefe, cheefe *n.* upper part of the shield, the principal part of the

escutcheon 2523, 2524, 3648; ruler 3649 [OF *chef*].

chefe, cheefe, cheffe *adj.* foremost, best, greatest 18, 530, 1404, 2297, etc.; head 208, 665, 1541, 1551; high 1363, 1873; fine 3041; noble 3058, 3650; **cheffeste** *superl.* greatest, noblest 3327 [from prec.].

cheftayne, chiftayne *n.* chieftain, leader 530, 1541, 1986, 2236, etc.; **cheftans, chiftaynes**, etc. *pl.* 18, 1323, 1406, 1872, etc. [OF *cheftayne*].

cheynes, cheynys. See CHAYNES.

chekefull. See CHOKKEFULL.

chekes, chekys *n. pl.* cheeks [OE *cē(a)c*].

chekyn *n.* offspring 4181 (*see note*) [OE *cicen*].

chekyrde *adj.* checkered 3267 [from AF *escheker,* chessboard].

chekke, cheekke *n.* setback, reversal 1539, 3000; attack, assault 1986, 2956 [OF *eschec*].

chele *n.* chill, cold 3391 [OE *c(i)ele*].

chere *n.* face, expression 2069, 2964 [OF *ch(i)ere*].

chese, cheese *v. trans.* to choose 682, 3347; **chosen, chosyn** *pp.* chosen, named 530, 690, 2731, 3348; distinguished 3327; seen, perceived 3648; *chese, chesez . . . the waye, chesen theire wayes,* etc., make their (one's) way, proceed, go 1225, 1873, 3914, etc.; *intr.* make one's way, go 1619; **cheses** *3 sg.* 2954; **chis** *pa. t.* 2217 [OE *cēosan*].

cheualere *n.* knight 208, 1551; **cheuelers** *pl.* 2116 [AF *chevaler*].

cheual(l)rye *n.* code of knightly conduct, valor 531; knighthood 18; group of knights, retinue of knights, entourage *169,* 1323, 1404, 1872, 2269, etc. [OF *chevalerie*].

cheual(l)rous *adj.* valiant, brave, bold 1362, 1399, 1540, 1619, 1880, etc.; warlike, bellicose 3538, 3604 [OF *chevalerous*].

cheueride *pp.* shivered, trembled 3391 [uncertain].

cheuys *2 sg.* achieve, triumph 3397 (*future*); **cheuede,** **cheuyde** *pp.* succeeded, triumphed 1117; *pp.* fared 1841, 4178; *wele had me chefede,* it would have gone well with me, I would have triumphed 869 (*see note*); **cheuede** *pa. t.* gained 3329 [OF *achever*].

chewyse *imper. pl.* take care of, provide for (yourselves) 1750 [OF *chevir*].

chiftayne. See CHEFTAYNE.

child(e) *n.* page, young nobleman 690, 2952, 2957, 2964, etc.; child 3552, 3576, 3649; **childire, child(y)re, children(ne), childyren** *pl.* young men 845, 1025, 1065, 1821, etc.; children, sons 850, 1051, 1206, 1607, etc. [OE *cild*, pl. *cildru*].

chillande *pres. p.* chilling 2965 [obscure; ?OE **ci(e)ldan*].

chymnes, chympnes *n. pl.* fireplaces, hearths, chimneys 168, 3041 [OF *cheminée*].

chyne *n.* spine, backbone 3390 [OF *eschine*].

chippe, chippes, chippe-burdez, etc. See SCHIPPE, SCHIPPEZ, SCHIPPE-BURDE.

chirches *n. pl.* churches 3039 [OE *circe*].

chis. See CHESE.

cho. See SCHO.

chokkefull, chekefull *adj.* chock-full 1552, 3604 [uncertain; perh,

rel. to OE *acēocian,* to choke].

chokkes *3 sg.* thrusts 2955 (*see note*); **chokkode** *pp.* 3603 [OF *choquier*].

choppe *n.* blow, stroke 1117 [from next].

choppe *v.* to chop, cut, hew 1406, 2237, 2269; **choppes** *3 sg.* 1823; **choppes** 3 pl. 2990, 4261; **choppode** *pa. t.* 2116; **chopped(e)** *pp.* 2368 (*with auxil. v. unexpressed*), 3390; *pp.* chopped up, minced 1026 [uncertain].

chosen, chosyn. See CHESE.

Christofre Daye. St. Christopher's Day, July 25, 2390.

chullede *pp.* kicked about, tossed about 1444 [OF *chouller*].

churlles *n. pl.* uncouth persons, louts 615; **churles** *sg. poss.* 4181 (*see note*) [OE *ceorl*].

cirquytrie, cirqwitrye *n.* arrogance, pride, presumption 2616, 3399 [OF *surcuiderie*].

cité(e), ceté(e) *n.* city 60, 440, 488, 601, 609, etc.; **cites, cetese, cetees** *pl.* 1337, 2609; capital 2419 [OF *cité*].

claye *n.* clay, mire 1839 [OE *clǣg*].

claymes, claymez *3 sg.* claims 287, 510, 1275, 1680, etc. [OF *clamer,* 3 sg. *claime*].

claymez *n. pl.* claims 1682 [OF *claime*].

clamour(e) *n.* clamor, uproar, commotion 1198, 2994, 3980 [OF *clamour*].

clappide, clappyde *pa. t.* clasped 956, 1137 [OE *clappan*].

claret *n.* claret, wine of a light-red color 200 [OF *claret,* adj.]

clarioune, claryoun *n.* a shrill trumpet, often used as a war signal 2718, 3563; **clarion(e)s**

pl. 1758, 1809 [OF *claron, clairon*].

claspande *pres. p.* clasping 4337 [from next].

claspes, clasppis *n. pl.* clamps, clasps 909, 1108 [uncertain].

clath-sekkes *n. pl.* sacks of cloth or clothing 733 [OE *clāþ* + *sæcc*].

clauer *n.* clover 3241 [OE *clæfre*].

clauerande *pres. p.* clutching, clawing 3324 [cf. Dan. *klavre,* clamber, ME *cleafer,* OE *clifer,* claw].

clede *pa. t.* clad, clothed 2713; **cled(d)e, cleede** *pp.* 217, 3334, 3684; *pp.* covered 3241 [ON *klœdr*].

clefe. See CLEUE.

cleffe *v.* to stick fast, cling 1312; **clewide** *pa. t.* 3268 [OE *cleofian*].

cleyffez. See CLYF(F)E.

clekes, clekys *3 sg.* seizes, grasps, pulls 1865, 2123; drags 1164 [OE **clæcan*].

clene *adj.* (of metals) pure, solid, brilliant 201, 217, 766, 1105, 1186, etc.; unsullied 4201; bright 1197; fair, fine 1589, 1603, 1997, 2013, 2019, etc.; clean 2710; healed 2713; *adv.* fully, completely 2302, 4177 [OE *clǣne*].

clenkkede *pa. t.* beat, bashed 2113 [cf. MDu *klincken,* OHG *chlingan,* etc.].

clenly, clenliche, clenlych(e) *adv.* excellently, faultlessly, elegantly 216, 654, 757, 2123, etc.; fully, completely 628, 850, 851, etc.; absolutely 581, 673; properly 1586, 4016; deftly, masterfully 1109 [OE *clǣnlīce*].

clensis *3 sg.* cleanses, cleans 2711 [OE *clǣnsian*].

clepid *pa. t.* summoned 3563 [OE *cleopian*].

clere *adj.* morally pure, guiltless 675, 1559; (of metals) pure, solid, brilliant 819, 909, 3099, 3269, etc.; gleaming, shining, sparkling 883, 2182, 2373, 3645, 4231, etc.; clear, bright 1601, 1998, 2711; beautiful 3045; good, fine 1780, 3190, 4265; shrill, loud 2718; free of danger 1640 [OF *cler*].

clereworte *n.* small clover 3241 [OE *clæferwyrt*].

clergiall *adj.* intricate, subtle 1758; **clergyally** *adv.* ingeniously, cleverly 200 [from next].

clergy(e) *coll. n.* clerics, scholars 809; clergy, churchmen 1215, 1245, 1316 [OF *clergie*].

clerkkes, clerkis *n. pl.* clerics, clergymen 2391, 3444 [OE *cleric,* from L].

cleue *v.* to cleave, cut, split 2993; **cleues** *3 sg.* 2182, 2201; **clefe, cleuede** *pa. t.* 1388, 2559; **clevede** *pp.* 3671 [OE *clēofan*].

clewes, clewez. See CLOUGHES.

clewide. See CLEFFE.

clyf(f)e *n.* cliff, promontory, steep, slope 883, 942, 2158; **clyf(f)ez, cleyffez, kleuys** *pl.* 1164, 2013, 2019, 2396 [OE *clif*].

clymbez *3 sg.* climbs, mounts 942; **clymbyd** *pa. t.* 1197; **clymbande** *pres. p.* 3324, 3422 [OE *climban*].

clynges *3 sg.* ?presses (see *OED* cling, v.¹ 9) 1865 [OE *clingan*].

cloke *n.* cloak 3470 [OF *cloke*].

close *n.* confinement 1586; mountain pass, valley, vale 1639, 3240 [OF *clos,* n.].

close *v.* to enclose, cover 1165; **closed** *pp.* 206, 2302; *close in,*

surround, hem in 2003 [OF *clore, clos-*].

closse *adj.* hidden, secret 1196 [OF *clos,* adj.].

clothes, clothys *n. pl.* apparel, outer clothing 1023, 2470; cloths 3099; ?pieces of cloth, pennons 3607 [OE *clāþ*].

cloughes, clewes, clewez *n. pl.* chasms, ravines, cliffs 941, 1639, 2013, 2019 [OE *clōh*].

clowde *n.* mist, fog 752; mass of rock, hill, mount 1197; **clowdes, clowd(d)ez** *pl.* clouds 799, 823, 3250 [OE *clūd*].

clowez *n. pl.* claws 783 [OE *clawu*].

clubb *n.* club 1105, 1109, 1132, 1186, etc.; **clubbez** *pl.* 2113 [ON *klubba*].

coblez. See CABILLS.

cofers, coferez, cofirs, cofres *n. pl.* coffers, chests 477, 733, 2283, 4206 [OF *cof(f)re*].

cogge *n.* ship 476, 756, 3634, 3644, etc.; **cogges, coggez** *pl.* 758, 3662, 3670, etc. [OF *cogue*].

cokadrisses *n. pl.* crocodiles (*or perh.* serpents, basilisks) *2283* (*see note*) [OF *cocatris*].

colde *adj.* cold 882, 944, 2773, etc.; *adv.* 2267 [OE *cald,* adj., *calde,* adv.].

coldis *2 sg.* chill, make cold 3518 [OE *cealdian,* *caldian*].

colour *n.* color, hue 1004; **colours, colurez** *pl.* 118 (*see note*), 819; complexion 3259; *pl.* heraldic bearings 217, 2305 [OF *colo(u)r*].

coloured(e) *pp.* colored 197, 3674 [OF *colo(u)rer*].

comande, comaunde *v.* to command 1271, 1585; **com(m)a(u)ndez** *3 sg.* 71, 1319,

1637, etc.; **coma(u)ndyd(e),
com(m)and(e), comande** *pa. t.*
156, 626, 839, 935, 1218, etc.
[OF *co(u)ma(u)nder*].

come *n.* arrival, coming, approach
1203, 1565, 1812; rush 1915,
2160 [OE *cyme*].

come *v.* come 131, 1274, 1584,
etc.; **com(m)es, com(m)ez** *3 sg.*
393, 799, 841, etc.; **com(m)ez**
3 pl. 1232, 1532, 1545; **com(e)**
pa. t. 80, 176, 192, etc.
commande *pres. p.* 3468; **comen,
com(m)yn** *pp.* 582, 987, 1198,
etc.; *pp.* born 865; *come to,* is
becoming, appropriate to, befits
1579; *come of,* became, befitted
1581 [OE *cuman*]. See COUNTRÉ.

com(e)ly, comliche, comlych(e)
adj. splendid, noble, fair, pleasing, beautiful 71, 834, 1053,
1192, 1199, 1203, etc.;
comlyeste *superl.* 537; **comlyly,
comlyli** *adv.* splendidly 3047,
4108 [OE *cȳmlic*].

comforthe *n.* comfort, support
3960 [OF *confort*].

comforth(e), comfurth(e) *v.* to
hearten, cheer, inspirit, brace,
encourage 830, 944, 1138, 1839,
3634; **comfort(h)es** *3 sg.* 395,
1565, 1724, 3199, etc.; **comforthes** *imper. pl.* 222; **comforthed** *pa. t.* 1560, 2712;
comforthede *pp.* 1203; assist, aid
1246; comfort 696, 2194, 4101;
comfurthes, comfourthes *3 sg.*
2196, 3131 [OF *conforter*].

comyng *vbl. n.* arrival 4022
[from COME, v.].

comly *adv.* in a seemly manner
3932 [OE *cȳmlīce*].

com(m)and(e), com(m)a(u)ndez,
etc. See COMANDE.

commandment(e), commaund-

ment(e), comandement *n.*
command, order 121, 581, 739,
1514, 4150, etc. [OF
com(m)aundement].

commons, comouns, comowns
n. pl. common people, citizens
274, 1215, 1245, 1316, etc.;
common soldiers 725 [OF
comon, commun].

comon *v.* to confer, consult 1580
[OF *comuner*].

companye *n.* company, assembly
of persons 1650, 1849, 2720
[OF *compai(g)nie*].

compas *n.* circumference, circle,
compass 3268, 3325, 4222; *in
compas,* all around, round about
3240 [OF *compas*].

compaste *pp.* encircled 3633 [OF
compasser].

conaunde. See CONYNGE.

condethe, condethes. See
COUNDYTE.

condycyon *n.* provision 1511
[OF *condicion*].

confessour *n.* confessor, priest
2193, 4314 [AF *confessour*].

confoundez, confundez *3 sg.*
brings to ruin, destroys 1245,
1922 (*for future*); **confundede**
pp. 1153 [OF *confondre, confundre*].

confusede *pp.* disturbed, agitated
123 [OF *confundre, confus-*].

conynge, conaunde *adj.* (*pres. p.*)
skilled, expert, intelligent 558,
3202; **cony[n]geste, konyngeste**
superl. 809, 3177 [from KANE].

connygez *n. pl.* rabbits 197 [OF
conil].

conquer(e) *v.* to get, acquire, gain,
win 3429; **conquerid** *pa. t.* 284;
conqueryde *pp.* 402; conquer
344, 641, 2393; *pa. t.* 24, 282,
2382; *pp.* 3084 [OF *conquerir*].

conquerour *n.* conqueror (generally referring to Arthur) 65, 71, 132, 216, 535, etc.; **conquerours** *pl.* 3407 [AF *conquerour*].

conqueste *n.* conquest 26, 43, 3425; **conquestez** *pl.* 3445 [OF *conquest(e)*].

constable *n.* constable 1585, 1590; **constabls** *pl.* 3087 [OF *conestable*].

contek(e) *n.* combat, struggle, battle 2721, 3669, 4177 [AF *contec*].

contena(u)nce. See CO(U)NTE-NAUNCE.

contré, contrée, etc. See COUNTRÉ.

conuaye *v.* to lead away, take away 1589, 1604 [ONF *conveier*].

cope-borde *n.* sideboard 206 [COPPE + BORDE].

copes *n. pl.* special garments of monks or friars 4334 [OE **cāpe*, ON *kápa*].

coppe *n.* wine cup, goblet 2750; *fig.* the drink taken in a cup 209, 892; **cowpes, coupes** *pl.* 210, 237, 3375 [OE *cuppe*].

coppe-full *n.* cupful 3378 [from prec.].

corage *n.* temperament, spirit, courage 536, 1725, 1922 [OF *corage*].

corageous *adj.* courageous 338 [AF *corageous*].

corkes *n.* carcass 1091 [OF *carcas*].

corne-bote *n.* payment, requital 1786 (*see note*), 1837 [OE *corn* + *bōt*].

corners *n. pl.* secret or remote places, hiding places 1640 [AF *corner*].

cornettes *n. pl.* cornets, trumpets 4108; *with cornettes,* to the sound of trumpets 1758 [OF *cornet*].

cornuse *n. pl.* horns 1809 [L *cornu*].

coronall, corenall *n.* golden circlet on a helmet 908, 1108, 3633; coronal, coronet 3258 [OF *coronal*].

coroun, corown, etc. See CROWN(E), n., CROWN, V.

corroumppede *pp.* (of language) corrupt, non-standard 3478 [OF *corompre*].

corsaunt *n.* the body of a saint, holy body 1154 [OF *cors saint*].

cors(e) *n.* body, corpse 1219, 1389, 1779, 2380, etc. [OF *cors*].

corven, coruen. See KERFES.

coseri *n.* barter, bargaining 1582 [from ME *coss,* to barter (of uncertain origin)].

cosyn(e), kosyn *n.* kinsman, cousin, relative 338, 343, 648, 864, 1218, etc.; **cosyns** *pl.* 50, 101 [OF *co(u)sin*].

coste *n.* coast 476, 834, 3898, 3905; region, place 877, 1787, 1867, 1893, 3111, etc. [OF *coste*].

cote, cotte *n.* kirtle, coat 1194, 1690, 3334 [OF *cote*].

couched *pp.* set, studded 909 [OF *coucher*].

co(u)ncell, counsaile *n.* counsel, advice 144, 259, 1023; judgment, wisdom 291, 1513, 3960; council 243, 344, 417, 626, 639, etc.; *in counsaile,* personally, face to face 648 [OF *concile, cuncile, conseil* etc.].

coundyte, cundit, condethe *n.* prescribed route, safe conduct 444, 475, 3148, 3483; **condethes** *pl.* conduits, pipes 201 [OF *conduit*].

coungé *n.* leave (to go) 479 [OF *congée*].

counsaile. See CO(U)NCELL.

counsayles *3 sg.* counsels, advises 305 [OF *conseiller*].

co(u)ntenaunce, contena(u)nce *n.* demeanor, expression, bearing 123, 222, 1649, 2120, 2313, etc.; conduct 536; display, splendor 542 [OF *co(u)ntena(u)nce*].

countere. See ENCO(U)NTRE.

countez *2 sg.* account 261; **countede** *pa. t.* counted 544 [OF *conter, cunter*].

countré, contré, contrée, cowntré *n.* country, territory, land 223, 623, 848, 1215, 1316, etc.; **contres, contreez, countrese, cuntrez** *pl.* 27, 627, 1244, 3425, etc.; the people of a particular region 727; countryside 1640; *to contré come,* return home 676 [OF *contrée*].

coupable *adj.* guilty, deserving of blame 1317 [OF *coupable*].

coupes. See COPPE.

coupylde *pa. t.* fastened 2336 [OF *coupler*].

course *n.* dinner course 176; passage, way 1770; **coursez** *pl.* 752; *pl.* charges, rushes 1681 [OF *cors, curs*].

coursere *n.* large, powerful horse ridden in battle 1388, 2166, 4010; **cou[r]sers** *pl.* 2115 [OF *corsier*].

courtays, curtais(e), curtay(e)s *adj.* gracious, courtly 21, 209, 417, 481, 987, etc.; generous, merciful 125 [OF *corteis, curteis*].

courte *n.* court 6, 543, 1198, 1512, etc.; *as adj.* 21 [OF *co(u)rt*].

coutere *n.* plate of armor protecting the elbow 2567 [OF **co(u)t(i)ere,* from *coute,* elbow].

couthe. See KANE.

couatys *n.* craving, covetousness 1580 [OF *coveitise*].

couenawnte *n.* covenant 3542 [OF *covenaunt*].

couent *n.* convent 1220, 4021 [OF *co(n)vent*].

couere *v.* to cover 1886; **couer(e)s** *3 sg.* 1110, 4243; **couerde** *pa. t.* 3378, 3995; **couerde, couerte, koueride** *pp.* 616, 1780, 2381; **couer(e)de** *pp.* caparisoned 1770, 2115, 3047; *pp.* canopied 3098; *pp.* plated *3633* [OF *covrir*].

couere, couerede, etc. See RE-COUER.

couerte *n.* concealment, hiding 1196 [from COUERE, *v.*].

couette, couaitte, coueite *v.* to wish, desire, covet 51, 1191, 3325; **couettes** *2 sg.* 1321; **cowayte** *pp.* 2397 [OF *coveiter*].

cowayte. See COUETTE.

cowarde *n.* coward 133, 2181; **cowardes** *pl.* 2882; *adj.* cowardly 2172; **kowardely** *adv.* in a cowardly manner 1923 [OF *couard*].

cowardys *n.* cowardice, fear 1693, 4186 [OF *couardise*].

cowchide *pa. t.* crouched, cowered 122 [OF *coucher*].

cowle *n.* cauldron 1051 [uncertain; perh. rel. to OE *cugle,* hood].

cowntas *n.* countess 3045; **cowntasses** *pl.* 4337 [OF *contesse, cuntesse*].

cowntere *n.* accountant 1672 [AF *countour*].

cownterez, cowntered. See EN-CO(U)NTRE.

cowpes. see COPPE.

cowpez *3 sg.* strikes, smites 799, 2059; **cowpen** *3 pl.* 2543 [OF *couper*].

cowthe. See KANE.

crachynge *vbl. n.* smashing 3669 [from CRASSECHES].

crafe *v.* to ask, demand, beg 1681, 3522 [OE *crafian*].

crafte *n.* skill, art 752, 3667; might, power 1107, 1560, 2267, 2393, etc.; *craftes of armes, kraftes of armes, etc.,* feats of arms, skill in warfare 24, 284, 1652, 2036, etc.; force of arms 1243, 2543 [OE *cræft*].

crafty, craftely, kraftly *adj.* skillfully done or made 211, 3336, 3351 [OE *cræftig, cræftlic*].

craftyly *adv.* skillfully 196; smoothly 600 [OE *cræftiglīce*].

crag(g)e *n.* crag (referring to St. Michael's Mount) 851, 858, 876, 882, 941, etc. [M Breton *cragg*].

crayers, krayers *n. pl.* small ships 738, 3666 [OF *craier*].

craysed *pp.* crushed, shattered 2150 [OF *acraser*].

cramede *pp.* crammed, loaded 477, 1051 [OE *crammian*].

cranes *n. pl.* cranes 196 [OE *cran*].

crasseches *3 pl.* smash, dash to pieces 3670; **craschede, crassched** *pa. t.* 1109, 2114 [onomatopoeic].

crauaunde *adj.* craven, cowardly 133 [OF *craventé,* with form infl. by *creaunt*].

Creatoure *n.* Creator, God 2196 [OF *creatour*].

creat(o)ure *n.* creature, being 143, 534, 859; **creatours** *pl.* 1064, 4102 [OF *creature*].

credens(e) *n.* credence 506; letters of credence, letters certifying the validity of information, credentials 88, 444, 3522 [OF *credence*].

creeste. See CRESTE.

creette. *n.* a sweet wine from Crete 200.

crepers *n. pl.* grapplers, grappling irons 3667 [from OE *crēopan*].

cresmede. See CRYSMED.

creste, creeste *n.* summit, top 882, 908, 942, 1108, 1133, etc.; **crestes** *pl.* heraldic crests 3605; **crestez** *pl.* crests of helmets 2114 [OF *creste*].

cretoyne *n.* a sauce made with milk 197 [OF *cretonée*].

creuell, crewell(e). See CRUELL.

crye *n.* shout, battle cry 1810 [OF *cri*].

crye *v.* to proclaim 3078; **cryes, cryez, kryes,** etc. *3 sg.* cries, weeps, cries out, shouts 1650, 1791, 1803, 1836, etc.; **criede, cryede** *pa. t.* 124, 858, 2120, 2772, etc.; **cryande** *pres. p.* 1137; *cryede appon,* called upon in supplication 3384 [OF *crier*].

crysmed, cresmede, krysomede *pp.* anointed with chrism 3185; christened, Christian 1051, 1065 [OF *cresmer*].

crispid *pp.* stiffly curled, waved 1003; **krispan[d]e** *pres. p.* curling 3352 [L *crispāre*].

crystall *n.* crystal 2381 *(see note)* [OF *cristal*].

Cristen, Cristyn *n.* Christian 1187, 3429; *uninfl. pl.* 2786; as Christians 4112 [OE *crīsten*].

cryst(e)nede *pp.* christened 2636, 3337 [OE *cristnian*].

Cristenly *adv.* in a Christian manner 1208 [from CRISTEN].

Cristyndome *n.* Christendom 534, 2036 [OE *cristendōm*].

Cristynmese, Cristymesse, Crystynmesse *n.* Christmas, Christmas celebration 64, 544, 839; *Crys-*

tynmesse Daye, Christmas Day
70, 3213 [CRISTEN + OE
mæsse].

crysum, krysom(e), krisome *n.*
chrism 142, 2447, 2636, 3435
[OF *crisma*].

cronycle *n.* chronicle, historical
account 3445; **cronicles, cronycles** *pl.* 274, 3218 [AF *cronicle*].

cros(s)e *n.* cross 284, 3335, 3336,
3428, 3434; *one crosse,* across
3667 [ON *kross*].

Crosse Dayes *n. pl.* the three days
preceding Ascension Day, 3212
(*see note*) [CROS(S)E +
DAY(E)].

crosselettes *n. pl.* crosslets, little
crosses 3336 [AF *croiselette*].

crossez *3 pl.* cross 738 [from
CROS(S)E].

crouell, crowell. See CRUELL.

**crown(e), crownne, croune,
coro(u)n(e), corown** *n.(lit. &
fig.)* crown, sovereignty 28, 291,
402, 673, etc.; **crounes, corowns**
pl. 51, 3269, 3647; head 1389
[OF *co(u)ro(u)ne*].

crown, coroun(e) *v.* to crown 678,
3185; **corounede, coround,
crown(n)ed(e), corownde** *pp.*
crowned 125, 142, 535, 1654,
2447, etc. [AF *corouner*].

crucifiede, crucyfiede *pp.* crucified
285, 3428 [OF *crucifier*].

**cruell, crouell, creuell, crewell(e),
crowell, krewell, krouell** *adj.*
fierce, stern 43, 118, 346, 536,
1271, etc.; *as n.* 3086; **kruelleste**
superl. 2749; harsh, hard, sharp
88, 132, 1831, 2059, etc.; **cruelly**
adv. harshly 2264 [OF *cruel*].

cruschen *v.* to crush, smash 1134
[OF *cruissir*].

cukewalde *n.* cuckold, general
term of abuse 1312 [OF **cucuald

(15th C. *cucuault*)].

cundit. See COUNDYTE.

cuntrez. See COUNTRÉ.

cunvayede *pa. t.* conveyed, escorted 482 [OF *conveier*].

cure *n.* care, duty 673 [OF *cure*].

cury *n.* food, cooking 1063 [OF
queverie].

curi(o)us *adj.* elaborate, intricate
61 (*see note*), 201, 211; sophisti-
cated, recondite, exotic 223 [OF
curio(u)s].

curlues *n. pl.* curlews 196 [OF
corlieu].

cursynge *vbl. n.* curse, damnation,
imprecation 1311 [from next.].

curs(s)ede *pp.* cursed 1064, 1273
[OE *cursian*].

curtais(e), curtay(e)s. See COUR-
TAYS.

curtaisie *n.* courtesy, nobility
1274, 1681 [OF *cortesie,
curtesie*].

dagges *3 pl.* pierce, stab 2102;
daggande *pres. p.* 3749 [rel. to
OF *dague,* dagger].

dagswaynnes *n. pl.* coarse cover-
ings of rough, shaggy material
3609 [uncertain].

day(e) *n.* day 73, 90, 92, 95, etc.;
uninfl. poss. 4305; **dayes** *pl.* 413,
447, 634, 3276, etc.; period of
time 318, 380, 3182; victory
2043; *þe dayes,* all the days 1447,
3067, 3885; *on a daye,* one day
2643 [OE *dæg*]. See DO, NEWȝERS
DAY, LAMMES(S)E DAY(E).

daynteez *n. pl.* dainties, delicacies
199 [OF *dainté, daintié*].

daynteuous *adj.* precious, valuable
4196 [from prec.].

daynttehely, deynttely *adv.* elegantly 723; ?with honor or ceremony 2643 [from OF *dainté*].

dale *n.* dale, bottom of a valley 2031, 2777, 3250 [OE *dæl*].

dalte, dalten. See DELE.

dame lady (as title) 233 [OF *dame*].

damesels *n. pl.* damsels 3044 [OF *dam(e)isele*].

dampnede *pp.* damned 3277, 3299 [OF *dam(p)ner*].

danke, dannke *adj.* damp 313, 3750 [unknown; cf. Sw dial. *dank,* moist place].

dare *v.*[1] *pres. t.* dare, make bold to 292; *subj.* 1343; **durste** *pa. t.* 135, 2812, 4048, 4131, etc. [OE *dearr, dorste*].

dare *v.*[2] to tremble or be paralyzed with fear, be in dismay, lose heart 4007; **dares** *3 sg.* 3225 [OE *darian*].

darielles *n. pl.* pastries, tarts 199 [OF *dariole*].

darte *n.* arrow, spear 3611; **dartes** *pl.* 2101 [OF *dart*].

dasschede *pp.* dashed, broken 2474 [?ON *daska;* cf. Sw *daska,* Dan *daske*].

daunce *n.* procession 408 [OF *dance*].

dauncesyng *vbl. n.* dancing 2030 [OF *dauncer*].

daungere, dawngere *n.* sovereignty, authority 579; danger 1935, 2935, 3060, 3067 [OF *dang(i)er*].

daweyng *vbl. n.* dawn, daybreak 1601 [OE *dagian*].

debles. See FY.

declarede *pp.* demonstrated 1321 [OF *declair(i)er*].

dede *n.*[1] deed, doing 1210; **dedes, dedez, dedis,** etc. *pl.* 13, 48, 256, etc.; task, duty 1737; *dedes of armes, dedis of armes,* etc., feats of arms 1563, 2936, 3320, etc.

[OE *dēd*].

dede *n.*[2] See DETHE.

ded(e) *adj.* dead 975, 1722, 2267, 2773, etc.; *as n.* 4017; doomed to die 2178 [OE *dēad*].

dede-thrawe *n.* the agony of death, death struggle 1150 [DEDE, n.[2] + THRAA].

de(e)pe *n.* deep, sea 761, 816, 3694; **depez** *pl.* depths 750 [OE *dēop*].

deesse *n.* dais 218 [OF *deis*].

defadide *pp.* faded away, withered 3304 [L *de-* + OF *fader*].

defawte *n.* failure to perform a duty 2939 [OF *defaute*].

defawtes *2 sg.* fail (to meet an obligation) 2928 [OF *defaillir,* 3 sg. *defaut*].

defence *n.* defense 300 [OF *defense*].

defendez *3 sg.* defends 797; **fendis** *imper. pl.* 4086 [OF *defendre*].

deffuse *n.* prohibition, ban 256 [OF *defois*].

degré *n.* throne, dais 84 [OF *degré*].

deynttely. See DAYNTTEHELY.

dele *v.* to mete out, allot, distribute, bestow (*often with pron. obj. unexpressed*) 332, 2400; **delte, dalte** *pa. t.* 49 (*see note*), 3088, 3527, 3614, etc.; **dalten** *pa. t. pl.* 2101; **delte** *pp.* 1216, 1277, 1564, 1728, etc.; dispose, settle 1278, 2936; *intr. pa. t.* contended, fought 3693 [OE *dælan*].

delygens *n. dide my delygens,* exerted myself to the utmost 1945 [OF *diligence*].

delitte, delytte *n.* delight, pleasure 422, 1970, 3387; **delyttes** *pl.* 253 [OF *delit*].

delyuer(e)de *pp.* dispatched, done away with 1548, 2081; saved, set

free 1688 [OF *delivrer*].

delte. See DELE.

demede, demyd(e) *pp. judged 3061*
(*see note*); considered 219,
1941, 3320, 3416, etc.; decreed,
ordained 1564, 4158, 4306 [OE
dēman].

demenys *3 sg.* leads, guides, directs 1988; *3 pl.* 4076 [OF *de-
mener*].

depayntide *pp.* depicted, painted
3355 [OF *depeindre*].

depe *adv.* deep, deeply 975 [OE
dēope].

depnesse *n.* depth 746 [OE
dēopnes].

dere *adj.*[1] beloved, dear 703, 974,
3518, 3956, etc.; *as n.* 712, 4006;
precious 4196; fine, noble, worthy
1216, 1601, 1940, 2643, etc. [OE
dēore].

dere *adj.*[2] bold, brave, hardy 1602,
2652, 2937, 3416, etc.; dread
4157 (*see note*) [OE *dēor*].

dere *v.* to injure, harm, trouble
1783, 3248, 3611; **derys** *3 sg.*
2099; damage 4200 [OE *derian*].

derefull *adj.* full of grief, sorrowful
4053 [OE *daru,* harm + *-full*].

derely, dereliche *adv.* dearly, at
great cost 1277; deeply 3379
[OE *dēorlīce*].

dereworthily *adv.* splendidly,
richly 3251 [OE *dēorwyrþlīce*].

derfe *adj.* terrible, dreadful, cruel
312, 332, 811, 2052, 2102, etc.;
derflyche *adv.* cruelly 3277 [ON
diarfr].

derygese *n. pl.* dirges 4017 [L
dirige].

derke *adj.* dark 754 [OE
de(o)rc].

derlyng *n.* favorite 4196 [OE
dēorling].

descendyd. See DISCENDIS.

despyne. See PORKE DESPYNE.

despysere *n.* despiser, scorner 538
[OF *despire, despis-*].

destaynede *pp.* ordained, destined
4157, 4306; *be destaynede* (*impers.*), it be destined 664, 4090,
4153 [OF *destiner*].

destyny, desteny, destanye *n.* fate,
destiny 704, 1563, 2401, 3436,
etc. [OF *destinée*].

destresse *n.* distress 2869 [OF
destresse].

destroyes (*3 pl.*), **stroye, struye** *v.*
to destroy, vanquish 561, 1262,
1927, 4039; **stroyen** *3 pl.* 3127;
distroyede *pa. t.* 3529, 4046;
**distroyede, dystroyede, de-
stroyede, destruede, stroyede,
struyede** *pp.* 1181, 1205, 1933,
2055, 2133, 2860, etc. [OF
destruire].

dethe, dede *n.* death 332, 1253,
1935, 2057, 2102, etc.; death
wound 4240 [OE *dēaþ;* ON
dauþr].

deuer *n.* duty 1940 [OF *deveir*].

Deuyll, Deuell *n.* Devil 1072,
1783, 2934 [OE *dēofol*].

devyse *v.* to divide, divide up, distribute 2400; **devisede, deuysede,
dyuysyde** *pa. t.* 49, 1349, 3088,
3527; **devysed** *pp.* 3573 [OF
diviser].

deuorande. See DEWORYD.

devottly, deuotly *adv.* devoutly,
earnestly 296, 347, 4040 [from
OF *devot*].

dewe *n.* dew, mist 313, 3248,
3750 [OE *dēaw*].

dewly *adv.* duly, properly 4006
[from OF *deü,* adj.].

deworyd *pp.* devoured 851 (*with
pron. obj. unexpressed*); **deuorande** *pres. p.* 2054 [OF
devorer].

diademe, dyadem(e)   *n.* diadem, crown 218, 3296, 3353 [OF *diademe*].

diamawndis   *n. pl.* diamonds 3297 [OF *diamant*].

dyaperde   *pp.* adorned with a diaper or fretwork pattern 3251 [OF *diapre*].

dictour   *n.* agent, deputy 712 [AF **dictour,* OF *dicteor*].

did(e).   See DO.

dy(e)   *v.* to die 664, 703, 1073, etc.; **diede, dyede** *pa. t.* 2960, 3217 [ON *deyja*].

dyghte   *v.* to dispose, put, arrange 1253; **dyghttes** *1 & 3 sg.* 2625, 3783; **dyghte** *pp.* 3610; **dighte** *pa. t.* clothed, dressed 3915; *pp.* 3251; *pp.* arrayed, decked, adorned 3297, 3353; *pp.* removed 3066; *refl. pa. t.* made (herself) ready, addressed (herself) to a task 3044; *pa. t.* directed (himself) 2970 [OE *dihtan*].

dyked   *pp.* covered, enclosed 975 [OE *dīcian*].

dym   *adj.* dark, gloomy 1723 [OE *dimm*].

dyn   *n.* din, noise 2031 [OE *dyne*].

dynned   *pa. t.* resounded 2031 [OE *dynian*].

dynnyng   *vbl. n.* noise, music 2030 [from prec.]

dynt(e), dyntt   *n.* force, power, assault 312, 1073, 1505, 3024, etc.; blow 1118, 2178, 2183; **d[i]nttez, dynt(t)ys, dynt(t)es,** etc. *pl.* 332, 787, 1127, 1253, etc. [OE *dynt*].

discendis   *3 sg.* descends 3250; **descendyd** *pa. t.* 408 [OF *descendre*].

dischayte   *n. in dischayte,* deceitfully 3789 [OF *deceyte,* perh. with infl. of *eschete*].

dyschargide   *pp.* unburdened (myself) through utterance 1322 [OF *descharger*].

dysches, dischees   *n. pl.* dishes 189, 1949 [OE *disc*].

discoueres, discoueris, diskoueres   *3 pl.* discover, come upon 2467, 2906; explore 3119; *imper. pl.* 1641 [OF *desco(u)vrir*].

discouerours, skouerours   *n. pl.* scouts 3117, 3118 [OF *descouvreur*].

disfegoures   *3 sg.* disfigures 2769 [OF *desfigurer*].

dyspens   *n.* spending, expenditure 538 [OF *despense*].

dispetouslye, disspetousely   *adv.* pitilessly, mercilessly 3159, 4126 [from AF *despitous*].

displayes   *3 sg.* displays 3925; **displayez** *3 pl.* 1618; **displayede** *pp.* 1605, 1633, 1712, 2011, etc. [OF *despleier*].

dyssauyde   *pp.* deceived, misled 683 [OF *deceivre, deceiveir*].

disseuere   *v.* to break up, divide into parts 1575; **disseuerez** *3 sg.* 1978; **disseueride** *pa. t.* 3529 [AF *deseverer*].

disspyszede   *pp.* insulted 269 [OF *despire, despis-*].

disspite   *n.* outrage, indignation 3163 [OF *despit*].

disspoylles   *3 pl.* destroy 4126 [OF *despoill(i)er*].

distroyede, dystroyede.   See DESTROYES.

dyverse, dyuers(e)   *adj.* various, many 49, 66, 2286, 2866, etc.; hostile, vicious 1935 [OF *divers(e)*].

dyuysyde.   See DEVYSE.

do, doo   *v.* to do, perform 712, 1683, 2042, 3057, etc.; **dosse** *2 sg.* 1954; **did(e)** *pa. t.* 1934,

2340, 3078, etc.; **don(n)** *pp.* 48,
1939, 1940, etc.; follow (advice)
1023; *3 pl.* celebrate 4333; *pp.* .
prepared 4017; give, bestow, confer 2322; *pp.* 1216; *dosse of,* remove, doff (clothing) 1023; *I
doo me one lordez,* I place my
case before lords 1934 (see *MED*
dōn 6[f]); *don of dawez, don
owte of lyfe,* put to death 2056,
2178 (*dawez = days*) [OE dōn].

doctours *n. pl.* learned men, legal
authorities 145 [OF *doctour*].

dogge *n.* dog. 4218; **doggez** *pl.*
2935 [OE *docga*].

dogge-son(e) *n.* offspring of a dog
1072, 1723 [DOGGE + SON].

doyng *vbl. n.* conduct, action
3884; **doyngs** *pl.* deeds, actions
20 [from DO].

dole, dule *n.* grief, sorrow, distress 256, 2777, 3067, 3299,
etc.; *of dule,* sorrowful 704 [OF
do(e)l, duel].

dolefull *adj.* doleful, sorrowful
2054 [from prec.].

doluen *pp.* buried 975 [OE
delfan].

Domesday *n.* Doomsday, Judgment Day 1278, 3442 [OE
dōmes dæg].

don(n). See DO.

dosse. See DO.

doubbyd(e). See DUBBEZ.

douce *adj.* dear 1251 [OF *douce*].

doughtynes(se) *n.* valor, bravery
1563, 3884 [from prec.].

dought(t)y, dowght(t)y *adj.* able,
worthy, valiant, brave 20, 1738,
2834, 3798; *as n.* 2777, 3024,
4241; **dought(t)yest(e)** *superl.*
most worthy, boldest, bravest
219, 1942, 2653, 3321, etc.;
doughttily *adv.* bravely, ably,
worthily 1939 [OE *dohtig*].

doun. See DOWN.

dout, dowtte *v.* to fear, doubt 312,
3061 [OF *douter*].

dowble *adj.* double, twice the
number 2569, 2834 [OF *double*].

dowblede *pp.* made double, increased twofold 3609 [OF
doubler].

dowblettez *n. pl.* doublets 2625
[OF *doublet*].

dowcherys. See DUCHERYE.

dowere *n.* endowment 3089 [OF
douaire].

dowght(t)y. See DOUGHT(T)Y.

down, downn(e), doun *adv.* down
101, 280, 313, 351, etc. [late OE
dūn(e)].

downkyng *vbl. n.* dampening,
moistening 3248 [unknown; cf.
Sw dial. *dänka,* to moisten; see
DANKE].

dowt(t)e *n.* doubt 2043; fear 3225
[OF *do(u)te*].

dowtte. See DOUT.

dowttouse *adj.* fearful, dreadful
3967 [OF *doutous*].

drafe. See DRYFFES.

dragges *n. pl.* barges 3615 [from
OE *dragan*].

dragon(e) *n.* dragon 760, 786,
811, 815; (as heraldic device)
2026, 2053, 2057; **dragouns** *pl.*
dragon ensigns 1252 [OF
dragon].

drawe *v. intr.* to protract, delay
550 (*see note*); **drawes** *2 sg.*
3968; **drawes** *3 sg.* goes, moves
1251, 4052; *drawes in,* draws up,
pauses 622; *trans.* drink, take a
draught 3379; *3 sg.* drives 2941;
drawen *3 pl.* draw, haul 3615;
3 pl. draw off (wine) 2028;
drawen *pp.* drawn 3924, (by
horses) 463; *drewe owt,* led off
2286 [OE *dragan*].

drawe-brigge *n.* drawbridge 2474 [prec. + BRIGGE].

dreche *v.* delay, stay, hang back 1504, 1722; **dreches** *3 sg.* 2940, 4052; **dreches** *3 pl.* 1254, 2154; **drecchede** *pa. t.* 754 [unknown].

drechede *pp.* tormented 811 [OE *drecc(e)an*].

dredde *adj.* afraid 20 [OE *ofdræd(d)*].

dred(e) *n.* fear, awe, dread 46, 579, 754, 1723, 2474; **dredis** *pl.* dangers 4034 [from next].

drede *v.* to fear, dread 829, 2935; **dredis** *3 sg.* 3010; **dredis** *3 pl.* 4085; **dredys** *imper. pl.* 3799; **dredde** *pp.* 3298; **dredis** *imper. s.* doubt 3060 [OE *drǣdan*].

dred(e)full *adj.* dreadful, awesome 760, 815, 829, 1252, etc.; **dredfully** *adv.* awesomely 2026 [from DRED(E), n.].

dredlesse, dredlez *adv.* without doubt, doubtless 1504, 2043, 4053 [from DRED(E), n.].

drefen. See DRYFFES.

dreghe *n.* duration 2915; *on(e) dreghe,* at length, finally 786, 3968; to a distance, afar off 787, 4219 [ON *drjúgr,* adj.]

dreghe. See DRYE, v.

dreghely *adv.* freely, unceasingly 2028 [from ON *drjúgr*].

drem(e) *n.* dream 829, 3224; **dremes** *pl.* 3223 [OE *drēam,* joy].

dremyd(e) *pa. t. impers.* 760, 815 [from prec.].

drenschen, drynchen *v.* to drown, overwhelm 761, 816 [OE *drencan*].

drerily, drerely *adv.* dolefully 2154, 2969 [OE *drēoriglīce*].

dresse, dresce *v.* to put in order, arrange, make ready, prepare (*often refl.*) 550, 1072, 2042;

dresses(se) *3 sg.* 2833, 2969, etc.; **dresses, drisses** *3 pl.* 2473, 3615; **dresside, dryssede, drissede** *pa. t.* 46, 579, etc.; *dressede one, drissede in,* placed, set in position, put on 1055, 2052; *dresses vp,* sets up, raises 2026; *pa. t.* dressed, clothed, adorned, arrayed 218, 3353; *pp.* 1252; *pa. t.* moved 786; deal 2401 [OF *drec(i)er*].

dreuen. See DRYFFES.

drye *adj.* dry 3249 [OE *drȳge*].

drye, dreghe *v.* to endure, suffer 704, 1546, 1632, 3437 [OE *drēogan*].

dryede *pa. t.* dried up 4171 [OE *drīgean, drȳgean*].

dryffes *3 pl. intr.* rush, move violently 2757; **dryfande** *pres. p.* 761, 816; **drefen** *pp.* drawn 3224; **drife** *pa. t.* endured, passed, went through 3276 (*see note*); *trans.* **dreuen** *3 pl.* impel, force 2914; **drafe** *pa. t.* 787 [OE *drīfan*].

Drighten, Dryghtten, Dryghttyn *n.* God, the Lord 1278, 3799, 4008, 4157, 4305, etc. **Dryght(t)yns, Dryghtynez** *poss.* 664, 1564, 4241 [OE *dryhten*].

drynchen. See DRENSCHEN.

drynke *v.* to drink 3379 [OE *drincan*].

drynkes, drynkyn *n. pl.* drinks 236, 2028 [OE *drinc*].

drynkles *adj.* without drink to quench one's thirst 4172 [from OE *drinc,* n.].

drissede, dryssede. See DRESSE.

dromedarie *n.* dromedary, riding camel, 2941; **dromondaries** *pl.* 2286 [OF *dromedaire*].

dromowndes *n. pl.* large, seagoing vessels 3615 [AF *dromund*].

droppe *v.* to drop, let fall 1504;
  drowppande *pres. p.* 4053;
  droppede *pp.* 3296 [OE *dropian*].

droughte, drowghte *n.* dryness,
  lack of moisture 3249, 4171 [OE
  drūgaþ].

droupe *v.* to languish 4007 [ON
  drúpa].

drownnes *2 sg.* overwhelm,
  smother 3968 [?OE *drūnian*].

drowppande. See DROPPE.

dubbez *3 sg.* dubs 622;
  doubbyd(e), dubbyd(e), etc. *pa. t.*
  48, 1738, 2642, 3614, etc.;
  dubbyde, dubbid(e), etc. *pp.*
  1728, 1942, 2029, 3417, etc.;
  pp. arrayed, adorned 3296, 3609
  [OF *aduber, adouber*].

ducherye *n.* duchy 2400, 2937;
  ducheres, ducheryes, dowcherys
  pl. 49, 1728, 3614 [OF *duché* +
  -erye (ME suffix from OF *-ier,*
  -er)].

duches, duchez *n.* duchess, lady
  974, 3044, 3089, 3251; (as
  title) 852 [OF *duchesse*].

duelle *v.* to dwell, live 3067;
  duellede, duellyde *pa. t.* 219,
  3321; **duelland** *pres. p.* 3443;
  duellyde *pp.* wandered, been
  away 1200; **duellis** *2 sg.* delay
  3967 [OE *dwellan*].

duke *n.* duke, nobleman 1738,
  1883, 2329, 2642, etc.; **dukes,**
  dukkez *pl.* 66, 145, 408, 578,
  etc. [OF *duc*].

dule. See DOLE.

dule-cotes *n. pl.* mourning cloaks
  4336 [DOLE + COTE].

durste. See DARE, v.¹

dussepere *n.* peer 2329, 2642;
  dusper(e)s, dus(s)zeperis, duzse-
  perez, etc. *pl.* 66, 145, 723, 1254,
  etc. [OF *douze pers*].

efte *adv.* again 470, 529, 2349
  [OE *eft*].

egerly, egyrly *adv.* eagerly, spir-
  itedly 337, 2246; fiercely 1125,
  1148, 1411, 1499, etc.; promptly
  1591 [from EGREE].

egge, eghge *n.* edge (of a sword)
  2567, 2958, 4194 [OE *ecg*].

eghelyng *adv.* on the edge, edge-
  ways 3675 [prec. + OE *-ling,* as
  in *bæcling*].

eghen, eghn(e). See EYGHEN.

egyrly. See EGERLY.

egle *n.* eagle (as heraldic device)
  360, 2067, 2245; **egles** pl. 1294,
  2027, 2339 [OF *egle*].

egree *adj.* eager 507 [OF *aigre*].

eye-liddis *n. pl.* eyelids 3953
  [next + OE *hlid*].

eyghen, eyghn(e), eghen, eghn(e),
  eughne *n. pl.* eyes 116, 358,
  426, 1083, etc.; **eye** *sg. 3282*
  (*see note*) [OE *ēagan*]. See
  MAUGER.

eyues, eyuy(e)s, eyuis, etc. See
  EUIS.

eke *adv.* also 44, 572, 674, 1157,
  etc. [OE *ēac*].

ekken *v.* to increase 2009; **ekys**
  3 sg. 3965 [OE *ēacan, ēcan*].

elbowe *n.* elbow 4245 [OE
  elnboga].

eldare. See OLDE, adj.

elde *n.* age, old age 4220; **eldes**
  pl. ages 301 (*see note*) [OE
  eldo].

elders, eldyrs *n. pl.* leaders, kings
  13; ancestors 99, 272, 293, 321,
  385, etc. [OE *eldra*].

eldeste. See OLDE, adj.

ells, elles *adv.* else, besides 215,
  825; **quasi-adj.** else, other 450,
  1014, 1191, 1209, 1320, etc.
  [OE *elles*].

emange. See AMONG.

eme   *n.* uncle 1347 [OE *ēam*].

emperour(e)   *n.* emperor 86, 265, 285, 286, 307, etc.; *uninfl. poss.* 1660; **emperours** *pl.* 276 [OF *empereor*].

empire, empy(e)re   *n.* empire, the Roman Empire 278, 359, 520, 643, 1308, etc. [OF *empir(i)e*].

enamelde   *pp.* enameled, colored 765, 2027, 2565, 3355 [AF *enameler*].

enangylls   *3 sg.* corners, surrounds so as to drive into an angle or corner 3781 [OF *en-* + *angle*].

enarmede   *pp.* plated 910 [OF *enarmer*].

enbraces, enbrassez   *3 pl.* strap on the arm 1753, 4111; **enbrassede** *pp.* 2459, 2518 [OF *enbracer*].

enbuschement, buschement   *n.* ambush, body of men waiting in ambush 1407, 3115, 3124 [OF *enbuschement*].

enbusches   *3 sg.* places in ambush 1981; **enbuschede, enbuschide** *pp.* placed or lying in ambush 1403, 1712 [OF *enbuscher*].

enclined(e)   *pa. t.* bowed 479, 1706 [OF *encliner*].

enclines   *n. pl.* bows 83 [from prec.].

enclosez   *3 sg.* surrounds, encloses, envelops 883, 1134; **enclosid, enclosed(e),** etc. *pp.* sealed 506, 4206; enclosed 616, 757, 849, 2396; surrounded 3238; circled 908 [from *enclos,* pp. of OF *enclore*].

encorownmentes   *n. pl.* coronations 4197 [OF *en-* + CROWN + *-ment*].

enco(u)ntre, encountire, encowntere, countere   *v.* to fight, meet face to face in combat 345, 1274, 1320, 1787, etc.; **cownterez** *3 sg.*

1848; **enconters** *3 pl.* 2158; **encontrede** *pa. t.* 1185; **cowntered** *pp.* 1893 [OF *encounter*].

encroche   *v.* to seize, capture 3212, 3426; **encrochez** *3 sg.* 1243; **encrochede** *pa. t.* 2036; **encrochede** *pp.* 3525, 3570; gain 4021 [OF *encrochier*].

encroyssede   *pa. t.* crossed, made the sign of the cross 4112 [OF *en-* + *croisier*].

ende   *n.* end 73, 2588, 3224, 4177; death 3400, 4253 [OE *ende*].

ende   *v.* to end, finish 3800, 4093; **endis, endys** *3 sg.* 4099, 4290; **endide** *pp.* 2930, 3957; die 4151; *3 sg.* 2255, 4342; **endyng** *pres. p.* 4170 [OE *endian*].

endelesse   *adj.* boundless, everlasting 3801 [OE *endelēas*].

endenttyd, endente   *pp.* (of a shield or coat of arms) surrounded with a border of notches or toothlike indentations 2052; inlaid, embossed 3297 [OF *endenter*].

endittede   *pa. t.* composed 3420 [OF *enditer*].

endoride   *pp.* glazed with the yolks of eggs *199* [OF *endorer*].

enewe.   See ENOWE.

enfeblesches   *3 pl.* grow feeble 2484 [OF *enfeblir, enfebliss-*].

enflureschit   *pp.* displayed flourishingly 198 [OF *en-* + FLORESCHE].

enforce, enforsse   *v.* to reinforce, strengthen 364; *refl.* try, make an effort 225 [OF *enforcier*].

engenderide, engenderde   *pp.* begotten 612, 843, 2111 [OF *engendrer*].

engendure   *n.* origin, engendering 3743 [OF *engendre*].

engynes, engeynes *n. pl.* siege engines, war machines, crossbows 2423, 2481, 3036 [OF *engin*].

engyste *v.* to appoint resting places along the route of a journey 335 [OF *en-* + OE *gieste*].

englaymes, englaymez *3 pl.* enslime 1131, *3684 (see note)* [OF *en-* + ME *gleim* (of obscure origin)].

engowschede *pp.* stout, fleshy 2053 [from OF *engoussé*].

engrelede *pp.* (of a shield or coat of arms) ornamented with curvilinear indentations 4182 [OF *engresler*].

enhorilde *pp.* bordered 3244 [OF *en-* + *ourler*].

enjoyne *v.* to enjoin, order 445; **enjoynes, enjoynys** *3 pl.* join battle 2897, 4109; **enjoynede** *pa. t.* came together 2087 [OF *enjoindre*].

enkerly *adv.* anxiously, earnestly, eagerly 507, 2066, 2222, 2839 [ON *einkar,* adj.].

enmy(e) *n.* enemy, foe 519, 565, 642, 1181, etc.; **enmyse** *pl.* 1205, 1240, 1411 [OF *enemi*].

ennelled *pp.* enameled, emblazoned with color 1294 [OF *en-* + *neeler*].

enoyntede, ennoynttyde, etc. See ANOYNTEDE.

enowe, enewe, inowe, inewe, ynowe, ynewe, *adj. (usually after n.)* many, in plenty, enough, abundant 45, 67, 199, 202, 232, 422, etc.; *adv.* fully, quite, sufficiently 300 [OE *genōg, genōh*].

enpeyrede *pp.* damaged 474 [OF *empeirer*].

enpoyson *n.* poison 213 [from OF *empoissoner,* v.].

ensege, ensegge *v.* to besiege, lay siege to 441, 1337; **enseggez** *3 sg.* 623; **ensegede** *pp.* 1696 [OF *enseg(g)er*].

enserches *3 sg.* probes (wounds) 4311; *3 pl.* search out 2466 [OF *enserchier*].

enserclede *pp.* encircled, surrounded *3942* [OF *en-* + OE *circul*].

ensure *v.* to assure 330, 439, 3734; make clear, guarantee, prove 1689, 2324 [AF *enseurer*].

entayllide *pp.* (of property) restricted or assigned by inheritance to certain heirs 3542 [OF *en-* + AF *tailé,* adj.].

entamede, attamede *pa. t.* ripped, pierced, tore open 2175, 2203; **entamed(e)** *pp.* wounded, torn 1160, 2708 [OF *attamer, entamer*].

entyce *v.* to provoke, incite 307 [OF *entic(i)er*].

entire, entre *v.* to enter 565; **enter(e)s** *3 sg.* 1499, 2007, 3076; **entres** *3 pl.* 4309; **entrede, entirde** *pp.* 1239, 4069; to make entry (into lands) as a formal assertion of ownership, to take possession 1967; *3 sg.* 2387; *pp.* 1691; **enters** *3 pl.* penetrate (a battle line) 4162; **enteride** *pa. t.* 2805; *pp.* begun, sat about 3448 [OF *entrer*].

enueryd *pp.* confirmed, attested, vouched for 1694 [OF *enverer*].

enverounes *3 pl.* surround, encircle 4124; **enuerounde** *pa. t.* 2051; **enuerownde** *pp. 3242;* **enverounde** *pa. t.* moved through the whole extent of an area 2094 [OF *environner*].

enuyous *adj.* malicious, invidious 2047 [AF *envious*].

Epiphanye *n.* the feast of the
Epiphany, January 6 415 [OF
epiphanie].

erberis *n. pl.* arbors 3245 [OF
(*h*)*erbier*].

ercheuesqes *n. pl.* archbishops 67
(*see note*) [OF *ercheuesques*].

er(e). See ARE.

erle *n.* earl, nobleman 1347, 1659,
1661, 1869; *uninfl. poss.* 3064;
erl(l)es, erlez *pl.* 67, 408, 576,
578, etc. [OE *eorl*].

erledoms *n. pl.* earldoms 42 [OE
eorldōm].

erles: *on erles,* in pledge 2687
[app. from OF **erles,* rel. to
erres].

erne *n. pl.* ears 1086 [OE *ēare*].

ernestly *adv.* truly, sincerely 2838,
4141; courageously, fiercely 2903
[OE *eornostlīce*].

errawnte *adj.* straying from the
proper course, deviant 2895 [OF
errant].

erroure: *in errour*(*e*), wrongfully,
unlawfully 1308, 1663 [OF *error,
errur*].

erth(e) *n.* the earth 3830; *in erthe,*
on earth, throughout the (whole)
earth 29, 161, 175, 219, 229,
etc.; ground 120, 784, 794,
1125, etc.; *a faire erthe,* even
ground, affording an equal
chance of success on both sides
972; land 577; burrow 109 [OE
eorþe].

erthely *adj.* temporal 1664, 4169
[OE *eorþlic*].

es. See IS.

eschape *v.* to escape 1020, 2957;
eschappede, eschappide, chapyde
pa. t. 1881, 2367, 4260;
eschapede, *pp.* 1117; *pp.* issued
3576 [OF *eschaper*].

escheffe *v.* to escape, move off,

move away 2301; **eschews** *3 sg.*
1116; **eschewes** *imper. pl.* 1750;
eschewede *pa. t.* 1881; *pp.* 1539
[OF *eschever*[1]].

escheue *v.* to perform, achieve,
accomplish, gain one's end 3347;
eschewede *pa. t.* 1620, 2956,
3000; **eschewede, escheuyde**
pp. 3021, 3027 [OF *eschever,*[2]
corruption of *achever*].

eschewes, eschewede. See
ESCHEFFE, ESCHEUE.

ese *n.* ease 3208 [OF *eise*].

este *adj.* eastern 577, 1740, 2200,
3210 [OE *ēast*].

Estyre, Esterne *n.* Easter 554,
1006 [OE *ēastre,* usually pl.
ēastran, ēastron].

eten *pp.* eaten 2716 [OE *etan*].

ethyns, ethenys *n. pl.* giants 4123
(*see note*), 4163 [OE *eten*].

ettyll *v.* to intend, purpose 554;
ettells, etles *3 sg.* 520, 3077
[ON *ǽtla*].

eughne. See EYGHEN.

euen, ewyn *n.* eve, evening 1006,
1594, 1788, 2933 [OE *ǽfen*].

**even, evyn(e), euen(e), euyne, ewen,
ewyn(n)(e)** *adv.* exactly, just,
right, straight 78, 618, 762, 774,
799, etc.; straightway, directly
453, 834, 3744; evenly 3241
[OE *efen, efne*].

euensang, euesange *n.* evensong,
vespers 894, 900 [OE *ǽfensang*].

euer(e), ewyre *adv.* ever, always,
forever, evermore 8, 59, 138,
155, 165, etc.; repeatedly 1149
[OE *ǽfre*].

euerilk, eueriche *adj.* every (*with*
a) 212, 2037 [OE *ǽfre* + *ilca,
ǽlc, ylc*].

euydens *n.* evidence 286 [OF *evidence*].

euyll *n.* evil 1117 [OE *yfel*].

evyn(e). See EVEN, adv.

euis, euys, eyues, eyuy(e)s, eyuis
n. sg. edge, border (of a forest)
1283 (*see note*), 1760, 1879,
2275, 2308, 2516, etc. [OE *efes*].

ewen, ewyn, etc. See EVEN, adv.

ewyre. See EUER(E).

excellente *adj.* noble, exalted
3781, 3800, 4161 [OF *excellent*].

excusede *pp.* excused, absolved
131 [OF *excuser*].

faamen. See FOOMEN.

face *n.* face, expression 121,
1079, 1103, 1115, etc.; **facez**
pl. 2149 [OF *face*].

fadire, fadyr(e) *n.* father 112,
2382, 2412, 2595, etc.; *uninfl.
poss.* 1169; **fadirs** *poss.* 4216;
fadyrs *pl.* ancestors 2033; a word
of respectful address, sir 2735
[OE *fæder*].

fadom *n. uninfl. pl.* fathoms 1103
[OE *fæþm*].

faees. See FOO.

faghte. See FYGHT(E).

faye *n.* faith, truth, religion 2860,
2862; *in fay(e),* in truth, by my
faith, assuredly 2842, 3073, 4252
[OF *fei*]. See FAITHE.

fay(e), fey(e) *adj.* doomed to die,
dead 121, 394, 428, 884, etc.;
as n. 517, 2143, 3927; *feye blod,*
lifeblood 4121 [OE *fæge*].

fayfully *adv.* truly, assuredly 1715
[from FAYE, n.].

faile *v.* to fail, miss, fall short
2860; **faylez** *3 sg.* 4271; **faillez**
3 pl. 585; **failede, faylede** *pa. t.*
1107, 3309, 3793, 3836; *3 sg.*
fades 751; *pa. t.* 486, 3594 [OF
faillir].

fayne *adj.* glad, happy 1160,
3073; eager 2764 [OE *fægen*].

faynt, feynte *adj.* weak, feeble

2947, faint 1874 [OF *faint, feint*].

faire, fayre *adj.* fair, beautiful,
goodly, fine 365, 425, 436, 438,
584, 631, 822; **faire** *compar.*
3306; agreeable 366; suitable,
advantageous, favorable 495,
1177; **faireste, fayreste** *superl.*
315, 861, 1709, 2151, etc.; *as n.*
2849 [OE *fæger*]. See ERTH(E).

faire, fayre *adv.* beautifully, splendidly 38, 62, 184, 197, etc.; courteously 838, 1938; well, excellently 870, 917, 1110, 1711, etc.;
completely, fully 3953 [OE
fægre].

fairely *adv.* gently, softly 954
[from prec.].

faithe, faythe: *in faith(e), in
fayth(e),* in truth, I swear 425,
526, 885, 1155; *in my faithe, be
my faythe,* on my faith, by my
faith, I swear 971, 3302 (*see
note*); *make faythe and faye,*
swear loyalty and faith 2862 [OF
feit, feid].

fayth(e)fully *adv.* truly, assuredly
1345, 1913; conscientiously 1735
[from prec.].

faithely, faythely *adv.* indeed, certainly, in truth 3864, 4031 [from
FAITHE].

faken *3 pl.* coil 742 [from ME
fake, a coil of rope (of obscure
origin)].

falded *pa. t.* bent 3308 [OE
faldan].

fall *v.* to fall, fall down, drop 803,
1147, 1874, etc.; **fallez, fallys,**
etc. *3 sg.* 313, 2207, 2707, etc.;
3 pl. 2797; **fell** *pa. t.* 759, 3309,
etc.; **fallen** *pp.* 667, 3270, etc.;
come to pass, happen, turn out
(*usually impers.*) *3 sg. subj.*
1006, 1749; *3 sg.* 2480, 2729,
4017; *pa. t.* befell 3828; *pp.* 870

one . . . falles, come upon 2506 [OE *fallan*].

falow *adj.* gray, dark 1402 [OE *falu*].

falowede *pp.* turned gray or pale 3954 [OE *fealwian*].

fals(e), falls *adj.* treacherous, faithless 1307, 2763, 2929, 3602, etc.; *as n.* 3739; *adv.* faithlessly, perfidiously 3776 [late OE *fals,* OF *fals*].

fals(s)ede *n.* falsehood, faithlessness 2860, 3918 [from prec.].

falterd. See FILTEREDE.

famows *adj.* famous 3303 [AF *famous*].

fan(n)de, fonde, fonode *v.* to try, attempt 557, 984; taste, sample 205, 3370, 3371; undertake 867; see that, take care 656 [OE *fandian*]. See also FYND(E), FOUND(E).

fannge *v.* to take, seize, grasp 425; **fangez** *3 sg.* 1005, 1249; **fongez, fongen** *3 pl.* 2799; **fongede** *pa. t.* 3308 [OE *fōn,* ON *fanga*].

fare *n.* track 393 [OE *faru*].

fare *v.* to go, move 3581; **fares, faris** *3 sg.* 788, 3519 [OE *faran*].

fareway(e) *n.* path, track 394; *in theire farewaye,* on their trail 1357 [prec. + WAY(E)].

farlande *n.* headland, bluff, promontory 880, 984, 1188 [OE *fore-* + LANDE, n.]

farly. See FERLY.

farrere. See FER(R)E, adj.

faste, feste *adj.* fixed, fastened 2142; swift, fast 2757; *adv.* fiercely 1076, 1115, 1383, 1494, etc.; violently 1143; straight 1037, 1401; swiftly 1441, 2226, 2584; close behind 1367, 2758, 4224 [OE *fæst* adj., *fæste* adv.].

faucetez *n. pl.* taps, faucets 205 [OF *fausset*].

faught(t)e, fawghte. See FYGHT(E).

fawcon, fawkon *n.* falcon 788, 4003; **fawcouns** *pl.* 925 [OF *faucon*].

fawe *adj.* dappled 747 [OE *fāg*].

fawntkyn *n.* child, infant 2440, 2736; **fawntekyns** *pl.* 845 [dim. of aphetic form of OF *enfant*].

fawte *n.* lack 160; fault 2737 [OF *faute*].

fax *n.* hair 1078 [OE *feax*].

feble *adj.* feeble, weak 2929; *as n.* feeble fare 226 [OF *feble*].

feche, feched, etc. See FETCHE.

feede *v.* to feed 2707; **fedde, feedde** *pp.* 4143; *refl.* eat 226; **fedys** *3 sg.* 1062 [OE *fēdan*].

feemen *n. pl.* vassals, servants 2488 [next + MAN].

feez *n. pl.* wages 2928 [AF *fee*].

feghte, feghttez, etc. See FYGHT(E).

fegure *n.* form, shape 781, 3301 [OF *figure*].

fey(e). See FAY(E), adj.

feyed *pa. t.* clasped, clutched 1114 [OE *fēgan*].

feyne *v.* to feign, dissemble 1913; flinch, falter 1147, 1734 [OF *feindre*].

feynyng *vbl. n.* flinching 225 [from prec.].

feynte. See FAYNT.

feyntly *adv.* timidly, in a cowardly manner 1734 [from FAYNT].

fekill *adj.* false, untrue 2860 [OE *ficol*].

felde, feelde *n.* field, battlefield 364, 388, 404, 452, 517, etc. [OE *feld*].

fele *adj.* many, countless, every

845, 1247 (*after n.*), 2143,
2450, etc. *as n.* 1496, 2092 [OE
fela].

fele *v.* to hide 3237 [ON *fela*].

felede *pa. t.* felt 1874 [OE *fēlan*].

feleyghes *n. pl.* the curved seg-
ments that form the rim of a
wheel 3308 [OE *felg(e)*].

feletez, felettes *n. pl.* loins 1158,
2174, 4237 [OF *filet*].

felewes. See FOLOWE.

fell *n.*[1] skin, hide 1081 [OE *fell*].

fell *n.*[2] rock, crag 2489, 2502
[ON *fjall, fell*].

fell *adj.* fierce, wild, savage, cruel
1401, 2769, 3692; **felly** *adv.*
fiercely 2141 [OF *fel*].

fell *v.* to fell, strike down, kill
973, 3739; **fellis, fellez** *3 sg.*
1247, 1249, 3827; **felles, fellis**
3 pl. 1496, 2805, 2945; *imper.*
pl. 4087; **felled(e)** *pa. t.* 1812,
2092, 2160; **fellide, fellyde**
pp. 1851, 3345, 3718, etc.; *fell*
hym o lyfe, kill him 1139; *fellyd*
them on lyfe, o lyfe, killed them
1899, 3906; *fellde owtte of lyfe,*
killed 2376 [OE *fellan*].

felly See FELL, adj.

felone *n.* wretch, villain, monster
3777, 4236 [OF *felon*].

felowez *n. pl.* companions 1381
[late OE *feolaga,* ON *félage*].

felschen *v.* to splash with water
1975 (*see note*); **flassches** *3 sg.*
slashes 4237; **fleschez** *3 pl.* flit,
dart about 926 [onomatopoeic].

fende, Fend(e), fente *n.* fiend,
monster, demon 871, 881, 954,
1038, 4249 (*see note*), etc.;
fendez *pl.* 612, 843, 2111; the
Devil 1062, 2761, 2763, 2862,
etc. [OE *fēond*].

fendis. See DEFENDEZ.

fenyste *pp.* finished 4254 [OF
fenir, feniss-].

fente. See FENDE.

fera(u)nte, ferawnte *adj.* iron-gray
1811, 2140, 2259, 2451, etc.
[OF *ferra(u)nt*].

fercostez *n. pl.* ships 743 [ON
farkostr].

ferde *n.* fear, terror 1875, 3069,
3237 [from next].

ferde *pp.* afraid 403, 526, 2438,
3227 [OE *fēran*].

ferdnesse *n.* terror, fear 121, 2258
[prec. + OE *-ness(e)*].

fere *n.* fear 2734, 3918 [OE *fēr*].

fere *adj.* safe, unhurt 2796, 3017
[ON *fœrr*].

feres, feris, ferys, ferez *n. pl.*
companions, fellows, peers 1578,
1608, 1789, 1884, 2072, etc.
[OE *gefēra*].

feryn(n)e, ferrom *adj.* foreign,
from afar 3578, 3711; *o ferrom,*
from a distance, at a distance,
some distance, afar 856, 934,
2100 [OE *feorran*].

ferynne *n.* fern 1875 [OE *fyrn*].

ferke, ferkke, ferken *v. intr.* to go,
proceed 1037, 1188, 2806, 4152;
ferkes *3 sg.* 2420, 2900, 3597,
etc.; **ferkes** *3 pl.* 2501; **ferkand**
pres. p. 1452; *ferke of,* go from,
leave 984; *ferkes ine,* goes on,
rides on 3002; hasten, move
quickly 2257, 3907; *3 sg.* 2071;
3 pl. 1811; *trans,* **ferkande** *pres.*
p. urging, driving on 2452 [OE
fercian].

ferly, ferlyche, farly *n.* marvel,
wonder 2440, 2484, 2842, 2947;
adj. strange, wondrous 925 [OE
fǣrlic, adj., ON *ferligr*].

fermes, fermez *n. pl.* revenues,
tributes 425, 1005 [OF *ferme*].

fermyson *n.* close season on deer: *fluriste of fermyson,* fattened through the close season 180 [AF *fermyson*].

fer(r)e *adj.* far 1176, 1232, 1442, etc.; *of ferre,* from afar 2096; *oo ferre,* far away 3907; *þe ferrere syde,* the other side 1496, 4237; *the farrere ȝate,* the gate on the far side 3068; **ferreste,** *superl.* most 2741 [OE *feorr*].

ferre *adv. compar.* farther 2873 [OE *feorr,* compar. *fierr, fyrr*].

ferrom. See FERYN(N)E.

fers(e) *adj.* fierce 1451, 1537, 1710, 1897, etc. [OF *fiers*].

fers(e)ly *adv.* wildly, fiercely, violently 1115, 1118, 2376, 3402, 4086 etc. [from prec.].

fersenesse *n.* vehement fury, savagery 3826 [from FERS(E)].

ferthe *adj. & n.* fourth 3412 [OE *fēorþa*].

ferthynges *n. pl.* farthings 3472 (*see note*) [OE *fēorþing*].

fesa(u)ntez *n. pl.* pheasants 198, 925 [AF *fesa(u)nt*].

fesede *pp.* put to flight 2842 [OE *fēsian*].

feste. See FASTE.

festenesse *3 sg.* delivers (a blow) 1118; **festenez** *3 pl.* fasten, tie 934 [OE *fæstnian*].

fetche, feche *v.* to fetch, bring back 1188, 2357; **fetches** *3 sg.* 3438; **fecchede** *pa. t.* brought forth, escorted 169; **feched, fechyd** *pp.* 111, 437 [OE *feccan*]. See also FETTE.

fetheris *n. pl.* feathers 2098 [OE *feþer*].

fette *v.* to fetch, bring back 557 [OE *fetian*]. See also FETCHE.

fettede. See FITT.

fetteled *pp.* arranged, set, fixed 2149 [perh, from OE *fetel,* girdle].

feulez. See FOWLE.

Feuerȝere *n.* February 436 [OF *feverier*].

fewe *adj.[1]* few 2162, 2742, 2850, 4031, etc.; *n.* 1881, 2257; **fewere** *compar.* 2887 [OE *fēawe*].

fewe *adj.[2]* hostile 2502 (*see note*) [OE *fāh*].

fewle. See FOWLE.

fewtée *n.* fealty, allegiance 112 [OF *feauté*].

fewters *3 sg.* thrusts (the lance) into its socket, ready for a battle charge 3775; **fewtrede, fewteride** *pp.* with lances at the ready, ready for battle 1711, 1756; *intr.* **fewters** *3 pl.* 2140 [from next].

fewtire, fewtyre *n.* a felt-lined rest or socket for a spear or lance, attached to the saddle 1366, 1769; *castez in fewter(e),* castis in fewtire, caste in fewtyre, etc., thrust(s) (the lance) into its socket, ready for a battle charge 1791, 1810, 1830, 2165, etc. [OF *feutre*].

fewtrede. See FEWTERS.

fy *interj.* fie! an expression of disgust 2778, 3777; *Fy à debles!* Fie on the devils! 2934 [OF *fy*].

fyche, fichene *v.* to pierce 2098, 2162; **fichede** *pa. t.* 4239 [OF *fich(i)er*].

fifte *adj. & n.* fifth 3306, 3414 [OE *fīfta*].

fyftene *adj. & n.* fifteen 837, 872, 983, 1005, etc. [OE *fiftēne*].

fifty, fyfty *adj. & n.* fifty 301, 365, 1402, etc. [OE *fīftig*]. See SICHE.

fyghte, feghte *n.* battle, fight 2143, 3001, 3582, 3689, etc. [OE *fe(o)hte*].

fyght(e), feghte *v.* to fight 303,

367, 404, 1345, etc.; **fyghttez, feghttis,** etc. *3 sg.* 789, 2091, 2232; **fyghttes, feghttez, feghtten,** etc. *3 pl.* **fight(t)es** *imper. pl.* 3740, 4086; **faghte, faught(t)e, fawghte** *pa. t.* 1174, 1898, 2164, etc.; **fyghtande, feghtande** *pres. p.* 4066, 4121, 4257; **fo(u)ght(t)en** *pp.* 1535, 2365, 2375, etc. [OE *fe(o)htan*].

fightyng *vbl. n.* battle, fighting 1885 [from prec.]

fygurede *pp.* created, formed 2151 [OF *figurer*].

fylede *pp.* defiled 978 [OE *fȳlan*].

fill *n.* fill, sufficiency 2822 [OE *fyllo, fyllu*].

fillez, fillis *3 sg. refl.* gluts, stuffs; **filled** *pp.* fulfilled 1032; *3 sg. intr.* fills up, bubbles up 1402 (*see note*) [OE *fyllan*].

filsnez *3 sg.* lurks 881 (*see note*) [from ON *fylgsni,* hiding place].

filterede, filtyrde, falterd *pp.* matted, tangled 780, 1078, 2149 (*see note*); contorted 1092 [OF *feltrer*].

fylth *n.* vileness 1032, 1071; gore, excrement 2782 [OE *fȳlþ*].

fynd(e) *v.* to find, discover, meet up with, encounter 226, 394, 884, 1966, etc.; **findis, fyndez, fyndys** *3 sg.* 945, 949, 1357, etc.; **fyndez, fyndys** *3 pl.* 836, 1647; **fande, fonde** *pa. t.* 1160, 2161, 2704, etc.; **founden, fonden, funden,** etc. *pp.* 92, 163, 311, 435, etc.; take note of 112 [OE *findan*]. See also FAN(N)DE, FOUND(E).

fyn(e) *adj.* fine 771, 1364, 2098, etc.; **fyneste** *superl.* 3371; pure 205 [OF *fin*].

fyole *n.* flask 2704 (*see note*) [OF *fiole*].

fyre *n.* fire 773, 789, 949, etc.; **fyrez** *pl.* 880, 945, 1975 [OE *fȳr*]. See WILDE.

fyrste *adj. superl.* first 176, 436, 949, etc.; *as n.: in þe firste,* in the front or foremost part (of the ship) 3677; *adv.* in the first place, firstly 393, 517, 1185, etc. [OE *fyr(e)st*]. See FLOUR(E).

firthe, fyrth(e) *n.* woodland, copse, meadowland, field 1409, 1708, 1850, 1875, 1897, etc.; **frithez** *pl.* 924 [OE *fyr(h)þ, gefyrþe*].

fyrthe *v.* to preserve, protect 3370; **frythes** *3 pl.* 2159; *imper. pl.* 1734; **frythede** *pp.* 656 [OE *friþian*].

fisch-halle *adj.* whole as a fish, sound as a fish 2709 [OE *fisc* + HOLE, adj.[1]].

fysnamye, fyssnamy *n.* physiognomy, face 1114, 3331 [OF *phisonomie*].

fiste, fyste *n.* fist 973, 2233, 4003 [OE *fȳst*].

fitt *v.* to array, marshal 2139 (*refl.*); **fittes, fittis,** etc. *3 sg.* 1755, 1989, 4082; **fittyde, fettede** *pp.* 2455, 4067; *fittez in,* lines up 2072 [obscure; perh. from ME *fit,* adversary (also obscure)].

fytz *n.* son of 337 [OF *filz, fiz*].

fyve, fyue, fyfe, fif *adj. & n.* five 844, 860, 1103, 1400, etc. [OE *fīf*].

flay *v.* to put to flight, frighten away 2779; **flayede** *pp.* 2441 [OE *flīgan, *flēgan (= ON *fleyga*)].

flayre *n.* flame, gush of fire 772 (*see note*) [uncertain].

flammande. See FLAWMES.

flanke, flawnke *n.* flank, the area between the ribs and the hip

1158, 2174, 2781; **flawnkkes** *pl.*
2100 [OF *flanc*].

flappes   *3 sg.* strikes with a sudden
blow 2781 [onomatopoeic].

flassches.   See FELSCHEN.

flate, flatte   *adj.* flat 2798, 3472
[ON *flatr*].

flatt-mowthede   *adj.* flat-mouthed
1088 [prec. + OE *mūþ*].

flawes, flawez   *n. pl.* sparks 773,
2556 [ON *flaga*].

flawmes, flawmez   *3 sg.* flames,
flashes 1037; *3 pl.* 2556;
flammande, flawmande *pres. p.*
flaming 945; bright, flashing,
brilliant, gleaming 198, 1365,
1494, 1975, 2555 [OF
flam(m)er].

flee   *v.* to flee 110, 2021, 3907;
etc.; **flees** *2 sg.* 2763; **flede, fleede,
fledde** *pa. t.* 494, 1432, 2730,
etc.; *pp.* 2488 [OE *flēon*].

fleet(e), flete   *n.* fleet 634, 822,
836, 1189, etc.; water 3692 [OE
flēot].

fleete   *v.* to float, float off, 803;
fletyde *pa. t.* 3602 [OE *flēotan*].

flemede, flemyde   *pp.* put to flight,
exiled 1155, 2738 [OE *flēman*].

flenges   *3 sg.* dashes, rushes 2762;
flyngande *pres. p.* 2757 [rel. to
ON *flengja*].

fleryand(e)   *pres. p.* grimacing,
sneering 1088, 2778 [uncertain;
cf. Norw & Sw dial. *flira,* Dan
dial. *flire,* to grin or laugh unbe-
comingly].

flesch(e)   *n.* venison 180; flesh,
meat 1032, 1089, 1092, 1160,
etc. [OE *flǣsc*].

fleschez.   See FELSCHEN.

fleterede   *pp.* dispersed (in every
direction), scattered 2097 [from
FLITT + OE *-er(e)*].

flethe   *n.* a stream of light 2482
[see note].

fletyde.   See FLEETE.

flye   *n.* fly 2441 [OE *flȳge*].

flye   *v.* to fly 4001; **flieghes** *3 sg.*
4002; **flyez** *3 pl.;* **flowe** *pa. t.*
2100; **flyeande** *pres. p.* 2451 [OE
flēogan].

flieghes.   See prec.

flyngande.   See FLENGES.

flynte   *n.* (*as adj.*) flint 3318 [OE
flint].

flysches   *3 sg.* slashes, cuts 2768;
flyschande *pres. p.* 2141 [ono-
matopoeic].

flitt   *v.* to fight, attack 2097 [OE
flītan].

flyttyng   *vbl. n.* strife, struggle
2099 [from prec.].

flode.   See FLOOD(E).

floynes   *n. pl.* small ships 743 [OF
flouin].

floke   *n.* troop, company 2849
[OE *flocc*].

floke-mowthede   *adj.* flat-mouthed,
like a fish 2779 [from FLUKE +
OE *mūþ*].

flones, flonez   *n. pl.* arrows 2097,
3619 [OE *flān*].

flood(e), flode   *n.* sea, ocean 773,
803, 1189, 3602, etc.; *as adj.*
461, 1147; flood 2706; flood tide
3718; river, stream 2798 [OE
flōd].

florenez   *n. pl.* florins, golden coins
885 [OF *florin*].

floresche   *v.* to brandish weapons
2555; **floresched(e), floreschte,
fluriste** *pa. t.* flourished 3246; *pp.*
fattened 180; embellished, decorated 771, 924, 1366, 1708, etc.
[OF *florir, flurir, fluriss-*]. See
FERMYSON.

flourdelice   *n. pl.* fleurs-de-lis, lilies
(heraldic) 3333 [OF *flo(u)r-de-
lis*].

flour(e)   *n.* flower 315; **flores,
florez, floures** *pl.* 924, 2508,

2694, etc.; the best, finest (of a people, of knights, etc.) 438, 556, 584, 837, etc.; nectar 2705; *fyrste flourez,* the prime of life, the bloom of youth 970 [OF *flo(u)r*].

flowes *3 pl.* flow 2706; **flowe** *pa. t.* streamed, issued 772 [OE *flōwan, flēow*]. See also FLYE, v.

fluke *n.* a flatfish, especially the flounder 1088 [OE *flōc*].

fluriste. See FLORESCHE.

foddenid *pp.* produced 3246 [OE **fōdnian,* from *fōda,* n.]

foynes *3 pl.* lunge, thrust 1494, 2141, 2163, 3689; **foynede** *pa. t.* 1898 [from OF *foine,* spear].

folde, foulde, fowlde *n.*[1] earth, ground 315, 1071, 2151, 3302 [OE *folde*].

folde *n.*[2] sheepfold, pen 2922 [OE *falod, fald,* etc.]

fole *n.* horse, steed 449; *uninfl. poss.* 2783 [OE *fola*].

foly *n.* folly 2412, 2432; mischief, harm 2737 [OF *folie*].

folily *adv.* foolishly 2841 [from prec.].

folke *n. pl.* people, men 365, 403, 438, 584, etc. [OE *folc*].

folowe *v.* to follow, pursue 2490, 2733; **folowes, folous** *3 sg.* 393, 1360, 1367; **foloes, felewes,** etc. *3 pl.* 1270, 2260, 2758, etc.; **folowede** *pa. t.* 982, 2454, 2756; pursued (*with pron. obj. unexpressed*) 856; *pa. t.* accompanied 807; *folowes in,* follows up 1118 [OE *folgian*].

fomand, foma(u)nde *pres. p.* foaming, frothing 780, 2233, 3307 [OE *fāman*].

fonde, fonden, fondez, fonode. See FAN(N)DE, FYND(E), FOUND(E).

fongez, fongen, fongede. See FANNGE.

foo *n.* foe, 1536, 1709, 3395; **faees** *pl.* 403 [OE *fāh*].

foode *n.* offspring, creature 3776 [OE *fōda*].

foomen, faamen *n. pl.* foes, enemies 303, 366, 1899, 1965, etc. [OE *fāhmann*].

foonde. See FOUND(E).

for, fore *prep.* for 91, 102, 2626, etc.; as 43, 65, 89, 290, etc.; by (in oath) 3981 (*see note*); of 162, 403; because of 117, 120, 121, 141, etc.; fit for 3143; for fear of 3721; for the sake of 126, 239, 433, 434, etc.; on behalf of 292, 3139, 3140, etc.; in exchange for *135,* 708, 1503, 1549, etc.; before, in front of 210, 314, 315, etc.; in spite of 426, 1483, 2225, 2540, etc.; *for to,* to, so as to 12, 58, 302, 404, etc. [OE *for*].

for, fore *conj.* for, because 110, 219, 261, 459, etc.; so that 4185 [OE *for þam þe*].

forbere *v.* to hold back 1913 [OE *forberan*].

forby *prep.* in comparison with 155 [OE *foran* + BY].

forbrittenede *pp.* utterly crushed 2273 [OE *forbrytian*].

force *n.* force 111, 437; *of force,* of necessity [OF *force*].

forced, forsede *pp.* ravished, violated 978, 1071 [OF *forcer*].

forchipe *n.* the fore part of a ship, prow 3678 [OE *forscip*].

forcyer. See FORSY.

fordremyde *pp.* worn out with dreaming 3392 [OE *for-* + ME *dreme,* v.].

forebreste *n.* front line, front rank 1494, 1990 [OE *forbrēost*].

forebrusten *pp.* burst, burst apart 2272 [OE *forberstan*].

fore-flude *n.* high tide, flood tide 494 [OE *fore-* + FLOOD(E)].

forelytenede *pp.* surrendered, abandoned 254 [OE *forlætan*].

foremaglede *pp.* utterly crushed 1534 (*see note*) [OE *for-* + AF *mangler*].

forestavne *n.* prow, stem *742* [OE *fore-* + *stæfn* (*see note*)].

forest(e) *n.* forest 452, 1363, 1401, etc.; **forestez** *pl.* 656, 1247, 2487 [OF *forest*].

foretoppe *n.* forelock 1078 [OE *fore-* + TOPPE].

foretrauaillede *pp.* worn out with suffering 806 [OE *for-* + OF *travaill(i)er*].

for euer, fore euer(e) *adv.* forever 111, 519, 549, 561, etc. [FOR, prep. + EUER(E)].

forfette *v.* to forfeit, give up, lose 437; **forfette, forfeted** *pp.* 585, 1155; subject to forfeiture 557 [from OF *forfait, forfet,* n.].

forfoughtten *pp.* wearied and worn out with fighting 3792, 4179 [OE *for-* + FYGHT(E)].

forgyffe, foregyffe *v.* to forgive 3488, 4324; **forgeffen** *pp.* 2184 [OE *forgiefan*].

forheued *n.* forehead, brow 1080 [OE *forhēafod*].

forjustede *pa. t.* struck down, overthrew in battle 2088; **forjuste, forjustyde** *pp.* 1398, 2134, 2895, 2908 [OE *for-* + OF *juster*].

formaylle *n.* female hawk 4003 [from OF *formel, formal,* adj.].

formede. See FOURMEDE.

forraye *v.* forage for food 2489; **forrayede** *pa. t.* 3017; **forrayse** *3 sg.* pillages, plunders, ravages 1247; **forrayede** *pp.* 3019 [prob. from next].

forreours, forriours *n. pl.* foragers, raiders 2450, 2752, 2901, 2945, etc. [OF *forreor, forrier,* from *forrer,* v.].

forsake, foresake *v.* to give up, withdraw, surrender 528, 1686; refuse 691; abandon, reject, renounce (*often with pron. obj. unexpressed*) 1945, 2734, 2926, 4142, etc.; **forsakes** *3 pl.* 2939; **forsaken** *pp.* 4182 [OE *forsacan*].

forsede. See FORCED.

forsett(e) *pp.* hedged in, obstructed, barred 1714, 1896, 1979, 2012, etc. [OE *forsettan*].

forsy *adj.* powerful, strong *3300, 3307;* **forcyer** *compar.* 1176 [from FORCE].

forsothe *adv.* in truth, indeed 487, 686, 1087, 1097, 1557, etc. [OE *forsōþ*].

forsterne *n.* the fore part of the stern 3664 [OE *fore-* + STERYNE].

fortethe *n.* front teeth 1089 [OE *fortēþ*].

forthe, furthe *adv.* forth, forward 262, 632, 1165, 1213, 1229, etc. [OE *forþ*].

forþer, forthire, forthyre *adv.* further, beyond this point 261, 340, 452, 478, 2666, etc. [OE *furþor*].

forþermaste, forthirmaste *adj. & n.* foremost, first 1365, 3330, [OE *furþra* + *mæst*].

forthes, forthis *3 sg.* goes forward, advances 1850, 2827 [OE *forþian*].

forthy, forethy, for(e)thi, forþi *conj.* therefore, for this reason 152, 225, 1010, 1034, 1172, etc. [OE *forþī, forþȳ*].

forthynkkes, forthynkkys *3 sg.* causes regret to 971, 4252

(*impers.*) [OE *forþencan*].

forthire   *v.* to supply 300; help, help out 1509 [OE *fyrþran*].

forthire, forthyre.   See FORÞER.

fortrodyn   *pp.* trodden down, trampled 2150 [OE *fortredan*].

fortune   *n.* fortune, destiny 1177, 1965, 2428, 3828, etc.; good fortune 3394 [OE *fortune*].

fosterde   *pp.* nurtured, trained, bred 300, 2761, 3776, 4143 [OE *fostrian*].

foster-modyr   *n.* foster mother, nurse 983 [OE *fōstormōdor*].

fote, fott(e), fute   *n.* foot (limb and measure) 461, 933, 1079, 1103, 1120, etc.; *uninfl. pl.* (measure) 801, 1855, 3309; **feete** *pl.* 771, 789; footing 1116 [OE *fōt, fēt*].

fotemen   *n. pl.* foot soldiers 1989 [prec. + MAN].

foulde.   See FOLDE n.¹

foule, full   *adj.* foul, vile 1092, 1114, 2099, 3237; **foulleste** *superl.* 781; *adv.* ill, badly 870, 1154, 1394, 2365 [OE *fūl*, adj.].

foully   *adv.* vilely 1062 [OE *fūllīce*].

found(e), foonde   *v.* to go, proceed, set out 452, 495, 1189, 2489; **foundez** *3 sg.* 1228; **fondez** *3 pl.* 747; **foundes, fowndes, fowndys** *3 pl.* hasten 2756, 3112, 4063; strike out, attack, fight 366; **foundide** *pa. t.* 1442, **fownden** *pp.* 3344 [OE *fundian*]. See also FAN(N)DE, FYND(E).

foure, fowre, fouur   *adj. & n.* four 1031, 2358, 2421, etc. [OE *fēower*].

fourmede   *pa. t.* created, born, formed 3808; **formede, formyde** *pp.* 526, 781, 861, 1061, 3227, etc. [OF *fourmer*].

fourte   *n.* fourth 3300 [OE *fēorþa*].

fourtedele   *n.* fourth part, quarter 946 [prec. + OE *dǣl*].

fourtene   *adj.* fourteen 1912 [OE *fēowertīene*].

fourtty   *adj. & n.* forty 2888, 2945 [OE *fēowertig*].

fowlde.   See FOLDE n.¹

fowle, fewle   *n.* bird 2071 (heraldic emblem), 4002; **feulez** *pl.* 926 [OE *fugol*].

fowly   *adj.* vile, filthy 1089 [OE *fūllic*].

fownde   *v.* to found, establish 3403 [OF *fonder*].

fowndes, fownden,   etc. See FOUND(E).

fowre.   See FOURE.

fra.   See FRO.

fraiez   *3 sg.* terrorizes *1248* (*see note*); **affrayede** *pa. t.* alarmed, frightened, frightened away 2804; *pp.* 2256 [OF *affrayer, effreer*].

fraynes, fraynez   *3 sg.* asks, inquires 337, 507, 954, 1441, etc. [OE *frǣgnian*].

fraist(e), frayste   *v.* (*often with pron. obj. unexpressed*) to seek out, search out 435, 881, 1038; test, try, make trial of 2821 (*expressing future*), 3691, 4195; **fraystez** *3 pl.* 3691; **fraistede** *pp.* 2774, 3582; *fraystez a furth*, crosses a ford 1227 [ON *freista*].

fraknede   *pp.* freckled, blotched 1081 [from ON *freknur*, n. pl.].

fransye   *n.* frenzy 3826 [OF *frenesie*].

frape, frappe   *n.* crowd, mob 2091, 2163, 2804; troop 3548, 3740 [OF *frap*].

frappez   *3 sg.* slaps, strikes 1115 [OF *frapper*].

fraunchez   *n.* immunity, asylum 1248 [OF *fra(u)nchise*].

frawde *n.* deceitfulness, insincerity 3918 [OF *fraude*].

frawghte *pp.* freighted, loaded 3547 [from ME *fraught,* n., MDu or MLG *vracht*].

frawnke *n.* enclosure 3247 [OF *franc*].

frechely. See FRESCHELY.

fre(e) *adj.* fair, noble 1711, 3247; without reservation 34 [OE *frēo*].

freeborne *adj.* freeborn 845 [prec. + *geboren,* pp. of OE *beran*].

freely, frely, frelich(e) *adj.* noble 970, 3371, 4059; fine 2488; fair 3330, 3808 [OE *frēolic*].

freely *adv.* easily, readily, freely 2072, 2140, 3346 [OE *frēolīce*].

freke *n.* man, warrior 557, 1174, 1364, 1966, 2709, etc.; **frek(k)es, frekez, frekis** *pl.* 742, 2260, 2822, 3677, etc. [OE *freca*].

freke, frekk(e) *adj.* eager, bold, daring, heroic 2139, 2454, 2759, 2821, etc.; *as n.* 3678; **frekkeste** *superl.* 1536, 2164, 4122; *as n.* 3690 [OE *frec*].

frekly(e), frekkly *adv.* eagerly, boldly, fiercely 556, 788, 1360; promptly 1451, 3927 [OE *freclīce*].

frely, frelich(e). See FREELY.

frem(e)dly, fremydly *adv.* unkindly, in an unnatural or hostile manner 1250, 2738, 3405 [from next].

fremmede *adj.* hostile, unfriendly 3343 [OE *frem(e)de*].

frenchepe *n.* harmony 656 [OE *frēondscipe*].

frendely *adj.* friendly 3343 [OE *frēondlic*].

frendez *n. pl.* friends, allies 836, 982, 1442 [OE *frēond*].

frendles *adj.* friendless 3305 [OE *frēondlēas*].

fresche *adj.* ready, eager, vigorous 364, 404, 2501; fresh 2491, 2759, 2944, 3581, etc.; freshwater 1227, 1497, 1535, 2258, etc. [OF *fresche,* fem, of *freis*].

freschely, frechely, frescheliche, fresclyche *adj.* eager, vigorous 2502; *adv.* eagerly, fiercely 1367, 1441, 1495, 2097, 2900, etc. [from prec.].

freschen *v.* to refresh, revive 1452 [from FRESCHE, adj.].

freson *n.* Frisian horse 1365 [OF *frison*].

freten *n.* See FRETTE.

fretyn *pp.* devoured 844 [OE *fretan*].

frette *pp.* rubbed 2708; *freten of* (*3 pl.*), rub off, tear off 2142 [obscure; perh. from OF **freiter* (= ModF dial. *fretter*)].

fretted *pp.* ornamented 1364 [OF *freter*].

Frydaye *n.* Friday 4057 [OE *frīgedæg*].

frykis *3 pl.* move briskly 2898 [OE *frician*].

frysthez *3 sg.* grants, sanctions 1248 [from OE *fyrst,* period of time, delay].

frithed *pp.* fenced in 3247 [from ME *firthe,* fence, hedge]. See also FIRTHE, FYRTHE.

frithez, frythes. See FIRTHE, FYRTHE.

fro, fra *prep.* from 3, 7, 47, 376, 446, etc.; *fro þe,* from which 1698; *conj.* from the time that, as soon as 3660 [ON *frá*].

froyt(e). See FRUYTE.

from *prep.* from 362 [OE *fram*].

fromonde *n.* alien, barbarian 1112 (*see note*) [cf. Norw dial.

framand, strange].

fronte, frount(e), frownt(e), frunt
n. forehead, face 1080, 1112,
2768, 3330; front 1850; front
line of an army 1495, 1711,
1756, 1990, etc.; *in a frounte,
on a frounte, on(e) frownte,* in a
battle line, in a fighting group
1811, 2455, 3690, 4067 [OF
fro(u)nt].

froske   *n.* frog, toad 1081 [OE
frosc].

frount(e).   See FRONTE.

frountere, frowntere   *n.* front
line 2861, 2898 [OF *frontier(e)*].

frowarde   *adj.* perverse, wicked
3345 [FRO + OE *-weard*].

frownt(e).   See FRONTE.

fruyte, froyt(e)   *n.* fruit, food
2492, 2707, 3370; **fruytes,
froytez** *pl.* 3246; products, bene-
fits 3346, 3403 [OF *fruit*].

frumentée   *n.* a milk pottage
served with venison 180 [OF
frumentée].

frunt.   See FRONTE.

frusche   *n.* rush, charge 2900 [OF
fruis].

fruschen   *pa. t. pl.* rushed violently
2804 [OF *fruissier*].

fude   *n.* food 160, 2486 [OE
fōda].

fulfill, fullfill   *v.* to carry out, ex-
ecute 2325; fill out 3438 [OE
fullfyllan].

full   *adj.* full 477, 747, 2705,
3578, etc.; *adv.* so, very, most,
quite, entirely 38, 39, 43, 117,
124, etc. [OE *full*].

full.   See FOULE.

full butt   *adv.* point-blank 1112,
2768 [from FULL, adj. + OF
buter, to strike].

fully   *adv.* fully, completely 73,
2742 [OE *fullīce*].

fulsomeste   *adj. superl.* most foul,
most odious 1061 [from FULL,
adj. + OE *-sum,* perh. with infl.
of FOULE].

funden.   See FYND(E).

furlang(e)   *n.* furlong, ⅛ mile
873, 946, 1538, 2152, etc. [OE
furlang]. See WAY(E).

furth(e)   *n.* ford 1227, 1525, 1714,
1897; stream 2144 [OE *ford*].
See FRAIST(E).

furthe.   See FORTHE.

fute.   See FOTE.

gaddes, gaddys   *n. pl.* spikes 3621,
3683 [ON *gaddr*].

gaderide, gadyrede.   See GEDYRE.

gadlynges, gadlyngez, gedlynges
n. pl. rascals, scoundrels 2443,
2728, 2854, 2884 [OE *gædeling*].

gafe, gaffe.   See GIFE.

gaye   *adj.* fine, splendid, magnificent 2854, 3759, 3868, 3937,
3943, etc. [OF *gai*].

gayliche, gaylyche   *adv.* brightly,
splendidly, beautifully, 912,
2655, 3462, 3684 [from prec.].

gayne   *v.* to benefit, profit, be of
use (to) 165; **gaynes** *3 sg.
impers.* 4303; **gaynez** *3 pl.* 1731
[ON *gegna*].

gayneste: *at the (þe) gayneste,*
by the shortest route 487, 1041,
1977, 3006, 3114, etc.; straightway 3374 [from ON *gegn,* adj.].

gayspand   *pres. p.* gaping 1462
[from ON *geispa*].

galaye   *n.* galley, warship 3724;
galays *pl.* 595, 3096 [OF *galie,
galee*].

galede   *pa. t.* sang 927 [OE *galan*].

galyard(e)   *adj.* high-spirited,
valiant, hardy 721, 1265, 1279,
1470, 2748, etc. [OF *gaillard*].

galte   *n.* swine 1101 [ON *galtr*].

gamen *n.* sport, game, (battle) play 2811; **gamnes** *pl.* delights, joys 1730, 3174 [OE *gamen*].

gan. See BEGYNNES.

ganggyng *vbl. n.* going, departure 706 [OE *gangan*].

gaped *pa. t.* opened (his) mouth wide, as if to bite 1076 [ON *gapa*].

gardwynes. See GWERDONS.

garett(e) *n.* watchtower 562, 3104 [OF *garite*].

garysone *n.* defense, watchtower, body of men stationed as a defense 3007; **garysons** *pl.* 4030 [OF *garison*].

garnescht(e), garneschit *pp.* garrisoned 563; armed, equipped for war 722; decorated, embellished 1000 [OF *garnir, garniss-*].

garnison, garnyson *n.* defense, watchtower, body of men stationed as a defense 2471, 2655, 3105; **garnysons** *pl.* 3620 [OF *garnison*].

garte. See GERE, V.

gas. See GO.

gate *n.* way, course, path 4144, 4308 [ON *gata*].

geant, geaunt(e), etc. See GYAUNT.

gedyre *v.* to assemble 592; **gadyrede** *pa. t.* amassed 594; **gaderide, gederyde** *pp.* 721, 3295 [OE *gadrian, gædrian*].

gedlynges. See GADLYNGES.

gemows *n. pl.* hinges 2893 [OF *gemeaus,* pl. of *gemel*].

genatours *n. pl.* horsemen, warriors on horseback 2897 [OF *geneteur*].

genitales *n. pl.* genitals *1123* [OF *genital*].

gentill, jentill, jentyll, ientill *adj.* noble, excellent, fine 115, 246,

372, 904, 987, etc.; *as n.* 2088; **gentileste** *superl.* most noble, most precious 862 [OF *gentil*].

gere *n.* equipment, armor 2539, 3007 [OE *gieru (= ON *gervi*)].

gere *v.* to make or cause something to be done or to go, order 3640; **gers** *3 sg.* 3592, 3921; **gerte, garte** *pa. t.* 1780, 1886, 1946, 1975, 3709 [ON *gorva, gæra*].

gerefawcon *n.* a large falcon 4004 [OF *gerfaucon*].

gers. See GERE, V.

gersoms *n. pl.* treasures, rewards 165, 1729 [OE *gærsum*].

gerte. See GERE, V.

gessande *adj.* (of a heraldic charge): situated on a background of another color *2521* (*see note*) [OF *gesant*].

gesserawnte. See JESSERAUNT.

gestes *n. pl.* stories of great deeds, especially metrical chronicles 2876 [OF *geste*].

getis *2 sg.* get, acquire 3450 (*future*); **getyn** *pp.* 886; *get owt,* call forth, send for 4029 [ON *geta*].

gettlesse *adj.* empty-handed, without booty 2727 [from ME *get,* n. (from prec.)].

ghywes *n. pl.* fetters, chains, or fastenings on a ship 3621 [obscure].

gyaunt, geaunt(e), geant(e) *n.* giant 825, 843, 1122, 1222, 2087, etc.; *uninfl. pl.* 559; **geauntes** *poss.* 245 (*see note*); **geauntez, gyawntis** *pl.* 375, 612, 2111, 2133, etc. [ONF *gaiant*].

gyde *v.* to guide 3791; **gydes** *3 sg.* 3005 [OF *guider*].

gydes *n. pl.* guides 3006 [OF

guide].

gye *v. refl.* to conduct or rule (oneself) 4; **gyede** *pa. t.* guided, led 3860 [OF *guier* (superseded later by *guider*)].

gif(f)e. See IF(E).

gife, giff(e), gyf(e), gyffe, ȝif(e), ȝiffe *v.* to give, grant, render 4, 102, 1060, 1179, 1305, 1503, etc.; **gyffes** *3 sg.* 1774; **gafe** *2 sg. subj.* 1018; **gafe** *pa. t.* 2628, 3707, 4297; **gaffe** *vp,* delivered, presented 85; **gifen, gyf(f)en** *pp.* 1202, 1729, 2687, 4277, etc.; *3 sg.* accounts 539 [ON *gifa*].

gifte *n.* gift 2645; **gyftes, gyftez** *pl.* 1503, 2628 [ON *gift*].

gilte, gylte *pp.* gilded 912, 3462, 3727 [OE *gyldan*].

girde, gyrde *v.* to strike, strike out, smite, thrust 3709; **girdes, gyrdez, gyrdis,** etc. *3 sg.* 1370, 1470, 1792, 2527, 2563, 2949, etc.; **gyrd** *pa. t.* 2971; **girde** *pp.* 3938; *3 sg.* rushes, starts, springs 3726; *pa. t.* 3850 [unknown; perh. rel. to OE *gierd, gyrd,* rod, staff].

girdill, girdyll, gyrdill *n.* girdle, 2704, 3220, 3458, 3727, 3923 [OE *gyrdel*].

girse. See GRESSE.

gladden *v. refl.* rejoice, make merry 928 [from GLADE, adj.].

gladdez, gladdis *3 sg.* makes glad or joyous 2883; cheers, heartens 2852 [OE *gladian*].

glade *adj.* glad, happy 489, 1386, 2525, 3863; **gladdeste** *superl.* happiest, most joyful 3876 [OE *glæd*].

glade. See GLYDE.

gladschipe *n.* gladness, joy, rejoicing 59, 928 [OE *glædscipe*].

glayfe *n.* lance, spear 3761 [OF *glaive*].

glase *n.* glass 3097 [OE *glæs*].

glauerande *adj.* chattering, babbling 2538 [obscure].

gledys *n. pl.* embers, live coals 117 [OE *glēd*].

glee *n.* merriment, gladness 59, 2852; music 489 [OE *glēo*].

glent *n.* blow, stroke 3863 (*see note*) [from next].

glentes, glentis, glenttys *3 sg.* moves quickly with a gliding motion, sweeps 2563, 2780, 4244 [of Scand orig.; cf. Sw dial. *glänta, glinta,* to slip, slide].

gleterand(e) *pres. p.* gleaming, glittering 595, 1280, 2853, 3097 [from ON *glitra*].

glyde *v.* to streak, swoop 4001; **glydande** *pres. p.* swooping 799; **glydez** *3 sg.* slides 1371; **glade** *pa. t.* 2972; **glides** *3 sg.* glides 3725 [OE *glīdan*].

gliftis, glyftes *3 sg.* gazes, looks 2525, 3949 [obscure; rel. to ModDu *glippen*].

glopyne *v. trans.* to frighten, terrify 2580; *intr.* **gloppyns** *imper. pl.* be frightened, fear 2853; **glopned** *pa. t.* gaped in amazement 1074; **glopyns** *3 sg.* is distressed or downcast 3949; **gloppynnande** *pres. p.* sorrowing 4329 [ON *glúpna*].

gloppynyng *vbl. n.* grief, distress 3863 [from prec.].

glored *pa. t.* glowered 1074 [ON *glóra*].

glorious *adj.* 1, 2852; splendid 207, 913 [OF *glorio(u)s*].

gloton *n.* glutton, vile wretch 1074 [OF *glutun, glouton*].

gloues *n. pl.* gauntlets, gloves 912, 3472 [OE *glōf(e)*].

gnawen *v.* to gnaw 464 [OE *gnagan*].

go, goo *v. intr.* to go, pass 213, 1279, 2540, 2727; **gos, gosse** *3 sg.* 3104, 3727; **gose** *imper. pl.* 1266; **gon(e)** *pp.* 413, 488, 2884, 3858, etc.; *gas in,* proceeds on, rides on 3006; *gone to noghte,* come to nought, been destroyed 1829; **gosse** *3 pl. quasi-trans.,* with WAY(E) 497 [OE *gān*]. See NEDES, n.

gobbede *adj.* haughty, proud 1346 [from OF *gobe,* adj.].

goblettez, gobelets *n. pl.* goblets 207; ?ornamental designs in the shape of goblets 913 [OF *gobelet*].

gobone *v.* to cut to pieces 4164 [from OF **gobone,* gobbet, piece].

God(e), Godd *n.* God 1, 14, 249, 369, 386, etc. [OE *god*]. See LOUE, n.

gode, gud(e) *adj.* good, excellent, noble 559, 563, 1077, 1368, 1387, etc.; *with a gud wyll,* gladly, willingly 4296 [OE *gōd,* adj.].

golde *n.* gold 182, 205, 214, 217, etc. [OE *gold*].

gole *n.* inlet 3725 [OF *gole*].

golet *n.* gullet, throat 1772 [OF *goulet*].

gome, gume *n.* man, warrior 85, 1353, 1372, 1731, 1773, etc.; **gomes, gomys** *pl.* 1461, 2538, 2748, 2943, 3683, etc.; (referring to a sword) warrior (*fig.*) 3709; being 1209 [OE *guma*].

gon(e). See GO.

gorge *n.* throat 3760 [OF *gorge*].

gorger *n.* gorget, a piece of armor covering the front of the neck 1772 [OF *gorg(i)ere*].

gorr(e) *n.* gore, excrement 1130, 1370 [OE *gor*].

gos, gose, etc. See GO.

gosomer *adj.* flimsy, inconsequential *2687* [OE *gōs* + *sumor*].

gossehawke *n.* a large, short-winged hawk 4001 [OE *gōshafoc*].

gouerne *v. refl.* to regulate one's actions, to conduct oneself (in a specified way), 4, 677 [OF *governer*].

gouernour *n.* ruler 1201 [OF *governeür*].

gowke *n.* cuckoo 927 [ON *gaukr*].

gowl(l)es *n.* red, scarlet (heraldry) 3646, 3759, 3945 [OF *goules*].

gowtes *n. pl.* designs in the shape of droplets (heraldry) 3759 [OF *goute*].

grace *n.* favor, mercy, blessing, grace 1, 1209, 1936, 2320, 2590, etc.; virtue, moral strength 4, 677, 1202, etc.; good fortune 3768, 3851 [OF *grace*].

gracious, gracyous *adj.* elegant, dainty 187, 3463; gracious, enjoying grace or favor 1468, 2851; **graciouseste** *superl.* 3877 [OF *gracio(u)s*].

gray(e) *adj.* gray, blue 1368, 2962, 3790 [OE *græg*].

grayhondes. See GREWHOUNDE.

graynes, graynez *n. pl.* beads, seed pearls 913, 3463 [OF *grain*].

graythe *v.* (*often refl.*) to make ready, fit out, equip 1279, 2539; **graythede, graythide** *pp.* prepared, arrayed 373, 589, 602, 3096, 3851, etc.; go, betake oneself, travel 1266, 2726, 3216, 3814, etc.; **graythes** *3 sg.* 1353, 1384, 2124, 2942; **graythes** *3 pl.* 4329; *graythes in sondyre,* shatters, falls into pieces 3761; *3 sg.* serves, deals 3105 [ON *greiþa*].

graythes *n. pl.* arms, equipment, gear 3620 [ON *greiþe*].

graytheste *adj. superl.* most excellent 1201 [from ON *greiþr*].

graythly, graythely(e), graythelyche *adj.* excellent 187; *adv.* excellently, splendidly 722, 1000 (*ironic*), 1468; promptly, readily 1369, 1384, 1387, 3476; earnestly 1774 [ON *greiþligr, greiþliga*].

grame *n.* anger, wrath 1077; trouble 3008 [OE *grama*].

granes. See GRONYS.

grante, graunte, grawnte *v. trans.* to grant, bestow (*often with pron. obj. unexpressed*) 2318, 2590, 2638, 2743; **graunt, graunted(e)** *pp.* 1202, 2820, 4298; *intr.* consent 2320 [AF *gra(u)nter*].

grape *v.* to grope, search 2725 [OE *grāpian*].

grapis *n. pl.* grapes 3243 [OF *grape*].

grassede *adj.* greased, greasy 1091 [from GREES(SE)].

graunt, grawnte, etc. See GRANT.

graue *n.* grave 951 [OE *graf*].

grauen *pp.* engraved, decorated 912, 3462 [OE *grafan*].

gree *n.*[1] favor, good will 2645; satisfaction, pleasure 2819; *to þi gree,* with your good will or favor, with your kindly feeling 1936; *of þe gre,* with good will 2748 [OF *gré*, from L *grātum*].

gree *n.*[2] victory 3706, 4298 [OF *gré*, from L *gradum*].

greefe. See GREFE.

grees(se) *n.* fat 658 (*see note*), 1101 [OF *gresse, graise*].

grefe, greefe, greffe *n.* pain, injury, harm 1373, 2562, 2590, 4324; misfortune 3851; threat 3007; rage, anger 1077, 3726, 3757; grief 1385, 1471, 2539, 3791 [OF *gr(i)ef*].

grefes, grefede, etc. See GREUE, *n.* & *v.*

grehownde. See GREWHOUNDE.

grene *adj.* green 722, 1266, 1281, etc. [OE *grēne*].

grenned *pa. t.* bared (his) teeth in anger 1075 [OE *grennian*].

gresse, girse *n.* grass 1131, 3944 [OE *græs,* ODan *græs*].

gret(e), grett(e) *adj.* almighty, mighty 1, 4228; **gretteste** *superl.* (*as n.*) mightiest 1469, 4164; great, large, huge 185, 256, 298, 539, 595, etc.; grand, magnificent 165, 207, 1280, 2628, etc.; **gretter** *compar.* 3243; angry, proud, arrogant 1352, 1936, 2225, 2540, 2580, etc.; boastful 2744 [OE *grēat*].

gret(e) *v.* to greet, salute 419, 1282, 2189; **gretis** *1 sg.* 3338; **gretes, gretez** *3 sg.* 955, 2185; **gretes** *3 pl.* 1233; **grette** *pa. t.* 84, 3476; *3 sg.* calls out, cries out 1774; *3 sg.* confronts, meets 1077, 1469 [OE *grētan,* wk.]

gretes *3 sg.* bewails, laments, weeps 2962; **grette** *pa. t.* 3790; **gretand(e)** *pres. p.* 951, 3912, 3950 [OE *grētan,* str.]

gretly *adv.* greatly, mightily 396 [from GRET(E), adj.].

grett(e). See GRET(E), adj. & v., GRETES.

greue *n.* grove, thicket 2540, 2726; **greues, greuez, grefes, greuys** *pl.* 927, 1874, 2881, 4256 [ON *græfa*].

greue, grefe *v. refl.* to grieve 705, 2686; *trans.* **greues** *2 sg.* vex, anger, offend, distress 2579; **greues** *3 sg.* 2443; **greues** *3 pl.*

2538; **greuede, greuyde** *pa. t.*
2124 (*with pron. obj. unex-*
pressed), 2205; **greuede, greuyde,**
gref(f)ede *pp.* 134, 266, 1022,
1173, 1282, 1423, etc.; *intr.*
pa. t. became enraged 1352;
pp. 2557, 3774 [OF *grever*].

greuous *adj.* arduous, difficult
497; grievous, harsh, hurtful 594,
2943 [OF *grevous*].

grewhounde, grehownde, grew-
hownde *n.* greyhound 1075,
3464, 4001; **grewhoundez, gray-**
hondes *pl.* 1730, 2521 (as
heraldic emblem) [OE *grīghund,*
greihund].

grychgide. See GROUCHE.

gryffoune *n.* griffon (as heraldic
emblem) 3869 [OF *grifoun*].

grygynge *n.* graying, breaking (of
day) 2510 [from ON *grýja,* to
dawn].

grym(e) *adj.* savage, cruel 2971,
3621, 3760; **grymmeste** *superl.*
3419 [OE *grimm*].

grymly(e) *adv.* grimly, cruelly
1471, 2558, 3813 [OE
grimmlīce].

gripe *v.* to seize, grip, grasp 3008;
gryp(p)es, grypys, gryppis *3 sg.*
1163, 1369, 2526, 2948, etc.
[OE *grīpan, grippan*].

grisely, grysely, gryeslye, gry[s]lych
adj. dreadful, ghastly, fearful
951, 1075, 1101, 1469, etc.; *adv.*
hideously, grimly 1373, 1462,
3912, 3950 [late OE *grislic*].

groffe: *one þe groffe, one grouffe,*
face downward, in a prone position 3850, 3944 [ON *á grúfu*].

grome *n.* groom, page 2526, 3489
[obscure].

groned *pa. t.* growled 1076 [OF
grognir].

gronys, granes *3 sg.* cries out in

pain 2562, 3912, 3950; **gronande**
pres. p. 1373, 3938 [OE
grānian].

grouche, gruche *v.* to complain,
bewail 705; grudge 2644, 2819;
grychgide *pa. t.* raged 2557;
grucchand(e) *pres. p.* glowering
1076; raging, wrathful 1353;
grieving, lamenting 1462 [ONF
gro(u)ch(i)er].

grouffe. See GROFFE.

grounde, grownde *n.* ground 1131,
1372, 1385, 1773, etc. [OE
grund].

grounden, grownden(e), grundyn
pp. sharpened, whetted 1281,
1371, 1461, 2972, etc. [OE
grindan].

growes *3 sg.* grows 315; **growen**
pp. 1101 [OE *grōwan*].

growndide *pa. t.* ran aground
3726 [from GROUNDE, n.].

gruche, grucchand(e). See
GROUCHE.

grundyn. See GROUNDEN.

gude *n.* advantage 706; **gudes,**
gudez *pl.* goods, possessions,
wealth 295, 1213, 1249 [OE
gōd, n.].

gud(e). See GODE, adj.

Gud Frydaye *n.* Good Friday
3431 [GODE, adj. + FRYDAYE].

gudly *adj.* goodly 3005; *adv.*
righteously 677 [OE *gōdlic*].

guyte *n.* child 2963 [app. a Scot.
var. of *get,* n. (from ON *geta,* v.]

gumbaldes *n. pl.* tasty morsels,
choice pieces of beef 187 [OF
grumel].

gume. See GOME.

guschez *3 pl.* gush 1130 [un-
known].

guttes, guttez *n. pl.* guts 1130,
1370, 2782 [OE *guttas*].

gwerdons, gwerddouns, gardwynes

n. pl. rewards 1729, 2820, 4277
[OF *guerdon*].

haa   *interj.* aha 133 [natural
interj.].
habydes, habyddez.   See ABYDE.
habite   *n.* the dress of a religious
order 3917 [OF *habit*].
had, hadde,   etc. See HAUE.
hafe.   See HEWYS.
haf(f)e.   See HAUE.
hayled.   See HALE.
hailsez   *3 sg.* greets 1058 [ON
heilsa].
haythemen, haythen.   See HETHEN.
haknays, hakenayes, hakkenays   *n.*
pl. horses kept for hire 484, 734,
2284 [from *Hackney,* Middlesex].
halde, haldes,   etc. See HOLDE.
hale, halle.   See HOLE, *adj.*¹.
hale   *v.* to haul 748; *intr.* **hayled**
pa. t. extended in space, reached
2077 (*see note to 2073–80*) [OF
haler].
halely.   See HOLLY.
halfe   *n.* half, part, side, direction
1079, 1120, 1980, 1991, 2077,
etc.; **halfes, halfez, halues** *pl.*
441, 1853, 2012, 2018, etc.; *the
four halues,* the four directions,
the four corners (of the earth)
1966; *adj.* 4091 [OE *half*].
haly.   See HOLY.
hall, hawle   *n.* hall, castle 268,
3879 [OE *hall*].
hally.   See HOLLY.
halowes   *3 sg.* shouts aloud 3319
[OF *halloer*].
hals   *n.* neck 764; **halses, halsez**
pl. 1798, 4120 [OE *hals*].
halues.   *See* HALFE.
hame-holde   *adj.* home-loving,
home-loyal 1843 (*see note*)
[HOM(E) + OE *hold,* faithful].
hand(e), hannde, honnde   *n.*

hand (*lit. & fig.*) 173, 1205,
1833, 2000, etc.; **handes, handys,
hondis,** etc. *pl.* 376, 678, 890,
950, etc.; *of handes, hondez,*
etc., *with handes, hondes,* etc.,
in action, in power, in fighting
ability, of deeds 290, 516, 532,
1939, 3810; *at hand,* near,
close by 2650; *at thyne honnde,*
near you, at your disposal 1807;
with (his) hondes, with his own
hands, by his own actions 2382,
2642 [OE *hand*]. See WRANGE.
hande-slynge   *n.* hand sling 3318
[prec. + SLYNGE].
handill   *v.* to hold, take hold of
4003; **handilez** *3 pl.* touch or
feel with the hands 1156 [OE
handlian].
handsomere   *adj. compar.* handsomer, better-looking 2128 (*see
note*) [prec. + OE *-sum*].
hang   *v.* to hang 2311; **hangede**
pp. 464 [OE *hangian*].
hannde-brede   *n.* handbreadth,
about six inches 2229 [OE
handbrædu].
hanseman   *n.* squire, page 2662;
hansemene *pl.* 2743 [OE *hengest,
hengst,* horse + MAN].
hape, happe   *n.* luck, lot, good
fortune 1937, 2446, 4315 [ON
happ].
happe   *v.* to have the good fortune
2630 [from prec.].
happen(e), happyn(n)(e)   *v.* to
come to pass, betide, befall, turn
out 825, 1657, 1668, 1751,
1965, etc.; **happyns** *3 sg.* 3743;
happenede *pa. t.* 1950, 3391,
3710, etc.; **happenede, hapnede,
happynede** *pp.* 870, 1154, 2365,
3304; *with dat. obj. expressed as
subject* 2436, 3436 [from HAPE].
happy(e)   *adj.* lucky, fortunate,

favored 1741, 2974; **happyeste**
superl. 3878 [from HAPE].

happynge *vbl. n.* fortune, good
fortune 3958 [from HAPPE].

har *n.* hair 1001 [OE *hær,* ON
hár].

harageous(e) *adj.* hot-tempered,
fiery 1645, 1742, 1834, 1878,
etc. [perh. OF **arageux,* rel. to
aragier, to become furious].

harawde, hawrawde *n.* herald
3013, 3029; **harawdez** *pl.* 2294
[OF *herau(l)t*].

harbergage. See HERBERGAGE.

hard(e) *adj.* harsh, severe, sharp
1119, 1146, 1180, 1832, etc.;
hardare *compar.* sharper 4194;
rough, rugged 3544; *adv.* hard,
tightly 1135 [OE *hard, hearde*].

harde. See HERE, V.

hardy *adj.* bold, hardy 4138;
hardieste, hardyeste *superl.* 3878;
as n. 1798, 3830 [OF *hardi*].

hardynes *n.* boldness, courage
3659 [from prec.].

hardly *adv.* assuredly, certainly
1084 [OE *heardlīce*].

hare. See HORE.

hares *n. pl.* rabbits 1444 [OE
hara].

harlott *n.* rogue, rascal, villain
2446; **harlottez** *pl.* menials, servants 2743, 2885; **harlotes** *pl.*
poss. harlots' 3643 [OF
(h)arlot].

harme *n.* trouble, difficulty 748;
harm, injury 875; **harmes** *pl.*
2110; pain, grief, sorrow 4176;
pl. 3319 [OE *hearm*].

harme *v.* to harm, hurt (*often
with pron. obj. unexpressed*)
2885; **harmes, harmez** *3 sg.*
1842, 2437, 2660 (*for future*)
[OE *hearmian*].

harnayse *n.* the defensive equipment of an armed horseman 2629
[OF *harneis*].

harpe *n.* harp 3318 [OE *hearpe*].

harrawnte *adj.* yelling, 2449
[from OF *harer,* to incite, set on
by shouting].

harske *adj.* rough 1084 [obscure;
cf. OSw *harsk*].

harte. See HERTE.

hartes *n. pl.* harts, stags 58 [OE
heorot].

has(e). See HAUE.

haste: *in haste,* posthaste, speedily, forthwith 158, 2631, 2663,
2886, 4315 [OF *haste*].

hastyly(e) *adv.* quickly, hastily
167, 484, 2436, 2701, etc. [from
OF *hasti,* var. of *hastif*].

hatche *n.* the deck of a ship
3704; **hatches, hetches** *pl.*
hatches, trap doors covering the
openings in a deck 3606, 3656,
3682 [OE *hæc, hec*].

hathell *adj.* noble, powerful, great
1659, 1662, 3501; **hathelest,
hathlieste** *superl.* 988, 2109 [OE
æþele, with infl. from *hæleþ*].

hathell *n.* man, knight 358 [OE
hæleþ, with infl. from *æþele*].

hathen. See HETHEN.

hatte *n.* hat 3471 [OE *hæt*].

ha(u)nche *n.* haunch, the leg and
loin together 1046, 1100, 1119,
1157; **hawnches** *pl.* 4167; *of þe
haunche,* from the haunch down
2208 [OF *ha(u)nche*].

haue, hafe, haffe *v.* to have 165,
275, 286, 324; etc.; **haue, haues,
has** *2 & 3 sg.* 673, 677, 711,
998, 1837, etc.; **has** *2 & 3 pl.*
12, 3536; **hade** *pa. t.* 982; **hadde**
pa. subj. 4035; *as auxil.* have
252, 402, 511, 709, 1065 (*after
pp.*), etc.; are 2847; **has(e)** *2 &
3 sg.* 100, 140, 812; **has** *2 & 3 pl.*

137, 267, 369, 1695, etc.;
had(d), hadd(e), etc. *pa. t.* 26,
28, 48, etc.; *pa. subj.* had, would
have 796, 869, 872, 1117, etc.;
consider 131; get, gain 827, take
1062, 1072, 1783, 1785; *3 sg.*
holds 3035 [OE *habban*].
hawberke *n.* hauberk, mail coat
1156, 2078, 2700; **hawberkes**
pl. 2552, 2984 [OF *hauberc*].
hawe *n.* fear, terror 3704 (*see
note*) [ON *agi*].
hawke *n.* hawk 1082 [OE *heafoc*].
hawle. See HALL.
hawnches. See HA(U)NCHE.
hawrawde. See HARAWDE.
hawtayne *adj.* arrogant 1058,
2612, 2910; courageous 3029
[OF *(h)altain*].
he *pron.* he 28, 32, 33, 38, etc.;
pleonastic 770; **hym** *acc.& dat.*
him, to him, for him 1, 32, 42,
55, etc.; = he 760, 790, 969,
1048, etc. (*see* Introduction,
pp.5-6); *refl.* himself 65, 783,
807, 902, etc.; **his, hys** *poss. adj.*
his 2, 6, 29, 33, etc. [OE *hē, him,
his*]. See THAT(E), rel. pron.,
THIS, HYM SELFE.
hedde *v.* to behead 2311;
heuedede *pp.* 463 [OE *hēafdian*].
heddys-men *n. pl.* leaders 281
[from next + MAN].
hede, hevede, heuede *n.* head
764, 1178, 1354, etc.; **hedys** *pl.*
3709; head or tip of a spear or
arrow 2077 (*see note*); *pl.* 3619;
chief 1344; *appon heuede*, headlong 262; *ouer hede*, impetuously,
rashly 2110 [OE *hēafod*].
hede-rapys *n. pl.* headropes, the
stays of a mast 3668 [prec. +
ROPES].
hedire *adv.* here 2614 [OE *hider*].
hedyrwarde *adv.* hither, in this

direction 25 [OE *hiderweard*].
hedlyngs *adv.* headlong 3829
[HEDE + OE *ling*, as in OE
bæcling, with adv. gen. ending].
hedoyne *n.* unknown 184.
heede, hede *n.* heed 2651, 2662
[from OE *hēdan*].
heghe. See HYGHE.
heghly. See HYELY.
heghte *adj.* eight 2830 [OE *eahta,
ehta*].
heghte, heghttez. See HIGHTE.
hey, heyghe. See HYE, HYGHE.
heyly *adv.* aloft 464 [OE *hēalīce*].
See also HYELY.
heyndly *adv.* courteously, kindly
15 [from HENDE].
heynne, hyen *adv.* hence, away
2436, 2582, 2744 [contr. of ME
hethen (ON *heþan*)].
heynȝous *adj.* heinous, hateful
268 [OF *haïnos*].
heythe. See HETHE.
heythen. See HETHEN.
hekes *n. pl.* horses of some type
734 (*see note*), 2284 [?OF
haque].
helded *pa. t.* bowed down, bent
down 3368 [OE *heldan*].
hele *n.* welfare, well-being, fortune
2630, 3958 [OE *hælu*].
hele *v.*[1] *intr.* to heal, recover 3688
(*for future*); **heles** *3 sg.* 2209
(*for future*); **helyde** *pa. t.* 1835;
trans. **helyd** *pp.* comforted 3030
[OE *hælan*].
hele *v.*[2] to cover, conceal 3286
[OE *helan*].
helych. See HYELY.
Helle *n.* Hell 3812 [OE *hel(l)*].
helm(e) *n.* helmet 1832, 2228,
2700, etc.; **hel(l)mes, helmys** *pl.*
730, 2113, 2137, 2459, etc.; *fig.*
men in armor 380 [OE *helm*].
helmede *pp.* helmeted, armed

1647, 3626 [OE *helmian*].

helpe *n.* aid, help 827, 1205,
2128, etc. [OE *help*].

helpe, helpen *v.* to help 1448,
1646, 2743, etc.; **helpede** *pa. t.*
1560; **holpen** *pp.* benefited, re-
warded 2631; *pp.* treated 2661
[OE *helpan*].

helpyng *vbl. n.* help, aid 2316
[from prec.].

helples *adj.* destitute 4284
[HELPE, n. + OE *-leas*].

hemmes, hemmez, hemmys *n. pl.*
hems, borders, edges 912, 1351,
1648, 2219, etc. [OE *hem*].

hende *adj.* gracious, courtly,
noble, gallant 167, 3486; *as n.*
1135, 1283, 2630; **hendeste**
superl. 3879; *as n.* 4127 [OE
gehende].

hente *v.* to seize, lay hold of 3485
(*future*); **hentes, hentez** *3 sg.*
1132, 2917; **hentes** *3 pl.* 2699;
hent *pa. t.* 3545; **hente** *pp.* 1842;
henttis *3 sg.* pulls 3459; *hente
owte,* drew (it) out 2973; *pp.*
experienced, suffered 3319 [OE
hentan].

herbariours *n. pl.* forerunners,
knights who go before and an-
nounce the approach of an army
2448 [OF *herbergeour*].

herberde *pp.* lodged 158, 166;
encamped, quartered 2650 [OE
herebeorgian].

herbergage, harbergage *n.* place of
lodging, lodgings, camp 1285,
2285, 2475, 3014 [OF *herbergage*].

here *adv.* here, in this place 4,
152, 471, 842, etc.; now 644,
668, 2020 [OE *hēr*].

here *v.* to hear 12, 2905, 3043;
heres *3 pl.* **herys** *imper. pl.* 25;
herde, harde *pa. t.* 1285, 1950,

3134 [OE *hēran*].

hereaftyre *adv.* after this, later on,
henceforth 685, 896, 1642, 3326
OE *heræfter*].

herede *adj.* covered with hair
1083 [OE *hǣr, hēr,* n.].

heretyke *n.* heretic 1307 [OF
heretique].

heritage, herytage *n.* inheritance,
birthright 359, 643, 1309 [OF
heritage].

herken(e) *v.* hear, listen (to),
hearken 3899; **herkenes,
herkynes** *imper. pl.* 15, 25; to
search out 1646 [OE *hercnian*].

herne-pane *n.* skull 2229 [late OE
hærne (ON *hjarne*) + OE
panne].

herons *n. pl.* herons 184 [OF
hairon].

herte, harte *n.* heart 251, 262,
264, etc.; **hertes, hertez** *pl.* 2725,
2855, 2911, etc.; courage 968;
pl. strength 4171 [OE *heorte*].

herte *v.* to cheer, encourage 1181
[OE *hiertan*].

hert(e)ly *adv.* courageously,
vigorously 2991, 3642 [from
HERTE, n.].

hertly, hertelyche *adj.* sore, severe
1835; dire, deadly 2551, 3686,
4127 [from HERTE, n.].

heslyn *adj.* hazel 2504 [OE
hæslen].

heste *n.* command 2294, 3368,
4307 [OE *hǣs*].

hetches. See HATCH.

hete, hette *v.* to promise, vow,
pledge 2127, 2631, 3030, 3369,
etc.; **highte** *pp.* called, named
2899 [OE *hātan, hēt, hēht*].

hethe, heythe *n.* heath 1834,
2108, 2308, 2660, 4176, 4248,
etc. [OE *hǣþ*].

hethely *adv.* scornfully 268 [ON

hæþiligr].

hethen, heþen(e), heythen, ha(y)then *adj.* heathen, pagan 1260, 1284, 1834, 2109, 2274, 2285, etc.; *as n., uninfl. pl.* 3704; *haythemen,* heathens, heathen men 2295 [OE *hæþen*].

hethynge *n.* scorn 1843 [ON *hæþing*].

hette. See HETE.

heuande. See HEWYS.

hevede, heuede. See HEDE.

heuedede. See HEDDE.

heuen, Heuen(e), hevyne, hewen, Hewyn *n.* Heaven 6, 285, 705, 863, etc.; heavens, sky 795, 4156; *vndire heuen riche, vndyr the heuene ryche,* under (all) the wide heavens, anywhere on earth 108, 2613, 3879 [OE *heofon*].

heuen: *heuen my herte,* rouse my heart to anger 1937 [OE *hafenian*].

hewe *n.* brilliance, luster 207, 913; **hewes, hewez** *pl.* hues, colors 768, 925, 2523, 3267 [OE *hēow, hīw*].

hewe *v.* to hew, cut, hack 2910, 3642; **hewes** *3 sg.* 1798, 2992; **hewes, hewen** *3 pl.* 1860, 2552, 3695, 4165, 4268, etc.; **hewede** *pa. t.* 1879 (*with pron. obj. un-expressed*), 2274, 4127; **hewen** *pp.* 1825, 2663, 3668 [OE *hēawan*].

hewede *pp.* fashioned, figured 3252 [OE *hīwian*].

hewede. See HEWYS.

hewen, Hewyn. See HEUEN.

hewys *3 sg.* heaves, lifts 4156; **hafe** *pa. t.* 1156; **heuande** *pres. p.* heaving, tossing 3704; **hewede** *pp.* 4091 [OE *hebban, hef-, hofe*].

hyde *n.* hide, skin 1085, 1157

[OE *hȳd*].

hyde *v.* to hide, conceal 2886; **hyd, hide** *pp.* 2316, 4175; **hyded** *pp.* covered 1001 [OE *hȳdan*].

hye, hey: *on hy(e), in hye, in hey,* in haste, quickly, forthwith, soon 166, 2108, 2109, 2128, 2275, 2449, etc. [from next].

hye *v.* to hasten 553, 1645, 2660, 2744 (*refl.*), etc.; **hyes** *3 sg.* 3013; **hyes** *3 pl.* 2475; **hyes** *imper. pl.* 2436 [OE *hīgian*].

hye. See HYGHE.

hyely, heyly, heghly, helych *adv.* quickly 2294, 2663, 2920, etc.; loudly 1058, 1286 [from HYE].

hyen. See HEYNNE.

hyghe, hye, hey, heghe, heyghe *adj.* high, tall, lofty 39, 158, 167, 499, etc.; mountainous 58, 620, 3014; steep 941, 3103; main 3467, 3485; great, grand 1284; haughty, proud 1646; *as n.* high, height 463, 1146; *on(e) heghe, one heyghe,* on high, on a height, at the height, upward 2476, 2651, 3324, 3857, etc.; **hegheste** *superl.* highest 3369, 3396; *adv.* high, high up, aloft 194, 769, 1037, 1119, etc.; greatly, strongly 1463; loudly 3122, 4115; proudly, haughtily 3715 [OE *hēh, hēah*]. See also HYE, HEY.

highte, hyghte, heghte *n.* height 2613; mountain peak 3106; **heghttez** heights, zenith 798 (*see note*); *one highte, on(e) heghte,* up, aloft 4156; all the way up 1157; above, on the heights 2295, 3605, 3626; *appon hyghte,* on high 3590 [OE *hēahþo, hēhþo*].

highte. See HETE.

hill, hyll *n.* mountain, mount, hill, cliff 1146, 1283, 3768; **hillys, hillez, hyllis, hyllys,** etc.

pl. 1226, 1259, 1292, etc. [OE *hyll*].

hillid   *pa. t.* buried 1120; **hillyd, hyled** *pp.* covered, glazed 184, 3606 [ON *hylja*].

hilte   *n.* hilt 1121, 4248; **hiltes, hiltez, hiltys** *pl.* (= *sg.*) 1056, 1149, 2239, 2310, 3358, etc. [OE *hilte*].

hiltede   *adj.* hilted, with a hilt 2274, 2911 [OE *hilted,* from n.].

hym.   See HE.

hymland   *n.* borderland 2503 [see note].

hym selfe, selfen, seluen, seluyn, selvyn   *pron. & adj.* he, himself, he himself, him, him and no other, the very person, his very person 1, 8, 10, 34, 46, 239 (*see note*), 244, 374 (*see note*), 433, 545, etc.; *reinf.* himself 71, 172, 216, 288, 338, etc.; *refl.* himself 54, 619, 785, 944, 1660, etc. [*him* + SELFE.]

hyndire   *adj.* rear 3626 [OE *hinder,* adv.].

hynnges   *3 pl.* hang 3473; **hyngede** *pa. t.* hanged 281; **hyngande** *pres. p.* overhanging 1083; **hynggyde** *pp.* hanged 3590 [ON *hengja*].

hynter   *n.* rear 3605 [OE *hinder,* adv., OHG *hintar,* adj.].

hippe   *n. uninfl. poss.* hip's 2613 [OE *hype*].

hyrdez   *n. pl.* flocks, herds 3245 [OE *hiord, herd*].

hir(e), hyr(e).   See SCHO.

hyres   *3 pl.* hire 484 [OE *hȳran*].

hirste   *n.* grove, copse 3369 [OE *hyrst*].

his, hys.   See HE.

hitt   *v.* to strike, smite, hit 2437; **hittez, hyttez, hyttis,** etc. *3 sg.* 1112, 1122, 1125, etc.; **hittes,**

hittis *3 pl.* 2991, 3686; **hitte** *pa. t.* 2173 [ON *hitta*].

hode   *n.* hood 3459 [OE *hōd*].

hodles   *adj.* hoodless, with head uncovered (as a sign of humility) 2308 [from prec.].

holde, halde   *v.* to keep, hold, possess, maintain 1842, 2311, 3768, 4150; **holdes, haldes, haldez, haldys** *3 sg.* 64, 636, 1667, 1770, etc.; **holdys** *imper. pl.* 15; **holden** *3 pl.* 4128; **helde** *pa. t.* 35, 53, 74, 1196, 3668, etc.; **holden, halden** *pp.* 543, 652, 1473, 1553, etc.; *haldys his awen,* maintains his position, holds his ground 3541; keep to 3485; *holdes wayes,* proceeds on (his) way, goes, travels 2986; *3 sg.* squeezes 1135; *pp.* gained 2037; *holde at,* hold to, carry out 4307; convene 424, 3214, 4005; *3 sg.* 3128; regard, consider 3480; *3 sg.* 3550, 3575; *pa. t.* 2613; *pp.* 40, 166 (*see* OSTE), 174, 387, 534, 2065, etc.; *intr.* take place (now) 340; **haldez** *3 sg.* is held 1512; *pa. t. refl.* remained in a state or condition 65 (*see note*) [OE *haldan*].

hole, holle, hale, halle   *adj.*[1] all of 545; (a) full, complete, whole 2108, 2275, 2449, 2651, 3107, etc.; *with hale strenghe,* with (a) full force 1260; well, healthy 2661; *adv.* fully, completely 1647, 3959 [OE *hāl*].

hole   *adj.*[2] hollow 1083 (*see note*) [OE *hol,* adj.].

holy, haly   *adj.* holy 297, 309, 348, 386 [OE *hālig*].

holle   *n.* hold of a ship 3687 [OE *hol,* n.].

holly, halely, hally   *adv.* all together 748, 3368, 3590; entirely

764, 1001, 1085; wholeheartedly, earnestly 4307 [from HOLE, adj.¹].

holpen. See HELPE, n.

holte *n.* wood, copse 1645; *as adj.* 1283, 1648, 1879, etc.; **holt(t)es, holtez, holtis** *pl.* 1259, 2504, 3544 [OE *holt*].

homage *n.* homage, allegiance 99 [OF *hommage*].

homagers *n. pl.* those who owe homage or fealty, those who hold lands by homage 3147 [OF *hommag(i)er*].

hom(e) *n.* home 2612, 2727, 3014, 3451 [OE *hām*].

homely *adj.* humble, plain 3471 [from prec.].

honden *v.* to take charge of, look after 3209 [from HAND(E)].

hondrethe. See HUNDRETH(E).

honeste *adj.* splendid, fine, sumptuous 3245 [OF *honeste*].

honnde, hondis, etc. See HAND(E).

honour *v.* to honor 1595 [OF *hono(u)rer*].

honourable *adj.* illustrious, esteemed 580, 1309, 1622, 1904, etc. [OF *hono(u)rable*].

honour(e) *n.* honor 400, 1293, 1328, etc. [OF *hono(u)r*].

honourliche *adj.* illustrious, esteemed 2298 [from HONOUR(E)].

hope *n.* hope, expectation 3958 [late OE *hopa*].

hope *v.* to expect 2209, 2885 [OE *hopian*].

hopes *n. pl.* valleys 2503 [OE *-hop*, as in *fen-hop, mōr-hop*].

hordes *n. pl.* treasures 3145 [OE *hord*].

hore, hare *adj.* hoary, gray 1082, 2504, 3544 [OE *hār*].

horne *n.* horn 2662 [OE *horn*].

hornez of olyfantez. See note to line 1286.

horreble, horrebill, orrible *adj.* hideous, frightful, fearful 1087, 1240, 4061 [OF *(h)orrible*].

horse, horsse *n.* horse 1372, 1773, 2051, etc.; **horses, horsses, horsez, horsys** *pl.* 153, 1358, 2235, *3721,* etc.; *uninfl. pl.* 463, 1549, 1730, 3136, etc.; *horses of armes, horsez of armez,* war horses 734, 2284 [OE *hors*].

horsede, horsyde *pp.* mounted on horseback, provided with horses 335, 1179, *1647, 2476, 2944* [OE *horsian*].

hostaye to make war 550; **ostayande** *pres. p.* 3502 [OF *(h)osteier*].

hoste, oste *n.* host, army 565, 1624, 1907, 1974, etc.; **hostes, hostez, ostes, ostez** *pl.* 617, 1240, 2008, 2888, etc. [OF *(h)oste*].

hotchen *3 pl.* hop, jump 3687 [perh. = OF *hocher*].

hott(e) *adj.* hot 1121, 1833 [OE *hāt*].

houndes *n. pl.* hounds, dogs 57, 464 [OE *hund*].

hourez. See OWRE.

hoursches *3 pl.* ?rush noisily 2110 [OE *hrȳscan,* to make a noise].

house *v.* to dwell 4284 [OE *hūsian*].

houes, houis, etc. See HUFE.

how *adv.* how, however 14, 22, 1044, 1349, 2347, 2393, etc.; by what right 509 [OE *hū*].

howes. See HUFE.

however *adv.* in what manner 1006 [prec. + EUER(E)].

howge. See HUG(G)E.

howndrethe. See HUNDRETH(E).

howntes. See HUNT.

howres. See OWRE.

howselde *pp.* given Communion 4315 [OE *hūslian*].

howsyng *vbl. n.* encampment, lodgings, pavilions 1284, 2285 [OE *hūsian*].

hufe *v.* to delay, stall 1688; **houez** *3 pl.* halt, pause 1283; **hufes, houes, houys** *3 sg.* waits, remains, lingers, stays, delays 1260, 2475, 2520, 2528, 2777, etc.; **houes, houis, houys,** etc. *3 pl.* 2084, 2118, 2122, 2220, etc.; **houede** *pa. t.* 2031, 3009, 3046; **houande** *pres. p.* 1648; **howes,** etc. *3 sg.* goes, proceeds, rides 915, 2010, 2824; *3 pl.* 377; *pa. t.* 3717 [?OE *hōfian*].

hug(g)e, howge *adj.* great, huge 583, 591, 606, 617, etc.; abundant 668 [OF *ahuge, ahoge*].

huke-nebbyde *adj.* hook-beaked, hook-nosed 1082 [from OE *hōc* + *neb(b)*].

hulke *n.* hulk, huge person 1058, 1085, 1121, 1149; **hulkes** *pl.* 4165 [OE *hulk*].

hunde-fisch *n.* dogfish, shark 1084 [OE *hund* + *fisc*].

hundreth(e), hondrethe, howndrethe *adj. & n.* hundred 844, 856, 930, 1440, etc.; **hundrethes, hun(n)-drethez** *pl.* 281, 1285, 1879, 2275 [OE *hundred, hundraþ*].

hunt *v.* to hunt 58 (*with* AT); **hunttes, howntes** *3 pl.* 2295, 4258 [OE *huntian*].

hurdace *n.* a wooden bulwark or other structure on a ship to protect the crew in battle 3626 [OF *hourdeis*].

hurdez *3 sg.* lies hidden, lurks 1010 (*see note*) [OE *hordian*].

hurles *2 sg.* rush 262 [obscure; cf. LG *hurreln*].

hurte, hurtte *n.* wound 1835, 2209, 2701; **hurtes** *pl.* 2661 [OF *hurt*].

hurte *v.* to wound 2427; **hurt(t)es, hurtez** *3 sg.* 1772, 2229, 2992, etc.; **hurte** *pa. t.* 2973; **hurte** *pp.* 3688 [from prec.].

I *pron.* I 16, 91, 138, 141, etc.; **me** *acc. & dat.* me, of me, to me, for me 9, 15, 136, 140, 143, etc.; *refl.* 360, 1034, 1322, etc.; **my, myn(e)** *poss. adj.* my 149, 164, 251, 264, 268, etc.; my own 678; *my selfe, selfen, seluen* myself, me, me and no other 937, 2320, 3796; to myself 324; *refl.* 151, 354; *reinf.* 445, 522, 554, 1034, etc. [OE *ic, mē, mīn, mē selfan*]. See ONE.

iche. See YSCHEWES.

iche, yche, ilke, ylke *adj.* each, every 589, 1004, 1006, 1093, etc.; *with* a 83, 194, 727, 776, etc.; **ilkone, ilkane** each, each one 279, 3691 [OE *ǣlc, ylc, ich(e),* etc.].

if(e), ȝif(e), ȝiff(e), ȝeffe, gif(f)e *conj.* if 104, 110, 164, 344, 420, etc.; whether 340 [OE *gif, gef*]. See BOT.

ilke *adj.* same, very 65, 232, 1311, 2323, etc. [OE *ilca*].

ilke, ylke, ilkone, ilkane. See ICHE.

ill *adv.* ill, badly 2904 [ON *illa, illr*].

imangez. See AMONG.

in *prep.* in, on 5, 8, 14, 19, 20, etc.; *in asseveration* 425, 526, etc.; to 494, 1515; into 561, 667, 759, 1450, etc.; through, throughout 651, 923, etc.; at 659, 897, 3201; toward 2169; inside 756; of 826 [OE *in*]. See KITHE, HYE, OSTE, SUYTE, SPECHE, TALE, n.².

inche *n.* inch 4245 [OE *ynce*].

income *n.* entrance, entry, arrival 2009, 2171 [from OE *incuman,* v.].

inewe, ynewe. See ENOWE.

Inglisce *n.* English 2529 [OE *englisc*].

injurye *n.* injury, wrong 663 [AF *injurie*].

In manus 4326 [see note].

inmette *n.* entrails, innards 1122 [OE *in-* + *mete*].

inns *n. pl.* inns 3041 [OE *inn*].

inowe, ynowe. See ENOWE.

insette *pa. t.* overcame, subdued 2038 [OE *onsettan*].

into *prep.* into 56, 57, 110, 379, 427, etc.; to 318, 3162 [OE *inn to*].

iren, iryn, yryn *n.* iron 1105, 1182, 1186, 2104, etc. [OE *īren*].

irous, irus, irows *adj.* hot-tempered, irascible 1329, 1592, 1957; **irouslye** *adv.* irascibly 2530 [AF *irous*].

is, es *3 sg.* is 16, 88, 89, 128, 129, 130, etc.; *for future* 683 (*with coll. n.*), 1328, 1816 (*with adv.*); *as auxil.* has 1239, 1419, 1782, 1870, 1892, etc.; *impers.* it is, there is 870, 1154, 1562, 2020, 2365, etc. [OE *is*].

ischewe *n.* offspring, progeny 1943 [OF *issue*].

yschewes *3 sg.* comes forth, sallies forth 610; **is(s)chewis, iche** *3 pl.* 1411, 3116, 4060 [from prec.].

it, itt, yt *pron.* it 88, 89, 258, 274, etc.; *indef.* 130, 150, 266, 385, 797, etc. [OE *hit*].

ythez *n. pl.* waves 741, 747, 763 [OE *ȳþ*].

iwis, iwys, iwysse *adv.* certainly, assuredly 322, 546, 2020, 2332, etc. [OE *gewisse*].

jaggede. See JOGGES.

jambé, jamby *adj.* sure-footed, nimble 373, 2894 [OF *jambé*].

japez *n. pl.* insults, jeers 1398 [obscure].

jentill, jentyll, ientill. See GENTILL.

jeryn *n.* a jacket or doublet, worn under mail 903 [OF *giron*].

jerownde *adj.* divided into triangular sections (heraldry) 2891 [from OF *gironé, geroné*].

jesseraunt, jesserawnte, gesserawnte *n.* coat of mail 904, 2892, 4238 **gesserawntes** *pl.* 2909 [OF *jasera(u)nt, jesseran*].

jocunde *adj.* cheerful, happy 2896 [OF *jocunde*].

jogges *3 sg.* slashes 2891, 2893; **jaggede** *pa. t.* slashed, cut 1123, 2087; **jaggede** *pp.* 2909; slashed or pinked along the edges for decoration 905 (*see note*) [obscure].

joy(e) *n.* gladness, delight, joy 2415, 3433, 3743, 3801, 4290 [OF *joie, joye*].

joyes *3 sg. refl.* rejoices 2896 [OF *joir*].

ioynez *3 pl.* encounter, meet in conflict 2112; **jonede** *pp.* 2890 [OF *joindre*].

joynynge *vbl. n.* encounter *2133* [from prec.].

ioynter *n.* joint 2893 [OF *jointure*].

joly *adj.* gallant, brave, spirited 3414; **jolyere** *compar.* more splendid 4110; **jolyeste** *superl.* most gallant 1658 [OF *joli(f)*].

jolyly, iolily *adv.* grandly, splendidly 245, 373; gallantly, boldly 2088, 4109 [from prec.].

jonede. See IOYNEZ.

journey, journé(e), journaye, jorné, jurnée *n.* a day's performance in fighting, battle, campaign, military expedition 340, 372, 374, 1161, 1398, 2134, etc.; *at journé,* at any battle 2875; jour-

ney 445 [OF *journee*].

jowell *n.* jewel, gem (*fig.*) 862 [OF *joel, juel*].

jugge *n.* judge 670 (God); **juggez, iuggez** *pl.* judges 246, 662 [OF *juge*].

juggede *pp.* adjudged 2877, 3744 [AF *juger*].

Iuny *n.* June 345 [OF *juin*, L *jūnius*].

jupon, jopown *n.* surcoat 905 (*see note*), 4238 [OF *jupon*].

jureez *n. pl.* juries 662 [OF *jurée*, oath].

jurnée. See JOURNEY.

iust: *iust to þe*, right up to, to the very 1123 [OF *juste*, adj.].

juste *v.* to joust, fight on horseback 374 [OF *jo(u)ster, juster*].

justere *n.* jouster, knight 3412; **justers** *pl.* 559 [from prec.]

justyfye *v.* to mete out justice to 663 [OF *justifier*].

justyng *vbl. n.* jousting, fighting 1657, 2875 [from JUSTE].

justis *n.* marshal 2890; **justicez** *pl.* judges, magistrates 246, 662 [OF *justice, justise*].

kaban. See CABANE.

kaghte. See CATCHEZ.

kay, kayes. See KEYE.

kaire, kayre, kayris, karede, etc. See CAIRE.

kaysere *n.* emperor 1651, 1959, 2266; **kayser(e)s** *pl.* 1894, 2391 [OE *casere* (from *Caesar*)].

kalander *n.* register 2640 [AF *calender*].

kalendez *n.* the first day of the month 345, 2371 [OF *kalendes*].

kambe *n.* comb 3351 [OE *camb, comb*].

kamells, kameles. See CAMELLEZ.

kampe *n.* warfare, battle, combat 3670, 3701 [OE *camp*].

kane, kwn *v.* can 2750; to express (thanks) 1565; **cowthe** *pa. t.* knew 3340; **couthe** *pp.* acquainted, familiar 21 [OE *cunnan*].

kare. See CARE.

karfuke *n.* crossroad 2003 [OF *carrefor, carrefours* (presence of *k* unaccounted for)].

karyage. See CARYAGE.

kariede, karyed. See CARYE.

karpe, karpes, etc. See CARPE.

kastys. See CASTE.

kaughte, kawghte. See CATCHEZ.

kaunt *adj.* stout 2195 [obscure].

keye, kay *n.* key (*lit. & fig.*), power 1867; a place which, from the strategic advantages of its position, gives its possessors control over the passage into or from a certain district, territory, etc. 3111; **kayes** *pl.* keys 3064 [OE *cǣg*].

kele *v. intr.* cool, grow cold 1839; *trans.* **keled** *pa. t.* 2712 [OE *cēlan*].

kelle *n.* decorative hair net or headdress 3258 [OF *cale*].

kembede *pa. t.* combed 3351 [OE *cemban*].

kemp *v.* to contend in battle 2633 [= MDu *kempan*].

kempis *n. pl.* warriors, men 1003 [OE *cempa*].

kene *adj.* bold, brave, fierce 47, 641, 1152, 1725, etc.; *as n.* 1785, 3086; powerful 1106, 3132; savage 3428, 3785; *as n.* 876; **kenere** *compar.* sharper, keener 4194; **keneste** *superl.* bravest, fiercest 2721; *as n.* 3490 [OE *cēne*].

ken(e) *v.* to tell, show, guide 876, 2619, 3521; **kend(e)** *pa. t.* 481, 1590, 2194 [OE *cennan*].

ken(e)ly *adv.* boldly, bravely 935, 1243, 2392; keenly, sharply 943, 1271, 1319 [OE *cēnlīce*].

kenetez *n. pl.* small hounds 122 [ONF *kennet*].

kepare *n.* guardian, regent 649, 709, 3512; **kepers** *pl.* lookouts, patrols 558 [from KEPE, *v.*].

kepe: *take kepe to, takez kepe on,* take custody of, take care, charge, or heed in tending, watching, or preserving 156, 1682, 2262, 4154; pay, take heed 3049, 3401, 3406; *tuke kepe,* took notice 2242 [from next].

kepe, keppe *v.* to keep, maintain, preserve 675, 1513, 1556, 1780, 3445, etc.; **kepide** *pa. t.* 4201 (*with pron. obj. unexpressed*); **kepede, kepyd(e)** *pp.* 2263, 4016, 4197, 4217, etc.; *pa. t.* sustained 3960; *pp.* acquired 998; seize 3484; take care, care for 3522, 4021; defend, guard 2181; *pp.* 563, 1586; keep watch 2003; **kepys** *imper. pl.* await 628, *pa. t.* 838, 919; *pp.* encountered, intercepted 2171; desire, wish 2398 [OE *cēpan*].

kerfe *n.* cut 4194; **carffes** *pl.* cuts, wounds 2713 [OE *cyrf* (from next)].

kerfes, kerues *3 sg.* cuts, carves, slices 2567 (*with pron. obj. unexpressed*), 4231; **corven** *pp.* cut up, cleft 3673; **coruen** *pp.* engraved, sculpted 211, 3335 [OE *ceorfan, cearfan*].

kest(e). See CASTE.

ketill-hatte *n.* a large, heavy helm that rests on the shoulders 3516, 3995; **ketell-hattes** *pl.* 2993 [ON *ketill* + HATTE].

kidd, kyde, kydd(e). See KYTH(E).

kyghte. See KITHE.

kill, kyll *v.* to kill, slay 2267, 2447, 3484; **killez** *3 sg.* 1390, 1822; **kyllede** *pa. t.* 2115; **kylled(e), killide, kyllyde,** etc. *pp.* 1065, 1106, 1187, etc.; *pa. t.* struck, beaten, smashed 1785, 1838, 3672 (*see note*); *pp.* 101, 1514, 1915, 2773, etc. [?OE **cyllan*].

kynd(e) *n.* nature, kinship 3867; *of kynd(e), o kynde,* by right of birth, by blood, 125, 3049, 3518, 3956, 4317; *as his kynde askes,* as his lineage demands 2385; family, clan 848 [OE *(ge)cynd*].

kynde *adj.* well-bred, courtly 21; **kyndeste** *superl.* 4102 [OE *(ge)cynde*].

kyndly *adj.* courteous, courtly 3883; noble 4188 [OE *cyndelic*].

kyndly, kyndely, kyndlyche *adv.* courteously, graciously 220, 714; properly, fittingly, solemnly 343, 395, 3185, 3521, 3994, 4148, etc.; kindly 2712; in a familiar manner 3506 [OE *cyndelīce*].

kyne *n.* kin, family 2618 [OE *cynn*].

king, kyng(e) *n.* king 26, 83, 88, 96, etc.; *uninfl. poss.* 1652, 3423, 4343; **kyngys, kyngis, kyngez,** etc. *pl.* 50, 101, 105, etc.; **kyngez, kyngys, kynges,** etc. *poss. sg. & pl.* 171, 206, 400, 1576, etc. [OE *cyning*]. See SELFE.

kyngdom *n.* kingdom 6; **kingdoms** *pl.* 27 [OE *cyningdōm*].

kyngryke *n.* kingdom 24, 1272; **kyngrykes, kyngrykez** *pl.* 649, 820 [OE *cyningrīce*].

kyns(e)mane, kynysemane *n.* kinsman 282, 1778, 3898 [*kyne* + gen. ending + MAN].

kirke, kyrke *n.* church 1219, 4016 [ON *kirkja*].

kyrnelles *n. pl.* crenelations, battlements 3046 [ONF *kernel*].

kyrtill, kyrtyll *n.* kirtle, tunic 998, 1024, 1191; **kyrtills** *pl.* 2312 [OE *cyrtel*].

kysses, kyssez, kyssis, kyssiz *3 sg.* kisses 697, 1779, 3952, 3970; **kyssede, kysside** *pa. t.* 714, 3516 [OE *cyssan*].

kystis, kystys *n. pl.* chests, coffers 2302, 2336, 2342, 2355 [ON *kista*].

kithe, kyth(e), kyghte *n.* country, land, homeland, one's own country 28, 542, 1004, 1512, *1653,* etc.; *in kyth,* with proper ceremony 142 [OE *cȳþþu*].

kyth(e) *v.* to display, demonstrate, perform 1652, 4193; **kidd, kyde, kydd(e)** *pp.* known, well-known, famed, great 65, 96, 232, 626, 654, 849, etc.; notorious, infamous 1272, 2177; declared 2640; avowed 3509 [OE *cȳpan, gecȳdd*].

kleuys. See CLYF(F)E.

klokes *n. pl.* claws, paws 792 [from OE *clyccan,* to clutch].

knaue, knaf(f)e *n.* boy, page, servant 2621, 2637; *as adj.* 850, 1025; **knaues, knafes** *pl.* 2632; knaves, villains 3484 [OE *cnafa*].

knawe, knawes, etc. See KNOW(E).

knees(s), kneys *n. pl.* knees 956, 2125, 2195, 4274 [*OE cnēo*].

knele *v.* to kneel 1024; **knelis** *3 sg.* 3951, 3993; *3 pl.* 3046; **knelyd(e)** *pa. t.* 680, 1199, 2312; **kneland(e)** *pres. p.* 1137, 4337 [OE *cnēowlian*].

knyfe *n.* knife 3852, 3856 [OE *cnīf*].

knyghte *n.* knight 124, 133, 649, 678, etc.; **knyght(t)es, knyght(t)ez, knyght(t)ys** *pl.* 48, 81, 94, 106,

115, etc. [OE *cniht*].

knyght(e)hode, knyghthede *n.* the whole body of knights 537; the character or qualities of a knight, chivalrousness, honor 1581, 1682, 2619, 3883; *for thy knyghthede,* for the sake of your honor 1320 [OE *cnihthād,* youth].

knight(t)ly, knyghtlyche *adj.* knightly, brave, noble 222, 506, 1218, 1649, 2395, 2750, etc.; **knyghtlyeste** *superl.* 291, 534; *adv.* in a knightly manner, nobly, bravely 402, 1692, 1707, 1724, etc. [from KNYGHTE].

knylles *3 pl.* toll bells 2353 [OE *cnyllan*].

know(e), knawe *v.* to acknowledge, recognize 864, 1003, 1581, 1672, 2304, 3522, 4185; **knawes** *3 sg.* 2639; **knewe** *pa. t.* 43, 3048, 3087, 3149, 3337, etc.; **knawen** *pp.* 1654, 1690, 2996, 3882; know 223, 1928; **knawes** *2 sg.* 3504; **knawes** *3 pl.* 1317; *pa. t.* 2177, 3866; **knowen** *pp.* 542, 809, 3259; *pp.* determined 1554; proclaim, declare 2637; *pp.* made known 475; encounter 2397 [OE *cnāwan*].

kombide *pp.* combed 1003 [from KAMBE].

konynge *vbl. n.* wisdom 3883 [from KWN].

konyngeste. See CONYNGE.

kosyn. See COSYN(E).

koueride. See COUERE.

kowardely. See COWARDE.

kraftes. See CRAFTE.

kraftly. See CRAFTY.

krayers. See CRAYERS.

krakede *pa. t.* cracked 3269 [OE *cracian*].

krewell. See CRUELL.

kryes. See CRYE, V.

krisome, krysom(e).   See CRYSUM.
krysomede.   See CRYSMED.
krispan[d]e.   See CRISPID.
kroke   *n.* a head of curly hair,
  locks 3352 [ON *krókr*].
krouell, kruelleste.   See CRUELL.
kuttes   *3 sg.* cuts, cleaves 2125
  [obscure; ?OE *cyttan*].
kwn.   See KANE.

lac(c)hen   *3 pl.* take 750; **lached,
  laughte, laghte** *pa. t.* 1515, 2226,
  2693, 2702, 4183, etc.; **laughte,
  laghte** *pp.* seized, grabbed, captured 874, 1817, 1826, 1902,
  2998, etc.; lift 2541; *pa. t.* 2292
  [OE *læccan*].
ladde   *n.* a man of low birth 4190,
  4302; **laddes** *pl.* 3535, 4093
  [obscure].
lade-sterne   *n.* lodestar, guiding
  star, especially the pole star 751
  [OE *lād,* journey + ON *stjarna*].
lady(e)   *n.* lady 855, 874, 1070,
  2189; **ladys, ladyes, ladysse** *pl.*
  713, 1255, 2866, 3081, etc. [OE
  hlǣfdige].
ladily   *adv.* befitting a lady 3254
  [from prec.].
laggen   *3 pl.* pause (?for a moment
  before charging) 2542 [obscure].
laghte.   See LAC(C)HEN.
laghttirs   *n. pl.* laughter (of several
  people) 2673 [OE *hleahtor*].
laid(e).   See LAYE, v.
laye   *n.*[1] faith, religion 2593 [OF
  lei].
laye   *n.*[2] water, sea 3721 [OE
  lagu].
laye   *v.* to lay 3279; **layes** *3 sg.*
  4268; **laide** *pa. t.* 2702; **laide** *pp.*
  460; **layes** *imper. pl.* cast down,
  lay low, kill 4093; **laid, layed**
  pa. t. 1814, 4166; *pp.* 1900,
  3278, 3293, 4276, etc.; *pp.*

abased, humbled 2083; *layes one,
  lays into,* attacks 2230 [OE
  lecgan].
layere   *n.* couch, bed 2293 [OE
  leger].
layke   *n.* game, sport 1599, 3386,
  4093 [ON *leikr*].
layne   *v.* to conceal, hide 419,
  2398 (*with pron. obj. unexpressed*), 2593 [ON *leyna*].
laysere   *n.* leisure 2430, 3095,
  4301 [OF *leisir*].
laythely.   See LOTHELY, adj.
layttede   *pa. t.* sought 254 [ON
  leita].
lake   *n.* lack, dearth 163 [cf. MLG
  lak].
lakes   *n. pl.* waters 960 [OF *lac*].
lakes.   See LOKKES.
lamede   *pa. t.* maimed, wounded
  4302; *pp.* 1600, 3281, 3723
  [from OE *lama,* adj.].
Lammes(s)e, Lammes(s)e Day(e)
  n. Lammas Day, August 1 92,
  349, 421, 3094 [OE *hlāfmæsse* +
  DAYE].
lande, londe   *n.* ground, land, territory, realm 253, 1255, 1270,
  1620, 2407, etc.; **lan(n)des,
  lan(n)dez, landys, londes,** etc. *pl.*
  58, 91, 98, 154, 224, 336, etc.;
  this land 701, *dry land* 840; *in
  lande,* throughout the land 2328
  [OE *land*].
lande   *v.* to land, go ashore 3720;
  londis *3 sg.* 3922; **landede** *pp.*
  3919 [from prec.].
lang, langere, etc. See LONG(E).
langage   *n.* language 3477 [OF
  langage].
lange   *v.* to belong, be loyal, attach
  3535; **langes** *3 sg.* 3490; **langes,
  langez, langys, longez** *3 pl.* 244,
  402, 465, 673, 1244, etc.; **langede,
  lon(n)gede** *pa. t.* 1901, 1907,

2305, 3080, 3083, etc.; *3 sg.* belongs, pertains 3667 [from OE
gelang, gelong, adj.].

lang(e), langere.   See LONG(E).

langour(e)   *n.* distress, sorrow 702,
4268 [OF *langour*].

languessande   *pres. p.* pining, sorrowing 4338 [OF *languir, lan-
guiss-*].

lannges   *3 sg.* longs, yearns 383
[OE *langian*].

lapynge   *vbl. n.* lapping 3235 [OE
lapian].

lappe   *n.* a piece of cloth 3286;
lappes *pl.* lappets, parts of a garment either hanging down or pro-
jecting so as to admit of being
folded over 3254 [OE *lappa*].

lappe   *v.* to enfold 3292; **lappede**
pa. t. encased 2300 [from prec.].

large   *adj.* long 801, 1095; ample,
wide, extensive 1598, 1640, 3330;
adv. freely, without restraint,
boldly 143, 1376, 1784, 2533,
2789, 3141, etc.; distant, at a distance, from a distance, as much
as 601, 1040, 1079, 1120, 1402,
1855, 2077, 2229, etc.; *at my
large,* freely, without restraint, at
my liberty 349, 421; *at the large,*
at the most 447 [OF *large*].

largesce   *n.* bounty, generosity 163
[OF *largece, largesse*].

larkes   *n. pl.* larks 2674 [OE
lāwerce].

lasschen   *3 pl.* dash, rush 2801
[obscure; perh. onomatopoeic,
like *dash, flash,* etc.].

laste   *adj. superl.* last 672; lowest 3278; *adv.* most lately, lastly
3588 [OE *lætest*].

laste   *v.* to endure 2407; **lastes,
lastez, lastis** *3 sg.* 855, 1570,
2351, 2364, etc. [OE *læstan*].

lat.   See LETE.

lates, latz, lotes   *n. pl.* looks, bearing, expression 118, 248, 536,
1076, 1462, 2054, etc. [OE *læte,*
ON *lát*].

lathe   *n.* trouble, annoyance 458
[OE *lāþ*].

latheliche.   See LOTHELY, adj.

latt(e), lattes.   See LETE.

laughe   *v.* to laugh, smile 1720;
laughes *3 sg.* 382, 1781; **laughen**
3 pl. 3698; **lughe** *pa. t.* 248 [OE
hlæhhan].

laughte.   See LAC(C)HEN.

launce   *n.* lance, spear 1379, 1820,
1831, 2167, 2168; **launces,
launcez** *pl.* 1459, 1754, 1813,
2462, etc. [OF *la(u)nce*].

launches, launschide,   etc. See
LAWNCHE.

launde, lawnde   *n.* field, meadow,
glade 1517, 2084, 2220, 2227,
2281, etc.; **laundes, laundez,
lawndez** *pl.* 2273, 2677, 2702
[OF *la(u)nde*].

laundon: *o laundon,* on the field
1768 [OF *landon*].

law(e)   *n.* law 996, 1268, 2407;
lawes *pl.* 430, 3093; rule, custom
371; faith, religion 14 [OE *lagu*
(from ON)].

lawe, laweste.   See LOWE, adj.

lawnche   *v. trans.* launch, set afloat
3921; **lawnches** *3 sg.* pierces,
slashes 3831; **launchez** *3 pl.*
heave (lead) 750; *intr.* **launches**
3 sg. springs, leaps, darts 2560;
launschide *pa. t.* darted [ONF
lancher].

lawnde, lawndez.   See LAUNDE.

leberall   *adj.* generous 2318 [OF
liberal].

leburde   *n.* the lee side of a vessel
3624 [ON *hlé-borþ*].

leche   *n.* slice of meat 194 [OF
lesche].

lechen   *v.* to cure, heal 2388 [from OE *lǣce,* physician].

lechyde   *pp.* cut into slices 188 [from LECHE].

lede   *n.*¹ man, warrior, knight 138, 430, 473, 1313, etc.; **ledis, ledys** *pl.* 2801, 3514, 3624, 3697, etc.; any man 1721; person, creature 854, 1035, 1102, 2326, etc.; **ledes,** etc. *pl.* 195, 2399, 2431, 2532, etc.; **lede** *pl.* people 997; **ledes** *pl.* nations 1902 [OE *lēod,* pl. *lēode*].

lede   *n.*² lead 2300, 3954; a lump of lead used to ascertain the depth of water 750 [OE *lēad*].

leders, ledars   *n. pl.* leaders, chieftains 2654, 3784, 3832 [from LE(E)DE].

ledyng(e)   *vbl. n.* leadership 3536, 3880 [from LE(E)DE].

lee   *n.* cover, shelter 1446 [OE *hlēo*].

le(e)de   *v.* to lead, conduct, carry 154, 241 (*with pron. obj. unexpressed*); **ledes, ledez, ledys** *3 sg.* 403, 1767, 3766; **ledys** *3 pl.* 233; **lede, ledd(e)** *pa. t.* 1515, 2293, 2832, 3380, etc.; **lede, ledd(e)** *pp.* 854, 874 (*with pron. obj. unexpressed*), 1827, 1903, 2998, etc.; treat, deal with 1268; **ledes** *3 pl.* 303 [OE *lǣdan*].

leefe.   See LEUE, n.

lefe, leefe, leue   *adj.* agreeable 350, 454, 1335, 2479; good 3093; *as n.* friend 1035; *compar. as adv.* **leuere** rather 872, 1344, 1573, 4159; *me ware leuer,* I would rather, I had rather 2648 [OE *lēof*].

lefe, lefede, lefte.   See LEUE, n. & v.²

lefte   *adj.* left 2000, 2560 [OE *left*].

lefull   *adj.* proper 130 [OE *lēafful*].

legemen.   See LIGEMANE.

legges   *n. pl.* legs 779 [ON *leggr*].

legyaunce, lygeaunce   *n.* loyalty, allegiance 244, 2594 [OF *lig(e)ance*].

legyon(e)s   *n. pl.* legions 605, 2000, 3784 [OF *legion*].

lele   *adj.* loyal, faithful 14, 420, 647, 1768, 1971, etc.; noble 2398, 3081 [OF *leal, leel*].

lelely, lel(l)y   *adv.* loyally, faithfully 672, 2328, 4149; carefully 1102; truly, actually 3084 [from prec.].

lemand(e)   *adj.* gleaming, shining 2462, 2463, 2672 [from OE *lēoma,* ray of light].

lemete   *pp.* delimited 457 [OF *limiter*].

lende   *v.* to tarry, remain, abide 1970; **lente** *pa. t.* lent, gave 2319 [OE *lendan*].

lendez   *n. pl.* loins 1047 [OE *lendenu*].

lene   *adj.* thin, wasted 3279; slim 3349 [OE *hlǣne*].

lenede   *pa. t. refl.* lay down, reclined 2703; **lenand(e)** *pres p.* leaning, reclining 2672; sprawling 1045 [OE *hleonian*].

lenge, lengen, lenghen   *v.* to stay, abide, tarry, delay, dwell 72, 128, 152, 349, 451, 996, 1588, etc.; **leng(g)es, lengez** *3 sg.* 129, 469, 476, 504, 693, etc.; **lenges, lengez** *3 pl.* 2670, 3209; **lengede** *pa. t.* 2612, 3285, 3505, etc.; *3 sg.* sits 1312; *3 sg.* lies 1219; *pa. t.* 2960; rested 3959; *3 sg.* belongs 1410, 2082; *3 pl.* 1479, 2190, 3057, 3130, 3584, etc.; *pa. t.* 1492, 1624, 1854, 2221, etc. lengthen 2845 [OE *lengan*].

lenge, lengere. See LONG(E).

lenghe *n.* height 1102; length 1126, 2532, 2823, 2874, 3254, etc. [OE *lengu*].

lenghen. See LENGE.

leppe *v.* to run, rush 2084; **lepys, leppyn** *3 pl.* leap 3696, 3697; **lepe** *pa. t.* 3427; **leppande** *pres. p.* 1460 [OE *hlēapan*].

lere *v.* to inform 1035 [OE *læran*].

lesyng *vbl. n.* loss 3079, 3721 [OE *-lēosan*, in compounds *belēosan, forlēosan,* etc.].

leskes *n. pl.* loins 1097, 3279 [of Scand. orig.; cf. MSw *liuske*].

lesse *n.* falsehood, deceit 139 [OE *lēas*].

lesse *adj.* less 1838; lesser 370 [OE *læssa*].

lesse *adv.* less 2300 [OE *læs*].

lesse *conj.* lest 2439 [OE *þe-læs-þe*].

lete, lette, lat(t), lat(t)e *v.* to let, allow 398, 420, 1139, 1189 (*with pron. obj. unexpressed*), 1321, 1733, 2694, etc; *lette hym,* may he 803; *lattes in sondre* (*with pron. obj. unexpressed*), disperses it 1819; **letande** *pres. p.* behaving, appearing 3831 [OE *lætan,* ON *láta*].

letherly. See LYTHERLY.

lette *n.* hindrance, obstacle 92, 458 [from next].

lett(e) *v.* to delay, detain 473, 2326; prevent, check 1269 (*future*); bar, impede 1972; quit, abandon, forsake 1721; forbear 4092; **let** *pa. t.* 3720 [OE *lettan*].

lett(e)res *n. pl.* letters, message 251, 505, 570, 2328 [OF *lettre*].

lettyng *vbl. n.* hindrance 371 [from LETT(E), *v.*]

leuetenaunte *n.* deputy 646 [OF *lieu,* place + *tenant,* holding].

leue, lefe, leefe *n.* leave, permission 370, 2082, 2321, 3432; *take leue, askes lefe,* etc., take(s) leave, depart(s) 72, 241, 349, 421, 693, 713, etc. [OE *lēafe*].

leue *v.*[1] to believe 702, 1097, 3287; **leues** *2 sg.* 2593 [OE *gelēfan*].

leue, lefe *v.*[2] to leave 429, 1340, 2850; **lefte, leuede** *pa. t.* 1432, 1516; **lefte, lefede, leued(e), leuyde** *pp.* left 394, 438, 517, 702, 848, 978, etc.; **leuyde** *pa. t.* gave up 4223; *pp.* given up 875, 3360, 3703; leave off 3063, 3980; **leues** *3 pl.* remain, stay 694; *pp.* 1177 [OE *læfan*].

leue. See LEFE.

leuenyng *n.* lightning 2463 [obscure].

leuere. See LEFE.

leueré *n.* lodgings, quarters 241, 3078 [AF *liveré*].

leues *n. pl.* leaves 1708 [OE *lēaf*].

leuez. See LIFE, v.

lyarde *adj.* gray 2542, 3280 [OF *liart*].

licence, lycence *n.* authority 997; permit to depart 457; *within thy lycence,* within the boundaries of your permit 474 [OF *licence*].

lye, lygge *v.* to lie, recline 3081, 3823; **lys, lygges, lyggez** *3 sg.* 805, 1060, 1834, 2293, etc.; **lyes, ligges, lyggez, lyggys,** etc. *3 pl.* 1372, 1380, 2295, 3040, etc.; *lye by,* lie with, have sexual relations with 855; *3 pl.* depend 459, 1184, 1773, 2108, 3927, etc. [OE *licgan,* ON *liggja*].

liege *adj.* sovereign 1220 [OF *l(i)ege*].

lyfe, lyffe, liffe, lyefe, lyue *n.* life 154, 459, 855, 875, etc.; **lyfez, lyvys, lyues** *pl.* 95, 1217, 2276;

appon liffe, on(e) lyfe, alive 430, 2311, 4146 [OE *līf*]. See PAYNE, BRYNG(E), FELL, V.

life, liffe, lyffe, lyf(e)   *v.* to live 1036, 1597, 1903, 3880, etc.; **lyffes, leuez** *3 sg.* 405, 537, 1731, 2326, etc.; **lyf(f)ede** *pa. t.* 3877, 3961; **lyffede, lyffyde** *pp.* 252, 868, 3387 [OE *libban*].

lifeliche   *adj.* strong 3427 [OE *līflic*].

lyfte   *n.* sky, heavens 4272 [OE *lyft*].

lifte, lyfte   *pa. t.* lifted, held up 1046, 3349 [ON *lyfta*].

lyfetym   *n.* lifetime 4159 [LYFE + TYM(E)].

lygeaunce.   See LEGYAUNCE.

ligemane, lygmane   *n.* vassal 420, 3080; **legemen, ligemen(e), ligge- men, lyggemen** *pl.* 605, 647, 694, 1518, 1768, 1901, etc. [OF *l(i)ege,* adj. + MAN].

lygge, lygges,   etc. See LYE.

liggemen, lyggemen.   See LIGEMANE.

lygham   *n.* body 3281, 3286; **lighames** pl. 4269 [OE *līchama*].

lyghte   *n.* light, daylight 486, 751, 2561, 3594 [OE *lēoht, līht*].

lyghte   *v. trans.* to lighten, make light 2846; **lyghttys** *3 pl.* 251; *intr.* **lyghttys** *3 sg.* grows light 368; **lyghttes** *3 sg.* lights, alights, dismounts 2441, 2693, 4058, etc.; **lyghttez** *3 pl.* 933, 2753; **lyghte** *pa. t.* 3594; **lyghttede** *pp.* 1782; *pa. t.* fell 3848; *lyghte lawe,* be brought down 1270; **lyghten- ande** *pres. p.* glittering, gleaming 2463 [OE *līhtan*].

lyghte   *adj.* clear, sparkling 2280 [OE *lēoht*].

lightly   *adv.* quickly, swiftly, sud- denly 3287, 3349 [OE *lēohtlīce*].

like   *adj.* like 3954, 4190 [OE *gelīc*].

lyke   *v. (usually impers.)* to please, delight, seem suitable *3 sg. subj.* 1581, 2651, 3401, etc.; **lykes, likez, lykez, lykys** *3 sg.* 32, 55, 69, 97, 107, etc.; **lykede, lykyde, lykid** *pa. t.* 267, 599, 1438, 1817, etc.; *as hym lykes, lykez,* to his delight 621; accord- ing to His will 671, 1278, 1561; *3 sg.* is proper to, befits 140, 803; *pa. t.* 84; be pleased 195; *3 sg.* likes, is pleased by 186, 2524; *pa. t.* 1448; **lykand(e)** *pres. p.* pleasant, agreeable 248, 498, 2406, 2677, 3109 [OE *līcian*].

likyng, lykyng   *vbl. n.* desire, wishes, pleasure, delight 130, 2673, 3095, 3381, etc.; *lykyng of lyfe,* pleasure in life, life's joy 701 [from prec.].

lykkyde   *pa. t.* licked 3234 [OE *liccian*].

lym(e), lymme   *n.* limb, leg 459, 1046, 1097; *fig.* safety 2318, 2321 [OE *lim*]. See PAYNE.

lympe   *v. intr.* happen, occur 1643; *trans.* **lymppen** *3 pl.* incur, suffer, meet with 3119; **lymppede, lympyde** *pa. t.* 292, 3415; **lymppyde** *pp.* 875 [OE *limpan*].

lynd(e)   *n.* linden tree 454, 486 [OE *lind*].

lynkwhyttez   *n. pl.* linnets 2674 [OE *līnetwīge*].

lyon(e)   *n.* lion 119, 139, 3831, 3881, etc.; **lyon(e)s, lyonez, lyouns** *pl.* 3234; (heraldic em- blems) 1818, 4183, 4190 [OF *lion*].

lyppe   *n.* lip 119; **lippis, lippys, lyppez, lyppys** *pl.* lips, mouth 772, 780, 1011, 1018, 1088, etc. [OE *lippa*].

lire, lyre   *n.*[1] face, complexion 3954, 4272 [OE *hlēor*].

lire   *n.*[2] flesh 3281 (*see note*) [OE *līra*].

liste   *n.* desire, longing 12 [ON *lyst*].

liste   *pa. t.* desired 4270 [OE *lystan*].

lysten   *v.* to hear 2532; lystynnys *imper. pl.* listen to, hearken to 371 [OE *hlysnan,* with infl. of *hlystan*].

lyth   *v.* to hearken, listen 12; lythes *3 pl.* 1810 [ON *hlýþa*].

lythe   *adj.* gentle, mild 1517, 1600 [OE *līþe*].

lytherly, letherly   *adv.* wickedly, viciously 1268; badly, miserably 1448 [OE *lȳþerlīce*].

lythes   *n. pl.* people 994 (*see note*) [ON *lýþir*].

lythyre   *adj.* wicked, evil 23 [OE *lȳþre*].

lytte   *n.* delay 550 (*see note*) [from ON *hlīta,* v.].

lyttill, lityll, littill, littyll   *adj.* little 448, 3278; *adv.* little 269, 994, 1021, 1029; *at(t) lyttill,* little 686, 2938; *n.* little 1719, 2728; *a littyll, a lyttill,* little, a little, somewhat, for a while 265, 378, 754, 758, 1116, 1423, etc. [OE *lȳtel,* adj. & n.].

lyue, lyues,   etc. See LYFE, n.

lyuer(e)   *n.* liver 2168, 2561, [OE *lifer*].

lywynge   *vbl. n.* living, manner of life 5 [LIFE, v.].

lofte: *on lofte,* prevailing 163; up, aloft, above, on high 942, 1197, 1459, 2331, etc.; atop (a horse) 916; *vpone, appon lofte,* through the air 2800; aloft 3623, 3696 [ON *loft*].

loge, lugge   *v.* to lodge, stay, rest 152, 421, 454; lugez *3 pl.* 2280;

luggede *pa. t.* 486; lugand *pres. p.* reposing, lolling 1045 (*see note*) [OF *logier*].

loyotour   *n.* ?embroidery [see Brock, Glossary, p. 174].

loke, luk(e)   *v.* to look, look about 135, 943, 1447 (*future*), 4050, etc.; lokes, lukes, lukez *3 sg.* 113, 943, 1084, 2430, etc.; lokede, lukede, lukyd *pa. t.* 138, 195, 1313, 4269; lukand *pres. p.* 3108; *3 sg.* stares, glares 4051; *pa. t.* 119; lokkes, etc. *3 sg.* appears 778, 1101; see to it, take care that 654, 663, 672, 675, etc.; lokez, lokis *imper. pl.* 1640, 4016; *lukkez to,* rely on 751; *lokes into,* look after, keep watch on 3585; *loke of,* look after 3722 [OE *lōcian*].

lokerde   *adj.* snarled 779 [ON *lokkr,* n.].

lokkes, lakes   *n. pl.* locks of hair 2149 (*see note*), 3280, 3630 [OE *loc*].

londe, londes, londis,   etc. See LANDE, n. & v.

long(e), lang(e), lenge   *adj.* long 252, 1269, 2226, 2542, etc. *as n. on lang(e),* at length, full length 1045, 2703; *at lenge,* along, all the distance 1903; langere *compar.* 550; tall 1103; *adv.* long, a long time 868, 1200, 3160, 3967; langere, lengere, lengare *compar.* 587, 693, 736, 889, 1055, etc.; earlier, some time ago 1840 [OE *lang, long, lengra*].

longes, longede,   etc. See LANGE.

loo   *interj.* lo! 974, 1349 [OE *lā*].

loos   *n.* praise, fame, good name 254, 474 [OF *los*].

lorayne   *n.* harness, trappings 1460 (*see note*); loraynes *pl.* 2462 [OF *lorain*].

lordchipe, lordechipe   *n.* domain,

estate, manor 460, 2399; **lord-chippes, lordcheppez, lord-chippez,** etc. *pl.* 253, 1727, 1970, 3293, 3387; authority, dominion 2319, 3536, 4276; **lordchipez, lordchips** *pl.* 646, 4288 [OE *hlāfordscipe*].

lorde, Lorde, louerde   *n.* lord, noble 72, 1282, 2074; **lordez, lordys,** etc. *pl.* 60, 152, 156, 220, etc.; (in polite address) 474; sovereign, master, ruler 23, 43, 65, 128, etc.; husband 700; God 255, 368, 813, 827, 1036, etc. [OE *hlāford*].

lordly(e), lordely(e), lordlyche, lord(e)liche   *adj.* noble 396, 1814, 1999, 2281, etc.; grand 1460; lordly, imperious 570, 2032, 3477; **lordlieste, lordlyeste** *superl.* most lordly 138, 3880; *adv.* in a lordly manner 1818, 2227, 2230, 2479, etc. [OE *hlāfordlic*].

lorne   *pp.* lost, ruined 1153 [OE *lēoran,* pp. *loren*].

losels   *n. pl.* good-for-nothings 252 [from *losen,* alt. pp. of OE *-lēosan*].

losse   *n.* loss 4051 [OE *los*].

los(s)e, lossen   *v.* to lose 1599, 2845, 3386; **loste** *pa. t.* 4270; **loste** *pp.* lost, destroyed 1518, 3287, 3293 [OE *losian*].

lotes.   See LATES.

lothely, latheliche, laythely   *adj.* loathsome, repulsive 778, 3234, 3279, 4302; hideous, gruesome 4166 [OE *lāþlic*].

lothelye   *adv.* hideously, dreadfully 2074, 3849 [OE *lāþlīce*].

lothen, lothyn   *adj.* rough, shaggy 778 (*see note*), 1097 [ON *loþinn*].

lott   *n.* lot 2082 [OE *hlot*].

loue, lufe, luffe   *n.* love 369, 3381;

for *Goddes lufe, for my lufe, for Cristez lufe, for Petyr luffe, for His lufe,* etc. for love of God, out of love for God, Christ, St. Peter, etc. 705, 1256, 1261, 1600, 2319, 4324, etc.; beloved 703 [OE *lufu*].

loue   *v.* to praise 369; **loued** *pp.* 4305 [OE *lofian*].

louede.   See LUFFE.

louely, lufly, lufliche   *adj.* fine, excellent 1459, 3623; lovely 2399 [OE *luflic*].

louelyly, louefly, luf(f)ly, luflye, lufflyche   *adv.* pleasantly, gladly, joyfully 248, 504, 2280, 2674, 3637, etc.; kindly, respectfully 2292, 3478 [OE *luflīce,* with infl. of prec.].

louerde.   See LORDE.

lowde   *adj.* loud 2531, 2673, 4269 [OE *hlūd*].

lowde, on(e) lowde   *adv.* loudly, aloud 124, 382, 858, 957, etc.; clearly 927 [OE *hlūde*].

lowe   *n.* flame 194 [ON *loge*].

lowe, lawe   *adj.* humble, lowly 154; low 1270, 4276; *on lawe, o lawe,* down, low down, on the ground 1517, 2281; shallow 3720, 3921; **laweste** *superl.* lowest 2431; *adv.* low down, on the ground 2672, 4093; all the way down 3253; softly 2677 [ON *lágr*]. See LYGHTE, V.

lowkkide   *pp.* locked 3953 [OE *lūcan*].

lowrande   *pres. p.* skulking 1446; mournful, forlorn 4338 [perh. from OE *lūrian*].

lowttes   *3 pl.* bow 505; **lowttede** *pa. t.* bowed to, paid obeisance to 2634, 3285, 3408 [OE *lūtan*].

lufe   *n.* rudder 744; the side of a ship toward the wind 750 [OF *lof*].

lufe, luffe.   See LOUE, n.

luffe *v.* to love, cherish, hold dear 1597; **luffes** *2 pl.* 12; **louede** *pa. t.* 14, 3292; **luffede** *pp.* 2866 [OE *lufian*].

lufly, lufliche,   etc. See LOUELY, LOUELYLY.

lugand.   See LOGE.

lugge, lugez.   See LOGE.

lughe.   See LAUGHE.

luyschen *3 pl.* rush, dash 1459; **luyschede** *pa. t.* 2226 [?echoic var. of LASSCHEN].

luke, lukes,   etc. See LOKE.

lukyng *vbl. n.* staring 129 [from LOKE].

lumpe *n.* throng, cluster of persons 1819, 2230; *in the lumppe,* in the mass, wholesale 1814 [obscure; rel. to ModDu *lomp,* rag, LG *lump,* coarse].

lunggez *n. pl.* lungs 2168 [OE *lungen*].

lurkede *pa. t.* hid, cowered 1446 [cf. Norw & Sw dial. *lurka*].

lussche *n.* stroke, blow 3848 [from LUYSCHEN].

lutterde *adj.* bowed, crooked 779 [unknown].

ma.   See MO.

mace *n.* mace, club 4210 [OF *mace*].

mache *n.* match 4070 [OE *gemacca*].

machede *adj.* matched, pitted against 1533, 2904 [from prec.].

ma dame *n.* madam 3057 [OF *ma dame*].

made *adj.* mad, distracted 4271 [OE *gemǣdd*].

mad(e).   See MAKE.

magestée.   See MAIESTÉE.

mayde, mayden, Mayden *n.* Maid (the Virgin Mary) 2872,

3648; maiden 3323; **maydens, maydyns, maydenys** *pl.* 3045, 3058, 3081, 3913 [OE *mægden*].

Maye *n.* the month of May 2371 [OF *mai*].

may(e) *v.* may, can, could 6, 323, 370, 387, 472, 516, etc.; **mowe** *3 sg.* may 3812; should 958; *periphr. subj.* 358; **might, myght(e)** *pa. t.* might, could 63, 195, 230, 270, 703, 4310 (*with v.* go *unexpressed*) [OE *magan, mæg, mihte*].

mailes, mayles, maylez, maylis, etc. *n. pl.* links of chain mail, mail 616, 769, 904, 1487, 1764, etc. [OF *maille*].

mayne: *with mayne,* with (all his) strength 4326 [OE *mægen*].

mayne, man *adj.* vast, wide, great 434, 4071; principal, most important 427 [from prec., with infl. from ON *megn,* adj.].

maynoyrede *pp.* worked over, tilled 2507 [OF *manovrer, mainoverer*].

mayntene *v.* to support, uphold 399; **mayntenyde** *pp.* 4278 [OF *maintenir*].

mayster *n.* master, chief, leader 4279; **maisters** *poss.* 2870; **maysters** *pl.* 3652; *maister man, mayster mane,* chief, leader, lord 938, 990 [OE *mægester,* OF *maistre*].

maisterede *pa. t.* overcame, defeated 2683 [OF *maistrier*].

maysterfull *adj.* powerful 3413 [MAYSTER + OE *-ful(l)*].

maiestée, magestée *n.* sovereignty, power 1236, 1313 [OF *majesté*].

make *v.* to make, do, create, perform, build 296, 308, 347, 379, 386, etc.; **mase** *3 sg.* 960; **mad(e)** *pa. t.* 50, 77, 83, 3385, etc.;

mad(e) *pp.* 812, 1066, 1304, etc.;
pa. t. made up 2884; *pp.* 3572;
make the somouns, serve thee
summons 91; *mad fewtée,* swore
fealty 112; *made joye,* rejoiced
1161; *made sorowe,* sorrowed
1437; *mad . . . manace,* men-
aced 3383; appoint 649; *pa. t.*
3132; *pp.* 709 [OE *macian*]. See
ROWT(T)(E).

makk *n.* fellow 1166 [OE *gemaca,*
ON *maki*].

malyncoly, malycoly *n.* fury 2204
(*see note*); 4209 [OF *melan-
colie*].

malle *v.* to strike, batter, smite
3038, 4037; **melles, mallis** *3 sg.*
2950, 3841; **mellyd** *pp.* battered
4210 (*see note*) [from OF *mal,
maul,* mace].

maluesye *n.* malmsey 236 [OF
malvasia].

man, mane *n.* man, one, person
129, 260, 1382, 2022, etc.; (in
direct address) 1314; **manys,
manns** *poss.* 76, 1046, 1210;
men(n), mene *pl.* 21, 157, 167,
178, 273, 2561 (redundant);
men *uninfl. poss.* 3429; *mane of
armes,* fighting man 3414; *men of
armes, armez,* men-at-arms,
fighting men 273, 364, 563,
1537, 1589, etc. [OE *man(n)*].

man. See MAYNE, adj.

manace *n.* menace, threat 426
[OF *menace*].

manacede *pa. t.* threatened 1383
[OF *menac(i)er*].

manere *n.* manor 4310 [OF
manoir].

manere: *on his manere,* in his
characteristic way, as is his wont
1383 [AF *manere*].

manhede *n.* dignity, standing 399,
434, 4278 [MAN + OE *-hǣde*].

many(e), mony *adj.* (*often after
n.*) many 22, 27, 253, 394, 517,
etc.; many a 252, 442, 1187,
1793, 1820, etc.; *n.* many 1357,
1467, 1669, etc. [OE *manig*].

manykyn *adj.* many sorts of, all
kinds of 3174 [prec. + OE
cynn].

manly, manliche *adj.* courageous,
valiant 2417, 4279; *adv.* courageously 4320 [MAN + OE *-līc,
-līce*].

manrede *n.* dependence 127 [OE
manrǣden].

marasse, marras, marrasse *n.*
marsh, swampland 1524, 2014,
2505 [OF *marais*].

marche *n.* frontier, boundary,
borderland, shore, edge 318,
1388, 2417; **marches, marchez,
marchys, merkes** *pl.* 344, 436,
461, 1147, etc. [OE *mearc*].

Marches *n.* Marquis *2950*
[OF *marchis*].

marchez-men *n. pl.* men of the
borderlands 1237 [MARCHE +
MAN].

mariners, marynerse *n. pl.* seamen, mariners 633, 3652 [OF
marin(i)er].

marre *v.* to harm, injure 2015;
merred(e), merride *pp.* 1238,
3555; *pp.* scarred, weakened
4220; *pp.* ruined, brought down
3322 [OE *merran*].

marschall *n.* marshal, high officer
of state 1233, 1235 [OF
mareschal].

Martynmesse *n.* the feast of St.
Martin, November 11, 3145
[*Martin* + OE *mæsse*].

martyre *n.* martyr 1221; **marters**
pl. 1066 [OE *martyr(e)*].

martyre *v.* to martyr, slaughter
560 [from prec.].

mase. See MAKE.

masondewes *n. pl.* hospitals or poorhouses 3038 [OF *meson-Dieu, maison-Dieu*].

mastes, mastez, mastys *n. pl.* masts 738, 3668, 3676 [OE *mæst*].

matyns *n. pl.* matins 4333 [OF *matines*].

mauger *n.* despite, displeasure 1588; *prep. mawgrée his eghne, maugrée theire eghne,* in spite of his (their) resistance, notwithstanding anything that he (they) may do 426, 1238 [OF *maugré*].

maundement *n.* command, order 1587 [OF *mandement*].

mawen *pp.* mown 2507 [OE *māwan*].

mawgrée. See MAUGER.

mawntelet *n.* a short cloak or mantle 3632 [OF *mantelet*].

me. See I.

mede *n.*[1] reward 1068; salvation 666, 3455, 4018 [OE *mēd*].

mede *n.*[2] plain, meadow 1290, 2506, 2671, 3465 [OE *mǣd*].

medill *n.* middle (of a person), waist 2205; **medills** *pl.* 4168 [OE *middel*].

medillerthe *n.* earth 2951, 3239 [after OE *middaneard,* with substitution of prec. for *middan-,* ERTH(E) for *eard*].

medil(l)warde, medylwarde *n.* the middle body of an army 1988, 2904, 3766, 4076, 4173 [MEDILL + -*warde,* after RERE-WARDE, AVANTTWARDE].

medowe *n.* meadow 3238 [OE *mǣdwe,* oblique case of *mǣd*].

meke *adj.* gentle, courteous, kind 3056; **mekely** *adv.* meekly, submissively 3145, 3455 [ON *miúkr*].

mekill, mekyll. See MYCHE.

meles, melis, melys *3 sg.* speaks, speaks to, talks 382, 679, 1781, 2872, 3056, etc.; **melys** *3 pl.* 2871; *meles with mouthe,* speaks directly to, speaks face to face with 1987 [OE *mǣlan*].

melion *n.* million 3244 [OF *million*].

mell(e), mele *v.* to mingle in combat 4071; **mellis, mellys** *3 pl.* 2904, 4173; to deal, treat, negotiate 938, 990; *3 pl.* get busy, occupy themselves 3652 [OF *me(s)ler*].

melles, mellyd. See MALLE.

melodye *n.* melody, song 242, 3174 [OF *melodie*].

men. See MAN.

mendement(e) *n.* relief, deliverance 989, 1236 [OF *amendement*].

mendynauntez *n. pl.* mendicants 667 [OF *mendinant*].

mene *v.* to remember, think on 2869; speak, tell 3556; **menys** *3 sg.* 3478, 3653; **menes** *3 sg.* means, signifies 692; **ment** *pa. t.* 977; **menede** *pa. t.* sorrowed, grieved 891 [OE *mǣnan*].

menewhile *n.* meantime 1231 [OF *me(e)n* + WHILLE].

mengen *3 pl.* mingle 4173; **mengede** *pp.* linked, attached 3632 [OE *mengan*].

menske *n.* honor, courtesy, graciousness 126, 399, 433 [ON *mennska*].

menske *v.* to honor, grace, favor 3145; **menskes** *3 sg.* 2871; **menskes** *3 pl.* 1303; **menskede** *pp.* 4018 [from prec.].

mensk(e)fully *adv.* faithfully 631, 2322; solemnly 940, 1233; with propriety 1988, 4076 [from

MENSKE, n.].

mercy *n.* mercy, compassion 127, 977, 1235, 3455 [OF *merci*].

mereswyne *n.* sea hog, porpoise 1091 [OE *mereswīn*].

mery *adj.* happy, cheerful 260; **meriere** *compar.* 3175; **meryeste** *superl.* 3239 [OE *myrge*].

merily *adv.* cheerfully, happily 3653 [from prec.].

merke *v. intr.* to proceed, advance 351, 427, 1588; **merkes** *3 sg.* 2670, 3595, 3773, 4310, etc.; **merkes** *3 pl.* 3767; **merkede** *pa. t.* 3238, 3556; give heed or attention 4320; *trans.* mete out 1068; *3 sg.* strikes, hits 2206; *merken in sondire,* strike asunder 4168; **merked, merkyde** *pp.* created, made 952, 1304 [OE *mearcian*].

merkes. See MARCHE.

merred(e), merride. See MARRE.

meruaile, meruayle *n.* wonder, marvel 2682, 2905 [OF *merveille*].

meruailles *3 sg. refl.* wonders, marvels 1314 [OF *merveillier*].

mervaylous, meruailous, meruayl(l)ous, meruelyous *adj.* wonderful, wondrous 236, 260, 428, 769, 1534, etc.; astonishing, surprising 3383; awesome 3595; **meruelyousteste,** *superl.* most marvelous, most wondrous 129 [OF *merveillos* + superl. ending with intrusive *t*].

message *n.* message 2322 [OF *message*].

messenger, messangere *n.* envoy, ambassador, messenger 126, 989, 3903; **messangers, messangerez** *pl.* 1232, 1532 [OF *messagier,* with intrusive *n*].

messes *n. pl.* masses 4018, 4333

[OE *mæsse*].

Messie *n.* Messiah 3998 [OF *messie*].

mette *n.* meat, food 2491; **metes, metez** *pl.* 75, 223, 230, 1298, 1948, 3196 [OE *mēte*].

met(t)e *v.* to meet, encounter 434, 560, 631; **metes, metis, metys** *3 sg.* 2199, 2204, 2950, 4209, etc.; **metis, metys** *3 pl.* 3766, 4014; **mett** *pa. t.* experienced 3223; *pa. t.* struck, smote 3841 [OE *mētan*].

mette *pp.* measured 2343 [OE *metan*].

mettewhile *n.* short time, short while 3903 [OE *mæte* + WHILLE].

meue *v. intr.* to move, march, go forth 2001; **moues** *3 sg.* 3102, 3840; **mouede** *pa. t.* stirred up, excited, provoked, angered 3771; **mouede** *pp.* 1383, 1584, 4024; *trans.* **mofes** *3 sg.* controls 3323; *pa. t.* set in motion, started 699 [AF *moveir, mev-*].

my. See I.

myche, mekill, mekyll *adj.* great, much, many 1166, 1214, 1351, 1426, etc.; most high 1236; so much 2707; *adv.* much, greatly 711, 1068, 1314, 1382, 2205, etc. [OE *micel, mycel*].

myddaye *n.* midday 952, 976, 1231, etc. [OE *middæg*].

myddes, myddys *n.* center, middle part 1293, 2176, 2206; central part, main part 2207 [var. of *inmiddes* (from OE *in middan,* by anal. with *tō middes*)].

myde-schelde *n.* the middle part of the shield 3841 [OE *midd-* + SCHELDE].

mydnighte *n.* midnight 3222 [OE *midniht*].

mydwaye: *in the midwaye,* halfway 2682 [OE *midd-* + WAY(E)].

mydwynter *n.* midwinter 77 [OE *midwinter*].

myghte *n.* might, power, force 426, 1069, 1210, 1303, etc.; **myghttis** *pl.* 4070; *of myghte,* mighty 1382, 1621. [OE *miht*].

myghte. See MAY(E).

myghty, myghtty *adj.* mighty, great 2683, 3197, 4077, 4221, etc.; *as n.* 2205; *myghtty with Criste,* mighty in Christ 940; **myghtyeste** *superl.* 603, 3413 [OE *mihtig*].

myghtyly *adv.* powerfully 4210 [from prec.].

mylde *adj.* gentle, meek 3323; *as n.* 976; gracious, merciful 1211, 2871, 3197, 3998, 4041, etc. [OE *milde*].

myldly *adv.* gently, courteously 679, 3056 [OE *mildelīce,* adv.].

myle *n.* mile 2532; *uninfl. pl.* 448, 478, 601, 1040, etc. [OE *mīl*].

mylke-whitte *adj.* pure white, white as milk 2287 [OE *milc* + WHITTE].

mynde *n.* memory, remembrance 1221 [OE *mynd*].

myn(e). See I.

myn(e) *v.* to demolish (a wall or fort) by digging away the foundations 351, 428 [OF *miner*].

mynistre *n.* servant 1235 [OF *ministre*].

mynystre *v.* to dispense 666 [OF *ministrer*].

mynsteris *n. pl.* churches 3038 [OE *mynster*].

mynstralsy *n.* minstrelsy 242 [OF *menestralsie*].

myracle *n.* miracle 1211; **miraclez** *pl.* 899 [OF *miracle*].

myrthe *n.* sweetness (of sound) 242; happiness, joy 3197; **myrthes, myrthis** *pl.* joys 3174, 4270; **myrthez** *pl.* causes for rejoicing 1532 [OE *myrhþ*].

myscaryede. See MYSKARIES.

myschance *n.* calamity, disaster 3028 [OF *mesch(e)a(u)nce*].

myschefe *n.* misfortune, need 667, 3437 [OF *mesch(i)ef*].

misdoo *v.* to harm, injure, wrong 126 [OE *misdōn*].

mysebide *v.* to injure, harm 3083 [OE *misbēodan*].

mysese *adj. as n.* unfortunate 667 (*see note*) [OF *mesaise*].

myshappen *v.* to meet with misfortune, come to grief 3454; **myshappenede** *pa. t. impers.* (it) fell out badly 3767 [OE *mis-* + HAPPEN(E)].

myskaries *3 sg.* comes to harm or misfortune, meets with death 2872; **myscaryede, myskaryede** *pp.* 1237, 1778 [OF *meskarier*].

mysse *n.* offense, injury 1315, 3057 [OE *miss*].

myste *n.*[1] need 2001 [shortened form of *mister* (OF *mest(i)er*)].

myste *n.*[2] mist 2506 [OE *mist*].

myx *n.* excrement, offal 989 [from OE *mixen, myxen,* dunghill].

mo, moo, ma *adj.* more 844, 856, 885, 1829, etc. [OE *mā*].

mobles *n. pl.* possessions 666 [OF *mo(e)ble*].

mode *n.* mood, feelings 3222, 3382; mind, heart 3454 [OE *mōd*].

Modyr(e) *n.* Mother, the Virgin Mary 2, 1211, 1559, 4041 [OE *mōdor*].

mofes. See MEUE.

moyllez *n. pl.* mules 2287 [OF *mul(e)*].

molde: *on(e) molde,* on earth 129, 977, 4279; on the ground 4326; in the ground 952; to the earth 3322; *in moldez,* in earth (*pl. = sg.*) 975 [OE *molde*].

mon *v.* must 813, 1155, 2436; shall, will 2186, 2820 [ON *mun*].

monée *n.* money, payment 2343 [OF *moneie*].

monethe *n. uninfl. poss.* month's 318 [OE *monaþ*].

mony. See MANY(E).

monkes *n. pl.* monks 4013 [OE *munuc*].

montayngnes. See MOUNTAYNE.

monte, montes. See MOUNTE.

moo. See MO.

more *adj. compar.* more, further, greater 114, 225 (*see note*), 491, 539, 540, etc.; *adv.* more, further, greater 141, 312, 314, 406, etc.; **moste** *superl.* most, greatest 524, 1955, 1987, 2124, etc. [OE *māra, māst*].

morne, morwen *n.* morn, morning 1223, 2306, 3116 [OE *morgen,* dat. sg. *morne*].

morne-while *n.* morning 2001; the hours after midnight 3223 [prec. + WHILLE].

mornyng *n.* morning 2506 [MORNE + -*ing,* by anal. with *evening*].

morthires *2 sg.* murder, slay 1315; **mourtherys** *3 sg.* 4259; **morthirede** *pp.* 976 [OE *myrþrian*].

mosse *n.* marsh, swamp 2014, 2505 [OE *mōs*].

moste. See MORE, MOTT(E).

mott(e), mot(t) *pres. t.* may, could, might 2162, 4104; *in forming periphr. subj.* 136, 227, 346, 467, 1306, 3517, etc.; **moste** *pa. t.* had to, must 250,

263, 449, 451, 1039, etc. [OE *mōt, mōste*].

mountayne *n.* mountain 854, 2670; **mowntaynes, mowntaygnes, montayngnes** *pl.* 3238, 3595, 4259 [OF *montaigne*].

mounte, monte *n.* mount, mountain 938, 990, 1096, 1221, 1397, etc.; **mount(t)es, mount(t)ez, mowntes, montes,** etc. *pl.* 307, 427, 551, 560, etc. [OE *munt,* OF *mont*].

mountede *pa. t.* soared 769 [OF *monter, munter*].

mournande *pres. p.* grieving, lamenting 4333 [OE *murnan*].

mourtherys. See MORTHIRES.

mouthe. See MELES.

moues, mouede. See MEUE.

mowe. See MAY(E).

mowntay(g)nes. See MOUNTAYNE.

mowntes. See MOUNT.

multitude, multytude *n.* multitude 2015, 2905, 4071 [OF *multitude*].

muskadell *n.* muscatel 236 [OF *muscadel*].

na. See NO, adj. and adv.

nay *adv.* no 1718, 2265 [ON *nei*].

naye: *a naye,* an egg 3283 [OE *æg*].

naylis *n. pl.* nails 3428 [OE *næg(e)l*].

nakyde *adj.* naked, bare 2248; unarmed 2433 [OE *nacod*].

nakyn. See NOKYN.

name *n.* name, reputation 523, 2083, 2619, 2638 [OE *nama*].

namede *pa. t.* called, named 1394, 2658, 3439 [OE *nemnan*].

nan(e). See NO, adj.

nauyll *n.* navel 979 [OE *nafela*].

nawntere. See AUENTURE.

ne   *adv.* not (*before v.*) 230, 692, 797, 829, 830, etc.; *conj.* nor 151, 261, 314, 426, 541, etc.; *with* NEUER(E) 2117; *with* NOGHTE 706; *with* NOTHYRE 10; **ne . . . ne** neither . . . nor 108, 161, 229, 2266, 2367, etc. [OE *ne*].

nedes, nedez, nedys   *n. pl.* errands, business 85, 263, 470, 522, 529, 1329, etc.; *gose on þer nedes,* do this errand (*lit.* go on these errands) 1266 [OE *nēd*].

nedes   *adv.* of need, necessarily 451 [OE *nēdes,* adv. gen.].

nedyll   *n.* needle (of a compass) 753 [OE *nǣdl*].

neghe   *adv.* almost, very nearly 2658 [OE *nēh*].

neghe   *v.* to draw near, approach closely 2433 [from prec.].

neynesom.   See SOM(E).

neke-bone   *n.* neck bone 2771 [OE *hnecca* + *bān*].

nere   *adj.* close, familiar 689; *adv.* at close quarters 1176; near 4105; nearly 805, 1127, 1135 [OE *nēr,* compar. of *nēh*].

nese   *n.* nose 2248 [orig. & rel. to OE *nosu* obscure; rel. to MDu & MLG *nese*].

neuer(e)   *adv.* never 76, 143, 183, 190, etc. [OE *nǣfre*].

neuewe   *n.* nephew 689 [OF *neveu*].

newe   *adj.* new 1815, 1829 [OE *nēowe*].

newe-made   *adj.* newly made 1809 [from OE *nēowe,* adv. + MAKE].

Newʒers Daye, Newʒere Daye, Newe ʒere   *n.* New Year's Day 78, 90, 522 [NEWE + ʒERE + DAY(E)].

nextte: *at the nextte,* directly, straightway 2422 [OE *nēxt,* superl. of *nēh*].

nyghes   *2 sg.* fall, get down, sink down 451 (*see note*) [OE *hnīgan*].

nyghte   *n.* night 451, 753, 754, 3065, etc. [OE *niht*].

nyghtgale   *n. uninfl. poss.* nightingale's 929 [OE *nihtegale*].

nynne   *n.* nine 3439 [OE *nigon*].

no, noo, non(e), nonne, na, nan(e)   *adj.* no 72, 89, 92, 126, 150, etc.; *double neg.* 76, 515, 542, 1169, etc.; *pron.* none, nothing, no one 406, 657, 982, 1217, 1562, etc. [OE *nān*].

no, na   *adv.* no 261, 312, 314, 403, etc. [OE *nā*].

noblay(e)   *n.* glory, splendor 76; royal garb 2433 [OF *noblei*].

noble(e), nobill, nobyll   *adj.* noble 18, 68, 125, 145, etc.; *as n.* 523; great 41, 512, 2394, etc.; splendid, fine, glorious 16, 180, 242, 259, 297, 348, etc.; **nobileste** *superl.* noblest 3439, 3935; **nobilly** *adv.* nobly, splendidly 1815 [OF *noble*].

noght(e)   *n.* nothing 223, 708, 1191, 1317, etc. [OE *nāht, nōht*].

noghte   *adv.* not, not at all, in no way 135, 270, 419, 449, 466, etc. [OE *nāht, nōht*].

noyes   *3 sg.* disturbs, troubles, grieves 1816, 2248 [OF *noire*].

noisez   *n. pl.* sounds 929 [OF *noise*].

nokyn, nakyn, nokins   *adj.* no sort of, not any 430, 2350 [NO, adj. + KYNE].

nombird, nowmberde   *pp.* numbered 2658, 2887 [OF *nombrer*].

nombyre, nowmbre, nowmbyre, nowmer   *n.* number 602, 884, 2831, 2884, etc.; **nowmbirs, nommers** *pl.* 591, 3935 [OF *nombre*].

nom(m)en   *pp.* taken, captured

1437, 1868, 1872, 1905, 2477, etc. [OE *niman*].

non(e). See NO, adj.

none *n.* noon, midday 78, 3176. [OE *nōn*].

nones *n. pl.* nuns 3539 [OE *nunne*].

nonis, nonys: *for þe nonis, for þe nonys,* for the nonce, indeed 1927, 3297 [OE *for þan ānum*].

nonne, noo. See NO, adj.

not. See WYT.

notaries *n. pl. poss.* notaries' 90 [L *notārius*].

notes, notez *n. pl.* notes, music 929, 1758, 2677, 4333 [OF *note*].

notez *3 pl.* employ, make use of 1815 [OE *notian*].

nothyng *n. as adv.* not a bit, not at all 2442 [OE *nā(n)þing*].

nothyre, noþer, nowthire *adv.* (*reinf. neg.*) neither, no more so 429, 2367; *conj. nothyre . . . ne, nowthire . . . ne,* neither . . . nor 10, 161 [OE *nawþer, naþer*].

notifiede *pa. t.* made known, announced 522 [OF *notifier*].

notte *n.* piece of work, matter, affair, business 1816 [OE *notu*].

now *adv.* newly, freshly 952 [OE *nēowe*].

now(e) *interj.* (as an introduction to solemn or religious verse) lo 1; *adv.* now 25, 90, 166, 257, 321, etc. [OE *nū*].

nowen. See OWNN.

nowmer, nowmbre, nowmberde, etc. See NOMBIRD, NOMBYRE.

nowthire. See NOTHYRE.

nurrée *n.* foster child, nursling 689 [OF *nurri*].

o. See OF(E), prep., ON(E), FERYN(N)E.

o *interj.* oh 3636, 3989 [natural interj.].

Occedente *n.* West, Western Europe 2360 [OF *occident*].

occyane *n.* ocean, the Atlantic 31 [OF *océan*].

oches *3 sg.* slices, cuts 2565; **ochen** *3 pl.* 3675; **ochede** *pa. t.* 4245 [OF *ocher*].

ocupies, ocupyes *2 sg.* occupy, hold 98; *3 sg.* 359, 643, 1308, 2360; *3 pl.* 577, 1663; **ocupyede** *pa. t.* 278 [OF *occuper* (source of *i* unknown)].

of(e) *adv.* off 328, 901, 1023, 1178, etc. [OE *of*].

of(e), off(e), oo, o *prep.* of 13, 17, 18, 21, etc.; for 249, 298, 300, 369, etc.; as 1691; from 194, 256, 271, 274, etc.; away from 718; at 302, 636, 1077, etc.; in 19, 180, 401, 536, etc.; on 1634; by, through 33, 516, 651, 843, etc.; over 2093; with 79, 193, 230, 444, etc.; as regards 913; concerning 948; *equiv. of gen.* 1, 2, 126, 137, etc.; *partitive* from, among, some of, some 281, 316, 333, 471, 523, etc. [OE *of*]. See BECAUSE, HAND(E), KYND(E), n., OLDE, n., SERUE, SUYT(T)E, WAY(E).

offende *v.* to offend 2412 [OF *offendre*].

offyce *n.* service, duty 691 [OF *office*].

offycers *n. pl.* officeholders, ministers 661 [AF *officer*].

offyre *v. intr.* to make an offering to God or to a saint 939 [OF *offrir*].

ofte, often *adv.* often 1697, 4274; repeatedly, continually 1779, 3155, 3290 [OE *oft* (in *often* with ending in imitation of inflexional *en*].

oghte　*n.* anything 1014, 1269
2802, 3248 [OE *a(wi)ht,
o(wi)ht*].

oken　*adj.* oak, oaken 2722 [OE
āc + *-en*].

olde, alde　*n.* former times, ancient
times 99, 689; *of olde,* since old
times 1348 [OE *ald*].

olde, alde　*adj.* old 986, 2829;
eldare *compar.* 4151; **eldeste**
superl. 2606, 3064; ancient,
past, former 13; *superl.* most
ancient 3408 [OE *ald, ieldra,
ieldest*].

olfendes　*n. pl.* camels 2288 (*see
note*) [OE *olfend*].

olyfaunte　*n.* elephant 2339;
olyfa(u)ntez *pl.* 1286 (*see note*),
2288 [OF *olifant*].

o lyfe.　See BRYNG(E), FELL, *v.*

on(e), o　*prep.* on 62, 70, 78, 92,
116, etc.; in 74, 392, 448, 656,
etc.; at 451, 2430; to 915, 1804,
2156; after 2260 [OE *on*]. See
LOFTE, LONG(E), LOWDE, adv.,
LOWE, adj., RAWE, SLANTE, PAYNE.

one, ane　*adj. & pron.* one (person) 861, 988, 1942, 1944, etc.;
a certain 2952, 2970; one hour
3222 [OE *ān*].

one　*adj.* alone, only 442, 597,
826, 937, 967, 1044, etc.; *þe
tone,* one, the one 3282 (*see
note*); *myn one, by myne one,*
(by) me alone, all (by) myself
704, 3230; none else but me
3578; *myselfe one,* myself alone
4035; *thyn one,* thee alone, by
thyself 466, 3479; *hym on(e),*
alone, him alone, by himself 81,
947, 1310, 1793, 2338, etc.; *be
oure one,* by ourselves, one to
one 1345; *be þam one, by them
one,* by themselves 3195 [OE
āna].

ones, onez, anes　*adv.* once, just
once 135, 326, 2818, 4191; ever
468; once and for all 298, 331,
345, 1274, 1320, etc.; *at(t)
ones, at(t) onez,* at the same
time, together, all together, as
one 179, 281, 592, 609, 755,
789, etc.; at one stroke 2254; at
once, right away, suddenly,
directly 492, 581, 1126, etc.
[OE *ānes*].

one-seeande　*pres. p.* looking (*in
absolute phrase with subj. following*) 525 [OE *on-* + SE(E), V.].

onon(e).　See ANON.

oo.　See OF(E), prep.

opyn.　See WYDE.

opynly　*adv.* plainly, clearly 828
[OE *openlīce*].

or, ore, are　*conj.* or 12, 110, 215,
295, 340, etc.; (*connecting two
words denoting the same thing*)
that is to say 860 [reduced from
oÞER].

or.　See AR(E).

ordayne　*v.* to appoint 661;
ordand *pp.* 1621; **ordaynede**
pa. t. drew up in order for battle
1991 [AF *ordeiner*].

ore.　See OR.

orfrayes, orfraeez　*n.* gold em-
broidery, ornamental work 902,
2142 [OF *orfreis*].

orrible.　See HORREBLE.

osay　*n.* a sweet wine from Alsace
202 [OF *aussay*].

ostage　*coll. n.* hostages 3187,
3205, 3208, 3589 [OF
(*h*)*ostage*].

ostayande.　See HOSTAYE.

oste:　*in oste holden,* given lodging
166 [OF (*h*)*osté*].

oste, ostes,　etc. See HOSTE.

oÞer, othir(e)　*adj. & pron.* other,
the other 224, 279, 289, 400,

732, 1869, etc.; *uninfl. pl.* others, all, the rest, all the others 45, 67, 146, 202, 238, etc.; more 778, 4219 [OE *oþer*].

oþer, owþer, owthire   *conj.* either 110; *or . . . owthire, or . . . oþer,* either . . . or, or . . . or 964, 2413, 3982 [OE *ō(w)þer*].

oþerwhile   *adv.* other times, sometimes 1145 [OE *ōþerhwīle*].

oundyde, ownd   *adj.* wavy, rippled 193, 765 [OF *ondé*].

our(e), our(e)s,   etc. See WE.

oute, owt(e), owtt(e)   *adv.* out 9, 480, 607, 701, 762, etc.; abroad 617; forth 1685; *owte ouer, owtt ouere,* outside, over, above 903, 2339; *owt(t)(e) of,* outside 996; from 3547, 3574, 4030; down from 1164, 3014 [OE *ūt*].

ouercharggede   *pp.* overborne by superior force, overrun 1749 [OE *ofer-* + OF *charg(i)er*].

ouer(e), oure, ower   *prep.* over, above, across 105, 289, 307, 427, 446, etc.; on 594 [OE *ofer*]. See OUTE, ALL.

ouergylte   *pp.* gilded, overlaid 207 [OE *ofergyldan*].

ouerhande   *n.* mastery 4300 [OE *ofer,* adj. + HAND(E)].

ouerkeste   *pa. t.* overturned, turned over 3932 [OE *ofer-* + CASTE].

ouerlaide   *pp.* covered, decked all over 3253 [OE *oferlecgan*].

ouerlyng(e)   *n.* overlord 289, 520, 710, 2602, etc. [OE *ofer* adv. + -*ling*].

ouerrane   *pa. t.* overran, overwhelmed 2035; ouerronne *pp.* 1206 [OE *ofer-* + RYN(E)].

ouerreche   *v.* to reach or get at (over an intervening space) 1508; ouerrechez *3 pl.* overhang 921 [OE *ofer-* + *rǣcan*].

ouerrydez   *3 pl.* trample, ride over (the fallen) 1430; ouerredyn *pp.* 1415, 1524 [OE *oferrīdan*].

ouersette   *pp.* overthrown, overcome 111, 2815, 4136 [OE *ofersettan*].

ouerswyngen   *3 pl.* strike down 1466 [OE *oferswingan*].

ouertake   *v.* to get at, reach, get hold of 3741 [OE *ofer-* + TAK(E)].

ouerwhelme   *v.* to overturn, overthrow 3261 [OE *ofer-* + OE **hwelman,* to roll].

ovyrefallys   *3 pl.* fall upon 3677; ouerfallen *pp.* overthrown 1154 [OE *oferfeallan*].

ower.   See OUER.

ownd.   See OUNDYDE.

ownn, awen   *adj. & pron.* own 171, 709, 1594, 1841, etc.; *in his awen,* on his own, to himself 997, 2389, 3092; *thy nowen,* thine own 1806 [OE *āgen*]. See HOLDE.

owre, owr(e)s.   See WE.

owre,   *n.* hour 3380; hourez, howres pl. 1031, 2709 [OF *(h)ore, (h)ure*].

owte iles, owte ilez, owtt illes   *n. pl.* outlying islands 575, 2359; the Hebrides 30 [OUTE + OF *i(s)le*].

owte landes, owte londes, owt londys   *n. pl.* outlying lands, foreign lands 2607, 2723, 3697 [OE *ūtland*].

owte mowntes   *n. pl.* outlying mountains, distant mountains 3909 [OUTE + MOUNTE].

owþer, owthire.   See OþER, adj. & pron., conj.

owtlawede   *pp.* outlawed, exiled, renegade 3534, 3780 [late OE *ūtlagian*].

owttray(e)   *v.* to overcome, over-

throw, crush 642, 2244;
owt(t)(e)rayede *pp.* 1952, 2617, 2840, 2848; outrage, injure, abuse 1010, 1328 [AF *outreyer*].

pacokes *n. pl.* peacocks 182 [OE *pēa, pāwa,* peafowl + *cocc*].

paye *v.* to please, appease, pacify 4049; **payes** *3 sg. impers.* 2646; **payede** *pp.* 230; *pp.* paid 1550 [OF *payer*].

paygaynys *n. pl.* pagans 4046 [L *pāgānus*].

payne, peyne *n.* penalty, punishment, pain 2329; **paynes, paynez** *pl.* 1546, 1632, 3498; *o payne,* under threat of penalty 1612; *in payne of ʒour lyvys, o peyne of ʒour lyfez, of payne of lyf and lym,* under threat of death, on pain of death 95, 1217, 3079 [OF *peine*].

paynyme *n.* paynim, pagan 1377; **paynym(e)s** *pl.* 2786, 2835, 3533, 4125, etc. [OF *pai(e)nime*].

payntede *pp.* painted, colored 3607, 3625 [OF *peindre*].

payses *3 pl.* poise, load 3037; **paysede** *pa. t.* bore down by impact 3042 [OF *peiser*].

payvese *n. pl.* large shields 3625 [OF *pavais*].

palaisez *n. pl.* palisades 1287 (*see note*) [OF *paleis*].

pales, palez, palesse *n.* palace 503, 636, 718, 3913 [OF *palais, paleis*].

palfray *n.* palfrey, steed 717; **palfrayes** *pl.* 3143 [OF *palefrei*].

palyd *pp.* enclosed with pales, encircled 1287; adorned with vertical stripes (heraldry) 1375 [OF *paler*].

pall(e) *n.* fine cloth, scarlet cloth 1288 [OE *pæll*].

palme *n.* a branch or sprig of the palm tree, carried by pilgrims 3475 [OE *palm*].

pape. See POPE.

Paradys(e), paradice *n.* Paradise, Heaven 3365; the earthly paradise 2039, 2706 [OF *paradis*].

pardone *n.* pardon 3497 [OF *pardon*].

pare *v.* to injure, damage 4047 (*see note*) [OF *empeirer, ampeirer*].

parlement *n.* council 146, 416, 636 [OF *parlement*].

parte *n.* portion, share 1217, 1341, 2039 [OE *part*].

parte *v. intr.* part, separate 7 [OF *partir*].

party *n.* part 212; **partyes** *pl.* companies of persons 1584, 1925; *pl.* areas, quarters 2596 [OF *partie*].

pas *n.* pace 3496 [OF *pas*].

passage *n.* departure, flight 1522 [OF *passage*].

passande *adj.* passant, walking and looking toward the dexter side, with the dexter forepaw raised (heraldry) 4184 [OF *passant*].

passe *v. intr.* to pass, go, go forth 446, 472, 568, 896, 2005, etc.; **passes, passez** *3 sg.* 1888, 3819, 3913, 4327; **passes** *3 pl.* 3003; **passede, paste** *pa. t.* 327, 527, 3120, etc.; **passede, paste** *pp.* 3010, 3106, 3394, 3524, etc.; *trans.* traverse 640; *pa. t.* surpassed 2831; **passande** *pres. p.* surpassing 2741 [OF *passer*].

pastorelles *n. pl.* shepherds, herdsmen 3120 [OF *pastoral*].

pasture *n.* pasture 3121 [OF *pasture*].

pasturede *pa. t.* pastured 183 [OF

pasturer].

pathe *n.* path, way, route 1635, 3010 [OE *pæþ*].

patriarkes *n. pl.* patriarchs 3807 [OF *patriarche*].

paumes *n. pl.* paws 776 [OF *paume*].

paunson *n.* breastplate 3458 (*see note*) [obscure; ?rel. to PAWNCE].

pauyllyons, pavelyouns *n. pl.* pavilions 2478, 2624 [OF *paveillun*].

pauys *adj.* of Pavia 3460 (*see note*) [from *Pavia*].

pauysers *n. pl.* shield-bearers 2831, 3004 [OF *pavissier*].

pawe *n.* paw, leg 776 [OF *powe*].

pawnce *n.* a plate of armor covering the abdomen 2075 [OF *pance,* abdomen].

pawnche *n.* abdomen, belly 2076 [ONF *panche*].

pece, pes, pesse *n.*[1] peace 356, 1542, 2411, 3058, etc. [OF *pais, pes*].

pece *n.*[2] piece, bit 3608; **peces, pecez** *pl.* 214, 1825, 2663, 3389, etc. [OF *p(i)ece*].

pechelyne *n.* haycock 1341 [see note].

peyne. *See* PAYNE.

pekill *n.* a preservative brine or vinegar, usually spiced 1027 [cf. MDu *pe(e)kel*].

pelid *pa. t.* beat, battered 3042 [uncertain].

pelours. *See* PYLOURS.

pendes *3 sg.* belongs, attaches, pertains 1612; **pendes** *3 pl.* 2624 [OF *apendre*].

penown *n.* pennon, banner 2917; **penouns** *pl.* pennons, streamers 2460 [OF *penon*].

pensell *n.* pennon, streamer, banner 2411; **pensells** *pl.* 1289, 2460 [OF *pencel*].

perced *pa. t.* pierced 2075 [OF *percer*].

perell, perelous. See PERILLE, PERILOUS.

peres, peris, perez *n. pl.* peers, noblemen 146, 416, 637, 1628, etc. [OF *per*].

perfournede *pp.* done, carried out 672 [OF *parfo(u)rnir*].

perille, perell *n.* peril, danger 1924, *2535; o perell,* taking risk or responsibility for the consequences 1612 [OF *peril*].

perilous, perelous *adj.* perilous, dangerous 569, 640, 777, 1258, etc. [OF *perillo(u)s*].

perischede *pa. t.* perished 1521 [OF *perir, periss-*].

perry(e), perrie *coll. n.* gems, precious stones 2461, 3461, 4184 [AF *perrie*].

persayfes *3 sg.* perceives, notices 4224; **persayuede, persayfede** *pp.* perceived, found out 1631, 2811 [OF **perceivre,* northern form of *percoivre*].

persewes, persewede. See PURSUE.

pertly. See APPERTLY.

peruertede *pp.* perverted, led astray 2786 [OF *pervertir*].

pesane *n.* armor for the upper breast and neck, gorget 3458 [OF *pisa(i)ne,* from *Pisa*].

pes(se). See PECE, n.[1]

peté *n.* pity 2812, 3043, 3180 [OF *pité*].

philosophre *n.* sage, man of learning 3394; **phylosophers(e), phylozophirs** *pl.* 807, 814, 3226 [OF *philosophre*].

pygges *n. pl.* the young of a porcupine 183 [OE **pigga*].

pighte, pyghte *pa. t.* set up 3625; *pp.* set up 1287, 1290, 2478; planted 3364; set, studded,

adorned 212, 3354, 3460 [?OE *piccan, *pihte].

pyke *n.* a pilgrim's staff 3475; **pykes** *pl.* points, claws 777 [OE *pīc*].

pyke *v.* to seize, take, capture 1636 (*with* VP); **pykes** 2 *sg.* 2534 (*future*) [OE *pican* or *pīcan,* derived from *picung,* n.].

pilgram *n.* pilgrim 3475 [OF *pelegrin,* antecedent form to *pelerin*].

pilgremage, pylgremage *n.* pilgrimage 327, 896, 3496 [OF *pelegrinage*].

pillion hatt *n.* a kind of felt hat usually worn by the clergy 3460 (*see note*) [from L *pīleus*].

pylotes *n. pl.* pellets, missiles 3037 [OF *pelote*].

pylours, pelours *n. pl.* spearmen, bowmen 2801, 3004 (*see note*) [from OE *pil,* dart, arrow].

pilouur *n.* plunderer, thief 2533 [from ME *pill,* to pillage (OE *pilian*), after OF *pilleur*].

pyment *n.* a drink made of wine, honey, and spices 1028 [OF *piment*].

pyne *n.* suffering, distress 3043 [OE *pīn*].

pynne *v.* to torture, torment 4047 [OE *pīnian*].

pype vpe *v.* to strike up music on pipes 4105 [OE *pīpian*].

pypez *n. pl.* pipes, wind instruments 2030 [OE *pīpe*].

place, plas *n.* place 446, 2049; **places, placez** *pl.* 569, 2004, 2477; dwelling, palace 518, 524, etc.; *pl.* 527; battleground 4047; *in place,* on the spot, at hand 1257 [OF *place*].

playne *adj.* clear, open 1290 [OF *plain*].

playne *v.* to complain 1217 [OF *plaindre, plaign-*].

playsterede *pp.* plastered 3042 [OF *plastrer*].

plant(t)ez. See PLAUNTE.

plas. See PLACE.

plasche *n.* pool, pond 2798 [OE *plæsc*].

platers *n. pl.* platters, plates 182 [AF *plater*].

platez *n. pl.* pieces of plate armor 2075 [OF *plate*].

plattes *3 pl.* set, place 2478 [OF *platir*].

plaunte *v.* to lay (a siege) 355; **plantez** *3 sg.* plants, sets, positions 2004; **planttez** *3 pl. refl.* 1635 [OE *plantian*].

plenerly *adv.* completely, fully 2608, 3498 [from AF *plener,* complete].

plenteuous *adj.* plentiful 1028 [OF *plentious, plentevous*].

plesande *adj.* pleasing, agreeable 11, 4049 [AF *plesant*].

plyande *pres. p.* bent, twisted 777 [OF *plier*].

plytte *n.* state, position 683 (*see note*) [OF *ploit,* inflected *pliht*].

plouers *n. pl.* plovers 182 [AF *plover*].

plumpe *n.* band, troop 2199 [uncertain].

plungede *pa. t.* fell down, went down 1522 [OF *plung(i)er*].

poyne *v.* to stitch, sew 2624 [OF *poindre, poign-*].

poyntes, poyntez *n. pl.* points 2554; dots, flecks 767 [OF *pointe*].

pomarie *n.* orchard 3364 [L *pōmārium*].

pome *n.* a ball or globe, usually of metal, signifying dominion 3354 [OF *pome*].

pomell   *n. uninfl. pl.* ornamental knobs 1289 [OF *pommel*].

pontyficalles   *n. pl.* pontiffs 4335 [L *pontificālis*].

Pope, Pape, pape   *n.* pope, the Pope 229, 2327, 3180, 3497; *uninfl. poss.* 2410 [OE *pāpa*].

pople, popule   *n. pl.* people 11, 52, 100, 509, 683, etc.; (fighting) men 1455, 1477, 1724, 1875, etc.; creatures 2675 [OF *po(e)ple*].

porke despyne   *n.* porcupine 183 [OF *porc,* swine + *espine,* spine].

porkes   *n. pl.* pigs, swine 3121 [OF *porc*].

porte   *n.*[1] port 446, 2609; harbor 746 [OE & OF *port*].

porte   *n.*[2] the left-hand side of a ship 3625 [obscure].

portes, portez   *n. pl.* portals, gates 503, 568; portholes 749 [OF *porte*].

possessione   *n.* legal control 2608 [OF *possession*].

poste   *n.* post, pillar 776 [OF *post*].

potestate   *n.* potentate, ruler 2327 [OF *potestat*].

postles.   See APOSTYLL.

pound, pownde   *n. uninfl. pl.* pounds sterling 2629, 3031 [OE *pund*].

pourpour.   See PURPUR(E).

pouerall   *coll. n.* poor people, peasants 3120 [OF *pouraille*].

pouere   *coll. n.* poor people 3540 [OF *povere*].

pouerté   *n.* hardship 1546 [OF *poverté*].

powdyre   *n.* powder 1027 [OF *poudre*].

powere   *n.* power, ability 684; fighting force, army 589, 1635, 1925, 2005, etc. [OF *poeir,*

pooir].

pownde.   See POUND.

pray(e)   *n.* booty, plunder 2534; prey, quarry 2754, 2787, 2814, 2844; **prayes** *pl.* 3003, 3010 [OF *preie*].

praye   *v.* to beseech, petition, entreat 4034; **prayes** *3 sg.* 3179; **prayes** *3 pl.* 1256 [OF *preier*].

prayere   *n.* prayer, prayers 2 [OF *preiere*].

praysede   *pp.* praised 711, 1382, 2596, 2865, etc. [OF *preis(i)er*].

prechynge   *vbl. n.* public religious service 638 [OF *pre(e)chier*].

precious, precyous(e)   *adj.* of great moral or spiritual worth 2, 3806; esteemed 2698; precious, rich 212, 500, 1027, 1288, etc. [OF *precio(u)s*].

preker.   See PRIKKERE.

prekes, prekys,   *etc.* See PRIKE.

prelat(t)e   *n.* prelate 229; **prelates** *pl.* 146, 416, 637, 4335 [OF *prelat*].

presant   *adj.* ready at hand, ready with assistance 1257 [OF *present*].

presante   *n.* present, gift 1021 [from PRESENTE, V.].

presence, presance, presens   *n.* presence, company (with connotations of ceremonial attendance) 94, 457, 638, 717, 1584, etc.; *in ȝour presance,* with you 687 [OF *presence*].

presente   *v.* to perform, represent 684 [OF *presenter*].

presoner(e).   See PRISSONERE.

preson(ne)   *n.* prison 1546, 1632 [OF *priso(u)n*].

presse   *n.* crowd, throng 1477, 1479, 1545; pressure, crowding together 1522 [OF *presse*].

pres(s)e   *v.* to importune, beseech

1021, 1583; **presses** *3 sg.* pushes forward, throngs 2787; **presses** *3 pl.* 604; **presede** *pa. t.* 2199; *presses to,* pushes forward, presses on 4224; *3 sg.* hastens 1374, 2698, 2917; **pressed** *pa. t.* 717 [OF *presser*].

preué *adj.* secret, hidden 2005 [OF *privé*].

preuely, preualye *adv.* secretly, discreetly 213, 896, 1609; stealthily, treacherously 2648 [from prec.].

price, pryce, pris, prys, prys(s)e *n.* value, excellence 1924; honor, glory, renown 2788; *adj.* worthy, excellent, choice, without peer 2, 94, 230, 355, 569, 688, etc.; main 3121 [OF *pris*].

prike *v.* to spur, ride 2844; **prykkes** *2 sg.* 2533; **prekez, prekys** *3 sg.* 718, 2156; **prekez** *imper. pl.* 1609; **prekes** *3 pl.* 503, 2464, 2754; **prek(k)ande** *pres. p.* 1545, 2836; **prykkyd(e)** *pp.* stabbed 2648; *pp.* stitched 3608 [OF *prician*].

prikkere, preker *n.* rider, horseman, skirmisher 1374, 2649 (*see note*); **prek(k)ers** *pl.* 355, 1479, 2835 [from prec.].

pryme *n.* the first time period of the day, 6–9 A.M. 95; *as adj.* 4105 [OE *prīm*].

prynce *n.* prince, ruler, sovereign 40, 229, 568, 589, 1258, etc.; *uninfl. poss.* 684, 1289, 2460; **pryncez** *pl.* 527, 1584, 1889, etc. [OF *prince*].

prior *n.* prior, superior of a religious house 4013 [late OE *prior,* from L].

pris, pryse, etc. See PRICE.

prys(e) *n.* prize 2649, 2751 [var. of PRICE].

prissonere, prys(s)oner(e), presoner(e) *n.* prisoner, captive 1478, 1519, 1543, etc.; **presoner(e)s** *pl.* 1583, 1636, 1888, etc. [OF *prison(n)ier*].

priste *adj.* ready, at hand 1021; eager, keen 4106; **pristly** *adv.* fiercely, eagerly 2762 [OF *preste*].

processe: *by* (*be*) *processe of tym*(*e*), in (due) course of time 356, 1258, 1340 [OF *proces*].

processione *n.* procession 4014 [OF *procession*].

professide *pp.* having taken the vows of a religious order 4013 [L *profitērī, profess-*].

profire, profyre *n.* trial (by battle) 1257; show of force 2857 [AF *profre*].

profire, profre *v. trans.* offer, tender 356; **profers, profres** *3 sg.* 3141, 3354; **profyrs** *3 sg.* proposes 3179; *intr.* offer battle 518, 2534, 2812; *3 sg.* 1376, 2533, 2789 [AF *prof*(*e*)*rir*].

profitabill *adj.* beneficial 11 [OF *profitable*].

pronounce *v.* to proclaim, make known 2328 [OF *pronuncier*].

prophetes *n. pl.* prophets 3807 [OF *prophete*].

protteccione *n.* protection, patronage 2410 [OF *protection*].

proudely, prowdly, proudliche, prowdliche *adv.* grandly, splendidly 1287, 1374, 3607; proudly 2728 [late OE *prūdlīce,* from OF *proud*].

proudeste. See PROWDE.

proue *v.* to test, try, make trial of 1341 (*with pron. obj. unexpressed*), 2751; **proues** *3 sg.* 1478; **proues** *3 pl.* 2464, 3037, 4106; **prouede** *pp.* 2596, 3143,

3533; **prouen** *3 pl.* sound (the depth) 746 [OF *prover*].

prouoste, proueste *n.* an officer charged with the apprehension and custody of offenders 1611, 1632, 1889 [OE *profost*, OF *provost*].

prowde *adj.* proud, haughty 2536; superb, splendid 2076, 3365; **proudeste** *superl.* 1479; *as n.* 2156 [late OE *prūt, prūd,* from OF *prout, proud*].

prowdly, prowdliche. See PROUDELY.

prowesche *n.* a daring feat or exploit 1958 [OF *pro(u)ece*].

psalmes *n. pl.* psalms 3420 [OE *(p)sealm,* from L *psalmus*].

purchese *v.* to procure, obtain 3497 [AF *purchacer*].

Purgatorie *n.* Purgatory 3498 [AF *purgatorie*].

purpos(se) *n.* resolution, decision 415, 687, 2843; *in purpos,* resolved 640 [OF *po(u)rpos*].

purpur(e), purpre, pourpour *n.* purple or scarlet cloth 1288, 1375, 3142, 4184 [OE *purpure*].

pursue *v.* to pursue, hunt down 4046; **persewes** *3 sg.* 2155, 2786; **persuede, persewede** *pa. t.* 1377, 1476 [AF *pursiwer, pursuer*].

purtrayede *pp.* represented *3607* [OF *pourtraire*].

purvayede *pp.* prepared, equipped, with provisions made 1925, 2477, 2832 [AF *purveier*].

purueaunce *n.* preparation 688 [OF *purveaunce*].

putte *v.* to put, place 683, 1924; *put of,* parry 2535; *put . . . atvndyre, putt . . . vndyre,* overthrown, laid low 2814, 3180 [OE *putian, pȳtan*].

quarte, qwerte *n.* health, good health 552 (*see note*) [ON **kwert,* neut. of **kwer-r,* quiet].

quartere *n.* last quarter (of the year) 552; **qwarters** *pl.* the four quarters of the body, the four limbs 3389 [OF *quart(i)er*].

quarterede *adj.* quartered, cut into four pieces 1736 [from prec.].

quytte *v.* to requite, pay back 1788 [OF *quiter*].

quod *pa. t.* said, spoke, cried 140, 259, 343, 368, 475, etc. [OE *cwæþ*].

qw-. See also WH-.

qwayntly, qwayntely *adv.* adroitly, nimbly 2103; cunningly 3261 [AF *queinte*].

qwarells *n. pl.* short, heavy arrows or bolts, shot by the crossbow 2103 [OF *quar(r)el*].

qwarters. See QUARTERE.

qwaste *pp.* smashed, crushed, dashed to pieces 3389 [OF *quasser*].

qwat(e). See WHAT(E).

qwene, Qwene *n.* queen 696, 2189; the Queen of Heaven, the Virgin Mary 2871, 3998, 4041 [OE *cwēn*].

qwen(n), qwhen. See WHEN(E).

qwerte. See QUARTE.

qwhyle, qwhills, etc. See WHILLE, WHIL(L)S.

qwyk(k)e *adj.* alive 3810 [OE *cwic*]. See WELLYS.

qwyn *adv. interrog.* whence 3503 [contr. of ME *queþen, wheþen* (ON *hvaþan*)].

qwythen *adv. interrog.* why not 4157 [see note].

raas *v.* to tear, wrench 362; **rasede** *pa. t.* 2984 [OF *raser*].

racches *n. pl.* hunting hounds

3999 [OE *ræcc*].

rade *adj.* afraid, frightened 1995, 2881, 3896 [ON *hræddr*].

rade. See RIDE.

radly, rathely, raythely *adv.* swiftly, readily, suddenly 237, 1529, 2880, 3815 [OE *hrædlīce, hræþlīce*].

radnesse *n.* terror, fright 120, 310 [from RADE].

raghte. See RECH(E).

raike, rayke *n.* way, path, course 1525, 2985 [ON *rák*, stripe, or OE *racu*, watercourse].

raike *v.* to go, walk, go off 2352; **raykes, raykez** *3 sg.* 889, 1057, 1762, 2179, etc.; **raykes** *3 pl.* 2920; **raykande** *pres. p.* 3469; **raykede** *pa. t.* coursed 237 [ON *reika*].

raylide *pp.* arrayed, adorned, set 3263 [OF *reiller*].

raymede *pp.* plundered, spoiled 100 [OF *raimbre, raim-*].

rayne *n.* rain 795 [OE *regn*].

raynedere *n. sg. & pl.* deer 922, 4000 [ON *hreindýri*].

raissede, raysede *pp.* raised, reared 2057; stirred up, fomented 3580 [ON *reisa*].

raythely. See RADLY.

rane. See RYN(E).

ranez *n. pl.* strips or ridges of land, furrows 923 [ON *rein*].

ranke, raunke *adj.* strong, noble, stout 1474, 1764, 2138, 2240, 2271, 3824, etc. [OE *ranc*].

rankour *n.* ill-feeling, bitterness 1666 [OF *rancor, rannkour,* etc.].

ransakes. See RAUNSAKE.

raply *adv.* quickly, swiftly 1763 [ON *hrapalliga*].

rappyd at *pa. t.* smote on, stamped on (*with pron. obj.* it, *referring to* erthe, *unexpressed*)

785 [onomatopoeic].

rared(e). See RORIS.

rasches *3 pl.* dash hastily or violently 2107 [prob. onomatopoeic, like *clash, dash*].

rasede. See RAAS.

raskaille *n.* rabble, mob 2881 [OF *rascaille*].

rathe *adj.* swift 2550; *adv.* swiftly, readily 1275, 1332, 1668, 2022, etc. [OE *hraþe*].

rathely. See RADLY.

raughte. See RECH(E).

raunke. See RANKE.

raunsake *v.* to ransack, probe, search thoroughly 4304; **ransakes** *3 sg.* 3939; **ransakes** *3 pl.* 1884; **rawnsakes** *imper. pl.* 3228 [ON *rannsaka*].

raunsone *n.* ransom 1528 [OF *raunson*].

raunson(e), rawnson(e) *v.* to levy ransom upon or for 176, 1508, 3275, 3540; **raunsound** *pa. t.* 293, 329; **raunsound** *pp.* 100; ransom, redeem, deliver 466; **raunsouns** *3 sg.* 549 (*future*); **rawnsonede** *pp.* 2667 [OF *ranconner*].

ravische *v.* to ravish, rape *3539;* **rauyschett** *pa. t.* 294 [OF *ravir, raviss-*].

rawe: *on(e) rawe,* in a row, in order, one after the other 238, 633, 1292, 1454, 3268; into position 2179 [OE *rāw*].

rawghte. See RECH(E).

rawmpyde *pa. t.* raged about 794 [OF *raumper*].

rawndoune: *on a rawndoune,* in a rapid, headlong course 2985 [OF *en un randon*].

rawnsakes. See RAUNSAKE.

rawnson(e), rawnsonede. See RAUNSON(E).

real(l)(e), ryeall, ryall(e), riall *adj.*
royal, noble, splendid 17, 74,
179, 221, etc.; majestic 921; *as n.*
royal person 53, 1656, 2180,
2987; **realles** *as n. pl.* 597; **realeste**
superl. most royal 175, 1410;
ryally(e) *adv.* royally, splendidly
1472, 3613 [OF *reial,* AF *rial*].

realtée *n.* pomp, magnificence,
splendor 155, 228, 423, 512;
ryalltes, ryalltez, royaltez *pl.*
1665, 3214, 4005; kingliness
1204 [OF *realté, roialté*].

rebanes *n. pl.* narrow bands of
fabric, used as trimming 3255
[OF *riban*].

rebawde *n.* one who uses offen-
sive or irreverent language 1333;
rebawdez *pl.* 1705; menial, low,
or base person 4283; *pl.* 1416
[OF *ribaut*].

rebawdous *adj.* coarse, scurrilous
456 [from prec.].

rebell(e) *adj.* rebellious 103, 510,
2040, 2402, etc. [OF *rebelle*].

rebuke *v.* to insult, outrage 1333;
rebuykyde *pp.* outraged, 867;
insulted 1705; **rebuyked(e), re-
buyk(k)yde, rebukkede** *pp.* re-
pulsed, checked, beaten down
1445, 2153, 2234, 2374; overthrown 4283 [AF *rebuker*].

rech(e) *v. intr.* to reach 549,
3372, 3375; **raughte** *pa. t.* 3352;
trans. **rechede, rechide** *pa. t.*
reached 488, 1090; **rechid** *pp.*
1043; **reches, rechez** *3 sg.* deals
or strikes (a blow) 792, 1111,
2252; **rechis** *3 pl.* 3754; *pa. t.*
4218; *pa. t.* gave 3350; to seize,
take 3492; *pa. t.* 1527, 1884; *pp.*
2666; *ra(u)ghte in,* pulled in,
caught up 2549, 2766, 2987;
rawghte on, put on 3456; approach closely, come as far as

2434 [OE *rǣcan*].

reches *n. sg.* opulence *3263* (*see
note*); *pl.* riches 3571; (all the)
riches 2667, 4131, 4229 [OF
richesse].

recheste. See RICHE.

reconsaillez *3 sg.* wins over, brings
into friendly relations (with himself) 3130 [OF *réconcilier*].

recouer, couer(e) *v. trans.* recover
from, get over 859; recover, re-
gain, win, reach, get 3425, 3434,
3639; **coueres, coueris** *3 sg.* 941,
3644; **couerd(e), coueride** *pa. t.*
274, 280, 858, 2195; **couerede**
pp. 28, 3085; *vpe . . . coueris,*
gets up, rises up 4274; *couerd vp,*
rose up, got up 124; *intr.* recover,
get well 1246, 1572 [OF
recov(e)rer].

recreaunt *adj.* craven, cowardly
2334 [OF *recreant*].

reddour(e) *n.*[1] fear, dread, terror
109, 485, 1418 [from ON *rædd,
redd,* frightened, by anal. with
next].

reddour *n.*[2] severity, harshness
1456 [ONF *reddur*].

rede, reed(d)e *adj.* red 392, 795,
1526, 2144, etc.; (of gold) 465,
995, 1528, 3262 [OE *rēad*].

red(e) *v.* to advise 550, 2369,
2438, 2745, etc.; interpret 3228;
red(d)e *pp.* read 3440; recognized
2921; reckoned 1677; **redyn** *pp.*
had control over [OE *rǣdan,
rēdan*].

reden. See RIDE.

redy(e) *adj.* ready, willing, eager
93, 311, 548, 2403, etc.; **redyare**
compar. 2665; straight 391;
redyeste *superl.* 2352 [OE
gerǣde].

redy *v. refl.* make ready 4137;
redyes *3 pl.* 1427 [from prec.].

redily, redyly, redely(e) *adv.*[1] readily, quickly, promptly 363, 1207, 1453, 1472, 1509, etc.; soon (ironic) 466; fully, freely 1526 [from REDY(E), adj.].

redily *adv.*[2] carefully, skillfully 3255 [OE *(ge)rǣd(e)līce*].

redyn. See RIDE.

reed(d)e. See REDE.

refresche *v.* to refresh, revive 2491 [OF *refrescher*].

refte, refede, rewede *pa. t.* robbed, took from by force 295, 959, 1475, 3315; **refte, refede** *pp.* 1206, 1733, 1820 [OE *rēafian*].

Regale of Fraunce 4207 [see note].

regestre *n.* registry, official records 113 [OF *registre*].

reght(e). See RYGHTE, n. & adv.

reghttes *3 sg.* puts in order, straightens 3815; **reghttez, ryghtten** *3 pl.* raise, lift up 1454, 3618 [OE *rehtan, rihtan*].

regne, ryngne *v.* reign, rule, hold sway, prevail 398, 422, 1705, 3214, etc.; **regnes, regnez, regnys, ryngnes** *3 sg.* 287, 310, 2266, 2348, etc.; **rengnez** *3 pl.* 865; **regnede, reynede, rengnede, ryngnede** *pa. t.* reigned, prevailed 175, 228, 293, 2034, etc.; **regnande** *pres. p.* 2665 [OF *regner*].

reherse, rehersen *v.* to recount, relate 3229, 3452; **rehersede** *pp.* 1666; **rehersys** *3 sg.* 3206 [OF *reherc(i)er*].

rehetes, rehetez *3 sg.* cheers, gladdens 411, 3198; **rehetede** *pa. t.* 221 [OF *reheter*].

reyne *n.* bridle 2549, 2987; **reynes** *pl.* reins 3164 [OF *reine*].

re(y)uere. See RYUER(E).

rejoyse *v. refl.* to delight (oneself) 4004 [OF *rejoir, rejoiss-*].

reke *n.* smoke 1041 [OE *rēc*].

rekeneste *adj. superl.* doughtiest, readiest 4081 [OE *recen*].

rekenyng, rekkynyng *vbl. n.* reckoning, account, settlement 102, 1678 [OE *recenian*].

rekke, rekken, rekkyn *v.* to count, reckon 378, 1275, 2040, 2404, etc.; **rekkenede,** *pp.* 3587; *pp.* recounted, related 3441; prove 2334; **rekkez** *3 sg.* values, sets store by 995; **roughte** *pa. t.* took care, heeded 3274 [OE *reccan*].

reklesse *adj.* rash, reckless 1670; *adv.* in a carefree manner, lightheartedly 922 [OE *rēcelēas*].

relayes *3 pl.* get a fresh relay (change of horses) 1529 [OF *relayer*].

releuis *3 pl. intr.* gather together, rally 2278; **releuyde** *pa. t.* 2234; *trans.* **releuede** *pp.* succored, delivered 1207 [OF *relever*].

relyes, relyez *3 pl.* rally, gather together 1882, 4291; **relyede** *pa. t.* 1391 [OF *relier*].

religeous, relygeous *coll. n.* those belonging to a monastic order, monks 3539 [OF *religious*].

relikkes *n. pl.* relics 4207 [OF *relique*].

relys *3 sg.* reels 2794 [prob. from OE *hrēol*, n.].

remembirde *pa. t.* recalled 3892 [OF *remembrer*].

remenaunt *n.* remainder, rest 1553 [AF *remenaunt*].

remmes, remys *3 sg.* cries out 2197, 4155; **remyd** *pa. t.* 3894 [OE *hrīeman*].

remmes. See REWME.

remowes *3 sg.* withdraws, draws back 1761; **remouede** *pa. t.* 1417 [OF *remo(u)ver*].

renayede *pp.* apostate, renegade 2913, 3572, 3892 [OF *ren(e)ier*].

renk(e) *n.* man, knight, warrior 466 (direct address), 1473, 1675, 2041, 2402, 2784, etc.; referring to Christ 3217; **ren(n)kes, ren(n)kez, renkys** *pl.* 17, 147, 2175, 2278, etc.; any man 3859; creature 1057 [OE rinc].

renkkes *n. pl.* courses, tracks 391 [OF *renc*].

rennen. See RYN(E).

renownd(e), renownnd *pp.* renowned, famed 1994, 2372, 2453, 2912, 3441, etc. [OF *renomer*, with infl. of next].

renownn, renoun *n.* renown, glory, fame 1732, 2033 [AF *reno(u)n*].

rente *n.* tribute, tax, revenue, money 465, 2405; **rent(t)es, rent(t)ez, rentis** *pl.* 103, 995, 1509, 1554, etc. [OF *rente*].

rente *pa. t.* rent, tore 2984 [OE *rendan*].

rependez *3 pl.* kick 2107 [OF *repenner*].

repent *v.* to repent 1332, 1392, 1669, etc.; **repenttes** *3 sg. impers.* 3453 (*future*); **repent** *pa. t.* 3894 [OF *repentir*].

Requiem *n.* requiem, dirge, mass for the dead 4332 [L *requiem*].

requit *pp.* paid up, made up 1680 [L *re-* + QUYTTE].

rere *v.* to cause to retreat 2810 [OF *arerer*].

rereage *n.* arrears 1680 [OF *arerage*].

rerebrace *n.* a plate of armor protecting the upper part of the arm (orig. protecting the back of the arm) 2566 [AF **rerebras* (*rere*, back + *bras*, arm)].

rerewarde *n.* rear guard 390, 1430, 1527, 1762, etc. [AF *rerewarde*].

reris, rerys *3 sg.* raises 3902, 4249; **rerede, reryde** *pp.* 562, 840, 4280 [OE *rǣran*].

resaywe *v.* to take delivery of, collect 3587 [ONF *receyvre*].

rescewe, reschewe, rescowe, reschowe *v.* to rescue 1752, 2243, 2784, 4131, etc.; **reschowede** *pp.* 363 [OF *rescourre, rescou-, reskeu-*].

rescowe, reschewe *n.* rescue 1953, 3859; **rescows, reschewes** *pl.* 433, 4137 [from prec.].

resonabillye *adv.* in a reasonable manner 1508 [from OF *reson(n)able, adj.*].

reso(u)n, resone *n.* reason, cause, justification 174, 295, 1668; a matter agreeable to reason 2041; right, justice 2404; wit, sense 3825; heraldic motto, emblem 2921 [OF *reso(u)n*].

restes, restez. See RISTE.

restreynede *pp.* checked, repressed 2041 [OF *restreindre, restrei(g)n-*].

retenue *n.* retinue 378; **retenuz, retenewys** *pl.* 1334, 1655, 2664, 2920, 3572 [OF *retenue*].

retournes *3 pl.* turn around, turn back 1395 [OF *retourner*].

reuaye, ryvaye *v.* to hunt or hawk along the banks of rivers 3275, 3999 [ONF *riveier*].

reuare. See RYUER(E).

reuell *n.* reveling, rioting 1667 [OF *revel*].

reuell *v.* to revel, make merry 1969, 3172, 3207, 3275 [OF *reveler*].

revenge, reuenge *v.* to avenge, take revenge for 2180, 2198, 3217, 3430, 3559; **reuengede,**

reuengyde pp. 1204, 2048, 4006 [OF *revenger*].

reuerence *n.* respect, deep regard, favor 412, 1331; *at þe reuerence of,* out of respect for, in honor of 389; majesty, glory 512, 3893 [OF *reverence*].

reuerence *3 sg.* honors 3201 [from prec.].

reuerssede *pa. t.* overturned, threw down, pulled down 2070; **reuersside** pp. lined 3255 [OF *reverser*].

reuertede *pa. t.* reversed, turned round 2918 [OF *revertir*].

reueste *pp.* arrayed in ecclesiastical garments 4334 [OF *revestir*].

rewdly. See RUYDLY(E).

rewe, rywe *v. trans.* to affect with sorrow, distress, grieve 1678 (*with pron. obj. unexpressed*); **rewes** *3 sg. impers.* 3272; injure 2439; *intr.* take pity 866 [OE *hrēowan*].

rewede. See REFTE.

rewfull *adj.* pitiful 1049; **rewfully** *adv.* pitifully 1523 [from next].

rewghe *n.* rue, sorrow 3859 [OE *hrēow*].

rewles, rewlys, rewllez, rewlis *3 sg.* rules, governs 509, 1675; **rewlyd** *pa. t.* commanded 2809; *refl.* conducts (oneself), behaves 1670; **rewlyde** *pp.* established rule, control over 52; arranges, arrays, sets in order 4080; **rewles, rewlys** *3 pl.* 726 (*with pron. obj. unexpressed*), 1455, 2136 (*refl.*); **rewlede** *pa. t.* 2023 [OF *riueler, riuler*].

rewme *n.* realm, kingdom 509, 637, 1207, 1276, etc.; **rewmes, rewmez, remmes** *pl.* 49, 52, 66, 425, 556, etc. [OF *reaume*].

rewthe *n.* pity, sorrow, grief 888,

2197, 2241, 3939, 3989, etc.; calamity, ruin 1430; *in rewthe,* ruinously 3753; *as adj.* ruinous 3453, 3560, 3894 [OE *hrēow,* with ending prob. from ON cognate *hryggþ*].

riall, ryall(e), etc. See REAL(L)(E).

ryalltes, ryalltez. See REALTÉE.

riatours *n. pl.* revelers 2034 [from RYOT(T)(E), v.].

rybbez, rybbys *n. pl.* ribs 1134, 1151, 2060, 2271, etc. [OE *ribb*].

riche, ryche *adj.* powerful, great, of high rank 37, 42, 87, 108, 174, 362, 387, etc.; *as n.* 238, 726, 1679, 1876; strong 3172; wide, vast 28, 833, 1455; (*all*) *þis werlde ryche,* all the wide world 401, 515, 533, 651, etc.; splendid, fine, glorious 37, 62, 178, 218, 361, etc.; **richere** *compar.* more powerful 203; more splendid 3363; **richeste, rycheste, recheste** *superl.* most powerful, greatest 147, 2270; *as n.* 865, 1429, etc.; most splendid 155, 3457; richest 2641; *adv.* richly 1287 [OE *rīce*].

richely(e) *adv.* splendidly, in a grand manner 173, 3189, 3493 [OE *rīclīce*].

rydde *adj.* violent, fierce 4117 [obscure].

ride, ryde *v. intr.* to ride, go 390, 1392, 1608, 1876, etc.; **rydes** *2 sg.* 2666 (*future*); **rydes, rydez, rydys** *3 sg.* 619, 918, 1386, 1409, etc.; **rydes, ryd(d)ez, ryden, reden** *3 pl.* 485, 1418, 1450, 1669, etc.; **rade, ro(o)de** *pa. t.* 920, 1530, 1953, 2795, etc.; *ryde in by Rone,* advance up the Rhone 1338; *3 pl.* parade 723; *3 sg.* floats 3601; take part

in a raid or foray 341; **ryddis**
3 sg. 3540; **rade** *pa. t.* 294, 853;
redyn *pp.* 100; *3 pl.* rush, charge
2549, 2903; *trans.* to traverse on
horseback 432; **reden** *pp.* ridden
over, occupied 2598 [OE *rīdan*].

ryders *n. pl.* horsemen 1996 [from
prec.].

ryeall. See REAL(L)(E).

rife *v. trans.* to tear apart, rend
362; **ryfez, ryvys** *3 sg.* 1474,
3824; **ryffes** *3 pl.* 2913; *intr. 3 sg.*
splits, rends 794 [ON *rífa*].

rigg *n.* back, spine 800 [OE
hrycg].

ryghte, reghte *n.* right, justice
287, 295, 510, 1275, etc.; *at*
(*all*) *ryghtys, ryghttez,* at all
points, properly 610, 894, 1439
[OE *riht*].

righte, ryghte *adj.* right-hand 173;
just 2041 [OE *riht*].

ryghte, reghte *adv.* accurately,
correctly 113, 3229; justly 820;
straight 889, 1057; full, very
3470; *ryghte as, reght as,* just as,
whatever 458, 1301 [OE *rihte*].

ryghtten. See REGHTTES.

ryghttez *3 sg.* rips, tears, cuts
1474; **rittes, rittez, rittis, rittys,
righten** *3 pl.* 1524, 2138, 3753,
3824, 4118 [perh. from OE
*rittan (= OHG *rizzan*)].

rightwis, ryghtwise *adj.* just,
righteous 866, 3989; **rightewissly**
adv. correctly, rightly 1554 [OE
rihtwīs, rihtwīslīce].

ryndes, ryndez *n. pl.* banks,
brakes 921 (*see note*), 1884,
3363 [perh. of Scand. orig.; cf.
Norw *rind(e)*, ridge, bank].

ryn(e) *v.* to run, rush 109;
rynnes, rynnys *3 sg.* 3123, 3758,
3829, 4000, etc.; **rynnys** *3 pl.*
3070; **rane, rynnyde** *pa. t.* 1526,

2881, 2965; **ronnen** *pa. t. pl.*
922; **rynnande** *pres. p.* 392;
rynnez *3 sg.* gallops 1799; flow,
flow out, gush 3990; *3 sg.* 31, 62,
540, 573, 737, 1121, etc.; *pa. t.*
920; *pres. p.* 795; **rennen** *pp.*
run, piped 200; *3 sg.* sinks, slides
1113, 2240, 2793, 2311 [OE
rinnan].

ryng(e) *v.* to ring 2840, 4332;
ryngez *3 sg.* 1763; **rungen,
rongen, roungen** *pp.* 462, 976,
1587 [OE *hringan*].

rynges *n. pl.* rings 4207 [OE
hring].

ryngne, ryngnes, etc. See REGNE.

rynisch *adj.* of the Rhine 203.

rynnes, rynnys, etc. See RYN(E).

rynsede *pp.* rinsed, cleansed 3375
[OF *rincer*].

riotous, ryotous *adj.* hotheaded,
fond of fighting 363, 379, 432,
1416, 1527, 1676, etc. [OF
riotous].

ryotte *n.* wildness, disorder 294;
revelry, mirth 412; **ryotes** *pl.*
3893; **riotes** *pl.* 388 [OF *riote*].

ryot(t)(e) *v.* to ravage, harry 341,
1276, 2403; *refl.* disport oneself,
frolic, revel, run riot 923, 1969,
3372, etc.; **ryottez** *3 sg.* 619;
ransack, search 1883 [OF *rioter*].

ripeste *adj. superl.* ripest 3372
[OE *ripe*].

rype vpe *v.* to rout out 1877; **vp
rypes** *3 sg.* searches out 3940
[OE *rӯpan*].

ryses, rysses, rysez *3 sg.* rises,
rises up 752, 2706, 3456, 3660;
ryses *3 pl.* 3704 [OE *rīsan*].

riste, ryste *v.* to rest, sleep, relax
108, 1969, 3207, 3373, etc.;
restes, rystez, rystys, etc. *3 sg.*
758, 1221, 1883, 2767, etc.;
rystez *3 pl.* 1300; **riste, risted,**

rystede *pa. t.* 53, 485, 3362; stay 423; *3 sg.* is tranquil 889; *3 sg.* comes to rest 2170; **ristes** *3 pl.* lie, are situated 3336; *trans.* **restez** *3 pl.* allow to rest, put to rest 1529 [OE *restan*].

riste, ryste *pp.* caparisoned, arrayed in trappings 1428, 2235 [OE *hrystan*].

rittes, ryttys, etc. See RYGHTTEZ.

ryvaye. See REUAYE.

ryve. See **arryfede.**

ryuer(e), reuare, re(y)uere *n.* river, stream 62, 424, 619, 920, 1292 [OF *riv(i)ere*].

ryues *n. pl.* rivets 1764 [OF *rivet,* pl. *rives*].

ryvys. See RIFE.

rywe. See REWE.

robbe *v.* to rob, plunder 3539 [OF *robber*].

roche *n.* rock 1146; cliff, rocky height 3601 [OF *roche*].

rochell *n.* wine from Rochelle, in western France 203.

Rode *n.* the Cross 3217, 3559 [OE *rōd*].

rode. See RIDE.

roggede *pa. t.* trembled, shook 784 [obscure; cf. Norw *rogga,* set in motion, shake].

royall *adj.* royal 3206, 4072 [OF *roial*].

royaltez. See REALTÉE.

roy(e) *n.* king 411, 1670, 2372, 3173, etc. [OF *roy*].

roll *v.* to revolve, turn round 3374 [OF *ro(u)ler*].

rollede *pp.* enrolled, recorded 2641 [from next].

rolles, rollez *n. pl.* official records, accounts 112, 1677, 2658, 4069 [OF *rolle*].

romawns *coll. n.* romances 3200, 3440 [OF *romans*].

romyez *3 sg.* bellows, cries out 888; **romede, romyed** *pa. t.* 784, 1124 [obscure; cf. Scot. *rummish*].

rongen. See RYNG(E).

ronnen. See RYN(E).

roo *n.*[1] roe, a small species of deer 922, 4000 [ON *ra*].

roo *n.*[2] wheel 3272 (*see note*), 3374 [OF *roe*].

roo *n.*[3] peace, calm, tranquillity 1751, 3362, 4304 [ON *ró*].

roode. See RIDE.

ropes *n. pl.* ropes 3601 [OE *rāp*].

roris *3 sg.* roars 2795; **rared(e)** *pa. t.* 784, 1124 [OE *rārian*].

roselde, rosselde *pp.* reddened (with blood) 2793 (*see note*), 2880 [OF *roseler*].

rosers *n. pl.* wild-rose hedges 923 [OF *rosier*].

rosse *n. pl.* roses 3457 [OE *rose*].

rossete *adj.* russet, reddish-brown (?red gold) 237 [OF *ro(u)sset*].

rosted *pp.* roasted 196 [OF *rostir*].

rostez *n. pl.* roasts 1049 [OF *rost*].

roughte. See REKKE.

rounde, rownde, rownnd(e) *adj.* round 388, 2792, (of shoes, as opposed to stylishly pointed) 3471; rolling 1292; coarse 3470 (*see note*), harsh, fierce 2439 [OF *roö(u)nde*].

Round(e) Tabyll, Rown(n)de Table, Rounnd Tabill, etc. Round Table 17, 53, 74, 93, 102, 147, 173, 389, etc. [prec. + TABLE].

roungen. See RYNG(E).

rowell *n.* the rim of a wheel 3262 [OF *rouel*].

rowes *3 sg.* rows, sails 3629; **rowes** *3 pl.* 729, 833; **rowede** *pa. t.* sailed 494 [OE *rōwan*].

rowm(e), rowmme   *adj.* roomy, spacious 391, 432; loose-fitting 3471; wide, broad 1454 [OE *rūm*].

rowte   *v.* behave riotously, revel, carouse 108 [OF *router*].

rowt(t)(e)   *n.* riot, stir 2879, 2983; *make rowtte,* rampage 379; disorderly retreat 1418; army, band, troop 390, 456, 719, 833, 1530, etc.; *in the rowtte, into þe rowte,* in, to the troop 1515, 2809; attendant company, retinue, train 1608, 1656 [OF *route*].

rubyes   *n. pl.* rubies 3263, 3463 [OF *rubi*].

ruyd(e)   *adj.* barbarous 1049; rude 1332; rough 1096; sturdy, firm, stout 1057 [OF *ruide*].

ruydly(e), ruydlyche, rewdly   *adv.* violently, savagely, roughly 785, 794, 1124, 1415, etc. [from prec.].

rungen.   See RYNG(E).

rusche   *v. trans.* to smash, shatter 1339; **rusches** *3 pl.* snatch 2550; *ruyssches down,* drive down, drive back 2913; **ruschede** *pa. t.* attacked 2792; *intr.* charge 2880; **ruschez** *3 sg.* 392; *pa. t.* 2879; **rusches, ruysches** *3 sg.* falls quickly or violently, plunges 2241, 2794, 2983; **ruschte** *pa. t.* 120 [AF *russher*].

rusclede   *pp.* gnarled, rugged 1096 [unknown].

sa.   See SO.

sable, sabyll   *adj. & n.* black (heraldry) 771, 1364, 2027, 2052, 2521 [OF *sable*].

sad(d)e   *adj.* sated, satisfied 847; **saddare** *compar.* stronger, more powerful 3289; *adv.* heavily, with force 3948 [OE *sæd*].

sadill   *n.* saddle 2202; **sadills, sadylls** *pl.* 1801, 1855 [OE *sadol*].

sadly, saddly, sadly(e)   *adv.* firmly, resolutely 331, 4089; vigorously, briskly 1685, 2466 [from prec.].

safe   *adj.* safe 1507 [OF *sauf*].

safe.   See SAUE, V.

sagge   *adj.* wise 814 [OF *sage*].

saghetyll   *v.* to make peace 330 [OE *sahtlian*].

say(e)   *v.* to say, tell, speak 292, 370, 519, 1330, etc.; **sais(e)** *3 sg.* 136, 227, 320, 357; **sais** *3 pl.* 2324, 3975; **saise** *imper. pl.* 1267; **said(e)** *pa. t.* said, spoke, told 140, 267, 308, etc.; **saide** *pp.* 2044 [OE *secgan*].

sayenges   *n. pl.* words, instructions 2325 [from prec.].

saile   *n.* sail 747; **sail(l)es, saillez** *pl.* 832, 3655, 3661 [OE *segl*].

saile   *v.* to sail 381, 635, 728; **saillez** *3 sg.* 818; **saillez** *3 pl.* 831; **sailede** *pa. t.* 598 [OE *seg(e)lian*].

saillez   *3 pl.* leap 744 [OF *saillir*].

sayne   *v. refl.* to cross (oneself), bless (oneself) 969; **sayn(n)ed** *pa. t.* 966, 1042 [OE *segnian*].

saynte, seynt(e)   *n.* saint 898, 937, 1169, 1171, etc.; **seyntez** *pl.* 502, 1163, 1168 [OF *saint, seint*].

sake: *for sake of,* on account of 141, 442, 1845, 3315, etc.; *for the sake of,* in the name of 2587, 2817, 3051, 3181, etc. [OE *sacu*].

sak(e)les   *adj.* blameless, guiltless, innocent 3399, 3986, 3992 [from prec.].

sale   *n.* hall 82, 91, 134, 159, 409, etc. [OE *sæl*, OF *sale*].

sall.   See SCHALL (E).

salte   *adj.* salt, briny 598, 898,

1337, 1422, 1457, etc. [OE *sealt*].

saluz *3 sg.* greets, salutes 87; **saluȝed(e)** *pa. t.* 82, 953 [OF *saluer*].

salue *v.* to heal, cure 932; **saluede** *pp.* saved 2907 [OE *sealfian*].

saluez *n. pl.* salves, ointments 2691 [OE *sealf*].

same *adj. & pron.* same 286, 3012, 3588 [ON *samr*].

sandes. See SONDE.

sandes, sonde *n.* messenger, envoy 513, 2511 [OE *sand,* message; gen. ending from next].

sandesmane *n.* messenger, envoy 1419; **sandismen** *pl.* 266 [prec. with gen. ending + MAN].

sange. See SYNGE.

sanke. See SYNKE.

sare. See SORE, adv.

satills *3 pl.* descend 2465 [OE **sætlan*].

saughte, sawghte *n.* peace, security 1007, 3052; *adj.* at peace, reconciled 1548, 3194, 4042 [late OE *seht, seaht;* ON **sæht, *saht*].

saul(l)e, sawle *n.* soul 666, 1062, 1072, etc.; **saules** *pl.* 7, 3739 [OE *sāwol*].

saunke *n.* blood 179 [OF *sanc*].

saue, safe *v.* to save, rescue, deliver, protect 1572, 2276, 2586, 3051, etc.; **sauede** *pp.* 2315, 3811 [OF *salver, sauver*].

saue *prep.* except 1558 [OF *sa(u)f*].

Saueoure *n.* Saviour 3805 [OF *sauveour*].

sawghte. See SAUGHTE.

sawle. See SAUL(L)E.

sawtere, sawtire *n.* psalter 3316, 3421 [AF *sauter*].

sawturoure *n.* saltire, heraldic

emblem in the form of a St. Andrew's Cross 4182 (*see note*) [OF *saut(e)oir*].

scathyll. See SKATHELL.

schadande *pres. p.* streaming, flowing 3845 [OE *scēadan*].

schafte *n.* spear, lance, shaft 2169, 3844; **schaftes** *pl.* 3748 [OE *sceaft*].

schaftmonde *n.* handbreadth, about six inches 2546, 3843, 4232 [OE *sceaftmund*].

schaylande *pres. p.* stumbling, walking in a shuffling manner 1098 [rel. to OE *sceol,* awry].

schake *v.* to go, move, rush 1213, 1992 [OE *sceacan*].

schakke *n.* charge, attack 1759 [from prec.].

schalyde *adj.* scaled 766 (*see note*) [OE *scealu, scalu*].

schalke *n.* man, warrior, knight 2170, 3628, 3842, 4232, etc.; **schalkes, schalkez** *pl.* 1857, 2333, 2456, etc.; creature 1098 [OE *scealc*].

schalke *n. as adj.* chalk 1226 [OE *calc*].

schalke-whitte. See CHALKE-WHITTE.

schall(e), sall *v.* shall, will, must 7, 16, 102, 395, 442, 566. etc.; **scholde, schulde, schoulde, sulde** *pa. t.* should, would, had to, might, could 72, 213, 214, 469, etc.; (*with v.* to be *unexpressed*) 736, 3475 (*see note*); (*with v.* to go *unexpressed*) 3231; (*with v.* to have *unexpressed*) 3381, 4331 [OE *sceal, sculon, sc(e)olde*].

schame *n.* dishonor, shame 20, 1719, 3400, 3715, etc. [OE *sc(e)amu*].

schamely *adv.* disgracefully,

shamefully 2616 [from prec.].

schamesdede   *n.* a shameful death 3 [SCHAME + DEDE, n.²].

schanke   *n.* shank, leg 3845; **schankez** *pl.* 1099, 1104 [OE *sc(e)anca*].

schape   *v.* frame, fashion 1324; to set oneself, prepare 342, 2588, 3400; **schoupe** *pa. t.* 3599; **schappes** *3 sg. impers.* befalls 1716 [OE *sceppan*].

schappely   *adv.* fitly, properly 2333 [OE *(ge)sceaplīce*].

schare.   See SCHERE.

scharlette   *adj.* scarlet 3459 [OF *escarlate*].

scharpe   *n.* sharp weapon 3842 (*see note*) [from SCHARP(P)E].

scharply(e), scharp(e)ly   *adv.* briskly, swiftly 725, 749, 1212, 2456, 4235; openly, plainly 2429 [from next].

scharp(p)e, charpe   *adj.* sharp 314, 1766, 2105, 2210, etc. [OE *scearp*].

schathe.   See SKATHE.

schawe.   See SCHEWE.

schawes   *n. pl.* thickets, copses, groves 1723, 1760, 1765, 1876 etc. [OE *sceaga,* ON *scaga*].

schede   *pa. t.* dispersed, scattered 2922; **schedde** *pp.* shed 3398 [OE *scēadan*].

scheen, schen(n)e   *adj.* beautiful, lovely 1760, 2676; shining, splendid 2429, 2457, 3628, 3747, etc. [OE *scēne*].

scheftys, scheften.   See SCHIFT(E).

schelde, schilde   *n.* shield 1110, 1184, 1193, 1380, etc.; **scheldes, scheldez, scheldis, scheldys** *pl.* 595, 1055, 1413, 1753, etc. [OE *scield, sceld*].

schelde   *v.* protect, shield 3;

scheldyde   *pp.* 1856 [OE *scildan, scieldan*].

scheltron(e), schiltrone   *n.* troops drawn up in battle array, phalanx 1856, 1992, 2106, 2922, 2940; **schiltroun(i)s, schiltrons** *pl.* 1765, 1813, 2210, 4115 [OE *sc(i)eldtruma*].

schenchipe   *n.* disgrace, ignominy 4299 [pp. of next + OE *-scip*].

schende   *v.* to harm, ruin 2435 [OE *scendan*].

schen(n)e.   See SCHEEN.

schepe   *n. pl.* sheep 2922 [OE *scēp*].

schere   *v.* to cleave, hew, cut, cut through, thrust through 2456; **scherys** *3 sg.* 3600; **scherde, schare** *pa. t.* 1856, 2545, 3843 [OE *sc(i)eran*].

scherenken.   See SCHRENKYS.

schethede   *adj.* sheathed 3852 [from OE *scǣþ,* n.].

scheuerede, scheueride   *pa. t.* 1813, 3748 [cogn. with MHG *schiveren,* MDu *scheveren*]. See SCHORTE.

schewe, schawe, schewen   *v. trans.* to see, behold 89 (*see note*), 191, 498, 815, 1086, 1252, etc.; look to 2588; decree, grant 642 (*see note*), 2244; **schewede** *pp.* 899; show, exhibit, display, show off (*often refl.*) 1183, 1195, 1290, 1325, 2335, etc.; **schewes** *3 sg.* 2429, 3715; **schewes** *3 pl.* 3714; *pp.* 828; *intr.* to perform openly, appear, make an appearance 1717; **schewede, schwede** *pa. t.* 3846, 4233, 4340 [OE *scēawian*].

schewynge   *vbl. n.* sign, revelation 3401 [from prec.].

schift(e), schyft(e)   *v. trans.* to dispose, put in order, arrange 1717;

schiftys, scheftys *3 pl.* 725, 2456; apportion, distribute, divide 1213; *intr.* withdraw, depart 1325; move about 3847; **scheften** *3 pl.* get into position 3627 [OE *sciftan*].

schilde. See SCHELDE, n.

schiltrone. See SCHELTRON(E).

schynbawde *n.* leg armor, greave 3846 (*see note*) [OE *scinu* + ?].

schippe, chippe *v. intr.* to embark 342, 3599; *trans.* **schippide** *pa. t.* loaded on a ship 491; **schyppede** *pp.* 736 [OE *scipian*].

schippe-burde *n.* shipboard 804; *within chippe-burdez,* on shipboard 1699 [prec. + BORDE].

schip(p)emen *n. pl.* seamen 749, 1212 [OE *scipmann*].

schippez, schippys, schyppes, chippes, chippis, chippys *n. pl.* ships 633, 743, 746, 3546, 3577, etc. [OE *scip*].

schire, schyre *adj.* bright, shining 1760, 3600, 3627, 3846, etc.; fair, noble 2169, 3714, 3844 [OE *scīr,* adj.].

schyremen *n.* inhabitants of a shire 1213 [OE *scīr* + MAN].

schirreues *n. pl.* chief officers of a shire 725 [OE *scīrgerēfa*].

scho, cho *pron.* she 655, 659, 715, 716, etc.; **hir(e), hyr(e)** *acc. & dat.* her, to her 653, 854, 978, 979, etc.; (referring to wind) 3662; **hir(e)** *refl.* herself 3044, 3916; **hir(e)** *poss. adj.* her 84, 659, 853, 855, etc.; *hire selfe refl.* herself 655; *hir selfe, hir seluen reinf.* herself 657, 4204, 4205 [prob. altered form of OE *sīo, sēo; hire* dat. of *hēo*].

schoderede, schoderide, schodirde, sc[h]odyrde *pa. t.* quivered, shook 2169, 3844; shuddered

4234; scattered 2106 [cogn. with MLG *schôderen*].

schokke *v. trans.* to move suddenly and swiftly, thrust, draw swiftly 4114; **schokkes** *3 sg.* 3816, 3852; *intr. 3 sg.* charges, rushes 4235; **schokkes** *3 pl.* 1759 [cogn. with MLG, MHG *schocken*].

scholde. See SCHALL(E).

schone *n. pl.* shoes 3471 [OE *sc(e)ōh,* late OE pl. *sc(e)ōn*].

schone. See SCHOUNE.

schonte, schontes, etc. See SCHUNTE.

schore. See SCORE.

schorte, schortte *adj.* short 2060, 3843, 3852; *at þe schorte,* quickly, forthwith 1325; *scheueride schorte,* broke off so as to leave nothing beyond the place of fracture 3748 [OE *sc(e)ort*].

schortly *adv.* quickly, soon 1716, 2588 [OE *scortlīce*].

schoten *3 pl.* shut, close 749 [OE *scyttan*].

schotte *n.* rush 2105; shot 2428; **schotys** *pl.* 3627 [OE *gesceot*].

schotte *v.* to rush, dart 1765, 1813, 4115; **schottis** *3 sg.* 3728; **schotte** *pa. t.* 2210; *pa. t.* fell violently 3847; shoot, pierce (*trans. & intr.*) 1857, 1992, 2545; **schottes** *3 pl.* 2426, 3685; *pa. t.* 2169; **schotand** *pres. p.* 1766 [OE *scēotan scotian*].

schotte-men *n. pl.* bowmen 2467 [prec. + MAN].

schoulde. See SCHALL(E).

schouldire, schuldyre *n.* shoulder 2688, 4232; **sco(u)lders, scholdirs, schuldirs, schuldyrs, schuldrez** *pl.* 766, 1094, 1157, 2546, 2993, etc. [OE *sculdor*].

schoune, schone   *v.* to shrink,
quail 314; seek safety by concealment or flight 1717, 1719;
schownes *3 sg.* hesitates 3599
[OE *scunian*].

schounte, schountes.   See
SCHUNTE.

schoupe.   See SCHAPE.

schove   *v.* to shove 3847;
schowand *pres. p.* thrusting,
knocking 1099 [OE *scūfan*].

schoue, schouen   *pa. t. pl.* shaved
2333, 2335 [OE *sceafan*].

schouell-foted   *adj.* shuffle-footed,
with a shuffling gait 1098
[*schouell*, v. (from prec.) +
FOTE (see *OED* shovel *v.*²)].

schowand.   See SCHOVE.

schownes.   See SCHOUNE.

schownttes.   See SCHUNTE.

schowttes   *3 pl.* shout, cry, call
1878, 4115 [from *showte,* n.
(perh. from SCHOTTE)].

schragges   *n. pl.* rags, tatters 3473
[unknown].

schrede   *pp.* shrouded 3991 [OE
scrȳdan].

schrede   *v.* to cut, hack 4167;
schrede *pa. t.* 2211; **schre(e)de**
pp. 2688; *pp.* scattered, powdered
767 (*see note*) [OE *scrēadian*].

schredez, schredys   *n. pl.* tatters,
ragged pieces of cloth 3473;
decorative gold threads or cut-
tings 905 [OE *scrēad(e)*].

schrenkys   *3 sg. intr.* shrinks,
dwindles 4234; **scherenken** *3 pl.*
2105; **schrinkande, schrenkande**
767 (*see note*), 1857; *trans.*
schrenkede *pa. t.* caused to
shrink, dwindle 2211 [OE
scrincan].

schrewe   *n.* shrew 2779 [OE
scrēawa, scrǣwa].

schryfe   *v.* to confess and receive

absolution 3400 [OE *scrīfan*].

schrifte   *n.* shrift, penance 2588
[OE *scrift*].

schrympe   *n.* crustacean (*fig.*, a
dragon, like WORME) 767
[from OE *scrimman,* dry up,
shrink].

schrynede   *adj.* enshrined 3991
[from OE *scrīn,* n.].

schrinkande.   See SCHRENKYS.

schrowde   *n.* garments, clothing
3628 [OE *scrūd*].

schulde.   See SCHALL(E).

schuldyre, schuldirs.   See
SCHOULDIRE.

schunte, schounte   *v.* to hang back,
delay, shrink 736, 1324;
**schuntes, schontes, schountes,
schownttes** *3 sg.* 1055, 3715,
3816, 3842; **schontes, schontez**
3 pl. 1759, 4114; **schonte** shrank
with dread 2106, 2428 [obscure;
perh. rel. to SCHOUNE].

schwede.   See SCHEWE.

scyence   *n. uninfl. pl.* branches of
knowledge 808 [OF *science*].

score, skore, schore   *n.* score,
twenty, twenty years 278, 380,
2344, 2358, etc. [ON *skor*].

scrippe   *n.* small bag, wallet,
satchel, especially one carried by
a pilgrim or beggar 3474 [OF
escrep(p)e].

seche, sechis.   See SEKE.

secounde, secunde   *adj.* second
2306, 3288 [OF *second*].

see   *n.*¹ throne, royal seat, dwelling
place of a monarch 63, 3291,
3350 [OF *sie*].

see   *n.*² sea 105, 381, 490, 492,
596, etc. [OE *sǣ*].

se(e)   *v.* to see, observe, look at
154, 387, 406, 880, etc.; **sees**
2 sg. 265; **ses, sees** *3 sg.* 720,
3468, 3941, 4312; **seese** *3 pl.*

1405; **saw** *pa. t.* 1295, 1872;
seen, sene, seyne *pp.* 381, 1697,
3985, 4177, 4341; establish 3183
[OE *sēon*].

seege *v.* to besiege, lay siege to
440; **seggede** *pa. t.* 3011 [OF
ass(i)eger].

se(e)le *n.* seal 87, 439, 478 [OF
seel].

segge, seegge *n.*[1] man, warrior,
knight 134, 1574, 3271, 4035;
seggez *pl.* 1420, 1422, 1951;
person, creature 1043 [OE *secg*].

segge, seegge *n.*[2] siege 355, 2478
[OF *s(i)ege*].

seggede. See SEEGE.

segnourry. See SEYNꝫOWRÉ.

seyne, syngne *n.* sign, mark,
heraldic emblem 2055, 2870,
3075 [OE *segn*].

seyn(e). See SYNE, SE(E).

seyngnour *n.* lord, overload 3313
[OF *seignor*, AF *segnour*].

seynt(e). See SAYNTE.

seynꝫowré, segnourry *n.* body of
lords 528; **seynowres** *pl.* 1577;
kingdom, domain 2419 [OF
seignorie].

seke *adj.* sick, wounded 1574
[OE *sēoc*].

seke, seche, seken *v. trans.* to
seek, make for, approach 1657,
1967, 2007, 2423, 2514, etc.;
sekes, sechis *2 sg.* 2591, 3507;
soghte *pa. t.* 3114; visit (a
"saint," i.e., a shrine, a holy
place) 898, 937; **sekes** *3 sg.* 1163
(with double meaning; *see note
to line 1171*); **sekes** *3 pl.* 502;
soghte *pp.* 1171 (with double
meaning; *see note*); advance
against, attack 105; look out for
4301; *intr.* move, go, advance
966, 1039, 1296, 1964, etc.;
sekez *3 sg.* 1500; **so(u)ghte** *pa. t.*
487, 720, 1041, 1977, etc.;

seke in by Sayne, advance up,
along the Seine 1336 [OE
sēcan, sōhte].

sekire, sekyre, sekere *adj.* secure,
safe, free from doubt or apprehension 478, 1173, 2423;
sure, steadfast, certain 551, 593,
818, 831, 1458, etc.; **sekerare**
compar. more steadfast 3289;
sekereste *superl.* most steadfast
1492, 1854 [OE *sicor*].

sekire *v.* to pledge 2585, 3804
[from prec.].

sekirly, sekyrly, sekerly(e) *adv.*
surely, assuredly, with full certainty 439, 969, 1008, 1420,
1550, etc.; steadily, relentlessly
441; faithfully 1042, 3499; carefully 1641; quickly, fast 3788
[OE *sicorlīce*].

sektour *n.* executor 665 [AF
executour].

selcouthe, selkouthe *adj.* unusual,
rare, strange 75, 1298, 1948,
3196; marvelous, wonderful
3421; sundry, various 3531;
selkouthely *adv.* marvelously,
exotically 3252 [OE *selcūþ*].

selden *adv.* seldom, rarely 1163
[OE *selden*].

sele. See SE(E)LE.

selfe, selfen, seluen, etc.: *þe King
selvyn, seluyn, seluen,* etc., the
King himself 96, 122, 176, 210,
etc.; *þe Fend seluen,* the Devil
himself 2862 [OE *self(a)*]. See
I, THOW(E), SCHO, WE, ꝫE, THEY,
HYM SELFE.

selkouthe, selkouthely. See
SELCOUTHE.

semblant *n.* aspect, appearance
410; show, display, splendor 75
[OF *sembla(u)nt*].

semble, sembles, semblede, etc.
See ASSEMBLE.

semes *2 sg.* seem, appear 962;

semes, semez, semys *3 sg.* 133
(*see note*), 139, 266, 969, 1162,
1418, etc.; *impers.* 1701, 2494;
semede, semyde *pa. t.* 123, 773,
777, 790, 952, etc.; were 193;
befitted, beseemed 170 [ON
sóma].

semly, semliche, semlyche *adj.*
goodly, fair, attractive 410, 655,
2457, 3947; *semly in syghte,*
lovely to look at 1949; **semliche,
semlyly** *adv.* beautifully, superbly
3316, 3787, 4064 [ON *sœmiligr*].

sen. See SYNE.

senatour(e) *n.* senator 80, 136,
170, 227, etc.; **senatours** *pl.* 97,
1295, 1625, etc. [OF *senatour*].

send(e) *v.* to send (*often with
pron. obj. unexpressed*) 355,
551, 556, 1007, 1330, 1438,
etc.; **sendes, sendis, sendys,** etc.
3 sg. 104, 570, 632, 3148, etc.;
sent, send *pa. t.* 3064, 3135,
4299, etc.; *sent to,* sent for 2924;
sent word to 3062; **sent(e)** *pp.*
529, 1012, 2614 [OE *sendan*].

sendell *n.* linen 2299 [OF *sendal*].

sene. See SE(E).

seng(e)ly, sengilly *adv.* alone 471,
2434, 2592, 3729 [from OF
single, sengle].

sent *n.* sense of smell, chiefly in
animals 1040 [from OF *sentir,* v.].

sent(e). See ASSENT(T)E, n. & v.;
SEND(E).

septre, ceptre *n.* scepter 511,
3186, 3350 [OF *ceptre, sceptre*].

sepulture *n.* sepulchre, tomb 4340
[OF *sepulture*].

sere *adj.* various, sundry 192,
1576, 1847, 2927, etc.; many,
several, every 441, 607, 1853,
1979, etc.; *adv.* separately, apart
3195 [ON *sér*].

serfe, serfed(e). See SERUE.

sergeantes of armes *n. pl.*

sergeants-at-arms, constables 632
[from next + ARMES].

sergeaunt *n.* servant, servant of
God or Satan 1173 [OF *sergent,
sarjant*].

serkylde *adj.* encircled, surrounded 3356 [from OE
circull, n.].

sertayne. See CERTAYNE.

serte *n.* merit 2926; **sertes** *pl.* 513
[OF *desert*].

serue, serfe *v.* to serve, furnish
1220, 2630; **seruez** *3 sg.* 968
(*future*); **serves, seruis** *3 pl.*
1168, 2748; **seruede** *pa. t.* 171;
servede, seruede, serfed, seruyde
pp. 79, 159, 443, 514, etc.; *of
. . . seruede, serfede with,*
served (wine or food) 209, 892,
1948; *pa. t.* dealt with 2230; *pp.*
dealt 2590 [OF *servir*].

seruece and suytte: formulaic expression describing attendance at
court and personal service due
from a tenant to his lord 3139
[OF *service,* AF *suite*].

serues *3 pl.* deserve 1315;
serfed *pa. t.* 1068 [OF *deservir*].

ses. See SE(E).

sessede *pa. t.* ceased 2132 [OF
cesser].

sesez *3 sg.* seizes 1500; **sesede** *pp.*
511; **seside** *pa. t.* gave possession
of 3065 (*with pron. obj. unex-
presse*d); *sessede . . . in,* in
legal possession of 2608 [OF
seisir].

sesyn *n.* possession 3588 [OF
saisine].

seson *n.* season 54, 624, 658,
1008, etc. [OF *seso(u)n*].

sessede. See SESEZ.

Seterdaye *n.* Saturday 1550, 3176
[OE *sætern(es)dæg*].

seþen. See SYTHIN.

setill *n.* seat, chair 3270 [OE *setl*].

set(t)e *n.* throne 1305, 3315 [ON *sǽti*].

sett(e) *v.* set, fix, place, lay 447, 1183, 1576, 4036, 4089; **settes** *3 pl.* 2481; **sett** *pa. t.* 3115, 3350; **sette** *pp.* 1946, 1963; appoint, assign 558, 644; establish, found 2407; **settez** *3 sg.* 3093; *pa. t.* 60; *pp.* 4043; *3 pl.* plant, put down 1458, 3746; *pa. t.* 1855; *pp.* 3421; *pp.* seated 97, 170, 3193, etc.; value 686, 2938; *sette be, settes by,* esteem(s), value(s) 406 (*see note*), 994; *sett be myn one,* esteemed over all others 3312; beset, batter 2423; *sett in, sett . . . on, sette . . . appon, settez on,* attack(s), assault(s) 1422, 1493, 1847, 2131, 4139 [OE *settan*].

seuen, seuyn *adj. & n.* seven 413, 440, 447, 808, etc. [OE *seofon*].

sevend *adj.* seventh 488 [OE *seofunda*].

seuenyghte *n.* one week, seven days 153, 380 (*uninfl. poss.*), 3176, 3182 [OE *seofonnihte*]. See DAY(E).

sewe *v.* to follow 3734; **sewede** *pa. t.* 3288; **sewande** *pres. p.* following 81; proceed, go, esp. with speed 2927 (*future*) [AF *suer*].

sewed *pa. t.* sewed, stitched 2299; **sewede** *pp.* 3317 [OE *siwan*].

sewes *n. pl.* pottages, stews 192 [OE *sēaw*].

sex *adj. & n.* six 354, 380, 471, 1040, 1855 [OE *siex*]. See SOM(E), SICHE.

sexte *n.* sixth 3316, 3416 [OE *sexta*].

sexten(e) *adj. & n.* sixteen 81, 105, 608, 634, etc. [OE *sixtȳne, siextȳne*].

sexty, sexti(e) *adj. & n.* sixty 179, 210, 448, 478, etc. [OE *sixtig, siextig*].

sexti-faulde *adj.* sixty layers of 2299 [prec. + OE -*fald*].

sybb(e) *adj.* kin, related, kindred 681, 3891, 3984; *me sybb,* kin to me 645 [OE *sibb*].

sybredyn *n.* relationship, kinship 691, 4145 [OE *sibrēden*].

siche, syche, suyche, swyche, swylke *adj. & pron.* such 76, 226, 228, 322, 403, etc.; *siche sex, syche fyfty, siche foure,* six (fifty, four) of such (as you) 967, 972, 1031 [OE *swilc, swylc*].

syde *n.* side, side of a person, rib 234, 1151, 1492, etc.; **sydes, sydez, sydys** *pl.* 1096, 1158, 2148, etc.; *syde wynde,* a wind blowing from one side of a vessel 598 [OE *sīde*].

sydlyngs *adv.* sideways, from the side 1039, 1043 [prec. + OE -*lings,* adv. suffix].

syen. See SYNE.

syghe *v.* to lament, sorrow, sigh 442, 3796; **syghede** *pa. t.* 3290; **sygh(e)ande** *pres. p.* 3794, 3891 [OE *sīcan*].

sighte, syghte *n.* sight, view 1043, 2512, 3289, 3717, etc.; *with sighte, with syghte,* with one's own eyes 968, 4036; *in syghte wyth,* in sight of, with a view of 1578; *in sighte to,* in the sight of 4294 [OE *siht*]. See SEMLY.

sygne *n.* an official mark of attestation, stamped on a document, seal 90; sign, symbol 3357 [OF *signe*].

syland(e) *pres. p.* gliding 1297; flowing 3794, 4340 [prob. of Scand orig.; cf. Norw & Sw dial. *sila*].

silke, sylke *n.* silk 3194, 3252,

3317 [OE *seolc*].

sylure *n.* canopy 3194 [OF *celure,* from L *cēlātūra*].

siluer(e), syluer(e), siluyre *n.* silver, 177, 198, 201, 477, 538, etc.; silver vessels 206, [OE *silfor*].

silueryn, sylueren *adj.* silver 185, 1949 [OE *silfren*].

symple *adj.* poor, weak, feeble 684, 967, 2739 [OF *simple*].

syn *n.* sin 3315, 3986, 3992 [OE *syn(n)*].

syne, synne, syen, seyn(e), sen *adv.* then, afterward 85, 188, 192, 282, 464, etc.; *conj.* since 127, 142, 526, 952, 1257, etc. [red. of SYTHIN].

syne(s)chall *n.* seneschal, person in charge of a king's household 1871, 1910 [OF *seneschal*].

synfull *adj.* sinful, wicked 3; *as coll. n.* sinners 2512 [OE *synnful*].

synge *v.* to sing 2510; **synges, syngys** *3 pl.* 3154, 4332; **sange** *pa. t.* 2676; **songen** *pa. t. pl.* 2674; sang out (ref. to song or chant accompanying work) 745 [OE *singan*].

syngyng *vbl. n.* singing 931 [from prec.].

syngne. See SEYNE.

singulere, synglere *adj.* (him) alone, apart from others 172; lone 3123; singlehanded 826 [OF *singul(i)er*].

synke *v.* to sink 1573, 3812; **sanke** *pa. t.* 3983; **synkande** *pres. p.* 3705; *pa. t.* weighed upon, weighed down 3948 [OE *sincan*].

synne. See SYNE.

synues *n. pl.* sinews 2708 [OE *seon(o)we, sionwe*].

sir(e), syr(e) *n.* lord, knight, sire 3134, 3288, 3312; sir (as title before name) 86, 88, 128, 156, etc.; (in polite address) 136, 227, 259, etc.; **sirs** *pl.* 222, 4084 [OF *sire*].

sister, syster *n. uninfl. poss.* sister's 645, 1945 [OE *swyster*].

syte, sytte *n.* pain, woe, sorrow 1060, 1305 [ON **sýt;* cf. Norw *sȳt*].

sythin, sythen, sythyn, seþen *adv.* then, next, afterward 56, 159, 184, 427, etc. [OE *siþþan*].

sythis *n. pl.* times 2216 [OE *sīþ*].

sitt *v.* to sit, be seated 1578; **sittez** *3 sg.* 1261; **satt** *pa. t.* 1044; **sitten, syttyn** *pp.* 511, 3291 [OE *sittan*].

sittande *pres. p.* fitting, appropriate, seemly 953, 1501; **sittandly** *adv.* fittingly, suitably 159 [from prec.].

skayles *3 sg.* attacks with scaling ladders, scales 3034 [OF *escaller*].

skayres *3 pl.* frighten, terrify 2468 [ON *skirra*].

skalopis *n. pl.* scallop shells 3474 (*see note*) [OF *escalope*].

skape *v.* escape 1562 [ONF *escaper*].

skathe, schathe *n.* hurt, harm, injury 292, 1643, 3119; matter for sorrow or regret 1841 [ON *skaþe,* OE *sc(e)aþa*].

skathell, scathyll *adj.* harmful, dangerous 32; *as n.* dangerous person 1642 [ON **skoþull,* rel. to prec.].

skathlye *adv.* with (only) damage or injury 1562 (*only in allit. phr. scape scathely*) [from SKATHE].

skewe *v.* to slip away, escape 1562 [OF *eskiu(w)er*].

skyfte *v. trans.* to manage, arrange, dispose, distribute 1643; **skiftez, skyftys, skiftis** *3 sg.* 32, 1561, 3034; **skyftes** *3 pl.* guide, direct 3117; *intr. 3 pl.* shift, move away 3118 [ON *skipta,* rel. to OE *sciftan*].

skilful *adj.* just 1561 [from next].

skyll: *by skyll,* by right, rightfully 32 [ON *skil*].

skippes *3 pl.* spring, move lightly and rapidly 3118 [obscure; rel. to MSw *skuppa, skoppa*].

skyrmys *3 pl.* skirmish 2467 [OF *eskermir, eskirmiss-*].

skyrttes *n. pl.* skirts 3473 [ON *skyrta*].

skomfite *n.* humiliation 2335 [OF *disconfit*].

skomfite *pp.* overthrown, defeated 1644 [OF *disconfire,* pp. *disconfit*].

skomfyture, skomfitoure *n.* defeat, overthrow 1651; victor, one who overthrows 1644 [OF *disconfiture*].

skore. See SCORE.

skorne *v.* to mock, deride, treat with contempt 1642; **skornede** *pa. t.* 1840 [OF *escarnir*].

skornefull *adj.* scornful, mocking 1840 [from OF *escarn,* n.].

skottefers, skotiferis *n. pl.* shield-bearers, squires 2468, 3034 [L *scutiferi*].

skouerours. See DISCOUEROURS.

skoulkery *n.* stealth, sneakiness 1644 [from *skulk,* v., of Scand. orig.; cf. Norw *skulk*].

skowtte-waches *n. pl.* sentinels, guards 2468 [OF *escoute* + OE *wæcce*].

skrogges, skroggez *n. pl.* bushes, underbrush 1641, 1642 [app. rel. to *scrag,* stump (orig. obscure)].

skulkers *n. pl.* people lurking about with hostile intentions 3119 [see SKOULKERY].

slade *n.* marsh, boggy land 2978 [OE *slæd*].

slayne. See SLEWE.

slakes *3 sg.* slackens, loosens 3220 [OE *slacian*].

slakkes *n. pl.* mud flats, shoals 3719 [of Scand. orig.; cf. Icel *slakki,* Norw *slakke*].

slante: *o slante,* aslant, on a slant 2254, 3854, 3923 [obscure].

slawe *adj.* sluggish, heavy 4044 [OE *slāw*].

slawyn *n.* a pilgrim's mantle 3474 [OF *esclavine*].

sleghe *adj.* skilled 2978 [ON *slǽgr*].

sleghte *pp.* rendered slack or relaxed 2675 [OE *slæccan*].

sleghte, sleyghte *n.* skill, dexterity 2675 (*see note*), 2977 (*see note*), 3220, 3418, 4045 [ON *slǽgþ*].

sleyghly. See next.

slely, sleygh(e)ly *adv.* skillfully 2975, 3855; covertly, secretly 4321; cunningly, shrewdly *3117* [from SLEGHE].

slepe *n.* sleep, slumber 2675, 3221 [OE *slēp*].

slepe *v.* to sleep 4044; **slepede** *pa. t.* 810 [OE *slēpan*].

sleppes *3 sg.* slips 2976; **sleppid** *pa. t.* 3854 [ON *sleppa*].

slewe, sloughe, slowghe *pa. t.* slew, slaughtered 23, 979, 2418, 4045; **slayne** *pp.* 1824, 2977, 3023, 4045, etc. [OE *slēan, pa. t. slōg, slōh,* pp. *slegen*].

slewthe *n.* sloth, languor 3221 [OE *slǽwþ*].

slydande. See SLODE.

slyke *adj.* such 3719 [ON *slíkr*].

slynge *n.* sling, hand sling 3418 [precise orig. not clear; cf. OF *eslingue,* MLG *slinge,* etc.].

slynges *3 sg.* throws, flings 3220, 3855; **slongen** *pp.* 2978, 4321 [prob. ON *slyngva*].

slippes *3 sg.* slips, slides 3923 [prob. MLG *slippen*].

slytte *n.* aperture, opening 3853 [OE *geslit*].

slyttes *3 sg.* slits, tears, slices 2254, 2975; **slitt** *pa. t.* 979 [OE *slītan*].

slode *pa. t.* slid, glided 3854; **slydande** *pres. p.* 2976 [OE *slīdan*].

slomyre *v.* to slumber, sleep 4044 [OE **slumerian* (= MDu *slummern,* MLG *slômeren,* etc.)].

slomowre *n.* slumber 3221 [from prec.].

slongen. see SLYNGES.

slope *n.* slope 2977 [from *aslope,* adv. (obscure)].

sloppes *n. pl.* muddy places, mudholes 3923 [OE **sloppe* (rel. to *slūpan*)].

slot(t)e *n.* the slight depression or hollow at the base of the throat 2254, 2975 [OF *esclot*].

slottede *pp.* pierced through the hollow at the base of the throat 3853 [from prec.].

sloughe. See SLEWE.

slowde *n.* sludge 3719 (*see note*) [uncertain].

slowghe. See SLEWE.

smyttes, smyttez *3 sg.* smites, strikes 1148, 2564 [OE *smītan*].

snell *adj.* ready, quick, eager 57 [OE *snell*].

so, soo, sa *adv.* so, thus 41, 62, 143, 174, 216, etc.; to such an extent, to the extent that 270, 441, 489, 675, etc.; (in asseveration) 136, 227, 346, 467, etc.; just so, if 2322; then 80 (*see note*); ever 4315; *as intensive* 503, 821, 908, 920, etc.; *so þat,* in order that 1507 [OE *swā*].

socoure *v.* to help, assist, aid 2276, 4139; **socour(r)ede** *pp.* 3811, 4140; shelter, protect 3137 [OF *socorre, sucurre*].

soda(y)nly, sodaynliche *adv.* suddenly 80, 1422, 2939, 3270, etc.; without delay, speedily, swiftly, soon 599, 632, 1493, 1980, 2481, 3053, etc. [from OF *sodain,* adj.].

softe *adj.* tender 3983 [OE *sōfte*].

softely *adv.* slowly, calmly 1297; gently 3350 [from prec.].

soghte. See SEKE.

soyte. See SUYT(.T)E.

soio(u)rne *v.* remain for a time 4027; stay 4042 [OF *sojorner*].

sola(u)ce *n.* pleasure, delight 75, 153, 239, 1336, etc.; contentment, satisfaction 192 [OF *so(u)las*].

sola(u)ce *v.* to delight, please, amuse 54, 354, 659; **solaces** *3 sg.* comforts 2512 [OF *solacier*].

solemply, solempnely, solempnylye *adv.* solemnly, with due ceremony 525, 1948, 3196, 3805 [from OF *solem(p)ne*].

solempnitée *n.* propriety 514 [OF *solempnité*].

solytarie *adj.* solitary, all alone 1576 [L *sōlitārius*].

som(e), somm(e), sum *adj.* a certain, one 134; some kind of 825; some 9, 2491, 3052; one or another 1750; *indef. pron.* some 1052, 1789, 2084, 2675; *sexsum, neynesom,* a company of six, nine 471, 523 [OE *sum*].

somercastell *n.* a movable tower used in sieges 3033 [OF *somer* + CASTELL].

somme *n.* sum, amount, number 448, 2347; **sommes, summes** *pl.* 606, 3136; **sowmes** *pl.* hosts 1627 [OF *so(u)me*].

sommonde, somounde, somond *pa. t.* summoned 1212; served a summons 525; *pp.* 140, 267 [OF *sumondre*].

somouns, sommons *n. sg.* summons 91; *pl.* commands, orders 104, 443 [OF *sumunse, somonse*]. See MAKE.

son, sone *n.* son 645, 1945, 3064, 3423; **sonnes** *pl.* 2995 [OE *sunu*].

sonde *n.* sand 3728, 3745; **sandes** *pl.* 3926 [OE *sond, sand*].

sonde. See SANDES.

sondyre, sondre, etc.: *in sondyre, sondre, sondire, sunder,* asunder, apart, in two, into bits, to pieces 362, 1123, 1151, 1388, 1482, etc. [OE *onsundran*].

sondirwise *adv.* asunder, separately 3529 [prec. + OE *wīse*].

son(e), sonne *adv.* at once, quickly, promptly, suddenly 170, 420, 508, 579, 814, etc.; soon 1282 [OE *sōna*].

songen. See SYNGE.

son(n)e, soone *n.* sun 1978, 2482, 2511, 2561, 3468, etc. [OE *sunne*].

Sonondaye *n.* Sunday 501, 2482, 3183 [OE *sunnandæg*].

soo. See SO.

soone. See SON(N)E.

sope *n.* light meal, quick meal 1890 [OE *sopp*].

soppe *n.* troop, band 1493, 2818, 3729, 3745, etc. [perh. ON *soppr*].

sore *n.* distress, pain, affliction 932 [OE *sorg*].

sore, sare *adv.* painfully, griev-ously 134, 266, 1173, 1392, 1574, etc.; **sorer** *compar.* more sorely 1163; madly, hotly 2263 [OE *sāre*].

sorowe *n.* sorrow, woe 383, 961, 1060, 1138, etc. [OE *sorg*].

sorowfull *adj.* sorrowful 1844, 3947, 3985, 4341; *as n.* 953 [OE *sorgful*].

sorte *n.* company, group of followers, troop 63, 410, 1575, 1854, 3531, etc.; **sortes** *pl.* 606 [OF *sorte*].

sothe *n.* (the) truth 1686, 2591, 2593, 2637, etc. [OE *sōþ*].

sothe *adv.* truly 3734 [OE *sōþe*].

sothely(e) *adv.* truly, certainly, in truth 172, 239, 817, 1007, 1789; rightly 319; utterly 1963, 4182 [OE *sōþlīce*].

sott(e) *n.* sot, one who stupefies himself with drinking or eating 847, 1044, 1060 [OF *sot*].

soughte. See SEKE.

sounde *n.* sound 490 [AF *soun*].

sound(e), sownde *adj.* steadfast, loyal 406; healthy, uninjured, untroubled 932, 1557, 1577, 4042, 4312; safe 4140; *adv.* without harm, safely 472 [OE *gesund*].

souppe. See SOWPE.

southe, sowþe *n.* south 728, *1041* (*see note*); *adv.* southward 1039 [OE *sūþ*].

soueray(g)ne, souerayne, soueraigne, soueraynge *n.* sovereign, king 82, 141, 239, 529, 1298, etc.; **soueraynes, souerayngez** *pl.* 1960, 2354, 3532; regent, viceroy 644; leader 1437, 1743, 3931; *adj.* sovereign, supreme 1167, 2419, 3499 [OF *so(u)verain*].

Sowdane *n.* Sultan 590, 596, 608, 1295, 1305, etc.; **Sowdanes** *poss.* 2816; **sowdanes** *pl.* 593, 607 [OF

soudan].

sowdeours *n. pl.* mercenaries 551, 2925, 2938, 3532, 3574, etc.; servants, vassals 593 [OF *soudier*].

sowe *n.* a movable structure used to cover men advancing to the walls of a besieged town or fortress 3033 [OE *sugu*].

sowmes. See SOMME.

sownde. See SOUND(E).

sowpe, souppe *v.* to sup, eat, feast 1298, 3805; **sowppes** *3 sg.* 1025; **sowpped** *pa. t.* 409; *refl.* **sowpand** *pres. p.* feeding, gorging himself 1044 [OE *sūpan*].

sowper. See SUPPERE.

sowte. See SUYT(T)E.

sowþe. See SOUTHE.

space *n.* distance 3265 [OF *espace*].

spayre *n.* the opening in the front of the breeches 2060 [unknown].

spakely *adv.* suddenly, quickly 2063 [ON *spakliga*].

spalddyd *pp.* splintered, split 3699 [= MLG *spalden*].

spanne *n.* span, a measurement of about nine inches 2060 [OE *span(n)*].

spare *v.* to spare 449; **sparis** *3 pl.* 3158; **sparede** *pp.* 269; be indulgent or merciful to 2414; *pp.* saved, stored up 3160; *spare for,* be sparing of 162 [OE *sparian*].

speche *n.* speech, words 221, 2416, 3508; *in speche,* out loud, publicly 269; *hir speche,* the opportunity of speaking or conversing with her 3908 [OE *sp(r)ēc*].

specyall *adj.* unique, uncommon 999 [OF *special*].

spede *v.* to hasten 449, 2416; **spedis** *3 pl.* (*refl.*) 3161; **spede** *pa. t.* 483, 1794; succeed, prosper 2414; **spede** *pp.* 3016 [OE *(ge)spēdan*].

spedily *adv.* quickly, speedily 3700 [OE *gespēdiglīce*].

speke *v.* to speak, utter 270, 1343, 2415; **spekes** *3 sg.* 1302, 2063, 3311, 4327; **spoken** *pp.* declared, called 538 [OE *sp(r)ecan*].

spekes *n. pl.* spokes 3264, 3311 [MLG *spēke*].

spekynngs *n. pl.* information, word, news 3163 [from prec.].

speltis *n. pl.* thin strips of wood or metal 3264 [rel. to *spelt,* to split (obscure)].

spencis *n. pl.* expenditures 3163 [OF *dispense*].

spende *v.* to expend 162; **spendis** *3 pl.* use up 3160; **spendyde** *pa. t.* gave out, passed out 235 [OE *spendan*].

spere *n.* spear, lance 1366, 1369, 1794, 2061; **speres, speris, sperys** *pl.* 1898, 2141, 2542, 2544, etc.; *as adj.* 3265; *spere-lenghe,* spear's length 3311 [OE *spere*].

speryt *n.* spirit, soul 4327 [OF *esperit,* AF *spirit*].

spycerye *coll. n.* spices 162 [OF *espicerie*].

spyces, spycez *n. pl.* spices 1027; spiced wines 235 [OF *espice*].

spille *v. intr.* to perish, be destroyed 2415; **spillis** *3 sg.* spills, is shed 4130; *trans.* **spillis** *3 pl.* destroy 3159 [OE *spillan*].

spirituell *n.* the spiritual authority, clergy 2414 [OF *spirituel*].

spytte *n.* outrage 270 [OF *despit*].

spleen *n.* spleen 2061 [OF *esplen*].

splent *n.* plate of armor 2061 [cf. MLG *splente*].

splentide *pp.* plated 3264 [from prec.].

spoylles *3 pl.* despoil, plunder
3159 [OF *espoillier*].
spoken. See SPEKE.
sponen *pp.* woven 999 [OE *spin-nan*].
spoures. See SPURS.
sprange, sprangen. See SPRINGEZ.
sprede, spradden *pa. t.* sprayed,
splattered 2062; dispersed 3158;
spread out 3310 [OE *sprǣdan*].
sprente, sprentyde *pa. t.* spurted
2062; sprinted 3310, 3700 [ON
spretta, older form **sprenta*].
springez *3 sg.* leaps 2062; **sprange**
pa. t. jumped up 3310; **spryngen**
3 pl. gallop, ride 3158; **sprangen**
pa. t. pl. 483; **sprongen** *pp.*
broken, split, burst into pieces
1794, 3699; *pp.* born 1943;
sprynges *3 sg.* spreads, spreads
out 3162; **springande** *pres. p.*
3265 [OE *springan*].
sprongen. See prec.
sproulez *3 sg.* sprawls 2063 [OE
sprēawlian].
spurs, spoures, spurres *n. pl.* spurs
448, 483, 2416 [OE *spura,
spora*].
sqwyere *n.* squire 1179 [OF
esquier].
stabbis *3 pl.* stab *3126* [un-known].
stablede *pa. t.* put (horses) into
a stable 3100 [OF *establer*].
stade. See STEDDE.
stake *v.* to pierce with a stake
1178. [OE *stacan*].
stale *n.* army, company, troop
(esp. one detached for recon-noitering or other special service)
377, 1355, 1435, 1932, 2080,
etc.; **stales, stalis** *pl.* 1980, 4134
[OF *estal*].
stalkis *3 sg.* follows 3466 [OE
*stealcian (inferred from *bisteal-*

cian, stealcung)].
stam, stamyn *n.* stem, prow 3658,
3664 [ON *stamn*].
stande, stannde *v.* to remain 552
(*see note*); **standez** *imper. pl.*
1748; **stode** *pa. t.* 3009; stand,
stand up 2117; **standes, standez,
stondys** *3 sg.* 1054, 1131, 1351,
3623; *standez, standis, stondez*
3 pl. 745, 2090, 3658; **stode**
pa. t. 2923; *pa. t.* made a stand
1489; *stodde for hym seluen,*
stood his own ground 4133 [OE
standan].
standerde *n.* standard, banner
2080 [OF *estandard*].
statte *n.* status, rank 157 [OF
estat].
staunche, stawnche *v.* to stanch,
stop (bleeding) 2577, 2584 [OF
estanchier].
stedde, stade *pp.* fixed, set, placed
1926; beset 2824; helped, aided
4132 [OE *steþja,* pp. *staddr*].
stede *n.¹* horse, steed 373, 376,
392, 915, etc.; *uninfl. poss.* 2823,
4038; **stedes, stedez, stedis, stedys**
pl. 335, 365, 611, 731, 934,
1280, etc. [OE *stēda*].
stede *n.²* place, spot, position
1748, 2824, 4038 [OE *stede*].
stekys *3 sg.* stabs, pierces 3822;
stekes *3 pl.* 3126; **stekede** *pa. t.*
1488 [OE *stician, stycian*].
stele *n.* steel 1371, 1474, 1764,
1861, etc. [OE *stȳle*].
stelen, stelyn *adj.* steel 1354,
1488, 2129, 2554 [OE *stȳlen*].
stepells *n. pl.* steeples *3040* [OE
stēpel].
stepes *3 sg.* goes, advances 1229
[OE *steppan*].
steppe *n.* step 4133 [OE *stepe*].
sterebourde, stereburde *n.* star-board 745, 3665 [OE *stēorbord*].

sterep, sterape *n.* stirrup 916, 2692; **sterapes** *pl.* 3823 [OE *stigrāp*].

steryn *adj.* brave, bold, steadfast 157, 735, 1793, 3823, etc.; *as n.* 377, 755, 1229, 1927, 2085, 2528, etc.; severe, fierce, cruel 1436, 2079 [OE *styrne, stierne*].

steryne *n.* stern, the rear part of a ship 3622 [ON *stjórn*].

sterynfull, sterenefull *adj.* brave, bold, fierce 2692, 3822 [from STERYN].

sterynly. See STERNLY.

sterys *3 sg.* guides, directs 917 [OE *stȳran, stēoran,* etc.].

steris, steride. See STIRE.

sternly, sterynly *adv.* boldly, fiercely 2130; heartily 745 [OE *styrnlīce*].

stertez, sterttes, stirttes, styrtez, etc. *3 sg.* leaps, jumps 1104; **sterte** *pa. t.* 916; rushes, hastens, goes 1152, 1355, 1932, 2692 [OE *styrtan*].

steuen *n.* voice 2531; cry, outcry 4269 [OE *stefn*].

stewede *pa. t.* checked, restrained 1489 [OE *stōwigan*].

stye *n.* path 3466 [OE *stīg*].

styffe *adj.* strong, rugged, massive, firm 1104, 3040, 3622, 3658, etc. [OE *stīf*].

styfflye *adv.* firmly, vigorously 376 [from prec.].

stiȝttelys. See next.

styghtyll *v.* to arrange, dispose 157; **stiȝttelys** *3 pl. 3622* [OE *stihtlian;* cf. OE *stihtan,* arrange].

still, styll *adj.* silent 15, 3466 [OE *stille*].

stynte *v.* cease, leave off 3127 [OE *styntan*].

stire, styre *v.* to move, stir 2823,

4038, 4133; **steris** *3 pl.* 2923, 3658; **stirrez** *imper. pl.* 1748; **steride** *pa. t.* disturbed, displaced 1793 [OE *styrian*].

stirttez, styrtez. See STERTEZ.

stode, stodde. See STANDE.

stokes *n. pl.* thrusts 1436, 2554 [perh. from OF *estoquier*].

stokkes *n. pl.* stakes, posts 3665 [OE *stoc*].

stomake *n.* stomach 2554 [OF *estomac*].

stonays *3 pl.* stun 2118; **stonayede** *pp.* 1933 [OF *esto(u)ner*].

stondez, stondys. See STANDE.

stone *n.* lodestone 753; **stones, stonys** *pl.* rocks 539, 3318, 3615; precious stones, gems 212, 215, 909, 1288, 2461, etc.; *pl.* 3142, 3256, 3262, etc.; *as adj.* 3040 [OE *stān*].

stone-dede *adj.* stone-dead 3823 [prec. + DED(E), adj.].

stoppede *pa. t.* stopped 2771 [OE *stoppian* (occurring only in *for-stoppian*)].

store *v.* to store up, stock, collect 2369 [OF *estorer*].

stotais, stotays *3 sg.* falters, totters 4271; comes to a stand 3467; makes a faltering stand 1435 [OF *estoteier*].

stour, stowre *n.* battle, fight 377, 1488, 1747, 1792, 2086, etc. [OF *estour*].

stowe *v.* to stow, pack 735; **stowede** *pa. t.* 3100 [OE *stōwigan*].

stownde *n.* moment, hour 3974; **stowndys** *pl.* 3888 [OE *stund*].

stownntyng *vbl. n.* stop, delay 491 [OE *styntan*].

stowre *n.* body of persons, troop 4039 [OF *estor*].

stowre. See STOUR.

stowttly *adv.* firmly, resolutely, vigorously 917, 2553, 3664 [from OF (*e*)*stout*].

strayte, straytt *adj.* harsh, severe, narrow, rugged 1230, 1933, 3101 [OF *estreit*].

straytez, strates *n. pl.* gorges, ravines 561, 3009 [OF *estreit*].

strake. See STRYKE.

strandes, strandez, strandys *n. pl.* streams, waters 598, 1227, 1337, 1422, 1457 etc.; waterfalls, cataracts 883, 947 [OE *strand*].

streynez, streynys *3 sg.* bridles, controls 917; grips, grasps tightly 2085 [OF *estreindre*].

streke *adv.* straight, directly 1792, 3101 [OE *strec,* adj.].

strekez *3 sg. intr.* runs, rushes, goes hastily 2085; **strekes, strekyn** *3 pl.* 3101, 3659; *trans. 3 sg.* stretches, pitches 1229 [OE *streccan,* 3 sg. *streceþ*].

strekyn. See STRYKE.

strem(e) *n.* water, stream 755, 1230, 2527, 3101, etc.; **stremes, stremez** *pl.* 629, 898, 1224, etc. [OE *strēam*].

strenghe, strenghte *n.* strength, fortitude, power, fighting force 258, 376, 796, 1260, 1489, etc.; **strenghes, strenghez, strenghis, strenghethis** *pl.* 1475, 1478, 1815, 3691, etc.; fortified place, fastness 1230, 1435, 1926, 2528; *pl.* 1827 [OE *strengu, strengþ*].

strenghely *adv.* firmly, stoutly 4096 [from prec.].

stret(t)e *n.* street, road 3040, 3467; **stretis** *pl.* 3127 [OE *strǣt*].

stridez *3 sg.* straddles, bestrides 916 [OE *strīdan*].

stryke *v. trans.* to strike, knock, smite 376, 561, 1178, 2553, *4039;* **stryk(k)es, strykez** *3 sg.*

788, 1124, 1471, 1480, etc.; **strykes, strykez, strykkys** *3 pl.* 1411, 2118, 4162; **strake** *pa. t.* 2080, 2129; *intr. 3 sg.* moves, goes, strikes out, charges 2086, 4225; **strekyn** *3 pl.* 755 [OE *strīcan*].

stryvynge *vbl. n.* conflict, struggle 3659 [OF *estriver*].

stroye, struye, struyede, etc. See DESTROYES.

studyande *pres. p.* meditating 3467 [OF *estudier*].

stuffe *n.* equipment, supplies 735, 3100; soldiers, reinforcements 2824 [OF *estoffe*].

stuffe, stuffen *v.* to furnish (troops) with support, reinforce 1932; **stuffede** *pp.* 4132; strengthen, fortify 2369; *pp.* protected 4096; **stuffede** *pa. t.* equipped 3616 [OF *estoffer*].

sturdely *adv.* violently, fiercely 1104 [from OF *estourdi,* adj.].

subarbe *n.* the area immediately surrounding a town 4043; **subbarbes, subarbis** *pl.* 2466, 3122 [OF *sub(b)urbe*].

subgettez. See SUGETT(E).

sucour(e), socure, socoure *n.* aid, help, assistance 1234, 1438; relief 3052; refuge, protection 2317 [OF *sucurs*].

sue *v.* to make legal claim to 91 [AF *suer*].

suerddes. See SWERDE.

suffre, suffyre, suffire *v.* to tolerate, put up with, allow 1701, 2817; (*future*) 141, 1548, 2587, etc.; **suffers** *3 sg.* 1167 [OF *sufrir*].

sugett(e) *n.* subject 87, 3138; **subgettez** *pl.* 2314 [OF *suget*].

suggourne *v. trans.* to rest or quarter (horses) 153, 501; *intr.*

stay, rest, relax 1335; **suggeourns, suggeournes, suggeournez** *3 sg.* 54, 354, 624, 3170; *refl.* entertain, amuse (herself) 655 [OF *sujourner*].

suyche. See SICHE.

suyt(t)e, soyte *n.* company of attendants, retinue 81, 179, 528; *in sowte,* in company 3941; *in soyte with,* in company with, together with 3931; *of suyte,* matching 210 [AF *suite*]. See SERUECE AND SUYTTE.

sulayne *adj.* alone 2592 [OF *solain*].

sulde. See SCHALL(E).

sum. See SOM(E).

summes. See SOMME.

sunder. See SONDYRE.

sundyre *v. intr.* to become separated or severed from something 7 [OE *sundrian*].

suppere, sowper *n.* supper, meal 897, 1022 [OF *super, soper*].

suppowell *v.* to support, assist, succor 2818 [AF *suppouail,* var. of *souspoial,* n.].

suppris(s)ede, supprys(s)ede, supprysside *pp.* taken by surprise, captured by sudden attack, undone 1420, 1845, 1951, 2612, 3797, etc. [OF *surprise,* pp. of *surprendre*].

surcott(e) *n.* surcoat 2434, 3252 [OF *surcote*].

surelye *adv.* certainly 330 [from OF *seür*].

surepel *n.* cover 3317 (*see note*) [AF *surepel*].

surgyon, surgyn *n.* surgeon, physician 2586, *4311* [AF *surgien*].

surrawns *n.* security, safety 3181 [OF *surance*].

surs *n.* rising 1978, 2511, 3468 [OF *surse*].

sustynaunce *n.* food, sustenance 846 [OF *sustenance*].

suteleste *adj. superl.* wisest, most expert 808 [from OF *soutil*].

swafres *3 sg.* staggers, totters 3970 [from Scand. stem *sveif-,* as in ON *sveifla,* to swing].

swayn *n.* man, youth 3360 [OE *swān,* ON *sveinn*].

swalters *3 sg.* wades, splashes 3924 [var. of ME *swatter,* v. onomatopoeic)].

swange *n.* groin 1129 [ON *svangi*].

swangen: *swangen in two* (*pa. t. pl.*), struck, divided by a blow 2146 [OE *swingan*].

swanke *pa. t.* worked, struggled 2961, 3361 [OE *swincan*].

swannes *n. pl.* swans 185 [OE *swan*].

swape *n.* stroke, blow 314 [unknown; perh. akin to ModE *sweep, swoop*].

swappes, swappez *3 sg.* strikes, thrusts, smites 1126, 1129, 1465, 2959, 2981, etc.; **swappez, swappen** *3 pl.* 1464, 2103 [unknown; perh. akin to ModE *sweep, swoop*].

swarthe *n.* greensward, turf 1126, 1466, 2145, 2960, *4246* [OE *swearþ*].

swathes *n. pl.* swaths 2508 [OE *swæþ, swaþu*].

swefen *n.* dream 812; **swefennys** *pl.* 3228 [OE *swefn*].

swefnyng *vbl. n.* slumber, sleep 759 [OE *swefnian*].

sweyftly. See SWIFT(E)LY.

sweys *3 sg.* sways, falls, moves, turns one's way 57, 4273; **sweys** *3 pl.* 1467, 3676 [ON *sveigja*].

swelte *v.* to die, perish 716, 813; **sweltes** *3 sg.* 2961; **swelltez** *3 pl.*

1466; **swelte** *pa. t.* 2982; *3 sg.*
swoons, faints 3969; **swelltande,**
sweltand *pres. p.* 1465, 2146 [OE
sweltan].

sweperly(e) *adv.* quickly, nimbly
1128, 1465 [OE *swiporlīce,* cun-
ningly].

sweppen *pp.* swept, mowed 2508
[unknown].

swerde *n.* sword *47,* 715, 1056,
1120, etc.; *as adj.* 1126, 2911;
swerdes, swerd(d)ez, suerddes *pl.*
314, 1253, 1414, 1494, etc. [OE
sweord].

swett(e), swete *n.* blood, lifeblood
2145, 3360, 3703, 4223 [OE
swāt, n., *swætan,* v.].

swet(t)e *adj.* sweet-sounding,
lovely 929; sweet-smelling 2508;
gracious 3969 [OE *swēte*].

swet(t)ly *adv.* pleasantly, smoothly
1297; lovingly, fondly 3970 [OE
swētlīce].

swyche. See SICHE.

swyers *n. pl.* squires 3703; *sg.*
poss. squire's 2959 [OF *esquier*].

swift(e)ly, swyft(e)ly, sweyftly *adv.*
swiftly, rapidly 1464, 2145,
2961, 2981, 2982, etc. [OE
swiftlīce].

swykede, swykkede *pa. t.* failed
1795, 3361 [OE *swīcan*].

swylke. See SICHE.

swym *n.* swoon 4246 [OE *swīma*].

swyng(e) *n.* sweep, stroke, blow
3360, 3676, 4223 [OE *geswing*].

swynne *n. pl.* boar 3232 [OE
swīn].

swyre-bane *n.* neck bone 2959
[OE *swēora, swīora* + *bān*].

swythe *adv.* quickly, suddenly
185, 715, 1128; rapidly, swiftly
920, 1949; immediately 4187;
as swythe, als swythe, forthwith,
immediately 409, 813 [OE
swīþe].

swoghe, swoughe *n.* murmuring,
sighing sound 759; movement,
sweep 1127; swoon 1467 [from
OE *geswōgen,* pp. of lost v.].

swoun: *in (a) swoun,* in a swoon,
in a faint 3969, 4273 [from OE
geswōgen].

swounes *3 sg.* swoons 715, 1127,
4246; **swounande** *pres. p.* 1467,
2960; sinks, falls 2982 [from OE
geswōgen].

swounyng *vbl. n.* swoon, faint 716
[from prec.].

swowyng *n.* sighing, murmuring
931 [from SWOGHE].

table *n.* table 545, 1301; banquet
table 1331, 1946, 3198, etc.;
tables *pl.* 3192 [OF *table*].

tachementez *n. pl.* appurtenances,
belongings 1568 [OF *attache-
ment*].

taghte. See TAWGHTE.

taile *n.* tail 801, 821 [OE *tægel*].

tak(e) *v. trans.* to touch, handle
1015; assume, take charge of 668;
take, seize 72, 144, 148, 275,
349, etc.; **takes, takez, takys, tase**
3 sg. 693, 713, 1890, 3724;
taken, tas *3 pl.* 2700, 3203; **tuke**
pa. t. 2282; **takyn** *pp.* 1543; lay
hold of, capture 3568; *3 sg.*
3151; *pa. t.* 328; *pp.* 852, 974,
1433, 1519, etc.; *3 sg.* summons
807; *pp.* reached 840; *pp.* received, taken in (with enjoy-
ment) 73; make 879, 992; *pp.*
415, 687; *intr.* to go, proceed,
strike out 307 [ON *taka*]. See
KEPE, WYNDE.

takle, takell *n.* gear, equipment,
weapons 2444, 3618, 3679 [cf.
MLG *takel*].

tale *n.*[1] tale, story 16, 3016 [OE
talu].

tale *n.*[2] count, reckoning 2933;

account 4094; *be tale, in tale,* in number 317, 335 [OE *tæl*].

talke *v.* to talk, speak 264, 1262, 3654; **talkes, talkez** *3 sg.* 698, 2575, 3887; exert influence 2409 [OE **talcian,* rel. to TALE, n.[1]].

talkyng *vbl. n.* talk, speech 2581 [from prec.].

talmes *3 sg.* falters, becomes faint 2581 [ON *talma*].

talounez *n. pl.* talons 800 [OF *talon*].

targe *n.* seal 89 (*see note*); **targez** *pl.* shields 732 [OE *targa*].

tarye to delay, tarry 1703, 2583; **taries, taryez** *3 sg.* 1890, 3593, 3899 [obscure; perh. rel. to OE *tergan,* to provoke].

tarsse *n.* silk of Tharsia 3189 [OF *tarse*].

tartes *n. pl.* pies 186 [OF *tarte*].

tas(e). See TAK(E).

taste *v.* to taste, try 186, 187 [OF *taster*].

tatterede *pp.* jagged, serrated *821* (*see note*) [of Scand. orig.; cf. Icel *töttur*].

taulde. See TELL.

tauernez *n. pl.* inns 1568 [OF *taverne*].

tawghte, taghte *pp.* trained, instructed 178; learned 3202 [OE *tǣcan, getǣht*].

taxe *n.* tax, tribute, revenue 2344, 2350, 2358, 2363, etc. [from OF *taxer,* v.].

tell, tellen *v.* to tell, say, speak 16, 1716, 2583, 2735; **tells, tellez, tellys** etc. *3 sg.* 1531, 1707, 1891, etc.; **telles, tellis, tellys,** etc. *3 pl.* 274, 279, 1251, 1396, etc.; **tolde** *pa. t.* 810; **taulde** *pp.* 2618; interpret 812 [OE *tellan*].

temez *3 sg.* empties 1801 [ON *tœma*].

temperall *n.* temporalty, temporal

authoriity 2409 [L *temporālis*].

tempeste *v.* to agitate, disturb violently 2408 [OF *tempester*].

templere *n.* Knight Templar 841 [AF *templer*].

temporaltée *n.* temporal or secular things, temporal authority 1570 [AF **temporelté*].

tende *adj.* tenth 73 [ON *tíonde*].

tenderly *adv.* tenderly 698; carefully, cautiously 3586 [from OF *tendre,* adj.].

ten(e) *adj. & n.* ten 545, 801, 1421, 2344, etc. [OE *tēn, tīen*].

tene *n.* woe, trouble 1956; *in tene,* woefully 1396 [OE *tēona*].

tenefull *adj.* grievous, painful 4280 [OE *tēonful*].

tenefully *adv.* painfully 272, 2345 [from prec.].

tenementez *n. pl.* buildings, dwellings 1569 [OF *tenement*].

tenes *3 pl.* grieve, afflict 264; **tende** *pp.* 1916 [OE *tēonian*].

tente *n.*[1] pavilion 889, 1946, 3015, 3192; **tentez, tentis, tentys,** etc. *pl.* 613, 732, 840, 1229, etc. [OE *tente*].

tente *n.*[2] attention, heed, care 4094; *take tente,* take care 3586 [OF *attent*].

tentyly *adv.* carefully 3618 [from OF *tentif,* adj.].

teraunt, terauntez. See TYRANTE.

teres, teris, terys *n. pl.* tears 698, 951, 3794, 3886, etc. [OE *tēar*].

terez *3 sg.* tears, tears open 800; **terez** *3 pl.* 1143 [OE *teran*].

termys *n. pl.* conditions, state 3654 [OF *terme*].

testament *n.* legacy, bequest 668 [OF *testament*].

tha(a), þa(a) *adj. & art.* (*pl.*) the, those 77, 157, 377, 425, 603, 629, etc. [OE *þā*].

thay(e), þai, þay, þam, thaym,

thaire, etc. See THEY, THIS.

than(e), þan(e), then *conj.* than 313, 315, 539, 540, 844, etc.; than if 1017; *adv.* then, at that time 53, 64, 124, 132, 200, etc. [OE *þænne, þanne*].

thanke *n.* thanks, gratitude 1565 [OE *þanc*].

thanke *v.* to thank 249, 4296; **thankes** *imper. pl.* 1209; **thankyde** *pp.* 1559 [OE *þancian*].

thare: *hym thare be,* he need be 403 [OE *þearfian*].

thare, þare, thareafter, þar(e)by, etc. See THER(E), THEREAFTER, THERBY, etc.

þareofe *adv.* of that, of it 2256 [OE *þǣrof*].

þarewith *adv.* with that, with it 4218 [OE *þǣrwiþ*].

thas, þas(e). See THOS.

that, þat *adj. & art.* the, that 24, 53, 54, 71, 249, etc.; *with n. pl.* 1425 [OE *þæt,* neut.].

that, þat *conj.* that 72, 92, 93, 174, 195, 265, etc.; so that 6, 108, 158, 160, 163, 213, 548, etc.; *pleonastic* 1006 [OE *þæt, þætte*]. See BY.

that, þat *pron.* that, it, that person 441, 515, 711, 903, 971, etc.; what 1196; anything that 3948 [OE *þæt*].

that(e), thatt, þate, þat(t) *rel. pron.* that, which, who, whom 10, 11, 12, 16, 18, 29, 61, etc.; those who 1067, 1987, 2118, 3057, 3126, etc.; that which, whatever 1570; all who 3827; He who (addressing God) 4277; when 26; of which 850; *that he,* who 230 [OE *þe,* replaced by prec.]. See WHEN(E).

the, þe *def. art.* the 2, 6, 7, 11, 17, 23, 26, etc.; these 2485 [OE *þe*].

the, þe *adv. with compar.* so much the, all the 141, 225, 1033, 3797, 3984, etc. [OE *þȳ, þē*].

thedyre *adv.* there, thither 2488 [OE *þider*].

the(e), þe. See THOW(E).

thee *n.* thigh 1046; **theese** *pl.* 1100 [OE *þēoh*].

theef(f)e *n.* villain, wretch 1150, 4253 [OE *þēof*].

thees. See THIS.

they, thei, thay(e), þey, þai, þay *pers. pron.* they 14, 22, 35, 43, 51, 70, 121, etc.; *pleonastic* 579, 1029, 2809, etc.; them, theym(e), thaym, þem, þa(i)m *acc. & dat.* them, to them, from them 11, 97, 103 (*see note*), 123, 169, etc.; *refl.* themselves 484, 485, 500, 579, etc.; þam *as nom.* they 729, 777; their(e), theyre, thi(e)re, thaire, thayre, þeire, þaire, þer *poss. adj.* their 13, 14, 19, 20, 157, 160, 168, etc.; *them selfe, þam selfen, þem seluen, þam seluen,* etc. them, themselves 599; *refl.* 923, 928, 1279, etc.; *reinf.* 276, 1521 [ON *þei, þeim þeir*].

theyne. See THOW(E).

theis, þeis(e). See THIS.

then. See THAN(E).

þer. See THIS, THEY.

þerappon *adv.* thereon, on it 459 [OE *þǣruppan*].

therby, þar(e)by *adv.* besides, in addition to 190; nearby 1186; by that 3337 [OE *þǣrbig*].

ther(e), theire, thare, þer(e), þar(e) *adv. demon.* there, in that place 60, 102, 354, 355, 430, 721, etc.; with that, on that, then 1837, 2435, 2987; *indef.* 92, 134, 163, 176, 192, 208, etc.; *rel.* where, wherever 51, 59, 63,

366, 446, etc.; when 273; which 921, 2289; *þere he standes,* as he stands there 1351 [OE *þǣr, þēr*].

thereaftyr, therafter, thereaftire, thareafter, etc. after that, then 159, 192, 235, 243, 484, 782, 980, 1115, etc.; accordingly 339 [OE *þǣræfter*].

therefore, tharefore, þerfore *adv.* accordingly, for that, for it 342, 550, 2042, 3277 [OE *þǣr* + FOR].

therein, tharein, þerin, þarein *adv.* within, in it, there 1220, 1242, 1254; in that affair, in that matter 1317 [OE *þǣrinne*].

thereon(e) *adv.* on it, on top 3266, 3355 [OE *þǣron*].

thereto, therto, theretoo, þareto *adv.* besides 181; for that purpose, to that end 347, 4040; to it, to that 1612 [OE *þǣrto*].

therevndyre, tharevndyre, þervndyr(e) *adv.* within, inside, underneath, beneath 213, 1156, 2303, 3245, 3606 [OE *þǣrunder*].

thes, þes(e). See THIS.

thewes *n. pl.* manners, customs 21 [OE *þēawas*].

thy, thi, þi, thie. See THOW(E).

thies, þies(e). See THIS.

thikke *n.* crowd, throng 3755; **thykkys** *pl.* 2216 [from next].

thikke, thykke *adj.* thick, massive 1100; 3294; **thikkere** *compar.* 1100 [OE *þicce*].

thin, thyne, etc. See THOW(E).

thynge *n.* thing 3890; **thyngez** *pl.* 1595, 3237 [OE *þing*].

thynk(e) *v.* to intend 3109; *imper.* think, consider 1726, 1732, 2033; **thynkes** *3 pl.* 323; **thoghte** *pa. t.* 3890; **thynk(k)es, thynk(k)ys, thynkkez** *3 sg. impers.* (it) seems

(to) 262, 350, 366, 431, 454, etc.; *pa. t.* 495, 2479, 2682, 3093, etc.; *as hym selfe thynkes,* as pleases him, as he likes 996; *me thynkes,* I expect [OE *þyncan*].

thirde, thyrde *adj. & n.* third 277, 3294, 3410 [OE *þridda*].

thire, þir(e). See THIS.

thyrle *v.* to pierce 1413; **thirllez** *3 sg.* 2167; **thirllede** *pa. t.* 1858, 3890; **thyrllede** *pp.* 2238, 2688 [OE *þyrlian*].

thyrtty, thretty *adj. & n.* thirty 317, 3295 [OE *þrītig, þritig*].

this, þis *adj. & art.* this, the 5, 9, 25, 65, 90, 134, 151, etc.; **the(e)s, this(e), theis, thies, theys, þes(e), þeis(e), þies(e), þis(e), thys, thire, þir(e), þer, þaire** *pl.* these, the 30, 52, 104, 152, 154, 167, 224, etc.; *pron.* this 846, 869, 2351, etc.; it 3569; *pl.* these (people) 831; *he this,* this man 3868 [OE *þis,* neut.; orig. of *thire,* etc. obscure].

thythen *adv.* thence, that place 4345 [ON *þeþan*].

thyʒandez. See TYDANDIS.

þof(e), þoffe. See next.

thoghe, þoghe, þof(e), þoffe *conj.* though, even though 109, 460, 477, 1329, 1703, etc.; that 2947 [ON *þó,* older *þoh].

thoghte. See THYNK(E).

thole *v.* to allow 676, 4022, 4150, 4317 [OE *þolian*].

thoos. See THOS.

thorow(e). See THROWGHE.

thorowely *adv.* in all respects, wholly 3294 [from THROWGHE].

thorowowte, thrughte *prep.* throughout, right through 390, 2170, 2986 [THROWGHE + OUTE].

thorughe. See THROWGHE.

thos, thoos, þose, thas, þas(e) *adj. & art.* those, the 42, 58, 156, 158, 220, 236, etc. [OE *þās*].

thourghe. See THROWGHE.

thourghegyrde, thurghegirde *pp.* run through, thrust through 1461, 3683 [THROWGHE + GIRDE].

thousande, thosaunde, tho(w)san(n)de, thosandez *adj.* thousand 301, 317, 335, 365, 1400 [OE *þūsend*].

thow(e), þow(e), þou *pron.* thou 93, 98, 100, 102, 103, 104, etc.; *with imper.* 452, 669, 3732; **the(e), thie, þe** *acc. & dat.* thee, of thee, to thee, from thee 87, 91, 104, 105, 127, etc. (*see note to line 133*); *refl.* 550, 675, 966, 969, 1013, 1071, etc.; *with imper.* 705, 829; **thy, thi, þi, thin, thyn(n)(e), theyne** *poss. adj.* thy, thine 91, 93, 94, 102, 106, 107, etc.; *thy selfe, thy seluen,* thee, thyself 319, 710, 817, 4145; *þi selfe, þe selfen, thi selfen,* etc. *refl.* 454, 456, 677, 830, etc.; *reinf.* 661, 1673, 2262, etc.; *of þi selfen, seluyn,* thine own 126, 1071 [OE *þū, þē, þīn*]. See ONE, adj.

thra, thraeste. See THROO.

thraa *n.* struggle, contest 249 [ON *þrá*].

thrange *n.* throng 2217 [OE *geþrang*].

thre *adj. & n.* three 1029, 1151, 1681, 2521, etc. [OE *þrēo*].

threppede, threpide *pa. t.* vied, competed 930; fought 2216 [OE *þrēapian*].

thrette *v.* to threaten, attack 3295; **thretys** *3 sg.* 249 [OE *þrēatian*].

thretty. See THYRTTY.

thryftye *adj.* worthy, successful 317 [ON *þrift,* n.].

þryng *v.* to torment, distress 804 (*see note*); **thryngez** *3 sg.* presses, squeezes 1150, 2217 [OE *þringan*].

thrystez *3 sg.* thrusts, presses, squeezes 1151; **thristis** *3 pl.* 3755 [ON *þrýsta*].

thryttene *adj.* thirteen 2216 [OE *þrēotīene*].

throly *adv.* fiercely, violently 1150, 2217; loudly 4332 [from THROO].

thronge *v.* to push, press 3755 [perh. from THRANGE or OE **þrongian*].

throo, thra *adj.* sturdy, bold, fierce 3294, 3295; **thraeste** *superl.* 3756 [ON *þrár*].

throstilles *n. pl.* thrushes 930 [OE *þrostle*].

throwen *pp.* thrown, flung 3694 [OE *þrāwan*].

throwghe, thrughe, thurghe, thourghe, thorughe, thorow(e) *prep* by means of 1, 5, 24, 215, 827, 1069, etc.; through 495, 499, 569, 1226, 1300, etc. [OE *þurh*].

thrughte. See THOROWOWTE.

thurghegirde. See THOURGHE-GYRDE.

thursse *n.* giant, monster 1100 [OE *þyrs*].

thus, þus *adv.* thus, so, in this manner 74, 148, 249, 286, 606, etc. [OE *þus*].

tydandis, tythdands, tythynngez, thyȝandez *n. pl.* tidings, news 264, 582, 1567, 3450, 3899 [OE *tīdung,* ON *tiþendi*].

tyde *n.* tide 737; **tydez** *pl.* hours 753; *þat tide,* then 3902 [OE *tīd*].

tyde *v.* to betide, befall, fall out

879; **tydd(e)** *pp.* 3451, 3654;
tyddes, tydis, tydys *3 sg. impers.*
1703, 3566; *future* 3741, 4227
[OE *tīdan*].

tykes *n. pl.* curs, mongrels 3642,
4258 [ON *tīk*].

til(l), tyll *prep.* to 6, 10, 34, 99,
130, 238, 496, 572, etc.; *till vs,*
for us 130; *conj.* until 413, 879,
985, 1011, 1554, etc. *tyll þat,*
until 325 [ON *til*].

tiltin *3 pl.* roll about, pitch up
and down 1144 [OE **tyltan;* cf.
OE *tealt,* unsteady].

tymbyrde *pp.* done, wrought 3742
[OE *timbr(i)an*].

tym(e) *n.* time, hour, occasion,
period 272, 897, 992, 1695, etc.;
tymms *pl.* 659; fitting moment
431, 1802, 3202; while 879; lifetime 1570, 2351, 2611, etc.; *at
this tym,* on this occasion 9; *of
alde tym,* of former days 13; *in
tym,* after a time 1917; *in his
tym, in þeire tym,* in his (their)
day, in his (their) lifetime 29,
3545; *in no manys tyme,* in no
one's day, never 76; *þat
tym(m)e,* then 328, 545, 1696,
2173; *þat tym þat,* at the time
that, when 810, 887 [OE *tīma*].
See PROCESSE.

tymede *pa. t. impers.* (it) hap-
pened, befell 3150 [OE
(*ge*)*tīmian*].

tyne *v.* to lose 2933; **tynnez** *2 sg.*
1954; **tynt(e)** *pp.* lost, destroyed
272, 770, 1917, 2345, 3566, etc.
[ON *týna*].

tyrante, tyraunt, teraunt *n.* tyrant,
oppressor, despot 842, 878, 991;
tyrauntez *pl.* 824, 2408; king,
ruler, prince 2574; **tirauntez,
terauntez** *pl.* 583, 1801 [OF
tiran(t ending from confusion

with pres. p.)].

tyrauntly *adv.* like a tyrant 271
[from prec.].

Tyseday *n.* Tuesday 3900 [OE
tīwesdæg].

tite, tyte, tytt(e) *adv.* quickly 737,
744, 841, 1891, 2574, etc.;
readily 3886 [ON *títt*].

tythdands, tythynngez. See
TYDANDIS.

title, tytle *n.* title, right 275, 2350,
2363 [OF *title*].

tittez *3 sg.* pulls, drags 1801 [ob-
scure].

to *prep.* to 11, 63, 69, 73, 85,
103, 307, etc.; *with infin.* 4, 8, 9,
12, 51, 54, 89, etc.; at 592, 2510;
toward 3717; for 160; of 593; as
1543; *conj.* until 73, 992, 1971,
3182, etc. [OE *tō*].

to *adv.* too 957, 967, 1200, 1267,
etc. [from prec.].

tobriste *v.* to burst asunder 3982
[OE *toberstan*].

todaye *adv.* today 852, 974,
1444, 1533, etc. [OE *tō dæg*].

**togedire, togedyre, togedirs,
togeders, togedyr(e)s, togederz**
adv. together, altogether 1000,
1050, 1078, 1099, 1141, 1144,
etc. [OE *to-gæd(e)re, to-gadere*
(*s* ending adv. gen.)].

toges, togers *n. pl.* cloaks, coats,
garments 178, 3189 [OF *toge*].

toile *n.* turmoil, strife, melee 1802
[OF *toil*].

toylez, toyelys *n. pl.* tools, gear
732; weapons 3616 [OF *toile*].

tolde. See TELL.

toll *n.* tribute, tax 1568 [OE *toll*].

tolowris *n. pl.* men who pull 3618
(*see note*) [from OE *tollian].

tomorne *adv.* tomorrow 1587
[OE *tō mor(g)ne*].

tone. See ONE, adj.

tonges *n. pl.* tongue-shaped extensions 821 [OE *tunge*].

toppe *n.* top, highest point 801, 1144; platform on the mast of a ship 744 [OE *top*].

toppe-castells *n. pl.* topcastles, fortified platforms at the top of ships from which missiles can be discharged 3616 [prec. + CASTELL].

torattys *3 pl.* scatter, rout 2235 [obscure; rel. to *rat,* scrap, rag (also obscure)].

torfere, tourfere *n.* hardship, misery, misfortune, woe 1956, 2582, 3451, 3741, 4191, 4280, etc. [ON *torfœra, torfœri*].

tornys, tornede. See TURNE.

toruscheez *3 pl.* disperse with force, rout 1428 [OE *to-* + RUSCHE].

tostonayede *pp.* utterly benumbed, stunned 1436 [OE *to-* + OF *estoner,* pp. *estoné*].

tother, toþer *adj.* other 234, 2208, 3409, 3430, etc.; *n.* other 2530, 3283, 3334, etc. [from *the tother* (from *that other*)].

touche, towche *v. trans.* to touch, strike, hit, wound 3747, 4116, 4191 (*with pron. obj. unexpressed*); **towchez** *3 sg.* 800; **towchede** *pa. t.* 770; **towchede** *pp.* 2570, 2575, 2770; **towchez** *3 pl.* tell, relate 1591; *3 sg.* pertains, relates to 1570; **towchande** *pres. p.* 263; to grab, grasp 360, 2067; *intr.* **towchide** *pa. t.* approached, drew near 841 [OF *tochier, tuchier*].

toun. See TOWN.

toure *n.* tower 245, 1890; **toures, towr(r)es, towrez** *pl.* 39, 499, 1569, 3151, 3153 [OF *tor, tur*].

tourfere. See TORFERE.

tourmente *n.* torment, suffering 810 [OF *tourment*].

tourmentez. See TURMENTTEZ.

tournez, tournede. See TURNE.

tourse. See TRUSSE.

towarde, towardes *prep.* toward 720, 1057, 1225, 1280, etc. [OE *tōweard, tōweardes,* adv. gen. ending].

towche, towchez, towchede. See TOUCHE.

towyn *3 pl.* haul, pull 3655 [OE *togian*].

town, toun *n.* town, city 355, 1569; **townnes** *pl.* 3151 [OE *tūn*].

town *adj.* urbane 178 [from prec.].

towres, towrez, etc. See TOURE.

towrythes *3 sg.* writhes violently 3920 [OE *tōwrīþan*].

traylede *pp.* dragged, haled 250 [OF *trailler*].

trayne *n.* trick, trickery, treachery 1630, 3901, 4192 [OF *traïne*].

trayne *v.* to deceive, trick 1683 [OF *traïner*].

trays *n.* way, track 4055 [OF *trace*].

traise *n.* to proceed, travel 1629 [OF *tracier*].

trayste *v.* to trust, believe, believe in 669; **traistez** *3 sg.* 1987, 2870; **traystede** *pa. t.* 1955, 3569 [ON *treysta*].

traistely, traystely *adv.* firmly, securely 1976, 3568 [from prec.].

traytour(e) *n.* traitor 886, 3712, 3741, 3782, 3856, etc.; **traytours** *poss.* 3928; general term of disapprobation, villain 886, 1214, 2017, 2173 [OF *traïtre,* acc. *traïtor*].

trayuellede. See TRAUELAND.

trappede, trappyde *adj.* caparisoned, in trappings 731, 1757, 2150, 3713, 3928 [from OF *drap,* cloth].

trauayle *n.* labor, toil 3566 [OF *travail*].

traueland, trauaylande *pres. p.* traveling 1630; vexing, troubling 1684; **trauaillede** *pp.* 1947; **trayuellede** *pp.* labored, toiled 2357 [OF *travaill(i)er, traveill(i)er*].

trebut(t)e. See TRIBUTE.

trecherye *n.* trickery, deceit 1684 [OF *trecherie*].

trees *n. pl.* trees 3244 [OE *trēo*].

tremlande *pres. p.* trembling 3899 [OF *trembler*].

trenchande *adj.* keen-edged, sharp 3856 [OF *trenchant,* pres. p. of *trenchier*].

treson(e) *n.* treachery 878, 1629, 2017, 3565, etc. [OF *traïson*].

tresour(e) *n.* treasure 668, 991, 1015, 1190, 1214, etc. [OF *tresor*].

trete *n.* trestle 3655 [OF *treste*].

tret(t)(e) *v.* to deal, bargain, negotiate 250, 263 (*see note*), 878, 991, 2932; **tretide, tretyd** *pp.* 407, 3191 [OF *tretier*].

treunt *v.* to steal off, depart 1976; **treunted** *pa. t.* 3900; **treunted** *pp.* 2017 [obscure].

trew, trewe *adj.* true, faithful, accurate, trustworthy 16, 3522, 3565, 3568, 3742, 4192, etc. [OE *trēowe*].

trewage *n.* tribute 2358 [OF *treuage*].

trew(e) *n.* truce 263 (*see note*), 879 (*see note*), 992, 2932, 3191 [OE *trēow*].

trewly *adv.* assuredly, without doubt 2610 [OE *trēowlīce*].

trewthe, trouthe, trowthe, trewghe, trowhe *n.* oath, word 164, 1063, 1314, 1807, 2585, etc.; truth 2127, 3437, 3929 [OE *trēowþ, trywþ,* etc.].

tribute, tributte, trybut, trebut(t)e *n.* tribute 114, 271, 275, 2344, 2350, 2357, etc. [OF *tribut*].

tryede *pa. t.* marshaled, arrayed 1947; **tryede** *pp.* chosen, selected 3782; *pp.* ascertained, determined 3437; *pp.* tested by experience, seasoned 3712 [OF *trier*].

trymblyde *pa. t.* shook, quivered 270 [OF *trembler*].

trine, tryne *v.* to march, go 1757, 3192; **trynes, tryn(n)ys** *3 sg.* 3592, 3901, 4055; **trynande** *pres. p.* 4189 [of Scand. orig.; cf. OSw *trina*].

trippe *v.* to prance 3713 [OF *tripper*].

trisen *3 pl.* hoist, haul 832 [MDu *trīsen*].

trist(i)ly, trystly, trystily *adv.* truly, faithfully, with trust 407, 2357; securely 731, 832; boldly 1262 [from *tristi,* adj., rel. to OE **trȳstan* or ON **trȳsta*].

trofle, trofull *v.* to trifle, dally 1702, 2932; **trofeland** *pres. p.* frivolous, mocking 1683 [from OF *trufle,* n.].

trome *n.* troop, body of men in battle array 3592 [OE *truma*].

trompede, trowmpynge. See TRUMPPEDE VP.

trompes, tromppez. See TRUMPPEZ.

trott *n.* trot 2757 [from OF *troter,* v.].

trouflyng *n.* trifling, dalliance 114 [from OF *trufle,* banter].

troumppes, troumppez. See TRUMPPEZ.

trouthe, trowthe. See TREWTHE.

trow(e) *v.* to believe, trust (in)
89, 250, 887, 1693, 3450;
trowes *2 sg.* 2581 [OE *trēowan*].

trowhe. See TREWTH.

trowmpynge. See TRUMPPEDE VP.

trufles *n. pl.* tricks, trickery 89
[OF *trufle*].

trumppede vp *pa. t.* rose to the
sound of trumpets 407; **trompede**
pp. trumpeted, accompanied by
trumpeting 3713; *with
trowmpynge,* with trumpeting,
to the sound of trumpets 3191
[OF *tromper*].

**trumppez, trompes, tromppez,
troumppes, troumppez** *n. pl.*
trumpets 1484, 1702, 3657,
4107; *with trumppez, with
trompes,* to the sound of trumpets
832, 1757, 1947 [OF *tro(u)mpe,
trumpe*].

trusse, tourse *n.* padding, cushion-
ing 616; trappings, baggage 3592
[OF *trusse, tourse*].

trvssel *n.* a furled sail 3655 [OF
troussel].

trussen *v.* to load, stow, pack up
1976; **trussez** *3 pl.* 731; **trussede**
pp. 1702; **trvssen** *3 pl.* truss, furl
3655 [OF *trousser*].

tuke. See TAK(E).

tumbellez *3 pl.* tumble, roll about
1143 [rel. to MLG *tummeln,* OE
tumbian, OF *tumber*].

tung *n.* language 1250; *with tunge,*
with one's own tongue, person-
ally, face to face 1891 [OE
tunge].

turky *n.* guinea fowl 186 [from
Turkey].

turmenttez *2 sg.* oppress, torment
1954; **turmentez** *3 sg.* 3153;
tourmentez *3 pl.* 824, 842 [OF
to(u)rmenter].

turne, turnne *v. trans.* to turn, revolve 1029; **turnes** *3 sg.* 2574;
turnez *3 pl.* 744; **tournede** *pa. t.*
1052; bring 1956; *3 sg.* over-
turns 3153; *intr.* to turn, go 431,
499, 2582, 4227; **tournez,
tornys** *3 sg.* 3015, 3150, 3593,
3887 (*refl.*); **turnede** *pa. t.* 3451;
turne in, move on, march on 583;
turnys in be, marches on along,
up 4056; *tornede agayne,* re-
turned 3203; **turnes** *3 pl.* roll
1143; *3 sg.* returns 1891; to re-
dound 706; change or reverse
position, shift 1788; *turnez owte,*
withdraws 1802 [OE *turnian,*
OF *to(u)rner*].

turnyng *vbl. n.* action of turning
around 2173 [from prec.].

tuskes, tuskez *n. pl.* fangs 791,
1075, 3234 [OE *tux*].

twys *adv.* twice 716 [OE *twiga,
twiwa,* with adv. gen. ending].

two, twa *adj. & n.* two 171, 301,
335, 807, 880, etc. [OE *twā*].

vgly *adj.* hideous, gruesome 1086
[from ON *uggligr,* to be feared
or dreaded].

vmbeclappes *3 sg.* embraces,
clasps 1779 [OE *ymbe* + OE
*clappian (erron. use due to
resemblance to OE
clyppan)].

vmbegrippys *3 sg.* grips, grasps
3758; **vmbegrippede** *pp.* 3944
[OE *ymbe* + GRIPE].

vmbelappez *3 sg.* surrounds, en-
compasses 1819; **vmbelappyde**
pa. t. 3785 [OE *ymbe* + LAPPE,
v.].

vmbrer(e) *n.* visor 943, 2247,
3952 [OF *ombrier*].

vnabaiste *pp.* undaunted 1378
[OE *un-* + AF *abahir, abaïss-*].

vnblysside *pp.* unhappy, made unhappy 962 [OE *unblissian*].

vnblythely *adv.* unhappily, grievously 1434 [OE *un-* + OE *blīþelīce*].

vnbrydills *3 pl.* unbridle (horses) 3509 [OE *un-* + OE *brīdlian*].

vncle *n.* uncle 2603 [OF *uncle*].

vnclede *pp.* unsheathed, naked 4202 [OE *un-* + CLEDE].

vnclene *adj.* unclean, foul 1063 [OE *unclǣne*].

vncouth(e), vncowthe *adj.* unknown, strange, alien 1902, 3449, 3514 [OE *uncūþ*].

vncouere *v.* to uncover 2710; **vncouerde** *pa. t.* ?unfurled their sails [OE *un-* + OF *covrir*].

vncowpyll *v.* to release (dogs) from being fastened together in couples, to set free for the chase 3999 [OE *un-* + OF *coupler*].

vncowthe. See VNCOUTH(E).

vnder, vndir(e), vndyr(e) *prep.* under, beneath, below, behind, under cover of 87, 108, 405, 439, 489, 537, 1259 (*after n.*), etc. [OE *under*]. See HEUEN, n., CRISTE, PUTTE.

vndirtakande *pres. p.* enterprising, bold 2723 [prec. + TAK(E), after *underniman*].

vndirtakande *vbl. n.* pledge, guarantee 3187 (*see note*) [from prec.].

vndon(e) *pp.* destroyed, brought to ruin 1722, 3752, 3778, 3966 [OE *undōn*].

vndron(e), vndroun *n.* the third hour of the day 462 (*see note*), 2840, 3077 [OE *undren*].

vnfaye *adj.* alive, unhurt 2796 [OE *un-* + FAY(E), adj.].

unfaire, vnfaire, vnfayre *adv.* unfairly, foully, ignobly 303, 779, 2171; hideously 1045, 1074, 2149; roughly 4226 [OE *unfægre*].

unfers *adj.* weak, subdued 4122 [OE *un-* + FERS(E)].

unfondyde *pp.* untested, untried 2485 [OE *un-* + FAN(N)DE].

vnfraistede, vnfraystede *pp.* inexperienced, untested 2736, 2861 [OE *un-* + FRAIST(E)].

vnfrely *adv.* unbeautifully 780 [OE *un-* + FREELY, adj.]

vnlawefull *adj.* lawless 473 [OE *unlagu*].

vnlordly *adv.* ignobly, dishonestly 1267 [OE *un-* + LORDLY(E)].

vnlordlyeste *adj. superl.* most ignoble 1313 [from OE *un-* + LORDLY(E)].

vnmade *pp.* unharvested 2507 [OE *un-* + MAKE].

vnmete *adj.* unequal, uneven 4070 [OE *unmǣte*].

vnquellyde *pp.* unvanquished 3810 [OE *un-* + OE *cwellan*].

vnreken *adj.* rough, savage 3754 [OE *un-* + OE *recen*].

vnresonable *adj.* unjust, outrageous 3452 [OE *un-* + OF *reson(n)able*].

vnryghttwyslye *adv.* unjustly 329 [OE *unrihtwīslīce*].

vnsaughte, vnsawghte *adj.* at odds, beset by strife, at enmity 1306, 1457; troubled, distressed 1910, 4140; **vnsaughtely, vnsaughtyly** *adv.* violently, with hostility 1501, 1847 [late OE *unseht*, ON *úsáttr*].

vnschaply *adj.* misshapen, deformed 1099 [cf. ON *úskapligr*].

vnsekyrly *adv.* insecurely, dangerously 966 [OE *un-* + SEKIRLY].

vnsemly *adv.* hideously, monstrously 1044 [ON *úsǣmiliga*].

vnsene *adj.* unseen 3114 [OE
un- + SE(E)].

vnslely *adv.* savagely, roughly 979
[OE *un-* + ON *slǽliga*].

vnsownde *adj.* suffering, stricken,
wounded 3931, 3942, 4088,
4294; *with adv. sense* 3290 [OE
ungesund].

vnsparely, vnsparyly *adv.* unspar-
ingly, generously 235; wastefully
3160 [OE *un-* + OE *spærlīce*].

vntenderly, vntendirly *adv.* un-
gently, violently 1144, 2575
[OE *un-* + TENDERLY]

vnto *prep.* to 47, 231, 351, 465,
470, etc. [OE **untō*].

vntrewe *adj.* faithless, treacherous
4227 [OE *untrēowe*].

vntrewely *adv.* treacherously 886
[OE *untrēowlīce*].

vnuenquiste *pp.* unvanquished
2049 (*see note*) [OE *un-* +
VENQUYSE].

vnwemyde *pp.* unblemished, im-
maculate 3801 [OE
ungewemmed].

vnwyn(n)ly *adv.* joylessly, woefully 955, 1481, 3562; harshly
1302 [OE *un-* + WYNLY].

vnwyse *adj.* reckless 3817 [OE
ungewiss].

vnwittyly *adv.* inadvertently, unin-
tentionally 3802 [from OE
unwittig, adj.].

vnworthye *adj.* unworthy 3554
[from OE *unweorþe*].

vnworthyly *adv.* treacherously
763 [OE *unweorþlīce*].

vpbrayde *v.* to censure, find fault
with, reprove 1930 [OE
upbregdan].

vp(e) *adv.* up 85, 124, 493, 740,
832, 840, etc. [OE *up*]. See GIFE,
V., RECOUERE.

vptyhes *n. pl.* ropes or chains by

which yards are suspended *3675*
(*see note*) [VP(E) + OE *tēah,
tēh*, n.].

vs. See WE.

vse *v.* to use 1843; **vsede** *pa. t.*
2627; **vsede** *pp.* accustomed 2847
[OF *user*].

Vtas of Hillary the feast of St.
Hilary 625 (*see note*) [AF
utaves].

vttere *adv.* farther off, away 2438
[OE *ūtor*].

vtterly, uttirly, vttirly *adv.* fully,
absolutely 31, 400, 3966 [from
OE *ūtera*, adj.].

vtters *v. intr.* speaks 418 [from
VTTERE].

vaile: *kawghte hir a vaile*, took
the veil, became a nun 3916 [AF
veile].

vayllede *pp.* covered, decked *2568*
(*see note*) [from prec.].

vayne *n.* vein 2570 [OF *vaine,
veine*].

vayne *adj.* fruitless, worthless 10
[OF *vain, vein*].

vale *n.* vale, valley 1981, 2007,
2046, 2094, 2876, etc. [OF *val*].

valiant(e), valya(u)nt, valyant(e)
adj. worthy, excellent, valiant
148, 299, 1726, 1958, 2025, etc.;
as n. 3164 [OF *vail(l)ant*].

value *n.* value, worth 41 [OF
value].

vassallage *n.* action, exploit 2048
[OF *vassal(l)age*].

vawewarde. See AVANTTWARDE.

velany(e) *n.* wickedness, villainy
298, 326 [AF *vilanie, vilenie,*
etc.].

velvett *n.* velvet 2569 [MedL
velvetum].

vencows. See VENQUYSE.

venemus, ven(n)ymous, venymos

adj. venomous, baneful, deadly 299, 772, 2570, 4124 [AF *venim(o)us*].

venge   *v.* to avenge 867; **vengede** *pp.* 298, 2264 [OF *veng(i)er*].

venym   *n.* poison 215 [OF *venim*].

venymos, ven(n)ymous.   See VENEMUS.

venyson   *n.* venison 3166 [AF *venison, venysoun*].

venquyse, vencows   *v.* to vanquish, defeat 1984, 4297; **venqwiste** *pa. t.* 2093; **venqueste, venquiste, venqwyste** *pp.* 325, 2065, 3765 [OF *veintre,* pa. t. *venquis*].

ventelde   *pa. t.* set sail 737 (*see note*) [OF *venteler*].

vernacle   *n.* vernicle, the kerchief of Veronica, with the imprint of Christ's face 297, 309, 348, 386 [AF *vernicle*].

vernage   *n.* a sweet white Italian wine 204, 3166 [OF *vernage*].

verrede   *pp.* flecked, stained 2573 [OF *vairier*].

verreilly, verrayely   *adv.* in truth, truly 308, 3765 [from OF *verai*].

vertely   *adv.* quickly, readily 3168 [after OF *vertement*].

vertue   *n.* power 215, 4297 [OF *vertu*].

vert(u)ous(e), vertouous, vertuus *adj.* virtuous, just, righteous 5, 3055; potent, powerful, with special power 204, 297, 348 [OF *vertuous, vertuos*].

vesage.   See VISAGE.

vesare, vesere   *n.* visor, vizard 910, 2572, 3054 [AF *visere*].

Vescounte, Vescownte.   See VISCOWNTE.

vesettez   *3 sg.* supplies, enriches 1726 [OF *visiter*].

vessell   *n.* (*uninfl. pl.*) household vessels, utensils 3071 [OF *vessel*].

vesture, vestoure   *n.* garment 2569; *uninfl. pl.* 3071; **vesturis** *pl.* 2572 [OF *vesture*].

vetaile   *n.* provisions, food 3071 [OF *vitaille*].

vetaile   *v.* to supply with provisions 353; **vetailles** *3 sg.* 3165 [OF *vitaill(i)er*].

viage   *n.* campaign, expedition 2037, 2493, 2863 [AF *viage*].

vice   *n.* flaw 911 [OF *vis*].

Vicounte.   See VISCOWNTE.

victor   *n.* victor 2065; **victoures** *pl.* 2863 [AF *victo(u)r*].

victorie, victorye   *n.* victory 827, 1984, 2037, 2093 [OF *victorie*].

vines, vynes   *n. pl.* vines, vineyards 3159, 3169, 3242, 3481 [OF *vine*].

violently   *adv.* profusely 2571 [from OF *violent*].

visage, vesage   *n.* face 137, 1983, 3055 [OF *visage*].

Viscownte, Vyscownte, Vicounte, Vescownte, Vescounte   *n.* Viscount 325, 1984, 2024, 2047, 2050, 2065; *uninfl. poss.* 3167 [OF *visconte*].

visez   *3 sg.* intends 3167 [OF *viser*].

visione   *n.* vision 828 [OF *vision*].

voyce   *n.* voice 2046; **voycez** *pl.* 2864 [AF *voice*].

voyde   *adj.* worthless, ineffective 10; devoid, free 911 [OF *voide*].

voide, voyde   *v. intr.* pass away, pass out 215; withdraw, give ground 309, 1974, 2049; **voydes** *3 sg.* 3764; **voyde** *pa. t.* 2094; **voydes** *3 sg.* empties, bleeds 2571; *trans.* **voydes** *3 pl.* withdraw from 3070; **voydez** *3 pl.* dismount from 3168 [OF *void(i)er*].

voute, vowt   *n.* expression,

demeanor 137, *2050, 3054* [OF *vou(l)t*].

wache *n.* sentry, guard 2499, 3035; **wac(c)hes** *pl.* 1356, 2480 [OE *wæcce*].

wache, wacchen *v.* to guard 547, 613; **wachede** *pp.* 1613 [OE *wæccan*].

wafull *adj.* woeful, miserable 950, 955, 4285 [from OE *wā,* n.].

wagande *pres. p.* stirring, shaking 3660 [OE *wagian*].

wage: *of my wage,* at my expense, in my service 302; **wages** *pl.* wages 2930 [ONF *wage*].

wage, wagge *v.* to pledge 333, 2967; hire, employ, engage 547, 1615; **wagen** *1 sg.* wager, bet 2445 [ONF *wagier*].

way(e) *n.* path, route, way, track 450, 473, 947, 1225, 1634, etc.; *as adj.* 1713; **wayes** *pl.* 391, 1796, 2005; **wayes** *adv. gen.* way 481, 497, 640, 1796, 1896, etc. *of waye,* away 873, 1538; *a furlange of waye,* a short time, the time it takes to walk a furlong 2091; *no waye,* in no way, not at all 3231 [OE *weg*]. See HOLDE.

wayfare *n.* course, way 1797 [prec. + FARE, n.].

wayfe *v.* to wander, stray, deviate 960 [ON *veifa*].

waykly *adv.* softly 697 [from ON *veikr*].

wayte, waytten *v.* to watch, look to, look out for 164, 1973; wait 1807; **wayt(t)es** *3 sg. refl.* watches with hostile intent 2979, 3770 [OF *wait(i)er*].

wakkenys(s)e, waknez *3 sg. intr.* awakens 257, 806, 3562; **wakkenyde** *pa. t.* 3392; *trans.*

wakkens *2 pl.* awaken, wake 2370 [OE *wæcn(i)an*].

walde. See WIL(L), V.

wale *adj.* excellent, noble, choice (general laudatory word) 741, 763, 2148 [ON *val,* act of choosing].

wale *v.* to choose, select 181 [ON *velja,* pa. t. *valdi*].

wale, walle *n.* wale, planks running the length of a ship 493, 740 [OE *walu*].

walewede *pa. t.* wallowed 3838 [OE *wealwian*].

walkes *3 sg.* walks, wanders 946, 3489; **walkede** *pa. t.* 3233; **walkande** *pres. p.* 3479; *pres. p.* moving (perh. with a slow, tossing motion, like that of waves) 762 [OE *wealcian*].

walkyn *n.* sky, heavens 787 [OE *wolcen*].

walles, wallez, wallis, wallys *n. pl.* 61, 167, 228, 280, 351, etc. [OE *wall*].

walopande *pres. p.* galloping 2147, 2827 [ONF **waloper,* OF *galoper*].

walowes *3 pl.* tumble, roll about 1142 [OE *wealwian*].

wan. See WYN(N)(E).

wandyrs *3 sg. intr.* flies, soars 798; **wanderande** *pres. p.* 763; *trans.* **wandyrde** *pa. t.* traversed 947 [OE *wandrian*].

wandreth(e), wan(e)dreth *n.* trouble, misery; distress 323, 384, 2370, 3157, 3524, 3889; **wonrydez** *pl.* 707 [ON *vandræþi*].

wandsomdly *adv.* wretchedly, miserably 4012 (*see note*) [perh. from WONDSOM].

wane *adj.* dark, gloomy 492 [OE *wann*].

wante, wannt(t)e *v. trans.* to lack,

lose, be deprived of 398, 653, 4019; **want(t)es** *3 sg.* 2486 (*impers.*), 4285; *intr.* to fail, give out 2445 [ON *vanta*].

wapen, wapyn(e) *n.* weapon 1106, 1119, 1188, 1193, 1390, etc.; *uninfl. pl.* 1281, 3673, 3692; **wapens, wapyn(n)s, wapynez,** etc. *pl.* 312, 332, 594, 1454, etc. [OE *wǣpen*].

warantizez *n. pl.* defenses, protections 1614 [OF *warentise*].

wardayne, wardane *n.* regent, guardian 650, 3523, 3554; **wardaynes** *pl.* 3090; defender, warrior, leader, general 2494, 2513, 2678, 2740, 3021 [ONF *wardein*].

warde *n.* post 2480, 3035; ward 2953; *in warde,* under guard 1613 [OE *weard*].

warded *pp.* guarded 1614 [OE *weardian*].

wardrop(e) *n.* dressing room, storeroom for armor and clothing 901, 2622, 4203, 4217 [ONF *warderobe*].

ware, warre, were *adj.* prudent, skilled, trained 19, 3692; prepared, on guard, watchful 1973, 3839; wary, cautious 546, 1616, 1808, 2370; *was warre,* became aware, noticed 2220, 2515, 2678, 2825, etc. [OE *wær*].

war(e). See WAS, WHERE.

warely *adv.* prudently, cautiously 4026 [OE *wærlīce*].

waresche *v.* to recover, heal 2186 [OF *warir, wariss-*].

warlawe, warlow, werlaughe *n.* monster, fiend 948, 958, 1140, 3771; **warlaws** *pl.* warlocks, sorcerers 613 [OE *wǣrloga*].

warme *adj.* warm, hot 2332 [OE *wearm*].

warne *v.* to warn 961, 965, 2499, 4223 (*with pron. obj. unexpressed*); **warnede** *pp.* 1616, 1808; **warnes** *3 sg.* denies, deprives 700 [OE *warnian*].

warpe, werpe *v.* to speak, utter 9, 150; **warp** *pa. t.* cast out, threw 901; **warpes** *imper. pl.* go hastily 2746 [OE *weorpan*].

warre. See next, WARE.

was, whas *pa. t. sg.* was 23, 40, 59, 61, 79, etc.; *with pl. subj.* 929, 1078, 1415, 1851, etc.; *with rel. or subj. pron. unexpressed* 338, 1485, 1628, 2761, etc.; *impers.* there was 76, 143, 190, 203, 543, etc.; there were 3174; which were 3678; *as auxil.* was, had been 932; had 1198, 3106, 3223, 2919, etc.; **were, ware, whare** *pl.* were 70, 174, 177, 191, 276, etc.; **were, ware, war, warre** *pa. t. subj.* were, would be, should be 73, 121, 134, 150, 477, etc.; *with sg. subj.* 976, 1938; *as auxil.* had, had been 602, 2260, 3192 [OE *wæs, wǣre, wǣron*].

waste: *in waste,* wastefully 150 [ONF *wast(e)*].

wast(e) *adj.* idle, vain 993; desolate 3910 [from prec.].

wasten *v.* to destroy 3835; **wastede** *pp.* 3802; **wastys** *3 sg.* lays waste 3156; **wastys** *3 pl.* waste 2444 [AF *waster*].

wasternne *n.* wasteland, wilderness 3233 [OE *wēstern* with infl. of WAST(E)].

wate. See WYT.

watere, wat(t)ire, watyre *n.* water, stream 540, 931, 1299, 1358, etc.; *as adj.* 2516; **waters, watyrs** *pl.* 3600, 3697, 4321 [OE *wæter*].

wathe, wawhte *n.* danger, peril 2668, 3480 [ON *váþi*].

wathely *adv.* dangerously, perilously 2090, 2186 [from prec.].

wathes *n. pl.* prey, game obtained in hunting 3233 [ON *veiþr*].

watyre-men *n. pl.* seamen 741 [WATERE + MAN].

watte. See WYT, WHAT(E).

wauering *vbl. n.* wandering, roving 2224 [prob. from ON *vafra*, to move unsteadily].

wawarde. See AVANTTWARDE.

wawhte. See WATHE.

waxe *n.* candlewax, candles 161, 4019 [OE *weax*].

waxe *v.* to grow 4322; **waxen** *3 pl.* 2947 [OE *weaxan*].

we, wee *pron.* we 6, 112, 114, 127, 128, etc.; *pl. of majesty* 3211; **our(e), owre** *poss. adj.* our 7, 112, 255, 293, etc.; *pl. of majesty* 282; **our(e)s, owr(e)s, ourez** ours 1912, 2043, 2737, 2859, etc.; **vs** *acc. & dat.* us, to us, for us 3, 4, 130, 131, 137, etc.; *pl. of majesty* 1943; *refl.* 4, 342; *vs moste,* we must 2491; *oure selfen,* ourselves 331, 1969, 3802 [OE *wē, ūre, ūs*].

weches *n. pl.* sorcerers 613 [OE *wicce*].

wedde, weddede, weddyde *pp.* wedded 700, 3550, 3575 [OE *weddian*].

wedes, wedez, wedis, wedys *n. pl.* clothes, garments 168, 500, 901, 1143, 1349, etc. [OE *wǣd, gewǣd*].

wedirwyns. See WYDERWYN.

wedowe *n.* widow, old woman 950, 4285; **wedewes** *pl.* 3154 [OE *weoduwe, widuwe,* etc.].

wee. See WE.

weend(e), weendes, etc. See WENDE.

weyde. See WYE, v.

weif(f)e. See WIF.

weilde, welde *v.* to rule, govern 650, 2967, 3090 [OE *wieldan, wyldan*].

weile. See WELL.

weyn *n.* wine 161 [OE *wīn*].

weyndes, weyndez. See WENDE.

weise, weysse. See WYSE.

wekyrly *adv.* nimbly 2104 [rel. to Icel *vakr,* nimble].

welcom *adj.* welcome 1200; (as greeting) 3339, 3517 [OE *wilcoma,* n.].

welde. See WEILDE.

wele *n.* weal, prosperity, good 401, 653, 3963, 4100; wealth 674 [OE *wela*].

well, wele, weile *adv.* well 170, 230, 321, 419, 663, etc.; to good, to advantage 3803; *well a, wele a,* a good 2758, 3113; *well wele,* full well, very well 3507 [OE *wel*].

well(e) *n.* spring, fountain, stream, well 540, 882, 947, 3376; *uninfl. pl.* 2705 [OE *wella*].

wellys *3 sg.* gushes, runs 3819; **wellyde** *pa. t.* welled up, bubbled over 3377; *wellyde all qwyke,* boiled alive 1736 [OE *wellan*].

welte *pa. t.* overturned, cast down 3152 [ON **welta* (Icel & Norw *velta,* MSw *välta*)].

welters, welterys *3 sg. trans.* tosses, rolls 1140; *intr.* rolls or twists the body, writhes 890; **welters** *3 pl.* 1142; **welterande** *pres. p.* tossing, lurching 2147 [cf. MDu & MLG *welteran*].

welthe *n.* good thing 161, 541, 653; wealth 2684; opulence 4331; gratification, satisfaction 231; **welthes** *pl.* goods 3157 [OE

wela, with *th* ending by anal. with *helthe*].

wende, weend(e) *v.* to go, journey, depart 302, 1299, 1959, 2445, 2493, etc.; **weyndez** *2 sg.* go (*future*) 450; **we(e)ndes, wendez, weyndes** *3 sg.* goes, is leaving 245, 614, 701, 2185, etc.; goes off 1355; goes back, rides back 2080; **wendez** *3 pl.* go forth 822; **weendes** *imper. pl.* go 2500; **went(e)** *pa. t.* 56, 231, 492, 695, 901, etc.; **wente** *pp.* come 3507 [OE *wendan*].

wenes, wenys, wenez *2 sg.* think, suppose, expect, hope 963, 1806, 2580, 2779; **wende** *pa. t.* 2121 [OE *wēnan*].

wenge *n.* wing 4002; **wenges, wengez** *pl.* 768, 819, 926 [ON *vængr*].

went. See WENDE.

wepe *v.* to weep, mourn 323, 3155, 3978, 4286; **wepede** *pa. t.* 1920; **wepand(e)** *pres. p.* 697, 2679, 3561, 3888 [OE *wēpan*].

wepyng *vbl. n.* weeping 707 [from prec.].

werdes, weredes *n. pl. as s.* fate, destiny 385, 3889 [OE *wyrd*].

were, werre *n.* battle, war, struggle, assault 22, 33, 257, 323, 333, etc.; *of wer(r)e,* through war, by battle, of battle 621, 685, 1657, 1681, 2137, etc.; *o werre,* at war 3480 [late OE *werre* (from OF)].

were. See WAS, V., WARE, adj.

werede: *werede owte,* exhausted, used up 2930 [OE *werian*].

weredes. See WERDES.

weres *3 sg.* raises, lifts 3054 [OF *vertir, ver-*].

wery *adj.* weary, miserable, sad 492, 812; *quasi-adv.* wearily

4012; miserably, grievously 806, 950, 3392, 3792 [OE *wērig*].

wery(e) *v.* to curse 699, 3155, 4286; **weries** *3 sg.* 3888; **weryd** *pp.* 959 [OE *wergan*].

weryede *pp.* worn out, exhausted 796 [OE *wēr(i)gian*].

werkes, werkys *n. pl.* actions, deeds 3, 19, 2915, 3453, 3560, etc. [OE *we(o)rc*].

werkkes *3 sg.* pains, hurts 2689; **werkand(e)** *pres. p.* racking, paining 1797, 2148 [OE *wærcan*].

werlaughe. See WARLAWE.

werld(e). See WORLDE.

werpe. See WARPE.

werraye, werreye *v. trans.* battle, make war on 657, 3448; **werrayes** *3 pl.* 3447; **werrayand(e)** *pres. p.* 2089, 2599; **werrayede** *pa. t.* 2045, 2215; *intr.* to make war 546 [OF *werreier*].

werre. See WERE.

werse *adj. compar.* worse 3082; **werst** *superl.* worst 3549 [OE *wyrsa, wyrsta*].

wesche *pa. t.* washed 231; **weschen** *pp.* 1301 [OE *wascan*].

west(e) *n.* west 3660; *adj.* west, western 77, 334, 336, 762, etc. [OE *west*].

weten, wette. See WYT.

wette *v.* to wet 2332 [OE *wætan*].

wh-. See also w-.

wham, whaym *pron.* whom, · whomever 770, 1202; *as n.* 186 [OE *hwǣm*].

whanne. See WYN(N)(E).

whare. See WAS, WHERE.

whas. See WAS.

what(e), whatt(e), watte, qwat(e) *pron. indef.* what, whatever 140, 162, 267, 370, 692, etc.; to what extent, how much 891; *interrog.* 2223; *what for,* what with, be-

cause of 3793; *whate . . . and,*
both . . . and 931 (*see note*);
whate so, whatever 1020; *adj.*
what, what kind of 154, 287,
510, 1275, etc.; which 318 [OE
hwæt].

whedire, whedyr(e). See
WHETHIRE.

whele *n.* wheel 3260, 3261, 3388
[OE *hwēol*].

when(e), whenn, qwen(n), qwhen
adv. rel. when, after, whenever 7,
48, 52, 63, 69, etc.; *when that,*
when þat, when 26, 313; as soon
as 582, 3587; as long as 423 [OE
hwænne, hwenne].

where, whare, ware *adv.* where,
wherever 107, 614, 803, 805,
1035 etc.; *whare so,* wherever
302, *whare þat,* where 948 [OE
hwǣr].

whethire *pron.* whichever 350;
conj. whether 2311, 2637, 2733
[OE *hwæþer, hweþer*].

whethire, whedire, whedyr(e), *adv.*
interrog. whither, where, wherever 962, 1548, 2533, 2931,
3231, etc. [OE *hwider*].

why *adv. interrog.* why, how 98,
100, 103, 2763, etc. [OE *hwȳ*].

whydyrwyns. See WYDERWYN.

whyeseste. See WYSE.

whilde. See WILDE.

whilke *pron.* which one 4194
[OE *hwilc*].

whille, qwhyle: *in a qwhyle, þat*
whille, in a short time, in a moment, quickly, suddenly 553,
3389 [OE *hwīl*].

whil(l)s, whilles, whylez, whylles,
qwhills, qwhylls, qwylls *conj.*
while, as, as long as, when 398,
406, 486, 855, 1197, 1335,
1590, etc.; until 2132, 3908,
4047; *prep.* until, up to the time

of 2511 (*see note*) [OE *hwīl,*
with gen. ending].

whilom *adv.* at times, sometimes
1145 [OE *hwīlum*].

whyne *adv. interrog.* why not 703
[OE *hwȳ + ne*].

whirles *3 sg.* whirls, turns, re-
volves 3388; **whirllide** *pa. t.* 3260
[OE *hwyrftlian,* ON *hvirfla*].

whitte *adj.* white, fair 3260; lustrous, shining 4183 [OE *hwīt*].

who, whoo *pron. interrog.* who
2726; *indef.* whoever 516, 1102,
1322, 2560; *who-so,* whoever, if
anyone 113, 205, 1084, 1843,
etc. [OE *hwā, swā-hwā-swā*].

wyde *adj.* wide 1796, 2089; *wyde*
opyn, at full length 2147 [OE
wīde].

wyderwyn *n.* adversary, enemy
2045; **whydyrwyns, wedirwyns**
pl. 2215, 3818, 3834 [OE *wiþer-*
winna].

wy(e) *n.* man, warrior, knight, person *515,* 695, 699, 891, 1616,
etc.; (in direct address) 164,
1807; **wyes(e)** *pl.* 56, 336, 533,
1300, etc. [OE *wiga*].

wye *v.* to weigh, hoist (anchors)
740; **weyde** *pa. t.* 493 [OE
wegan].

wieffe, wyefe. See WIF.

wielde *n.* muscle 2689 [OE
weald].

wyesly, weisely *adv.* attentively,
carefully 1613; wisely, prudently
1974, 3507; cleverly, cunningly
2599 [OE *wīslīce*].

wyes(s)(e), wiese, etc. See WY(E),
n., WYSE.

wi(e)t. See WYT.

wif, wyf(f)e, weif(f)e, wyefe, etc. *n.*
woman, wife 652, 674, 955, 986,
2191, etc.; **wyfes** *poss.* 864;
wyfes *pl.* 294 [OE *wīf*].

wyghte *adj.* valiant, fierce, strong 1140, 1615, 2137, 2514, etc.; **wyghttere** *compar.* 964; **wyghteste** *superl.* 290, 336, 532; **wyghtly(e)** *adv.* keenly, fiercely 553; swiftly 740 [ON *vigr,* neut. *vigt*].

wyghte *n.* man, creature 959 [OE *wiht*].

wyghtemen *n. pl.* warriors [WYGHTE, adj. + MAN].

wyghtnesse, wightenez *n.* valor, courage, might, power 258, 516, 796, 1358, 2214 [from WYGHTE, adj.].

wikkede, wykkyd(e) *adj.* savage, vicious, wicked 3232, 3447, 3523, 4322 [from OE *wicca*].

wyld(e) *n.* game 181, 657 [OE *wild, wilder,* pl. *wildru*].

wilde, wylde, whilde *adj.* wild, savage 188, 960, 3232, 3446, 3523, etc.; *wylde fyre,* destructive fire, conflagration 797 [OE *wilde, wildefȳr*].

wildernesse *n.* wilderness 3910 [OE **wild(d)ēorness* (= MDu, MLG *wildernisse*)].

wile *v. refl.* get (away) by stealth, steal (away) 3908 [from next].

wilez *n. pl.* tricks 1504 [OE *wīl*].

wilfully *adv.* willfully, obstinately 151, 3835 [from WILL, n.].

wylily *adv.* cunningly, craftily 2746 [from WILEZ].

will, wyll *n.* desire, pleasure 33, 339, 620, 692, etc.; will, purpose, determination 664, 1057, 1564, 3774, etc.; testament 672; favor, good will 3340 [OE *willa*]. See GODE, adj.

will *adj.* wayward, wild, bewildered 3836 [ON *villr*].

wil(l), wyll *v.* to wish, want, want to 896, 937, 1190, 1556, 2223,

etc.; **walde, wold(e)** *pa. t.* 877, 1359, 1927, etc.; bid, command 652; *auxil. future tense* will, shall 319, 515 (*with v.* do *unexpressed*), 546, 553, 670, 2406 (*with v.* go *unexpressed*); *pa. t.* would 339, 342, 528, 716, etc. [OE *willan, wolde, walde*].

willed *adj.* bewildered, perplexed 3230 [WILDE adj., with infl. of ON *villr*].

wil(l)nez *2 sg.* desire, wish, crave 961, 2224, 3479 (*wiith v.* go *unexpressed*); **wylnez** *3 sg.* 384 [OE *wilnian*].

wynch *v.* to wince, flinch 2104 [AF *wench(i)er*].

wynde *n.* wind 1788, 3600, 3660; *tuke wynde,* caught (their) breath 1359 [OE *wind*]. See SYDE.

wyndowes *n. pl.* slits in the visor of a helmet for vision and air 911 [ON *vindauga*].

wyne *n.* wine 203, 540, 2028, 2714, 3166, etc.; **wynes** *pl.* 1028 [OE *wīn*].

wynly, wynlyche *adj.* delightful, delectable 181; *adv.* splendidly 671; courteously 2185, 3338 [OE *wynlic, wynlīce*].

wyn(n)(e) *v. trans.* to get, gain, capture, conquer 516, 2444 (*future*), 2751, 3908, etc.; **wynnys** *2 sg.* 965 (*future*); **wynnys** *3 sg.* 621, 3104, 3124, etc.; **wynnys** *3 pl.* 2470; **wan(e), whanne** *pa. t.* 22, 33, 115, etc.; **wonn(e), won(n)en, wonnyn** *pp.* 26, 618, 651, 820, 887, 1214, etc.; *pp.* destroyed 3053; *intr.* go, depart 468 [OE *gewinnan,* ON *vinna*].

wyn(t)er(e)s, wyntres, wynteris, wynnttyrs, etc. *n. pl.* winters, years 278, 614, 846, 1174, 2344, etc.; **wyn(n)t(t)er, wyntyre**

uninfl. pl. 440, 872, 983, 1009, etc. [OE *winter*].

wirche, wyrche. See WIRKE.

wirchip(e), wyrchip(p)(e) *n.* honor, respect, veneration, glory 10, 150, 164, 401, 468, 541, etc.; **wyrchippis** *pl.* 22; credit 3977; one who constitutes a source or ground of honor 700; *зour wirchip,* your honor 2739 [OE *weorþscipe*].

wirchipe, wyrchipe *v.* to honor, worship, treat with respect 3340; **wirchipid, wyrchipide** *pp.* 320, 685; give glory to 397; **wyrscheppez** *3 sg.* 1059; *pp.* praised 257 [from prec.].

wirchipfull, wyrchipfull *adj.* worthy 333, 1299, 1356, 2218, 2231, etc.; loyal, trusted 650, 1614; honorable 2601 [from WIRCHIP(E), n.].

wirke, wyrk(e), wirche, wyrche *v.* to work, do, act, perform, carry out 130, 149, 339, 692, 1030, 1384, 1629, etc.; **wirk(k)es** *2 sg.* 2432, 4026 (*future*); **wyrkkes, wyrkez** *3 sg.* 1267, 1393, 1468, 1790; **wirkes, wirkkys** *imper. pl.* 4099, 4100; **wyrkes** *3 pl.* 663, 1426, 1430; **wroghte** *pa. t.* 322, 326, 3157, etc.; **wroghte** *pp.* 2622, 3524, 3567, 4025, etc.; *wroghten on* (*pa. t. pl.*), set on 2137; make, create, produce, effect 3803; *3 sg.* 1797; *pa. t.* 1796, 2089, 3154; *pp.* 3495, 3552; *pa. t.* appointed 3090 [OE *wyrcan, wrohte*].

wyrscheppez. See WIRCHIPE.

wyse, wyes(e), wyesse, wiese, weysse, weise *adj.* prudent, experienced, skilled 19, 149, 1973, 2514, 2680, 2745, etc.; **wyseste, whyeseste** *superl.* 290, 532,

2496; wise 806, 2185 [OE *wīs*].

wyssdome *n.* experience, skill 2600 [OE *wīsdōm*].

wysse *v.* direct, guide, lead 9; rule 813; **wysse** *3 sg.* 671 [OE *wissian*].

wysse, wiste, wyste. See WYT, v.

wit, witt(e), wytt(e) *n.* knowledge, sense, intelligence, wisdom, science 149, 959, 2020, 2739, 2745, 3090; skill 741, 2600, 4287, 4297; *his witte changede,* his brain reeled 2571 [OE *(ge)witt*]. See CASTE.

wyt, wi(e)t, wette *v.* to know 420; **wat(t)e** *1 sg. pres.* 533, 2224, 4203; **wat(t)e** *2 sg. pres.* 692, 3393, 3549; **wotte** *2 pl. pres.* 4100; **not** (= ne wot) know not 977; **wist(e), wyste** *pa. t.* 339, 891, 3231, 3792, etc.; **wyten** *pp.* 869; **wysse** *pp.* famed 685; observe, witness 708 (*see note*); **weten** *pp.* 2966; find out, discover 948, 958; *pa. t.* 3919 [OE *witan, wāt wiste*].

wythall *adv.* in addition, besides 1521 [after OE *mid alle*].

withdrawes *3 pl.* withdraw 2154, 2473; **withdrewe** *pa. t.* 4219 [WITH(E) + DRAWE].

with(e), wyth(e) *prep.* with, along with, possessing, accompanied by 8, 39, 56, 57, 59, 61, etc.; against 1174; by, through, by means of 22, 47, 90, 111, 115, 167, 169, etc.; to, toward 66; for 192, 3052; on 1025, 3257; on the side or with the party of 1327, 2729 [OE *wiþ*].

within, wythin *prep.* in, within, inside, into 167, 228, 301, 318, 380, 440, 634, etc.; *adv.* inside 758 [OE *wiþinnan*].

wytholdez *2 sg.* withhold 103

[WITH(E) + HOLDE].

withowte, withowten, withowttyn, wythowttyn, etc. *prep.* without 114, 139, 225, 295, 491, 748, etc.; outside of 849, 997, 3589; beyond 884, 2825, 3068; this side of 461; *adv.* afar 3017 [OE *wiþūtan*].

wythsytte *v.* to resist, oppose 104 [OE *wiþsettan*].

withstonden *1 pl.* offer resistance, bear up 1747; **withstonden** *pp.* 1926 [OE *wiþstandan*].

withthy *conj.* provided 2587, 2591 [WITH(E) + OE *þȳ*].

witter *v.* to inform, report to 1239 [ON *vitra*].

wytterly *adv.* certainly, without doubt, truly 324, 3549 [ON *vitrliga*].

wittnesse *uninfl. pl.* witnesses 3552 [OE *witnes*].

wlonke *adj.* proud 3154; fair, fine *as n.* 3338 [OE *wlonc*].

wo, woo *n.* woe, distress 708, 2966, 3393, 3553, 3561, etc.; *adj.* woeful, grieved, wretched 2684, 2979, 3820 [OE *wā*].

wode, wodde *n.* wood, forest 1266, 1281, 1300, 1359, 1713, etc.; **woddes, woddez** *pl.* 1974, 2504; *as adj.* 2219, 2516, 2825, 3376, 4060, etc. [OE *wudu*].

wode *adj.* mad 3837 [OE *wōd*].

wodely *adv.* madly, furiously 2827 [OE *wōdlīce*].

wodewyse *adj.* mad, raging 3817 [WODE, adj. + OE *wīse*].

wokes *n. pl.* weeks 354 [OE *wucu*].

wolde. See WIL(L), v.

wolfe-heuede *n.* wolf's head 1093 [OE *wulf* + HEDE].

wolfes, wolues *n. pl.* wolves 3232, 3446 [OE *wulf*].

woman *n.* woman 3978; **women** *pl.* 3554 [OE *wīfman*].

wombe *n.* belly 768 [OE *womb*].

wonde, woonde *v.* to hesitate, shrink 1615, 3494; **wondis, wondys** *3 sg.* 3820, 3833 [OE *wandian*].

wondes, wondez, wond(d)ede, etc. See WOUNDE, WOUNDES.

wondire, wondyre *n.* wonder, amazement 1166, 1342; *had wondyre of,* were surprised, amazed at 2681; **wondyrs** *pl.* marvels, miracles 2514; distress, anguish 3793; **wonndyrs** *pl.* horrors, horrible deeds 322 [OE *wundor*].

wondyre *adv.* wondrously 2515 [from prec.].

wondirfull, wondyrfull *adj.* wondrous, awesome 768, 3834 [OE *wundorful*].

wondyrlyche *adj.* awesome 1357 [OE *wundorlic*].

wondirliche *adv.* wondrously 3377 [OE *wundorlīce*].

wondis, wondys, wondide, etc. See WOUNDE, WOUNDES.

wondsom *adj.* beset with difficulty 3836 (*see note*) [of Scand. orig.; cf. MSw *vandsamr*, difficult].

wone *n.* dwelling place 1300, 4204; city 2472 [ON *ván,* expectation, with infl. of next].

wonn *v.* to dwell, live 3910; **wonnys** *3 sg.* 3551; **wonte** *pp.* accustomed 4217 [OE *wunian*].

wonndyrs. See WONDIRE.

wonn(e), won(n)en, etc. See WYN(N)(E).

wonnynges *n. pl.* dwellings *3157* [OE *wunung*].

wonrydez. See WANDRETH(E).

wonte. See WONN.

woo. See WO.

woonde. See WONDE.

worde *n.* utterance, speech, words 9, 3549; **wordes, wordez, wordis, wordys** *pl.* words, message 88, 104, 132, 150, 260, etc.; renown, reputation, notoriety 3162; *pl.* 2397 [OE *word*].

worde *v. imper.* speak out 3393 [from prec.].

worlde, werld(e) *n.* world, earth 398, 541, 671, 891, etc.; **wer[l]dez** *poss.* 674; earthly life 5; fortune, good fortune 2189 (*see note*) [OE *weorold*].

worme *n.* serpent, dragon 796, 798 [OE *wyrm*].

worows *3 sg.* (*future*) dooms, afflicts with calamities 958 [OE *wyrgan,* *wurgan].

worthe *v.* to be, become 959, 1306, 4088, 4104; *indef.* 992; happen, come to pass, befall 3553, 3778 [OE *weorþan*].

worthy(e) *adj.* honored, honorable, worthy 233, *1302*, 1920, 3962, 3991; **worthyeste** *superl.* 290, 532 [OE *wyrþe, wyrþig*].

worthily, worthilyche, wortheliche *adj.* worthy, honorable, exalted 695, 2191, 2669; *adv.* nobly 2231; wondrously 2547 [OE *weorþlic, weorþlice*].

wotte. See WYT, v.

wounde *n.* wound 2177; **wondes, wondys, woundez** *pl.* 1469, 2148, 2562, 2690, 2711, etc. [OE *wund*].

woundes, wondes, wondis, woundis *3 sg.* wounds, injures 2090, 2215, 3818, 3834; **woundez** *3 pl.* 707; **wounded, wondide, wondyd** *pa. t.* 1796, 2231, 3152; **woundede, woundyde, wond(d)ede, wondide,** etc. *pp.* wounded, stricken, hurt 137, 1415, 1434, 1523, 1558,

etc.; *woundes noghte,* do not take offense 2739 [OE *wundian*].

wraite *pa. t.* wrote 3904 [OE *wrītan*].

wraythe. See WRYTHES.

wrakfull *adj.* vengeful, angry 3818 [from OE *wræc,* vengeance].

wrange: *on the wrange hande,* from the wrong side 1480 [ON *rangr*].

wreche, wriche wryche *n.* wretch 1064, 1273, 2778, 4185; **wreches, wrechis** *pl.* 1446, 2913, 3572 [OE *wrecca*].

wrechyd *adj.* miserable, unhappy 5 [from OE *wrecca,* adj.].

wreke *n.* harm, injury 3839 [OE *wræc*].

wreke, wreken *v.* to avenge, revenge 151, 3771; **wroken, wrokyn** *pp.* 2225, 2968; give vent or expression to 321, 385, 2548; **wrekes, wrekys** *3 sg.* 2213, 3821 [OE *wrecan*].

wrethe *n.*[1] rage, wrath, indignation 151, 321, 385, 1737, 2225, 2548, 3821, etc. [OE *wræþþo, wræþ(þ)u*].

wrethe *n.*[2] fold, crease 1093 [OE *wriþa*].

wrethide *pa. t.* angered 2191 [OE *wræþan*].

wriche, wryche. See WRECHE.

wryng(e) *v.* to wring 3977, 4286; **wryngez** *3 sg.* 890; **wryngen** *3 pl.* 3155; **wryngande** *pres. p.* 950, 2679, 3920 [OE *wringan*].

wrystill *v.* to twist, writhe about, wrestle 1141; **wristeles** *3 sg.* 890 [OE *wrǣstlian*].

wrythe *v.* to flourish 4322 [OE *wrīþan,* var. of *wrīdan*].

wrythes, wryththis *3 sg.* writhes, twists, twists and turns 1920, 2214; **wrythyn** *3 pl.* 1141;

wraythe *pa. t.* 1093 [OE *wrīþan;* pa. t. perh. infl. by ON **wreiþ,* pa. t. of *wriþa*].

wroghte, wroghten.   See WIRKE.

wroken, wrokyn.   See WREKE, v.

wrothely *adv.* madly, furiously, wildly 1141, 1480, 2214 [OE *wrāþlīce*].

wrotherayle *n.* ill fortune, disaster 3154 [OE *wrāþ,* evil + *hælu,* fortune].

ȝa *interj.* yea, indeed 993, 1033, 2579 [OE *gēa, gē*].

ȝaldsons *n.* sons of jades, whoresons 3809 [ON *jalda* + SON].

ȝalowere *adj. compar.* yellower 3283 [OE *gealo, gealu*].

ȝapely *adv.* readily, promptly 1502 [OE *gēaplīce*].

ȝate *n.* gate 3068; **ȝates, ȝatez** *pl.* 2039, 2471, 3072, 3121 [OE *geat*].

ȝe *pron. sg. & pl.* you 12, 226, 250, 399, 402, etc.; *with imper.* 702, 1097; **ȝow(e)** *acc. & dat.* you, to you, for you, etc. 16, 364, 397, 644, 681, etc.; *as nom.* 250; *refl.* (for) yourself, yourselves 15, 225, 226, 682, 2369, etc.; **ȝour(e), ȝowre** *poss. adj.* your 95, 153, 339, 627, etc.; **ȝoures** *pron.* 3798; *ȝour selfe(n), ȝowre selfen, ȝour seluyne,* etc., you, you yourself, yourselves, etc., 826, 1682, 4086, etc.; *refl.* 222, 1750, etc.; *reinf.* 1735, 1928 [OE *gē, ēow, ēower*].

ȝeffe.   See IF(E).

ȝelde *v. refl.* to give (oneself) up, surrender 1502; **ȝeldes** *3 sg.* 3809; **ȝelden, ȝolden** *pp.* surrendered 1870, 3063; defeated 2334; *pp.* given out 2482 [OE *geldan*].

ȝeme *v.* to care for, have charge of, govern 3554; **ȝemes, ȝemez** *3 sg.* 647, 938, 990, 1069, 1585, etc.; **ȝemes** *3 pl.* 2354; *3 sg.* keeps, follows 430; protect, preserve (from injury) 1503 [OE *gēman*].

ȝerde *n.* yard 3254, 3280 [OE *gerd*].

ȝere *n.* year 552, 3144; **ȝeres** *pl.* 614, 2599, 2622; *uninfl. pl.* 2925 [OE *ge(a)r*].

ȝermys *3 sg.* wails, cries 3911 [OE *gierman*].

ȝerne *adv.* eagerly 3325, 4189; quickly, directly 1794 [OE *georne*].

ȝernes, ȝernez *3 sg.* lusts after, longs for 1032, 1502; **ȝernede** *pa. t.* 2343 [OE *giernan*].

ȝeȝes *3 sg.* cries out *3911* [OE *gēgan*].

ȝif(f), ȝife, etc. See IF(E), GIFE.

ȝis(e) *adv.* yes 2324, 2585, 2589 [OE *gīse*].

ȝit(t)(e) *adv.* yet, still 847, 1128, 1140, 1351, etc.; hereafter 1107, 4004; now (while there is still time) 3406 [OE *gīt, gīet*].

ȝolden.   See ȝELDE.

ȝole *n.* Yule, Christmas 2628 [OE *gēol*].

ȝolke *n.* yolk 3283 [OE *geolca*].

ȝomane *n.* yeoman, a high-ranking servant 2628 [red. from OE *gongman*].

ȝondyr, ȝondire *adv.* yonder 2720, 3809, 4189 [cf. OE *geond,* MLG *gender*].

ȝone *adj.* yon, yonder, those, that 299, 336, 341, 344, 641, etc. [OE *geon*].

ȝour(e), ȝow(e), ȝowre, ȝoures, etc. See ȝE.

Index of Names

Absolon Absalom 2868.
Achinour one of Cador's men
  1824.
Acres Acre, the site of an im-
  portant battle during the Cru-
  sades 903.
Affrike, Affryke, Aufrike, Awfrike
  Africa 574, 1869, 2607, 3933.
Akyn Aachen 496.
Aladuke, Alyduke, Alidoyke one
  of Cador's men 1793, 1824,
  1916.
Alexander(e), Alexandire Alex-
  ander the Great 3408; *uninfl.*
  poss. 2602, 2634.
Algere 2837, 2847.
Alymere 4078.
Almayn(e), Almaygne Germany
  45, 496, 555, 618, 2387, 3210,
  3596.
Amazonnes Landes the land of
  the Amazons 584.
Ambyganye 572 (*see note*).
Anyou Anjou 42.
Antele 2829, 2837.
Araby a mountain in Wales 1175
  (*see note*).
Argayle, Orgaile, Orgayle Argyll
  30, 3534, 3934, 4123.
Arraby Arabia 576.
Arthur(e) King Arthur 26, 172,
  288, 305, 470, 508, 519, 618,

625, 868, 900, 986, 1015, 1125,
1145, 1148, 1222, 1327, 1591,
1593, 1662, 1938, 1952, 2008,
2290, 2360, 2386, 2426, 2626,
3076, 3084, 3135, 3147, 3205,
3500, 3504, 3716, 3965, 4079,
4135, 4170, 4262, 4309, 4342;
as battle cry 1412, 1490, 2245,
2246, 2529, 2802; **Arthurs, Arthures, Arthurez** *poss.* 1674,
2838, 4068; *uninfl. poss.* 496,
988, 1009, 1309, 2255, 4113,
4216.
Asye Asia 574.
Askanere one of Cador's men
  1739.
Aungers King of Scotland and
  brother of Lot 288.
Awguste Autun 1967 (*see note to*
  1964), 2386 (*see note*).

Babyloyn Babylon 586.
Bayon(e) Bayonne 38, 2379.
Bayous. See note to line 587.
Baldake ?Baghdad 586.
Barflete, Bareflete Barfleur 629,
  835, 1182, 1223.
Basill Basle 907.
Bawdewyne the Thyrde Baldwin
  the Third, an ancestor of Arthur,
  otherwise unknown 277.
Bawdwyne Baldwin, one of

Cador's men 1606, 2384.

Bedvere, Bedwere   Bedevere 893, 1162, 1264, 1606, 1744, 2238, 2379; *uninfl. poss.* 1170.

Bedwar   ?Bedevere 2384 (*see note to 2371–85*).

Bedwyne   *uninfl. poss.* Bedwin's 1408 (*see note*).

Belyn   Belinus, an early king of Britain and brother of Brennius 277.

Berade   2384.

Berill, Beryll, Berell   Berill 1264, 1433, 1605, 1771, 1775, 1914.

Boice, Boyce, Boys   Boice 1263, 1378, 1426, 1433, 1456, 1483, 1485, 1605.

Brabane   Brabant 36.

Brene   Brennius, an early king of Britain and brother of Belinus 277.

Bretayne   Brittany 852.

Bretayn þe Brode, Bretayn þe Brade, Bretayn(e) þe Braddere, Bretayne þe More   Britain 55, 106, 1017, 1699, 2095, 2330, 2362, 2577, 2855, 2519, 3579, 4328, 4346.

Bretayn the Lesse, Bretayne þe Lyttyll   Brittany 36, 304.

Bretons, Bretouns, Bretowns   Britons 1348, 1403, 1407, 1414, 1423, 1431, 1449, 1484, 1617, 1753, 1862, 2121, 3695, 4104, 4111, 4130, 4345; *pl. poss.* Britons' 1011, 4289; **Bretowne** British 3508.

Bryane   1606.

Brut, Borghte   Brutus, legendary descendent of Aeneas and founder of Britain 1698; *uninfl. poss.* 1695.

Burdeux   Bordeaux 38.

Burgoyne   Burgundy 36, 1017, 1241, 2383.

Cador(e), Cadour   Cador 247, 259, 481, 1602, 1637, 1706, 1718, 1724, 1777, 1784, 1790, 1804, 1830, 1836, 1848, 1870, 1886, 1892, 1921, 1922, 1928, 2002, 2265, 2385 (*see note to 2371–85*), 4264; **Cadors** 4188 (*see note*).

Caerlyon, Karlyon, Karelyone   Caerleon 61, 3512, 3916.

Cayme   Cain 1311.

Cayous, Kayous, Kayon   Kay 156, 209, 892, 1152, 1194, 1864, 1997, 2157, 2165, 2171, 2177, 2380 (*see note to 2371–85*); *poss.* 2264.

Caliburne, Calyburn, Calaburn, Collbrande   Arthur's sword 2123, 2201, 4193, 4230, 4242.

Came   Caen 2380, 2385.

Capados   Cappadocia 580.

Cardyfe   Cardiff 2498.

Carlele, Carelele   Carlisle 64 (*see note*), 476, 480, 839.

Carous   *1908* (*see note*).

Castell Blanke   1225 (*see note*).

Catrike   Catterick 482.

Chartris   Chartres 1619.

Chastelayne, Chasteleynne   2952, 3028.

Cheldrike   an ally of the Duke of Lorraine, slain by Chastelayne 2954.

Chestyre   Chester 3914.

Childrike   a heathen king, allied with Mordred 3537.

Cyprys   Cyprus 596.

Clarent(e)   Arthur's ceremonial sword 4193, 4202.

Clarybalde   2497.

Clegis, Clegys   Cliges 1604, 1638, 1649, 1671, 1692, 1706, 1828, 1865, 1997, 2157, 2497, 3635, 4265.

Clemente   1828.

**Cleremonde, Cleremown(n)de,
  Clarymownde** 1603, 1638,
  2157, 2497, 3635, 4265.
Cleremus 1603, 1638.
Clyme an unknown locality 1639.
Clowdmur 1604.
Collbrande. See CALIBURNE.
Coloine Cologne 623 (*see note*).
Combe Como 3110, 3128, 3149.
Constantyn Arthur's kinsman and
  heir 4316.
Constantyne, Costantyne Cotentin,
  the Cotentin Peninsula 628, 848,
  1187, 2373.
Constantyne The Emperor Con-
  stantine 282.
Cordewa Cordova 1866.
Cornett(e) Corneto 600, 1909.
Cornwalle, Cornewaile, Cornewayle,
  Kornewayle Cornwall 247,
  1637, 1777, 1848, 2002, 2262,
  3897; *A Cornewale,* Cador's
  battle cry 1791.
Cradoke, Craddoke 3487 (*see
  note*), 3511, 3517.
Crasyn an unknown locality 3045.
Crete Crete 204, 580.
Crist(e), Cryste Christ 136, 227,
  257, 285, 296, 308, 320, 346,
  347, 405, 467, 482, 537, 676,
  714, 809, 940, 1107, 1138,
  1220, 1506, 1559, 1566, 1575,
  1671, 1718, 1785, 1786, 2184,
  2265, 2316, 2511, 2587, 2620,
  2633, 2721, 2785, 3029, 3051,
  3385, 3426, 3491, 3517, 3803,
  3811, 3917, 3961, 4022, 4040,
  4070, 4101, 4150, 4154, 4317;
  Cristes, Cristez *poss.* 3980, 4324.
  See VNDER, LOUE, n.

Damaske Damascus 578.
Damyat Damietta, a seaport in
  Northern Egypt 578.
Danmarke, Danemarke, Danamarke

Denmark 46, 3752, 3783, 3936.
Danmarkes, Danamarkes, Danes
  Danes 3528, 3610, 3694.
Danuby The Danube 622.
Dauid King David 3416.
Dolfyn, Dolphyn Dauphin 2970,
  3023.
Dolfinede Dauphiné 2653.
Dorsett Dorset 4052.
Douere Dover 3066.
Duchemen Germans 1251, 2030,
  2101, 2653, 2834.

Ector Hector 2603, 2635, 3409;
  Ectores *poss.* 4343.
Egipt Egypt 576, 2200.
Elamet an unidentified locality
  575 (*see note*).
Ermyngall 1825.
Ermonye Armenia 573.
Errake 4075, 4161, 4263.
Esex Essex 1740.
Estriche Austria 45; Austrian
  3933.
**Ewayn(e), Ewan fitz Vryence,
  Ewayne fytz Vriene** Ywain, son
  of Urien 337, 357, 2066, 3973,
  4075, 4136, 4161.
Ewayn(e), Ewayne fitz Henry
  Ywain, son of Henry 1558, 1572,
  4262.
Ewandyre, Ewaynedyr An ally of
  Lucius 1622, 1868, 1904.
Ewfrates Euphrates 573.
Ewrope þe Large the greater part
  of Europe 574.

Famacoste Famagusta 2761.
Fawuell Florent's horse 2765.
Federike 2899.
Feltemour an ally of Lucius 1382.
Feraunt, Ferawnt a knight fight-
  ing for the Duke of Lorraine
  2760, 2765, 3405.
Ferawnt(e) one of Arthur's knights

Hamptone Hampton 3031.
Hardolfe, Hardelfe one of Cador's followers 1741, 3583.
Hardolfe a pagan knight 2974.
Hawyke Hawick 3541.
Henawde Hainault 35.
Henguste Hengest 3545 (*see note*).
Herygall one of Cador's men 1742.
Heryll one of Cador's men 1742.
Holaund Holland 35.
Hors Horsa 3545 (*see note*).
Howell King of Brittany 1180.
Howell one of Cador's men 1741, 3583.
Humbyre the Humber 3541.

Idrus, Idirous, Idrous, Idrus fitz Ewayn Idrus, son of Ywain 1439, 1490, 1498, 1510, 4078, 4135, 4141.
Ile of Aueloyne Isle of Avalon 4309 (*see note to 4303*).
Inde India 573.
Inglande, Yngland(e) "England"; Britain 283, 710, 724, 1412, 2359, 3500, 3685.
Ioneke one of Cador's men 1739, 1868, 1905.
Irelande Ireland 31, 2359, 3534, 3909.
Irische, Iresche Irish 3934, 4123, 4163.
Irritayne an unidentified locality 575 (*see note*).

Iene. See GEEN.
Ierant 2890.
Ierodyn ? Jordan 905.
Ierusalem Jerusalem 3433; *uninfl. poss.* 3415.
Iewe Jew 2895.
Ihesu Jesus 863.
Ioatall 2877.

Iolyan 2889.
Ionathal *2112* (*see note*).
Iosephate Jehosaphat 2876.
Iosue Joshua 2605, 3414.
Iudas Judas Maccabeus 2605, 3412.
Iulyus Julius 2877.
Iulius Cesar, Iulyus Cesare Julius Caesar 115, 3410.

Kayon, Kayous. See CAYOUS.
Karlyon, Karelyone. See CAER-LYON.
Karolus Charlemagne 3423.
Kentt Kent 3542.
Kornewayle. See CORNWALLE.

Latyn Latin 3478.
Launcelot(t), Lawncelott, Lawncelot de Lake Lancelot 368, 1720, 1999, 2073, 3638, 4266.
Leo an ally of Lucius 1971.
Lettow(e) Lithuania 605, 2167, 3784.
Lewlyn Llewellyn 1826; **Lewlyns** *poss.* 1826.
Lyby, Lebe Libya 1625, 1767, 1817, 1827; *as adj.* 1781, 1803, 1900.
Lyonell Lionel 1516, 2227, 3637, 4266.
London 2418.
Lor(r)ayne Lorraine 350, 429, 2531, 2652, 2997, 3092, 3432; the Duke of Lorraine 2398, 2418, 2833; *as battle cry* 2800, 2874.
Lott, Loth(e), Lottez Lot 382, 1999, 2081, 3637, 4266 (*Lottez* app. a Latin form, like *Cayous*).
Lowell 1516.
Lowes 4266.
Lucerne 3094.
Lucius, Lucyus, Lucius Iberius "Emperor of Rome" 23, 86 (*see*

note), 128, 251, 383, 419, 460, 504, 570, 1267, 2016, 2032, 2074, 2220.

Lumbard(d)ye, Lumberd(d)ye Lombardy 135, 350, 429, 498, 1972, 2406, 2654, 2997, 3108, 3585, 3594.

Lusscheburghe Luxembourg 2388.

Macedone Macedonia 603.

Makabee Maccabee 3413.

Marches of Mees Marquis of Metz *2950*.

Marie the Virgin Mary 2869, 3998, 4041.

Marrake, Marrike Merrake 4077, 4209, 4220, 4267.

Marschalle de Mowne 1397.

Mauncez 1918.

Mawrell 1918.

Mawren 1918.

Meyes, Mees Metz 2417, 2950.

Melan(e), Meloyne Milan 351, 428, 3134, 3144.

Meneduke 1919, 4077, 4267.

Mentoche 1919.

Myghell. See SAYNT MIGHELL.

Mordrede, Modrede, Mordrede the Malebranche Mordred 645, 679, 711, 3555, 3569, 3766, 3772, 3840, 4062 (*see note*), 4174, 4221, 4226; *uninfl. poss.* 4259, 4320.

Mounte Bernarde Mt. St. Bernard 566.

Mount God(d)ard(e) Mt. Gotthard 497, 562, 2655, 3104.

Mownttagus Montagues 3773.

Nauerne Navarre 55.

Nazarethe Nazareth 591.

Nylus the Nile 591.

Norma(u)ndye Normandy 44, 834.

Norwaye Norway 44, 3935.

Orcage an unidentified locality 572 (*see note*).

Orgaile, Orgayle. See ARGAYLE.

Orient, Oryent(e), Oryentte Orient, East 571, 774, 1623, 1906, 2289, 3461, 3502.

Origg 1825.

Orkenay, Orekenay, Orkkenaye Orkney 30, 3934, 4163. ,

Ouergne Auvergne *42* (*see note*).

Owghtreth Utred 234 (*see note*).

Pamphile Pamphylia, an ancient district in Asia Minor 588.

Parys, Paresche Paris 1340, 1609, 1631, 1888, 2647.

Paule St. Paul 2413.

Pavy(e) Pavia 568, 3141.

Pawnce Pallanza 3140.

Peghttes, Peyghtes Picts 3533, 4125.

Peyters. See PETYRSANDE.

Perse, Perce Persia 588, 1377, 1520, 1544.

Peter, Petyr, Petire St. Peter 2413, 2724; *uninfl. poss.* 1256; as oath 2646, 2883. See LOUE, n.

Peter, Peryr, Petir(e) a Roman senator 1419, 1476, 1519, 1543, 1610, 1631.

Petyrsande, Peyters Petrasanta 40, 352.

Pys(e), Pis Pisa 352, *500,* 3141.

Plesaunce Piacenza 3140.

Porte Iaffe Jaffa 1520, 1544, 2039.

Portyngale Portugal 1028 (*often used as adjective, as here*).

Pounte Tremble, Pownte Tremble Pontremoli, in northern Italy 327, 352, 3140.

Preter Iohne Landes Prester John's lands 588 (*see note*).

Swecy an unidentified locality 2958.

Swetherwyke Sweden 47.

Swyan 2958.

Swynn 47 (*see note*).

Tambire the Tamar 3902.

Tartary Tartary 582.

Thebay Thebes 583.

Tolouse, Tholus Toulouse 39, 1567.

Towell 1916.

Treyntis the Trent 4056 (*see note*).

Troye Troy 887, 1696, 2603, 2635, 3409, 4343.

Troys Troyes 1629.

Turky Turkey 582.

Turkys Turks 1917.

Turoyn Touraine 39.

Turry Turin 234 (*see note*).

Tuskane, Tuskayne, Tuschayne Tuscany 328, 431, 499, *2408,* 3150, 3586, 3593.

Vnwyn Unwin 2868.

Vryence. See EWAYNE.

Vter(e) Uther 29, 521, 1310, 4216.

Vtolfe an ally of Lucius 1622, 1868, *1904.*

Valence, Valewnce Valence 41, 2047.

Valyantt, Valyant of Vyleris a Welsh king (*see note to 320*) 1982, 2064.

Venyce, Venyse Venice 204, 2025.

Vertennon Vale 3169.

Vicounte of Rome 325.

Vyenne Vienne 41.

Viterbe, Vale of Viterbe Viterbo, Valley of Viterbo 326, 353, 2025, 2048, 3164.

Vryell 1744.

Wade 964 (*see note*).

Waynor(e), Waynour. See GAYNOUR.

Wales, Walis, Galys Wales 33, 2890, 3862.

Walyngfordhe Wallingford 4203, 4217.

Walsch(e) Welsh 320 (*see note*), 2044.

Walschelande Wales 334.

Waltyre, Walthere 2495, 2680.

Watlyng Strette Watling Street 450 (*see note*).

Wawayne. See GAWAYNE.

Wecharde, Wycherd *2680 (see note),* 2495.

Westfale, Westuale, Westwale Westphalia 621, 2656, 2826.

West Walys West Wales 322.

Wychere, Whycher 2678, 4025.

Wyghte Wight 334.

Wynchestre Winchester 4011.

Ʒorke York 636, 3911.

Bibliography

Amours, F. J. *Scottish Alliterative Poems*. Edinburgh: Scottish Text Society 27 and 38, 1897.

Anderson, J. J. *Patience*. Manchester: Manchester University Press, 1969.

Andrew, S. O. "The Dialect of *Morte Arthure*." *RES*, 4 (1928), 418–23.

———. "Huchown's Works." *RES*, 5 (1929), 12–21.

Arnold, I. D. O. "Malory's Story of Arthur's Roman Campaign." *Medium Aevum*, 7 (1938), 74.

Banks, Mary M., ed. *Morte Arthure*. London: Longmans, Green, 1900.

———. "Notes on the 'Morte Arthure' Glossary." *MLQ*, 6 (1903), 64–69.

Benson, Larry D. "The Alliterative *Morte Arthure* and Medieval Tragedy." *TSL*, 11 (1966), 75–87.

———. *Art and Tradition in Sir Gawain and the Green Knight*. New Brunswick: Rutgers University Press, 1965.

———, ed. *King Arthur's Death: The Middle English* Stanzaic Morte Arthure *and* Alliterative Morte Arthure. Indianapolis: Bobbs-Merrill Company, Inc., 1974.

Bessinger, Jess B., Jr. Review of George Kane's *Piers Plowman: The A Version*. *JEGP*, 60 (1961), 571–76.

Billings, Anna Hunt. *A Guide to the Middle English Metrical Romances*. New York: Yale Studies in English 9, 1901.

Björkman, Erik. "Alliterative Text." *Anglia*, 39 (1915), 253–67.

———. "Etymological Notes." *JEGP*, 5 (1903–05), 501–04.

———. "Merc. onsien 'facies.' " *Englische Studien*, 48 (1914–15), 115–23.

———, ed. *Morte Arthure*. Heidelberg: Carl Winters, 1915.

———. "Notes on the 'Morte Arthure' and Its Vocabulary." In *Minneskrift af Forna Lärjungar Tillagnad Professor Axel Erdmann på Hans Sjuttioårsdag den 6. Febr., 1913*. Uppsala: Almqvist und Wiksell, 1913.

Borroff, Marie. *Sir Gawain and the Green Knight: A Stylistic and Metrical Study*. New Haven: Yale University Press, 1962.

Branscheid, P. "Über die Quellen des Stabreimenden Morte Arthure." *Anglia*, 8 (1885), 179–236.

Brink, August. *Stab und Wort im Gawain: Eine Stylistische Untersuchung*. Halle: M. Neimeyer, 1920.

Brock, Edmund, ed. *Morte Arthure*. London: E.E.T.S. O.S. 8, 1871 (Revision of Perry); rpt. 1961.

Brown, J. T. T. *Huchoun of the Awle Ryale and His Poems*. Glasgow: J. Maclehose, 1902.

Bruce, J. D. "Development of the Morte Arthure Theme in Medieval Romance." *Romanic Review*, 4 (1913), 403.

――――. *The Evolution of Arthurian Romance*. Göttingen: Vandenhoeck and Ruprecht, 1923.

Cassidy, Frederic C. "How Free Was the Anglo-Saxon Scop?" In *Franciplegius: Medieval and Linguistic Studies in Honor of Francis Peabody Magoun, Jr.* Edd. Jess B. Bessinger, Jr., and Robert P. Creed. New York: New York University Press, 1965, pp. 75–85.

Chambers, E. K. *Arthur of Britain*. London: Sidgwick and Jackson, 1927; rpt. 1966.

Clark, George. "Gawain's Fall: The Alliterative *Morte Arthure* and Hastings." *TSL*, 9 (1966), 89–95.

Dichmann, Mary E. "Characterization in Malory's 'Arthur and Lucius.'" *PMLA*, 65 (1950), 877–95.

――――. "The Tale of King Arthur and the Emperor Lucius." In *Malory's Originality: A Critical Study of Le Morte d'Arthur*. Ed. R. M. Lumiansky. Baltimore: Johns Hopkins Press, 1964.

Eagleson, Harvey. "Costume in the Middle English Metrical Romances." *PMLA*, 47 (1932), 339–45.

Elliot, Ralph W. "Landscape and Rhetoric in Middle English Alliterative Poetry." *Melbourne Critical Review*, No. 4 (1961), 65–76.

Finlayson, John. "Arthur and the Giant of St. Michael's Mount." *Medium Aevum*, 33 (1964), 112–20.

――――. "The Concept of the Hero in 'Morte Arthure.'" In *Chaucer und Seine Zeit: Symposion für Walter F. Schirmer*. Ed. Arno Esch. Tübingen: Max Niemeyer, 1968.

――――. "Formulaic Technique in *Morte Arthure*." *Anglia*, 81 (1963), 372–93.

――――, ed. *Morte Arthure*. London: Edward Arnold, 1967.

――――. "*Morte Arthure*: The Date and a Source for the Contemporary References." *Speculum*, 42 (1967), 624–38.

――――. "Rhetorical *Descriptio* of Place in the Alliterative *Morte Arthure*." *MP*, 61 (1963), 1–11.

――――. "Two Minor Sources for the Alliterative 'Morte Arthure.'" *NQ*, 9 (1962), N.S., 132–33.

Fischer, Joseph. "Die Stabende Langzeile in den Werken des Gawain-dichters." *Bonner Beiträge zur Anglistik*, 9 (1901), 1–64.

Fischer, Joseph, and F. J. Mennicken. "Zur Mittelenglischen Stabzeile." *Ibid.*, 139–54.

Gardner, John., trans. *The Alliterative Morte Arthure, the Owl and the Nightingale, and Five Other Middle English Poems*. Carbondale: Southern Illinois University Press, 1971.

Gates, Robert J., ed. *The Awntyrs off Arthure at the Terne Wathelyne*. Philadelphia: University of Pennsylvania Press, 1969.

Gist, Margaret A. *Love and War in the Middle English Romances*. Philadelphia: University of Pennsylvania Press, 1947.

Göller, Karl H. *König Arthur in der englischen Literatur des späten Mittelalters*. Göttingen: Vandenhoeck and Ruprecht, 1963.

――――. "Stab und Formel im Allitierenden *Morte Arthure*." *Neophilologus*, 49 (1965), 57–67.

Gordon, E. V., ed. *Pearl*. Oxford: Clarendon Press, 1953; rpt. 1963.

Gordon, E. V., and Eugène Vinaver. "New Light on the Text of the Alliterative *Morte Arthure*." *Medium Aevum*, 6 (1937), 81–98.

Griffith, R. H. "Malory, *Morte Arthure*, and *Fierabras*." *Anglia*, 32 (1909), 389–98.

Gross, Laila. "The Meaning and Oral-Formulaic Use of *Riot* in the Alliterative *Morte Arthure*." *Annuale Mediaevale*, 9 (1968), 98–102.

Halliwell, J. O., ed. *The Alliterative Romance of the Death of King Arthur*. London: Brixton Hill, 1847 (75 copies).

Holthausen, F. Review of Banks' edition of *Morte Arthure. Beiblatt zur Anglia*, 12 (1901), 235–37.

———. "Zum Alliterierenden Morte Arthure." *Ibid.*, 24 (1913), 250–52.

Hulbert, J. R. "The 'West Midland' of the Romances." *MP*, 19 (1921), 1–16.

Imelmann, Rudolph. *Laʒamon: Versuch über Seine Quellen*. Berlin: Weidmann, 1906.

Johnson, James D. *Formulaic Diction and Thematic Composition in the Alliterative Morte Arthure*. Unpbl. Diss. University of Illinois, 1969.

Kane, George. *Piers Plowman: The A Version*. London: Athlone Press, 1960.

Keiser, George R. "Edward III and the Alliterative *Morte Arthure*." *Speculum*, 48 (1973), 37–51.

Kelly, F. H., and Schwabe, R. *A Short History of Costume and Armour, Chiefly in England*. 1931; rpt. New York: B. Blom, 1968.

Kittner, Heinz. *Studien zum Wortschatz William Langlands*. Halle: Max Niemeyer, 1937.

Krishna, Valerie. "Archaic Nouns in the Alliterative *Morte Arthure*." *NM* 76 (1975), 439–45.

Lawrence, J. *Chapters on Alliterative Verse: A Dissertation*. London: H. Frowde, 1893.

Lawrence, R. F. "The Formulaic Theory and Its Applications to English Alliterative Poetry." In *Essays on Style and Language: Linguistic and Critical Approaches to Literary Style*. Ed. Roger Fowler. London: Routledge and Kegan, 1966, pp. 166–83.

Loomis, R. S. *Arthurian Legends in Medieval Art*. Oxford: Clarendon Press, 1938.

———. *Arthurian Literature in the Middle Ages*. Oxford: Clarendon Press, 1959.

———. *The Development of Arthurian Romance*. New York: Harper and Row, 1964.

———. "Edward I, Arthurian Enthusiast." *Speculum*, 28 (1953), 114–27.

Lord, A. B. *The Singer of Tales*. Cambridge, Mass.: Harvard University Press, 1960; rpt. New York: Atheneum, 1965.

Luick, Karl. "Die Englische Stabreimzeile im XIV, XV, und XVI Jahrhundert." *Anglia*, 11 (1889), 585–97.

———. Review of Mennicken's "Versbau und Sprache in Huchowns Morte Arthure." *Beiblatt zur Anglia*, 12 (1901), 33–49.

Lumiansky, Robert M. "The Alliterative *Morte Arthure*, the Concept of Medieval Tragedy, and the Cardinal Virtue Fortitude." In *Medieval and Renaissance Studies*. Ed. John M. Headley. Chapel Hill: University of North Carolina Press, 1968, pp. 95–118.

MacCracken, Henry N. "Concerning Huchown." *PMLA*, 25 (1910), 507–34.

Madden, Frederick, ed. *Syr Gawayne*. London: Bannatyne Club, 1839.

Magoun, F. P., Jr. "The Oral-Formulaic Character of Anglo-Saxon Poetry." *Speculum*, 28 (1953), 446–67; *Ibid.*, 30 (1955), 49–63.

Matthews, William. *The Ill-Framed Knight: A Skeptical Inquiry into the Identity of Sir Thomas Malory*. Berkeley: University of California Press, 1966.

———. *The Tragedy of Arthur: A Study of the Alliterative Morte Arthure*. Berkeley: University of California Press, 1960.

———. "Where Was Siesia-Sessoyne?" *Speculum*, 49 (1974), 680–86.

McIntosh, Angus. "The Textual Transmission of the Alliterative *Morte Arthure*." In *English and Medieval Studies Presented to J. R. R. Tolkien*. Ed. Norman Davis and C. L. Wrenn. London: Allen & Unwin, 1962, pp. 231–40.

———. Review of Ogden's *Liber de Diversis Medicinis*. *RES*, 15 (1939), 336–38.

Mennicken, Franz Joseph. "Versbau und Sprache in Huchowns Morte Arthure." *Bonner Beiträge zur Anglistik*, 5 (1900), 33–144.

Morris, R. *Early English Alliterative Poems*. London: E.E.T.S. O.S. 1, 1869.

Neilson, George. "Contributions to Old English Literature: Three Footnotes." In *An English Miscellany Presented to Dr. Furnivall*. Ed. W. P. Ker, A. S. Napier, and W. W. Skeat. Oxford: Clarendon Press, 1901, pp. 382–85.

—————. *Huchown of the Awle Ryale*. Glasgow: J. Maclehose, 1902.

Newstead, Helaine. "Arthurian Legends." In *A Manual of the Writings in Middle English, 1050–1500*. Ed. J. Burke Severs. New Haven: Connecticut Academy of Arts and Sciences, 1967, Fasc. 1, pp. 44–46; 233–34.

Oakden, J. P. *Alliterative Poetry in Middle English*. Vol. I. *The Dialectical and Metrical Survey*. Vol. II. *A Survey of the Traditions*. Manchester: Manchester University Press, 1930–35; rpt. as one volume, Hamden, Conn.: Archon Books, 1968.

Offord, M. Y., ed. *The Parlement of the Thre Ages*. London: E.E.T.S. O.S. 246, 1959; rpt. 1967.

Ogden, Margaret S., ed. *The Liber de Diversis Medicinis*. London: E.E.T.S. O.S. 207, 1937.

O'Loughlin, J. L. N. "The English Alliterative Romances." In *Arthurian Literature in the Middle Ages: A Collaborative History*. Ed. R. S. Loomis. Oxford: Clarendon Press, 1959, pp. 520–27.

—————. "The Middle English Alliterative *Morte Arthure*." *Medium Aevum*, 4 (1935), 153–68.

Parks, G. B. "King Arthur and the Roads to Rome." *JEGP*, 55 (1946), 164–70.

Parry, Milman. "Studies in the Epic Technique of Oral Verse Making. I. Homer and Homeric Style." *Harvard Studies in Classical Philology*, 41 (1930), 73–147. II. "The Homeric Language as the Language of an Oral Poetry." *Ibid.*, 53 (1933), 1–50.

Perry, George, ed. *Morte Arthure*. London: E.E.T.S. O.S. 8, 1865.

Schaar, Claes. "On a New Theory of Old English Poetic Diction." *Neophilologus*, 40 (1956), 302.

Schröder, Edward. "Zur Datierung der Morte Arthure." *Anglia*, 60 (1936), 396.

Schumacher, Karl. "Studien über den Stabreim in der Mittelenglischen Alliterationsdichtung." *Bonner Studien zur Englischen Philologie*, 11 (1914), 1–213.

Sievers, Eduard. "Old Germanic Metrics and Old English Metrics." Trans. Gawaina D. Luster. Rpt. in *Essential Articles for the Study of Old English Poetry*. Ed. Jess B. Bessinger, Jr., and Stanley J. Kahrl. Hamden, Conn.: Archon Books, 1968, pp. 267–88.

Stevick, R. D. "The Oral-Formulaic Analysis of Old English Verse." *Speculum*, 32 (1962), 387.

Tatlock, J. S. P. "Contemporaneous Matters in Geoffrey of Monmouth." *Speculum*, 6 (1931), 206–24.

—————. *The Legendary History of Britain*. Berkeley: University of California Press, 1950.

The Thornton Manuscript. Intro. D. S. Brewer and A. E. B. Owen. London: Scolar Press, 1975.

Tolkien, J. R. R., and E. V. Gordon, eds. *Sir Gawain and the Green Knight*. Oxford: Clarendon Press, 1925. 2d. ed. Norman Davis, 1967.

Trautmann, Moritz. "Der Dichter Huchown und seine Werke." *Anglia*, 1 (1878), 110–49.

—————. "Zur Kenntnis und Geschichte der mittelenglischen Stabzeile." *Anglia*, 18 (1896), 83–100.

Van der Ven-Ten Bensel, Elise. *The Character of Arthur in English Literature*. Amsterdam, H. J. Paris, 1925; rpt. New York: Haskell House, 1966.

Vinaver, Eugène. "From Epic to Romance." *Bulletin of the John Rylands Library*, 46 (1964), 476–503.

—————. "Malory's 'Morte Darthur' in the Light of a Recent Discovery." *Ibid.*, 19 (1935), 438–57.

Vorontzoff, Tania. "Malory's Story of Arthur's Roman Campaign." *Medium Aevum,* 6 (1937), 99–121.

Waldron, R. A. "Oral-Formulaic Technique and Middle English Alliterative Poetry." *Speculum,* 32 (1957), 792–804.

Watts, Ann Chalmers. *The Lyre and the Harp: A Comparative Reconsideration of Oral Tradition in Homer and Old English Epic Poetry.* New Haven: Yale University Press, 1969.

Whallon, William. *Formula, Character, and Context: Studies in Homeric, Old English, and Old Testament Poetry.* Washington: Center for Hellenic Studies; distr. by Cambridge, Mass.: Harvard University Press, 1969.

Williams, W. Llewelyn, ed., *Giraldus Cambrensis: The Itinerary through Wales and the Description of Wales.* London: J. M. Dent, 1930.

Wilson, R. H. "Some Minor Characters in the *Morte Arthure.*" *MLN,* 71 (1956), 475–80.